Furscience

A Decade of Psychological Research on the Furry Fandom

INTERNATIONAL ANTHROPOMORPHIC RESEARCH PROJECT
IARP
FURSCIENCE.COM

Furscience
A Decade of Psychological Research on the Furry Fandom

Edited by

Courtney N. Plante
Bishop's University

Stephen Reysen
Texas A&M University-Commerce

Camielle Adams
University of Calgary

Sharon E. Roberts
Renison University College, University of Waterloo

Kathleen C. Gerbasi
Niagara County Community College

International Anthropomorphic Research Project
Commerce, Texas, USA

ISBN-13: 978-0-9976288-3-8

Commerce, Texas, USA
Cover Art by @echoofjustice

Table of Contents

Acknowledgments

Furscience is, and has always been from its very start, a collaborative effort. And, just like a Broadway show, it's easy for an audience watching from the outside to forget that the actors on stage represent just a fraction of all the people needed to make a production happen!

In this spirit, we at Furscience would like to collectively thank all the people who've helped us to get where we are today, without whom this book would not be possible. We'll endeavor to recognize every person who's helped us along the way, but realize that it's a herculean task: Furscience represents the cumulative contribution of hundreds of people (not to mention tens of thousands of furries who've generously given their time and effort for free to help us with our research). Despite our best efforts, we will almost certainly forget to mention people. This oversight should be seen as a reflection on the frailty of the human memory and on our humble recognition of how many people we owe a great thanks to, and not as our being ungrateful for everything that so many people have done to help us over the years!

Kathy Gerbasi

I would like to extend a huge thanks to all of the research assistants we've worked with over the years, without whom there would never have been any furry research! In alphabetical order, and to the best of my ability to recall, they are Charlie Aquilina, Ashley Borelli, Eric Broeker, Troj Brueghel, Mike Cline, Carlos Darby, Emma Verratti DeChellis, James Ducas, Erika Edwards, Caitlin Fulle, Tim Gadawski, Anthony Hartman, Rebecca Hewitt, Justin Higner, Dan Kish, Elise Koepke, Darryl Lockie, Jared McCaffrey, Brian Mendel, Nick Paolone, Anthony Paterno, Adam Privitera, Tristan Puffer, Jennifer Raymond, Isaia Sciabarrasi, Joe Vullo.

In addition to the aforementioned individuals, most of whom have been my students, and the thousands of furries who have participated in the research over the past 10 years, I would also like to especially thank Laurence "Green Reaper" Parry, William Conde, Michael Brenner, and Douglas Muth (Giza) for their continued support and interest in furry research and Simona Ghai for her amazing transcription abilities.

Courtney "Nuka" Plante

I began this undertaking as a graduate student, at a time when my confidence in the project was shaky and when I wasn't sure whether what I was doing would kill my career prospects or not. In that regard, I'd like to extend a big thanks to my graduate school supervisor, Dr. Richard Eibach, and to his partner Dr. Steve Mock, both of whom helped to develop the research skills I still use today and who helped me to balance my eagerness and enthusiasm to run off and do this wacky line of research with the need to stay grounded and pragmatic. In this same vein, I'd also like to thank my colleagues, in particular Kathy, Stephen, and Sharon. I consider myself to be the luckiest graduate student who ever lived because of them; while most graduate students only have one supervisor, I was lucky enough to have four mentoring me through a tough time in my life. Any success I have today can be attributed to their combined efforts.

I'd also like to thank the furries I've met over the years who've been instrumental in either directly helping with our research or who've helped me personally as a person who does furry research. This includes, but is in no way limited to, the Alberta Furries, the Waterloo Furries, and the UW Bronies Club. In particular, I'd like to thank Edolon, who introduced me to Kathy in the first place, Kaa, who was instrumental in both moral support and helping set up and run a computerized experiment at a furry convention. Thank you to the podcasts Fur What it's Worth and Furcast, both of whom were early supporters of our research and helped us to disseminate our findings to furries around the world! Similarly, thank you to Greenreaper for helping us to signal boost our findings on Flayrah and for being such an enthusiastic supporter of our work.

Thank you to all of the convention staff who've helped us to conduct research at their conventions, including accommodating all of our strange requests. This includes a myriad of staff members at Texas Furry Fiesta (e.g., Istanbul, Glass), Anthrocon (e.g., Kage, Giza), Further Confusion (e.g., Carbon), Oklacon (e.g., Lenny and Andy), Furnal Equinox, Canfurence, Eurofurence, Fur-Eh, and Furality (e.g., Alofoxx)!

I'd also like to thank the numerous furry scholars, many of whom have provided valuable input, feedback, perspective, and criticism of our work, which has only helped to make it better! This includes Troj, who's been a fantastic soundboard against which to bounce clinical ideas, Hazel (Bobbi) Ali Zaman, who always provides excellent perspective and pushes us to consider a more phenomenological look at our work, Yerf, whose criticism has been a productive creative friction, and to Camielle (Kirisis) Adams, who, in addition to editing this book and offering invaluable perspective and research ideas on political science and BIPOC issues, I also consider to be a dear friend!

Finally, I'd like to extend a huge thanks to my friend and fellow furry Ocean, who's single-handedly the person most responsible for both my journey into the furry fandom and into what would eventually become Furscience!

Sharon Roberts

There are so many people who have worked behind the scenes to make Furscience possible. If not for the institutions, journals, and funding agencies who saw the promise in our early work, we would not have succeeded. Thank you to our funders for assisting us with some of the many research projects that are presented in this book: Renison University College for seed funding; start-up grants from the University of Waterloo; thank you to The Bob Harding and Lois Claxton Humanities and Social Sciences Endowment Fund; and a heartfelt thank you to SSHRC for the ability to say: This research is supported in part by funding from the Social Sciences and Humanities Research Council. So, thank you so much, Tom, for teaching me how to write better grant applications. Live long and prosper, friend.

I am grateful for the many conventions and their incredible staff who have helped us succeed, many of whom have already been mentioned by my colleagues. However, a personal thank you from me and Malicious Beaver goes out to the organizers of Anthrocon, CanFURence, ConFuzzled, Eurofurence, NordicFuzzCon, Furnal Equinox, Oklacon, Furality, Owomacon, Texas Furry Fiesta, Furpoint, VancouFur, Alamo City Furry Convention, Further Confusion, and Furry Pinas. We are so grateful for these partnerships and friendships. We also give a heartfelt thank you to many wonderful people in the furry community who have worked tirelessly with Malicious Beaver in the background on all kinds endeavors. There are so many of you, but we send a special thanks to Dr. Conway, Arc Husky, Jacob, Tempe O'Kun, Cheetah Spotty Cat, Jyanon, GerMANshep, Trax, Arrkay, Andy, Lenny, and Moms of Furries. Your guidance, generosity, and kindness are so appreciated by both of us.

Thank you to our dedicated students, research assistants, and Furscience volunteers: Chelsea, Kayla, Abigail, Marie-Michelle, Scott, Roula, Rebekah, Simona, Kendra, Jacklyn, Kim, Iona, Anna, Charles, Troj, Dawn, Asher, and many others.

I feel such gratitude when I think of Professor James Côté. Thank you for investing so much energy and time in my education and for continuing to mentor me through my entire academic journey. What a privilege it has been for me to learn from you over the past quarter century. Also, thank you so much for your feedback and encouragement regarding the Furry Fandom Identity Resolution Model (FFIRM), which is making its debut in Chapter 24 of this book.

My heartfelt thank you goes to our Creative and Communications Director, Malicious Beaver, for your endless dedication to Furscience and me. And, thank you to my fellow Furscience colleagues—my dear friends. I am so grateful for your patience and wisdom. I feel so fortunate to have had the chance to help write this story of Furtuity.

Finally, thank you to the amazing furry community that has made us feel so welcomed in furry spaces. As I tell the students in my Research Method course, participants who share the details of their lives are offering researchers the most precious of gifts. Learning about the ebb and flow of so many furries' lives has been a remarkable privilege. Thank you to the furry fandom for participating in our many studies and supporting this research. We are grateful.

Stephen Reysen

Thank you to Tanner McCarter, Jessica Gamboa, Amanda Gamboa, and Jessie Kierbow who have been on our Texas Furry Fiesta crew for many years (and hopefully many more to come). Also, thank you to students who have helped in the past: Catherine Schroy, Jamie Snider, Jason Lloyd, and Justin Miller. Lastly, thanks to Eduardo Soliz.

Elizabeth Fein

I'd like to acknowledge Jennifer Bradley, Ben Gaddes, José G. Luiggi-Hernández, and Gabriela Mena Ibarra.

Camielle Adams

Wow, I never thought that I would be making this type of statement for a non-fiction publication, but here I am. Life has certainly sent a variety of tests and challenges my way, but I'm very grateful to have been presented with all of the unique opportunities that I have been given. I hope with each and every publication I'm asked to participate in, my works enlighten and invigorate others to further explore and seek out their understanding. Remember, if we all do one thing each day that positively impacts someone else, then little by little, we can change the world.

First and foremost, I would like to thank The Creator for my talents and my ability to endure while this thing I call my life unfolded around me. I would also like to thank my loving husband, Ocean, for his love and late-night snacks. Really and truly, I would be so lost without him. He truly is the moon to my sun. I would also like to thank my godparents, Tonae & Earle, Irene, and Cathy for their encouragement and for checking in on me while things have been so rough at times. Likewise, many thanks to my cousin, Elaine, who sent me many prayers of strength and patience. I would also like to thank Dr. Courtney "Nuka" Plante for including me in this endeavor. It's been a lot of fun and as a lifelong nerd, this research and editing has been an awesome experience.

Last but certainly not least, I would like to thank my mother, Dee, for laying the groundwork for me as a kid to view knowledge, research, and just reading as a fun and engaging activity. Though you're no longer with us, your legacy and love can be felt at every summit that I reach, now and forever. Remember to hug dholes!

Part 1
What *is* All of This?

Chapter 1
An Introduction to the Book
Courtney "Nuka" Plante

You know those moments in life where you just *stop*, look around, and ask yourself "How the heck did I get here?"

That's what this book is: A chance for us, the members of the Furscience team, to take stock of where we are and how we got here.

Let me explain.

Since 2011 we, a team of social scientists who call ourselves Furscience, have been scientifically studying the furry fandom—conducting online and in-person surveys, interviews, focus groups, and experiments to better understand what makes furries tick.[1] In the time since then, we've conducted dozens of studies on tens of thousands of furries from around the globe, on subjects such as what motivates furries, furry well-being, relationships in the furry fandom, furries' attitudes toward animals, the functions of fursonas, identity formation and maturation in fandom spaces, and fandom conflict, to name just a few. When we began, there was relatively little psychological literature on the subject of furries at a time when a lot of news outlets, television shows, and haters online had a lot to say about furries. And so we did what all good academics strive to do: we published our research to try and bring knowledge to a subject people cared about.

We published our research in academic journals, book chapters, and online on our own website in a relatively piecemeal fashion. Scientific journal articles and book chapters represented a deep dive into very specific, thin slices of furry behavior while our website regularly showed off the results of our most recent studies. We did this for the better part of a decade, gradually accumulating a bigger and bigger pile of published articles and chapters and growing our online repository of findings by tacking on each new study like a post-it note on an increasingly busy office whiteboard. With each passing year, we focused on putting out more articles and adding more data to our website, with little time to do anything else because as soon as we finished analyzing the data from one study, we were already putting together the materials for the next study—there was always one more convention to go to, one more sample to get.

---

[1] As we explain in Chapter 3, some individual members of our team have been conducting studies since as early as 2006, but we didn't unite as the Furscience team until 2011!

And then, in 2020, the world was brought to a screeching halt by a global pandemic. Quarantines put a stop to furry conventions for the better part of two years, as well as to regular academic activities. As professors, we were still holding online classes but, aside from that, we, like the rest of the world, were all stuck in a holding pattern, waiting for the pandemic to end. The breakneck cycle of data collection, analysis, planning, and then more data collection stopped along with everything else. With no conventions to attend, we suddenly found ourselves with some uncharacteristic free time on our hands.

That's when we took a step back and realized that, in more than a decade, we'd never really stopped to put all the pieces together, to take a holistic look at all of our data. After any given study, we'd harvest the juiciest and most exciting tidbits of information to share in publications and on our research website, but we never really went back to do the slower, more methodical drudgework of science: poring over some of the more mundane, but nevertheless important, findings. We were so eager to think about future studies that we never stopped to compare our current findings to the ones that had come before.

In short, the pandemic gave us a sense of perspective and the opportunity to sit down with our data and pore over it in a way we'd never done before. We finally had a chance to look at more than 30 studies comprised of thousands of questions given to tens of thousands of furries and, in doing so, began to see the broader trends and patterns that only emerge from a holistic look at a body of research.

That's what this book is: it's the most complete picture of all the research we've compiled to date on the furry fandom. It's our most holistic look at the psychology of the furry fandom, the story with the most interconnected, overlapping, interweaved narratives and subplots that we've written. We're using the whole buffalo, from head to toe, pulling together all of our findings and looking at them not in isolation, but with an eye for seeing the big picture that they all contribute to.

So, why bother doing this after a decade?

We'd be lying if we said it wasn't at least a *little* self-serving. After all, a decade is a long time for those irritating itches in the backs of our minds to accumulate, that annoying sense of "I really should go back and take another look at the data, just to make sure I haven't missed anything" piling up with each additional study. Getting to thoroughly comb through every piece of data we've ever collected and organizing it has been a refreshing experience—sort of like finally setting aside a Sunday afternoon to declutter that messy closet or organize that junk drawer!

It's also been a fantastic opportunity for us to reach out and seek the perspective and expertise of those who are better studied on specifics than ourselves. While we may be "experts" when it comes to furry, we are generalists when it comes to many of the topics described in this book (e.g., race, sex, gender, the history of the fandom, political beliefs). As such, while Furscience provided all of the data, experts have generously helped to interpret and contextualize our findings within their respective fields, providing important history or theoretical frameworks within which to understand our findings. This is why we've opted for a more "edited collection of chapters" approach to this book rather than a "the same authors write every chapter" approach—it allows us to benefit from the years of experience and expertise of other scholars!

A third reason for writing this book is to give back to the furries who have given so much to us over the years. Our work at Furscience would be impossible if not for the generous time of literally tens of thousands of furries who've spent time completing our studies—not to mention the countless others who've helped to signal boost our research, provide useful critiques, and suggest new research topics and interpretations of our findings. In fact, this was a big impetus for the book being self-published and released for free digitally—because we truly feel that we've entered into a partnership with the furry fandom, and so it's only right and fair that every furry be able to benefit maximally from this community effort.

The final purpose of this book is to be a one-stop shop for anyone who's curious about furries to learn more about the furry fandom and its denizens. We've tried to balance the depth and breadth of our coverage to make this book as relevant to newcomers to the fandom as it is to decades-long aficionados; as useful to journalists and concerned parents as it is to academics, and as accessible to laypersons as it is to furry lifestylers and professionals. And while it might seem, on the face of it, a bit presumptuous for us to assume that such a wide range of people would read our book and get something from it, this is exactly what we've seen over the years from our Furscience website: every week we receive e-mails from furries looking to know more about the fandom they're a part of, journalists writing stories about furries and wanting to get the facts straight,[2] parents wanting to better understand their child's new interest, and students and professors writing

---

[2] This is a welcome change from the early 2000s, where much of the media discourse on furries was based on unsubstantiated stereotypes and hearsay.

papers about the fandom. If nothing else, we hope that this book expands the reach of our data and can help make it easier for people seeking to learn more about the furry fandom to do so!

We've carefully curated and organized our findings into chapters in this book in a way that both has a logical flow of ideas from chapter to chapter (e.g., with facts building upon other facts) and allows readers who are only interested in one specific subject to quickly and easily find what they're looking for. In this first part of the book, we start with the very basics, briefly summarizing the story of how the furry fandom came to be, as well as the story of where the Furscience team comes from and how we conducted the research that we summarize throughout the rest of this book.

In Part Two, we look at concepts and behaviors that are fundamental to the furry fandom. This includes defining what a furry is (or, rather, showing how difficult it is to nail down a definition of what a furry is) and describing what it means to identify as a furry. We also look at core behaviors that are nearly universal in the furry fandom (i.e., creating a fursona, consuming and creating content) or which, at the very least, are associated frequently enough with the furry fandom that they warrant discussion (e.g., fursuits, pornography). We also discuss important fandom-related concepts such as the blurred lines between furries and other fandoms, the hodgepodge of different subgroups within the furry fandom, as well as the presence of drama and conflict in fandom spaces.

In Part Three, we take another approach to understanding furries, this time looking at the people who comprise the furry fandom. This includes looking at demographic features that are fairly distinct or that play an important role in the character of the furry fandom (i.e., its fairly young age, its predominantly LGBTQ+ composition, etc.). We also dedicate chapters to giving voice to those whose presence in the fandom is often overlooked or brushed over with the homogenization of the furry fandom, including racialized individuals, transgender people, and women. We also provide additional context for the chapter on drama and conflict by delving into the religious and political beliefs of the furry fandom to see how an understanding of furries' fundamental values and principles helps us to better understand why the fandom is the way that it is (e.g., progressive values).

In Part Four, we shift our focus to the psychological processes driving furries and furry behaviors. We consider individual differences between people and how they manifest in furry-specific behaviors and delve into the question of what compels furries to be furries in the first place. We also consider the role of animals in furries' lives, including the distinction between liking or being a fan of an animal and identifying as an animal, a distinction commonly overlooked by laypersons outside the furry fandom. Along these same lines, we also address a variety of misconceptions people have about the furry fandom and how this contributes to stigma toward the furry fandom, as well as the impact this stigma has on the well-being of furries (and how the fandom provides a buffer against this stigma). We also shine a spotlight on some very specific psychological concepts highlighted by the furry fandom, including the significant prevalence of neurodiverse furries and the role of furry in helping people navigate the increasingly tumultuous pathway to adulthood.

We sincerely hope that, as you read, you're instilled with the same curiosity and passion to find out more about this weird and wonderful fandom that we are![3] It's that indescribable need to take very seriously this subject which people so easily trivialize or dismiss out of hand as silly or pointless. And, if nothing else, perhaps this book will help you to understand why, when we're so frequently asked "Why are you, a bunch of actual, serious scientists, doing a study at a furry convention of all places?", we always give the same answer:

"For science!"[4]

---

[3] Okay, it's probably unlikely that most of our readers will feel compelled to dedicate a decade of their life to scientifically studying furries the way we have—but hey, if you are, drop us a line! We're always looking for collaborators!

[4] Yes, this is the actual reason why we are called Furscience.

Chapter 2
Furry 101: A (Brief) History of the Furry Fandom
Joe Strike

"Furry" is new; it's also very, very old.

When I say "Furry is new," I'm referring to what is generally known as the "furry fandom." This ever-expanding community of people who are enthusiasts of anthropomorphic animal characters has only been around since the closing decades of the 20th century.

But furries' enthusiasm for imaginary beings who straddle the human and non-human animal worlds goes way back. In fact, it predates civilization itself!

Take for example the *Lion-Man*, or *Löwenmensch*, carved from a mammoth tusk by an anonymous Ice Age sculptor some *40,000 years ago.* This twelve-and-a-quarter-inch tall sculpture depicts an upright figure with a lion's head on an essentially human body and is quite possibly the very first piece of art ever created.

A teenager by comparison, the cave painting known as *The Sorcerer* dates back a mere 140 centuries. Discovered beneath the French countryside, *The Sorcerer*, like his older brother the *Lion Man*, is a therianthrope—a combination of man and beast. Standing on human legs, a gently curving tail adorns an otherwise human rump. His upper arms are pressed tightly against his torso while his forearms, thrust straight out, end in paws. His head sports antlers, tufted animal ears—and a pair of human eyes, round and looking over his shoulder, as if startled.

One can ask whether *Lion Man* and *The Sorcerer* were intended to represent half-human, half-animal deities, or were perhaps representations of shamans or shapeshifters, beings at home in both the human and animal worlds.

A clearer picture emerges in the better-known anthropomorphic gods of Egypt, namely Anubis, the jackal-headed deity who judged whether a deceased soul was worthy of entering the afterlife. His fellow gods included the falcon-headed Horus, Sobek, the crocodile river god, the feline goddess Bastet, and a veritable menagerie of others. Greek mythology is similarly littered with half-goat satyrs, human/equine centaurs, and the bull-headed minotaur. In India, the monkey god Hanuman and the benevolent elephant-headed deity Ganesha are revered, while China's legendary anthropomorphic beings include Sun Wukong the Monkey King (a notorious trickster) and

Japan's include shape-shifting and often passing-for-human kitsune foxes and tanuki raccoon dogs.

In Indigenous cultures the world over, we can find countless examples of rituals and ceremonies honoring specific animals—those who had supernatural abilities or those from whom they descended. Native Americans donned bison hides and performed the Buffalo Dance in hopes of a successful hunt and they wore eagle feathers and danced in honor of the sacred animal whose domain extended beyond the clouds. The shamans of the Pacific Northwest Nootka tribes dressed in bear skins and bear masks to "abduct" children in a ceremony bestowing adult privileges. Mesoamerican and African tribes created and wore masks of animals and human/animal hybrids for reasons ranging from religious ceremonies to intimidation of the enemy during war.

This stands in stark contrast to modern society, in which we've lost some of the intimate, direct, and even spiritual connection our ancestors had with the non-human animal world. Our relationship with that world has become mediated, denatured: cages and moats separate us from the beasts we gawk at in zoos and nature preserves. Film and TV documentaries transform animals' lives into narratives that we view safely from the comfort of our living rooms and movie theaters. The animals we rely upon for sustenance are raised and slaughtered in factory farms far from our squeamish eyes. For many of us, the closest we come to a flicker of our primal connection to animals is manifest through our domesticated companion animals, the dogs, cats, and miscellaneous critters we occasionally choose to share our homes with.

While animals have *always* had a central role in the lives of humans, the nature of that role has shifted over time. In earlier times, animals were integral to humans' spiritual and cultural lives, foundational to their systems of meaning. Today, they have been reduced to mere commodities or symbols: sports team mascots, corporate logos, advertisements[1], and, most presently relevant, cartoon characters whose antics we laughed at as children over a bowl of cereal on Saturday mornings.

The roots of these cartoon critters predate modern animation and television. Aesop (or the various ancient authors whose works are now

[1] From 2009 through 2020 photo-realistic, CGI-animated hamsters promoted the Kia Soul in a series of humorous TV commercials. A Kia executive remembers the advertising team arriving in full-body hamster suits to present the campaign. In 2007, the French soft drink Orangina began an advertising campaign centered on CGI-animated and quite attractive anthropomorphic animals; many of the commercials had adult and even erotic undertones.

credited to him) gave animals human sapience and speech as a means to tell moral tales that shed light on our human foibles and failings (the expression “sour grapes”, for example, comes from the fable of the fox who decided the out-of-reach grapes were sour and not worth the effort acquiring them.) Other examples can be found throughout literature, such as *The Canterbury Tales*, a 14th-century staple of college English Literature courses, and the “The Nun’s Priest’s Tale”, a story about a vain rooster deceived by a wily fox that would not be out of place as a Disney animated feature.[2]

Over time, fairy tales gave way to “funny animal” comic books starring both recognizable, A-List Looney Tunes and Disney superstars and, even more prominently, long-forgotten characters like Barney Rooster, Foxy Fagan, and Dizzy Dog. These characters cavorted in silly, colorful stories that (once you track them down online) would not be out of place today. They were admired by plenty of fans who would grow up to continue to be fans, including Ken Fletcher, an influential science fiction artist and a major contributor to the early furry fandom:

“My parents bought Little Golden Books and things like that before I was in kindergarten and read them to me. Funny animal comics too, like Bugs Bunny and Uncle Scrooge, and secondary comics like [those with] Andy Panda. When I was five or six, they gave me a subscription to *Walt Disney’s Comics and Stories*. I started to read before kindergarten. I recognized my first word in an Andy Panda comic: ‘BOOM’—a very distinctive, large explosion filling a panel. Once the idea lit up in my brain, I was able to learn reading by phonetics pretty quickly.”

Reed Waller, who worked with Fletcher and who similarly played an influential role on the early furry fandom, had a similar story “My parents read comics to me and [books] like *Treasure Island* and *Tom Sawyer*, whatever they thought might interest me. They kept reading me comics because I responded to them and seemed fascinated by the interaction of story and art; good judgment on their part. Their intent was to raise themselves a creative genius. They continued to read to me constantly, until I was reading to them, and drawing comics of my own. As long as I [can] remember, I wanted to be a cartoonist when I grew up.”

Ken and Reed’s paths crossed in the local Minneapolis sci-fi scene. “I’d see him at least once a month or more,” remembers Ken, “hanging out in people’s apartments. He seemed like just another guy in person, but we both

---

[2] The studio spent years trying to adapt the story into a feature before abandoning the project; instead, concept art for the film became the illustrations of a charming children’s picture book, *Chanticleer and the Fox*.

had the 'wiggle the eyebrows' persona hidden away until we trusted other people.

"I was impressed—he was just as weird or weirder [when it came to] cartooning ideas as I was. He seemed to have more natural ability to do the drawings than I did. We were certainly compatible in terms of what our general interests were. And one of the things we discovered [was that] we both liked animal comix—and enjoyed drawing them too."

Ken and Reed realized they were kindred spirits who appreciated each other's work and shared a fondness for funny animal comics, classic Looney Tunes, Fleischer animation, and underground comic artists like Robert Crumb and Vaughn Bodē. "Soon," Reed recalls, "Ken and I were regular contributors of humorous art to science fiction fanzines around the world."

Ken and Reed began to plan their own publication, one devoted to funny animals; not a fanzine but an APA—an "Amateur Press Association"—that only its contributors would receive.

"We dedicated ours to funny animal cartoons," Reed explains, "because it was the main bond between us. We were both sad that funny animals and humorous comics, in general, had died a horrible death because of the new 'seriousness' of 1970s comics like Frank Miller's 'Dark Knight' Batman—we felt they were an endangered species. We were uninterested in swords and sorcery or dark fantasy. We were cutting our teeth on Monty Python's Flying Circus, the Firesign Theater,[3] and underground comix—anarchist humor."

"We were kind of aware that we weren't alone," recalls Ken, "that there were people out there with the same interest in reconstructing, reusing funny animal tropes from the 1930s and forties who felt themselves as isolated as we did."

Ken and Reed created a one-page flyer and a sample "issue zero" promoting their planned APA. They distributed copies at the local comics convention, made use of Ken's contact list ("I'd been an active fan since 1968; at that point, I had accumulated eight years' worth of addresses"), and reached out to artists in fanzines and APAs doing funny animals (as well as to others they guessed were funny-animal friendly.) "If they're doing science-fiction aliens but doing them funny-animal style, they're probably sympathetic; let's send them an issue and see if they respond to it."

[3] The Firesign Theater was a troupe of four young L.A. comedians who created a series of surreal countercultural and extremely funny LP comedy records in the style of 1940's radio dramas.

The sample issue's cover, a joint effort by the pair, was inspired by the final panel of a 1950s *MAD* magazine spoof of the era's *Today* show.[4] Their cover depicts a chimpanzee, but their chimp was a parody of *MAD*'s parody. Dressed in a Star Trek tunic, the chimpanzee mimicked Mr. Spock's split-fingered Vulcan salute. They also adopted the *MAD* chimp's one word of dialog—"Vootie"—as their APA's title: *Vootie.* Its subtitle read "The APA of Funny Animal Fandom," while the Spock-chimp warned potential readers "NO HUMANS ALLOWED!!" They gave their publication a tongue-in-cheek political edge, declaring it "the official organ of the Funny Animal Liberation Front."

As Ken and Reed hoped, issue Zero had attracted a healthy roster of funny animal fan artists. Shepherded by a series of editors, *Vootie* ran from 1976 through 1983, producing thirty-seven issues along the way.

Those thirty-seven issues were the first stirrings of what would eventually evolve into the furry fandom.

A new, bigger and better APA was born from the ashes of *Vootie.* Just as that publication appropriated a nonsensical word spoken by a comic book chimp as its title, the new APA named itself *Rowrbrazzle* after a pseudo-profanity often bellowed by Albert Alligator, the *Pogo* comic strip's cigar-chomping saurian. Amateur artists, writers, and enthusiasts network like never before through the publication. *Rowrbrazzle*, which began as a funny-animal-centric publication, gradually evolved into a furry-themed one and attracted an assortment of fellow former *Vootie* contributors, high-profile anthro fans, and, due to its being based in Los Angeles, animation professionals like Jerry Beck (a founding member of the Cartoon Network advisory board) and Chris Sanders (director of *Lilo and Stitch*). Even though its distribution, like *Vootie*'s, was limited to its contributors, the publication soon achieved legendary status within the furry fandom. Put simply: if you were in *'brazzle*, you had it made—you were an art god.[5] If you weren't, you

---

[4] From 1953 to 1957, a chimpanzee named J. Fred Muggs was *Today*'s on-camera mascot. There was supposedly no love lost between host Dave Garroway and the chimp; the *Mad* parody concludes with "J. Fred Gluggs" usurping "Dave Garrowunway" as the show's host and appropriating his palm-in-the-air "peace" sign-off.

[5] A waiting list of artists (including me) eager to join *Rowrbrazzle* soon accumulated. I was finally accepted in 1990, when membership was increased from fifty to sixty contributors. I never considered myself an "art god," merely a mortal, half-way decent cartoonist lucky enough to see his scribbles in print alongside the work of vastly more talented artists.

wanted to see the work that was. In fact, members who were willing to let other furs xerox pages of their copy suddenly acquired lots of friends.

If *Vootie* and its successor *Rowrbrazzle* laid the foundation for the furry fandom, construction on its first floor began at the 1980 World Science Fiction Convention in Boston, when funny-animal fans discovered a portrait in the convention's art show of a sci-fi character named Erma Felna. While fans might have seen high-tech, hardware-heavy environments before in space-themed anime, what they likely hadn't seen was this sort of environment inhabited by an anthropomorphic cat.

Vootie contributors and miscellaneous animation fans at the convention were drawn to the painting—and to its creator, Steve Gallacci. They soon discovered that the piece wasn't a one-off: Steve had bought several other paintings and a briefcase full of sketches and notes for an anthropomorphic deep-space epic, something he'd been doodling for years. "For whatever reason," Steve later wrote in the third person, "his plopping in their midst as an unknown with all that material in hand was some kind of gosh-wow." Steve invited the crowd to his hotel room to look over the art he had brought and chat about their mutual interest in all things anthro. It was the first meeting of what would come to be known as a "Gallacci Group." For the next several years, whenever a convention brought them together, a Gallacci Group would spontaneously form. Almost all of those who attended were artists who brought their sketchbooks along, brimming with their own animal creations. They would talk about Erma, trade sketches, and share opinions on their favorite sci-fi movies and cartoon characters. They would discuss their own ideas for anthropomorphic epics late into the evening until Steve had to toss them out to get some rest before the convention festivities resumed in the morning.

When *Rowrbrazzle* launched in 1984, the artists gathered around Steve—and Steve himself—were an immediate talent pool for the new APA. Thanks to *Rowrbrazzle*, they didn't have to wait until the next convention to interact with one another; they could share their thoughts and opinions with everyone at once, every three months, via the APA. That same year, Steve shared Erma with the world at large via his newly published anthology comic *Albedo Anthropomorphics*. As with *Rowrbrazzle*, Erma fans didn't have to wait until the next convention to catch up with her adventures.

With *Rowrbrazzle*, the Gallacci Groups would gradually come to an end, although their creative energy and the momentum they had started would continue to gather momentum.

* * *

Just off Trask Avenue in Garden Grove, California, there exists a large ranch house that looks, more or less, like any of the other large ranch houses lining the street. There is one difference, however: an enormous tree stump, at least ten feet tall, stands in the middle of its front lawn. A sign affixed to it depicts a weasel-like animal in a high-stepping Michigan J. Frog pose, sporting a top hat and diamond-tipped cane, with a pair of antennae sprouting from his head. He's framed above and below by the words "PRANCING SKILTAIRE."

"Skiltaires are an alien species I created, based on Earth weasels and other mustelids. They're semi-biped, have a natural electro-generative 'battery,' electrostatic range sensing, and a kind of tele-empathy. I created them in 1969 when I was in high school because I was tired of all the aliens in science fiction that were just slightly different humans—and I happened to really like weasels."

The speaker is Mark Merlino who, together with his partner Rod O'Riley, owns the house known as The Prancing Skiltaire, their home for more than thirty years. Someday, there may be a historical marker attached to a tree stump as well, an engraved brass plaque reading, "Home of Mark Merlino and Rod O'Riley, creators of the Furry Fandom." This may only be a slight exaggeration. Furry has its origins at the junction of cartoon animals, anime, and science-fiction content, and it was Mark and Rod who were at the center of it all, and who ultimately named the result.

"I was a senior in high school when I met Mark," Rod O'Riley recalls. "Our science-fiction club went on a field trip to a sci-fi convention. I thought conventions were all about costuming; this was the first one I'd been to that had an art show. I was already a weasel fanatic when I saw Mark's skiltaire art in the show. When I met him, I asked why his otters had antennae. He started explaining them to me, and when he mentioned he was running the video room at the convention, I asked him if he had any *Kimba*[6] episodes."

Mark did indeed have *Kimba* episodes on hand. Rod then asked if the same held true for *The Amazing 3*—a much more obscure series than the widely distributed show about the white lion cub. "I think I have some," Mark replied.

It was the beginning, as the expression goes, of a beautiful friendship, which eventually led to an ever-more beautiful partnership as Mark and Rob became Furry's number-one power couple.

---

[6] *Kimba the White Lion* was an anime series based on a manga from the 1950s and which some have suggested was a source of inspiration for Disney's *The Lion King* due to similarities between the two.

Mark held monthly screenings of cartoons from his extensive collection at the Los Angeles Science Fiction Society's clubhouse. Fred Patten, the editor of *Rowrbrazzle*, a reviewer of furry books and anime films, an editor of furry short story anthologies, and an animation historian, was a regular attendee. Patton's appreciation and participation in all things fannish went back decades, when he cosplayed the Golden Age Flash at the 1962 Worldcon (his costume was perfect, right down to the wings adorning Jay Garrick's boots and World War I helmet.) Fred described himself as "the biggest funny animal fan around" who learned to read when he was four from newspaper comic strips and *Walt Disney's Comics and Stories*.

Fred, Mark, and others organized the screenings into an animation fan club. On Saturday, May 21, 1977, four days before the premiere of the original *Star Wars* movie, the first official meeting of the Cartoon/Fantasy Organization—the C/FO—was held with a program consisting entirely of *Kimba* and giant-robot TV episodes, another anime specialty.

The C/FO screenings also attracted funny-animal fans, there for anime series starring anthropomorphic characters like Kimba, *The Amazing 3*'s Bonnie Bunny, and *Fables of the Green Forest*'s Johnny Woodchuck. Many of the attendees hadn't met each other previously; the C/FO screenings were their first chance to network with other anime fans who also enjoyed anthro characters—people destined to become some of the earliest members of furry fandom.

At a 1985 "Westercon," Mark and his partner, Rod O'Riley, decided it was time to throw a funny-animal room party. They needed a name for the event, something to put on the flyers publicizing it. It didn't take them long to decide the gathering would be a "Prancing Skiltaire" party, in honor of Mark and Rod's Garden Grove residence.

The event itself was a fairly low-key affair, with Mark screening videos from his voluminous cartoon collection, including the funny-animal fan favorite, *Animalympics*. New faces joined the regulars, people who had been drawing or imagining their own anthros, but who never had a crowd to hang out with before. They perused each other's sketchbooks and traded opinions on all things anthropomorphic between occasional glances at the *Looney Tunes* episodes currently onscreen.

Building upon the success of the event, Mark and Rod hosted funny-animal-themed parties at other conventions in the following months. They attracted more fans, almost none of whom had expected to find others who shared their distinct interest in anthropomorphic animals.

When it came time for the next Westercon, Mark and Rod decided to call their party by a different name. They decided that the 1986 iteration of the party would officially be known as a "furry party."

They decided on the term "furry" instead of "funny animals" for a few reasons, the most apparent of which was the fact that not all of the cartoons were "funny," with the case of Erma Felna being a prominent example. Other adjectives had been floating around, including "fluffy" and "fuzzy" among them. Mark credits a former Skiltaire resident and self-proclaimed non-furry known as "Dr. Pepper" (no relation to the soft drink) for the adjective furry.[7] Mark and friends blanketed Westercon and subsequent conventions with flyers featuring attractively drawn anthro characters promoting furry parties. The fans who attended started calling both themselves and their anthropomorphic characters "furries," and their shared interest was dubbed the "furry fandom." From that point onward, the adjective was indelibly cemented to the noun. As Rod O'Riley put it years later, "We didn't start [the] furry fandom, we just introduced it to itself."

The premiere furry party was a success, and a tradition was born: Furry parties (and the illustrated flyers promoting them) became a mainstream tradition at science fiction conventions.

Encouraged by the growing attendance at these furry room parties, Mark, Rod, and a few others organized a furries-only convention dubbed "ConFurence" to be held in January 1989 in Costa Mesa, California, not far from the Skiltaire. Its official title was "ConFurence Zero." It wasn't a real convention so much as it was a dry run for an *actual* ConFurence they had hoped to run a year later. Sixty-five furs from all over North America (and one from Australia) showed up to mostly lounge around the lobby of the Costa Mesa Holiday Inn. The program book (more of a pamphlet, really) featured statements from Mark ("Some people criticize Furries as 'wish-fulfillment' or a mask we wear to hide ourselves. My experience leads me to believe the opposite is true. Your Furry is the face that lies behind the mask [you] wear in everyday life") and from Rod ("We are not, as it turns out, a new fandom. We are an old, very basic fandom that has been waiting its turn to proudly shout its name in public."). Others contributed an assortment of

---

[7] An Australian fur and an American one who are friends have each told me the *other* first used "furry" in a 1983 fanzine. Thirty-plus years later, it seems less important who said it first. Maybe Dr. Pepper had read that particular fanzine when coming up with the adjective, or perhaps it was just a case of furry minds thinking alike.

furry art to the pamphlet and even a tutorial on how to "Make Your Own Tail."

For those sixty-five furries, the lure was irresistible. What could be better than a furry party that lasted the entire weekend? They would get their answer one year later when, in 1990, the first "official" ConFurence attracted 130 furs. Year by year, the numbers kept rising as word spread: 250 for ConFurence 2 in 1991, over 400 for ConFurence 3. By ConFurence 9 in 1998, attendance peaked at 1,250 furs—an increase of over *1800%* over a decade. The furry fandom had arrived—and it wasn't going away.

* * *

Most people—including most furs—don't realize that, despite the attention given to fursuits as the most iconic and recognizable aspect of the furry fandom today, furry was started by cartoonists and fans of funny animals, animation, and anime. Fursuits came along later, once the fandom was well-established.[8]

In fact, it was a bit of a surprise to cartoonists when fursuiters started showing up in growing numbers at conventions, with some seeing them as interlopers invading "our" art-centric fandom. In hindsight, it really shouldn't have been a surprise that fursuits became a popular form of anthro self-expression. After all, costume contests and masquerades have been part of sci-fi, comic, and anime conventions since their inception, and overlap prominently with the LARP (live-action role play) and Renaissance Faire communities. It would, if anything, be an anomaly to find that there weren't at least some fans of anthropomorphic characters who would be interested in expressing themselves in the same way. However, the pendulum may have arguably swung too far in the opposite direction, with many people (including younger furs) believing that one *has* to own and wear a fursuit to be considered a furry. To be sure, fursuits are now an established and sizeable presence in the furry community, although they are hardly cheap (see Chapter 8 for more on this).

In Furry's early years, there were a handful of fursuit builders with the skill to craft fursuits for those who were interested in them. Today, hundreds of makers exist, offering all manner of customization options. The best of

---

[8] One could argue that fursuits were present at the beginning of it all, even if they weren't a focal point. There was a single fursuiter at ConFurence Zero—a professional Disneyland mascot performer who showed up not as one of Walt's creations, but as a "Bambioid," a sexy outer-space deer partial to knee-high leather boots!

these makers have waiting lists that are longer than a year, with some holding auctions for a slot in their waiting list.

For those who can't afford a suit, or for whom they prefer a more do-it-yourself approach—there are countless tutorials, online resources, templates, and tools available. It is easier than ever for novice builders to hone their skills through practice and the sharing of knowledge in the community. In fact, many professional makers got their start constructing their own suits, only to become skilled enough to take on clients themselves.

*　　　　*　　　　*

Midwest FurFest and Anthrocon—America's two largest furry conventions—both grew out of (or outgrew) the mainstream science fiction conventions that had originally hosted their "furry track" of anthro-themed programming. Anthrocon—born in 1997 as "Albany Anthrocon"—gradually pulled furry attendees away from Philcon, due to its exclusive focus on furry content. Likewise, Midwest FurFest originated as the furry track at Chicago's Duckon convention.[9]

We can find an illustrative example of the variety of responses of the general public to furry conventions by looking at these two conventions. Midwest FurFest (or MFF as it's known for short) has a larger attendance than Anthrocon (due to its proximity to Chicago's O'Hare airport, a destination for direct flights from countries around the world). Nevertheless, MFF's presence goes largely unknown in the nearby metropolis.

In contrast, Anthrocon has been held in the heart of Pittsburgh at its downtown convention center every year since 2006 and has been embraced by the city in a way that furry has not been embraced by any other city in the world; banners celebrating Anthrocon hang from the city's lampposts, while the local media give the furry convention glowing coverage. Parents bring their kids downtown to take their photo posing with the fursuiters, while the convention's fursuit parade, which previously only looped through the convention center, now makes its way outside the building to entertain the thousand-plus Pittsburghers who wait hours to enjoy the magical sight of an endless procession of fantastical animals marching by. In 2022, Anthrocon and the city added a furry block party to the festivities, giving people the opportunity to mingle with the fursuiters on the street fronting the convention center.

*　　　　*　　　　*

---

[9] Despite its name, *Duckon*, had nothing to do with ducks, anthropomorphic or otherwise.

We started this chapter by pointing out that an interest in anthropomorphic animals has been a fairly universal part of the human condition for as long as the historical record has existed. Over time, humans have gradually seemed to distance themselves from the natural world, and have seemed to lose some of that connection to animals.

Furries, however, may represent a counterpoint to this broader trend, one that, while starting in the United States in the 1970s and 1980s, has spread to become a global phenomenon. Furry conventions are now held worldwide, including in Mexico, Canada, England, France, Germany, Hungary, Belgium, Austria, Russia, The Netherlands, Brazil, Argentina, Australia, Japan, China, and South Korea – to name just a few countries. Its global appeal may represent a return, or at least a lingering sense of familiarity, of that primal interest to understand ourselves and the world we inhabit by blurring the divide between humans and those we inhabit this planet with.

Chapter 3

Furtuity: The Story of Furscience[1]

Kathleen Gerbasi, Courtney "Nuka" Plante,
Sharon Roberts, Stephen Reysen, Elizabeth Fein

Albert Bandura was one of the most influential psychologists of the second half of the 20th century. In his work, he discussed the role of fortuity and chance encounters in life, stating that "under certain conditions... fortuitous events set in motion constellations of influences that alter the course of lives" (Bandura, 1982, 1998, p. 95). Fortuity is one of those things we only seem to recognize in hindsight, and it's through this lens that we reflect on the history of how our furry research team, Furscience, developed and the role of "*furtuity*" in how we got here.

Dr. Gerbasi and Our First Study

In truth, the real credit for the origins of Furscience could well be given to *BoB the DoG. BoB* was a gigantic, intensely social golden retriever who greeted everyone he met with a big grin and a warm wag. *BoB* became part of Dr. Gerbasi's family largely through chance. He was the last of his litter and an outcast because his size violated breed standards.[2] Because of *BoB's* engaging personality, he and Dr. Gerbasi were invited to visit the local nursing home throughout the 1990s so that *BoB* could share his joy with everyone who wanted to meet him. *BoB* was ultimately recognized for his service by being named Western New York Nursing Home Volunteer of the Year!

But what, you may ask, does *BoB* have to do with furry research?

While Dr. Gerbasi has been a lifelong "dog" person[3] and animal lover, she had not followed the developing research on Animal Assisted Therapy or any of its related phenomena (now broadly referred to as Animal Assisted Interventions; Fine, 2010). Dr. Gerbasi did, however, become curious about the state of scientific knowledge on the health benefits of associating with non-human animals as a result of her work accompanying *BoB* as a nursing

---

[1] This chapter is dedicated to the memory of Dr. Penny L. Bernstein, without whose support, interest, enthusiasm and Kent State (Stark) University's institutional review board, this furry research team would have never begun.

[2] Because *BoB* was an enormous dog for his breed, he was readily recognizable. *BoB* was a local celebrity, and Dr. Gerbasi thinks he could have probably been elected mayor of the village where they took their walks, if only their official residence had been within the village limits!

[3] No offense to cats, it's just that Dr. Gerbasi is very allergic to them!

home visitor.[4] Eventually, she enrolled in an online course offered by People-Animals-Nature (PAN) through DePaul University.

After taking the course, Dr. Gerbasi became interested in the field of anthrozoology more broadly.[5] As a social psychologist, she was already focused on the scientific study of how humans think about, influence, and relate to one another, and so, given her life-long interest in all species of animals, it was only natural for her to be drawn to anthrozoology; it was easy for her to imagine that relationships between humans and non-human animals may share a number of similarities with relationships between humans. Numerous studies show that to be the case, on subjects as varied as attachment, abuse, empathy, and social support, to name just a few (e.g., Angantry, 2011; Arluke et al., 1999; Carlisle-Frank & Frank, 2006; Greenebaum, 2004; Herzog, 2010; Julius et al., 2013; Topál et al., 1998).

As part of her growing interest in anthrozoology, Dr. Gerbasi led an archival study on the immense growth of HAS from the 1980s through the 1990s (Gerbasi et al., 2002). She discovered that the number of HAS dissertations had more than doubled in that time and that 27 different academic disciplines had produced doctoral dissertations in HAS (e.g., psychology, sociology, anthropology, geography, philosophy, nursing, and agriculture). She also observed that the study of HAS was a somewhat risky business at the time, in that most HAS dissertations did not come from high-prestige universities. Or, to put it another way, in high-status universities, where young scholars face the plight of "publish or perish," studying a newly emerging field might be a career killer.

Because of her growing interest in anthrozoology and her 2002 article, Dr. Ken Shapiro invited Dr. Gerbasi to become the moderator for an online HAS discussion group sponsored by Psychologists for the Ethical Treatment of Animals (PsyETA), known today as the Animals and Society Institute (http://www.animalsandsociety.org/main/). In her capacity as group moderator, Dr. Gerbasi responded to requests for information that other list members had left unanswered. It was in this context that Dr. Gerbasi had her first fortuitous encounter with furries.

---

[4] And later Dan and Sparky, two of her other canine family members who took turns with *BoB*!

[5] Anthrozoology is defined as the study of the relationships or interactions between humans and other species of animals, also referred to as Human-Animal Studies (HAS). And while the study of Animal Assisted Interventions (AAI) is a part of anthrozoology, anthrozoology is a much broader field.

One day early in the 2000s, a request came through the HAS online group asking if anyone knew anything about furries. Dr. Gerbasi waited a day or two for someone to respond. Alas, no one did. Ever a dutiful scholar, Dr. Gerbasi turned to a psychological database to see if there were any published psychological articles on the subject of furries—something she knew nothing about herself—only to find nothing.[6] She followed her fruitless *PsycINFO* search up with a more general Google search for information about furries. The most popular response was an article on furries published in *Vanity Fair* (Gurley, 2001). Unaccustomed as Dr. Gerbasi was to reading *Vanity Fair*, she was pretty shocked by the claims being made about furries in the article, which seemed to be based on very limited observations and interviews with a small number of furries. As a social psychologist and now a budding anthrozoologist, the study of furries represented the ultimate merging of her two areas of academic interest—an exciting prospect!

At the time, Dr. Gerbasi was teaching at Niagara County Community College, which is part of the State University of New York system. As a fairly small, teaching-focused college, conducting research was not typically part of the job description. As such, unbound by the "publish or perish" mentality of bigger departments, she had the freedom to study whatever she wanted as long as it didn't impact her teaching and department responsibilities. As luck would have it, Dr. Gerbasi was also teaching a research methods class at around the same time she was "learning" about furries from *Vanity Fair*. Her students were fascinated by the idea of learning about furries and tried to find any peer-reviewed journal articles that might explain what the *Vanity Fair* article was describing. Despite acquiring a sizable stack of journal articles on fetishes,[7] they concluded that these articles had little to say about furries or the furry fandom specifically.

A few years later, another chance encounter —"an unintended meeting of persons unfamiliar to each other" (Bandura, 1982, p. 748)—would find Dr. Gerbasi. As she was sitting in an office, Justin Higner, a student of the anthropology professor with whom Dr. Gerbasi shared an office, came looking for the anthropologist, who happened to not be in. Justin had a large

---

[6] Well, *almost* nothing—she *did* find an article on "the furry ceiling," proposed by Raupp (2002) to describe the rather limited reference to non-human animals in clinical psychology. She was pretty sure, however, that this was not what the inquirer was asking about.

[7] Dr. Gerbasi dreaded the phone calls from her college's interlibrary loan department, which would usually start with, "Dr. Gerbasi, we have another fetish article for you!"

art portfolio with him and asked if Dr. Gerbasi wanted to see his artwork. Not wanting to be rude, she agreed and took a look.

Dr. Gerbasi nearly fell out of her chair at what she saw! It looked, to her, like furry art. She asked Justin if that's what it was, and he said yes, confirming that he was, himself, a furry. Both were astonished—he, that Dr. Gerbasi recognized furry art, and she, that she had finally met a real furry! Dr. Gerbasi gently suggested that Justin might want to take her Psychology of Human-Animal Relations course, sweetening the deal by letting him write a paper about furries. He accepted and took the course in the fall of 2005. And, as promised, he did get to write a paper about furries. Justin also asked Dr. Gerbasi if she thought the college would send him to a furry convention. When asked why he thought the college would send him to a furry convention, he simply replied because he wanted to go to one. While Dr. Gerbasi was absolutely certain that the college would not send him to a furry convention, it gave her the idea to look into where the nearest furry convention was. In another bout of fortuity, she discovered that Anthrocon was relocating to Pittsburgh, Pennsylvania, less than a four-hour car ride away from her college.

Of course, ethical guidelines dictate that one cannot simply show up at a convention and start collecting data without permission to do so from the convention itself. The chair of Anthrocon was Dr. Samuel Conway, known in the furry fandom as Uncle Kage. Fortuity struck again, as Dr. Conway was, himself, a research scientist (albeit a chemist, not a psychologist), and understood the scientific method and the importance of data collection. He also clearly understood how the media worked and was open to a scientific perspective on furries to shed light on the more sensationalized approach to furries that the media frequently took. Dr. Gerbasi explained to Dr. Conway that she would let the data do the talking and that this would be one of the first psychological studies of furries[8]—and would finally give psychologists

---

[8] We should clarify here that this was one of the first empirical, psychological studies of furries, but it was not the first, nor was it the only attempt to study furries happening at around this time. We'd be remiss if we didn't mention David Rust's 1998 survey of the furry fandom—a survey which, while not conducted through a university or published in a peer-reviewed journal, nevertheless represents one of the first attempts of furries to study their own fandom. It was followed up by a replication not long after Dr. Gerbasi's first Anthrocon study (Evans, 2008), as well as with a large-scale general survey of the furry fandom by Alex Osaki (2008) and with work by Rossmassler and Wen (2007). An in-depth compilation of scholarly writing on the furry fandom is beyond the focus of this chapter, but has been

a peer-reviewed article about furries, rather than having to rely on outlets like *Vanity Fair*.

Dr. Conway agreed to let the research team attend Anthrocon and attempt to collect survey data, although he warned that almost no furries would want to complete the survey. Ever an optimist, Dr. Gerbasi figured there was no way to know if furries would take a survey unless someone tried! Dr. Conway also mentioned that, on the off chance some furries *did* complete the survey, there was no way to assess whether the participants constituted a representative sample (see Chapter 4 for more on this). Dr. Gerbasi assured him that, as a social psychologist, she was well aware of sampling issues and how they can impact a study's validity, and Dr. Conway seemed relieved to hear that.[9] Dr. Gerbasi was certain that she had cleared the most difficult hurdle.

Boy, was she wrong.

Another significant hurdle was obtaining ethics approval to conduct the study from an Institutional Review Board (IRB). In modern social science, it's essential to protect the well-being of one's participants, something that requires a review by an ethics committee. Unfortunately, Dr. Gerbasi's small community college didn't have an IRB. When Dr. Gerbasi looked for a free-standing, for-profit IRB, the price they quoted for a review was in the ballpark of $25,000—completely out of the realm of possibility. She then approached her biologist/anthrozoologist friend, Dr. Penny Bernstein, whose specialty was human/cat relations. Fortuitously, Dr. Bernstein was interested in collaborating on a study about furries, and her college, Kent State in Canton, Ohio, did have an IRB. Hurdle number two was cleared!

Yet another challenge came from the fact that, despite being a half-day drive from her college, Dr. Gerbasi was not going to be anywhere near Pittsburgh when Anthrocon was being held in 2006; she would be at her daughter's Ph.D. graduation ceremony that weekend on the other side of the country, at Stanford University. As such, Dr. Gerbasi needed a colleague who was willing to travel to Pittsburgh, attend Anthrocon, and run the study that Dr. Gerbasi had set in place. Enter Professor Laura Scaletta, another psychology professor at Niagara County Community College. She was not

---

compiled by the furry scholar yerf on their website: https://yerfology.wordpress.com/furry-in-academia/

[9] Dr. Conway mentioned that, in his line of work, which involved molecules instead of people, one never has to worry about molecules refusing to participate!

only up for the adventure, but helped design the survey and took several student assistants to Anthrocon to collect the data.[10]

The survey itself was designed to test the assertions made by Gurley in the *Vanity Fair* article, as well as to test whether there was a correlation between being a furry and various psychological variables. Dr. Scaletta hypothesized that if furries really believed they were not human or did not want to be human, this might be an indicator of a personality disorder. Dr. Gerbasi's thinking at the time was that if furries did not think they were human or if they wanted to be non-human, it seemed somewhat analogous to Gender Identity Disorder (GID), as it was referred to at the time (American Psychiatric Association, 2000), insofar as both seemed to involve feelings of discomfort with one's body.[11] As such, the survey included indicators of possible personality disorders, items adapted from a measure of GID, and questions developed from the *Vanity Fair* article (e.g., furries have beards, wear glasses, are gay men, work in fields involving computers, do not think they are humans, and do not want to be humans.)

This first study (Gerbasi et al., 2008) illustrated one of the best things about science: it was full of surprises! Perhaps the biggest surprise was the fact that furries were willing to participate in our study at all. More than 200 furries—10% of Anthrocon's attendance that year—participated in the study! Another big surprise was the fact that, when it comes to measures of personality disorder indicators, they were much more likely to be ascribed to college students than they were to furries. Finally, the study showed that there might be something to the idea that some furries—particularly those who didn't consider themselves to be 100% human and who wanted to be 0% human, were more likely to say that they didn't feel entirely comfortable in their own bodies.[12]

---

[10] Among the assistants was, of course, Justin, the furry anthropology student from Fall 2005!

[11] We note that Dr. Gerbasi was working within the frameworks of the time. As we point out in Chapter 20, we don't pathologize people who feel like they are not completely human, and we now know that people who do not identify as human are actually therians or otherkin, not furries. Moreover, the comparison to GID was only done to make a comparison to a condition that involved feelings of dysmorphia, or discomfort with one's own body, not to suggest that they had the same mechanisms or were the same thing at all!

[12] Of course, the study also found that most furries do not fall into this category, and do see themselves as fully human and would not choose to become non-human!

In the following year, Dr. Gerbasi submitted a poster about the original furry study to the Society for Research in Identity Formation (SRIF; Gerbasi, Paolone et al., 2007) and also offered a panel discussion on the topic (Gerbasi, Harris, & Jorgensen, 2007). She invited Dr. Conway to participate as an expert, but he was unavailable on the scheduled date. Instead, Dr. Conway put her in touch with some highly-regarded furries in the Washington, DC area where the conference was being held. She met with Karl Jorgensen and Brian Harris, who not only participated in the panel discussion at SRIF, but they generously gave Dr. Gerbasi a ton of great advice on how to get more people to participate at Anthrocon[13] and introduced her to the concepts of otherkin, therianthropy, and the therian identity, topics which would become the eventual focus of her work in the furry fandom.

At Anthrocon 2007, Dr. Gerbasi conducted a modified replication of the first study. Not long after, she wrote what would become the first piece of empirical psychological research on the furry fandom, *Furries From A to Z*, (Gerbasi et al., 2008).[14] By 2008, Dr. Gerbasi was running another study at Anthrocon, this time including a measure of finger length ratios based on prior research suggesting that it's a proxy measure for testosterone and, by extension, sex and sexual orientation (Putz, 2004). This would become known as the great Xerox machine adventure, a valiant attempt to measure furries' finger digit ratios by photocopying so, so many hands and then calculating finger length ratios from it.[15] 2008 was also the year that Dr. Gerbasi began presenting a panel at Anthrocon, reviewing the findings from

---

[13] One piece of advice was to give a prize for participating in the study. Since the research had no source of external funding, this seemed infeasible. Karl and Brian pointed out that it didn't have to be: furries *love* having ribbons to put on their convention badges, and ribbon is quite affordable! Dr. Gerbasi found the most eye-catching multicolor paw print ribbon she could and, since then, it's been a staple of our research, a small token of appreciation to furries who complete our survey. It also served to advertise the research project because it prompted other furries to ask how they, too, could get a ribbon!

[14] The article was published in the journal *Society & Animals*, for which Dr. Gerbasi owes a great debt of gratitude to Dr. Ken Shapiro, the journal editor, for being open to the publication of research about furries. While the topic of furries, anthropomorphism, zoomorphism, and anthrozoomorphism clearly fit within the parameters of a HAS publication, he was probably going out on a limb accepting an article on such a novel topic!

[15] Sadly, this methodology turned out to be too messy and imprecise, and yielded nothing of interest.

previous years, discussing that year's hypotheses, and seeking feedback and ideas for future studies—the start of a tradition that we continue to this day.

It was during one of these sessions that a furry asked us about autism in the furry fandom (see Chapter 23 for more on this). Following up on this suggestion, in 2009 Dr. Gerbasi attempted to measure the characteristics of people on the autism spectrum using a measure called the ASQ (Baron-Cohen, 2001). This caused some problems with the Kent State IRB, as the fact that we wanted to measure traits of autism suggested, to them, that we were studying an "at-risk" population that needed special consideration. Cutting it far closer than she would have liked, Dr. Gerbasi got IRB permission the day before Anthrocon, and the study went off without a hitch.[16]

Enter: Dr. Courtney "Nuka" Plante and Dr. Stephen Reysen

Another moment of monumental fortuity would occur not long after, in 2010. Dr. Gerbasi was asked to present her research at the very first Furnal Equinox furry convention in Toronto, Canada.[17] After completing her presentation and chatting with the audience, one attendee said, "My friend has to meet you, he wants to study furries too!" Dr. Gerbasi gave him a copy of her 2008 furry article from her car to pass onto his friend and asked him to have his friend contact her.

The friend in question was Dr. Courtney "Nuka" Plante who, at the time, was not a doctor but, rather, a new graduate student in Social Psychology at the University of Waterloo in Waterloo, Ontario, Canada. Like many young graduate students, he was trying to figure a lot of things out about himself and this new life he had chosen, which had taken him from his home in Edmonton, Alberta, and across the country for his studies. One of the things he was trying to figure out was what he should study for his thesis project, as he felt directionless. He'd been told to focus on the things that most interested him, but for him, that was playing video games and, as he'd only

---

[16] Funnily enough, the results did not support the hypothesis that furries were particularly represented on the Autism spectrum, at least as measured by the ASQ. These findings would later be contradicted by much of our future research on the subject years later.

[17] The Canadian border crossing guard was initially suspicious when Dr. Gerbasi said she was crossing to attend a furry convention. When asked to provide proof, Dr. Gerbasi showed them a copy of *Furries From A to Z* that she happened to have in the car. It was enough to convince them, and she was allowed to proceed.

recently discovered, furries.[18] And while there were ample examples of researchers studying video games, he didn't know of any psychologists studying furries.

That is, until Dr. Plante's furry friend, Edolon, excitedly returned, research paper in hand. He skeptically read the paper, half-expecting it to be little more than an opinion piece or some unsubstantiated claims about furries—as that was pretty much the only thing anyone had to say about furries in popular media at the time. To his surprise, however, this seemed like the "real deal," and he quickly got in touch with Dr. Gerbasi.

This is how Dr. Plante and Dr. Gerbasi ended up working together at Anthrocon 2010. They broadened the focus of the study, including measures of dehumanization (a topic of interest for Dr. Plante at the time) and fanship (see Chapter 6; Reysen & Branscombe, 2010), which was a topic of interest for Dr. Gerbasi. To measure fanship, she used a scale developed by Dr. Stephen Reysen, an up-and-coming expert in fan psychology. She contacted Dr. Reysen for permission to use the scale in the relatively novel context of furries, and he enthusiastically supported the idea. A few months later, he contacted Dr. Gerbasi to let her know that there was a furry convention near him in Texas called Texas Furry Fiesta and that he could put together a team to study furries there. They agreed, and Dr. Plante tagged along with Dr. Reysen to his first study at Texas Furry Fiesta, a tradition that could continue for more than a decade afterward. Not long afterward, Dr. Plante proposed dubbing the collaboration the International Anthropomorphic Research Project (IARP),[19] and the team ran their first large-scale online survey of furries, their largest study to date, with more than 5,000 participants!

---

[18] Dr. Plante had begun calling himself a furry as an undergraduate, where he met his first furry friend, Ocean, who had helped him discover that there were others like him. He eventually became part of the furry fandom and started going by his fursona's name, Nuka.

[19] The name was somewhat out of necessity, to give their research project a bit more credibility. To that point, whenever they were asked about their research, they had to describe it as "research on furries"—a subject that wasn't taken very seriously at all. By calling themselves the IARP, they reframed their research as an international collaboration between social scientists studying anthropomorphic phenomena (really, just putting big words together to make it sound more complex than "research on furries")—it was enough to give it the air of credibility, even if it was a mouthful to say!

Dr. Sharon E. Roberts

2011 would be a year just as filled with furtuity as 2009 and 2010 were! Dr. Plante, still a graduate student, was saddled with one of the most soul-draining tasks foisted upon graduate students: exam proctoring.[20] At one point, he found himself proctoring a final exam for Dr. Sharon Roberts, a sociology professor. Being from different fields and working out of buildings on the opposite side of campus from one another, the two had never crossed paths. When Dr. Plante showed up before the exam, he was expecting to make small talk with Dr. Roberts as a matter of politeness before settling into the boring task.

It was during this idle chit-chat that Dr. Roberts asked him what he was currently researching. While he was accustomed to hearing this question, the truth was that he was working on a dozen different projects, most of which were fairly mundane compared to his furry research. Normally, he would describe one of the more mundane projects, if only to avoid a raised eyebrow and skepticism about the validity of whatever they were doing in the social psychology department. Maybe it was his exhaustion, or perhaps the sheer boredom from a week of proctoring exams, but on that day Dr. Plante chose to tell Dr. Roberts about his weirdest line of research, just to get a rise out of her, especially if she had heard anything about furries in the popular.

Dr. Roberts had indeed heard of furries and was immediately *very* excited. Her main source of information about furries was the infamous CSI episode, *Fur and Loathing* (see Chapter 21 for more on this), but, rather than weirding her out, it had only intrigued her as a researcher—she had always been interested in studying furries, though she'd never had the opportunity.[21] As a person who seizes upon an opportunity when it presents itself, Dr. Roberts became the fourth co-founder of the IARP in the 15 minutes it took to set up the exams in the room.

---

[20] For the uninitiated, university final exams take place over approximately two weeks at the end of a semester, seven days a week, from morning until late in the evening. Each of these exams needs to be monitored not only by a professor, but by additional proctors who patrol the room and monitor for cheating. To a graduate student trying to pay for a trip home for Christmas, it means 30-40 hours spent walking around eerily silent rooms full of terrified undergraduate students writing exams. It's about as exciting as it sounds.

[21] In a distinct *lack* of furtuity, Dr. Roberts had presented some of her own research at the biennial Society for Research on Identity Formation (SRIF) conference in 2001, 2003, 2005, 2009, 2013, 2015, and 2017. One of the only years she missed, 2007, was the year in which Dr. Gerbasi presented her furry research!

That fortuitous meeting completely shifted Dr. Roberts' career trajectory, as the furry research had done for everyone else on the team. From that point forward, furries were an important focus for her data collection, publishing, and funding pursuits. To her, the data spoke volumes about how the furry community was unfairly maligned by much of the media. She directed her energy towards evidence-based, anti-stigma efforts and saw an opportunity to forge a win-win partnership with the furry community, conventions, and the media that would be central to the success of the IARP's research and dissemination. To this end, Dr. Roberts forged a number of important collaborations and sought out several key opportunities for the project—reflecting something Dr. Plante once said of her: "If you send her off on her own at a convention, she'll come back with a new collaboration."[22] She was the driving force behind the team getting a number of important research grants, which has helped to fund much of our efforts.[23]

The Birth of Furscience

During 2013-2015, the IARP saw growing success as we published our findings in numerous outlets (Gerbasi et al., 2015; Mock et al., 2013; Plante et al., 2014a, 2014b, 2015a, 2015b; Reysen 2015a, 2015b, 2015c; Roberts et al., 2015a, 2015b, 2015c). This was *not* an easy task, but the more we published, the stronger our grant applications became. Likewise, the more our work was funded by our institutions and government-led funding agencies,[24] the more we were able to conduct more ambitious projects and publish that work in a wider range of outlets.

Despite this success, there was a feeling of discontent about the inability of our work to make an impact on public discourse. Despite our ever-growing body of peer-reviewed research—research that handily refuted the stigmatizing sentiments put forth in sensationalistic media—we recognized that we had a limited ability to hold court in the "attention economy" if all

---

[22] From her own perspective, Dr. Roberts sees it as a matter of "the harder you work, the luckier you get." As an illustrative example, she knew that she wanted to study trauma and resilience in the furry fandom, but also knew that her lack of qualification would make it hard to do so. She solved that problem by getting a Master of Social Work Degree in 2021—something she completed while simultaneously working fulltime as a professor.

[23] Tom Barber, who an awards officer at the University of Waterloo, was also a *tremendous* help to the IARP as we secured larger and larger grants.

[24] A big shoutout to Canada and the Social Sciences and Humanities Research Council of Canada (SSHRC) for helping to fund a significant portion of our research!

we brought to the table was peer-reviewed scholarship in its original format.[25] Ultimately, publishing our work in scientific journals wasn't making a difference in the real world because it wasn't getting into the hands of the people who needed it the most. If we were going to make a difference in reaching the public and injecting our research into the media narrative, we had to go beyond traditional methods of disseminating and mobilizing our findings.

One day, while Dr. Roberts and Dr. Plante were sitting together in Dr. Roberts' office, musing about how to get our research into the hands of more people, this conversation happened:

Dr. R: *"Maybe we could create some kind of public communication video series with a YouTube station!"*

Dr. P: *"You mean a YouTube channel?"*

Dr. R: *"Yeah! It should have 'furry' in its name."*

Dr. P: *"It should have 'science' in its name. Furries love science. Whenever they walk past our table at a convention or we give them one of our surveys they yell 'For Science!!!' at us."*

Dr. R: *"It's Furry Science."*

Dr. P: *"It's Furscience!"*

In fact, in 2015, we documented these musings in a chapter written for *Furries Among Us*:

> *"Despite evidence that they function well psychologically... furries nevertheless perceive and experience significant stigma from the world around them. Our one clinical paper is not going to change this reality substantially... furries are regularly misrepresented in popular media as sexual deviants, immature, or deserving of mockery... At this point, the IARP is working on finding alternatives to the mainstream media. We have begun the process of collecting and producing our own media footage that tells the story rooted in science, not conjecture, prejudice, or "informed" by screenwriters bent on sexing up a story to play on people's fears and distrust of the unknown or the different. We have several projects on the go that we plan to release as we gain funds. One is Just Like You* which is an anti-stigma outreach for anthropomorphic communities. These will be original public service announcement commercials designed to help the public become interested in learning more about the furry fandom. The second project is Furscience—an*

[25] Say what you will about scientific reading, but it's not exactly "light" reading, nor is it easily accessible to the general public—most articles are unfortunately locked behind paywalls put up by journals themselves.

original educational show designed to provide an accurate public [friendly] account of the furry fandom. None currently exists. The raw footage (furries' Speaker's Corner interviews), which is partially collected, will be fused with existing data/research to produce a quirky, factually accurate media outreach/education project... We hope that the work that we do will continue to inform the public about furries..." (Roberts et al., 2015c, pp. 166-168).

Looking back on the seeds of the Furscience vision—to insert our research into the public domain—evokes many kinds of emotions. They were big dreams with the odds stacked against us. We wanted to change minds with information that opposed much of the public's preconceived misunderstanding of furries and their fandom. But our facts needed to be more than just true—they needed to compete with the multimillion-dollar visual spectacle and sensationalistic narratives. We also needed the media to be able to find us—four researchers spread across a continent whose work was largely published behind restrictive paywalls wasn't going to cut it. What we needed was some expertise that none of us possessed.[26]

Enter Malicious Beaver

Malicious Beaver, the furry moniker of our Creative and Communications Director (CCD), has helped shape the launch of the IARP's rebrand into *Furscience*, which would be the public face for our team's evidence dissemination to furries, the non-furry public, scholars, and the media in general. He'd been "beavering away" quietly behind the scenes of the IARP since 2011, although he officially became our CCD in 2016 with the goal of helping us communicate our findings to the public and beyond, and to go where furries often didn't want to go—directly to the media. However, he recognized the need to do so on our terms—armed with facts presented in a compelling way that was easy to understand.

With more than a decade of experience in marketing, communications, art direction, brand and concept development, Malicious Beaver helped Furscience reach broader and more diverse audiences, not just by putting our facts against the internet's (or whoever's) fiction of what a furry is, but by showcasing and packaging our facts in a way that makes the truth about

[26] It's rather unfortunate that many researchers in general, including several on our own team, are so bad at self-promotion. Perhaps it's because of the imposter effect, the tendency for experts to feel inadequate or to underestimate their competence because of a growing awareness of how much they don't know (Bravata et al., 2020), but it would be nice if experts could sometimes speak with at least some of the volume that uninformed pundits do.

furries more interesting and worth writing about. Beaver was able to articulate a brand and communications strategy that distilled our foundational peer-reviewed data into messages that the mainstream media could more easily understand, find compelling, and which would make accurately writing about furries easier and more eye-catching than rehashing the same old, overused, fictionalized, and sensationalized stereotypes. His overall brand strategy for Furscience has been to present complex concepts without sacrificing accuracy, making them visually and rhetorically compelling to compete with less substantive, clickbait headlines. Our Furscience brand is more than just a logo: it's a visual identity purpose-driven to convey both the seriousness of the science surrounding furries and how fun furries can be.

New Areas of Research and New Additions to the Team

For years we were in dire need of a clinical psychologist on our team, given the numerous areas of research we wanted to study (e.g., autism, mental health) but fell outside our team's general area of expertise (i.e., social psychology, anthrozoology, sociology). Once again, fortuity struck! Ideally, we were looking for a fairly new Ph.D. faculty member who had yet to fully establish a research program—as was the case with Dr. Plante, Dr. Reysen, and Dr. Roberts when they joined the team. To this end, Dr. Gerbasi scoured the faculty pages of psychology departments in and around Pittsburgh, given that Pittsburgh is where our team conducted its largest annual convention study—meaning it would be less of an ask for a new faculty member to travel to Anthrocon to do research with us. To Dr. Gerbasi's amazement, she found Dr. Elizabeth Fein, a new assistant professor at Duquesne University in Pittsburgh. She was a clinical psychologist with a background in Anthropology (which was also on our wish list) whose doctoral dissertation involved work with adolescents on the autism spectrum. When Dr. Gerbasi reached out to her, she was enthusiastic about the work and agreed to come aboard the team.

As a clinical psychologist and anthropologist, Elizabeth had long been interested in the power of roleplay, myth, and creative subcultures to help people transform themselves and their lives. Having come of age as a young adult in the goth scene, she knew that close-knit communities could be built around aesthetic and symbolic systems. In her dissertation research with youth on the autism spectrum, some of which took place at a summer camp for live-action role-players (LARPers), she'd learned how transformative it can be to join together with others through shared imaginative mythologies, to re-imagine oneself and the possibilities of one's world. (For more on this work, you can check out her book, *Living on the Spectrum: Autism and*

Youth in Community.) When she was approached by Dr. Gerbasi about joining a research team studying furries—a group who, themselves, engaged in shared imaginative experiences, created alternative identities, and had a significantly higher proportion of people on the autism spectrum (see Chapter 23)—it was a tremendous opportunity for her to continue her work.

Dr. Fein went to Anthrocon for the first time in 2016, where she was entranced by the furries (and even more by therians and otherkin!) who sat with her for hours on the floor of the convention center, human bodies awkwardly folded into whatever quiet corners they could find, taking the time to tell her their life stories. The Furscience research team had already built up a great deal of trust with the community, which made it easier for her to earn their trust and be greeted with the gentle playfulness that characterizes much of the furry fandom.

Since that first year, Dr. Fein has worked alongside many graduate students from the Duquesne Ph.D. program (Ben Gaddes, José Luiggi-Hernandez, Gaby Mena-Ibarra, and Jennifer Bradley), she's interviewed dozens of furries on the autism spectrum and their families and friends, and has held numerous focus groups on autism at Anthrocon. She's also been working alongside Dr. Gerbasi on better understanding therians and otherkin, as well as with her neuroscientist colleague, Alex Kranjec, and his team of graduate students (Erick Guzman, Lou Lammana, and John Dall'Aglio) to see if furries, therians, and otherkin respond differently to a "bodily illusion" involving a rubber hand. Most recently, she's been conducting online surveys to better understand the experiences of therians and otherkin who may not make it out to furry conventions, but who, nevertheless, have a lot to say about their experiences.

Conclusion

Albert Bandura was really onto something when he talked about the importance of fortuity in our lives. The book you're holding[27] is a testament to that fact—it's the culmination of the many fortuitous happenings, large and small, that changed the trajectory of each member of the Furscience team. It's every chance conversation, small coincidence, split-second decision, and opportunity that presented itself over the past decade and allowed us to forge our myriad interests into a harmonious collaboration.

This chapter didn't need to be in this book. We could have easily excluded it and jumped straight into talking about our methodology and the countless studies and results we've obtained over more than a decade of

---

[27] Or, more likely these days, looking at on a screen!

studying furries. However, we're frequently approached by furries and scholars alike who've seen what we've been able to do at Furscience and exclaim that they could *never* do what we do. We want our story to inspire others to see that the Furscience team is, at the end of the day, just a group of curious people whose passions and curiosity have led us to find like-minded others who share that interest. Importantly, when each of us started along this shared journey, taking the plunge and capitalizing on those fortuitous moments that presented themselves, we had no idea where it would lead us. Dr. Gerbasi had no idea, when she agreed to be a forum moderator, that it would lead to her trailblazing work doing studies at furry conventions. Dr. Plante had no idea when he decided to e-mail a person he hadn't met after reading her paper, that it would lead to a decade-long collaboration. Dr. Reysen had no idea when he agreed to let his scale be used by a researcher he'd never heard of before, that it would lead to his noticing a nearby furry convention only months later and lead to dozens of research papers and book chapters. Dr. Roberts didn't know, when she chose to make small talk with her exam proctor, that his answer would launch her into a research and activism-filled career. And Dr. Fein didn't know when she was completing her dissertation work on LARPers, that she would eventually springboard from that into studying furries, of all things!

If nothing else, we hope this story inspires others to be bold and pursue their interests, even if it's not clear at all where they may take you. For us, our mutual interest has led to science-based advocacy and knowledge mobilization efforts, helping furries to learn more about their fandom, and scholars and the media alike to better understand this commonly misunderstood group. This shared goal has compelled us to make our work visible and to use the tools of social marketing, community, and media partnerships to be educational partners for the furry community.

And while none of us could have expected where the work would eventually take us, we'd be lying if we said we weren't surprised by the impact our work has had! While we'll never be able to single-handedly change public discourse, competing, as we are, with multi-billion dollar corporations, we have had measurable success in disseminating our findings to the public, who can now find our work simply by doing a Google search using common keywords (e.g., furries, what are furries).[28] We're also proud to have been the fact-checking source for countless media articles, correcting the record when it comes to everything from the belief that furries are people

[28] More often than not, Furscience pops up in the top five results! This isn't an accident or coincidence, as Malicious Beaver can tell you!

who wear fursuits and believe that they're animals to rumors about furries using litterboxes in school during the 2022 US election cycle (e.g., *New York Times, NBC News, Reuters, Snopes, Politifact, Guardian, Daily Beast, New York Post*).

So take a page out of Bandura's book and be on the lookout for the little opportunities that present themselves to you. You never know how a small conversation, a quick e-mail, going to an event, or putting yourself out might change your life—or the lives of those around you—for the better!

References

American Psychiatric Association. (2000). *Diagnostic and statistical manual of mental disorders* (4th ed., text rev.).

Angantyr, M., Eklund, J., & Hansen, E. M. (2011). A comparison of empathy for humans and empathy for animals. *Anthrozoös, 24*(4), 369-377. https://doi.org/10.2752/175303711X13159027359764

Arluke, A., Levin, J., & Ascione, F. (1999). The relationship of animal abuse to violence and other forms of antisocial behavior. *Journal of Interpersonal Violence, 14*(9), 963-975. https://doi.org/10.1177/088626099014009004

Bandura, A. (1982). The psychology of chance encounters and life paths. *American Psychologist, 37,* 747-755. https://doi.org/10.1037/0003-066X.37.7.747

Bandura, A. (1998). Exploration of fortuitous determinants of life paths. *Psychological Inquiry, 9,* 95-99. https://doi.org/10.1207/s15327965pli0902_2

Baron-Cohen, S., Wheelwright, S., Skinner, R., & Clubley, M. E. (2001). The autism-spectrum quotient (AQ): Evidence from Asperger syndrome/high-functioning autism, males and females, scientists and mathematicians. *Journal of Autism and Developmental Disorders, 31*(1), 5-17. https://doi.org/10.1023/a:1005653411471

Bravata, D. M., Watts, S. A., Keefer, A. L., Madhusudhan, D. K., Taylor, K. T., Clark, D. M., Nelson, R. S., Cokley, K. O., & Hagg, H. K. (2020). Prevalence, predictors, and treatment of imposter syndrome: A systematic review. *Journal of General Internal Medicine, 35*(4), 1252-1275. https://doi.org/10.1007/s11606-019-05364-1

Carlisle-Frank, P., & Frank, J. M. (2006). Owners, guardians, and owner-guardians: Differing relationships with pets. *Anthrozoös, 19*(3), 225-242. https://doi.org/10.2752/089279306785415574

Evans, K. (2008). *The Furry Sociological Survey*. Accessed on June 2, 2023 from https://gwern.net/doc/psychology/2008-evans.pdf

Fein, E. (2020). *Living on the spectrum: Autism and youth in community.* NYU Press.

Fine, A. H. (Ed.). (2010). *Handbook on animal-assisted therapy: Theoretical foundations and guidelines for practice* (3rd edition). Academic Press.

Gerbasi, K. C., Anderson, D. C., Gerbasi, A. M., & Coultis, D. (2002). Doctoral dissertations in human-animal studies: News and views. *Society & Animals: Journal of Human-Animal Studies, 10*(4), 339-346. https://doi.org/10.1163/156853002320936782

Gerbasi, K. C., Paolone, N., Higner, J., Scaletta, L. L., Bernstein, P. L., Conway, S., & Privitera, A. (2008). Furries from A to Z (anthropomorphism to zoomorphism). *Society & Animals: Journal Of Human-Animal Studies, 16*(3), 197-222. https://doi.org/10.1163/156853008X323376

Gerbasi, K. C., Paolone, N., Higner, J., Scaletta, L. L., Privitera, A., Bernstein, P., & Conway, S. (2007). *The Furry Identity*. Poster presented at Society for Research on Identity Formation. Sterling, VA.

Gerbasi, K. C., Harris, B., & Jorgensen, K. (2007, March 25). *Furries: Why do some humans grow up wanting to assume a non-human identity?* Interactive Session at Society for Research on Identity Formation, Sterling, VA.

Gerbasi, K. C., Plante, C. N., Reysen, S., & Roberts, S. E. (2015). The origins of the international anthropomorphic research project. In T. Howl (Ed.), *Furries among us: Essays on furries by the most prominent members of the fandom* (pp. 102-105). Thurston Howl Publications.

Greenebaum, J. (2004). It's a dog's life: Elevating status from pet to 'fur baby' at yappy hour. *Society & Animals: Journal of Human-Animal Studies, 12*(2), 117-135. https://doi.org/10.1163/1568530041446544

Gurley, G. (2001, March). Pleasures of the fur. *Vanity Fair*. Retrieved from http://vanityfair.com/culture/features/2001/03/furries200103?currentPage=1

Herzog, H. (2010). *Some we love, some we hate, some we eat: Why it's so hard to think straight about animals.* HarperCollins Publishers.

Julius, H., Beetz, A., Kotrschal, K., Turner, D., & Uvnäs-Moberg, K. (2013) *Attachment to pets: An integrative view of human–animal relationships with implications for therapeutic practice*. Hogrefe Publishing.

Mock, S. E., Plante, C. N., Reysen, S., & Gerbasi, K. C. (2013). Deeper leisure involvement as a coping resource in a stigmatized leisure context. *Leisure/Loisir, 37*(2), 111-126. https://doi.org/10.1080/14927713.2013.801152

Osaki, A. (2008). State of the fandom. *Furry Research Center*. Retrieved June 2, 2023 from https://commons.wikimedia.org/wiki/File:Furry_Survey_2008.pdf

Plante, C., Roberts, S., Reysen, S., & Gerbasi, K. (2014a). "One of us": Engagement with fandoms and global citizenship identification. *Psychology of Popular Media Culture,* 3(1), 49-64. https://doi.org/10.1037/ppm0000008

Plante, C., Roberts, S., Reysen, S., & Gerbasi, K. (2014b). Interaction of socio-structural characteristics predicts identity concealment and self-esteem in stigmatized minority group members. *Current Psychology, 33,* 3-19. https://doi.org/10.1007/s12144-013-9189-y

Plante, C. N., Roberts, S. E., Reysen, S., & Gerbasi, K. C. (2015a). "By the numbers": Comparing furries and related fandoms. In T. Howl (Ed.), *Furries among us: Essays on furries by the most prominent members of the fandom* (pp. 106-126). Thurston Howl Publications.

Plante, C., Roberts, S., Snider, J., Schroy, C., Reysen, S., & Gerbasi, K. (2015b). "More than skin-deep": Biological essentialism in response to a distinctiveness threat in a stigmatized fan community. *British Journal of Social Psychology, 54*(2), 359-370. https://doi.org/10.1111/bjso.12079

Putz, D. A., Gaulin, S. J. C., Sporter, R. J., & McBurney, D. H. (2004). Sex hormones and finger length: What does 2D:4D indicate? *Evolution and Human Behavior, 25*(3), 182-199. https://doi.org/10.1016/j.evolhumbehav.2004.03.005

Raupp, C. D. (2002). The 'furry ceiling:' Clinical psychology and human-animal studies. *Society & Animals: Journal of Human-Animal Studies, 10*(4), 353-360. https://doi.org/10.1163/156853002320936809

Reysen, S., & Branscombe, N. R. (2010). Fanship and fandom: Comparisons between sport and non-sports fans. *Journal Of Sport Behavior, 33*(2), 176-193.

Reysen, S., Plante, C. N., Roberts, S. E., & Gerbasi, K. C. (2015a). Ingroup bias and ingroup projection in the furry fandom. *International Journal of Psychological Studies, 7,* 49-58. https://doi.org/10.5539/ijps.v7n4p49

Reysen, S., Plante, C. N., Roberts, S. E., & Gerbasi, K. C. (2015b). A social identity perspective of personality differences between fan and non-fan identities. *World Journal of Social Science Research, 2,* 91-103. https://doi.org/10.22158/wjssr.v2n1p91

Reysen, S., Plante, C. N., Roberts, S. E., & Gerbasi, K. C. (2015c). Social identity perspective of the furry fandom. In T. Howl (Ed.), *Furries among us: Essays on furries by the most prominent members of the fandom* (pp. 127-151). Thurston Howl Publications.

Roberts, S., Plante, C., Gerbasi, K., & Reysen, S. (2015a). The anthrozoomorphic identity: Furry fandom members' connections to non-human animals. *Anthrozoos, 28*(4), 533-548. https://doi.org/10.1080/08927936.2015.1069993

Roberts, S., Plante, C., Gerbasi, K., & Reysen, S. (2015b). Clinical Interaction with Anthropomorphic Phenomenon: Notes for health professionals about interacting with clients who possess this unusual identity. *Health and Social Work, 40*(2), e42-e50. https://doi.org/10.1093/hsw/hlv020

Roberts, S. E., Plante, C. N., Reysen, S., & Gerbasi, K. C. (2015c). Marginalization of anthropomorphic identities: Public perception, realities, and "tails" of being a furry researcher. In T. Howl (Ed.), *Furries among us: Essays on furries by the most prominent members of the fandom* (pp. 152-168). Thurston Howl Publications.

Rossmassler, L., & Wen, T. (2007, May). *Furries are people too: Social and cognitive factors in unique social communities.* Poster presented at the Seventh Annual Stanford Undergraduate Psychology Conference, Stanford.

Rust, D. J. (2001). The sociology of furry fandom. *The Darken Hollow.* Retrieved June 2, 2023 from https://web.archive.org/web/20120303084029/http://www.visi.com/%7Ephantos/furrysoc.html

Topál, J., Miklósi, Á., Csányi, V., & Dóka, A. (1998). Attachment behavior in dogs (Canis familiaris): A new application of Ainsworth's (1969) Strange Situation Test. *Journal of Comparative Psychology, 112*(3), 219-229. https://doi.org/10.1037/0735-7036.112.3.219

yerf. (n.d.). *Furry in academia.* Accessed on June 2, 2023 from https://yerfology.wordpress.com/furry-in-academia/

Chapter 4
A (Not Too Painful) Introduction to Research Methods

Courtney "Nuka" Plante

If you're getting ready to read this whole book, we should probably warn you: you're about to get hit with a lot of data. Like, a *lot*. More than a decade of studies and tens of thousands of participants worth of data. To put that into perspective: if you were to multiply each of those thousands of participants by the (on average) two hundred or so questions in a given study, we're talking 5-10 million points of data.

It's a lot to take in at once, and it can be a bit intimidating to try and make sense of, especially if you're not accustomed to poring over scientific research. Don't worry if you feel that way—that's half the reason why we've included this chapter in the book! It's a chance to get your feet wet with some of the basics when it comes to data collection, analysis, and interpretation, sort of like easing you into the pool instead of throwing you head-first into the deep end and watching you flail around.

But, as we've said, that's only *half* the reason we've included this chapter!

The other reason we've included this chapter is to help our readers become informed skeptics. Of course, you can be skeptical about anything without too much effort. I could choose, for example, to simply disbelieve everything I've ever been told about gravity, insisting that any tendency for me to be drawn toward the ground is a coincidence or the result of my willing this to be the case. I imagine you'd feel pretty comfortable dismissing my skepticism as contrarianism or plain old ignorance, but could you precisely explain *why* I was wrong? If I were to argue that you couldn't *prove* gravity was a universal force because you couldn't observe everything everywhere in the universe—wouldn't there be a kernel of truth embedded in my statement? Or what if I claimed that I had a no-gravity experience one time when you weren't looking—isn't it possible? And sure, maybe I recently had my heart broken by a physicist and am being paid by an organization that profits when people believe that gravity isn't real—but can you *prove* that this is what's causing my skepticism?

As it turns out, not all skepticism is equal, nor should all skepticism be extended unlimited charitability. Sometimes skepticism is dishonest, done in bad faith by someone who's motivated by something other than arriving at truth. Other times, skepticism is ill-informed, grounded in falsehoods and misinformation. At the end of the day, there's little we can do in this book to stymie the first type of skepticism: if someone's reading this book with the goal of misquoting, misrepresenting, and selectively focusing only on data that fits their pre-existing beliefs about furries while ignoring or challenging anything to the contrary, we can't stop them.[1] Instead, this chapter aims to address the second type of skeptic, the one who, despite having the best of intentions, simply lacks the skills and knowledge to be an informed, critical consumer of research. We believe that a little knowledge can go a long way toward helping these folks, and we want to give them the tools to become skilled consumers of science.

In full disclosure, our intent isn't entirely altruistic. That is to say, we *do* have an ulterior motive for wanting to instill some scientific literacy in our readers: it's to help us do better science. Indeed, many of our best ideas have come from those who critique our methods, challenge our findings, and suggest new approaches to avoid our shortcomings.[2] We wouldn't be scientists if we didn't enjoy nerding out about ways to improve our methods, analyses, and conclusions! But skepticism and criticism are only helpful if they're informed. Imagine, for example, telling a video game designer that their video game sucks. The designer, obviously, has a vested interest in wanting to improve their video game, and so they press you for details: what was bad about it? Was it the pacing? The writing? Was the core gameplay loop uninteresting or lacking in interesting variety? Did it rely too much on random chance, depriving players of the chance to influence the outcome? Was the difficulty curve too steep?

"No, it just, y'know, sucked."

Unfortunately, criticism of this sort is painfully common, and we've witnessed plenty of it over the years from skeptics whose criticisms or outright dismissals of our work hinged on misunderstanding basic scientific principles. This is why we'd like to help readers learn to form better, more precise arguments for their skepticism and to better discern which of their criticisms are valid and which are relatively trivial. As we'll discuss at the end of this chapter, a bit of scientific literacy can help us avoid throwing babies out with the proverbial bathwater and prevent the sort of all-or-nothing, black-or-white thinking that characterizes criticism of scientific research from those who don't do research themselves.

---

[1] Indeed, the author of this chapter has seen more than his fair share of this sort of "motivated reasoning" from people "just asking questions," both when it comes to his research on furries and when it comes to his research on the especially hot-button topic of media violence!

[2] And believe me, there are *always* ways we could have done a study better!

And hey, if nothing else, this chapter will teach you a few concepts and fancy words so you can flex your critical thinking at the next dinner party![3]

Thinking Like a Scientist

As the name of this book suggests, we've taken a scientific approach to the understanding of furries and the furry fandom. But what, exactly, does this mean? What makes an approach scientific, and what makes this approach different from other means of knowledge acquisition (e.g., trusting one's gut feeling, relying on word-of-mouth, or learning about something from the media)?

To start, take a moment and think about what comes to your mind when you picture science. Chances are, you're probably picturing people wearing white lab coats in a laboratory. Maybe they're using microscopes or transferring colorful liquid from one test tube to another using a pipette. Perhaps you're imagining a data scientist staring at a sea of numbers on a monitor or a neuroscientist pondering a scan of a brain.

Images like these often focus on the superficial trappings of science; that is, they focus on specific scientific fields (e.g., physics, chemistry, biology) and the tools those fields employ (e.g., computers, scanning devices, fancy beakers). But just because you're using these devices, that doesn't mean that what you're doing is science. For example, a chef can don a white coat and mix up a sauce in customized glassware using fancy tools to achieve precise measurements. Would we consider the chef to be doing science?[4] Conversely, you can do science without fancy tools, with little more than a pencil and paper; asking a group of people to fill out and return a survey to test a hypothesis can be science. It might not involve million-dollar machines or a laboratory, but gathering data to test hypotheses is the backbone of science!

At its core, science is a very particular way of acquiring knowledge. Of course, there are lots of ways you've learned the things you have: by listening to what your parents have told you, by watching television or reading a newspaper, by interpreting moral lessons in stories, and even by intuition and a gut feeling. Each of these ways of knowing has its respective strengths and weaknesses—some are fairly quick and easy to do, but can't

---

[3] It's also worth noting that the concepts we're teaching you in this chapter apply to far more than just our research on furries. Scientific literacy skills can be applied when reading scientific research from almost any scientific field!

[4] To be sure, scientifically-derived principles are at play in cooking and baking, including chemistry and physics. But the act of baking is not, itself, doing science, for reasons we soon shall see!

always be counted on. Some are riddled with bias, but have the benefit of being fairly commonly agreed upon by others in society.

Science is really just another way of acquiring knowledge, albeit one that involves a very specific way of thinking.[5] We can characterize scientific thinking as having at least five different facets:[6]

1. Forming models and theories based on empirical observation and prior research.
2. Systematic, unbiased observation to test hypotheses.
3. A willingness to rigorously re-test the consistency of one's findings.
4. An open-minded willingness to be wrong and to actively seek falsification.
5. Nuanced, multivariate, probabilistic thinking.

Scientists Form Theories and Models

Let's start with the first point: scientists observe the world around them and read the existing literature to be aware of what others have found. They then try to integrate all of this available information into a model or framework that consistently explains how some facet of the world works. These models may vary in scale and complexity, from models of the structure of atoms to models of human motivation to models of entire cultures and economic systems. What they all have in common, however, is that they are all grounded in empirical reality; scientists make observations themselves or note the findings of other scientists and develop models consistent with these observations that also make predictions about what scientists can expect to find in the future.

Predictions are a critical part of scientific thinking. Good scientific theories not only explain the world, but they also make predictions about it. A model that explains everything, but predicts nothing, is practically useless. As an illustrative example, let's imagine I was watching customers walk in and out of a pet store. One by one, I observe customers walking into the store and, one by one, they walk out of the store with either a cat or a dog. After a few dozen customers, I might propose a model to explain which customers walk out with cats and which walk out with dogs. Perhaps I suggest that when customers walk into the store, they pass through an invisible energy field that puts the idea into their head to get a cat or a dog. As such, the

---

[5] Note that science is a *process*, not merely a heap of facts. Some facts may be derived through the scientific process, but a textbook full of scientifically-derived facts is not, in and of itself, science; it is the output or consequence of doing science!

[6] This is far from a complete list, but it represents some of the most important characteristics of scientific thinking.

people who walked out with cats passed through this unseen barrier, had "cat" put into their mind, and got cats, while those who got dogs passed through the same unseen barrier, which put "dog" into their mind, and they got a dog instead.

A strength of my model is that it perfectly explains 100% of my observations: to this point, I have observed nothing in the behavior of customers that contradicts my model. Despite this, for all intents and purposes, my model is entirely useless. Why? Because my model can't help me predict whether or not the next customer who walks into the store will walk out with a cat or a dog. I can't see this barrier for myself, nor do I know how or why this barrier influences people. In other words, my model makes me no better at predicting the pet-purchasing behavior of the next customer than someone just flipping a coin that says "cat" on one side and "dog" on the other side.

In short, if a scientific model can't predict anything about the world, then it contributes nothing to our knowledge of the world.[7]

Now let's consider what a scientific model might look like in the same situation. Imagine if, as people were going into the pet shop, I gave them a quick personality test to measure their level of extraversion. After a few dozen customers, I begin to notice a pattern: those who scored higher on the extraversion scale walked out of the store with a dog, while those who scored lower on the scale walked out with a cat. From here, I devise a model that proposes that extroverts tend to like dogs, whose personalities tend to be more outgoing, while introverts prefer cats, whose personalities tend to be more independent and less attention-seeking. Unlike my invisible energy field model, however, I can now make predictions about the behavior of future customers based on this model. I can give a customer my personality test before they walk into the store and, based on the results of that test, I can make an informed guess about whether they are more likely to walk out of the store with a dog or a cat. And, if there's any truth to this new model, it should outperform the energy field model and the person flipping a coin when it comes to accurately guessing whether the customer will walk out of the store with a dog or a cat.

Scientists Test Hypotheses

Science isn't just about forming models, it's about *testing* them.[8] Part of the craft of science is in devising practical ways to gather information in a

[7] Case in point: I could easily replace the invisible energy field with pixie dust and it would be just as informative. The interchangeability of these models shows us how untethered to reality they are.

systematic and unbiased manner. Systematic, in this case, means gathering data in a planned and controlled fashion, and designing a study to maximize its ability to effectively test our hypotheses. For example, we may run our pet-purchasing study at different pet stores in different parts of the country to test whether our findings are consistent across the country or are limited to the customers at one store. It also involves trying to control for external factors to ensure that nothing influences the results of the study (e.g., the pet shop having a "free cat" day while you try to collect data, which might incentivize people to choose cats over dogs regardless of their personality).

A good scientist will also be motivated to be unbiased in the way they collect, analyze, and interpret data. After all, the only way to be certain of one's model is to expose it to cold, hard reality to see whether it sinks or swims. If the researcher gave customers the personality test and then followed the extrovert into the store to convince them to buy a dog, then it would be impossible to know whether dog-buying behavior was driven by extraversion or by being hounded[9] by a scientist in the store. In this case, the scientist's influence might help them find data consistent with their model, but these sorts of biases end up producing models that don't hold up to scrutiny and which, over time, are replaced by models that better reflect reality (e.g., accurately predict the behavior of customers who aren't harassed by scientists in a pet shop). For this reason, scientific thinking *necessitates* systematic and unbiased data gathering.[10]

Scientists Test and Retest

Being a good scientist means being difficult to please; it's not enough to find evidence that supports your model once. Scientists are an incredibly skeptical bunch, always worried that a finding may have been a fluke. Returning to our pet store example, if I were to determine that a single

---

[8] We're focusing primarily on experimental studies in our examples, but these same principles can also apply to the gathering of open-ended, exploratory data as well, something we'll discuss later in this chapter! For now, we'll say that researchers who specialize in gathering open-ended, qualitative data (e.g., case studies, long-form interviews) often do so to form models that are later tested by quantitative researchers. They are similarly hurt by being non-systematic or biased in their approach to data collection.

[9] Pun definitely intended.

[10] We're talking about scientific thinking as an ideal here. In practice, scientists have biases that may cloud their deliberate or inadvertent judgment. This is one of the reasons why the peer-review process is so important, a point we bring up later. For now, we'd just like to point out that science in practice may not always live up to the ideal of science.

customer was an extrovert and then watch them walk out of the store with a dog, I might conclude that my model is correct. However, it is entirely possible that the next customer to walk into the store may be an extrovert and, nevertheless, choose a cat, something that would go against the prediction of my model. For this reason, it would be in my best interest to sit by the door of the pet store for a while, subjecting my model to test after test, customer after customer, to see how consistent it is.

But a diligent scientist won't stop there. After all, who can say that the results weren't simply a quirk of this particular pet store? With this in mind, I might set up tests of my model at every pet store in town. If, after running all these tests, the evidence still points in favor of my model being correct, then I can be reasonably sure it probably wasn't a fluke, and that my model accurately predicts pet-buying behavior in most people in most places.

But why stop there? An especially diligent researcher would consider the possibility that they, themselves, might be biasing the results—after all, they're the ones with a model to test. As such, they might ask other researchers in the field to run the study themselves, at their pet stores, to see whether the model holds up even when tested by other researchers. They might even go one step further, testing how well the model holds up over time. Perhaps they might run another test of the model at pet stores 20 years later to see whether the model still predicts pet-purchasing behavior or whether the model's usefulness was limited to one particular point in time or for one specific generation.[11]

Scientists are Willing to be Wrong

Building upon our previous point, scientific thinking requires openly embracing the likelihood that one might be incorrect. If a scientist doesn't seriously consider the possibility that their model could be wrong, it becomes impossible to truly test their model. For example, if I were convinced that my model of pet-purchasing behavior was correct and refused to believe that it might be wrong, I might find excuses to conveniently disregard evidence suggesting that my theory is wrong. If I saw an extrovert walk out of a pet store with a cat instead of a dog, in opposition to my model, I might dismiss

[11] This is why scientists often balk at the idea that a scientific model or theory is "just a theory," implying that it has little to no predictive power or that it hasn't been held up to intense empirical scrutiny. In lay conversation, we often use the terms "theory" or "model" to suggest baseless suppositions or crude approximations. In reality, the most renowned scientific theories and models are subjected to a degree of scrutiny and testing that would stagger (and probably bore to tears) anyone who doesn't have an especially keen interest in the subject.

the observation by saying "Well, clearly that person is an introvert, they must have filled out the survey incorrectly!" In doing so, I could protect my model from any evidence suggesting that it's incorrect, no matter how much that evidence piles up![12]

This principle of skepticism and a willingness to be wrong is so fundamental to scientific thinking that we build it into scientific practice by default. For example, scientists design studies and test hypotheses around the assumption that their model is, in fact, *incorrect*. They are trained to interpret the results of a study as showing no support for their model *unless* the data show quite conclusively otherwise (e.g., less than a 5% chance of being wrong). In other words, if the data from a study were to come out such that there was a 50/50 chance that the model was either right or wrong, scientists would err on the side of skepticism and treat this as evidence that the model is incorrect. Even if the data came out with 90/10 odds in favor of the model being correct, scientists will still treat this as evidence that the model is wrong, as a 10% chance of being incorrect is still considered too large to be acceptable.[13]

And the skepticism doesn't end there! We've acknowledged that scientists may be biased and have some incentive to find support for their models. To account for this, scientists have built a self-correcting mechanism into the publishing process called "peer review." In a nutshell, highly-credited, prestigious outlets for scientific research require that any piece of research wanting to be published must first be scrutinized by other experts in the field. This scrutiny includes subjecting the study to questions about its methodology and analysis,[14] requests for additional studies, and challenging the study's conclusions with alternative explanations. The intended result of this process is for low-quality, biased, or dubious findings to be filtered out, leaving behind only the strongest studies that hold up to scrutiny from the top

---

[12] Scientists are often pressured to find support for their models by the allure of prestigious awards or, as is unfortunately common, the threat of losing their jobs if they don't contribute sufficiently to their field. These pressures can undermine a scientist's impartiality and hurt the pursuit of science.

[13] This is, of course, an oversimplification of how hypothesis-testing works in practice, but it's good enough for our purpose, since we assume most readers don't want to delve into the finer points of null hypothesis statistical tests and Bayesian estimation.

[14] And, in recent years, scientists are even required to make their data available so that other scientists can analyze it themselves and look for irregularities or evidence of tampering.

minds in the field. While the peer-review process is often grueling, intimidating, and far from perfect, it represents a level of self-criticism that one rarely finds with other ways of gathering knowledge.[15]

Scientists Recognize the Complexity of the World

A final characteristic of scientific thinking, one interwoven throughout the previous characteristics, is that it accounts for complexity and nuance through probabilistic thinking. Probabilistic thinking is a tricky topic for people to wrap their heads around, especially if they have little formal training in statistics. In a nutshell, it refers to the idea that our world is complex, and therefore one can expect a degree of random chance in almost everything. For example, while there's a good chance it will rain if there are dark, stormy-looking clouds in the sky, there is a chance it might not rain. Weather is a complex system, after all; thousands of variables interact to determine the weather in a given area at a given time. Scientific models cannot possibly account for every one of these variables, but scientists do the best they can using the models they have while recognizing that there is a chance the predictions generated by their model might be incorrect. Based on a handful of variables, a scientist might predict that there's an 80% chance of rain today, recognizing that there is a 20% chance the model could be wrong.

Those unaccustomed to probabilistic thinking often fall prey to black-and-white, all-or-nothing thinking. You probably know people who get angry at the local weather report when it rains on a day that was predicted to be sunny. This is because we live our lives one day at a time, interacting with one person at a time, in one situation at a time; we care about individual outcomes, like whether a sick relative will recover or die, whether our favorite football team will win or lose the next game, or whether the value of our stock will go up or down in value.

Scientists don't develop models to predict individual people or events, however. Because the world is such a complex place, scientists know they won't be able to perfectly predict 100% of outcomes. Instead, they develop models to predict general tendencies, trends, and overall patterns in the data. Returning to our pet store example, we can imagine an extrovert walking into the pet store and purchasing a cat instead of the dog that we would have

---

[15] The peer-review process, while essential to science, is far from perfect. For example, reviewers may have their own biases, which can prevent high-quality research from being published (or allow lower-quality research to be published, if it supports the reviewer's model or theory). Papers can also find themselves rejected for reasons other than the quality of the study (e.g., because it was deemed uninteresting, overly niche, or too similar to a paper that's already been published).

predicted. What can we conclude from this? On its face, we might conclude from this single example that the model is wrong.

In reality, however, *countless* variables impact whether a person walks out of the store with a cat or a dog: their personality traits, the size of their apartment, prior history with cats and dogs, the availability and cost of cats and dogs in the store, allergies to cat or dog hair, social acceptability of cats or dogs in the area—the list is endless. A model that could perfectly predict pet purchasing behavior would need to take all of these variables and more into account and would be impossibly complex to build. Even with the combined effort of thousands of researchers and data from millions of people to develop such a model, it would be impossible to guarantee that the model would be 100% correct every time.

So, is the solution to simply abandon the whole practice of trying to predict anything complex, like pet-purchasing behavior, stock prices, weather patterns, or a person's likelihood of survival? Hopefully, you realize the answer is no. Even if a model is not *perfectly* predictive, it can still be useful. Imagine, for example, that a person's extraversion score, while not perfectly predictive of pet-buying behavior, could correctly predict their choice of pets 75% of the time. While far from perfect, it's a vast improvement over being correct 50% of the time by just randomly guessing. Likewise, if you knew the weather forecast for tomorrow was predicting an 80% chance of rain, you probably wouldn't go out of your way to plan a picnic for tomorrow, even if there is a 20% chance the model might be wrong. Imperfect models can still be valuable!

What's more, scientists can *improve* the predictive ability of their models by adding variables. Extroversion scores might make our theoretical model 75% accurate at predicting pet ownership, but maybe, if we consider a few more variables, like age, income, and whether they had a dog or a cat in their past, we can improve our model's accuracy to 85%—not too shabby! And with additional variables in the model, the accuracy of the model may improve even more!

Because the world is complex, there is seldom a single cause for anything in this world, whether it's a stock market boom, a bridge collapsing, or a patient unexpectedly recovering from a disease. This is why it can sometimes be maddeningly frustrating to get a clear answer from a scientist, especially if your question has to do with a single event or a person. A doctor can tell you that 75% of people with a particular disease end up dying from it, but they can't tell you for sure whether your sick grandfather will be one of those 75% or not.

This is what we mean when we say that scientific thinking involves probabilistic thinking and understanding complexity and nuance: it's a very different way of thinking than most people are accustomed to, one that doesn't come naturally. In fact, every facet of the scientific way of thinking—forming empirically derived models, coming up with ways to test and re-test those models, embracing and actively seeking out evidence that one might be wrong, and appreciating nuance and probabilistic thinking in those models—are skills that need to be taught to scientists through years of education and practice. In the same way that athletes spend years learning how to think strategically about their sport, mechanics spend years learning how parts of an engine work together, and artists spend years learning how to make the image in their head come to life on the canvas, scientists have to be taught how to think scientifically.

And sure, it's a lot of work learning to change the way you think, but when it comes to explaining how this complex world of ours works, humans haven't found a better, more reliable way to acquire this knowledge than through science.

Study Design: Exploration, Description, Correlation, and Causation

As mentioned in the previous section, one of the most important activities that scientists engage in is the systematic collection of data. This is usually done when forming new theories and models or, in later stages of research, when testing how well models hold up to scrutiny. Regardless of the specific goal, scientists employ carefully designed studies to do the job. And, just as an athlete, artist, or mechanic has to choose the right tool for the job, scientists must choose which of a variety of different study types is appropriate for the task at hand.

For simplicity's sake, let's break down the different goals a scientist may have into four types: exploration, description, correlation, and causation. Each of these goals has a different set of requirements and will require different tools to accomplish. To use an analogy, a screwdriver, while useful for screwing in a screw, isn't an especially good hammer, even if it might be able to partially do the job of a hammer in a pinch. It would be silly to judge the usefulness of a screwdriver based on its ability to hammer something into place since it was never designed for that purpose. Even if a mechanic may find themselves using a screwdriver more than a hammer, there are jobs where a screwdriver just won't get the job done, and on those days, a hammer is the best fit for the job.

The same can be said for our four different types of goals: a study designed for the purpose of exploration may not be especially useful at testing correlation or causation, while a study built to test causal direction may be poorly suited for basic exploration. While this may seem obvious in the abstract, it's a point I often have to explain to students and laypersons alike, many of whom latch onto one type of study as being the ideal, with all others being deemed inferior because they are not the preferred type of study. This tendency persists even when another study design would be vastly more appropriate for the purpose being considered. Keep this in mind as we proceed through this section: there are no "perfect" studies, only studies whose strengths and weaknesses make them better suited or less suitable for a particular task. It's okay to have a fondness for screwdrivers, but realize that you may occasionally need a hammer to get the job done!

Goal: Exploration

To start, let's consider the task of exploration. Exploration often represents a scientist's first foray into a topic. Oftentimes, it's a subject that few others have looked at, meaning the scientist may have little existing theory or data to draw upon for guidance. In such circumstances, scientists may find themselves so unfamiliar with the subject that they're not even sure where to begin. What are the right questions to ask and are there any existing models that are appropriate?

Let's imagine that a scientist wants to study a subculture about which relatively little is known. For our purpose, let's use the example of the community of players who play the *Dark Souls* series of video games.[16] There may be existing research on related topics (e.g., people who play other genres of video games, research on gamer culture more broadly), but our intrepid scientist finds nothing specifically on the subject of *Dark Souls* fans. The scientist's ultimate goal is to better understand *Dark Souls* fans, but, not being a fan themselves or a member of the culture, it's hard to even know where to begin. Would it be appropriate to apply models of gamer motivation that were derived from other video game fan communities (e.g., fans of real-time strategy games) to this community, or would such a model be woefully inadequate at explaining what compels *Dark Souls* fans? Is there anything unique about the *Dark Souls* genre that makes its fans distinct from other types of fans? Is there any special vocabulary or knowledge that the researcher needs to know to make sense of the sorts of responses *Dark Souls*

---

[16] For readers who are unaware, the *Dark Souls* franchise is a series of 3rd-person action roleplaying games in which players fight their way through dark, destroyed, fantasy-themed worlds filled with larger-than-life enemies. The franchise is renowned both for its infamous level of difficulty as well as for the memes generated by its fanbase.

fans might provide? Without knowing the answer to these sorts of questions, it's hard for the scientist to gain a foothold in this area of research.

This is why researchers may want to start their initial foray into a topic with exploratory research. In this type of research, the emphasis is on getting a handle on the important ideas, research questions, and idiosyncrasies of a topic. As one might imagine, thinking about relevant questions to ask at this stage of the process can be tricky, as the researcher may lack important terminology or knowledge of the group, its composition, or its history. As an example, an unaware researcher might ask *Dark Souls* fans to describe their favorite driving/vehicle section from the series, only to find out that the question makes no sense in a genre that *has* no vehicle or driving sections. Without talking to a few fans of the series or learning more about the game in advance (e.g., by playing it or watching videos of it for themselves), there would be no way for our scientist to know this!

For this reason, exploratory research rarely involves the use of highly specific, targeted questions. Instead, researchers approach the topic with a broad range of very general questions and an emphasis on passive, open-minded observation rather than active, targeted testing of a specific hypothesis. Studies ideally suited to this purpose include field observation, focus groups, individual interviews, and surveys with open-ended (qualitative) questions.[17] Our scientist could sit down and watch a few players playing *Dark Souls* while taking notes and making observations (they could even try it themselves). Alternatively, they could interview a few *Dark Souls* players and ask them very broad, open-ended questions about the game and their experience playing it, recording the responses to see whether common themes, important terms, relevant research questions, and new ideas emerge.

Goal: Description

Having nailed down some of the basic concepts in a field through exploratory research, our scientist may shift into descriptive research. Descriptive research seeks to measure and accurately describe the state of a phenomenon. At this point, the researcher isn't looking to test or explain anything, but rather to document the phenomenon as it is and accurately capture it on relevant dimensions. Returning to our *Dark Souls* example, our researcher might take the information they gathered from their interviews

---

[17] Qualitative questions refer to open-ended questions designed to elicit detail-rich responses from respondents. This is often contrasted against quantitative measures, which involve gathering numeric data (e.g., counting the number of times a respondent does something or a response on a 7-point scale).

and decide that some of the important variables worth studying include the number of games played in the series, the number of hours played per game, the number of messages players post in a *Dark Souls* forum, and the number of friends they have who also play the *Dark Souls* games. If these were topics that came up again and again during interviews, the researcher may want to get an accurate picture of how several players measure up on relevant variables.

To satisfy this goal, the researcher may design a simple survey to give to a large number of *Dark Souls* players. In an effort to try and get as accurate a snapshot of the *Dark Souls* fan base as possible, they may try to cast an especially wide net, gathering data on thousands of *Dark Souls* fans from around the world. Each player would be asked, through the survey, a set of fairly basic questions inspired by the exploratory research, almost like a census of players. From this data, the researcher might gain a basic understanding of the characteristics of a typical *Dark Souls* fan, as well as how much variability exists within the fan community when it comes to this subject. In a nutshell, it gives them a snapshot of the state of the *Dark Souls* community.

Goal: Correlation

As a next step, our scientists may want to go beyond the data they've collected so far to construct a model to represent *Dark Souls* fans. This model would draw inferences from the existing data, suggesting connections and forming hypotheses about players and their behavior. Perhaps the researcher notices, for example, that people who play the game a lot also seem to be the same people who post about their accomplishments in forums and are also the first to offer help to newer players. From this observation, the researcher wonders whether there might be a link between these two concepts, and sets out to test whether their casual observation holds empirical water. They may be able to test this hypothesis statistically, based on the data they already have, or they may have to run an additional study that more precisely measures the variables in question; instead of asking players if they post in forums, researchers may ask them to quantify what percentage of their forum posts are dedicated to helping newer players. Or, rather than asking about the approximate number of hours they've played, the researcher may ask more precise questions about the exact number of hours played on their account, or ask players how many hours they have played in the past week as a measure of their current tendency to play.

Regardless of how they measure the variables in question, the point of this research is to test for correlations—that is, to measure two or more variables quantitatively and test whether there is statistical evidence for a connection between them. At the end of the day, correlational research boils down to testing whether the researcher can state with confidence that two different variables co-vary with one another: If you know what a person's score on Variable X is (e.g., number of hours played), can you predict, with a reasonable degree of accuracy, what their score on Variable Y is (e.g., frequency of helping newer players).

Goal: Causation

Assuming our scientist finds empirical support for their hypothesis in the study above (e.g., a statistically significant correlation between two variables), the final step to understanding the phenomenon is to be able to explain *why*. Sure, they found that players who play more are also the same players who help newcomers, but why is this the case? One possibility is that playing more hours of the game *causes* people to become more helpful, perhaps because one needs to become skilled themselves before they can teach the skills to another player. The reverse causal direction represents another possibility: perhaps players who help other players get a warm, fuzzy feeling from doing so, which drives them to want to keep playing the game, which ultimately helps them hone their skills. A third possibility is also true: maybe those who have friends that play *Dark Souls* are more likely to help others (e.g., their friends) and are *also* more likely to play more because they can talk with their friends about the game—in this case, there is no actual causation happening, but rather the *illusion* of causation caused by some third variable being related to the two correlated variables (e.g., having a friend who plays).

From a statistical perspective, finding a significant correlation cannot tell us which of these possible causal directions is true; it could be any one of them, or it could well be all of them. This is a significant limitation of correlational studies—they can only tell us *that* two variables are related, not whether one *causes* the other to occur. In order to go to the last step and establish causal direction (and, thus, explain how or why something happens), additional steps are needed. Specifically, scientists need to be able to establish temporal order—that is, they need to be able to show that changes to one of the variables comes *before* changes in the other variable—and they need to be able to rule out possible alternative explanations which may create the illusion of causality where there is none.

Fortunately, while correlational studies (e.g., surveys) fall short, there *is* a type of study specifically designed to test causal direction: experiments. An experiment is designed to allow researchers to rule out all possible alternative explanations and to show not only that two variables are related, but also to test whether one variable causes changes in the other to occur.

Unfortunately, the drawback of experiments is that they can be difficult to do, and often involve artificially controlling circumstances to ensure a pure test of causality. Without going into too much detail, the core of an experiment is the random assignment of participants to one or more conditions or levels of the variable you believe to be the "causer" variable.[18] In a medical experiment testing the effectiveness of a drug, for example, participants are randomly assigned to get a certain amount of the drug; some participants may get none of the drug (the control condition), some may get a little bit of the drug (a treatment condition), and some participants may get a lot of the drug (another treatment condition). In our *Dark Souls* study, we might get some gamers who have never played *Dark Souls* before and randomly assign them to either play no *Dark Souls* or to play a bunch of *Dark Souls*.

After this manipulation, the researchers look for a change in the outcome variable, the variable thought to be *caused* by the first variable.[19] In the drug trial, researchers might measure a person's health or recovery after manipulating the amount of the drug they get. In our *Dark Souls* example, the scientist might give participants a chance to cooperate with another new player to see whether they work together and help the other player. The logic of the experiment is this: if we notice a difference between the conditions, we can say that the manipulated variable *caused* the change in the second variable to happen, since it came *before* the second variable. In other words, it doesn't make sense to say that the recovery *caused* an increase in the amount of medicine a person received, because the recovery came afterward. Likewise, we can't say that helping other players came first because we *know* that the gameplay came first; we designed the experiment specifically to ensure that this was the case!

Astute readers might recall that part of the requirement for establishing causation involves ruling out alternative explanations. How can an experiment do that? How do we know, for example, that we didn't coincidentally put people who were going to recover on their own in the "get the medicine" condition and people who were bound to get sicker in the "no medicine" condition? Likewise, how do we know that we didn't just put the more helpful people in the "play *Dark Souls*" condition and all the jerks in the "no play" condition?

---

[18] In technical parlance, this is referred to as the "independent variable."
[19] This variable is known as the "dependent variable."

This is where we see the importance of random assignment. By assigning people to their conditions randomly, the participants in the different conditions are, in the eyes of statistics, completely equal. If we truly assigned people at random, then it should be incredibly unlikely that all of the healthy people wound up in one condition, or all of the helpful people wound up in one condition, purely by chance. Imagine taking a room full of people, flipping a coin, and randomly assigning the heads to one side of the room and the tails to the other side of the room. If you did this, how likely is it that, by pure coincidence alone, all of the blonde-haired people wound up on one side of the room while all of the brown-haired people wound up on the other side? Is it possible? Sure. But is it likely? No.[20] This is why, as long as participants were randomly assigned to their condition, we can assume the conditions are equal at the start of the study.

And why is it so important that the two conditions are the same at the start of the study? If we assume that the conditions are the same at the start of the study, and then they are different at the end of the study (e.g., more healthy people in the drug condition, more people cooperating with new players in the playing condition), the *only* possible explanation is the one single difference between the groups: our manipulation. This logic is what allows experiments to rule out all possible alternative explanations. However, as you've seen, it also requires a fair amount of planning and control and is often, though not always, going to be harder to run than, say, emailing a single survey out to thousands of people online.

To summarize this section: scientists have a variety of tools available to them in the form of different study designs. Some designs are perfectly designed to gather rich, detailed content straight from the mouths of participants without any researcher interference or bias. These studies, which are ideally suited for exploratory studies, do not lend themselves well to describing the average tendency or variability of a phenomenon (e.g., a group of people), nor do they allow researchers to measure correlations between variables or test causal explanations. Survey studies often build upon this initial exploratory research, allowing researchers to describe a phenomenon and measure correlations between variables, and can be easily

---

[20] In fact, the likelihood of this happening by chance becomes smaller with each additional person in the room. It's easy to imagine how, if there were only four people in the room, you might coincidentally assign the two brunettes to one side and the two blondes to the other side by random chance alone. But, if there were 200 people in the room, the odds of this same thing happening due to chance alone are astronomically small: the equivalent of flipping 200 heads in a row on a fair coin!

scaled up to large samples of a population. However, they typically lack the ability to determine causation and typically reduce all of the complexity and nuance of a participant's response or experience down to a handful of numbers on a scale. Finally, experiments can do what none of these other studies are able to do—establish causal explanations between variables—but they are often very limited in terms of scope (e.g., only being able to look at a small handful of variables at a time) and are often more limited than correlational studies when it comes to sample size.

As we mentioned before, it would be silly to say that any of these study designs are inherently "better" or "worse" than any other design. Without considering the context in which they are being used, we can't say whether experiments are more valuable than interviews or whether correlational studies are more useful than focus groups or observation. Doing so would be akin to saying that hammers are better than screwdrivers without knowing whether the task involves driving in a nail or screwing in a screw.

Being an informed skeptic means considering the context and purpose of the research being conducted before deciding the appropriateness of a particular study design. This is the lesson overlooked by many a layperson and college student who dismiss qualitative studies out of hand simply because they aren't experiments. As you read about the research in this book, keep in mind the types of questions being answered and the sort of study that would be ideally suited to that particular task. In doing so, you'll avoid many of the common pitfalls of casual skeptics and be better able to weigh in on the merits and weaknesses of the research being discussed.[21]

A Pain-Free Lesson in Basic Statistics

We can feel the collective shudder of readers who saw the heading of this section and opted to skip over it to the next section. So kudos to you, brave

[21] To help with this task, much of the research being presented in this book is descriptive in nature, aiming to describe the state of the furry fandom as it is (e.g., demographics). There is also a lot of research aimed at initially exploring, in a very broad and open sense, various facets of the furry fandom (e.g., what is a furry?). Finally, there are a smaller number of topics which look for correlations between variables (e.g., identifying as a furry and well-being). While many of these studies seem to lend themselves naturally to questions about causal direction, in many instances we cannot manipulate the predictor variable in question (e.g., manipulating whether or not a person is a furry), which makes it impossible to conduct true experiments—and test causal hypotheses—on these topics. We address such limitations later in this chapter.

reader, for being one of the few who decided to tough it out and give a section on statistics a gander. Hopefully, you won't be disappointed!

The number of people who almost certainly skipped over this section reflects a general fear of mathematics, one that many of the authors of this book recognize both in the general population and in our own undergraduate students. Unfortunately, whether we like them or not, statistics abound in the world around us. If you've ever read an opinion poll in the weeks leading up to an election, you've been exposed to statistics. If you've ever read an advertisement for a product that claimed to clean 20% better than the leading competitor or to kill 99.9% of germs, you've encountered statistics. If you've ever seen the batting average of your favorite baseball player, you've seen statistics.

The omnipresence of statistics wouldn't be such a bad thing, in and of itself, if we left their interpretation to the experts.[22] In reality, however, statistics are often misapplied, misunderstood, and misrepresented—sometimes deliberately and sometimes not—leading to confusion at best and, at worst, mistrust and disinformation. Speaking to this idea, we've encountered more than a few lay skeptics of our work who, after looking at summaries of our findings, decided that they disagree with our conclusions—not because they have any specific criticism of our methodology or its theoretical underpinning, but simply because they don't understand how the statistics came to be, what the statistics mean, or assume that the statistics were deliberately manipulated to mislead them.

This is precisely why we're attempting to lift the veil and dispel some of the intrigue and apparent mysteriousness of statistics here. To be sure, we've deliberately chosen to keep our display of statistical procedures and outputs to a minimum throughout this book to improve its readability. That said, every single finding we present in this book is underpinned by at least one statistical analysis.[23] We hope that, with a little bit of explanation, we can help create more informed readers who are better able to critically evaluate our findings for themselves and who, when skeptical, can challenge the

---

[22] While we're at it, we could also probably stand to leave medicine to the doctors, psychology to the psychologists, teaching to the teachers, and climate science to the environmental scientists.

[23] In fact, inquisitive readers are welcome to contact us if they wish to take a look "under the hood" and look at any of the statistical analyses that went into this book! More often than not, it's other scientists who want us to "show our work," but we're happy to do so for anyone who wants to see it for themselves!

findings on substantive grounds, rather than out of a general mistrust of statistics.

Descriptive Statistics—Central Tendency

With our goal stated, let's begin with the simplest type of statistics—the type most readers are likely to be familiar with—descriptive statistics. Descriptive statistics are a way to condense a bunch of data into a simple, easy-to-understand summary. The most common and intuitive of these statistics refer to central tendency, that is, a summary of what is typical, most prevalent, or most likely in a sample.

One of the most common statistics relating to central tendency is an average. An average, or mean, is calculated mathematically from the data, the result of adding up all the values and dividing by the number of values. Averages are a fairly simple way of approximating what is typical in a group and are fairly intuitive to understand. If, for example, I were to tell you that the average person in a room has $20 in their pocket, you would probably have a basic understanding of the amount of spending power (in cash) that the people in the room have. You also probably understand that just because the *average* person has $20 in their pocket doesn't mean that *everyone* has exactly $20 in their pocket; some people may have only $10, while others may have $30.[24] In fact, it's possible that no one in the room has $20 in their pocket, and the room is instead comprised entirely of an equal number of people with $10 in their pocket and $30 in their pocket. Either way, if you want to sell something to the people in the room, knowing what the average person is able to spend in cash would be useful information.[25]

---

[24] Despite the intuitiveness of this principle in a simple example like this, people often forget this idea in other contexts. If, while giving a talk, I were to say that the average furry is in their early-to-mid 20s, a fairly common response is for an older furry to argue that *they* are much older than this. This tendency may underpin some peoples' distrust of statistics, feeling like an average score doesn't reflect their own experience and must, therefore, be trying to cover up or deny their experience. To be sure, statistics of central tendency do, by design, speak only about common experiences and fail to display the full range of responses. The problem is not with the calculation of the statistic, however, nor is it incorrect that the average represents the group's central tendency. Instead, the skeptic's problem may lie in their desire to see the full range of responses, which is perfectly defensible, especially when it comes to overlooking underrepresented minorities. This only emphasizes the importance of being able to precisely voice the source of one's concern, to avoid throwing blame in the wrong direction.

[25] Of course, in other contexts, you might not be at all interested in central tendency. For example, in conjunction with the previous footnote, you may be more interested

When it comes to summarizing central tendency, averages aren't the only game in town. Other statistics similarly describe central tendency, albeit in slightly different ways. For example, the mode refers to the most common value in a group. If, for example, most people had $20 in their pocket, with some people having $10 and an equal number having $30 in their pocket, we could say that the modal value is also $20, the same as the average. But one can also imagine other datasets where a few extremely high or low values pull the average score up, making the average less useful. If, for example, everyone in the room had $20 in their pocket, but one person in the room had $50,000 in their pocket, the average amount of pocket money in the room would be much higher than $20—perhaps closer to $1000. As a vendor, however, it would probably be more useful for you to know that most people in the room only have about $20, allowing you to better adjust your prices or to more appropriately stock your store with goods in the $20 range.

Another alternative is to consider the median value of a group—that is, the "middle" value of the group. If you can imagine lining up all the values from smallest to largest, the median score would be the score directly in the middle of the line-up. For example, if there were 5 people in the room, the amount of money on the person with the 3rd highest amount of money (the middle score between 1 and 5) would be the median score. The median is another way to assess the central tendency of a group in a way that's immune to extremely high or low values. Returning to our previous example, it wouldn't matter if the person with the most money in the room had $50 or $50,000 in their pocket, the person with the 3rd-most money would remain the same. For this reason, the median and mode scores are sometimes used to describe the central tendency of a dataset when extremely high or low values are present as a more representative way of showing the state of a typical person in the sample.

Descriptive Statistics—Variance

So far, we've spoken about statistics of central tendency. These are, by far, the statistics most laypersons will be familiar with. After all, they represent the sorts of statistics most people are interested in: How much does the average person in your workplace make? Which candidate did most people vote for? How tall is the average athlete in the NBA? However, there are other important dimensions to consider when looking at a dataset. For

---

in the full range of available money in peoples' pockets. For such a research question, we might say that a measure of central tendency isn't especially helpful. It's not a bad statistic or an erroneous statistic, it's just not the statistic that's best suited to answering the specific question that you're interested in.

instance, in a room where the average person has $20, does everyone in the room have exactly $20 in their pocket, or are there differences in how much every person has? If so, how big are these differences? It might be useful to know, for example, whether the amount of money in peoples' pockets varies from $15-$25 or whether it varies from $0-$40.

What we're describing here is variance: the amount that scores differ around the central tendency. In a sample with absolutely 0 variances, everyone would have the exact same score. As variance goes up, so too does the distance between scores and the central tendency. With greater variance, we expect people to differ more from the average score and to differ from it by a greater amount. In fact, we can even calculate the *average* amount that a typical person differs from the average score, a value known as the standard deviation.[26] For example, if the average amount of money in the pocket of people in a room is $20 with a standard deviation of $1, we can say that the average person differs from $20 by about $1. If we compare this to a room with an average amount of money of $20 and a standard deviation of $10, we can say that people in the second room are more likely to have $10 or $30 in their pockets than people in the first room. Another way to put is that both rooms have an average of $20 per person, but the second room is "noisier" in that peoples' scores vary more around that central tendency.

Inferential Statistics—t-Tests

To this point, we've seen how we can use descriptive statistics to summarize the general shape of a dataset. For example, without looking at a spreadsheet full of numbers, you know that there is more money in a room with an average amount per person of $50 than there is in a room with an average amount per person of $10. You also know that you'll probably be closer to estimating the amount of money in a given person's pocket in a room with a standard deviation of $1 than in a room with a standard deviation of $5. Applied to the real world, we can use measures like these to predict which states are the most likely to vote for one political party or another (or which will be a toss-up) and to know which restaurants are probably going to lead to a better dining experience (e.g., based on online ratings).

And, if we only ever used statistics to concisely describe phenomena in the world around us, that would be pretty darned useful. However, we can also use these statistics in a much more powerful way. Using a category of statistics called *inferential statistics*, we can go beyond merely describing a

---

[26] It's slightly more complicated than that, but for present purposes, this gets the point across!

dataset and start answering more complex questions about it. For instance, descriptive statistics typically only looks at a single variable at a time (e.g., age), and so they're fairly limited in the types of questions we can ask (e.g., how old is the average furry?) But what about questions that involve associations between two or more variables?

For example, let's suppose we want to answer the question "who's better at science, anime fans or sports fans?" This is a question that involves two variables: a person's science skill and the fan group one belongs to. By involving more than one variable, it becomes a much more interesting, but complex, question to answer. One way to test it would be to get a sample of anime fans and a sample of sports fans, give them a science test, and see which group performs better. Pretty straightforward, right? Let's say we did that: we grabbed 5 anime fans and 5 sports fans, gave them a science test, and found that anime fans scored an average of 70% and sports fans scored an average of 60%. What would we conclude from this?

At first glance, the answer seems pretty obvious: the anime fans seem better at science, since they scored, on average, higher than the sports fans. But remember, our question wasn't "who is better at science, a *sample* of anime fans or a *sample* of sports fans"—we want to make a claim about *all* anime fans and *all* sports fans. As we'll discuss in a later section of this chapter, it's pretty much impossible for us to measure *all* anime fans and all sports fans. As such, we're stuck trying to draw conclusions about which group is smarter based only on these two samples.

Still, you might argue, our samples seem to suggest that anime fans were smarter, so what's the problem? Well, what if we were to grab another random sample of 5 anime fans and another sample of 5 sports fans? Would we expect anime fans to win again, or is it possible that sports fans might win next time?

Let's imagine some possible datasets, this time with variance information in addition to central tendency. Let's imagine, for example, that the anime fans' scores looked like this (70%, 68%, 69%, 71%, and 72%) and the sports fans' scores looked like this (60%, 58%, 62%, 61%, 59%). What does this suggest? Well, we can see that the anime fans scored an average of 70%, and every anime fan in our sample scored pretty close to that. We can also see that sports fans scored an average of 60%, and every sports fan scored pretty close to that. So, if we were to grab another 5 anime fans and another 5 sports fans, what might we expect? Well, given how little variability we found in the scores, we might reasonably expect another set of anime fans to score pretty close to 70% and another set of sports fans to score pretty close to 60%, since there doesn't seem to be much variability in their scores here.

Now, imagine a different dataset. This time, anime fans' scores looked like this (70%, 95%, 45%, 100%, 40%) and sports fans' scores looked like this (60%, 100%, 20%, 90%, 30%). The averages are the same as the previous dataset: an average of 70% for anime fans and 60% for sports fans. But if we were to pull 5 new anime fans and 5 new sports fans, would you expect the averages to stay the same? Probably not. With so much variability in these scores, there's every reason to believe that our next set of anime fans may well contain several people who fail, while the next set of sports fans may contain a lot of people who did really well.

In other words, our question about which group is better at science is more complex than at first glance: it's not enough to just compare the average scores of the two groups and see which is higher. We also need to consider information about the variability of the group scores to see whether we might expect the same result if we were to run the study again, or whether we would expect a different result next time. This is, at its core, the logic behind a type of statistical test known as a *t*-test: comparing how big the difference is between the average of two groups compared to how much variability is in the two groups. If there is a big difference between the group averages and if there is relatively little variability in each group's scores, we can conclude that, yes, one group's scores are *statistically significantly* higher than the other group, meaning we would expect to find the difference again and again if we were to keep sampling from those populations.[27] This is the same underlying logic behind many of the group comparisons in this book (e.g., comparing furries to anime fans), and when we claim that one group scored higher than the other, we are typically doing so based on this logic.[28]

---

[27] There is, of course, more to the test than this, but this is the basic logic of the test. For something to be considered *statistically significant*, scientists have to show that a difference between the groups that's *this big* with variance *this low* could *only* happen due to random chance 5% of the time or less, which is where you may have heard the expression "$p < .05$."

[28] We don't show the underlying statistical analyses, including *t*-scores and *p*-values, or their equivalents in ANOVAs—a variant of this logic that involves comparisons between two or more groups—to avoid overwhelming readers with numbers. Nevertheless, for each statement where one group scored higher than another, an analysis like this was run to test and support the point.

Inferential Statistics—Correlations

Inferential statistics can also be used to answer other types of questions. For example, earlier in this chapter we described studies designed to test questions about correlation—the extent to which we can predict a person's score on one variable by knowing their score on another variable. In theory, if two variables are correlated, it means that we should be able to predict, better than chance, a person's score on Variable Y by knowing their score on Variable X. If this is true, then we can say variables X and Y are correlated. If not, we would say that they are not correlated.

We describe correlations using a numeric score that ranges from -1 to +1. Correlations with a positive value are called positive correlations. They describe a relationship between two variables where, as scores on one variable increase, scores on the other variable also increase. As an illustrative example, imagine two variables: a person's age and the amount of pain they have in their back. As scores on one variable go up (i.e., age), so too do scores on the other variable (i.e., back pain). In other words, older people in our study would be expected to have more back pain, while younger people in our study likely have less back pain. If this is true, then the two variables can be said to be positively correlated. This means that if I know a person is older, then I can estimate that, in all likelihood, they have more back pain than a typical younger person in the study.

A negative correlation describes the exact same relationship, only the direction is different; as scores on one variable go up, scores on the other variable go down. As an example, imagine how many miles you've driven your car and the value of the car. If we sampled a bunch of different cars, we would imagine that, all else being equal, the cars that have been driven farther are probably worth less money. As one variable goes up (i.e., mileage), the other variable goes down (i.e., value).

Finally, we describe no correlation at all with a value of 0. This means that knowing something about one variable tells us next to nothing about their score on a second variable. As an example, imagine a person's age and their liking of chicken soup. Chances are, a person's liking of soup changes very little over time, meaning that if we know a participant is young, this tells us nothing about whether they like or dislike chicken soup. Knowing this person's age tells us nothing about their liking of chicken soup, meaning that these two variables are not correlated with one another.

The basic logic behind a correlation is fairly simple: the more accurately we can predict someone's score on Y based on their score on X, the more strongly correlated the two variables are. If a correlation is sufficiently strong, we can conclude that it's probably "real," and not simply a fluke or a product of luck or noise in the data. On the other hand, if a correlation is extremely weak (e.g., a person's age tells us almost nothing about their liking of chicken soup), we can conclude that any perceived association between the variables is simply due to random chance, and that, in reality, there is probably no association between the two. Another way to think about it is like this: if a correlation is quite strong, we can reasonably conclude that it probably didn't happen by accident. If we were to run the study again and again, we'd probably find that older people consistently have more back pain than younger people and that this wasn't a fluke caused by happening to find a unique sample of old people with bad backs or a rare sample of young people with no back pain. If a correlation is quite weak, on the other hand, we generally conclude that, in all likelihood, if we were to run the study again, we probably wouldn't find evidence for it again, meaning that there isn't actually a real association between the two variables.[29]

Throughout this book, you'll see countless examples of us describing two variables as being associated with one another (e.g., the more strongly one identifies with other furries, the more likely they are to attend furry conventions). In nearly all of these cases, we're describing associations between variables that were calculated using the logic of correlational analysis discussed above. As is the case with our discussion of the logic of *t*-tests and with our discussion of descriptive statistics as a whole, we hope that, armed with a better understanding of what these statistics are, where they come from, and what they mean, some of the confusion, spookiness, and mistrust of them can be alleviated.

Operationalization: What Are We Measuring?

As we mentioned earlier in this chapter, an important part of the scientific process is collecting data in a systematic way to form or test theories and

---

[29] Once again, the actual calculations and underlying statistical procedures are more complex than is described here, but this is sufficient to help you understand the logic behind many of the analyses in this book. Behind every discussed association between two variables is a correlation analysis that was run to test for the significance of the association. It is worth noting that with a large enough sample size, even fairly weak correlations can be statistically significant. For example, if we find a weak, but significant correlation in a sample of 10,000 people, it's unlikely to be a fluke in a sample this size—we can fairly safely conclude that if we got another large sample, we'd probably find a similarly weak correlation. Generally, larger sample sizes are needed to detect weaker correlations through the random noise in a dataset.

models about how the world works. At first glance, this seems like a pretty simple thing to do; once you've decided on the type of study you're running (e.g., an interview, a survey, an experiment), just go out and measure the thing you want to measure using an appropriate measurement device. You use a ruler if you want to measure distance and a thermometer when you want to measure temperature—what could be simpler than that?

As it turns out, there's a lot more to measurement than you might think. Sure, measurement is simple when we want to measure physical, tangible things. If I want to measure the height of a person, all I need to do is stand them next to a ruler or run a tape measure up alongside them to get their height. If I want to take that person's temperature, just plunk the thermometer in their mouth for a minute or two.

But what if I want to measure the person's aggression?

Aggression is an abstract concept. I can't bore a hole into a person's skull and drop in a ruler to measure their aggression. I can't observe the physical mass of the aggression in their head, because it has no physical form. We can all agree that aggression, as a concept, exists. We can talk about individual differences in aggression (e.g., Tom is more aggressive than Steve.) But how do we assign numbers to it when we can't see, touch, or weigh it?

It'd be easy to shrug this off as a rare, isolated problem, but the reality is that a *lot* of the science we do requires the measurement of the abstract, the intangible, and the unseeable. If we were to restrict ourselves only to the things we could see, feel, touch, hear, or smell, we would have to abandon much of the social sciences, including psychology, sociology, political science, and economics. And while some people might be okay with abandoning these "softer" sciences, this approach would also require us to do away with large swaths of the "hard" sciences as well, including physics, chemistry, and biology.[30] Hopefully, you're not ready to give up on science just because not everything lends itself readily to measurement!

Operationalization: Indirect Measurement

Okay, so how do we measure what we can't see, touch, or experience with our own senses? Well, the next best thing is to measure the phenomenon we're interested in through proxies—that is, by-products or residual effects of the thing we're actually interested in. Returning to our aggression example, I might not be able to measure Tom and Steve's aggression directly, but I can measure indicators and outcomes of their

---

[30] Can you "measure" evolution—the backbone of modern biology—with a ruler? Has anyone "seen" a quark with their own eyes, or touched dark matter?

aggression! I can count the number of fights Tom and Steve have been in or the number of holes they've punched in the wall. I can measure the volume of their voice when they get frustrated or count the number of times they've threatened another person. I can measure spikes in their heart rate, changes in the conductance of their skin, and increases in their breathing rate as they get angry. I can even ask them to rate their anger on a scale from 1 to 10 or ask people who know them to rate how aggressive they are on average.

Skeptical readers might argue that these by-products of aggression are still not aggression itself and that this whole endeavor feels too removed from the thing we want to measure to count as a proper measure. This critique is often directed toward the social sciences, like psychology, where it is often necessary to measure by-products, self-reported feelings, or behavior and infer the variable of interest from these measures. But what if we told you that the same use of indirect or proxy measures happens all the time in the hard sciences without the same outcry?

For example, think about a typical mercury thermometer. It's about as simple a measure of temperature as you can get: when a room is hot, the volume of mercury in a sealed tube increases, causing it to rise, and when it gets cold, the volume contracts, causing its level to fall. Almost no one would argue that this is an invalid way to measure temperature. In fact, most of us use such thermometers to measure the temperature on a cold winter day to decide what to wear or to determine whether a loved one is running a fever.[31]

But just what *is* temperature? Put in simple language, temperature is the average speed of the particles bouncing around in a region. In hotter places, the particles move faster on average, while in colder areas, the particles move slower on average.[32] This being the case, a "direct" measure of temperature would detect and calculate the average speed of the particles in an area. But that's not what a mercury thermometer does. Instead, a mercury thermometer measures temperature indirectly, through an increase in the volume of a known mass of mercury inside of a sealed space. When the average velocity of the mercury particles is faster, the volume of mercury

[31] Actually, most of us these days probably use a digital thermometer, which bases measurements of temperature on a thermocouple, but the overarching principle being discussed here still applies—it just happens to be easier to explain the inner workings of a mercury thermometer!

[32] And, at absolute zero, the lowest possible temperature, particles cease to move at all, which is why there can be no temperature lower than absolute zero—there is no less possible movement than *no* movement!

expands to fill the space and we see its level rise. As a result, we have an indirect measure of particle speed via the volume of a mass of mercury.

As another example of indirect measurement in the "hard" sciences, we turn to neuroscience and the measurement of brain activity. Functional magnetic resonance imaging, or fMRI, is used by researchers and clinicians alike to measure localized brain activity. In a nutshell, fMRI measures which parts of the brain increase in activity during a specific period (e.g., while doing a memory task). It's used by neuroscientists to better understand the functions of specific parts of the brain and by clinicians to determine if and where unusual brain activity may be occurring. If a certain part of your brain lights up while you're remembering the faces of people you know, we might conclude that part of the brain is responsible for face recognition or the storage of face information.

But what, exactly, is being measured in fMRI? Is it *actually* measuring "brain activity"? In a word, no. Brain activity is the firing of neurons—millions of tiny electrochemical reactions. These individual reactions aren't what's being measured in fMRI, however. Instead, fMRI relies on the blood-oxygen-level-dependent (BOLD) signal—a measurement of oxygen use and blood flow in a region of the brain. In other words, neuroscientists *infer* that an area of the brain is more active if there is an increase in blood flow and oxygen use in that particular region.[33] As an analogy, this would be like inferring that a house is being built somewhere in a neighborhood because you notice an increased number of construction vehicles driving by on the otherwise quiet road. You may not see the construction itself, but you can see evidence that construction is going on nearby.

Just to be clear, inferring temperature from mercury levels and brain activity through increased blood flow aren't *bad* assumptions to make! These are perfectly defensible, practical ways to measure these phenomena. But they *are* indirect ways of measuring them—no different, in principle, than measuring aggression through its by-products. If we wouldn't dismiss physics for using mercury thermometers or biology for using fMRI, it would be fairly arbitrary to draw the line at indirect measures of psychological constructs like aggression simply because they rely on using indirect measures.

---

[33] This is, of course, an oversimplification of a very complex process, but we only need to get the basics across for this example!

Operationalization: Psychometrics and Limitations of Measurement Devices

Okay, so let's assume we've accepted that indirect measures are an appropriate way to measure abstract or intangible phenomena. We now run into a new problem: *which* indirect measure should we use? Returning to our aggression example, we suggested numerous different ways to measure aggression: frequency of violent behavior, bodily response, self-reported feelings of anger, and reports of aggression from others. Which one of these should we use in our study? This is a question about operationalization—a fancy-sounding word that refers to the way a researcher decides to measure something in their study. In other words, each of these different approaches represents a different operationalization of the variable "aggression."

Scientists spend a lot of time thinking about operationalization when designing their studies. This is because there are, in theory, countless ways to operationalize any given variable. At the end of the day, the ways to operationalize a given variable are limited only by the creativity of the scientist. This doesn't mean, of course, that every operationalization is equally useful! Some measurements are better suited for specific purposes, just like some tools are better suited for specific jobs. For example: measuring how many holes a person punches in a wall might be a good tool for measuring very high levels of physical aggression in extremely violent people, but may prove fairly useless when it comes to distinguishing more mundane, day-to-day levels of aggression.[34] Likewise, asking a person to report how angry they feel could be a fairly straightforward way to measure their level of aggression here and now, but it's vulnerable to participants lying. And while we certainly *could* ask the classmates and co-workers of someone to rate how aggressive that person is, this assumes some people know the person in question, and that they would be easy to track down and willing to participate in the researcher's study.

While some of the limitations of a particular operationalization are pretty obvious, others can be fairly subtle. For example, imagine the survey question "How many times have you threatened someone or gotten into a fight?" At first, it may seem like a pretty simple, straightforward way to measure aggression: People who score higher on this question are probably more aggressive than people who score lower on this question. However, the wording of the question creates a problem known as a double-barreled

---

[34] As an analogy, imagine using a scale designed to weigh trucks to try and measure the weight of a feather. This is a problem of sensitivity: The feather is probably too light to even register on the truck scale!

question; the question is asking about two separate concepts at once. Imagine two people answering this question, one who has threatened people 10 times but never actually gotten into a fight, and one who has gotten into 5 serious physical fights, but never once threatened a person.[35] The first person would score higher (10) than the second person (5) on this measure, even though most of us would probably agree that getting into 5 serious physical fights is probably more aggressive than making 10 idle threats, but never actually acting on those threats.

To illustrate another example of how the wording of a question can subtly undermine its utility, imagine if we decided to measure a person's aggression by asking them the question "Do you consider yourself to be an aggressive person?" What does a response to this question mean? On the one hand, we probably want to say that a person who scores high on this measure is probably more aggressive than someone who scores low on this question. But is that *actually* what the question is measuring? What if a person was quite aggressive, but didn't consider their actions to be aggressive? A violent person who decides that their actions were always in self-defense and, thus, don't count as aggression, would score low on this scale, even though an outside observer might consider this person to be highly aggressive based on their behavior. In this case, the question is measuring someone's *belief* about a phenomenon, rather than the actual phenomenon itself.[36]

As a final example, let's imagine that we want to thoroughly assess a person's aggression. As such, we give them a 500-question survey, with each question asking them about all manner of aggressive behavior: getting into gunfights, knife fights, fights with broken bottles, arguments with loved ones, arguments with family members, breaking windows, punching walls, knocking down doors, and so on. Such a measure would certainly be thorough and would undoubtedly make nuanced distinctions between different types of aggression. However, the questionnaire is also

---

[35] The second person might even say that they don't make threats, they *act*!

[36] A similar problem arises in other fields as well. For example, in my research methods classes, I often ask students to design a study to test the hypothesis that playing violent video games increases players' aggression. Numerous students will include a question such as "Have violent video games made you more aggressive?" on the survey. Despite *appearing* to measure the phenomenon in question, this question only measures whether people *think* violent games have made them more aggressive; it says nothing about whether or not violent games actually *have* made people more aggressive (something which could be true regardless of whether or not people think it's true!).

prohibitively long—no one wants to answer 500 questions about the same subject.[37] As a result, participants may drop out of the study halfway through or may stop paying attention to the questions and haphazardly answer without thinking about them.

These examples illustrate just some of the considerations psychologists have to consider when designing their measures, through a field known as psychometrics. In fact, this is a significant part of learning to be a scientist: learning what tools are out there, the tradeoffs in their respective strengths and weaknesses, and how to design and validate new measures when existing measures are insufficient. Ultimately, scientists are trained to recognize that there is no such thing as a "perfect" measure. At the end of the day, their job is to choose or create a measure that works sufficiently for their intended purpose. This is how a good skeptic should determine the value of a measure in a study: does it do what it's intended to do in an adequate fashion? Does it get the job done with reasonably few drawbacks? Can you think of a better way to measure the variable that doesn't introduce the same or additional problems?

Untrained skeptics often treat the existence of a flaw in a measure as reason enough to dismiss the measure or the study as a whole without considering the scope of the flaw or whether it could reasonably be expected to impact the study's conclusions. The author of this chapter has seen, far too often, studies being completely dismissed or trivialized by critics who point out that a measure was imperfect, and therefore could not be trusted or should not have been used. By this logic, however, any study can be ignored so long as it measures something since all measures are imperfect.

As an illustrative final example, let's take the simplest of measurement devices: a ruler. On the surface, it seems pretty hard to criticize a ruler: it's simple to use and it can tell us fairly reasonably how long something is or how far apart two things are. But if we were truly determined to invalidate a study, we could argue that a ruler is an inadequate way to measure length and distance. After all, we could argue, a metal ruler can expand and contract based on the ambient temperature of the room. This introduces errors in our measurement and can cause us to overestimate or underestimate lengths and distances. Even if the researchers were to use a wooden ruler or a tape measure, we could nevertheless argue that humidity levels, stretching, or warping of the devices over time could make them sufficiently unreliable for the task at hand. Moreover, rulers require a degree of interpretation: is this

[37] Ironically, such a measure might even make participants a bit more aggressive by the end of it!

object 6.1 inches long or 6.2 inches long? Depending on the angle of the viewer and the thickness of the lines on the ruler, we could argue that there is room for researcher bias in interpretation to creep into the measure and make it unsuitable for use as such.

Hopefully, we can all see that this example is a fairly silly one. All of the critiques of the ruler are valid, but we can also probably agree that the scope and nature of the concerns likely don't warrant dismissing a study out of hand just because the scientists running the study used a ruler—with all of its imperfections. In fact, even a warped, damaged, or numberless ruler could be a reasonably good measurement if used properly. For example, while a ruler with no numbers might not be able to tell us precisely how tall something is, we could nevertheless creatively use it to compare the relative length of two different objects. Imagine, for example, that one person is "five rulers" tall and another person is "six rulers" tall. In this case, the ruler is useful as a measure of relative height, even if it's not useful as a measure of absolute height: It can still tell us which person is taller. Likewise, the tendency of a ruler to expand or contract in different conditions becomes a fairly moot point if we conduct our measurements in consistent settings (e.g., keeping the temperature and humidity at steady levels throughout the study).

To summarize this section, scientists rely on tools to measure the world around them, whether the things they're measuring are tangible or abstract. When possible, scientists try to use or adapt previously existing measures, but other times they are forced to create something new for their intended purpose. Regardless, measures will always be flawed in some way—there is no such thing as a perfect measure. Measures always involve trade-offs, with researchers having to use their experience and training to make informed decisions about these trade-offs so they can employ the most appropriate measurement device for the task at hand. As such, an operationalization that might be ideal in the context of one study might be wholly inappropriate in another study. While it's definitely worth scrutinizing the measures used by researchers in their studies and keeping their strengths and limitations in mind when interpreting their results, it's important to not dismiss a study out of hand just because a measure is flawed or isn't the measure that you would have used. Instead, consider the nature of those limitations, whether there is reason to believe that the limitations might have systematically affected the results of the study, and think critically about the scope and magnitude of the flaw before deciding whether there should be caveats attached to a study's conclusions.

Sampling: Who Are We Studying?

Scientists seek to build models and develop theories to explain the world around them. This is why they conduct studies: to gather data about the world and how it works and to test hypotheses generated by their models. However, inherent in this approach is the fact that scientists, while trying to understand the world as a whole, are unable to study it in its entirety. Physicists can conduct experiments to test their models in laboratories on Earth but rarely have the ability to conduct the same test on Mars, let alone in another galaxy. Likewise, chemists can conduct experiments involving various compounds in various conditions, but they lack the time and resources to test every compound in every concentration in every possible environmental circumstance. Biologists can conduct drug trials to test the effectiveness of a treatment for a disease in a sample of willing participants, but they will never be able to test the effectiveness of the treatment in every single human being on the planet.

All of these examples illustrate a problem called generalization or external validity: scientists want to draw broad conclusions about the world based on studies of a subset of that world. The issue is pervasive across all of science, from psychology to physics. Ultimately, scientists in these fields do the best they can, sampling the world around them and using the results of that sample to make inferences about how the rest of the world works.

But what if our sample is an imperfect representation of the world? What if, for example, a chemist's laboratory study fails to represent conditions in an especially hot or especially cold part of the world? What if a biologist's treatments work for people of one age group, but not another? What if the results of a physics experiment work in controlled laboratory conditions, but yield entirely different results in the complex and messy real world? In such cases, one could argue that the conclusions scientists draw about the world from their study may be, at best, somewhat inaccurate and, at worst, completely wrong.

Sampling: Generalizing From Samples to Populations

To better understand the issue of generalizability, we should first introduce some important terms. The term population refers to the group or circumstances that we would ideally like to be able to draw conclusions about. Doctors, for example, might want to draw conclusions about the effectiveness of their treatments for all humans. A sociologist, on the other hand, might want to draw conclusions about working-class Americans, while an archeologist might limit their generalizations to the inhabitants of one small Mesoamerican tribe who lived in a particular region one thousand years ago.

In contrast to a population, a sample refers to a subset of instances or exemplars drawn from the population of interest and used as a stand-in or representation of the population as a whole for a study. In other words, a sample is the people I was able to get for my studies. In an ideal world, the sample would be the same as the population; scientists would prefer to sample the entirety of a population so they wouldn't have to make inferences or engage in guesswork about the population! If we wanted to calculate the average age of every person in Canada, the only way to do so perfectly would be to collect age information about every person currently living in Canada and then calculate the average.

Practically speaking, this is impossible, even under the best of circumstances. The census is a concerted effort by the government to gather information about every person in the country. Despite having millions of dollars of resources and hundreds or even thousands of employees behind it, a census will never be able to gather data on *every* Canadian, for reasons ranging from some people refusing to complete it[38] to people getting missed due to having no fixed address.

Because it's nearly impossible to study every member of a population, scientists do the next best thing: they gather a sample. From the sample, they make informed estimates and build models about the population. For example, if a researcher were unable to measure the average age of every Canadian, they might gather a sample of several thousand Canadians and calculate the average age of their sample. This would be used as a stand-in or approximation of the average age of all Canadians.

Sampling: Imperfect Samples

It's important to note, right out of the gate, that all samples are imperfect. Even if we were to measure the age of every single person in the country of Canada except for one person who refused to answer, and were then to calculate that average, it would not represent the *exact* average age of all Canadians. That final person's age would shift the average of all Canadians ever-so-slightly if it could have been included, meaning its absence does impact the data. Of course, this doesn't mean that the *estimated* average will be drastically inaccurate. If the average age was gathered from every

---

[38] I once had a job working in a Statistics Canada call center. It was my job was to call people who had refused to do their census and attempt to convince them to do so. Suffice to say, I was not always successful, even though people risked a fine and jail time for refusing to fill out their census!

Canadian except for one, we would expect our estimate to be extremely close to the average age of all Canadians. The point, however, is that by being a sample and not the entire population, a sample will always be an estimation of the population and not the actual value of the population. Samples will always be imperfect, by their very nature.

However, just because an estimate generated from a sample is imperfect, that doesn't mean it can't be close enough to be useful. This is the goal of scientists: to generate estimates from their samples that are close enough to their population of interest that they can be useful. The trick to doing this effectively is fairly simple, at least in principle: gather a sample that's as representative (i.e., similar) to the population as possible. For example, if a population consists of 20% senior citizens, then a good, representative sample would similarly be made up of 20% senior citizens. If the sample doesn't represent the makeup of the population it's supposed to be a stand-in for, this raises significant problems, regardless of how large the sample is. To illustrate this principle, imagine if someone were to gather a sample of Canadians, but the sample was made up only of 100,000 senior citizens and no one else. Chances are fairly good that this sample's average age would be an *overestimation* of the actual average age of the population of Canada. This is because the sample does not perfectly represent the makeup of the Canadian population; it's missing all of the children, young adults, and middle-aged people.

Okay, so scientists should do their best to create a representative sample. But herein lies the next problem, a familiar refrain at this point: it is almost impossible to get a perfectly representative sample. To illustrate why, let's imagine that, instead of measuring the average age of Canadians, we wanted to measure how positive the average Canadian feels about maple syrup, on a scale from 1-10. Let's be generous and assume that we were able to get a sample that was *perfectly* representative of the age breakdown of Canadians: our sample has the *exact* same proportion of 12-year-olds, 13-year-olds, 14-year-olds, et cetera as the population of Canada. In this case, we could say that the sample is perfectly representative of Canadians when it comes to age. However, age isn't the only relevant variable to consider in this study. For example, a person's attitude toward maple syrup might depend on which province the person lives in, on their socioeconomic status, cultural background, or medical history, just to name a few variables! So now, to have a perfectly representative sample, we not only need to have the same proportion of 14-year-olds as the population of Canada, but we also have to have the same number of upper-middle-class, 14-year-old, second-generation

Portuguese immigrants with a gluten allergy as there are in the Canadian population.

Hopefully, this example illustrates how nearly impossible it is to obtain a perfectly representative sample of a population across all variables of interest. Instead, the best researchers can do is to accept that their samples will always have a degree of error in them, and recognize that the estimates and models they derive from these will necessarily be somewhat inaccurate. The goal is to come reasonably close to representing the population on the variables that are the most theoretically relevant. If we're estimating the population's age, for example, it's more important for our sample to represent the generational breakdown of the population than it is to represent the religious breakdown of the population.

Sampling: Size and Random Sampling

So what can scientists do to maximize the representativeness of their sample? The best thing they can do, from a statistical standpoint, is to obtain a large, random sample of the population. A large sample matters, since it increases the likelihood that relatively small subgroups will be represented in the sample. As a bit of a silly example, imagine if we gathered a random sample of 5 Canadians and used this to estimate the age of the average Canadian. Given how rare 105-year-old people are, it is statistically unlikely that our random sample of 5 people will happen to include a 105-year-old person by sheer chance. Likewise, if a particular racial group makes up 1% of the population, it's unlikely that any members of that group will make it into a random sample of 5 people. As a result, the sample could give the impression that the racial group simply doesn't exist, effectively erasing them from consideration in the estimation or model being developed.

Okay, so a large sample is a more representative sample. But size, in and of itself, isn't the only thing that matters.[39] A random sampling technique is just as important, if not more important, than size when it comes to a sample's ability to represent a population. From a statistical perspective, if every person in a population has an equal likelihood of being included in a

---

[39] In fact, size generally becomes less and less important as it increases. The increase in sample size from 100 to 200 people, for example, is *far* more impactful than the increase in sample size from 10,100 to 10,200 people when it comes to a sample's representativeness! This is why sample sizes of a few thousand people, properly randomly sampled from a population, can be a fairly good representation of a population of hundreds of millions of people—one quickly sees diminishing returns in representativeness from simply increasing one's sample size.

sample, then a reasonably sized sample drawn from that population should be a fairly good representation of that population.

To illustrate why random sampling is so important, imagine pulling marbles out of a hat. The hat contains 100 marbles, half of which are green and half of which are blue. To represent pure random sampling—every marble having the same chance of being pulled out of the hat—imagine that the marbles are all the same size. If you were to pull 20 marbles out of the hat blindly, you should, according to statistical principles, end up with a sample that consists of an approximately equal number of green and blue marbles—accurately reflecting the 50/50 split of marbles in the hat (the population).

But what if the blue marbles in our hat were four times the size of the green marbles? In other words, the blue marbles take up more space in the hat and are easier to reach when grabbing marbles. If we then grabbed 20 marbles blindly from *this* hat (without paying attention to their size as we grabbed them), we'd almost certainly end up with more blue marbles than green marbles, simply because the blue marbles were easier to reach than the green ones. As a result, our sample, made of mostly blue marbles, would be far *less* representative of the 50/50 split of blue and green marbles in the hat. This is why researchers need to have both a large and randomly drawn sample of the population.

Sampling: Techniques and Practical Considerations

These are ideals to be strived for whenever researchers sample from a population, but there are also practical tradeoffs to consider. For one thing, scientists are often limited in terms of money, time, and resources. It's easy to tell a scientist doing a phone survey to sample 100,000 people, but if they only have the funding to pay a single research assistant for two weeks, they might be lucky to end up with a few hundred participants at best. Likewise, mailing out a survey to millions of people seems like an easy way to reach a large group, but it also requires paying postage for millions of letters, something which is beyond the budget of many researchers.

Clever readers might land on another alternative: the internet. Posting a survey online is a relatively cheap and easy way to reach a large group of people at once. Indeed, the advent of the internet has, in many ways, dramatically increased the ability of researchers to recruit participants affordably. However, it also runs afoul of the second consideration: random sampling. Recall that purely random sampling means that every person in a population has an equal chance of being recruited into the study. So what happens if the only way to get into our study is by accessing it online?

For one thing, the study, by definition, excludes anyone who does not have access to a computer, along with anyone unable or unwilling to do an online survey. This could mean that our decision to recruit participants online has led to a bias in our sample, which now underrepresents older people and people who cannot afford to own or access a computer. Likewise, if we chose to recruit people by phone, we may well be leaving out people who do not own a phone, people who are socially anxious and dislike answering their phone, and people who work during the day and may not be able to answer the phone at the time when we're calling.

Difficulties in random sampling can occur in other ways. To avoid technology barriers, we may choose to recruit people in person, go out to large, public spaces, and recruit people at random. This carries with it its own set of problems, however: It may exclude people who are unable to leave their homes (e.g., due to physical or psychological conditions). This approach will also favor people who live in the area while reducing the likelihood of sampling people who live farther away. Researchers must also consider the language of the study itself: an English-only survey will necessarily exclude those who don't speak English.

When you put it all together, it quickly becomes apparent how difficult obtaining a representative sample of a population can be. Scientists routinely conduct studies with smaller samples than they would like and sample in non-random ways that introduce bias. This isn't because researchers are oblivious to these issues or because they are deliberately trying to sabotage or bias their studies. Remember, scientists spend years learning about these topics and would prefer to develop models and calculate estimates that most accurately reflect the world around them. It's in their best interest to have as representative a sample as possible. Unfortunately, practical limitations often necessitate trade-offs when it comes to recruiting a sample for a study.

It's important to understand the principles of sampling, representation, and generalization when critiquing research. All too often, people criticize research[40] by attacking a study's sample size without thinking critically about the points they're raising. I frequently see critics argue that a study's sample size is too small despite the study having thousands of participants—a fairly herculean feat in many fields! Likewise, critics are often quick to disparage sample sizes without knowing *why* a small sample size is a problem and without showing evidence that a study's sampling methodology is systematically biased or non-representative. And even in cases when a

---

[40] Especially research whose conclusions they dislike or disagree with!

study's sampling strategy isn't random,[41] critics often can't explain why this is a problem or how these particular biases would undermine the study's findings.[42]

We'll end this section by pointing out that nearly every study ever conducted arguably suffers from imperfect sampling. Pointing this out does not, in and of itself, invalidate a given study. Instead, it should be thought of as a caveat, a consideration when interpreting the study's findings. Think of these problems as existing on a sliding scale that goes from "minor problem" to "major problem." Rather than throwing out a study simply because the sampling methodology was imperfect, instead consider how big a problem the sampling is, and how it might impact the study's conclusions. In many cases, the implication is that the study might not be able to generalize to an *entire* population, but only to a subset of the population (e.g., only younger people, only English-speaking people, only North Americans, etc.) In other cases, an oversight in sampling might warrant a follow-up study being done to address the exclusion of a significant group or to test whether the same results can be found in other, more inclusive samples.

As we'll see in the next section, however, skeptics should be hesitant to outright dismiss or trivialize a study unless there are blatantly egregious problems that seriously undermine the study's ability to draw conclusions.

The Perfect Study Fallacy: How We Learn Anything From Flawed Studies

If you've made it this far in the chapter, chances are you may be having a bit of an existential crisis when it comes to science. It's the same crisis every science graduate student feels when they learn that every study they've ever heard about was plagued with flaws and limitations: every design is flawed, every measure is limited, and every sampling technique is imperfect. How can we know *anything*?

Do not despair—we promise, there is a light at the end of the tunnel! In fact, we've already alluded to it somewhat throughout this chapter. The solution? Converging evidence! In a nutshell, we can be increasingly confident in a finding, despite the flaws of the study from which it came, if we can find more evidence for it in additional studies.

---

[41] Few, if any studies can claim to have a *perfectly* random sampling strategy.

[42] As a silly example: if a study looking to estimate a population's age failed to include people who had freckles, one could argue that this *is* a limitation to the sample's representation of the general population. However, you'd be hard-pressed to explain how, exactly, this oversight systematically changes the estimate of the population's age (e.g., are freckles related to age in any way?).

But wait, how does that work? If we have to be skeptical about the results of a single flawed study, how do additional flawed studies help us out of the problem? Doesn't the pile of problems and limitations just compound on itself and give us *more* reason to be skeptical?

Not necessarily! As an analogy, let's imagine a brick wall. There are hundreds of structural weaknesses in a brick wall because it's made up of small, individual pieces (bricks). The gap between any two bricks represents a potential structural weakness, a place where the wall could come apart and collapse under its own weight. Collapse would, indeed, be likely if we were to simply stack bricks on top of one another, 20 feet high. But that's not how we build brick walls, is it? We intersperse the bricks, staggering their placement so that the seam between two bricks on one layer is covered up by a brick on the layer above it. The wall is designed so that each brick provides structural support for the layers above and below it, precisely at their weakest points.

Scientists do something analogous when it comes to research. We know that no one study can do everything. By its very nature, designing a study, operationalizing variables, and choosing a sampling strategy will always involve trade-offs; some studies need to be done on a shoestring budget. Others have a larger budget but are pressed for time. Still others sample from a highly dedicated, but small sample. Others allow for the recruitment of a large sample, but the study can't be long, lest participants become bored. Some designs allow researchers to calculate average tendencies and correlations between variables, but oversimplify reality by relying on numeric scales, while others collect rich, detailed, nuanced data, but at the cost of being unable to conduct statistical analyses.

Knowing that these different strengths and weaknesses exist, we can run a series of studies that complement the strengths and weaknesses of one another. For example, our first foray into a topic might begin with an open-ended, exploratory study on a small number of participants. While this study can collect detail-rich information and guide the development of future questions, it suffers from a small sample size and the inability to calculate averages or correlations between variables. In a follow-up study, however, we might create survey questions based on the initial interviews and give them out to a large number of participants. Such a study would make up for the limitations of the previous study (e.g., a small sample size, inability to calculate statistics) while presenting its own limitations (e.g., inability to determine causal direction). As a third study in a series, we might design an experiment where we experimentally manipulate one of the variables and randomly assign participants to conditions to see whether that variable is causally linked to the other variable in our observed correlation. This study might suffer from a smaller sample size than the survey study, but it makes up for it by being able to do what the survey study cannot: establish causal direction. Just like a brick wall, the weaknesses of any one study in the set are offset by the strengths of the other studies. If one study used a too-long measure of some variable, a follow-up study might use a shorter measure. If one study only sampled participants online, a second study might recruit participants in person. If one study used qualitative data, a follow-up study might collect quantitative data.

To better understand this principle of converging evidence, it's helpful to apply the philosophical concept of Occam's razor[43] to our interpretation of a body of research. In this case, let's imagine that we have ten hypothetical studies, each using a different methodology, sampling technique, and set of measures, all of which reach the same conclusion: playing video games puts people in a better mood. Which of these two possibilities is more likely?

A. All ten of the studies were inaccurate, reaching a conclusion that does not match reality. In each case, the faulty conclusion came about for different reasons: sometimes as a result of research bias, other times as a result of sheer coincidence in the sample obtained, and sometimes as a result of participants wishing to sabotage the study. The point is, ten different studies each came to the same, incorrect solution for ten different reasons.

B. All ten of the studies are correct, reaching the same conclusion because it's true that playing video games puts people in a better mood.

According to Occam's razor, we should prefer the second possibility, as it requires the fewest assumptions. Sure, if a single study reaches a conclusion,

---

[43] For those who don't know, Occam's razor argues that the simplest explanation, or the one that requires the fewest assumptions or unknowns, is the preferred one. For example, imagine I were to make myself a plate of chicken wings and leave them on the table while I grab a soda. Upon returning, I find that the chicken wings are gone. I don't know for sure what happened to the chicken wings, so I come up with some plausible theories. One theory is that my cat jumped up on the table and ate them. Another possibility is that an extradimensional being teleported in, stole my wings, and teleported them away. While both theories are possible, for the latter theory to work, I would have to presuppose that a race of extradimensional beings exists and that they have transporter technology—two things I cannot be sure about. In contrast, I do have a cat and she has been known to eat chicken. As such, according to Occam's razor, I should prefer the first explanation, as it requires the fewest assumptions or appeals to unknown entities.

we should be cautious in how we interpret that conclusion. There's plenty of reason to suspect that one or more of the study's specific details might have conceivably led to an erroneous conclusion, and flukes can always happen. But with each additional study that reaches the same conclusion, it becomes increasingly unlikely that the conclusion reached was simply a fluke. Ultimately, if we're able to reach the same conclusion using a different sample, different measures, and different study designs, this is strong evidence that the finding is a fairly robust and resilient one. After all, we're all pretty convinced that gravity exists precisely because anyone can drop anything anywhere on Earth and show that it falls toward the ground. Likewise, if we can find a link between two variables despite measuring those variables in different ways and using different samples, that's a reasonably good sign that we've tapped into a real effect!

For this reason, a good scientist will rarely base the entirety of their conclusion about a subject on the results of a single study. Sure, a single study provides a bit of evidence and is certainly better than no evidence whatsoever. However, scientists aren't in the business of basing the future progress of an entire field on the results of a single study, precisely because they know that every study has flaws, quirks, limitations, and the possibility of sheer dumb luck. This means, somewhat to the disappointment of amateur science enthusiasts everywhere, that science is far more like a slow, gradual accumulation of evidence than it is a race to be the first one to run the *definitive* study that single-handedly *proves* a theory to be true.[44]

This is also why scientists are often at odds with the media whenever television shows and newspapers report on the results of a study: rather than contextualizing a study as being one piece of a much bigger puzzle, or as a first step in a line of research, media outlets talk about individual studies as

---

[44] In fact, scientists and entire scientific fields often find themselves in trouble when they get too far ahead of themselves and forget this. Numerous scientific fields, including social psychology and medicine, to name just a couple, have been dealing with a "replication crisis" in which many of its high-profile studies (many published in top-tier scientific journals) have failed to be reproduceable by other researchers. This problem would be far less likely if more time was dedicated to testing and re-testing prior findings to avoid the possibility that the originals were a fluke or the result of a quirk in the design, analysis, or sample. Unfortunately, there is also significant pressure on researchers to constantly be churning out new and exciting research, as well as pressure from scientific journals to publish new work, rather than replications of prior work. Thankfully, as these issues are brought to light, changes are being made to these fields to slow down the pace of science and ensure that studies are being properly replicated.

"definitive proof" or as "the nail in the coffin." In reality, scientists spend years becoming familiar with a body of research so they can better judge how any single study fits into the broader context and appreciate where the bulk of the evidence is pointing on a given topic.

It's important to keep all of this in mind as you evaluate the research being discussed in this book. Throughout this book, we'll be making numerous claims about furries and the furry fandom based on our research. Some of our findings are well-substantiated trends and patterns we've observed across dozens of studies for more than a decade. Other findings are more tentative, especially when the only evidence for them is from the results of a single study.

As always, we encourage readers to be skeptical of our findings and critical of the conclusions we've reached, especially if they run counter to evidence from other studies or if the claims themselves seem extraordinary or far-fetched. However, at the end of the day, a good scientist goes where the data leads them and is compelled to believe what the preponderance of the evidence shows. Thus, if ten studies suggest that X is true, while only one study opposes it, the scientist should probably be siding with what the ten studies conclude, even if they have reservations or a wish to see further tests to explain what happened with that one unusual study. Similarly, if only a single study supports a conclusion, it's perfectly fine to be skeptical of that study and its conclusions. However, if there is no evidence or other studies to oppose the study's conclusions, then one is limited in their ability to dismiss the study. For example, if one study concluded that people prefer chocolate over vanilla and there is no other study on the subject, I could certainly critique the study's findings or question its methodology. However, without collecting my own data or finding another study that showed the opposite, I wouldn't be in a position to say "Psh, I think this study is wrong—therefore people must prefer vanilla over chocolate!" Data rules supreme when it comes to science, and even a single, imperfect study wins out over no evidence at all. If nothing else, this is all the more incentive for skeptics to run their own studies and throw their hats into the scientific ring.

The Present Research

As we wrap up this chapter on research methods, it's time for us to show our work, so to speak, and introduce the studies and methodologies upon which this book is based. Specifically, this book is based on 30 studies run by the Furscience team between 2011 and 2022 (see Table 4.1), with a combined sample size of just under 25,000 furries from more than 80 different countries and across six different continents.[45] A detailed account of each study's methodology could be its own book in and of itself, so we'll limit our discussion to the broad strokes and general methodology employed across our studies.

First, all of our studies are designed months before they are carried out. This usually entails a meeting between the researchers involved (the Furscience team, as well as other interested collaborators) to discuss research questions of interest. These research questions usually come from a few different places. Sometimes they are replications or extensions of previous studies, reflecting a desire to test the generalizability or resilience of a previous finding. Another source of research questions is prior theory, where we draw upon existing theoretical frameworks developed in our respective fields (e.g., social psychology, fan studies, sociology) and apply them in the context of furries.[46]

A third place we draw research questions is from furries themselves. When we present our research findings at conventions or online, we often get questions, critiques, or suggestions from furries in attendance. Many of our most interesting studies have stemmed directly from furries asking us to test a hypothesis, providing us with an alternative explanation to explore, or simply asking us to measure a variable or phenomenon we'd never considered before.[47] Sometimes these ideas stem from furries who are, themselves, scientists, but other times they come from furries who simply stumble upon a really interesting question from their curiosity or from a critique of our work that they'd like to see us address.

---

[45] It's worth noting that these are not the only studies the Furscience team ran during this time. In fact, in total we've run closer to 50 separate studies in that time. The studies not included in this book were largely exploratory studies consisting of a handful of individual interviews or focus groups. These studies were largely done with the intent of generating research questions for other studies. They're not included in this book because the studies based upon those interviews and focus groups *did* make it into the book instead.

[46] These theories were typically not developed with furries in mind, but it's often interesting to apply them to a furry population. Sometimes this can be done to test the resilience of a theory by looking for evidence for it in a sample that's very different from the one in which it was originally tested. Other times, theories might lead to interesting or unexpected hypotheses when applied to furries.

[47] I can confirm that furries themselves are my favorite source of research questions, since the questions are so often unexpected or come from a completely different perspective than my own!

Once we've settled on our set of research questions, we next decide on the study's design and determine the best way to operationalize all of our variables of interest. These two steps often go hand-in-hand, as our operationalizations may be limited by our methodology. For example, if we decide to do an online study, we are limited in the types of questions we can ask by virtue of needing to be able to program the survey using online survey software. Likewise, if we choose to do a survey study, we need to consider the length of the survey itself; asking respondents to complete a 500+ question survey while at a convention is pretty much out of the question, as respondents would almost certainly get bored and prefer to be doing anything else at a convention besides filling out our survey. This means we sometimes have to use shorter measures of our variables of interest, accepting the trade-off of precision and nuance in favor of being able to fit everything we want in the study. Even so, we're often forced to drop topics from our studies simply due to the length of the survey itself.

The workhorse of our study designs is the survey study, which makes up most of our studies. These survey studies are typically run online or at a furry convention (or, sometimes, both at the same time, which allows us to directly compare furries recruited online to furries recruited at a convention). For surveys run at conventions, we obtain permission from the heads of the convention months in advance, informing them about our plans and, if they wish to see it, letting them see our survey itself. We set up a plan for data collection during the convention, which usually consists of passing physical copies of the survey out to furries who are interested in participating at the convention (e.g., while standing in the registration line, furries standing around in common areas, or furries who approach our table in the vendor's area). Online surveys, on the other hand, typically involve programming the survey online and pilot-testing it to work out bugs and mistakes beforehand before preparing links that we can post on social media and on furry websites and forums (with permission from the administrators).

While survey studies comprise the bulk of our studies, they are not the only types of studies we conduct. Sometimes we'll conduct focus groups or individual interviews at conventions. In this case, we prepare a set of basic, open-ended interview questions beforehand. Furries sign up for the interview or focus group at our table in the convention's vendor hall and meet up with us in a separate, private room for the interview. These interviews are typically recorded (with the participant's permission), and the interviewer asks questions, takes notes, and engages in a dialogue with participants. These can range from 15 minutes to over an hour in length.

We also occasionally conduct experimental studies. These vary in complexity and the degree of setup and control required. For example, a simple experiment might involve randomly assigning participants to get one version of a survey or another, which has different questions, different information, or a different order of questions to let us test hypotheses about how such manipulations affect the way furries respond to other questions. Other times, experiments require a more elaborate set-up. This might include, for example, setting up a portable computer lab on-site at a convention, allowing us to manipulate the sorts of stimuli furries are exposed to and rate their responses to, or memory of, them.

Once we've designed our studies, they next go through an ethical review at one or more of our institutions' review boards. Here, an interdisciplinary team of scholars reviews our proposed study with an eye for potential problems and concerns. The ethics board considers issues such as whether participants are being given enough information up-front to make an informed decision about participating, how participants' information is going to be kept secure, whether any of the questions or methodologies will expose participants to potentially upsetting or disturbing content, and establishing contingencies for what to do in case a participant has an averse response to something in one of our studies.

After approval, we then run the study. This might take place over a single weekend at a convention or it could take place over a month or two online. Once the data is collected, however, we begin the process of analyzing the it.[48] Our analyses range in complexity from basic summary statistics (e.g., averages) to *t*-tests, correlations, and more advanced inferential statistics (e.g., regression, ANOVA, path analysis, factor analysis, structural equation modeling).[49] From there, our results make their way into several different outlets. First, we publish summaries of most of our findings (the ones we

---

[48] In the case of in-person surveys, the additional step of data entry is required—a process which often takes dozens or even hundreds of hours to complete, depending on the size of the sample and the number of questions involved! This work is usually carried out by myself or, in rare circumstances, by undergraduate or graduate research assistants.

[49] It would be far beyond the scope of this book to try and explain all of these other statistical analyses. We mention them here for readers who are fairly adept at statistics and who want to know a bit more about the sorts of procedures we conduct. While we don't show any of these more advanced statistics in this book, many of them were used to generate the summaries in this book and are shown in greater detail throughout many of our published papers.

think that the average furry will be most interested in) on our research website.[50] Second, we put together talks that we give both online and in-person at many furry conventions every year. Third, we often write up book chapters and pieces to be included in collections of writings on the subject of furries. Finally, a subset of our research that we think will be most interesting to academics in our field is written up for publication in peer-reviewed scientific journals, where it can be scrutinized by other scientists.

As we go through the rest of this book, we'll regularly refer back to the source of our findings, such as whether they're supported by data we collected at a single online study in a particular year or across a dozen studies recruiting furries online and in-person at conventions over five years. Each time we do so we're making it clear that the findings presented here are not mere opinion or speculation, but grounded in empirical research. We make a point of providing the number of studies, the basic methodology involved, and the year involved to allow readers to contextualize the findings for themselves. If, for example, a conclusion is based on a single convention study from 2011, readers may want to read the conclusion with the caveat that the data are more than a decade old at the time of this book's writing. As such, it's possible that the responses of the average furry may have changed a bit. Likewise, if we indicate that a finding was based on furries surveyed at a convention, readers may want to keep in mind that furries who attend conventions may be in a better situation financially than furries who are recruited online, by virtue of their being able to afford to go to a convention in the first place.

We hope that this chapter has given you the basic tools needed to be a more informed consumer of the research in this book. Remember that our goal isn't to speak as an unquestioned authority on furries. Instead, we're presenting the findings of a decade-long program of research on a fairly specific set of scientific perspectives (e.g., social-psychological, sociological, political science, fan studies). The findings are not beyond criticism—as is

[50] This step is especially important to us. Given that furries are the source of many of our research ideas, and given that so many furries have been so generous in volunteering their time to participate in our studies, we consider it both an obligation and a point of pride to make the findings available to furries without paywalls, in plain, easy-to-understand language. Additionally, having this information made easily accessible and public also allows the media and others interested in learning more about furries to find our research and learn about furries based on the results of scientific research, rather than being forced to rely on opinion pieces and media misconceptions.

the case with any scientific study—and we would encourage readers to keep in mind the concepts we've discussed about study design, sampling, variable operationalization, and statistics in mind as they read through this book. We also hope that readers have learned a bit about how to be an informed critic—to learn when some criticisms represent significant problems and when they are fairly insubstantial. In doing so, we hope to spark a productive discussion about our work, including suggestions for future studies to build upon what we've done here while avoiding the throwing of babies out with the bathwater.

Table 4.1. Summary of all Furscience studies conducted between 2011 and 2022 that are discussed in this book.

Study Location	Study Year	Participants	Summary of Topics
Furry Fiesta (Convention)	2011	182 Furries	Demographics, Therianthropy, Furry Displays, Fursonas, Furry Identity, Species Identification, Furry Motivation, Self-esteem, Gatekeeping, Belongingness
Online	2011	3042 Furries	Same as Furry Fiesta 2011
Anthrocon (Convention)	2011	742 Furries	Demographics, Therianthropy, Furry Identity, Fursonas, Species Knowledge and Attitudes, Furry Activities, Furry Culture, Furry Subgroups, Non-Furry Interests, Artists/Writers, Fursuits, Path into Furry, Personality, Perceived Prejudice, Self-esteem, Well-Being, Species Identification, Identity Development, Furry Activities, Magical Thinking, Furry Disclosure
Online	2011	859 Furries	Same as Anthrocon 2011
Furry Fiesta (Convention)	2012	320 Furries 138 Sports Fans (Control Group)	Demographics, Furry Identity, Fursonas, Personality, Perceived Prejudice, Self-Esteem, Fantasy, Entitlement, Identity Development, Essentialism
Online	2012	582 Furries	Same as Furry Fiesta 2012
Anthrocon (Convention)	2012	908 Furries	Demographics, Therianthropy, Brony, Furry Identification,

		805 Non-Furries (Online Control Group)	Furry Prejudice, Fursona, Species Identification, Bullying, Fantasy, Self-Esteem, Well-being, Identity Development, Global Citizenship, Animal Knowledge
Furry Fiesta (Convention)	2013	281 Furries 179 Sports Fans (Control Group)	Demographics, Personality, Furry Identification, Brony, Therianthropy, Species Identification, Fantasy, Perceived Prejudice, Motivation, Identity Development, Anthropomorphizing Non-Human Things, Well-Being, Self-Esteem, Purpose in Life, Furry Disclosure, Pornography
Anthrocon (Convention)	2013	702 Furries	Demographics, Therianthropy, Brony, Furry Identification, Fursonas, Well-Being, Species Identification, Magical Thinking, Self-Esteem, Identity Development
Furry Fiesta (Convention)	2014	216 Furries	Demographics, Therianthropy, Brony, Furry Identification, Furry Trajectory, Actual / Ideal Self (Experimental Manipulation), Fursonas, Furry Merchandise, Self-Esteem, Well-Being
Anthrocon (Convention)	2014	1031 Furries 3159 Anime Fans (Control Group) 421 Fantasy Sports fans (Control Group)	Demographics, Therianthropy, Furry Identification, Furry Consumption, Artist / Writer, Friends, Personality, Fantasy, Entitlement, Social awkwardness, Identity Development, Well-Being, Furry Stigma, Furry Disclosure, Nerd Scale, Motivation, Fan Overlap, Furry Prejudice, Fandom Comparison, Fursonas
Furry Fiesta (Convention)	2015	214 Furries	Demographics, Furry Identification, Therianthropy,

(Main Study)			Fursona Similarity (Experimental Manipulation), Emotions, Self-Esteem, Fursonas, Prototypicality, Divisive Fandom Issues, Artists, Well-Being
Furry Fiesta (Convention) (Experiment)	2015	69 Furries 108 Undergrads (Control Group)	Rating of Furry/Non-Furry Porn, Human and Furry Face Memory
Anthrocon (Convention)	2015	814 Furries Included a Post-Con Follow-up Study	Demographics, Fursona, Well-Being, Identity Development, Brony, Therianthropy, Furry Identity, Fursonas, Species stereotypes, Furry Drama, Emotions, Fantasy, Friends, Furry Activities, Experience at / After a Furry Convention
Furry Fiesta (Convention)	2016	288 Furries	Demographics, Furry identification, Therianthropy, Fursonas, Well-Being, Self-Esteem, Fursona Species, Giving / Getting Help, Bullying, Empathy, Shared Fate with Furries, Furry Prejudice
Anthrocon (Convention)	2016	1045 Furries	Demographics, Therianthropy, Brony, Furry Identification, Gatekeeping, Drama, Furry Consumption, Species Stereotypes, Physical Touch, Well-Being, Identity Development, Neurodivergence, Nerd Scale, Furry Prejudice, Maturity, Fursonas, Fursuit, Emotions, Self-Esteem, Motivation, Species Identification, Emotional Intelligence
Furry Fiesta (Convention)	2017	270 Furries	Demographics, Subgroups, Furry Identification, Fursona Species, Technology Use,

			Coping problems, Self-Esteem, Well-Being, Purpose in life, Locus of Control, Sexism, Spending Habits, Forgiveness, Drama, Pluralistic Ignorance, Need to belong, Furry Disclosure, Furry Stigma, Furry Culture, Bullying, Entitativity, Furry Conflict
Anthrocon (Convention)	2017	795 Furries	Demographics, Furry Identification, Therianthropy, Technology Use, Fursonas, Fursona Attitudes, Other Fan Interests, Elitism / Gatekeeping, LGBTQ+ Acceptance, Fursuits, Spending, Personality, Well-Being, Fantasy, Attitudes toward Animals, Species Identification, Personality, Empathy, Ageism, Connected to Nature, Dreaming
Online	2017	1556 Furries	Demographics, Species Stereotypes and Memory (Experimental Manipulation), Subgroups, Furry Identification, Furry Activities, Fursuits, Spending, Immersion, Motivation, Status, Furry Disclosure, Fandom Conflict, Alcohol Use, Fursonas, Fursona Attitudes, Therianthropy, Gatekeeping, LGBTQ+ Acceptance, Furry Drama, Giving / Getting Help, Non-Furry Interests, Media Preferences, Empathy, Entitlement, Openness about Sex, Personality, Well-Being, Neurodivergence, Identity Development
Furry Fiesta (Convention)	2018	329 Furries	Demographics, Subgroups, Furry Identification, Spending, Furry-Related Sacrifices, Fandom Cohesion, Gatekeeping,

			Entitlement, Status, Conformity, Spending, Attitudes Toward Animals, Fursona, Animal Welfare, Fursona Copying
Anthrocon (Convention) and Online	2018	1102 Con furries 102 Online furries	Demographics, Convention Attendance, Furry Identification, Therianthropy, Fursonas, Elitism, Fursuits, Fursuit Attitudes, Furry Stigma, Self-Esteem, Fantasy, Animal Attitudes, Species Identification, Personality, Friends; Furry as Fetish, Connection to Nature, Neurodivergence, Identity Development, Furry Prejudice, Fury Disclosure, Acceptance of Fandom, Well-Being, TV Media Preferences
Furry Fiesta, Furnal Equinox (Conventions)	2019	612 Furries	Demographics, Subgroups, Furry Identification, Charity, Values, Fursona copying, Fantasy, Independence, Bullying, Loneliness, Anthropomorphizing Non-Human Entities, Animal Identification, Fursona, Self-Esteem, Well-Being, Global Citizenship, Furry as a fetish, Neurodivergence, LGBTQ+ Acceptance
Anthrocon (Convention) / Eurofurence (Convention) Online	2019	1428 Furries (Anthrocon) 589 Furries (Eurofurence) 558 Furries Online (English + German)	Demographics, Furry Identification, Conventions, Subgroups, Therianthropy, Fursona, LGBTQ+ Acceptance, Personality, Neurodivergence, Identity Development, Well-Being, Bullying, Furry Activities, Fantasy, Identification with Furry Characters, Individualism, Furry Prejudice, Other Fan Interests, Self-Esteem, Empathy

Online I	2019	1171 Furries	Demographics, Furry Identification, Partner Furry Identification, Fursona, Fursuits, Furry Conventions, Motivation, Sexual Attraction to Furry, Immersion, Therianthropy, Pornography, Fetishes
Online II	2019-2021	1445 Furries	Demographics, Therianthropy, Well-Being, Addiction, Disability, Fan Identification, Fursona, Identity Development, Purpose in Life
Furry Fiesta (Convention)	2020	520 Furries	Demographics, Furry Identification, Fursona, Other Fan Interests, Fan Activities, Playfulness, Harmony-Seeking, Self-Concept Clarity, LGBTQ+ Acceptance, Well-Being, Self-Esteem, Neurodivergence, Fandom Trends, Elitism, Commitment to Fandom, Gatekeeping
Online	2020	454 Furries	Demographics, Subgroups, Furry Identification, Furry Partner, Spending, Commissions, Covid, Well-Being, Generation Gaps, Media Influence, Fandom Trajectory, Furry Activities, Appeal of Furry Characters, Passion, Individualism, Bullying, Loneliness, Anthropomorphizing Non-Human Entities, Animal Attitudes, Therianthropy, Well-Being, Attachment
Online	2020 / 2021	186 Furries 188 *Star Wars* Fans (Control Group)	Demographics, Furry Identification, Subgroups, Well-Being, COVID-19, Coping, Fandom Activities, Magical thinking, Self-Esteem, Need for Cognition, Locus of Control, Generational Gaps, Furry Partners

Online	2021	1694 Furries	Demographics, Subgroups, What is Furry, Fursonas, Race Attitudes, Gender Attitudes, Marginalization, Attachment, Generational Divide, Social Support, Intrafandom Conflict, Politics in Fandom, Authenticity, Bullying, Motivation, Emotions, Furry Identification, Fan Activities, Leisure Activities, Polyamory
Furry Fiesta (Convention) Online	2022	363 Furries at Furry Fiesta 238 Furries Online	Demographics, Furry Identification, Subgroups, Fursonas, Intrafandom Conflict, Furry Stigma, What is a Furry, Self-Concept Clarity, Need for Uniqueness, Conformity, Gender Dysphoria, Fursonas, Pornography, Fetishes, Well-Being

Part 2
Furries Doing Furry Things

Chapter 5
What's a furry?

Courtney "Nuka" Plante[1]

Before diving deep into more than a decade of research on furries, we should probably start by figuring out what, precisely, we mean by the term "furry." After all, if you and I are working with different definitions of what a furry is, then our findings, based on our definition, might not be relevant to the group you're thinking about, based on your definition. To avoid that sort of mix-up, let's take a moment (or, rather, a chapter) to make sure we're on the same page!

At first glance, it might seem pretty simple to define what a furry is. After all, if you ask a bunch of self-described furries to define what furry is, it's likely they'll all be able to do so pretty easily. However, there's a saying in the furry fandom: if you ask ten furries to define what furry is, you'll end up with eleven different answers. This is the first hurdle we have to overcome: while furries can define what a furry is, they might not all do so in the same way. Is furry a fan interest, akin to anime fans, science fiction fans, and sports fans? Is it a lifestyle, reserved only for those who've dedicated significant time and resources to their pursuit of "furry?" Is it an indicator of behavior or consumption habits—are the "real furries" the ones who own fursuits, go to conventions, or produce furry content themselves? Is it a mindset, a particular way of thinking? Is it a label you can apply to yourself whenever you feel it's appropriate, or can someone else decide that you're a furry despite your protestations? Is it none of these things, or all of the above?

More importantly, who gets to make that decision?

As we begin this chapter we'll state, up-front, that we are neither authority figures nor arbiters on matters such as these. At the end of the day, we cannot decree what furry is or ought to be for anyone, nor can we empirically derive a definition of what furry is, even with all the data in the world. As you'll see, there are far too many definitions, some of which are completely contradictory, for us to be able to come up with a definition of furry that every furry would agree with.[2]

---

[1] We'd like to give special thanks to yerf, a furry scholar who helped to significantly streamline and improve this chapter with their input!

[2] For another take on the complexity of defining furry, see yerf's 2020 piece *On Furry*.

A practical person could ask whether all this hair-splitting is merely an exercise in pedantry. While it's true that, to at least some extent, where we draw the line between "furry" and "non-furry" might not seem all that important, it does have some practical importance for our studies. For example, if we don't have at least a working definition of what furry is, how can we know whether the participants in our furry studies "count" as furries? Our studies about the psychology of furries would be invalid if we ended up including a significant number of people who, by all accounts, aren't "real" furries. Alternatively, if we ended up systematically excluding people from our studies who *are* furries, then we would also have a potentially invalid study since it's not a study of furries so much as a study of a certain type of furry.

In short, we're left in a bit of a pickle. We need to have a working definition of furry for our research, one that includes people whom most would consider to be furries while also excluding those whom most would not consider to be furries. Ideally, the definition would also have some face validity with furries themselves—that is, it's a definition that would make sense to most furries.

Later in this chapter, we'll discuss the working definition that we at Furscience have come up with for use in our work. But before we do that, let's first take a closer look at how furries themselves conceptualize the term furry to see if there are really eleven different answers for every ten furries. Maybe, just maybe, we can find some common ground.

What is Furry: An Open-Ended Question

We've been studying furries since at least 2010, and in that time we've studied hundreds of different facets of furry identity, the furry fandom, and furry psychology. However, it wasn't until 2021 that we realized, upon having it pointed out to us by our critics, that we had yet to ask furries the simplest of questions: tell us what furry is, in your own words. Oh sure, we've asked furries on many occasions whether X, Y, or Z were important parts of what it meant to be a furry and we've asked them to pick from a list of options which terms best described what it meant to be a furry. However, these were all options and lists generated by us, the researchers.[3] To address this issue, we decided to go back to basics in an online study in 2021, where we asked more than a thousand furries to answer, in their own words, what being a furry meant to them.

---

[3] To be charitable, the lists weren't completely arbitrary, nor did they come out of nowhere—they were based on observations of furries, informal conversations with furries, and input from at least one of the team members who, themselves, is a furry.

The result was more than a thousand responses of varying length and detail. As awesome as all this detail-rich data was, it was also pretty unmanageable and difficult to draw any conclusions from. If we were to simply copy all of those responses here, it would not only inflate the length of this book considerably, but readers would also probably be left feeling a bit perplexed as to how to get a handle on it all, wondering what, if anything, they should be taking away from all of this information. What we needed was a way to condense and summarize all of this information into something that could be easily parsed.

To this end, we went through all of the responses and coded them, extracting recurring themes and organizing them based on common categories. At the end of it all, we were left with dozens of different themes, although many of them were rare enough to be considered outliers (e.g., identified by two or three furries out of a thousand). Here, we'll focus our attention on the most common themes, namely the sixteen themes that were brought up spontaneously by at least 2% of the sample. These themes, as well as their prevalence in the sample, are shown in Table 5.1.[4]

In the following sections, we'll delve more into each of these specific themes, looking at representative quotes from our furry participants to illustrate the nuances of each theme's meaning. Before we do, however, it's worth pointing out that no one theme was expressed by the majority of furries. To put it another way, there doesn't seem to be a single conceptualization of what it means to be a furry that most furries agree with, at least not when it comes to spontaneously using that conceptualization in their definition of what it means to be a furry.

Astute readers may also notice that the percentage of responses, when added up, greatly exceeds 100%. This is because many furries' responses fell into more than one category. This suggests that, in addition to there being no singular conception of what a furry is, individual furries tend to have a multifaceted and complex understanding of what it means to be a furry.

---

[4] We conducted a similar study ten years earlier—back in 2011—where we asked respondents to define what furry is. Some of the themes extracted from those responses were quite similar in content and prevalence to the themes extracted ten years later: A group (47.1%), fans of anthropomorphic animal characters (42.4%), an expression of true self (26.2%), fursuiting (14.0%), a hobby (13.4%), and escapism (4.7%).

Table 5.1. Common themes extracted from an open-ended question asking respondents to describe what being a furry meant to them. Some responses could be categorized into multiple themes.

Theme	% of Responses
Fandom / Community / Group	45.2
Interest in Anthropomorphic Animals	39.6
Inspiration / Self-Expression	22.3
Art / Writing / Content Consumption	20.1
Fursonas and Wish Fulfillment	18.7
LBGTQ+ Space and Acceptance	11.4
A Hobby / Leisure Activity	10.8
An Identity / Label	6.2
Self-Discovery / Self-Acceptance	4.3
Interest in Fursuits	4.7
Escapism	4.7
A Job / Content Creation	4.3
Sex / Kink	4.2
Fascination with Actual Animals	2.6
Activities / Events	2.3
Social Support	2.0

Furry is About Community / Fandom

The single most common theme in furries' responses conceptualizes furry as a community that they can belong to. These communities are often described as highly valued and significant and, in some cases, are comparable to family.

"A friendly community that helps fulfill socializing needs as well as a welcoming supportive community for creative endeavors."

"A sense of community and belonging."

"A way to connect with people in ways I probably never would have or with the same level of outreach."

"At its core, it's a community of accepting people to hang out and talk with, and I value that a lot."

"Being a furry is everything to me. It serves as my found family. The majority of my friends are furry and 75% of all of my romantic partners have all been furries as well."

Like other social groups, the furry community is organized around a common interest. Whereas some communities organize around a shared religious or political belief, shared geographical location, or shared features or traits, furries seem to be united by a shared, fan-like interest in media featuring anthropomorphized animal characters—for more on this, see the next section. This shared fan-like interest would make them a fandom—a fan community. In fact, some furries even made a direct comparison between furries and other fandoms.

"An internet community, like anime or bronies, where people go when they can't otherwise socialize."

"Being part of a community of people that I have actual interest in and can enjoy socializing with, not just socializing because I have to like work. Having genuine common interests rather than mere common experiences/backgrounds."

"[Being] a furry means, to me, [being] involved in the furry community. Be it by following or supporting artists drawing anthropomorphic animals, supporting people declaring themselves furries (such as streamers, [muscians], cloth sellers...), participating in furry communities (discord, telegram, ...), etc."

Many furries also seem to intuitively distinguish fanship—being a fan of something—and fandom—being part of a community of fans.[5] Importantly, many furries see the fandom or community aspect of furry to be more important than the fan interest itself, in some cases going so far as to explicitly say that they didn't consider themselves to be a furry until they were part of the furry community.

"Being part of an inclusive fandom, united by their shared love of anthropomorphic animals. To me being a furry is more about the community than liking anthros."

---

[5] We discuss these concepts at length in Chapter 6.

"Part of being a furry is sharing your interests with other furries. I had interests [sic] in the fandom for a long time (since childhood) but never really interacted with the fandom until about 2 years ago. It wasn't until I began to interact with and befriend other furs that I truly began to self identify as a furry."

As a final note, some furries described furry itself as a catalyst for social interaction, a way to facilitate or ease the task of interacting with others by providing them with something in common to talk about. In other words, in line with the idea that the community is more important than the interest itself, furries may use furry as a tool to facilitate social interaction and belonging to a group.

"A feeling of knowing I can always find likeminded [sic] people and join local communities quickly and feel welcome."

"Furs are like meeting prescreened strangers, it feels more comfortable to talk too [sic], because we already have a shared common interest and larger social groups are great to meet new people."

"It means having a community of individuals interested in the same topics, but beyond that, not much. My friends are my friends because we share mutual interests, etc., beyond the fandom. The fandom just provides a foundation upon which to build real interactions."

Furry is an Interest in Anthropomorphic Animals

The second-most common theme to emerge in furries' responses recognizes furries as people who share a specific interest in anthropomorphized animals and in media featuring these characters—what we might call "fanship," in contrast to "fandom" above. In many cases, furries recognize this as the only necessary criterion for being a furry and as being sufficient, in and of itself, to warrant being called a furry.

"An interest and appreciation of anthropomorphic animals."

"Enjoying artistic depictions of sapient characters with both human and animal characteristics."

"An interest in anthropomorphic animals. If you're interested, you are to a degree, a furry."

"It's just an interest in anthropomorphic animal characters. I don't feel there's any other qualification for it."

"Someone who enjoys cartoon/anthropomorphic animals. It's really as simple as that and you enjoy finding others with the same interest as you."

Other furries make a distinction between "mere" liking of media featuring anthropomorphized characters and a more intense, fan-like interest in the content. In other words, to some, liking media featuring anthropomorphized animal characters isn't enough to make a person a furry. According to these furries, a person only counts as a furry if they meet certain conditions (e.g., a certain level of interest, engaging in particular fan behaviors, or identifying with this interest).

"A fan of anthropomorphic animal characters. It's on a basis of self identification [sic], so you can be a fan of anthro characters but not a furry if you choose."

"Being a fan of anthropomorphic animals, and calling yourself one. If those two conditions aren't met, then you're not a furry."

"Having a strong interest in anything 'defined' as 'furry', such as anthropomorphic animals/creatures, art of said animals/creatures. Having this interest beyond common media is also a key factor, you can like Zootopia and the relevant fanart without being a furry, but if you express further interest for example by creating a Zootopia OC[6], I would call that furry territory."

"It's partly about being a fan of anthropomorphic media, but also the way you engage with it. There's no hard dividing line. Simply liking Zootopia or The Lion King, for example, doesn't make one a furry. But if you make an OC, if you roleplay, if you seek out saucy fan art, and if the focus shifts from anthropomorphic works to the concept of anthro characters

---

[6] "OC" refers to an "original character," that is, a character created by a fan to exist non-canonically in a fictional universe.

themselves -- then it's edging toward furry territory. I think this question can be applied to lots of fandoms, with similar results."

Finally, some furries pointed out other distinctions they consider important when deciding what does or doesn't constitute being a furry. The first response below, for example, highlights a distinction sometimes made in the furry fandom between "furries" and "scalies," with the latter representing furries whose fursona species is a creature with scales instead of fur, such as a reptile. As pointed out in the second response, many furries, while recognizing such distinctions, are nevertheless willing to consider anyone with a fursona or a strong interest in anthropomorphized animals to be a furry regardless of the species of their fursona or favorite animal.

"A fan of anthropomorphic animal fiction/fantasy in art or writing, as well as other mediums. Almost exclusively warm blooded furred living creatures."

"Being a fan of or having an uncommonly keen interest in cartoon animals. Cartoon animals are not exclusively found in cartoons, as they can also be found in real life mascots or in storybooks. The phrase 'cartoon animal' here also is not exclusive to real life [sic] animals, and can include fictional or alien species as well. A good definition for 'cartoon animal' used here would be 'any being with a human-like intellect that is not a human.' A person with an uncommonly keen interest in sentient trees is just as much a furry as a person with a wolf fursona."

Furry is About Self-Expression and Inspiration

One of the most universal behaviors engaged in by furries is the creation of a fursona, a representation of oneself, typically as an anthropomorphized animal character.[7] For some furries, the creation of a fursona is an act of self-definition or self-expression, being able to highlight aspects of themselves that they consider to be ideal or being able to be seen in a way that they might otherwise not be seen in their day-to-day life. The importance of this ability to self-express can, for some furries, be the central or defining feature of what it means to be furry.

---

[7] For more on fursonas, including data supporting this point, see Chapter 7.

"The ability to declare who and what you are, irrespective of the general public opinion, without judgement or prejudice from your peers."

"A better self, a freer self that can be free from social constraints, and at the same time a psychological support, the true side of yourself, or the side that you want to be."

"A means [to] better understand and express parts of myself I wouldn't have a place for otherwise."

"Being a furry means expressing a more complex or deep identity than is possible through other means. In a way I think of it like my gender, a core piece of how I understand and view myself. It's a way to express both what I am and what I would like myself to be."

"It means feeling a special affinity towards anthropomorphic animal characters (whether humanoid with animal features or animal in form with human features such as human speech, human facial expressions, etc.). For me, this is an important part of my identity. Although I don't have a fursona that I regularly use, and although I also don't dress up in a fursuit, and although I don't believe that I actually am an animal at heart, I'm drawn to these anthropomorphic animal characters in a deep way. When I look at them, they produce a feeling of recognition, like I'm seeing a part of myself. For this reason, I tend to avoid expressions such as 'furry fandom' that imply that furriness is a casual interest or hobby like watching anime or playing games."

"To me, it's about being able to express parts of myself that aren't easy to express physically. Using certain species as a container or expression medium for myself, I feel like I've found ways to communicate to others what kind of person I am in ways that don't feel natural when communicating without the vocabulary of furry. That shared vocabulary makes it easier for me to connect to people, and seems to help people open up to me and express their own quirks and individuality too."

In a related vein, therians and otherkin—people who identify in whole or in part as non-human animals—may, to perhaps an even greater extent, conceptualize furry in terms of its usefulness as a way to express a non-human part of themselves.[8]

"Furry represents a radical approach to species which recognizes that it, just like gender and race, is a construct. while it can be as 'serious' and integral as otherkin and therian identities, it is simultaenously [sic] more deliberate and more playful, and not beholden to the same kind of narratives. i started out in furry spaces back when there was a hard distinction between 'fandom' and 'lifestyler', and moved on to otherkin & therian communities because at the time i wasn't finding people for whom nonhumanity was as serious and integral as it was for me, but over time i've [sic] come back round to mostly aligning with furry (when not simply using 'alterhuman' as an umbrella term) as the boundary between 'just a hobby' and 'legitimate identity' seems to have dissovled [sic]."

"It gives me a way to express myself in a non-human form. For me, seeing myself as a human actually causes my discomfort and dysphoria, so it provides a sense of relief from this. It also has introduced me to lots of cool people!!"

For other furries, the concept of furry as self-expression is less about drawing attention to a facet of their identity and more about drawing inspiration from furry content itself or using the idea of anthropomorphized animals as a catalyst for their own creative processes.

"Being a furry for me means to express myself and my creativity"

"It helps me to deeply feel the beauty behind the furry art while I am learning how to draw and visiting art museum every weekends [sic]. It's furry arts and amazing furry artists that remind me to draw, which I abandoned at least 10 years ago because of school works [sic]. I just picked up drawing half a year ago and I took it seriously after I graduated from my master school, it feels really fulfilling while leaning [sic] and creating in drawing."

"It is a great opportunity to see cool art and develops my own characters. Gods wonder can show through many mediums and art is one of them.

[8] For more on therians, see Chapter 20.

Great furry art is an example of the wonderful creativity that God has given us."

"It's like a second life. I have enjoyed mostly dragons since I have memory, but I didnt have friends to enjoy such passions, the fandom gave me that. To feel related to other people, I made a lot of friends and I became an artist myself, I discovered my creativity and nowadays I work full time as a furry artist too."

Furry is About Furry Content

Similar to the earlier theme about being a fan of anthropomorphic animals, some furry respondents mentioned a specific interest not just in anthropomorphic animals as a broad concept, but interest specifically in artwork, shows, video games, and other media featuring these characters.

"At it's core, a furry is someone with an affinity for anthropomorphic animals. I really enjoyed animated movies and tv [sic] shows with animal characters, had a bit of a fascination with certain irl animals, and always thought getting into mascotting would be fun."

"Being a fan not just anthropomorphic animals in media, but also of the art & culture that's developed within the furry community."

"Being a fan of works (art, stories, movies, songs, etc.) where animals are given humanlike qualities."

"Having a strong interest in Anthropomorphic animal characters in art, video games, TV & Movies, literature."

Also similar to respondents who spoke about furry as a broader interest in anthropomorphism, furries were often quick to point out that an interest in art and media was only one part of what it meant to be furry, overlapping with, and often overshadowed by, social or self-expressive facets of being a furry.

"A. That a person is a fan of anthropomorphic art and/or media B. And that a person would like to identify as a member of the furry fandom"

"An appreciation for character design and stories which involve creatures with human intelligence but more than human bodies. An

appreciation for biology and science and animal behavior/facts/diversity and an ability to connect those things to oneself and one's self expression. An appreciation for art, design, symbolism, and self freedom through more than just human imagery."

"Appreciating anthropomorphic animals in art and other media, and engaging in the community; Appreciating furry art, especially if one appreciates it moreso than other... genres? of art."

"I originally joined the furry community out of curiosity and it's since then became a part of me although I haven't been able to attend many event's it has given me the chance to meet all sorts of people and open my mind to all walks of life. I came for the art but stayed for the community even during it's [sic] down time [sic] where I live."

Furry is About Fursonas and Wish Fulfilment

Conceptually related to the earlier concept of self-expression, some furries specifically identified having a fursona as an essential part of what it means to be a furry. Importantly, fursonas were often discussed in the context of the furry fandom as a whole, being a way to not only represent oneself as an anthropomorphic animal character but to do so in the context of others, with a fursona perhaps facilitating such interactions.

"A person who runs a persona that is of an anthropomorphic character."

"Belonging to a community of generally creative and accepting people, where each person is not defined by their actual appearance, sex, or occupation but rather that of their character/fursona. As a transgender autistic guy, being a furry allows me to be myself without even being considered unusual."

"Having an anthropomorphic character/persona that you use as an alternate identity that you can use as an extension of yourself online or around other furries."

Many furry respondents also indicated specifically that their fursonas were not just anthropomorphized animal representations of themselves, but that they also represented idealized versions of themselves, a point we'll return to in Chapter 7 on fursonas. For now, it is sufficient to point out that many furries saw the ability to be a better self through their fursona as a defining feature of what furry meant to them, in some cases treating being a furry and one's fursona as the same thing.

> *"A method to cover up the nonidealities of natural character, express personality, and make connections."*

> *"A new way to reflect myself, to describe myself, to be someone I want to be."*

> *"Its [sic] an identity, one that serves to place all the things you don't possess as a person on your new persona, or fursona, and giving someone who might not be as confident a mask to be who they want to be."*

> *"It's pretty much a lifestyle queer choice of 'that design is attractive, yes I like' and then realizing everybody wishes we could have just been Anthros. At least God shoulda gave us a tail."*

> *"Being a better version of myself, of who I want to be but with a fun character to represent myself."*

> *"I'm not quite sure, being a furry provides me with an identity that I feel more comfortable in than my own. Not in the sense that I don't belong to my mortal human self, but a fursona lets me anonymise [sic] the qualities of myself that I desire, and showcase my best traits as a perfect cultured mask to enjoy in the company of others."*

Furry is a Space for LGBTQ+ Acceptance

As we'll cover in Chapters 15 and 16, demographically speaking, the furry fandom is a predominantly queer space, with the majority of its members being LGBTQ+. The prevalence of LGBTQ+ folk and the fandom's progressive attitudes toward these topics have not escaped the notice of some who see these as defining characteristics of what it means to be furry. In fact, in some cases, furry respondents saw the queerness of furry space as being more important to being furry than media featuring anthropomorphized animals.

> *"Being Openly Queer, Kink Friendly. without it i wouldn't of discovered who i truly [sic] was."*

"A great community of LGBT+ people who support each other and share their creativity and experiences."

"Community. Creativity. A sense of family, acceptance, a queer majority space which reflects the values that should be forefront in society."

"Difficult to sum up in any short form, but the most important part would be an identity for my unique outlooks on my queerness and neurodivergence."

"An 'excuse' for community and belonging. The 'anthropomorphic animals' part could be substituted for anything else, but the kindness and queerness of the furry community couldn't."

"To me, it's more than just necessarily enjoying anthropomorphic characters, it's about subverting cultural norms, being a part of a space where the identity you put out is you, where people can be unabashedly queer and find solace in the fact that you know there are others like you because those people surround you and are a part of your life. It's powerful."

For others, instead of LGBTQ+ being the defining feature of the furry fandom, they recognize the significance of queerness to furry spaces without necessarily seeing it as the defining or central feature of the space. Instead, the queerness of furry space is more of a by-product or secondary facet of furry space.

"Having an interest in art and content depicting anthropomorphic animal characters. It's intersectionality of queer individuals, BIPOC, and disabled individuals is an important part of the culture and scene."

"Making friends easily over a hobby most are passionate about, having a space to meet LGBTQ folk, and having a creative outlet."

"A community that's incredibly accepting of queer identities without that being the focal point."

Finally, many respondents described furry as a safe space for them, a place free from judgment where they can live authentically and without fear of reprisal or aversive consequences for being themselves—something they might not otherwise experience in their day-to-day lives.

> *"A place to feel accepted and be embraced in all my weirdness, and my queerness."*

> *"Being a furry allows me to express myself in ways that I may not have the confidence to do otherwise. I like being in fursuit and behaving as I think my character would. Although he isn't much different than me in terms of personality, he's more confident and outgoing. I can make new friends in the fandom and learn new thigs[sic] from them! We might not even have much in common, but furries are just happy to talk to you. The fandom is very accepting and lets me feel like I can be myself and explore free of judgement. The art is fantastic too!"*

> *"Exploring my identity in a safe and supportive environment with other like-minded people, creating a fun fuzzy version of myself that makes me happy, and accepting others at face value no matter who they are."*

> *"It means I have a safe place where I can be myself and meet people outside of the normal toxic environment I grew up in."*

> *"It's a safe space where everyone should be able to feel comfortable with themselves, and chat with similar people to help feel better if they need help."*

> *"That in some way I am choosing to focus on things that make me happy and getting to have an identity I'm actually comfortable with rather than one that is put upon me by societal expectation or capitalist greed. I not only get to have a safe and unique space but I get to help make it what it is for others, too."*

Furry is a Hobby or Leisure Activity

Many of the themes above focus on the important functions or significance of furry as part of its definition. Unexpectedly absent from these themes are descriptions of furry as a hobby or leisure activity. This isn't to say that furries don't consider furry to be a hobby—far from it. For example, a number of furries primarily conceptualized furry as a hobby, something to be contrasted against their day-to-day routine or work life.

> *"A creative hobby."*

> *"A fun hobby."*

> *"It's a hobby and a way of getting a break from my day-to-day routines. It gives me a sense of belonging to a group outside of places like work or studies."*

> *"It's a hobby. Something I find is a fun distraction from every day life."*

It is notable, however, that among many who consider furry to be a hobby, the term is often used to connote not taking furry all that seriously, or to distinguish their own experience as a furry from more intense or involved furries—a distinction somewhat akin to the distinction between "casual" and "hardcore" fans. This can often be seen with furries adding qualifiers such as "just a hobby." Some directly contrast it against being a lifestyle, while others spoke about how they were once more involved, but that their interest has waned to that of a "mere" hobby.

> *"Being a furry is a hobby, i am aware that it is much more for others but not for me, yes i do like to participate in cons, suitwalks etc. but i keep my for example workspace free from furry things."*

> *"It's a hobby among many others, now, but it has still strongly shaped my social life in the past couple decades."*

> *"Just a hobby and I like the porn."*

> *"It's a hobby to me, not a lifestyle. I enjoy furry art, stories, comics, and other visual media. I have a small group of online friends who share this interest, and most of whom I follow on social media also share the interest. Personally, I enjoy developing and writing about furry characters, as well as roleplaying. I consider myself a 'furry' due to these interests, but more on the margins of the definition. I don't attend furmeets or conventions, nor do I present or identify as a furry in my real-world life."*

Nevertheless, at least one furry seemed to suggest that furry's status as a hobby did not detract from its significance in their life, suggesting that not every furry would agree with the idea that furry being a hobby or leisure activity trivializes its importance.

> *"It's my lifestyle, my hobby and my main source of happiness."*

Furry is an Identity or a Label

In earlier themes, we've alluded to the idea that, for at least some furries, identifying as a furry is distinct from having an interest in anthropomorphic animals or a particular type of media. In other words, to some furries, an interest in media featuring anthropomorphic animal characters is not sufficient to warrant being called a furry—not unless the person themselves chooses to use this interest as part of a label for themselves.

> *"A person who is interested/likes anthropomorphic/personified animals and creatures, but has to identify themselves as a furry."*

> *"An enjoyment of media, usually visual art, depicting animals with some level of anthropomorphism, as well as making such enjoyment a part of one's identity."*

> *"Being a fan of anthropomorphic characters, but namely - it's a label that anybody can put on themselves. I find it very fluid. People can be as involved as they want - they're still furry if that's how they identify."*

> *"Being a Furry means having an affinity for anthropomorphic characters in media. To grow up with and have an intimate relationship with the media to a point where it becomes apart [sic] of your personality. The media we consume eventually becomes apart [sic] of us."*

> *"Being part of the community and sharing experiences and fantasies with its members. Having an actual interest in anthropomorphic animals, enough to make it a part of my identity and dictate how I express myself."*

Others spoke less about what causes furry to become part of one's identity, instead preferring to focus on the importance of furry for their sense of self.

"A important part of my identity."

"Being a furry is a core part of my identity and interests."

Speaking to the importance or centrality of furry to some, a few respondents indicated that furry was an essential part of who they were. Or, to put it another way, furry isn't something they do or became; it's part of who they are and who they have always been, with the implication being that they have little control over the fact that they are furry and could not change it even if they wanted to. These respondents may well agree with the idea that furries are born, not created.

"Hard to say. I could tell you long and wide about the community of course, but otherwise, for me at least, this asks for meaning for something that just is. I am a furry, basically always have been. This isn't like a brand of car I choose over its competitors."

"It's just who I am. I can't stop being a furry any more than I can stop being tall."

Furry is About Self-Discovery and Self-Acceptance

Related to the earlier theme of fursonas, some furries indicated that beyond merely representing avatars or idealized versions of themselves, the fursonas associated with being a furry allow them to actively explore and discover parts of themselves that they might otherwise have been unable to explore, either for lacking the means or language to do so, or simply from having never been asked to consider aspects of themselves that they had taken for granted.

"An honest exploration of myself in the form of self created anthropomorphic creatures representing myself/some part of myself, and their/my interactions with others."

"Being a fur is about exploration of self and community. It's being able to show vulnerabilities that maybe you couldn't before cause you're doing it through the safety of your Sona. It's about letting yourself loose, and being real fluffy while doing so."

"I use my furry personas to help me deal with my emotions and discover my personality, dividing parts of myself across my OCs helps my struggles with understanding myself."

"It means identifying with some kind of non-human creature, at a basic level. It also means using animals as a proxy to explore the nature and possible expressions of identity, and rethink/challenge a lot of cultural social rules and traditions."

"It's both a hobby and part of my identity. Many of my online interactions are with other furs. In viewing other people's furry art, I feel like I get to explore everyone else's expressions of identity and thus also reflect on my own identity."

Other furries indicated that in addition to facilitating self-exploration, or perhaps instead of it, furry allows them to accept parts of themselves that they might otherwise be ashamed or frustrated about.

"Being myself without feeling bad about making a mistake."

"Finding comfort in and inspiration from sapient animal-like characters (inhuman but not subhuman), having that interest as a common ground for bonding with other furries, favoring works of fiction that include such characters (e.g. Beastars, Zootopia, Warriors), being attracted to such characters for their animal-like features (soft fur, pawpads [sic], fluffy tails, perky ears, etc.), and using such characters to explore and affirm my identity (including self-image and sexuality) in the face of the alienation of the human world."

"It has helped me accept myself for who I am, and discover things about myself that I otherwise would not have."

"It's a way of expressing yourself with the use of animal personas. For me personally, I've always identified as something non-human since I was 7, the furry fandom opened up a new avenue for me to express my non-human side with the help of my fursona as an extension of my identity and explore what it is like to be a different species. I met a lot of wonderful people in this community through this wonderfully open and accepting avenue of expression, letting me come more to terms with and closer to

being my ideal self, both in terms of species identity, as well as sexuality and gender."

Furry is About Fursuits

As an offshoot of furries defining furry in terms of an interest in media featuring anthropomorphic animal characters, many also indicated that one manifestation of their interest involves dressing up as a furry character. Sometimes this is done with a desire for self-expression, other times it's because furries find it fun to do. Notably, it was rare to find participants for whom their concept of furry was tied solely to fursuits; instead, fursuits often emerged as one of several facets of being furry.

"A way to enjoy and share the fun of anthropomorphic animals via suiting and artistic expression."

"Likeing and dressing up as an anthropomorphic animal."

"Simply liking anthro characters, and for me, enjoying fursuiting."

"The furry fandom is one of my special interests as an autistic person. i make fursuits on the side and draw furry art almost exclusively. i've been in the fandom for a large part of my life and it makes me very happy."

"Obsessed with mascots for a kid, it's a chance to let my ego run wild in goofy outfits that do something to my brain. It's a way of life and gives me agency."

"Interest in anthropomorphic animals, bringing joy to other people (for example while suiting), being part of an open and welcoming community."

"Self-expression and the ability to express various parts of yourself through art, music and costume."

"The love of anthropomorphic animals in TV shows/movies, comics, etc. Being able to create and become your persona of an anthro animal, and being able to pretend and act as such. Fursuiting to fully become my creation."

Furry is About Escapism

One of the appeals of fictional genres (e.g., fantasy, science-fiction), and, indeed, one of the appeals of media in general is its ability to give viewers a temporary escape, whether it's from the mundane tedium of their day-to-day life or, in some cases, to escape from something far more insidious and troublesome. When asked what furry was to them, some furries pointed directly to the opportunity for escapism that their interest in furry provides.

> *"A hobby, an escape, to be someone else for a while someone I actually like and want to be."*

> *"It means having an interest in anything with anthropomorphic animals and being able to share your excitement with people all over the world who feel the same way. But more than that, it means being able to enter into an alternate universe from time to time, one where dogs work in hospitals and martens go into space and blue cats give lectures on psychology. It's a ridiculous and whimsical fandom, and I love it."*

For some, the escapism was less about seeking out something fun or a break from the tedium of day-to-day life and was more about escaping something particularly upsetting, troublesome, or even traumatic in their lives.

> *"Being able to escape being human sometimes. To be happy and dumb without life problems."*

> *"An escape from the terrible feelings of reality."*

> *"1. Camouflage to evade harm/unload pressure from real life. 2. Punchbag to avoid committing actions causing damage or bad influence in real life. 3. To satisfy personal Science Fiction/Fiction hobby.; a chance to escape from the disappointing real world."*

> *"It helps me discover my identity as a living person. It can also be an escape from the trauma that occur in my life."*

Speaking to the utility that such escapism affords, some furries mentioned that part of their conceptualization of furry includes the benefits they glean from being given these opportunities to escape.

"Being able to escape and let loose for a bit... it's my unofficial therapy..."

"It's hard to explain. It's difficult to always act 100% human and fit into all the societal normals [sic], at the sake of giving up things that help destress/mental state. Being a furry allows [one] to shed some of the human ideas and in a relatively safe way adopt some of society's less accepted behaviors that can help"

Of course, we should also note that not every furry who sees furry as a means of escapism conceptualizes it as an all-or-nothing break from reality. For some, furry is less about completely escaping from reality and more about supplementing or infusing reality with aspects of their interest—they maintain a firm presence in reality, rather than actively trying to avoid or escape it.

"Being a furry means appreciating an alternate universe where we can be silly, fluffy, cartoonish versions of ourselves and having the opportunity to bring some of those aspects into our own reality, while still remaining grounded as humans."

"I like to say being a furry means witnessing the blurring of the line between reality and the fictional, strange world of anthro animals. You commonly get this experience when you interact as your furry avatar or fursona (if you have one) with other antho [sic] animals online or in person in [sic] conventions/meets while wearing furry costumes (fursuits) or make-ups, etc."

Furry is a Job for Me

Furry content is created in a fairly decentralized way, in the sense that furry content is not produced by a single company that gets to dictate what does and does not count as canon (e.g., *Star Wars*, *Harry Potter*), but rather is the product of numerous independent artists and content creators.[9] For that reason, it makes sense that at least some furries would base their conceptualization of furry around their content creation for the fandom, as more of a job than as a fan interest or means of self-expression—although it

[9] For more on this, see Chapter 9.

is certainly possible for furry to be more than one thing for a person. Responses seem to suggest, however, that while some furries see their content creation and their interest in furry as going hand-in-hand, others see it as a job and recognize that they could be producing content in another context in a fairly interchangeable fashion.

> *"My partner is furry, I'm working fulltime [sic] creating furry art and I'm happy that way. Without furry fandom my life would be very sad."*

> *"An audience for my art and a way to make friends."*

> *"Furry has given me community, helped me discover my identity, friendship, romance... The support of the furry writing community also helped me get an agent and become a full-time, award winning author!"*

> *"It's everything to me, its a strong part of my personality my day to day [sic] life. It's what I do for a living too."*

> *"I enjoy costuming and seeing nice artwork, but I'm not as involved anymore. I'm a passive furry, as I've found my art appreciated more in other fandoms and found more friends in these places to than furry."*

> *"Money! Furry doesn't mean as much to me as others."*

> *"To be completely honest, absolutely nothing. If it disappeared overnight, I wouldn't give that much of a damn with the exception of 'where do I get money from' since I'm an artist."*

Furry is Sexual or a Kink

One of the more common presumptions that laypersons have about furries is that furries are motivated, first and foremost, by a fetish-like attraction to animals, fursuits, or anthropomorphic animal characters (Brooks et al., 2022; See also Chapter 8 on fursuits or Chapter 21 on furry stigma). Participants' responses both support and oppose such presumptions. They may be true in the sense that at least some furries are motivated, at least in part, by an interest in erotic content pertaining to their furry interest. On the other hand, conceptualizing furry as a kink is relatively rare compared to the conceptualizations we've seen above, and when sex is involved, it usually represents only one facet of a more complex conceptualization of what it means to be furry.

"An interest in anthropomorphic art, costumes, and a culture of sex and kink positivity"

"Being a furry is having a fascination and enjoyment with anthropomorphized animals, often also involved with being artistic, or sexual."

"Being a furry to me means enjoying, consuming, and taking part in anthropomorphic media that one finds delight in. That can range from NSFW art in the most deeply lurid sense, to a more soft, completely SFW adoration."

"Being sexually attracted to anthros; Furry genre is not automatically sexual, but it is intrinsically erotic. This means artistic works definable as furry do not always involve sexual contents, but (some of) its intrinsic characteristics tend to erotism, carnality and naturism."

"Having an interest in animals with human characteristics, fetishized or not."

"There's a (non-sexual) feeling I get when I look at anthropomorphic animals and fursuits that other people don't. I'm sexually attracted to furry art too, but they're different feelings. That's what makes me a furry."

Others spoke not about sexual attraction to furry media per se, but rather about furry spaces as being inclusive, sex-positive and kink-positive spaces.

"Being a furry allows me to express myself more freely not only with my interests, but with my sexual preferences and kinks."

"Being able to have a community of PoC/Queer people that share my interests, that I can bond with, and having an artistic outlet. There's also porn, kink and fetish interests I want to express and share."

"Expressing and enjoying Kinks/Paraphila with other Furries."

"love of furry characters. shared subcultural context. normalized diversity. friendly non-sexual contact. sex-positivity and kink friendliness."

Not every respondent saw furries and their openness to sexuality in a distinctly positive light, however.

"It's a collection of people that formed a community around a fetish, or it was at first. Now it's a distinct subculture with high instances of queerness, neurodiversity, poor mental health, and poverty. I'm not sure where it comes from but childhood cartoons combined with puberty seems likely for the hypersexualising children's cartoons. The community is comprised of social outcasts and pariahs or people who never found anywhere to belong. It's like an island of misfit toys, except people into plushies want to fuck 'em."

It is also worth mentioning that many respondents who incorporated sex as part of their conceptualization of furry indicated that they did not consider themselves to be especially involved in the furry community or did not identify strongly as a furry themselves. One respondent indicated that pornography was a bigger part of their interest in furry at the outset, but, as time went on, their interest broadened and became more multifaceted. This may suggest that, for at least some furries, their initial interest in furry content may have been motivated by erotic content, but, over time, they may gradually come to develop a broader, more nuanced and complex conceptualization of furry—a point we discuss in greater detail in Chapter 19.

"Just a hobby and I like the porn."

"Nothing deep. I just like art and porn."

"Not much, honestly. Mostly the porn and a certain group of people."

"To me, being a furry involves components of interaction on the furry community such as having a fursona and/or engaging primarily with furry erotic materials. I don't identify as a furry, but I do have erotic interest in anthropomorphic animal characters in sexual situations."

"When I first started dipping my toes in the fandom I mostly viewed it as a porn thing, but as I became more involved I came to believe it more a community of radical self discovery, exploration, definition and celebration."

Furry is About an Interest in Actual Animals

Given that many furries have an interest in anthropomorphic animals, a point we found evidence for earlier in this section, it might make sense that furries are also interested in non-human animals in general—that is, non-anthropomorphic animals. The data suggest that this may be the case for at least some furries, who see their interest in anthropomorphic and non-anthropomorphic animals as going hand-in-hand, part of the same underlying interest.

"Someone who is a fan of an animal (or animals), realistic or imaginary, and consistently uses an animal (or animals) to represent themself."

"Fan of anthropomorphic animals and finding animals cute."

For others, their interest may reside more firmly in a broader interest in non-human animals or a desire to change human nature.

"An expression of my connection to and identification with animals. Opportunity to connect with others with similar interests."

"It means to love animals and care for them the same way you would treat a human, since you are also an animal."

"Being a little more in touch with the animal side of human nature, and the acknowledgement [sic] that animals are awesome and human society can be pretty boring and needs spicing up."

"Loving and relating to animals maybe more than you do other people."

As mentioned, the number of furries that indicated an interest in real animals was far lower than the number of furries that indicated an interest in anthropomorphic animals. Speaking to this point, one participant indicated being disappointed to discover that furries, as a group, seemed to not be especially interested in non-human animals.

"It is definitely a huge part of my life. I in no way believe that I am (or my spirit) is an animal, but I have always had deep connections with animals my entire life. It was a relief initially to find a community of other people who felt the same way, but actually I feel that many furries are only surface-level interested in real animals. So it is starting to become a bit alienating to me."

Furry is about Furry-Themed Events and Activities

While many furries indicated a general interest in anthropomorphic animals or a particular interest in some specific activity (e.g., art, fursuiting), other furries conceptualized furry, at least in part, in terms of activities collectively engaged in by the furries community (e.g., conventions, meet-ups). For at least some furries, active participation in furry events is a component of what it means to be a furry.

"A group of friends I can count on and events to go to."

"A wonderful, diverse and welcoming community, a hobby, and very close friends. Also an annual de-stressing with attending Confuzzled."

"Being a silly character on the internet and going to silly public events."

"Community, friendship and a chance to costume at events."

"I like art I guess, I like being in this fandom, love being social, and I love spending time with like minded people. I guess you could say going to a furry con is like a break from the whole adult life, you can be you around these people, their [sic] less likely to judge you, their [sic] very accepting."

Furry is About Social Support

In this final theme, we explore the role that social support plays in some furries' conceptualization of what furry is to them. To be sure, there is ample evidence to suggest that the furry fandom provides a tremendous amount of social support to furries, a point we establish in detail in Chapter 19 and have made elsewhere in published articles (Roberts et al., 2015). For now, it's enough to say that a number of furries benefit from the sense of belongingness and community provided by the furry fandom, especially insofar as it helps provide them with a sense of resilience and support during difficult times. While this was seldom the only facet of being a furry that they recognized, it was noted as being among other important parts of the concept of furry.

> *"A shoulder to cry on and adorable characters in my novels."*

> *"As a furry, I can interact with many people with many difference from me, which help me learn a lot. Furry also helped me get through a difficult period in my life."*

> *"Being a furry – to me – means quite a lot to me. For one it lets me express myself as who I really am, as well as how I identify myself, not having to hide parts of my personality out of fear from getting rejected for being myself. Furthermore, it means very much being around and talking to people who are very accepting, which helps me with socializing as well as getting through phases of – sometimes – very deep depression. In other words it lets me feel that I'm worth something."*

> *"Being a furry means having a great community to rely on in my times of need, and fantastic FRIENDS to share my life with."*

> *"Being a furry saved my life, so it means community, friendship, love, and a safe place."*

> *"Being a part of a community that are fans of themselves and the works they create. The kindness and openness of the fandom is important as well. I've never seen so much money raised for good causes in such a short amount of time."*

> *"Being part of a community endorsing and housing acceptance for all. A more open social space, and a more progressive one than what's typically found elsewhere. Support is plentiful. Animal people are comforting and interesting."*

Summary: What is Furry—Open-Ended Responses

By now it should be apparent that furry, as a concept, is multifaceted and nuanced. No single definition of furry can fully capture the wide range of experiences that furries have with the term. For instance, conceptualizing furry solely as a "fandom" overlooks the fact that there are many furries for whom furry is a solitary hobby they engage in separate from the broader furry fandom. Defining furry solely as an interest in media featuring anthropomorphized characters overlooks the fact that many furries consider furry to be a deeply held and significant part of who they are. Focusing solely on furry as an inclusive or safe space for LGBTQ+ furries overlooks the fact that some furries may simply be looking for an entertaining form of escapism from the mundanity of their job while focusing solely on furry as a kink or fetish overlooks the fact that the furry community is often a source of social support and belongingness for some furries, for whom the fandom becomes like a second family.

At the end of the day, we must content ourselves with the fact that we will only ever have imperfect, limited, or flawed definitions of what furry is—whether to conceptualize it as a personal identity, as a fan group, as a means of self-expression, as a hobby, or even as a political statement. Despite this lack of a universal definition, however, it is still possible to extract useful, if imperfect working definitions of the term. For instance: Many of the studies Furscience carries out are done from a social-psychological perspective, which emphasizes group identity and the cultures that develop around groups of fans. While furry is not *only* a fandom or a social group, and may not even be a fandom or social group for all furries, we can nevertheless answer questions about some facets of furry by construing furry as a fandom.[10]

This also means that it's entirely possible to understand furry from several different theoretical perspectives and through a number of different academic lenses. For instance, a communications and media scholar might focus specifically on questions about the transmission of furry culture through different media. A literary scholar might focus on the content of furry artwork or furry stories and the use of anthropomorphized animals as an allegory for human culture. A sex researcher might focus on attitudes toward pornography and the impact of kink-positivity on furries' sexual behavior. Scholars from race and gender studies could look at issues of intersectionality within the furry fandom and study the informal power dynamics at play in online and in-person furry spaces.

The point is that there is no one "right" way to conceptualize furry, and scholars will ultimately conceptualize furry in the way that is most

---

[10] This is sort of akin to a physicist being told to "assume the plane is a sphere and that wind resistance doesn't exist" for the purpose of testing a physics model. While the model being tested is more simplified than reality, it's nevertheless possible to make fairly reasonable predictions about reality from a flawed and imperfect model!

appropriate for their own line of research. Ultimately, the most complete picture of furry will arise from a consideration of these different perspectives and the light they can shed on the topic through their unique approaches and perspectives—much like how a complete picture of how the human body works involves an understanding of physics, chemistry, cellular biology, anatomy, medicine, and psychology. We'll point out that the perspective that we at Furscience take generally tends to involve conceptualizing furry as a fandom and as a social identity, but this is far from the only way furry can be conceptualized, nor does this mean that the findings we obtain through this approach represent the sum of all knowledge available about furries.

With that in mind, let us finish this chapter by taking a look at some closed-ended data from some of our other furry studies to see whether their findings correspond with what we've observed in the open-ended data.

What is Furry: Fixed Responses

In a closed-ended response format, rather than asking respondents to describe what furry is in their own words, we provided them with a list of themes and asked them to indicate the extent to which each theme is or is not an important part of what it means to be furry on a 7-point scale (1 = *not important at all*, 7 = *very important*). These themes were drawn from a combination of prevalent stereotypes about furries and from observations and conversations with furries at furry conventions. The themes were presented to two different samples of furries in 2011: one sample that was recruited in-person at a large furry convention and another that was recruited online through various regional furry forums and popular online furry websites. Their average response to each category is presented in Table 5.2.

First, it is worth noting that while these themes do not perfectly overlap with the themes extracted from the open-ended data in the 2021 study, the same general pattern of responses was found: the sense of community and being a fan of furry-themed art and content emerged as being two of the most important themes underlying furry. While art was equally important to both online and convention furries, community was slightly more important to furries recruited at a convention.

Going down the list, other similar trends emerge. For example, themes of openness and acceptance were also important to online and convention furries, aligning with the themes of LGBTQ+ acceptance and feeling free to self-express without fear of being rejected or ostracized that were expressed in the open-ended data. Fursuits were also somewhat important, just as they were in the open-ended data: neither the most nor least important facet of being a furry. Sex was also somewhat lower on the list in terms of importance, paralleling the fact that sex was only the 13th-most common theme extracted from the open-ended data and, in both cases, seemed less important to the conceptualization of furry than activities such as fursuiting.

Table 5.2. Respondents' average rated importance of various themes to what it means to be furry in a sample of furries recruited at a convention and a sample recruited online. * Indicates a theme where the two samples differed statistically significantly from one another.

Theme	Conv. Avg.	Online Avg.
Community*	6.6	6.5
Art	6.5	6.6
Openness / Acceptance*	6.3	6.1
Internet Groups	6.1	6.0
Conventions*	6.1	5.9
Local Meet-Ups	5.8	5.7
MUCKs / Roleplaying*	5.2	5.0
Making Fursuits*	5.2	4.8
Writing	5.2	5.3
Wearing Fursuits*	5.0	4.6
Music*	4.4	4.1
Gaming*	4.3	4.0
Sex	3.6	3.5
Drama / Social Conflict*	3.2	2.8

One notable difference did emerge between the open-ended data and the closed-ended data. Specifically, in the closed-ended data specific furry activities, including going to conventions and meet-ups and interacting with other furries in online groups were placed fairly high in terms of their importance. In the open-ended data, these specific activities were far less common in terms of the frequency with which they were mentioned as being part of what it means to be furry.

The closed-ended data also offer some interesting context to the themes extracted from the open-ended data. For example, asking furries explicitly about the role of MUCKs and roleplaying revealed that they are a fairly important part of furry, even if this was only fairly rarely mentioned spontaneously by furries in their open-ended responses. The closed-ended data also reveal that not all furry content is seen as being equally important. Specifically, art (usually connoting visual artwork in fan spaces) is seen as more important or central to furry than writing or music, a point that did not emerge in the open-ended data. Finally, the closed-ended data help to dispel a common misconception that drama is a unique or inextricable part of what it means to be furry, a point we'll return to again in Chapter 12.

Will the Real Furry Please Stand Up?

To this point, we've addressed the general question of what constitutes furry: the multitudinous themes and interacting facets that combine to make furry what it is. However, another provocative, conceptually related question emerged as we were studying gatekeeping and elitism in the furry fandom, a topic we discuss in Chapter 12. Specifically, we were interested not just in how furries define the concept of furry, but also the criteria they use to distinguish "real furries" from people who, in their judgment, should not be considered furries.

Based on feedback provided to us by furries and from our observations of furries, we came up with a list of 11 different criteria that we thought furries might use to distinguish "real furries" and those who are not furry.[11] In a 2022 study, we recruited a sample of furries in person at a furry convention and a separate sample of furries recruited online and asked them each to rate the importance of each of the different criteria for distinguishing real furries from fake, superficial, wannabe furries using a 7-point scale (1 = *not important*, 7 = *very important*). The results are shown in Table 5.3.

As the data in the table reveal, one item was a clear frontrunner in terms of its importance for distinguishing authentic furries from superficial furries: whether someone loves furry content. To put it another way, most furries would seem to agree that a "fake" furry is one who lacks a genuine love of furry content. This finding coincides with earlier findings, both from open-ended and fixed-response studies, suggesting that an interest in content featuring anthropomorphic animals is seen as one of the more important and defining features of furries. It is also noteworthy that the second-most important item across the two samples is the extent to which someone interacts with other furries, something which hints at the other most commonly indicated facet of being a furry: the sense of community or fandom. In this case, however, it would seem that furries see it as far less important when it comes to determining whether someone does or does not "count" as a furry.

[11] This could include so-called "wannabe furries," "bandwagon furries," or people who might be erroneously labeled as furries by outsiders.

Table 5.3. Respondents' average rated importance of various items when determining who is or is not a "real furry" in a sample of furries recruited at a convention and a sample recruited online. * Indicates an item where the two samples differed statistically significantly from one another.

Theme	Conv. Avg.	Online Avg.
Love of furry content	5.7	5.8
Interacts with other furries	4.0	3.7
Proudly furry, even when it's unpopular*	4.0	3.6
Loves discussing details of furry content	3.3	3.1
Attends in-person furry events*	2.8	2.3
Spends time and money on a furry-themed collection*	2.5	2.1
Knows the history/people in furry culture	2.4	2.6
Produces furry content	2.4	2.2
Been a furry for a long time	2.3	2.1
Dresses up like a furry (e.g., fursuit)*	2.3	2.0
Integrates furry into their day-to-day life	2.3	2.2

We can point out a few other noteworthy trends from these findings. For one thing, it seems that specific activities do not "make the furry," so to speak. For example, attending furry events, collecting furry merchandise, producing furry content, and wearing a fursuit are generally not seen by furries as defining features of what makes a person a furry. While responses to the questions earlier in this chapter suggest that these may be a part of furry culture or represent one possible manifestation of a person's general interest in furry-themed content, these activities, in and of themselves, are not necessary for a person to be a furry.

Another point worth noting is that the label of furry does not appear to be grounded in the extent or magnitude of one's engagement in furry activities. For example, knowing a lot about furry history, having been a furry for a long time, or being a so-called "lifestyler" who incorporates furry into their day-to-day life (e.g., being "openly furry" and wearing a collar at work) does not seem necessary to "prove" that one is a furry. To put it another way, furry seems to be more about the genuineness of one's felt love of furry content itself than it is about their ability to demonstrate devotion to the interest by displays of knowledge or trivia about their interest. It would seem that both new and long-time admirers can be equally likely to be seen as furries.

Conclusion: Furry to the Bone

As we finish up this chapter looking at the multifaceted nature of what it means to be a furry, we want to leave you with one additional wrinkle to add just a bit more complexity to the emerging picture of what it means to be a furry. The results are drawn from a study we published in a journal article looking at how furries responded to threats to their furry identity (Plante et al., 2015). Specifically, furries in the study had the distinctiveness of their fan interest threatened by suggesting that, when you get right down to it, furries are no different than any other fan group.[12] Two versions of this threat were used, a strong and a weak version. In the strong version, furries were compared to a fan group with whom furry could be argued to share a lot of conceptual overlap: anime fans. In this case, the threat was a potentially viable one. In the weak version, furries were compared to a fan group with whom furries had very little conceptual overlap: sports fans. Given this lack of conceptual overlap, it is unlikely that the threat was seen as being especially viable. Finally, there was also a control group for comparison, in which furries were not compared to any other fan group.

Furries were also asked some questions about furry, either by itself or as compared to the other fan groups (i.e., anime, sports), including questions about how stigmatized furries are and how strongly the participant identified as a furry. Most importantly, after the threat, furries were also asked to indicate whether furry was something biologically essential—that is, whether being a furry was something they were born with, something inextricably tied to them that couldn't be taken away from them. The results showed that, all else being equal, the furries who were the most likely to believe that furry was something hard-wired into them were furries who were compared to anime fans (high-threat), who saw furry as highly stigmatized, and who identified most strongly as furry.

One possible explanation for these findings is that furries who identify strongly as furries and who perceive furry as being "under attack" by being

[12] A lack of distinctiveness represents a possible threat insofar as it threatens potential erasure of one's group identity. As an example, one can imagine what would happen if someone were to tell a Canadian that Canadians, as a group, were basically the same as people from the United States of America. The implication of this statement is that there is no need for "Canadian" to be seen as a distinct category and, as such, it can be safely absorbed into the category of "American." Doing so would eliminate any distinctiveness that comes from being Canadian, something which might be especially upsetting to a Canadian who identifies strongly with these unique or distinct elements.

lumped into a similar fandom may shift their views on where furry comes from (i.e., something hard-wired into them, something they're born with) to defend the distinctiveness of furry. In other words, rather than allowing furry to be consumed by another fan interest and having their distinct identity erased, furries may appeal to furry as something essential that cannot be changed or erased: furries and anime fans are not the same because furry is something you're born with, something inside of furries that anime fans simply lack. This would imply that you can't simply absorb furry into another fan group, because being furry is a difference that's innate and immutable, as unchanging as one's height.

The point of the study, and the reason it's being brought up here, is not to suggest that furry is defined by anything biological or immutable. We do not mean to suggest that "furry" is some innate, unalterable essence within the genes or the bodies of furries. Instead, the study demonstrates that furries' beliefs about what furry is may change in response to what's happening around them. A threat to the distinctiveness of their fandom can cause furries to shift their beliefs about what makes a furry a furry in the first place.

As if defining a furry wasn't complex enough! In addition to being multifaceted and distinct to every furry, now we need to contend with the fact that, even within a single furry, the definition of what a furry is can shift within a matter of minutes depending on what's going on around them!

So what are we to conclude from this—that the task of trying to define furry is too complex and should be abandoned?

Not at all! We can, for example, point to trends and general tendencies that seem to be fairly consistent across furries as a group. Most furries would agree, for example, that whatever furry is, it's probably tied, at least in part, to a person's interest in being part of a group of like-minded people who share an interest in content featuring anthropomorphized animal characters. This conceptualization is unlikely to be agreed upon by all furries, of course, but this is probably a common conceptualization of what it means to be a furry. But we should always be mindful of the considerable variation that exists around this average tendency: "furry" can be imbued with tremendous significance for some furries, including elements of their self-expression, sexuality, escapism from day-to-day life, and with specific activities (e.g., fursuiting, creating content). This is almost certainly the reason why asking different furries often yields similar, but distinct definitions as to what it means to be furry. And, as we've seen in this final section, this also explains why some furries' responses to this question may change from situation to situation.

While we may not be ending this chapter with a clear, universally-accepted definition of furry, what we have emerged with is a definition that, at least for practical purposes, is "good enough" to allow us to consider furries as a group with some common beliefs, norms, interests, and values. It also allows us to anticipate that, going forward, we are likely to see considerable variability between different furries. This chapter is, if nothing else, a cautionary tale against treating all furries identically, as a single, homogenous entity. To do so would be to destroy much of the rich texture, depth, and complexity that, in many ways, makes furry so interesting in the first place.

References

Brooks, T. R., Bennett, T. N., Myhre, A., Plante, C. N., Reysen, S., Roberts, S. E., & Gerbasi, K. C. (2022). "Chasing Tail": Testing the relative strength of sexual interest and social interaction as predictors of furry identity. *The Journal of Sex Research.* Advance online publication. https://doi.org/10.1080/00224499.2022.2068180

Plante, C. N., Roberts, S. E., Snider, J. S., Schroy, C., Reysen, S., & Gerbasi, K. (2015). 'More than skin-deep': Biological essentialism in response to a distinctiveness threat in a stigmatized fan community. *British Journal of Social Psychology, 54*(2), 359-370. https://doi.org/10.1111/bjso.12079

Roberts, S. E., Plante, C., Gerbasi, K., & Reysen, S. (2015). Clinical interaction with anthropomorphic phenomenon: Notes for health professionals about interacting with clients who possess this unusual identity. *Health & Social Work, 40*(2), e42-e50. https://doi.orfg/10.1093/hsw/hlv020

yerf. (2020). *On furry.* Retrieved on June 2, 2023, from https://yerfology.files.wordpress.com/2020/08/on-furry_yerf.pdf

Chapter 6
Being Furry: Fanship versus Fandom

Stephen Reysen, Courtney "Nuka" Plante

What comes to mind when you hear the word "fan?"[1] Chances are, you're probably thinking about a person engaging in behavior related to an interest that they're passionate about—wearing interest-related clothing, watching or producing interest-related media, and hanging out with others who share that particular interest.

This notion of fans as a collection of fan-related behaviors represents a fairly typical conceptualization of what it means to be a fan. Indeed, it makes sense that most laypersons would think to define fans based on the most visible, recognizable, and iconic behaviors that fans engage in. But this isn't how a psychologist—specifically a social psychologist—thinks of a fan. To a social psychologist, a fan is more than a bundle of specific behaviors. To a social psychologist, a fan is a person who identifies with a particular interest, and it's this identity that shapes the way they think, feel about, and act in the world.

While it might seem like trivial hair-splitting to distinguish fan identity from the behaviors fans engage in, coming to think about being fans in terms of their identity has proven to be one of the most important and fruitful avenues for psychologists to research and ultimately understand what makes fans tick. By thinking about a fan as an identity, one attaches a sense of significance and gravitas to fan interests, implying something far more than a mere aesthetic preference: it's a filter through which fans perceive the world, convey information to others, frame their values and beliefs, and make decisions about their behavior.

As an illustrative example of what we gain by thinking about fans as an identity, let's imagine what we can learn about a person based on another identity they may have: their identification with a particular political party. Most of us would reasonably assume, based on which political party someone identifies with, that we have at least some insight into that person's worldview. We can probably make a reasoned inference about the policies they would support, the people they consider to be allies and enemies, and their behavior in certain circumstances (e.g., in the voting booth) just by knowing whether they identify with a more conservative or liberal political party. Moreover, we understand that this identity is not necessarily static or

---

[1] *Other* than a device with oscillating blades used to circulate air!

fixed, but rather something that can change, both within an individual over time (e.g., changing party affiliation) and more broadly, as something whose cultural meaning may shift (e.g., the policies of Republicans and Democrats shifted dramatically across the 20th century).

By considering "fan" as an identity, we are implying that many of the same psychological principles that drive other identities (e.g., political affiliation, gender) are also at work in fans. In the present chapter, we'll delve into the implications of this approach by first reviewing the most popular theoretical perspective on fan identity—the social identity approach. Next, we'll make an important theoretical distinction by splitting the concept of fan identity into two parts, fanship, and fandom. Lastly, we'll illustrate the importance of thinking about fanship and fandom as separate facets of fan identity by showing how they differently predict important beliefs and behaviors for the furries in our studies.

What is the Social Identity Perspective?

The social identity perspective is the result of combining two separate psychological theories, one called, appropriately enough, social identity theory (Tajfel & Turner, 1979), and the other called self-categorization theory (Turner et al., 1987). Put simply, social identity theory talks about what happens when people think of themselves as members of a group, while self-categorization theory outlines when people are the most likely to see themselves as members of a group. While these are, technically speaking, two distinct psychological theories and experts in the field might get a bit caught up in the minute differences between them, most researchers recognize that the theories complement one another quite well and prefer to treat them as two parts of a social identity perspective.

Okay, but why should anyone who's not a social psychologist care about this social identity perspective? Chances are you picked this book up to learn some interesting facts and trivia about furries, not to get lost in dense psychological theory! Trust us, we haven't included this chapter just to flex all the reading we had to do in graduate school.[2] In fact, we think the social identity perspective is so important to being able to understand furries, that we've put this chapter near the beginning of the book. Indeed, much of what follows is consistent with, and can be best understood through, a social identity perspective.[3] And we're not the only ones who think so: this

[2] … okay, maybe there's a *hint* of that going on, but only a little bit, we promise!

[3] As an analogy, imagine that you're looking at a gallery of artwork created by five different artists. One way to learn about the pieces is to memorize a bunch of trivia about each piece separately (e.g., date, artist, style, etc.). At the end of the day, you'd

perspective has been used across academic disciplines to explain behavior within groups (e.g., how fans and non-fans alike behave), and to explain behavior between groups (e.g., how non-fans behave toward fans and vice-versa).

With that in mind, let's take a moment to see for ourselves what insights we might glean from this social identity perspective that academics can't seem to stop talking about.

Social Identity Theory

Tajfel and Turner (1979) were interested, like many social psychologists at the time, in understanding what caused groups of people to fight with one another. Popular theories at the time argued that groups typically came into conflict because the world is limited in its resources, meaning that if one group got something that they wanted, it usually came at the cost of another group not getting (or losing) that very thing (Sherif, 1966; Sherif et al., 1961). Intuitively, this makes a lot of sense: examples abound of groups fighting over something they both want, be it countries warring over land or two different little league soccer teams competing for a trophy and a pizza party.[4]

But Tajfel and Turner made a provocative suggestion: maybe groups don't need a reason to be at odds with one another. Maybe they would disagree, compete, or outright fight with one another simply because they were told that they were different from the other group. They suggested that the very act of categorizing people into groups was enough, in and of itself, to lead to intergroup conflict.

Their idea didn't just spontaneously exist, of course. It was an observation based on a series of studies using what they termed the minimal group paradigm. In these studies, participants entered a laboratory and were divided into groups in about as random a way as you can get: they were shown a screen covered in dots and were asked to estimate how many dots were on the screen. Those who overestimated were put into an "over-

---

be left with a set of scattered facts about these specific pieces, and nothing more. But if you had an organizational framework, a way of understanding the style, techniques, and history of each artist, you would be able to look at each piece of art in this gallery (and in others) and be able to predict which piece was made by which artist, as well as to be able to make inferences about when it was made and what might have inspired the piece. This framework ties together the scattered facts and trivia and allows a deeper understanding of the subject.

[4] At least, we assume winning the championship comes with a pizza party. Neither of the authors of this chapter were especially athletic growing up!

estimator" group while those who underestimated were put into an "under-estimator" group (but, in reality it was random assignment to groups).

Participants were then escorted off by themselves and given a task: they had to decide how to assign points between the over-estimators and the under-estimators. Importantly, they were told that they, themselves, would not be the recipient of any of these points—they had no skin in this game, so to speak. They were told that these points had monetary value, but that they would not be receiving any of it themselves. Their only choice was whether members of their group (called the ingroup) should receive more money than members of the other group (called the outgroup). It's also worth noting that participants never actually got to see or interact with other members of their group. For example, while a participant might have been told that they were a dot over-estimator and that they were part of a group of over-estimators, they never actually met any of their fellow over-estimators. The participants were also told that their decision would be anonymous, meaning that they could neither be praised nor condemned by the other participants in the study based on their decision. They would simply make their decision and then leave the lab, where they would never again have to think about their group.

This entire procedure was done to ensure that participants had no self-interest in the decision and that the groups to which they were assigned were entirely meaningless.[5] Under such circumstances, there would seem to be no reason for participants to favor their ingroup over the outgroup when it came to giving out points. After all, they wouldn't personally profit one way or another, and it wasn't like they had anything in common with the people in their group (aside from supposedly sharing the same tendency to over- or under-estimate the number of dots on a screen). Nevertheless, the results of the study showed that most people gave preferential treatment to "their" group, giving more points to the ingroup over the outgroup. If being put into a group truly had no impact on peoples' behavior toward group or non-group members, we would expect the same number of points to be given out to members of both groups. Instead, people showed a tendency to favor their ingroup, even if it was a group they had only just learned about, knew next to nothing about, and didn't personally stand to benefit from.[6]

---

[5] To drive this point home even more concretely, in one version of the study the participants were outright told that they had been assigned to the groups at random and that they were completely meaningless.

[6] Participants probably couldn't justify being *completely* one-sided in their allocation of points, but they could probably play dumb and sweep a small amount of ingroup favoritism under the rug as a coincidence.

These findings formed the backbone of *social identity theory*, which, in a nutshell, states that people want to identify as part of distinctly positive groups, and will spend time, effort, and resources to do so. As we saw in the studies above, people willingly favored the group that they were part of, contributing to the idea that it paid to be part of this group and that they were, fortunately, part of the winning group, the group that one would want to be part of. Their actions also contributed to a widening of the gap between ingroup and outgroup members, adding one more difference between the groups and making the distinction between them clearer.

But what does this have to do with fan groups? The study above applied to a completely arbitrary group with whom someone shared nothing in common, but fan groups—and indeed most of the groups to which we belong—are far from random, and we have far more in common with other group members than the over-estimators did with their group mates.

The logic of the argument goes like this: if we can find ingroup favoritism, outgroup derogation, and a desire to increase group distinctiveness in largely meaningless groups, these same tendencies should be present, but even stronger, in groups that *are* meaningful and significant to us. In other words, fans should show these same underlying tendencies, but even stronger, especially when their identity as a fan is on their mind. This is exactly what fan researchers have found. For example, Platow and colleagues (1999) went to soccer games and set up charity booths that were either related to the home team, the away team, or neither and found that fans donated more money to the charity whose collectors wore symbols of the home team. In another study of sports fans, Levine et al. (2005) made fans think about their favorite team before sending them across campus to a different building. While walking to the other building, participants saw a person fall and hurt themselves. Importantly, the injured person was either wearing a shirt of the participant's favorite team, a rival team, or a neutral shirt. The researchers found that fans were more likely to help the person if they wore a shirt of their favorite team. We've also observed ingroup favoritism in the furry community, where furries rated their fursona species as having far more positive characteristics than the other nine species being studied.

Some fairly influential early research on fan behavior has shown some of the other ways these group processes can impact the way people think, feel, and behave. One such phenomenon is known as *basking in reflected glory* (Cialdini et al., 1976). In this study, the researchers took note of how likely students were to wear school-themed clothing (e.g., hoodies, t-shirts) after their school's football team won or lost a game. They found that after a victory, students were more likely to wear symbols of their school as compared to after a loss. Why? Remember, according to social identity theory people are motivated to be part of groups that are distinct and positive. So if a person's school wins a sporting event, they can siphon off some of that glory for themselves (i.e., basking in the reflected glory of the team) and get a self-esteem boost from being part of the winning group. In contrast, a loss represents a threat to one's self-esteem, since people typically don't want to be seen as losers—and so they keep the school hoodie in the laundry hamper.

Skeptical readers might find themselves questioning the interpretation of these results. Isn't it a bit of a stretch to say that wearing one's school hoodie after a victory means that the person is identifying more strongly with the school community? Fortunately, some follow-up data can speak to this skepticism. As part of the same line of research, the psychologists called up students after a victory or loss and asked them if they knew the results of the recent game. Specifically, the researchers were looking at the choice of words students used when describing the results: did they use the words "we" or "us" to describe the outcome (suggesting a shared identity with the team), or did they use the words "they" to differentiate themselves from the team? Turns out, after a loss, students were less likely to use the words "we" or "us" (e.g., "they lost") than they were after a victory (e.g., "we won").

Findings like these suggest that fans identify with a particular fan interest, just as people identify with other group identities, to help them forge a positive identity, one that lets them draw self-esteem from their group.[7] While the above research suggests that people identify with groups because of this positivity, other research suggests that the distinctiveness afforded by a group—the fact that it helps you to feel different from others—may be just as important, if not more important (Mlicki & Ellemers, 1996). In our research, for example, we manipulated whether furries were compared to sports fans (a dissimilar group), anime fans (a similar group), or made no comparisons at all (control condition; Plante et al., 2015). When the distinctiveness of furry as a social identity was threatened (e.g., when furries were said to be the same as anime fans), highly identified furries were especially likely to get defensive and respond by insisting that being furry was something hard-wired into them, something biological and innate that

---

[7] If you find yourself wondering how this can be the case when some fan groups are stigmatized, which would seem to, if anything, hurt one's sense of self-esteem, see Chapter 21 and Chapter 22, where we talk about this at length.

made them categorically different from other people. Findings like these are consistent with a social identity perspective and show the utility of understanding furries specifically, and fan groups more generally, as group identities.

Social identity theory also makes other important predictions about what happens to people when you make them think about their group identity. For one thing, people tend to treat members of other groups as all being the same while seeing the distinctiveness and variability of members of their groups—a phenomenon called *outgroup homogeneity*. This may lead to the application of stereotypes to members of other groups (e.g., anime fans are all geeks and nerds) while taking offense to the suggestion that members of one's own group are all the same (e.g., all furries have wolf fursonas).

As a test of this *own-group bias*, a tendency to recognize and distinguish individuals from one's own group better than members of an outgroup (see Meissner & Brigham, 2001), we ran a study where we pitted furries and college undergraduates against each other in a memory test for fursuit faces, furry art faces, and human faces (Reysen et al., 2018). We showed participants images from each of these categories at the beginning of the study and then, after distracting them for a few minutes, we showed them additional images, some of which were the same as before, and others that were brand new. The results showed that while furries and students were equally good at distinguishing human faces from one another, furries were especially good at distinguishing fursuit and furry art faces. These findings emphasize the fact that people tend to treat all outgroup members as being the same (e.g., college students being unable to distinguish fursuit and furry faces), while ingroup members are more likely to process ingroup information more deeply and make these sorts of distinctions. It's just another example of how understanding furry as a social identity can help to provide context, perspective, and an explanation for a phenomenon that, by itself, would be little more than a weird, quirky piece of trivia about furries.

Taken together, the above findings illustrate how social identity theory can help us to make sense of a wide range of behaviors, be it in fan groups more broadly or in furries specifically. However, social identity theory is only half of the theoretical backbone underpinning the social identity perspective. Let us now briefly turn our attention to the second half of this perspective.

Self-Categorization Theory

After helping Tajfel develop social identity theory as a graduate student, Turner continued to advance the theory. Alongside his colleagues, the work eventually gave way to what we now call *self-categorization theory* (Turner et al., 1987). According to this theory, people do not have a single identity but instead shift between a variety of identities from situation to situation. For example, when we are in the classroom, the authors of this chapter think of ourselves as professors, psychologists, or researchers. But at the end of the day, when we return home, our most relevant group identity switches. At home, Stephen may think of himself as a spouse or as an anime fan, while Courtney may think of himself as a furry or as a gamer. Turner and his colleagues proposed that these different identities are not all equal but instead differ in their level of abstraction and inclusiveness. At the most concrete level is one's identity, their sense of individuality or uniqueness, what makes them different from the person sitting next to them. At higher levels of abstraction is one's group identity as compared to other groups of comparable size—for example, a furry comparing themselves to an anime fan—or comparing one's group to broader, more inclusive groups—for example, a furry compared to all of humanity.

How inclusive one's identity is in a given moment, while abstract as a concept, can have real-world consequences. For example, earlier we mentioned the research by Levine et al. (2005) in which fans were more likely to help an injured person if they were wearing a shirt of their favorite soccer team. In a follow-up study, rather than making participants think about themselves as fans of their favorite team before they went on their walk, the researchers instead had them think about themselves as part of the broader, more inclusive category of "soccer fan," in which all soccer fans were part of the ingroup, not just fans of their favorite team. In this condition, participants were now likely to help both the person with their favorite team's shirt and the person wearing the shirt of the rival team. In effect, by activating a more inclusive group identity in the participants' minds, the researchers redrew the boundaries of who was and wasn't part of the participants' ingroup, which had a notable impact on their behavior toward others.

But we rarely have a researcher standing over our shoulder telling us which of our many social identities we should be thinking about. So what, in a given circumstance, determines which of our social identities will be on our minds? As it turns out, there are two factors at play. The first factor is called *accessibility*. Accessibility refers to whether someone has a prior history or experience adopting that identity. To illustrate this, neither of the authors of this chapter are Chinese. As such, a Chinese identity is not accessible to either of us. It is not within our repertoire of available identities and so it will not suddenly spring to our minds in a given situation—there are no circumstances under which either of us will suddenly start to think of ourselves as Chinese.[8] The second factor is the *fit* of the identity, which refers to whether the situation is one in which there are groups or stereotypes around us that direct us into thinking of ourselves as part of a particular social identity. So if, for example, Stephen is an anime fan and he walks past an anime-themed store in the mall, this may activate this particular identity in his mind.

Once an identity is on our mind, we begin to think of ourselves less as individuals and more as a member of a group, a process called *depersonalization*. When we are depersonalized, we start to act less and less as unique individuals and give over more of our decision-making to the beliefs, norms, and values of the group. For example, if a stereotype of sports fans is that they are argumentative and boisterous, an otherwise mild-mannered and quiet person who is a sports fan may become uncharacteristically loud and confrontational when surrounded by fellow sports fans. Put simply, when we're thinking about ourselves as members of a group, we tend to act more in line with how members of that group are expected to act.

Armed, at last, with a basic understanding of the social identity perspective and an appreciation of how being a fan affects the way we think, feel, and behave, we can now turn our attention to the question of what, precisely, it means to identify as a fan.

Identification: Fanship and Fandom

To this point, we've talked about being a fan as if fan identification were a single concept. However, Tajfel and Turner (1979) make a distinction between a social identity and a personal identity. They define a social identity as the degree to which one feels a sense of psychological connection to other members of a group (e.g., emotional connection, shared values, a common sense of identity). One can see how this would apply to fans who share a sense of community with other fans. But fans can also identify with the interest itself, independent of other fans of the interest. For example, one might really enjoy watching a particular television show while having no interest whatsoever in the fan community and the memes and culture that

---

[8] If, on the other hand, one of us were to suddenly find out that we were adopted and that our extended family was Chinese, and if we were to go to China and spend 30 years living there, a Chinese identity might begin to become accessible to us.

surround it.[9] Reysen and Branscombe (2010) use the term fanship to refer to the degree of psychological connection one feels to an object of interest (e.g., "I love anime") and the term fandom to refer to a psychological connection with a fan group (e.g., "I love the anime community"). While fanship reflects a personal identity that can be used to distinguish one person from another (e.g., "I am a bigger anime fan than you"), fandom is a social identity that embeds oneself within a fan group, distinct from other fan groups.

Fanship

Most psychology research examining fans has tended to focus on sports fans. We suspect this is due to the popularity of sports (e.g., a whole section of the news is dedicated to sports), but also because, generally speaking, it's easier to find sports fans to study than it is to find members of more niche fan groups.

This is why, when Wann and Branscombe (1993) developed their measure of fanship, they did so by sampling sports fans. However, a drawback of this approach is that it led to the development of a measure of fanship that included items that were only relevant to sports fans. For example, participants were asked to indicate how important it was to them that their favorite team wins games. While this question may well assess the fanship of sports fans, the question itself cannot easily be adapted to other fans (e.g., furries, anime fans).

To address this problem, Reysen and Branscombe (2010) developed a measure of fanship that could be used for fans of any interest. While the original scale was eleven items long, it was eventually reduced to a three-item version (or, if space on the survey is really tight, a single-item version) which asks participants to indicate the extent to which they agree with a statement like "I strongly identify with being a furry" from 1 = *strongly disagree* to 7 = *strongly agree* (Postmes et al., 2013; Reysen et al., 2013).

In nearly all of our furry studies, we include a measure of fanship. We find that, from year to year, there are small fluctuations between samples concerning their average fanship score, but, on average, it tends to be fairly high—exactly what you'd expect to find in a sample of fans (see Figure 6.1). What's more, fanship scores tend to consistently be higher than scores on a similar measure of fandom, which we discuss in the next section.

---

[9] One of the authors of this chapter feels this way about the television show *Rick and Morty*, being an avid viewer of the show while having little to no interest in identifying as part of the fan community which has formed around the show.

Fandom

In the same way that psychological research on fans was dominated extensively by research on sports fans, it was also heavily dominated by research on fanship to the detriment of research on fandom. As such, there are comparatively few studies in psychology looking specifically at the variable of fandom identification. What little research does exist suggests that fandom is an important social identity; science-fiction fans (Obst et al., 2002a, 2002b) and fans across a range of interests more broadly (Chadborn et al., 2018) report identifying more strongly with their fan communities than they do with their local neighborhoods. Yoshida et al. (2015) assessed fanship and fandom in a longitudinal study of Japanese soccer fans to find fandom is a stronger predictor of game attendance.

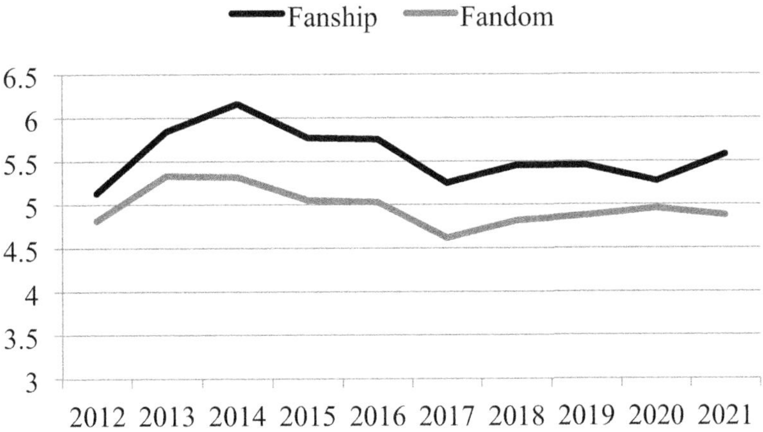

Figure 6.1. Furries' ratings of fanship and fandom across time. 7-point Likert-type scale, from 1 = *strongly disagree* to 7 = *strongly agree.*

When it comes to measuring fandom identification, there are a number of measures available from social identity theory which, while not developed specifically for use with fan groups, can easily be adapted for use in this context (see Reysen et al., 2013). As with fanship, we mostly use a three-item measure, though we'll occasionally use a single-item measure of fandom if space gets tight; in both cases, the measure asks participants to indicate their agreement with a statement like "I strongly identify with other furries in the furry community" (Postmes et al., 2013; Reysen et al., 2013).

Pitting Fanship and Fandom Against One Another

At first glance, it's easy to think that the distinction between fanship and fandom is trite and meaningless. After all, studies show that fanship and fandom are fairly highly correlated, meaning that people who score high in one tend to also score high in the other (Plante et al., 2021; Reysen & Branscombe, 2010). Even so, the same studies also suggest that, while highly correlated, fanship and fandom are conceptually distinct. This is important because, as the rest of the research in this chapter will show, knowing whether we're talking about fanship or fandom is important when talking about the potential consequences or implications of one's fan identity.

As an illustrative example, in a study of the brony community,[10] Edwards et al. (2019) allowed both fanship and fandom scores to simultaneously predict fan behaviors. In doing so, they were able to measure the association of one variable with fan behavior while statistically controlling for the other one. In doing so, they found that fanship was positively associated with purchasing official merchandise, displaying fan symbols (e.g., wearing a shirt with a symbol), identification with a character from the show, and feelings of entitlement as a fan. In contrast, fandom was positively associated with watching fan-made content, talking to friends about the show, purchasing fan-made products, creating content oneself, attending a fan convention, and watching reruns of the show. In other words, despite being similar to one another, fanship and fandom uniquely predicted different fan behaviors.

To show that this wasn't a coincidence, Reysen et al. (2021) conducted a similar study with anime fans. They found, in line with the brony research, that fanship predicted collecting official merchandise, watching anime, looking at fan art, reading news and reviews, playing anime-related games, listening to J-pop, obsessing about anime, feeling immersed while watching anime, and dreaming about anime—all behaviors indicative of content consumption and being a fan of the content itself. Fandom identification, on the other hand, was associated with spending money on conventions, reading fanfiction, talking with others about anime, posting in online anime forums, and having more friends who also like anime—all behaviors associated with the fan community.

Together, the brony and anime data suggest that when pitted against one another, fanship tends to be related to consumption of the object of interest. Fandom, on the other hand, tends to be related to social aspects of fan

[10] Bronies are (typically adult male) fans of the television show *My Little Pony: Friendship is Magic*.

engagement. Relatedly, because fandom is related to forming and maintaining social relationships with others, it is also connected to better well-being, while fanship is typically not. Indeed, when fanship and fandom are included in the same statistical model, fandom is more likely to be associated with positive outcomes (e.g., well-being), while fanship is more likely to be associated with negative outcomes, such as excessive or obsessive behavior.

Fanship and Fandom and Furry Beliefs and Behaviors

At long last, we can now turn our attention to our research looking at whether fan identification (fanship or fandom) can help us to predict psychologically important thoughts, feelings, and behaviors in furries.

Similar to the research described above, we conducted a series of analyses in which fanship and fandom simultaneously predicted a number of outcome variables. Within each of the tables, values with an asterisk indicate a statistically significant trend, with more asterisks indicating a greater degree of confidence in the finding (* $p < .05$, ** $p < .01$). Positive values indicate a positive association (e.g., as fanship scores go up, so too does the other variable), while negative values indicate a negative association (e.g., as fanship scores go up, the other variable goes down).

It should be noted that each of the analyses below represents data taken from a multitude of studies over the past decade. In some cases, we used single-item measures of fandom and fanship, while in other cases we used a three-item scale. Some of these analyses are based on samples recruited in-person at furry conventions while others represent data collected online. Given how many different results are presented here, for ease of presentation we have left out information about which result came from which study, although this information is available upon request from interested readers who wish to get in touch with the authors.

Furry Activities

As shown in Table 6.2, furries' fanship scores predicted being a furry for a longer period of time while, if anything, fandom scores were associated with being a furry for less time.[11] Fanship, relative to fandom, was more

[11] One possible explanation of this finding may be that younger furries may identify more with the surrounding fandom while older furries feel less of a connection to the fandom. Given that, demographically, the furry fandom is comprised of fairly young furries (see Chapter 13), it might make sense that, as furries get older, they may feel less of a sense of connection to the current furry fandom, which is more likely to be comprised of furries younger than themselves. To this end, we also discuss issues of ageism and generational differences in the furry fandom in Chapter 12.

strongly positively associated with open and avid consumption of furry content, including watching and reading furry related-materials, wearing furry-related apparel, being more likely to own a fursuit, having furry-related dreams, immersion in furry-related media, disclosing one's identity, and liking furry pornography. Fanship was also more positively associated with negative behaviors, such as problematic purchasing behavior (e.g., buying more merchandise than one has money for). Fandom scores, in contrast, were more positively associated with group-related behaviors, including interacting with other furries online, attending local meetups, and attending furry conventions. Finally, the results reveal some variables where both fanship and fandom identification predicted outcomes to about the same extent: reading news/blogs/reviews, talking with friends about furries, interacting with furries in person, and frequenting furry-related websites.

Motivation

We'll discuss the motivations that compel a person to be furry in greater depth in Chapter 19. For now, however, we'll quickly look at whether fanship and fandom are differently associated with a furry's underlying motivation to be a furry. As shown in Table 6.3, fanship scores were more strongly positively associated with being motivated by aesthetics (e.g., liking of the style/content), economic motivations, escapism, the attention that being furry provides, and sexual interest. Fandom scores, in contrast, were more strongly associated with being motivated by a desire for belongingness, a sense of family, a desire to experience positive / beneficial stress, and the entertainment provided by being a furry. Notably, both fanship and fandom predicted the extent to which self-esteem is a motivator to be part of the fandom to about the same extent.

Table 6.2. Regressions with fanship and fandom predicting fan-related activities.

Variable	Fanship	Fandom
Years Furry	.20**	-.10**
Watch / Read Material	.28**	.06*
Read News / Blogs / Reviews	.17**	.13**
Talk with Friends about Furries	.19**	.18**
Interact with Furries in person	.14**	.17**
Interact with Furries Online	-.04	.35**
Dress Furry-Apparel	.30**	.10**
Attend Local Meetups	.10	.18**
Number Furry Websites	.19**	.13**
Number of Conventions	.04	.10**
Number Fursuits	.14**	-.003
Furry Dreams	.24**	.12*
Immersion in Furry Media	.27**	.16**
Disclose Identity	.33**	.09**
Problematic Purchasing	.22**	-.26**
Liking Furry Porn	.14**	.07*

Table 6.3. Regressions of fanship and fandom predicting motivations.

Variable	Fanship	Fandom
Belongingness	.19**	.47**
Family	.18**	.28**
Aesthetic	.21**	.03
Self-Esteem	.25**	.25**
Economic	.16**	.01
Eustress	.19**	.30**
Escape	.22**	.11**
Entertainment	.02	.23**
Attention	.22**	.10**
Sexual Attraction	.23**	-.04

Individual Differences

We'll discuss individual differences between furries such as personality and fantasy (Chapter 18), as well as how furries develop a healthy sense of identity (Chapter 24) later in this book. For now, we want to briefly highlight the association between fanship and fandom scores and these measures of individual differences (e.g., what makes one furry different from another).

As shown in Table 6.4, fanship scores were more negatively associated with emotional stability and components of identity resolution (i.e., integration, differentiation, productivity), meaning that those who scored higher in fanship tended to have less stable emotions and had a less developed sense of identity. Fanship scores were, relative to fandom scores, more positively associated with how furries engage in fantasy, including fantasy proneness (e.g., blurring the lines between fantasy and reality), negative fantasy engagement (e.g., problematic fantasy behavior), having a pathological personality, anxious attachment style (e.g., relationship insecurity), and shyness.

Table 6.4. Regressions with fanship and fandom predicting individual difference measures.

Variable	Fanship	Fandom
Extraversion	-.05	.19**
Agreeableness	.01	.13**
Conscientiousness	-.05	.08
Emotional Stability	-.14**	.11*
Openness	-.01	.18**
Fantasy Proneness (Creative)	.18*	.09
Fantasy Proneness (Childhood)	.15	.08
Negative Fantasy	.18**	-.06
Positive Fantasy	.26**	.39**
Primary Psychopathy	.07	-.14**
Pathological Personality	.16**	-.18**
Anxious Attachment	.13*	-.10
Avoidant Attachment	-.06	-.13*
Integration	-.23**	.36**
Differentiation	-.14**	.21**
Productive	-.13**	.12*
Worldview	.04	.02
Shyness	.13**	-.16**
Magical Thinking	.10	.21*
Magical Ideation	.12*	.13**

In contrast, compared to fanship scores, fandom scores were more positively associated with greater extraversion, agreeableness, emotional stability, openness to new experiences, positive fantasy engagement (e.g., healthy fantasizing activities), identity resolution (i.e., integration, differentiation, productive), and magical thinking. Fandom was also less likely than fanship to be associated with psychopathy, pathological personality, and shyness.

Taken together, the results suggest that extreme levels of fanship may be an indicator of psychological maladaptation or dysfunction in a way that doesn't seem to be the case for fandom scores. To put it another way, when one thinks about an obsessive fan, they are probably imagining a fan who is excessively high in fanship, not a fan whose fandom identification is high. We'll return to this idea in Chapter 19 and Chapter 22 when we talk about social support and the benefits of the furry fandom for building social support and resilience.

Identity and Intragroup Variables

In a 2015 paper, Roberts et al. proposed three ways in which furries could experience a sense of connection to their favorite/fursona species: identification (e.g., "I was born with this connection to my non-human species"), liking (e.g., "I am preoccupied with my species"), and spiritual connection (e.g., "I feel that I have a mystical connection to my non-human species"). As shown in Table 6.5, fanship scores were more strongly positively associated than fandom scores with all three types of connection. Or, to put it another way, one's fandom identity says very little about the extent to which they feel a sense of connection to their fursona / favorite non-human animal species. In a similar vein, fanship scores were, relative to fandom scores, more strongly positively associated with one's fursona spilling over into furries' everyday life.

In a 2020 paper, Plante et al. suggested that when it comes to elitism in fan groups, there are two dimensions: inflating one's sense of self and looking down upon others (see Chapter 12). Fanship was positively associated with both, whereas fandom identification was not associated with self-inflation and, if anything, was negatively associated with derogation of other furries. Fandom scores were also more likely than fanship scores to be positively associated with helping other furries within the community, the feeling that they are of higher status than others in the community, and with feeling that all furries share a common fate (e.g., if the fandom does well, then everyone benefits). Taken together, these findings again suggest that fandom identification, unlike fanship identification, is much more tied to feelings and behaviors that pertain to the broader furry community, and generally suggests a more healthy and beneficial association with furry than is the case with fanship.

Table 6.5. Regressions of fanship and fandom predicting identity and intragroup variables.

Variable	Fanship	Fandom
Fursona Identification	.57**	-.10**
Fursona Liking	.59**	-.04*
Fursona Spirit	.43**	-.02
Fursona Spillover	.26**	.11**
Intragroup Helping	-.03	.26**
Intragroup Status	.02	.30**
Willingness to Sacrifice	.22**	.21**
Common Fate	-.004	.40**
Subgroup Gatekeeping	-.01	-.17**
Elitism Self-Inflate	.38**	.06
Elitism Other-Derogate	.25**	-.28**
ID-Acceptance Concerns	.20*	-.13
ID-Concealment Motivation	-.001	-.24**
ID-Identity Uncertainty	-.55**	-.13
ID-Internalized Negativity	-.17*	-.36**
ID-Difficult Process	-.02	-.37**
ID-Identity Superiority	.20*	.10
ID-Identity Affirmation	.23**	.61**
ID-Identity Centrality	.67**	.06

Building off the work of Mohr and Kendra (2011), we adopted a measure that assesses various dimensions of being a member of a stigmatized minority group.[12] Specifically, the measure contains eight dimensions: *acceptance concerns* (feeling that others may not accept me due to being a furry), *concealment motivation* (desire to hide one's furry identity), *identity uncertainty* (feeling uncertain if one is a furry), *internalized negativity* (rejecting one's furry identity), *difficult process* (the process of becoming a furry was difficult), *identity superiority* (perceiving furries as better than non-furries), *identity affirmation* (affirming one's furry identity), and *identity centrality* (being a furry is central to one's identity). Fanship scores, relative to fandom scores, were associated with greater concern that others would reject them for being furry, with less uncertainty about whether they were a

[12] The original measure was designed to assess feelings toward being a member of a sexual minority. Given that most furries are LGBTQ+ (see Chapter 15 and Chapter 16), many furries are likely to be familiar with the feelings tapped into in this measure.

furry, with the feeling that furries were superior to non-furries, and with perceiving furry to be a central part of one's identity. Fandom, in contrast, was more associated with greater disclosure, less negativity, perceiving the process of becoming a furry as being an easy one, and with affirming one's furry identity. In short, fanship and fandom scores are differently associated with different aspects of being a member of a stigmatized minority group, although fanship tends to be associated with the more negative aspects of this stigmatized group identification.

Well-Being

As has been suggested throughout the chapter, we suspect that fandom, as compared to fanship, is more strongly and positively associated with well-being, given that it is associated with the social aspects of fan engagement and given that group identification may contribute to a sense of social support and resilience provided by the fandom (see Chapter 19 and Chapter 22).

While there is no one single measure of "well-being," researchers often employ a variety of different measures to assess different facets of the broader concept of well-being (for a review see Linton et al., 2016). As shown in Table 6.6, fanship, as compared to fandom, tends to be associated with lower self-esteem, lower satisfaction with life, less of a sense of purpose in life, and greater depression, anxiety, stress, and psychological distress. Fandom, on the other hand, is associated with greater self-esteem, satisfaction with life, purpose in life, flourishing, relationship well-being, personal growth, environmental mastery, self-acceptance, and body satisfaction, and is negatively associated with depression, stress, loneliness, and psychological distress. These findings support the idea that fandom identification is much more strongly positively associated with well-being, regardless of what facet of well-being is being considered, than is fanship.

Miscellaneous

In this final section, we cover some variables that didn't necessarily fit in the other sections, but which may nevertheless be of interest to readers.

As an example, Amiot and Bastian (2017) developed a measure to assess one's felt connection to animals (e.g., "I feel solidarity toward animals"). As shown in Table 6.7, fanship scores were more strongly associated than were fandom scores with one's felt connection to animals, suggesting that the sense of community associated with fandom may not extend to non-human animals.

Fanship scores are also more likely than fandom scores to be positively associated with feeling that one has a phantom body part (e.g., tail, feathers), while fandom scores are more positively associated with identifying as a nerd, feeling empathy for others, and being a less individualistic, more collectivistic person.

In a 2003 study, Vallerand et al. (2003) developed a measure of passion that distinguishes between *obsessive passion*, an excessively felt pressure to engage in one's interest (e.g., "I am emotionally dependent on furry activities"), and *harmonious* passion, feeling a sense of choice and control over one's interest (e.g., "For me, furry activities are a passion that I still manage to control"). In a pattern consistent with prior findings in this chapter, fandom scores were more strongly associated with harmonious passion than were fanship scores, with the reverse being true for obsessive passion.

Table 6.6. Regressions of fanship and fandom predicting well-being.

Variable	Fanship	Fandom
Self-Esteem	-.30**	.37**
Satisfaction with Life	-.18**	.24**
Purpose in Life	-.20*	.34**
Depression	.12*	-.18**
Anxiety	.11*	-.06
Stress	.21**	-.20**
Flourishing	-.02	.25**
BBC Physical	-.03	.17**
BBC Psychological	-.10*	.31**
BBC Relationships	-.11*	.16**
Loneliness	.14*	-.19**
Ryff-Autonomy	.01	-.01
Ryff-Environmental Mastery	.003	.17**
Ryff-Personal Growth	-.01	.16**
Ryff-Positive Relations	-.06*	.26**
Ryff-Purpose in Life	.003	.13**
Ryff-Self-Acceptance	-.05	.14**
Optimism	-.18	.38**
Psychological Distress	.34**	-.19*
Body Satisfaction	-.14	.19*

Table 6.7. Regressions of Fanship and Fandom Predicting Miscellaneous Variables

Variable	Fanship	Fandom
Solidarity with Animals	.21**	.11**
Nerd Identification	.04	.10**
Empathy	.10	.21**
Phantom Limb	.22**	.10
Individualism	.05	-.11*
Collectivism	-.05	.14*
Harmonious Passion	.27**	.50**
Obsessive Passion	.44**	.16**

Conclusion

This chapter began with a theoretical deep dive into what it means to identify as a fan. After reviewing the social identity perspective and seeing how useful it can be to understand fan identity as a social identity, we distinguished between the concepts of fanship and fandom. Past research (Edwards et al., 2019; Reysen et al., 2021) has shown that fanship tends to be associated with consumption of the fan interest and, at its extreme ends, with obsession, excess, and maladaptation. Fandom identification, in contrast, tends to be associated with the social facets of fan interests and with moderation and well-being. The results of our studies in the furry fandom largely followed this same pattern, with fanship being associated with consumption and negative variables (e.g., obsessive passion, elitism) and fandom being associated with social facets of fan interest and well-being. Given that fandom is typically omitted from research in fan psychology more generally, and given that the most memorable exemplars of fan behavior also tend to be the most extreme and maladaptive, the present results speak to the importance of assessing not only how strongly fans feel connected to the object of their interest, but also assessing the connections they form with their fan communities, which may represent a protective factor against obsession and excess. This healthy, protective aspect of fan identity is often overlooked, both by researchers and by laypersons alike, and may be part of why fans of unusual interests—such as furries—so frequently find themselves stigmatized.

The findings of this chapter will be echoed time and again throughout this book as we return to many of these topics in future chapters. For now, however, it is most important to take away the fact that fanship and fandom are distinct concepts and the fact that furry is a fan interest with a fairly strong social component and sense of community for many furries and, as such, it may be a source of stability, resilience, and well-being for all but the most extreme, obsessive, or secluded members.

References

Amiot, C. E., & Bastian, B. (2017). Solidarity with animals: Assessing a relevant dimension of social identification with animals. *PLoS ONE, 12*(1), e0168184. https://doi.org/10.1371/journal.pone.0168184

Ashmore, R. D., Deaux, K., & McLaughlin-Volpe, T. (2004). An organizing framework for collective identity: Articulation and significance of multidimensionality. *Psychological Bulletin, 130*(1), 80-114. https://doi.org/10.1037/0033-2909.130.1.80

Chadborn, D., Edwards, P., & Reysen, S. (2018). Reexamining differences between fandom and local sense of community. *Psychology of Popular Media Culture, 7*(3), 241-249. https://doi.org/10.1037/ppm0000125

Cialdini, R. B., Borden, R. J., Thorne, A., Walker, M. R., Freeman, S., & Sloan, L. R. (1976). Basking in reflected glory: Three (football) field studies. *Journal of Personality and Social Psychology, 34*(3), 366-375. https://doi.org/10.1037/0022-3514.34.3.366

Doosje, B., Ellemers, N., & Spears, R. (1995). Perceived intragroup variability as a function of group status and identification. *Journal of Experimental Social Psychology, 31*(5), 410-436. https://doi.org/10.1006/jesp.1995.1018

Edwards, P., Chadborn, D. P., Plante, C., Reysen, S., & Redden, M. H. (2019). *Meet the bronies: The psychology of adult* My Little Pony *fandom*. McFarland & Company.

Hinkle, S., Taylor, L. A., Fox-Cardamone, D. L., & Crook, K. F. (1989). Intragroup identification and intergroup differentiation: A multicomponent approach. *British Journal of Social Psychology, 28*(4), 305-317. https://doi.org/10.1111/j.2044-8309.1989.tb00874.x

Leach, C. W., van Zomeren, M., Zebel, S., Vliek, M. L. W., Pennekamp, S. F., Doosje, B., Ouwerkerk, J. W., & Spears, R. (2008). Group-level self-definition and self-investment: A hierarchical (multicomponent) model of in-group identification. *Journal of Personality and Social Psychology, 95*(1), 144-165. https://doi.org/10.1037/0022-3514.95.1.144

Levine, M., Prosser, A., Evans, D., & Reicher, S. (2005). Identity and emergency intervention: How social group membership and inclusiveness of group boundaries shape helping behavior. *Personality and Social Psychology Bulletin, 31*(4), 443-453. https://doi.org/10.1177/0146167204271651

Linton, M.-J., Dieppe, P., & Medina-Lara, A. (2016). Review of 99 self-report measures for assessing well-being in adults: exploring dimensions of well-being and developments over time. *BMJ Open, 6*(7), e010641. http://dx.doi.org/10.1136/bmjopen-2015-010641

Meissner, C. A., & Brigham, J. C. (2001). Thirty years of investigating the own-race bias in memory for faces: A meta-analytic review. *Psychology, Public Policy, and Law, 7*(1), 3-35. https://doi.org/10.1037/1076-8971.7.1.3

Meyer, I. H. (2003). Prejudice, social stress, and mental health in lesbian, gay, and bisexual populations: Conceptual issues and research evidence. *Psychological Bulletin, 129*(5), 674-697. https://doi.org/10.1037/0033-2909.129.5.674

Mlicki, P. P., & Ellemers, N. (1996). Being different or being better? National stereotypes and identifications of Polish and Dutch students. *European Journal of Social Psychology, 26*(1), 97-114. https://doi.org/10.1002/(SICI)1099-0992(199601)26:1<97::AID-EJSP739>3.0.CO;2-F

Mock, S. E., Plante, C. N., Reysen, S., & Gerbasi, K. C. (2013). Deeper leisure involvement as a coping resource in a stigmatized leisure context. *Leisure/Loisir, 37*(2), 111-126. https://doi.org/10.1080/14927713.2013.801152

Mohr, J. J., & Kendra, M. S. (2011). Revision and extension of a multidimensional measure of sexual minority identity: the Lesbian, Gay, and Bisexual Identity Scale. *Journal of Counseling Psychology, 58*(2), 234-245. https://doi.org/10.1037/a0022858

Obst, P., Zinkiewicz, L., & Smith, S. G. (2002a). Sense of community in science fiction fandom, part 1: Understanding sense of community in an international community of interest. *Journal of Community Psychology, 30*(1), 87-103. https://doi.org/10.1002/jcop.1052

Obst, P., Zinkiewicz, L., & Smith, S. G. (2002b). Sense of community in science fiction fandom, part 2: Comparing neighborhood and interest group sense of community. *Journal of Community Psychology, 30*(1), 105-117. https://doi.org/10.1002/jcop.1053

Pepitone, A. (1981). Lessons from the history of social psychology. *American Psychologist, 36*(9), 972-985. https://doi.org/10.1037/0003-066X.36.9.972

Plante, C. N., Reysen, S., Brooks, T. R., & Chadborn, D. (2021). *CAPE: A multidimensional model of fan interest.* CAPE Model Research Team.

Plante, C. N., Reysen, S., Chadborn, D., Roberts, S. E., & Gerbasi, K. C. (2020). 'Get out of my fandom newbie': A cross-fandom study of elitism and gatekeeping in fans. *Journal of Fandom Studies, 8*(2), 123-146. https://doi.org/10.1386/jfs_00013_1

Plante, C. N., Reysen, S., Roberts, S. E., & Gerbasi, K. C. (2016). *Furscience! A summary of five years of research from the International Anthropomorphic Research Project*. Furscience.

Plante, C. N., Roberts, S., Reysen, S., & Gerbasi, K. (2014). Interaction of socio-structural characteristics predicts identity concealment and self-esteem in stigmatized minority group members. *Current Psychology, 33*(1), 3-19. https://doi.org/10.1007/s12144-013-9189-y

Plante, C. N., Roberts, S. E., Snider, J. S., Schroy, C., Reysen, S., & Gerbasi, K. (2015). 'More than skin-deep': Biological essentialism in response to a distinctiveness threat in a stigmatized fan community. *British Journal of Social Psychology, 54*(2), 359-370. https://doi.org/10.1111/bjso.12079

Platow, M. J., Durante, M., Williams, N., Garrett, M., Walshe, J., Cincotta, S., Lianos, G., & Barutchu, A. (1999). The contribution of sport fan social identity to the production of prosocial behavior. *Group Dynamics: Theory, Research, and Practice, 3*(2), 161-169. https://doi.org/10.1037/1089-2699.3.2.161

Postmes, T., Haslam, S. A., & Jans, L. (2013). A single-item measure of social identification: Reliability, validity, and utility. *British Journal of Social Psychology, 52*(4), 597-617. https://doi.org/10.1111/bjso.12006

Reysen, S., & Branscombe, N. R. (2010). Fanship and fandom: Comparisons between sports fans and non-sports fans. *Journal of Sport Behavior, 33*(2), 176-193.

Reysen, S., Katzarska-Miller, I., Nesbit, S. M., & Pierce, L. (2013). Further validation of a single-item measure of social identification. *European Journal of Social Psychology, 43*(6), 463-470. https://doi.org/10.1002/ejsp.1973

Reysen, S., Plante, C. N., Roberts, S. E., & Gerbasi, K. C. (2015). Ingroup bias and ingroup projection in the furry fandom. *International Journal of Psychological Studies, 7*(4), 49-58. http://dx.doi.org/10.5539/ijps.v7n4p49

Reysen, S., Plante, C. N., Roberts, S. E., & Gerbasi, K. C. (2018). Fan and non-fan recollection of faces in fandom-related art and costumes. *Journal of Cognition and Culture, 18*(1-2), 224-229. https://doi.org/10.1163/15685373-12340024

Reysen, S., Plante, C. N., Chadborn, D., Roberts, S. E., & Gerbasi, K. (2021). *Transported to another world: The psychology of anime fans.* International Anime Research Project.

Reysen, S., & Shaw, J. (2016). Sport fan as the default fan: Why non-sports fans are stigmatized. *The Phoenix Papers, 2*(2), 234-252.

Roberts, S. E., Plante, C. N., Reysen, S., & Gerbasi, K. C. (2016). Not all fantasies are created equal: Fantasy sports fans' perceptions of furry, brony, and anime fans. *The Phoenix Papers, 2*(1), 40-60.

Roberts, S. E., Plante, C. N., Gerbasi, K. C., & Reysen, S. (2015). The anthrozoomorphic identity: Furry fandom members' connections to nonhuman animals. *Anthrozoös, 28*(4), 533-548. https://doi.org/10.1080/08927936.2015.1069993

Sherif, M. (1966). *Group conflict and cooperation: Their social psychology.* Routledge & Kegan Paul.

Sherif, M., Harvey, O. J., White, B. J., Hood, W. R., & Sherif, C. W. (1961). *Intergroup conflict and cooperation: The Robbers Cave experiment.* The University of Oklahoma.

Tajfel, H., & Turner, J. C. (1979). An integrative theory of intergroup conflict. In W. Austin & S. Worchel (Eds.), *The social psychology of intergroup relations* (pp. 33-47). Brooks/Cole.

Turner, J. C., Hogg, M. A., Oakes, P. J., Reicher, S. D., & Wetherell, M. (1987). *Rediscovering the social group: A self-categorization theory.* Blackwell.

Vallerand, R. J., Blanchard, C., Mageau, G. A., Koestner, R., Ratelle, C., Léonard, M., Gagné, M., & Marsolais, J. (2003). Les passions de l'âme: On obsessive and harmonious passion. *Journal of Personality and Social Psychology, 85*(4), 756-767. https://doi.org/10.1037/0022-3514.85.4.756

Yoshida, M., Heere, B., & Gordon, B. (2015). Predicting behavioral loyalty through community: Why other fans are more important than our own intentions, our satisfaction, and the team itself. *Journal of Sport Management, 29*(3), 318-333. https://doi.org/10.1123/jsm.2013-0306

Chapter 7
Fursonas: Up Close and Fursonal

Courtney "Nuka" Plante[1]

Whenever I attend a psychology conference, I find myself lost in a sea of professionally-dressed colleagues. We all wear name tags that prominently feature our name, the university where we work, and our current title or rank (e.g., associate professor, Ph.D. student). Whenever I attend a furry convention, I can't help but notice a few similarities to this experience: all the attendees are, likewise, wearing convention badges that state their title or rank (e.g., sponsor, dealer) alongside their name and, in some cases, other information about them (e.g., country of origin).

Differences do start to emerge before long, however. For one thing, while there are names on the badges at both events, the names at the furry convention rarely are legal names (e.g., "Nuka," "Dr. Shazzy"). Another difference is the bigger, more prominent badge frequently found adjacent to the official convention badge, the one featuring an anthropomorphic animal character. The character may or may not share features with the attendee (e.g., similar hairstyle, glasses, style of dress), but it will almost certainly be unique, even amidst a sea of other anthropomorphic animal characters.

In this chapter, we're focusing our attention on these anthropomorphic animal characters, also known as fursonas—the name, image, and character a furry uses to represent themselves in physical and online furry spaces. As we'll see, the appearance and meaning embedded within these characters are as varied and distinct as their owners' fingerprints.

What is a Fursona?

Before we delve too far into the specifics of fursonas and their integral role in furry culture, we should first take a moment to define what we mean by the term fursona. Is a fursona a self-representation in furry spaces or is it a character being roleplayed? Is it an ideal self-being embodied in the real world, or an opportunity to indulge one's darker, more basic instincts? Is it all of these things, or none of the above?

As it turns out, like with the definition of furry (see Chapter 5), there is no single, agreed-upon definition of what a fursona is. At best, we can say that fursonas tend to have animal-like features (or, in some cases, are completely feral animals) and have a name associated with them. Beyond these generally agreed-upon features, however, consensus quickly breaks down.

---

[1] We'd like to thank Dr. Hazel (Bobbi) Ali Zaman for the input on this chapter and for the numerous discussions we've had on this topic!

Table 7.1. Common themes extracted from an open-ended question asking respondents to describe the nature of their fursona and any functions it fulfilled. It was possible for some responses to be categorized into multiple themes.

Theme	% of Responses
Represents / Expresses Me	49.4%
An Avatar, Mascot, or Online ID	21.7%
Idealized Version of Me	21.2%
A Way to Interact / Connect with the Fandom	16.9%
Reflects Certain / Specific Personality Traits	14.8%
A Focus for Creativity, Fantasy, or Art	12.9%
The "Real" or "Authentic" Me	8.0%
A Different Self, an Alter-Ego	7.7%
A Means of Coping or Self-Improvement	7.2%
Allows me to be Something I Can't / Shouldn't Be	6.4%

To illustrate this point, we asked nearly 1,700 furry respondents in a 2021 study to explain, in an open-ended fashion, what their fursona was to them and whether it fulfilled any particular function. We read each and every response and then extracted, coded, and organized the themes that came up the most often. The result was 24 different categories of responses, the ten most common of which are shown in Table 7.1.

Rather tellingly, not a single theme was endorsed by more than half of furries. Or, to put it another way, there was no single definition of what a fursona is or does that was spontaneously produced by the majority of furries.[2] Instead, the results reveal that fursonas are a lot of different things to a lot of different furries.

Of course, any time you try and group or combine responses into categories, you're necessarily going to lose some of the important nuance in those responses.[3] To reduce this problem and avoid imposing our interpretation on participants, we present some representative quotes from the respondents themselves for each of the themes in Table 7.1.

[2] This doesn't mean, of course, that most furries wouldn't agree with some of these conceptualizations if they read them on a page. But it can be informative to see what people come up with on their own, as that's a fairly good representation of what concepts or themes are most prominent in their mind.

[3] For a wonderful example of all of the nuance and "messiness" that accompanies a fursona, please see Zaman (2023).

My Fursona Represents or Expresses Me

The most common theme to emerge was that one's fursona was them, or at the very least a representation or expression of some facet of themselves. As seen in several of the following quotes, this theme often overlaps with other themes from the list.

> *"For me, the dragon is just like me without a human form."*

> *"Essentially me but fluffy - no weird backstories or lore involved."*

> *"For me it simply represents myself, not some character that I'm trying to play. Maybe in a way slightly 'idealised' but not to the extreme."*

> *"For me, my fursona (the most important) is a mental representation of me, normally when i think of me like doing something apart from real world situations i think of me as my fursona, at least in apereance [sic]. this does not mean i belive [sic] thats my interior self or my true form or something like that, its just the form i see myself or the form i like to think of myself."*

> *"He's not better than me, but he's easier to be than me. Also he has a better haircut.; He's just.. me. He's me if I was an anthro. Another form of expressing myself; He's the personality I had as a kid that I feel I've buried away or otherwise lost touch with."*

> *"I have opted to form my sona as if it were me, just a kangaroo, as that is what I feel most furries do. Its meant to visualize themselves as if they were their favorite animal. My fursona has the same first name as me, the same scars, and I even gave him the same pronouns, height, weight, and sexuality as me. Like I said, it is meant to be me, but a kangaroo."*

> *"My fursona, an otter, is basically a representation of myself: funny (I hope...), playful, caring, enjoys swimming and easily distracted. I guess I can say it's like my inner child came out to play in the form of an otter."*

Of course, one's fursona need not be a perfect representation of oneself, nor does the relationship need to be simple or consistent across contexts:

"My fursona is the gateway and creative outlet to the furry world. I identify with him, but at the same time he is seperate from me. I draw him in ways that come to mind and these include things that I personally might shy away from. The merging of his personality and my own is particularly true when I am in my fursuit and my fursona and I become one. I definitely notice a change in my behavior and the way I interact with people. My fursona is a part of me and I am a part of it."

In a point we'll return to later in this book, transgender furries may find it especially helpful to express facets of their gender identity through their fursona:

"A way to express myself and my trans-ness, since deer have visible traits (antlers) to help denote my transition."

"My fursona allows me to freely express myself and my gender identity without fear of being outed or misgendered. It allows me to feel comfortable with my body and presentation."

"It is me! I have two because I am genderfluid. I have my female and my male and since I mainly present and am female she is my main. But my fursonas are very much me and apart [sic] of me. It is what I see myself as most [of] the time as well."

My Fursona is an Avatar, Mascot, or Online ID

While the furries in the previous section may have considered their fursonas to be indelibly tied to their sense of self, others describe seeing their fursonas in a much more functional manner, as a tool with a practical purpose when it comes to interacting with others—especially in online spaces. Some, for example, emphasized the utility of having a fursona as an alias to preserve their anonymity.

"An avatar to talk with people and allow me some form of anonymity."

"He's a form of self-expression with the benefit of anonymity. I can be more open about myself without doxxing myself."

"Buffer that allows online anonymity. I can be myself without fear of people being able to Find Out Who I Really Am and attack me for it. It

allows me to socialize where I wouldn't have the courage to do otherwise."

"He is how I represent myself and also allows a level of anonymity to express myself safely."

"My fursona is a mascot for my internet presence. I don't have to share my real name, face, age, or gender, because people treat the character as me. It keeps me safe."

"To me, my fursona is an extension of myself. In many ways I am him and he is me! Though in several aspects he may be a little more outgoing, attractive and spontaneous than I am but for the most part we are the same creature just in different skins. He also gives me some semblance of anonymity online when I want to share my feels about things such as politics and government so I don't get in trouble with my employer."

"My fursona is just a character that I like to pretend to be. One purpose it serves is to present myself in an anonymous way online and in art/music. A benefit of this being that I feel better protected from criticism towards myself as a person - it instead feels directed towards this character. It also allows me to express myself in ways through a character that is divorced from any of my own flaws and life experiences. Not that I feel this gives me an excuse to behave disrespectfully. But I don't believe that I have a fursona mainly for its utility, I mostly just have it because I want to have it."

For others, their fursonas served the function of a brand or logo.

"He mostly serves as a representation for me online, as an avatar, as part of my brand as a personality online."

"I have two 'fursonas' - both are merely names and associated artistic representations. One focuses on PG related material, the other on adult related material."

"I think it's a name/brand for me. It plays a similar role of a nick name when I communicate with furries on the internet."

"It helps me project myself and is a useful tool for marketing. Human faces do not look as attractive compared to a mascot/minimalist logo."

My Fursona is an Idealized Version of Me

Rather than focusing on the function of their fursonas, some furries emphasized the form of their fursona. In such cases, it was far more likely for furries to describe their fursonas as embodying an ideal or a more perfect, desirable self.

"He's me, more-or less. Represents me online and within furry, and is somewhat me as I'd want to be. Younger, healthier, fitter, ... smaller."

"It offers a more tangible way to interact with the aspects of myself that I like and want to cultivate more in my daily life. It represents my kind, curious, fun, silly, spontaneous, nature-loving(and often chaotic) side."

"He's what I want to be. Strong and confident."

"[My Fursona] is the perfect being in my eyes. She is divinity, prideful and powerful, capable of making the most of her unique talents and experience. She is confident, caring, and capable. These are things that I aspire towards myself, but I recognize that I can never be as perfect as [My Fursona] is."

As the last quote suggests, for some, describing their fursona as ideal also involves an explicit contrast of their fursona against less desirable aspects of themselves.

"It serves as the ideal me, the me that went above and beyond to accomplish the things I was to [sic] lazy or cowardly to try and do while reflecting my personality at any given time."

"Fursona is essentially myself with a few improvements in areas which I feel lacking in like social skills"

"Fursonification of myself with usually better abilities and less flaws."

Many respondents also indicated that, beyond merely representing an ideal, their fursonas were something they were actively striving to become more like.

> *"My fursona functions in two ways. Firstly, as I would assume is the case with most people, my fursona is meant to be an extension of myself that I use as a form of self expression. Second, however, I model my fursona's personality on things I would like to embody myself, giving them traits I want to have, usually as a method of self improvement. For example, right now I am trying to work on my organizational skills, so I decided that my fursona is a well-organized individual. It's sort of a visualization exercise."*

> *"It is an inspiration to develop in my self traits that I consider valuable. Traits like self-sufficiency, fitness, confidence. It is an idealized version of my self that allows me to experience a type of "power fantasy" about what I can be."*

> *"My fursona is a bigger, bolder, more confident version of myself. It enables me to project as a more confident, bubblier, character, that I wish to personify full-time."*

> *"My fursona is a dragon, and his primary purpose is to help bring aspects of myself to the front and amplify them that I enjoy. By acting like my fursona, within societal norms, I can bring confidence and a bit more extraversion to my normal every day."*

> *"My fursona is an ideal representation of myself; who I would be if I had no limitations, both in the physical and mental space. To that end, I'm significantly fitter both physically and mentally fitter than I was before I was a furry because he gave me an ideal to work towards - something I could never picture if I was looking at myself."*

> *"It's another imaginary self that is typically a slightly better me. Though I'm not particularly eager to make this fursona magical and powerful, I prefer it to be as close as myself. This fursona has my future dream job to be a professor, intellectual, scholarly, knowledgeable, yet also funny, cute, or flamboyant. It has become my life goal in some way."*

"Extension of my identity: in some ways idealized, but mostly a candid reflection of myself In some ways, I use it as a role model to guide my own decisions (e.g. my alter-ego is relatively fit, therefore i will exercise to match it)"

"He is my ideal, dream and goal self. He is a normal animal, but he pushes me to study hard to achieve my dream"

My Fursona is a Way for Me to Interact or Connect with the Fandom

Having already discussed furry not just in terms of fanship, but also as a fandom (see Chapter 6), it comes as no surprise that many furries see their fursona as a way to facilitate interaction with the rest of the furry fandom. Perhaps seeking to "do as the Romans do," many furries may feel compelled to create fursonas upon entering the fandom, noticing that most other furries have a fursona (see later in the chapter for more on this). As such, many furries see their fursonas as a vehicle for creating common ground with other furries. Some, however, speak somewhat negatively about the felt need to do this, pointing to possible feelings of peer pressure due to the fandom's norms or expectations that furries are supposed to have a fursona.

"An avatar to present myself as within the fandom. It's only a means to blend in and participate better within furry spaces, but I'm first and foremost a human."

"It's a mechanism for self expression [sic] that aligns more closely with my experience of being other-than-human, primarily for use in social spaces so this experience of mine is immediately legible to other furries and therians."

"It's just a tool for other furries to get to know me and to call me."

"It's mostly an avatar. It suits my aesthetic tastes. Through it, I can engage with other anthro characters in a consistent setting populated by animal people."

"As for the reason I use them, I'd say they just serve the functional purpose of creating an actual identity on the internet for my person, since otherwise I wouldn't exist in the community. That's one of the very few things I did to adopt furries' 'customs and traditions'."

"Uh its basically my key to the fandom. Without [fursona name], I'm not accepted. But at the same time she is just me."

"From the very start, a "fursona" was something I needed simply because not having one while enjoying other aspects of the furry fandom caused too many questions and snarky comments from the fandom members."

Others emphasized that their fursona helped them to interact with other furries by reducing their social anxiety or shyness when meeting new people, perhaps by providing a sense of distance or disconnect from the situation.[4]

"Gave me the confidence to get over my stage fright and performing in front of people. I explain it to many as a way of people not to judge you for your personal flaws. If your [sic] performing or interacting with a group and you stumble, make a mistake it's just a silly cat making a mistake, not more harsh critisism [sic] if you were in 'Human Form'."

"My fursona is a blank slate, I'm less anxious to talk to people I've never met and might not meet again."

"My fursona is a self insert [sic]. My sona is me. I feel more comfortable speaking with furries as my sona."

"It allows me to take (positive, social) risks among furries than I wouldn't in other settings."

"Not so much a fursona, as in, a named character that I would puppet. It's more of a mask that I put on (in the same sense that I put on a mask to go to work or visit family, the masking is not furry-specific) that feels nice to wear and interact through."

---

[4] Media researchers have long recognized the impact of creating social distance on disinhibiting people—that is, causing them to act in ways that they might not otherwise due to anxiety or fear of repercussions. This is certainly the case in online interactions, where the feeling of anonymity or invisibility offered by using a pseudonym or having one's actions seen as being untraceable allow people to express opinions or behave in a far more outgoing way than they might face-to-face (Suler, 2004).

My Fursona Reflects Certain/Specific Personality Traits

While many furries indicated in an earlier section that their fursonas were an expression of themselves, others are more specific in describing a particular facet or aspect of themselves that their fursonas represent. Rather than being a holistic representation of themselves, some furries create fursonas that represent one facet of themselves.

> *"My fursona basically communicates my aesthetics in terms of color scheme aka dark and broody. Also has ear clipped to communicate childfree/desire to be sterilized, and maned lioness which does occur in nature suggests transgender without necessarily having to out myself."*

> *"I have 5. 4 of them represent different sides of me. For example, one is anxious, reserved, clumsy, and shy. Another is sporty, sarcastic, loud, and spontaneous. Another is fun, caring, a hugger, and supportive. The last of the 4 is antisocial, irritable, numb, and down. My 5th fursona is essentially all of these into one character. She is my main fursona and I connect her personality/etc to me."*

> *"I have a few mains, but my big one, my dragon, is my sense of happiness. I use this fursona to bring smiles to people, they're meaning is to make people happy. Colorful and full of life, definitely a kind look for anyone to look towards for help, or a friend."*

> *"I have three fursonas , one for id , one for ego ,one for superego."*[5]

> *"I really did little more than choose my favorite animal with my favorite colors. Now I realize I can somewhat relate to a cat-like personality."*

---

[5] In case you've never taken an introductory psychology course, the terms "id," "ego," and "superego" were used by Sigmund Freud to refer to different aspects of the self (Freud, 1923; Freud & Jones, 1922). The "id" can be thought of as one's inner five-year old, a manifestation of every urge or impulse (however inappropriate) they might have. In contrast, the "superego" represents one's inner scolding parent, the internalization of all of society's rules and laws to guilt and shame you for failing to live up to them. Finally, the ego can be seen as a proverbial chariot driver, trying to balance the impulsivee whims of the id with the unreasonable sternness of the superego.

"It's intent is to capture [a] certain aspect of me and reflect it in an artistic sense within fantasy elements. Specifically, my character captures an heroic, spotlighty/performer and my goofy everyday self."

"My fox fursona is my kind personality that express my generosity towards other. My cat fursona is my angst personality with [a] bit of rebellious. My horse fursona is my mellow and loyal personality with a hint of sarcasm."

"My fursona basically communicates my aesthetics in terms of color scheme aka dark and broody."

"My fursona is an extension of my own personality, but without the depression and anxiety I normally suffer from."

My Fursona is a Focus or Catalyst for Creativity, Fantasy, or Art

Some furries describe their fursonas as a sort of muse, a catalyst for their own acts of fantasy or creativity.

"A fantastical and somewhat idealized version of myself that I have crafted a story around. I enjoy imagining him in different situations, and imagining myself as him."

"There's a lot I'd love to do in life, and I like to picture my characters in worlds that I dream of."

"2/3 of my fursonas [fursona names] are character's [sic] I made for an ongoing illustration project I've been working on for years in my own time."

"The first and flagbearer of the original species I've poured my heart and soul into."

"It's partially a face I present to the others in the community as representative of myself, and partially a conduit for imagination and daydreaming."

"My fursona is a character to draw, write about, and roleplay as. He's basically a creative outlet."

"My fursona is me if fantasy tropes (magic, talking animals, etc.) were real. I like making stories about them that reflect real life with fantastical elements!"

For other furries, a fursona is a means through which to experience or commission content, a way to immerse themselves into, or otherwise experience content. This can sometimes go hand-in-hand with the fursona as a muse or catalyst for creativity, as seen in the last few quotes.

"My Fursona I consider like a part of me yet is different. The main function of her is a medium to get art with other fursonas with."

"An expy in artworks."[6]

"Mascot of me as a [sic] animal person and as a self-insert into furry art."

"A character to design, identify with, and buy art of."

"Both a mascot for my art as well as something I can get drawn in cool styles by other artists."

"It's a character for me to make art creation or buy art pieces."

My Fursona is the Real Me

In an earlier section, we saw that some respondents saw their fursona as a representation or expression of themselves. This suggests that these respondents have a sense of self upon which their fursona is based. In contrast, the participants in this section indicated that their fursona was not an expression of themselves, but rather it *was* them: a more authentic, genuine self. To some, the "self" they express in day-to-day life is a symbol or façade, while the fursona is the *real* them.

"It is me as I see my true self. We are identical in values and temperament. Its [sic] just a more accurate visual form of me."

---

[6] An expy refers to an "exported character"—a character used as a stand-in or representation of another character in a piece of fiction.

"It is part of my identity, a deeper more intimately related part of me that explains & shows a deeper part of me."

"It is the real me without filters imposed by society. It is a cartoon animal representation of myself that I can use to express myself more freely."

"It is what I would be if one's internal image were able to manifest. Beyond that there is no difference between it and myself."

"My Fursona is me. I am only wearing a costume once I get out of my fursuit."

"An identity that takes off the social mask to be honest with other people."

"My fursona means the world to me. She is me. The real me. Who I consider myself to be, if not trapped in the current means of reality."

"My Fursona is more so a truesona. I see her as myself, but as a [fursona species]!"

Many of the respondents in this section also indicated that they identify as therians or otherkin, groups we discuss in greater detail in Chapter 20. For now, it is sufficient to say that these respondents identify, in whole or in part, as not entirely human and, as such, their fursona—if they even choose to use that word—may be less a matter of allegory or symbolism and be more accurately described as their authentic selves.

"As a therian, I have feelings of being something else that are [sic] very difficult to reconcile with my physical body. I don't know where those feelings come from or why, but I can't get rid of them, so my fursona helps me present an alternate image of myself that lines up better with those feelings. It's kind of like a self-actualization, not just in terms of personality or wish-fulfillment attributes, but in species as well."

"I am my fursona, my fursona is me. I identify as a wolf. I am species dysphoric/trans species. It is a way to express my true self."

"I identify as a dog therian more than a furry, so I wouldn't call my dog identity a 'fursona' as it is not a constructed character (just as my nationality isn't a "countrysona"). Dogness is simply a facet of my personality and selfhood. I have considered creating a more deliberate fursona for roleplay, fun, or other such expressive purposes."

"I'm otherkin, so my fursona isn't just a sona, it's who I really am. I'm a chakat stuck in a human body, and my fursona is the real me that I see myself as."

"My fursona is also my otherkin identity. I have always thought of and represented myself as this kind of being, even before I knew of the furry fandom or otherkin."

"Our human body is the façade."

My Fursona is a Different Self or Alter-Ego

In stark contrast to the previous section, some furries indicate that their fursona is largely untethered to who they are. Instead, the appeal of a fursona is in its ability to represent something different or distinct from themselves.

"A facade to hide who I truly am."

"A different type of me cuz I can be anything I want."

"A fursona is like a second personality or alter ego that either reflects their personality or is completely different from how they act normally since they are free to express themselves."

"Hiding my real self behind a cute amnimol [sic] figure."

"It's an alter ego. It's another me I can trust without limit."

My Fursona is a Means of Coping or Self-Improvement

For some furries, their relationship with their fursona is less about identifying with their fursona per se and more about their fursona's function as a means of coping with or processing trauma or other undesirable life circumstances, either through escapism or as a means of making those struggles abstract or symbolic.

"A way to process childhood trauma by mirroring there [sic] experiences with my own but through a fantasy lens. Making it easier to discuss because it's 'not real'."

"He is how I represent myself. I can hide a lot of my insecurities, when I have 'someone else' to show publicly. It helps. He also helps me escape when the world is to [sic] much. I can close my eyes, and walk through his world instead. The cuddles there are soothing."

"A version of me that is able to be what I want to be but can't due to mental issues such as depression, OCD and anxiety."

"I have many fursonas, I just switched my mains. They all have a specific use and meaning to me, my old one was created with a stoic and intimidating vibe. She was created as a coping mechanism due to abuse and neglect. My main was adopted to be a vent character for my issues with emotional repression, but she's now to help me learn self confidence [sic], to be my expressive, and to take up space."

"I RP[7] *as werewolves who have aspects of my personal demons as a way of dealing with them."*

"My dog fursona is a shell of my childhood that I try to forget but keep around to heal and process my childhood trauma thru [sic] them."

"My main sona (a draft horse) is basically a [sic] ideal inner veiw [sic] of who I want to be just in animal form. I have struggled with self worth [sic] & social anxiety all my life due to an abusive childhood and my oc gives me a healthy escape from the things that contribute to my depression and other issues in my daily life."

In line with a point mentioned earlier in this chapter, many transgender furries indicate that their fursona has proven to be an effective way for them to cope with feelings of dysmorphia or confusion about their gender identity.

"A detached fictional character helping to work out gender confusion"

---

[7] RP refers to "roleplay."

"My first fursona is how I would wish to be, I sometimes pretend to be it because it makes me happy, I imagine myself as my fursona and am my fursona in my dreams (I believe it also helps me cope with gender dysphoria)."

"My fursona is a representation of myself and how I'd like to be, however they've also served as a beacon of hope in some dark times, and having a fursona has permitted me to express my gender more freely than would otherwise be possible. My fursona is extremely important to me."

"My fursona was how I worked through my feelings on my transistion [sic]... he changed before I did."

Also noteworthy is the fact that several neurodivergent furries mentioned the utility of their fursonas to aid in communication or simply to provide comfort.

"I don't -have- a fursona, it is a part of me whom I sadly cannot show like I can a certain style of clothes on the street. As somebody on the autism spectrum, the changes in my looks, be it clothes or fursona's appearance, are helpful for communicating certain dispositions and moods. My fursona is my extra facial expression, my added body language."

"My fursona is a comfort character. I have autism so certain activities and things are difficult to express and this is a happy healthy way I can do it. Having something represent me and the happy side of me is comforting!"

"[sona name, species] is my main sona. He serves as a representation of what my thoughts and intentions are versus what is shown in the twisted form my autism, depression, and anxiety can sometimes make them present. In [layman's] terms, he's me without any mental disorders to twist my actual feelings and intentions."

My Fursona Allows Me to Be Something I Otherwise Can't Be

In this final category, furries described their fursonas as a form of wish fulfillment, being able to be something or do things that would be impossible in their day-to-day life. For some, this represents the catharsis of having an outlet for behavior that might be considered inappropriate or unusual (e.g., for a person of their age, or simply for violating social mores) in reality.

> *"He allows me to voice all that stuff in my head that wouldn't feel comfortable coming out of my own mouth."*

> *"To present/express/release the desire of dominance which is definitely unreasonable/ harmful/ undo-able in real life."*

> *"He's me, he's my representation. I can explore and express things and ideas with him that aren't possible in my real life. So he's pretty much a solid mix between myself and my fantasies. I wouldn't do everything I let him do."*

> *"My fursona is my souls [sic] shadow, every part of my personality I usually keep hidden in order to be socially acceptable to normies."*

> *"My fursona both allows me to project my gender identity (as male) more freely, as well as my genuine personality which isn't considered desirable in mainstream society. My fursona is withdrawn, sometimes bizarre and socially clueless, and hardly speaks, whereas I'm expected to have good communication skills (despite my autism) in order to survive in this world."*

> *"A way to let out my inner child forget about acting how the world expects me to and just be stupid, impulsive, and plain have fun."*

> *"Just a cute character that I look at and recognize [sic] as 'me' somehow. Personality wise, Me, but more confident and able to get away with being silly and playing because she's a cute animal and I'm an adult who would be embarrassed."*

For others, a fursona represents the ability to embody a physical form or engage in acts that would be physically impossible as a human being.

> *"It's effectively an ideal version of myself in terms of body, looks, hair, personality being visually expressed. It's myself in ways that aren't acceptable to the rest of society and visualized in a way that is completely unique to me."*

"My fursona is pretty much the same as me in personality, but with a body I wish I had and the ability to do things I wouldn't be able to do as a human."

So… What is a Fursona?

Having looked at the open-ended data above, it should be apparent that no single definition of fursona can fully capture the wide range of possible forms and functions that fursonas represent. Instead, we can speak about fursonas in terms of general tendencies, things that are true for many, but not all furries. Generally speaking, fursonas are comprised of one or more non-human animal species that are often, though not always, inspired by a combination of the furry's own traits as well as features or characteristics that they consider to be ideal. These fursonas are often used in fandom spaces as an avatar through which to interact with other furries. Fursonas can serve a variety of purposes, with some being little more than a logo or a way to ensure anonymity, others being used as a muse or catalyst for fantasy, others still representing an authentic self, and, finally, as a means of self-improvement or resilience in the face of adversity.

Now that we appreciate how much variability there is in how fursonas manifest, the rest of this chapter will focus on some specific research questions we've asked about fursonas. Some of these are questions inspired by existing psychological theory, while others are questions asked by furries and non-furries alike who want to know more about this aspect of the furry fandom.

Fursona Species

When you encounter a fursona for the first time, be it as a profile online, on the badge of another furry at a convention, or as a fursuit in a parade, one of its most salient features is its species. After all, most fursonas are a different species from their owner (i.e., they're not human).[8] And, given that humans tend to notice things that are unique or different (Jeck et al., 2019), it would make sense that a furry would notice species before, say, the clothing a fursona is wearing or its name since these other features are things we would expect to see in humans.

With this in mind, let's take a look at which fursona species furries tend to choose for their fursonas. In theory, if furries chose their fursona species for entirely idiosyncratic reasons, one would expect every possible fursona

---

[8] Having studied more than 20,000 furries, we don't recall ever seeing a "human" fursona.

species to be prevalent with about the same frequency. Or, to put it another way, if there were no biases or external forces systematically influencing fursona choice, then one might expect to find just as many wolves, cats, dragons, birds, and insects among fursona species because there would be no reason why one species should be more prevalent among the others. If, instead, some fursona species emerge with greater frequency than others, it may be that fursona species choice is influenced by systematic biases or cultural pressures, something we might be able to predict.[9]

We gathered data on furries' fursona species across a series of five different online and convention studies from 2017-2022, giving us a fairly broad look at the fursona species commonly chosen by a diverse group of furries. Respondents in each study were given a list containing a large number of different species and asked to check off which species (one or more) represented the species of their current fursona (or if they had more than one, the fursona with which they most strongly identified).[10] The results for the prevalence rate of the most popular species are presented in Table 7.2

The first thing worth noting from the table is that approximately one-quarter of fursona species were not captured in our list of common fursona species labels. A manual look through the open-ended data revealed a wide range of species that were too rare to be given their own checkbox in future studies.[11] Taking these participants into account, along with participants who chose the "unique" or "custom" species option, we can say that a sizable minority of furries have a fursona species that is very unlikely to be chosen by any other furry.

---

[9] At least theoretically, if not practically! Of course, it's impossible to know all of the thousands of variables that subtly influence a person's fursona species—from chance experiences at a zoo to a story they read in school to peer pressure from other furries. But we should be able to at least consider some of the bigger influences and account for at least some of the variability in fursona species!

[10] The list of species was inspired by the content submission systems of prominent furry art websites, which ask users to indicate the species in the submission. Of course, the options do not represent all possible species, but, they do represent the species most frequently present in art. Participants were also permitted to write in a species that wasn't in the list.

[11] Practically speaking, the question needs to be limited to avoid becoming unreasonably long. For example, if the list included more than 500 different options, it would take up several pages and be impractical to add to an in-person, paper-based survey at a convention. Even online, it's unlikely that participants would want to scroll through a list of hundreds of options on the off chance that their own fursona species was listed somewhere in it.

Table 7.2. Prevalence rate of fursona species across five online and convention samples of furries from 2017-2022. Ranges with a single number indicate species where the option to choose that particular species was only present in one study.

Rank	Species	Range (%)	Avg. (%)	Rank	Species	Range (%)	Avg. (%)
1	Other	24.0-29.7	26.1	26	Other Bird	0.7-2.9	2.1
2	Wolf	16.5-19.9	19.1	27	Otter	1.1-2.6	2.0
3	Fox	14.6-16.8	16.0	28	Horse	1.3-2.3	1.9
4	Hybrid	12.9-17.5	14.4	29	Goat	0.7-2.4	1.7
5	Dragon	10.5-15.4	13.5	30	Sergal	0.9-2.8	1.7
6	Dog	10.1-15.1	12.5	31	Bat	1.5	1.5
7	Housecat	6.4-9.8	7.7	32	Mouse/Rat	0.7-2.1	1.5
8	Other Big Cat	4.1-7.0	5.8	33	Red Panda	1.4	1.4
9	Mythical	3.6-6.8	5.3	34	Skunk	1.2-1.7	1.4
10	Tiger	3.3-6.0	4.5	35	Gryphon	0.7-1.7	1.3
11	Shapeshifter	3.5-5.5	4.4	36	Taur	1.2	1.2
12	Unique / Custom	1.8-5.8	3.8	37	Dinosaur	0.4-1.5	1.1
13	Deer	2.5-4.0	3.4	38	Shark	0.7-1.7	1.0
14	Rabbit	2.7-4.6	3.2	39	Kangaroo	0.9-1.4	0.9
15	Hyena	2.3-4.6	3.0	40	Bull / Cow	0.5-1.7	0.9
16	Lion	2.0-3.5	2.8	41	Ferret	0.9	0.9
17	Bear	2.2-3.2	2.7	42	Snake	0.2-1.4	0.9
18	Snow Leopard	1.7-3.6	2.6	43	Unicorn	0.4-1.1	0.8
19	Coyote	2.6	2.6	44	Raven	0.2-1.4	0.7
20	Were-	1.5-3.5	2.6	45	Owl	0.2-1.0	0.7
21	Reptile	1.8-3.3	2.4	46	Crow	0.3-1.1	0.7
22	Raccoon	2.1-3.4	2.4	47	Squirrel	0.3-1.1	0.6
23	Monster	0.0-3.2	2.2	48	Phoenix	0.3-0.9	0.6
24	Pokemon	1.3-3.9	2.1	49	Insect	0.0-1.2	0.6
25	Protogen	2.1	2.1	50	Hawk	0.5	0.5

We also note that about 14.4% of furries indicated that their fursona was not comprised of a single species, but rather was a composite of two or more different species. Or, to look at it another way, the vast majority of furries create fursonas that are comprised of a single species.

These notes aside, let's look at some of the most popular fursona species. The table reveals that wolves are fairly consistently the single most popular fursona species, making up approximately one-fifth of all fursona species. Not far behind them are foxes, the second-most prevalent fursona species. Dragons and dogs are in a fairly close battle for third, while housecats trail behind in a distant fifth place. Other notably popular species include big cats (e.g., tigers, snow leopards), deer, rabbits, hyenas, and bears.

More important than which particular species emerged as the most popular, however, is the fact that some species emerged as more popular than others. Wolves, for example, are more than fifty times more prevalent than hawks, on average. This would seem to shoot down the idea that furries choose their species entirely haphazardly: a difference in prevalence this big would be unlikely to happen without systemic biases or external influence.

An Explanation for Fursona Species Choice

After presenting this data to furries and non-furries alike, we commonly get the follow-up question "Why these species in particular?" It's a difficult one for us to answer, for at least two different reasons. First, it's unlikely to have a single answer. As we mentioned earlier, a person may choose their fursona species for any number of reasons, none of which are mutually exclusive. Someone might decide to choose a cat fursona because of a combination of the popularity of cats in popular culture (e.g., internet videos of cats), their own familiarity with cats (e.g., having a pet cat), exposure to cats in the media they consume (e.g., the feline character Luna from the anime series *Sailor Moon*), stereotypes about cats that resonate with their personality (e.g., cats as indifferent and independent), and the fact that cats are already a fairly popular fursona species in the furry fandom. Second, even if we did try to assess all of these different possible sources of inspiration for a fursona, there is little reason to believe that participants themselves are aware of the reasons why they chose their fursona species.

As an illustrative example, imagine I we were to ask you to explain why you chose the brand of laundry detergent that you most recently purchased.[12] You could probably give me one or even several explanations: it works well, it's affordable, you like the way it smells, it's the brand you grew up with, it was on sale... These are all plausible explanations, and may well have played a role in your decision. However, it's also likely that factors completely outside your awareness may have influenced your decision: the color of the bottle, a recent commercial that played on the radio, the product's position on the shelf (e.g., at eye level versus on the bottom of the shelf), its relative scarcity (e.g., there were only one or two bottles of that brand left on the shelf), or having recently heard words related to the brand's name (e.g., ocean-related words increasing your likelihood of purchasing Tide-brand detergent).[13] Psychological studies have repeatedly shown that

[12] Feel free to substitute this with another common household product if you haven't purchased laundry detergent recently!

[13] If you think this last one in particular is silly, it was actually shown to occur in a study by Nisbett and Wilson (1977) where they found that showing people a list of

we're often unaware of the actual reasons underlying the decisions we make, although we are fairly good at coming up with plausible-sounding reasons after the fact (Haidt, 2001; Nisbett & Wilson, 1977).

What does this mean for furries and their fursona's species choice? Well, we're sure that if we asked them to, furries could give us all sorts of explanations for why they chose the fursona species they did. At the end of the day, however, we'd have no way of knowing if these were the actual reasons why they chose their fursona species or just the reasons furries *think* they chose their fursona species.

Even if we can never know for sure what drove a furry to choose a particular species for their fursona, we can, at the very least, speculate on some plausible-seeming influences, especially given that we know the most popular fursona species. For example, cats and dogs are the two most popular species of pets (see Chapter 20 for more on this), and also happen to be among the most popular species chosen. This might suggest that positive face-to-face experiences with a particular species may play a role in fursona species choice. Of course, one could argue that most furries probably don't have first-hand experience with some of the other species on the list, like wolves, foxes, and dragons, so there must be other explanations as well.[14]

Another possibility is the stories we tell and the media we consume. Species like wolves, foxes, dragons, and lions play a prominent role in our stories, both contemporarily (e.g., Disney movies like *Zootopia*, which features wolves, foxes, and rabbits, and films like *How to Train Your Dragon*, which prominently features dragons) and historically (e.g., folklore, spiritual beliefs, legends). With psychological studies showing that the more we're exposed to something, the more we generally tend to like it (Moreland & Beach, 1992), it would seem that being exposed to species, either face-to-face or through media, is a plausible explanation for why certain species emerge consistently as the most frequently chosen by furries for their fursonas.[15]

---

ocean-related words, as compared to a control group with non-ocean words, made them more likely to choose Tide over another brand!

[14] Dragons, in particular, will need some additional explaining, given that their non-existence makes it especially tough for someone to have a first-hand experience with them!

[15] Consistent with the explanations in this section, a pair of studies we ran in 2011 found that furries, regardless of their fursona species, believe that they know significantly more than the average person about their fursona species. Whether furries *actually* knew more about their species was not something we tested, but the

Before we finish this section on fursona species choice, let's take a look at some of our research on other facets of fursona species choice. For instance, across a set of four online and convention studies, furries were about 10-14 times more likely to agree than to disagree that a person's fursona species choice was something they had control over. To put it another way, furries overwhelmingly agree that a person's fursona species is a deliberate choice and not something they have no control over.[16] In other studies, furries generally agreed that choosing a fursona was something that takes work (e.g., wasn't a decision made lightly), and most agreed that they had spent a lot of time crafting the details of their fursona.[17]

Predator versus Prey Fursona Species

Perceptive readers might have noticed that many of the most popular fursona species could arguably be considered to be predators (e.g., wolves, dragons, big cats). In contrast, species we would traditionally think of as prey species (e.g., rabbits, deer) seem far less common in the list. To directly assess this, we asked furries in a series of six studies to indicate whether they thought of their fursona as a predator or prey species, doing so in a variety of different ways across studies. For example, when given a single, forced choice between "predator," "prey," "both," or "neither," furries were 4-6 times more likely to say that their fursona species fell under the category of predator rather than prey, while nearly a quarter of furries opted for "both" and another quarter chose "neither." In other studies, furries were given the opportunity to select either predator or prey (or both): 47.4-55.2% called their fursona a predator species, while 14.6-15.2% called their fursona a prey species. Finally, on a 1-7 scale ranging from 1 = *completely predator* to 7 = *completely prey*, furries averaged 3.25, showing a tendency toward predator species. Taken together, these studies suggest that while many furries choose fursona species that are not obviously predator or prey species, when the

---

data *does*, at very least, hint at the possibility that furries may feel they have more exposure to information about their fursona species, whether through first-hand experience, media, or research, which might explain why they feel confident in proclaiming themselves to be more of an expert than the average person.

[16] As we'll see in Chapter 20, therians may represent an exception to this.

[17] Of course, "details" may include more than just choosing a fursona species. Another important decision furries make is the color of their fursona species—whether to go with a "natural" color or a more cartoonish color. A pair of 2011 studies of convention and online furries found that most opted to go with a natural color, with 39.3-41.3% choosing, instead, to go with a non-natural color (e.g., a blue husky).

species does clearly fall into one category, predator species are much more common than prey species.

In fact, this biased preference toward predator species extends beyond one's fursona choice. In one study, furries were shown 12 pairs of animals and were asked to choose, for each pair, which animal they liked more. Notably, each pair contained one common predator species (e.g., hawk, shark, polar bear, snake) and one common prey species (seal, rabbit, rat, deer). Furries chose the predator species over the prey species an average of 8.5 times out of 12, showing that furries generally showed a preference for predator species over prey species even when not choosing one for their fursona.

When we present these results to furries, we're often asked to study whether there are differences between furries who choose predator species for their fursonas and furries who choose prey species for their fursonas. In a pair of studies in 2016-2017 we did just that and found some small differences between the two groups. First, we noted that furries with predator and prey fursonas had more in common than they had differences. Among the small differences we did observe was the fact that furries with predator fursonas tended to have higher self-esteem (but not higher well-being in general). Likewise, furries who preferred predator species over prey species (not as a fursona, but simply as a preference) scored slightly higher on measures of aggression and psychopathy. Of course, these differences were fairly small and need to be contextualized against the fact that furries in general scored fairly high on measures of self-esteem and fairly low on measures of aggression and psychopathy. In other words, it would be wrong to say that furries who prefer predator species are violent or lack remorse and empathy—they're simply, on average, slightly more likely (but still unlikely) to be violent or display a lack of remorse or empathy—a drop in the proverbial bucket.

Popular Fursona Species

Another question that arises when furries choose their fursona species is whether to go with a more "popular" or "trendy" fursona species or to pick a lesser-known species. Anecdotally, furries tell us that the popularity of different fursona species waxes and wanes with trends in popular media (e.g., a spike in lion fursonas after *The Lion King*, a spike in foxes and rabbits after *Zootopia*). While we've been largely unable to notice these sorts of trends in our findings (given how 'noisy' fursona species data is because of all the factors that influence fursona choice), we have, at the very least, noted the emergence of a few new species in our list over time. For example, approximately two percent of furries have a protogen fursona—a fictional species that only came into existence in the mid-2010s, suggesting a fairly rapid growth in its prevalence that some might consider to be a "trend."[18]

With such trends in species popularity being possible, we've asked participants questions about whether they created their fursonas based on "popular" species in the fandom, leaving it up to them to decide what, precisely, counts as a "popular" species and whether their fursona species counts as a popular species. Across studies, we found little evidence that furries' choice of a "popular" fursona species says anything about the furry themselves. For example, a pair of 2011 studies found that fursona species popularity was completely unrelated to how strongly a furry identified as a furry, dispelling the idea that newer furries or furries who were only somewhat interested in the fandom would simply choose a popular fursona species to be "trendy."[19] About the only difference we were able to find comes from a 2016 study of convention-going furries which found that those who went out of their way to choose an unpopular fursona species (not just a not-popular species, but a species the respondent deemed "unpopular") scored slightly higher in anxiety and slightly lower in self-esteem. Choosing a popular fursona species was unrelated to measures of well-being or self-esteem.

Finally, while it may be the case that a furry's choice of a popular or unpopular fursona species says very little about them, the same cannot be said for furries who choose to create fursonas that are heavily inspired by, or which blatantly "copycat"[20] details of another furry's fursona. In a study that we published in a scientific journal, furries were asked to imagine how they would feel about a hypothetical person who either copycatted their personality/style (e.g., the way they dressed, their mannerisms) or who copycatted specific details of their fursona (Reysen et al., 2019). The results revealed that while furries would only be mildly bothered by someone copying their sense of style or personality, they would be far more angry about someone else copying specific details from their fursona and would

[18] One could also consider the growth of the "Dutch Angel Dragon" species in the fandom throughout the 2010s to represent another trend, albeit one that failed to reach the same level of prevalence as did protogens.

[19] Converging evidence from a pair of 2017 studies found that self-identified "popufurs" were no more likely than non-popufurs to choose a popular fursona species, shooting down the idea that popular furries might become popular by choosing popular fursona species.

[20] No pun intended.

treat that person's fursona as being illegitimate. This opposition to copying another furry's fursona was fairly consistent regardless of how strongly one identified with being a furry, meaning that even those who were only somewhat into furry or those who were fairly new to the fandom agreed that it's a bad idea to copy specific details from another person's fursona. This could plausibly be due to the fact that furries feel a strong sense of connection to their fursona. A 2015 study we conducted at a furry convention found that 83.6% of furries agreed that their fursona was a meaningful component of themselves, while our 2019 convention study similarly found that furries were 14 times more likely to agree than to disagree that their fursona was a meaningful and important part of who they were. Given how much of themselves furries put into their fursonas, it makes sense that they'd be bothered to see aspects of their fursona copied onto someone else's character.

Connection to Fursona Species

Given what we've discussed in the previous section about the possible reasons driving furries' fursona species choice, it should follow logically that furries probably feel a sense of connection to their fursona species. To better understand the potentially multifaceted nature of this connection, we asked furries, in an open-ended question on a 2011 convention study, to describe their connection to their species. After coding their responses, the most common category was a general liking of the species, an almost fan-like appreciation for it—a feeling endorsed by just over half of furries (52.3%). Another common response from 9.2% of furries was a sense of spiritual or innate connection to the species. In short, furries were far more likely to choose a fursona species that they thought was cool, interesting, or which they generally held in positive regard, while a minority of furries felt a stronger, deeper connection to their fursona species.[21]

To more directly compare the nature of furries' felt connection to their fursona species we developed a scale called the Species Connection Scale. The scale pitted three different ways of identifying with one's fursona species against one another: liking of a fursona species (e.g., "I really enjoy this species"), feeling a sense of spiritual connection to a fursona species (e.g., I feel that I have a mystical connection to this species"), and identifying

---

[21] The same study also found that the stronger one's felt connection to their fursona species was, the more they felt they knew about that particular species. If nothing else, this may suggest that furries may "do their homework" or have a genuine understanding of the species they choose for their fursona, rather than deciding on a fursona species that they have only superficial knowledge about.

as a member of your fursona species (e.g., "I was born with this connection to this species").[22] Across 12 separate online and convention studies from 2011 to 2018, furries consistently scored highest on the "liking" items (being two to four times more likely to agree than to disagree with the items on it on average) and the lowest on the "identification" scale (being two to four times more likely to disagree than to agree with the items on it on average), with scores on the "spiritual" scale falling between the two, but generally being disagreed with. Consistent with the open-ended data above, the species connection scale seems to reiterate that most furries simply like their fursona species rather than feeling a mystical connection to their species or actually identifying with it.

One might wonder whether there's any point to these comparisons: does it *really* matter if a furry chooses a cat fursona because they *like* cats rather than actually identifying *as a cat*? As it turns out, it's a difference that matters. In a pair of studies published in a multidisciplinary journal of human-animal interaction, we looked at data from more than 6,000 furries, including their responses to the Species Connection Scale and to questions about their perception of animals, attitudes toward animals, and even the respondents' mental health (Roberts et al., 2015). The study found that the nature of one's connection to their fursona can predict additional information about the person. Specifically, the extent to which one *liked* their fursona species was associated with an increased tendency to anthropomorphize the species (i.e., to see them as more capable of having human-like emotions), something that wasn't the case for feeling a spiritual connection to one's fursona species, and which was the *opposite* for identifying with one's fursona species, which was associated with less anthropomorphizing of the species. The study also found that the extent of one's liking their fursona species said little about one's well-being or self-esteem. In contrast, feeling a greater sense of spiritual connection was positively associated with greater self-esteem and well-being, while identifying more strongly as a member of one's fursona species was just the opposite, associated with less self-esteem and less well-being.

In short, while furries generally feel a strong connection to their fursona species, the nature of this connection differs from furry to furry, and this is far from a trivial difference.

---

[22] The latter two dimensions overlap fairly strongly with the concept of therianthropy, which we discuss in Chapter 20.

The Nature of a Fursona

Earlier in the chapter we reviewed furries' responses to an open-ended question asking them to describe the nature and function of their fursona. In this section we'll take a closer look at some additional questions in this vein, including furries' relation to their fursonas, the extent to which fursonas resemble actual animals or anthropomorphized animals, and the extent to which furries create their fursonas themselves or are heavily inspired by outside sources.

Identifying With One's Fursona

Recall that many furries responded to the open-ended question about what a fursona is by implying, or in many cases explicitly stating, that their fursona was significant and meaningful. To be able to meaningfully compare the prevalence of these attitudes among furries, we can also look at data from studies that took a quantitative approach using scales and numeric data. For example, we ran a pair of studies, one online and one in-person, asking furries to indicate the extent to which they agreed or disagreed that their fursona was less like a significant, meaningful character and more like an abstract idea without details like a personality or backstory. As Figure 7.1 shows, furries across both studies disagreed with the idea more than they agreed with it, with average scores ranging from 2.9-3.6 across the studies. This finding is consistent with the open-ended data and the fact that, for most furries, their fursona represents something significant and meaningful to them.

As a follow-up to these results, we can ask whether the significance or meaningfulness of furries' fursonas stems from the fact that furries identify with their fursonas as an aspect or facet of themselves. Psychological research suggests that our concept of "self" is not a simple matter of "me" versus "everything that's not me." The "self" is a mental construct made up of all the thoughts, beliefs, attitudes, concepts, groups, and ideas that come to mind when you think about yourself. For example, as a Canadian, being from Canada is part of who I am. Even though I am, technically speaking, a distinct entity from the country of Canada, Canada is one of many concepts that become activated in my mind when someone says my name. Over time, the concept of Canada has become an inextricable part of how my mind represents my sense of self. Psychologists refer to this concept as the *inclusion of other* in self (IoS), a phenomenon frequently studied in the context of including significant others (e.g., romantic partner) into one's own self-concept (Aron et al., 1991, 1992).[23]

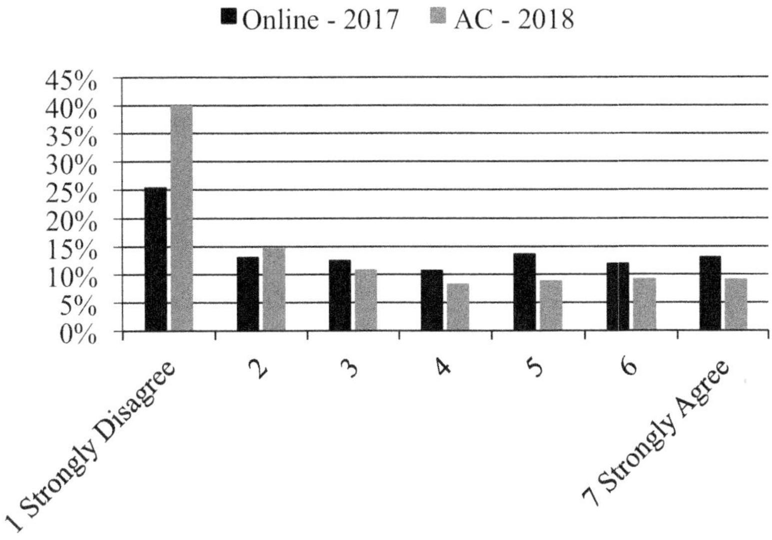

Figure 7.1. Extent to which an online and convention sample of furries agree that their fursona is abstract and lacking details such as a personality or backstory.

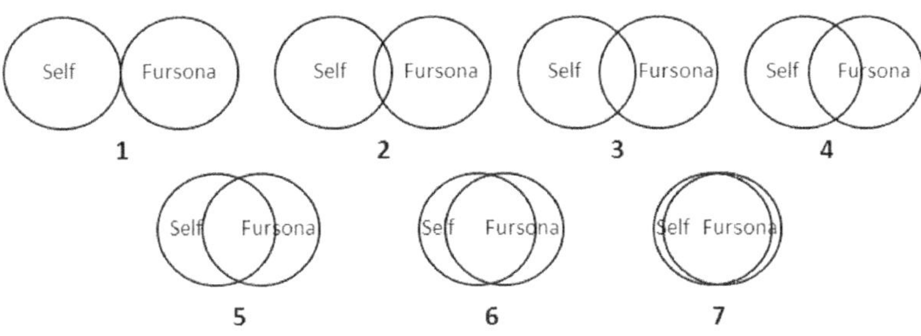

Figure 7.2. Adaptation of the Aron et al. (1992) inclusion of other in self-measure for use with furries and their fursonas.

---

[23] Colloquially, we say things like "you complete me" or "they're my better half" as an illustrative example of how we come to include romantic partners in our sense of who we are.

While the concept of IoS sounds abstract or metaphysical, psychologists have devised a fairly simple and intuitive way to measure it. Using a series of seven figures, each containing a set of increasingly overlapping circles, one that represents you and that represents another concept, participants are asked to indicate how strongly they feel like another person, entity, or concept fits into their sense of self (Aron et al., 1992). As seen in Figure 7.2, we adapted the measure to refer to furries and their fursonas as a way of measuring the extent to which furries consider their fursonas to be part of who they are. Those who answer lower on the scale are essentially stating that they and their fursona are distinct entities (e.g., a furry who creates a fursona using a random fursona generator or simply to provide them with some anonymity online). In contrast, furries who score high on the scale may feel that they and their fursona are one and the same, or that there is no way to disentangle who they are from who their fursona is.

So how did furries respond on this scale assessing the overlap between themselves and their fursonas? Across two studies we ran at furry conventions in 2014 and 2015, furries scored, on average, just above a 5 on the scale. Or, presented another way, furries were four times more likely to choose a score above the midpoint of the scale than they were to choose a score below the midpoint of the scale. It was also found that the more strongly one identified as a furry (fanship), the higher they tended to score on this IoS scale.[24]

While the results of this IoS data would certainly seem to suggest that furries identify, at least in part, with their fursonas, the scale itself is not a direct measurement of identification. For that, we can turn to a series of eleven online and convention studies run between 2014 and 2022 in which we asked furries to indicate, across various measures, the extent to which they identified (or did not identify) with their fursona. The results of the studies were clear and consistent: furries consistently scored high on measures of identification with their fursona, being anywhere from 5-13 times more likely to agree than to disagree with statements about identifying with their fursonas. This was true regardless of the particular scale used in each study. What's more, across every measure the highest level of agreement was always the most commonly-selected response.

---

[24] In contrast, identifying with the furry fandom was unrelated to this tendency. This may be because the concept of fanship is about one's own identity, something which overlaps conceptually with their fursona. In contrast, fandom is about the groups to which one belongs, something less clearly tied to a fursona.

All in all, the data seem to suggest that furries' fursonas may be meaningful and significant for them, in no small part, because they strongly identify with their fursonas. In a sense, furries imbue or infuse their fursonas with themselves, treating them as extensions of themselves, which would explain why fursonas become so meaningful to them.

Fursona as a Representation of Ideal and Actual Self

Now that we've shown that most furries identify strongly with their fursonas, we can move on to asking more nuanced questions about the nature of this identification. One possibility alluded to in the open-ended responses earlier in this chapter is that fursonas represent an idealized version of the self that a furry can strive toward. This idea is, in fact, consistent with a significant body of psychological research showing that people hold many different representations of themselves and often compare these different selves to gauge whether they are living up to their own standards and the standards set by others (Higgins, 1987). Two such self-representations are a person's "ideal" self and their "actual" self—who they would like to be and who they actually are at present, respectively. The same research suggests that the more a person's actual self fails to line up with their ideal self, the more likely they are to feel a sense of sadness or disappointment.

So, do furries see their fursonas as their idealized selves? The short answer is yes. Across six different studies, we found that furries, on average, consistently agreed that their fursonas were an idealized version of themselves—whatever that meant to them.[25] In fact, across samples, furries were 2-12 times more likely to agree than they were to disagree that their fursona represents their ideal self. Perhaps most telling, the single most commonly selected response on the surveys was consistently the highest possible level of agreement, as seen in Figure 7.3 below.

Okay, so most furries see their fursonas as an idealized version of themselves. But what about their actual selves—do fursonas pull double duty by also representing who furries are at this very moment? After all, many furries also indicated in their open-ended responses that their fursonas were imbued with aspects of their personality and quirks.

Indeed, we found evidence for this as well. When we asked furries directly whether they agreed or disagreed that their fursona represents their actual selves, furries in three different convention studies typically agreed

---

[25] Importantly, we didn't define what an "ideal self" meant to furries, since "ideal" will mean something different to everyone. Some people want to be astronauts, some want to be athletes, some want to be rock stars, and some just want to find happiness in a tranquil, relaxing existence. Who are we to say which of these is "more ideal?"

with this statement as well, as seen in Figure 7.4, with the strongest possible agreement being the single most popular response in each of the three studies.

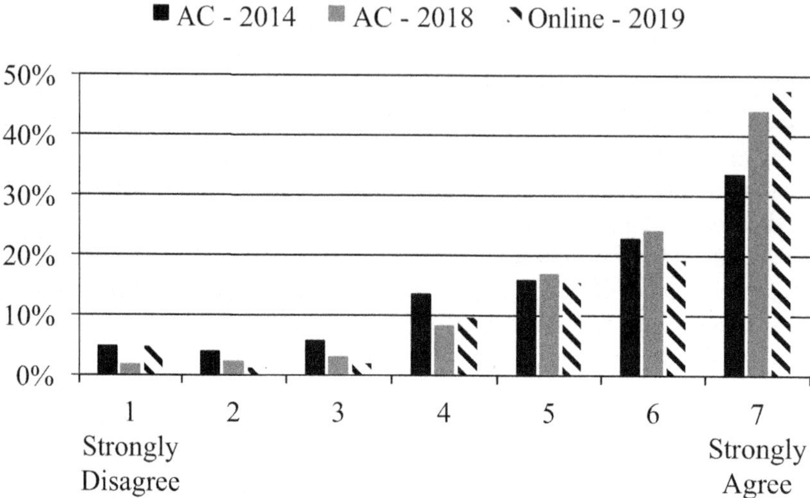

Figure 7.3. Extent to which furries in online and convention studies agree that their fursona represents their idealized self.

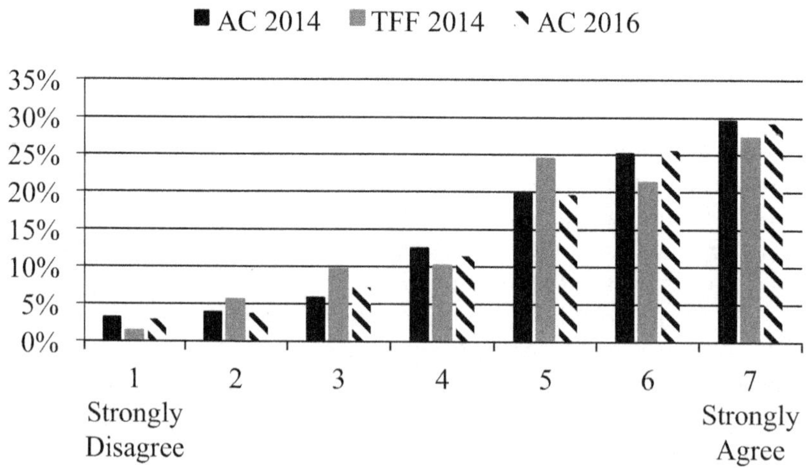

Figure 7.4. Extent to which furries in three different convention studies agree that their fursona represents their actual self.

To summarize, a typical fursona is an amalgamation of who furries currently are and who furries wish they could be. Given what we said about the discrepancy between actual and ideal self, you might imagine this could tell us something about furries and their well-being. Additional studies suggest this is the case. On the one hand, across numerous studies, we found no consistent evidence that, by itself, having a fursona that represents one's ideal self is associated with well-being. However, in a 2014 study, furries who were frustrated that they were not *more* like their fursonas—a discrepancy between actual and ideal self—scored higher on a measure of depression—exactly what prior research would predict (Higgins, 1987).[26]

Fursonas as a Different Mindset

One sentiment expressed by some furries in the open-ended data is that their fursona is not a representation of themselves so much as it's a mask they put on to be in a different headspace or an alternate mindset that they try to get into. This might be analogous to a person playing a roleplaying game because it lets them experience the world as a hero or a villain, a noble or a peasant, or as a traveler from a distant world.

Is this how some furries use their fursonas? To test this, we asked furries in a pair of online and convention-based studies to indicate their degree of agreement or disagreement with the idea that their fursona is a different mindset that they try to get into. Responses were fairly mixed, with a slight tendency for participants to disagree with the item more than they agreed with it, although the single most common response was the highest degree of disagreement. In other words, furries were fairly divided on the issue, with more furries strongly disagreeing with the assertion than strongly agreeing with it. This is largely in line with the open-ended data and with the above findings showing that, for most furries, their fursonas *are* them, at least in part. While a fursona may offer some furries a chance to be something different, this doesn't appear to be the function of a fursona for most furries.

Anthropomorphizing Fursonas

Let's move away from questions about whether a fursona represents oneself to dive deeper into the association between fursonas and non-human

---

[26] We've done additional studies which add even more nuance to these findings. For instance, one study found that furries who create fursonas that bear no resemblance to who they are currently tend to score lower on measures of well-being than furries whose fursonas represent their actual self. Another set of studies found that relatively few furries create fursonas that represent the *worst* parts of themselves, and that those who do also tend to score significantly lower on measures of psychological well-being.

animals. As we saw in the species prevalence data, virtually all furries who create fursonas base them on some kind of non-human animal species, real or otherwise. But remember that furries are interested in *anthropomorphized* animals. As such, it seems plausible that furries would tend to have fursonas that are not *just* animals, but animals that have anthropomorphized features, at least to some extent.

To measure this degree of fursona anthropomorphization, we asked attendees at a 2016 furry convention to indicate, on a 7-point scale ranging from 1 = *completely feral* to 7 = *completely anthro*, the extent to which their fursona was anthropomorphized. The results, shown in Figure 7.5 below, reveal a strong tendency toward creating highly anthropomorphized fursonas, with the strongest degree of anthropomorphism being the most popular response by far. In contrast, very few furries indicated that fursonas were completely feral in nature. A follow-up analysis found no evidence that furries who have more feral or more anthropomorphized fursonas identify more strongly as furries or with the furry fandom, so we cannot use the degree of anthropomorphization as a predictor of "how furry" someone is.[27] At the moment, the decision to have a more anthropomorphized or feral fursona seems to boil down to aesthetic preference, although future research is needed to rule out other possibilities.

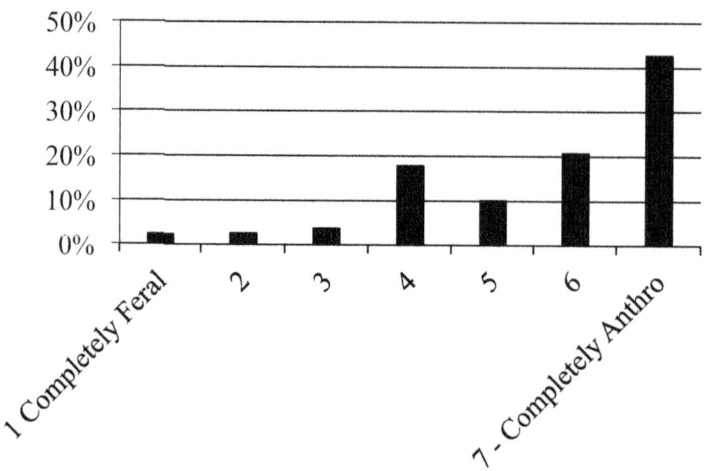

Figure 7.5. Extent to which furries described their fursonas as feral or anthropomorphized.

[27] Although a follow-up analysis did reveal that self-identified therians have more feral fursonas than do non-therian furries.

Fursona Source: Self- or Other-Generated

To finish off this section on the nature of one's fursona we turn briefly to a 2014 convention study in which furries were asked to indicate, in a pair of questions, the extent to which their fursona was something they created themselves and the extent to which their fursona was adopted or modified from another source. Given that there is a seemingly growing market of "adoptable" characters for sale by artists, as well as the fact that many furries have been inspired to join the fandom based on specific media (for more on this, see Chapter 19), it seems at least somewhat plausible that furries may draw inspiration for their fursonas, in part or in whole, from outside sources.

As Figure 7.6 shows, however, furries overwhelmingly agreed that their fursonas were self-created and that they were not created by, or modified from an outside source. This is consistent with previously discussed findings showing that furries imbue their fursonas with a lot of themselves and place a great deal of time, work, and significance into the creation of their fursonas, as well as with findings suggesting that furries look down at the idea of taking specific details from another character for use in their fursona. Taken together, these findings point to furries seeing their fursonas as distinct, unique characters rather than as something inspired by some other source, something which is far more common in other fandoms, such as science fiction or anime, where cosplaying and roleplaying as established characters are far more common and normalized (Reysen et al., 2021).

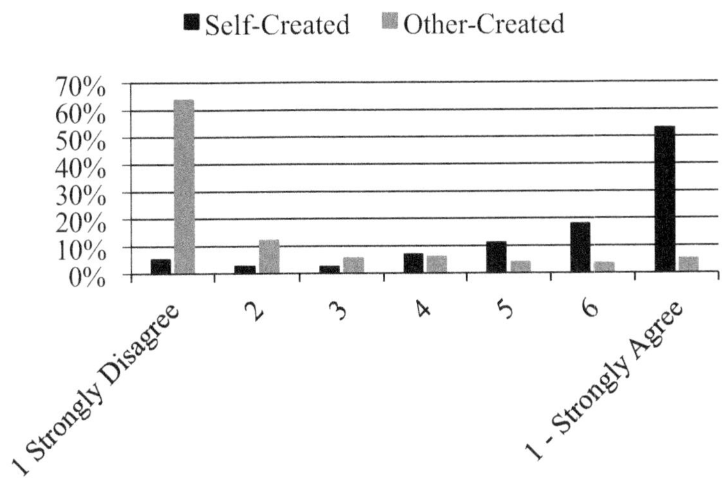

Figure 7.6. Extent to which furries at a convention agreed that their fursonas were self-created or adopted/modified from another source.

Similarity to One's Fursona

Earlier in this chapter, we found evidence that furries generally consider their fursonas to be an amalgamation of who they currently are and who they would like to become. In this section, we'd like to ask a conceptually related question: do furries see themselves as being similar to their fursonas, and, if so, how? After all, furries might say that their fursona is a representation of who they are, but is this in a strictly symbolic sense, or is it literal? As an example, if I'm playing a video game, the character I'm controlling is a representation of me in the game world, regardless of whether the character looks like me or not.[28] In other words, the similarity of a fursona to a furry and the fursona's ability to represent some facet of a furry may be overlapping, but distinct concepts.

With this in mind, let's look at furries' feelings of similarity to their fursonas, and how this similarity manifests. We asked furries in three different studies to indicate whether they agreed or disagreed with a statement about feeling very similar to their fursona. The results, shown in Figure 7.7, are remarkably consistent across studies and show that furries feel very similar to their fursonas. These findings are also very consistent with the pattern of findings shown in Figure 7.4, suggesting that feeling similar to one's fursona may well overlap with seeing one's fursonas as a representation of their actual self.

But let's dive a bit deeper into what it means to feel similar to one's fursona. Furries put it in their own words in one of our early 2011 studies, when participants were asked to describe how they felt similar to their fursona. After coding the responses and grouping together similar responses, the most common similarity noted was psychological similarity (34.0%)—that is, being similar to their fursona in terms of personality or ways of thinking about and seeing the world. The next most common category of similarity was behavioral similarity (11.8%)—believing that one's fursona would act in a similar manner to how furries, themselves, would act in a given situation. The third most common category was physical similarity (7.2%)—sharing physical traits in common with one's fursona, including hairstyle or body shape. Taken together, these results suggest that the similarity furries feel to their fursonas tend to be psychological in nature

[28] Of course, if one's in-game character looks, thinks, and behaves in a manner consistent with the player, the character is probably going to be seen as a more faithful representation of the player, and this may, in turn, make the game feel more immersive! The point still stands, however, that a character can represent someone even if they are in no way similar to that person.

(e.g., personality, behavior), rather than based on the physical appearance of one's fursona.

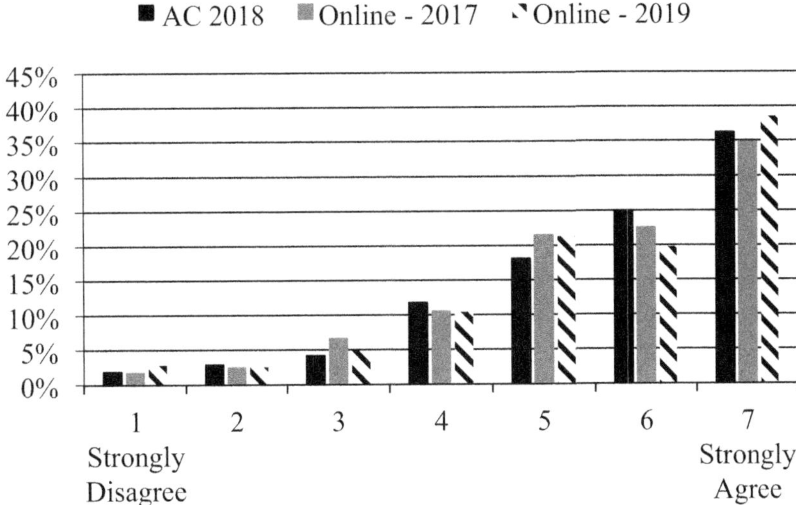

Figure 7.7. Extent to which furries in three different studies agree that they feel very similar to their fursona.

To more rigorously test this idea we can look at data from seven different online and convention studies that asked respondents to indicate, on a set of three 7-point scales ranging from 1 = *not similar at all* to 7 = *identical*, the extent to which they felt physically, psychologically, and behaviorally similar to their fursonas. Mirroring what was found in the 2011 open-ended data, participants scored highest on the measure of psychological similarity, with average scores ranging from 5.5-5.9 across the seven studies and an overall average score of 5.7. Behavioral similarity was a close second, with average scores ranging from 5.2-5.7 across the seven studies and an overall average score of 5.5. Finally, the lowest average score was for physical similarity, which ranged across the studies from 4.1-4.4 with an overall average of 4.3. In other words, both open-ended and numeric data suggest that furries feel a greater sense of psychological similarity to their fursonas than they do physical similarity.

In some of our other studies, we've asked other questions about fursona similarity. For example, a 2022 study found that, regardless of whether one considers psychological, behavioral, or physical similarity, convention-going samples of furries score higher, on average, than online samples of furries.

Other studies find that more highly identified furries (fanship) also tend to feel more similar to their fursona, while fandom identification was unrelated to how similar one felt to their fursona. In a pair of 2022 studies, we found that furries are about 5-10 times more likely to feel that they have become more similar to their fursonas over time than they are to feel they have become less like their fursonas over time.

Finally, in a 2014 cross-fandom study we found that furries felt a greater sense of psychological, behavioral, and physical similarity to their fursonas than anime fans felt toward the characters they cosplayed as and as compared to fantasy sports fans concerning the teams they managed in their fantasy leagues. In other words, the connections furries feel with their fursonas are distinctly strong in a way that may have few analogs across other fandoms.

Number of Fursonas

Up until now, we've focused our attention on the particulars of fursonas, describing and characterizing them at length. In the rest of this chapter, we'll move away from the specifics of fursonas to talk about fursonas more broadly. An example of this is the question of whether furries only have one fursona, or whether they may have more than one (or, indeed, none at all!).

To begin, we'll consider some data we've collected across eight furry surveys, some online and some in-person at conventions, from 2011-2022. Across the studies, the number of furries saying that they have never had a fursona ranges from 2.4-11.9%, with an overall average of about 6.2%. Or, to put it another way, approximately 94% of furries say they have had a fursona. As we'll see in Chapter 9, compared to the wide range of other fan-related activities furries engage in, creating a fursona may be one of the most universal activities that furries engage in!

So, if it's true that most furries have a fursona, do they only have one? We've seen how much time and effort many furries put into crafting significant, deeply meaningful fursonas infused with aspects of themselves. And given that our personality stays relatively stable once we reach adulthood (Atherton et al., 2021), it would make sense that furries would create a fursona that represents themselves and then stop there. But what does the data suggest?

Looking at the same eight studies mentioned above, we find, consistent with our hunch, that the single most common response across every study was to have one fursona throughout one's life. Having said that, the number of participants choosing "1" ranged from 30.2%-49.3% across the studies, meaning that there was no sample in which more than half of participants said they had only ever had one fursona. Instead, between 43.5 and 67.3% of furries across samples said that they have had more than one fursona over time, with the average furry having had 2.0-2.7 fursonas across samples, or an overall average of 2.3 fursonas.[29]

One possible interpretation of this data is that most furries have changed their fursona at least once over their time in the fandom. This sort of "serial fursona" model suggests that furries create a fursona that they use until they decide to create another one to replace it. Another possibility, however, is that furries may have more than one fursona at a given time. This "simultaneous fursona" model suggests that furries may create and identify with multiple fursonas at a time, perhaps to represent different facets of themselves, different moods or mindsets, or to simply for use in different contexts (e.g., roleplaying, fursuiting, social media).

To compare these two models we turn to data from six studies representing furries both recruited online and at conventions. Across the studies, an average of 30.0-40.4% of furries said that they currently have more than one fursona, with furries having, on average, 1.8-2.2 fursonas at a given time.[30] These data "split the difference" between the two models and suggest that both are probably occurring: some furries who've had more than one fursona have changed or replaced their fursona with a new one, while others simply add additional fursonas to an existing pool or create multiple fursonas at the same time—although the precise motivation underlying both models remains to be studied.

To finish up this section, we can look at specific questions from surveys across the years to help us add some nuance to these findings. For example, a pair of studies found that furries were six times more likely to disagree than to agree that they change their fursonas regularly; moreover, the strongest level of disagreement was the most common response to this question. In other words, consistent with what we've already found, even when furries do change their fursonas, it is rarely seen as a routine or common occurrence.

Finally, data from a pair of 2022 studies has found that the average furry has had their current fursona for 5.5-6.7 years. While the most common

---

[29] Follow-up analyses reveal that the number of fursonas a furry has had is unrelated to whether they were recruited online or at a convention, nor does having more fursonas mean that furries feel less attachment or sense of connection to those fursonas. The number of fursonas one has is also generally not a good predictor of how strongly someone identifies as a furry or with the furry fandom.

[30] As before, there seems to be no evidence suggesting that furries recruited online or in-person at conventions differ with respect to how likely they are to have more than one fursona at a given time.

response to the question was 1-2 years, 46.7-47.9% of furries said that they have had their current fursona for five or more years. These findings once again coincide with prior findings suggesting that fursonas are deep and significant for many furries and that they are neither replaced haphazardly nor on a whim for most furries, given that a typical fursona is kept for several years.[31]

Beliefs About Fursonas in General

A recurring theme throughout this chapter has been the fact that many furries identify with their fursonas as a significant and meaningful representation of themselves. Knowing that this is the case for themselves, we can ask whether furries might assume the same is true for other furries. To test this possibility, we asked furries in a pair of 2012 studies to indicate, on a scale ranging from 1 = *strongly disagree* to 10 = *strongly agree*, the extent to which they agreed that, in general, someone's fursona probably says a lot about who they are. Importantly, this question asked about fursonas in general, rather than asking participants about their own fursonas.

The results across the two studies, shown in Figure 7.8, reveal that furries have fairly mixed opinions on the subject. Furries' average score of 6.2 in both studies suggests a slight tendency toward agreeing that a fursona tells you a lot about a person. This could be the result of furries projecting onto others from their own experience, acknowledging the significance and meaning of their own fursonas while also recognizing that this may not be the case for all furries. An alternative explanation has to do with how furries interpret the specific wording of the statement: while a person's fursona may be significant and meaningful, simply looking at a fursona without any additional information may not prove especially useful to an outsider when it comes to learning more about a furry. Just because your green fox fursona is imbued with significance and meaning for you doesn't mean that I'll be able to discern anything about you by looking at your green fox fursona by itself. Of course, further research is needed to determine which of these two interpretations best explains the results, or whether some third explanation would fit the data better.

---

[31] In fact, one of our 2017 studies found that the longer someone had been a furry for, the *less* likely they were to consider even just making changes to their current fursona. If nothing else, furries' fursonas may become more deeply-entrenched and stable as a representation of the furry over time, with younger, newer furries being the ones to more readily change a details about a fursona or to add a new one altogether.

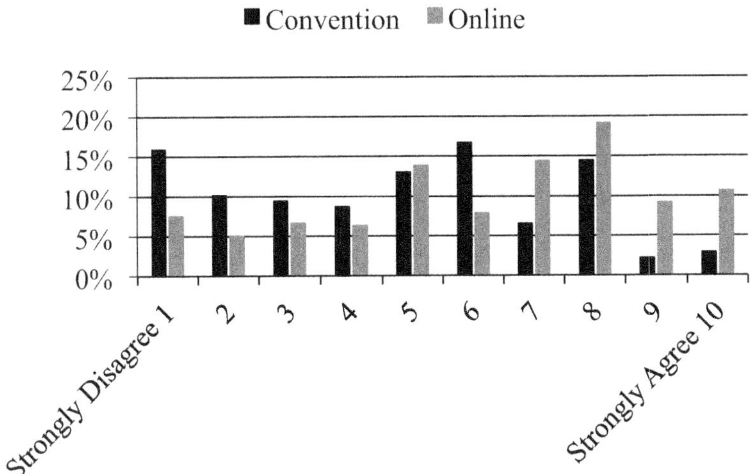

Figure 7.8. Extent to which furries agreed that a person's fursona can tell you a lot about that person.

A related question in the same pair of studies also asked furries whether they agreed or disagreed that another person's fursona species influences how well the participants would get along with the person. We initially asked the question based on misconceptions that laypersons have about the organization of the furry fandom. For example, we've been asked by interviewers whether furries who have dog fursonas prefer to hang out with other furries with dog fursonas and hate furries who have cat fursonas, based on the old adage that cats and dogs do not get along. To be fair, the idea is not wholly unfounded, as many furry conventions *do* host species-specific events (e.g., equine meet-ups). However, such events are the exception rather than the rule at a furry convention, with the novelty being that they are one of the only times at a furry convention when a room will be full of just one type of fursona species. In contrast, throughout the rest of the convention, and, indeed, in most online spaces, furries with all manner of fursona species interact fairly harmoniously—or, at the very least, do not seem to discriminate against one another based on fursona species.

This fact is borne out in the data from our pair of studies, shown in Figure 7.9. Whereas the results from the previous question indicate a fair degree of indecisiveness about whether a fursona can tell you something about a person, furries largely disagree that a person's fursona would influence their interaction with that person, with average scores ranging from 3.1-3.2 across the two samples. As a noteworthy caveat to the data, follow-up analyses revealed that furries who most strongly identified with their own fursonas were also the most likely to say that another person's fursona species would impact their willingness to interact with them. The reason for this is, at present, unknown, although one possibility may be that furries who identify strongly with their fursonas may be more aware of, or likely to hold, stereotypical beliefs about particular fursona species, meaning they assume certain things to be true about a person with a particular fursona species and that this might feed into their decision to avoid that person.

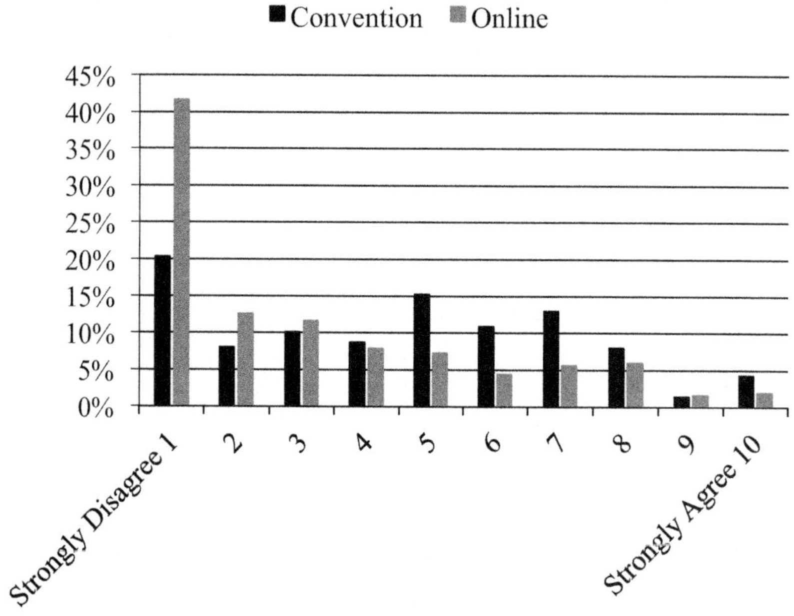

Figure 7.9. Extent to which furries agreed that a person's fursona would influence their interaction with that person.

With this possibility in mind, we asked participants attending a 2016 convention to indicate, in an open-ended fashion, whether there exist any stereotypes about their fursona species and, if so, to state what those stereotypes were. Looking at some of the most popular fursona species, some consistent stereotypes were reported by participants, including the stereotype that wolves are loyal, foxes are sly, dragons are strong, cats are lazy, and rabbits are shy. While far from a formal and thorough study on the existence of species-specific stereotypes in the furry fandom, the data at least suggest that some species-specific stereotypes do exist and that furries, themselves, are aware of the stereotypes about their own fursonas. This would seem to suggest that it is at least plausible that some furries would take these stereotypes into account when deciding on a fursona species to represent themselves and when deciding whether they wanted to interact with another person based on that person's fursona species.

In a related follow-up study from 2017, we also tested whether there was any merit to the species stereotypes: is it true, for example, that furries with wolf fursonas are more likely than other, non-wolf furries to apply the label of "loyal" to themselves? We found evidence that approximately half of the measured stereotypes seemed to hold at least some empirical water; furries with wolf fursonas were significantly more likely than furries without wolf fursonas to consider themselves to be loyal, dragons were more likely to consider themselves to be strong, and foxes were significantly more likely to consider themselves to be sly. Of course, this also means that just as many stereotypes were not supported by the data, suggesting that while stereotypes may exist for some popular fursona species, there is only modest evidence suggesting that there is any truth to them.

We can consider one more possible explanation for the finding that furries might take a fursona species into account when deciding whether to interact with a fellow furry. This explanation is less about endorsing stereotypes about another species and more about furries tending to give preferential treatment to others who share a fursona species as them. There is considerable evidence, both from our studies and from other social psychological research, suggesting that, due to self-serving biases, furries should have a fairly high opinion about their fursona. For example, we found, in a 2014 convention study, that furries spend a moderately high amount of time thinking about their own fursona species, far more than they spend thinking about other species. Likewise, we saw earlier in this chapter that furries consider themselves to be especially knowledgeable about their own fursona species, suggesting that, at the very least, they like their fursona species enough to spend time learning about it. Finally, a significant body of psychological research suggests that all else being equal, people tend to prefer and give better treatment to people who are part of *their* group as compared to people who are part of a different group (Tajfel, 1970; Tajfel et al., 1971, 1979). Taken together, this would mean that furries should tend to prefer other furries who share their fursona species over other furries who do not.

In short, it is at least plausible that part of the reason why some furries may treat another furry differently based on their fursona species is because they are prone to giving preferential treatment to those who have fursonas similar to their own. In other words, it might not be that furries are activating stereotypes about other species so much as they might simply like another person who shares the same fursona species as they do, thinking they share something in common (e.g., "we foxes are a sly bunch") and having the human tendency to give special treatment to others in one's ingroup (e.g., "we foxes need to stick together!").

Of course, as with many questions in this chapter, more research is needed to determine which of these explanations best explains this phenomenon.

Fursona Functions

In this last section, we'll briefly revisit a topic that we introduced earlier, namely the question about the function of a fursona. Given how ubiquitous fursonas are in the furry fandom, it would make sense that some furries develop fursonas, in no small part, to fit in with what they see other furries doing.[32] This is fairly consistent with prior research showing that when we belong to groups, we often internalize the values and norms of the group, which may include behaving in accordance with how other group members behave (Turner et al., 1987). In the case of furries, this might include creating a fursona to be like the other furries.

Of course, fitting in with other furries may not be the only reason to create a fursona, or, at the very least, it may not be the only benefit that comes from having a fursona. As was indicated by many furries in the open-ended data that we started this chapter with, furries may benefit from having a fursona, whether it's using a fursona as a role model, leaning on a fursona as a crutch for social anxiety, or exploring and expressing facets of themselves that they might otherwise be unable to express.

To test these various functions, we asked furries recruited at a 2015 convention to complete a measure that asked them to indicate, on a scale from 1 = *strongly disagree* to 7 = *strongly agree*, how much they agreed that their fursona fulfilled a number of different functions for them. The results, shown in Table 7.3, reveal that fursonas can fulfill a multitude of different functions, although not every function is equally common. For example,

---

[32] I can personally attest to the fact that this was the case for me. At my first furry meet-up, I was asked about my fursona. At the time, I didn't have a fursona, or even know what a fursona was, prompting me to go home that night and create one before the next meet-up!

furries were significantly more likely to agree that their fursona helped to facilitate social interaction than they were to say that their fursona allows others to see a more authentic side of themselves. The prevalence of these different functions generally lines up with the prevalence of the themes mentioned in the open-ended questions at the start of the chapter.

Table 7.3. Furries' agreement that their fursona fulfilled several specific functions, assessed as an average score on a 1-7 scale. Scores above 4 indicate agreement with the item.

Function	Average
Helps me meet people I couldn't have met otherwise	6.1
Lets me try out a different way of being	5.2
Inspires me to act more kindly or compassionately toward others	5.1
Allows me to become greater and better than myself	4.9
Helps me accept myself as who I am	4.9
Lets people see "the real me"	4.7
Inspires me to be more assertive in my life	4.6
Often helps me through difficult times in my life	4.4
Inspires people to treat me more kindly	4.4

A follow-up analysis from the same study revealed that furries who identified more strongly as furries (but not necessarily with the furry fandom) were more likely to say that their fursonas were functional for them. Or, to put it another way, furries whose interest in furry is not especially strong may not be as likely to experience the benefits from their fursona that more highly-identified furry would experience.

We also took a more focused look at one particular fursona function: helping furries through difficult times in their life. We assessed this item across three separate studies and found that furries fairly consistently agreed more than they disagreed with this item, with average scores ranging from 4.3-4.8 across samples, and with furries being 1.5-3 times more likely to agree than to disagree with the statement. Furries for whom their fursona represented their ideal self were especially likely to agree with this statement.

Finally, we asked a few additional questions based on inquiries and research questions provided to us by some furries. Specifically, we were asked by furries who had a range of different physical and psychological disabilities whether or not this factored into the creation of their fursona. For example, one hypothesis was that furries with a disability might create fursonas with the same disability, given that many furries incorporate elements of themselves into their fursonas. Others hypothesized the opposite, that a furry with a disability might prefer to create a fursona who did not have the disability as a way to have others interact with them without being aware of their disability.

As Table 7.4 illustrates, furries with disabilities largely disagreed that their disability significantly impacted the creation of their fursona and also disagreed that their fursona fulfilled any function specific to their disability. Instead, it seems likely that furries with disabilities are no different from furries in general with respect to the functions that their fursona fulfills and the underlying factors that drive the creation of their fursonas.

Table 7.4. Agreement with items pertaining to one's fursona and their disability among furries who self-identified as having a disability, assessed as an average score on a 1-7 scale. Scores above 4 indicate agreement with the item.

Item	Average
My fursona helps me to forget my disability	3.5
My fursona hides my disability from others	2.6
My fursona has the same disability that I have	2.5
My fursona helps me to see my disability in a different light	2.4
My fursona helps to educate others about my disability	2.1
My fursona helps me to explain my disability to others	1.9
My fursona has a condition or disability that differs from my own	1.6

Conclusion

We began this chapter with a fairly basic understanding of what a fursona was, as a layperson might conceptualize it: an animal-themed character with an associated image, name, and some distinguishing characteristics. By allowing furries to describe the nature of their fursonas in their own words, however, it quickly became apparent that fursonas are, for many furries, much more than just an avatar, nickname, or way of maintaining their anonymity.[33] Moreover, we saw that there really is no one, singular

[33] We also saw that, for at least some furries, a fursona really was nothing more than a logo, avatar, or way to remain anonymous!

conceptualization of a fursona. Instead, we recognize that fursonas vary considerably in the form they take (e.g., their species, sharing traits with their creator), but also in their relation to their creator (e.g., identifying with one's fursona) and in the functions they fulfill.

Alongside this variability in fursona form and function, furries themselves also vary considerably in their beliefs about fursonas, including the extent to which furries believe that someone else's fursona can be a valuable source of information about a person and whether or not another person's fursona species might impact decisions about whether to interact with the person. And while furries as a whole generally disagreed with the idea of letting their interactions with another furry be dictated in whole or in part by that person's fursona species, stereotypes do exist about those with particular fursona species, only some of which are grounded in any sort of demonstrable fact, and these stereotypes may impact how furries feel about others, whether furries themselves want to acknowledge it or not.

Throughout this chapter, we've also put to rest some common misconceptions that people have about fursonas. For example, while laypersons may believe that furries identify *as* the non-human animal species represented by their fursona, the available evidence suggests the opposite: while most furries have a particular admiration for their fursona species and many know an inordinate amount about them, relatively few would say that they identify as a non-human animal. Laypersons may also believe the furries choose their fursona species fairly randomly, or change them on a whim, neither of which is supported by the data; furries tend to put a great deal of time and thought into the development of their fursonas and, while some may have more than one fursona simultaneously and many have changed their fursonas over time, furries are generally unlikely to change their fursona species with any sort of regularity. Moreover, rather than fursona species being a fairly random choice, a handful of species are especially likely to be chosen, including species that are commonly represented in media we consume (e.g., wolves, foxes, dragons) or with which furries are likely to have first-hand experience (e.g., dogs, cats).

It's hard to put all of this together into a single, coherent statement that encompasses what fursonas are for all furries, but that, in itself, is worth knowing. While there may not be a single, agreed-upon conceptualization of a fursona that all furries agree upon, having a fursona remains one of the most universal behaviors engaged in by furries and, despite the vast differences in what their fursonas are to them, furries seem remarkably adept at effectively navigating fandom spaces full of these characters and the complexities that this brings with it.

References

Aron, A., Aron, E., N., Tudor, M., & Nelson, G. (1991). Close relationships as including other in the self. *Journal of Personality and Social Psychology, 60*(2), 241-253. https://doi.org/10.1037/0022-3514.60.2.241

Aron, A., Aron, E. N., & Smollan, D. (1992). Inclusion of other in the self scale and the structure of interpersonal closeness. *Journal of Personality and Social Psychology, 63*(4), 596-612. https://doi.org/10.1037/0022-3514.63.4.596

Atherton, O. E., Grijalva, E., Roberts, B. W., & Robins, R. W. (2021). Stability and change in personality traits and major life goals from college to midlife. *Personality and Social Psychology Bulletin, 47*(5), 841-858. https://doi.org/10.1177/0146167220949362

Freud, S., & Jones, E. (Ed.). (1922). *Beyond the pleasure principle.* (C. J. M. Hubback, Trans.). The International Psychoanalytical Press. https://doi.org/10.1037/11189-000

Freud, S. (1923). The ego and the id. In J. Strachey et al. (Trans.), *The standard edition of the complete psychological works of Sigmund Freud* (Volume XIX). Hogarth Press.

Haidt, J. (2001). The emotional dog and its rational tail: A social intuitionist approach to moral judgment. *Psychological Review, 108*(4), 814-834. https://doi.org/10.1037/0033-295x.108.4.814

Higgins, E. T. (1987). Self-discrepancy: A theory relating self and affect. *Psychological Review, 94*(3), 319-340. https://doi.org/10.1037/0033-295X.94.3.319

Jeck, D. M., Qin, M., Egeth, H., & Biebur, E. (2019). Unique objects attraction attention even when faint. *Vision Research, 160,* 60-71. https://doi.org/10.1016/j.visres.2019.04.004

Moreland, R. L., & Beach, S. R. (1992). Exposure effects in the classroom: The development of affinity among students. *Journal of Experimental Social Psychology, 28*(3), 255-276. https://doi.org/10.1016/0022-1031(92)90055-O

Nisbett, R., & Wilson, T. (1977). Telling more than we know: Verbal reports on mental processes. *Psychological Review, 84*(3), 231-258. https://doi.org/10.1037/0033-295X.84.3.231

Reysen, S., Plante, C. N., Roberts, S. E., & Gerbasi, K. C. (2020). My animal self: The importance of preserving fantasy-themed identity uniqueness. *Identity, 20*(1), 1-8. https://doi.org/10.1080/15283488.2019.1676245

Reysen, S., Plante, C. N., Roberts, S. E., Gerbasi, K. C., & Chadborn, D. (2021). *Transported to another world: The psychology of anime fans.* International Anime Research Project.

Roberts, S. E., Plante, C. N., Gerbasi, K. C., & Reysen. S. (2015). The anthrozoomorphic identity: Furry fandom members' connections to nonhuman animals. *Anthrozoös, 28*(4), 533-548. https://doi.org/10.1080/08927936.2015.1069993

Suler, J. (2004). The online disinhibition effect. *Cyberpsychology & Behavior, 7*(3), 321-326. https://doi.org/10.1089/1094931041291295

Tajfel, H. (1970). Experiments in intergroup discrimination. *Scientific American, 223*(5), 96-103. https://www.jstor.org/stable/24927662

Tajfel, H., Billig, M., Bundy, R., & Flament, C. (1971). Social categorization and intergroup behavior. *European Journal of Social Psychology, 1,* 149-178. https://doi.org/10.1002/ejsp.2420010202

Tajfel, H., & Turner, J. C. (1979). An integrative theory of intergroup conflict. In W. Austin & S. Worchel (Eds.), *The social psychology of intergroup relations* (pp. 33-47). Brooks/Cole.

Turner, J. C., Hogg, M. A., Oakes, P. J., Reicher, S. D., & Wetherell, M. S. (1987). *Rediscovering the social group: A self-categorization theory.* Blackwell.

Zaman, H. B. A. (2023). Furry acts as non/human drag: A case study exploring queer of colour liveability through the fursona. *Queer Studies in Media & Popular Culture, 8*(1), 99-114. https://doi.org/10.1386/qsmpc_00090_1

Chapter 8
Fursuited for Success

Courtney "Nuka" Plante

Close your eyes and imagine a typical furry. No, really, do it. Don't worry, we'll wait for you: imagine what an average furry looks like.

What did you picture? If you're a furry, you might have been cheeky and just imagined yourself or a close friend who happens to be a furry. We're willing to bet, however, that many readers, furry or otherwise, imagined someone wearing something animal-themed, anything from a pair of ears and a tail to a kigurumi[1] to a full-body mascot-style costume—what furries would call a fursuit.

If this is what came to your mind when you imagined a furry, you're far from alone. Most people, furry or otherwise, would probably imagine something similar when asked to picture a typical furry, someone dressed in some kind of animal-themed outfit. Don't just take our word for it: Look at how news stories about furries describe them:

> *"members of the local 'furry' community, meaning they attend group events dressed in elaborate animal costumes"* (Walker, 2016, para. 1).

> *"the furry fandom, [a] subculture in which members enjoy making art and dressing up as anthropomorphized characters"* (Dickson, 2022, para. 1).

> *"he's also a furry—a member of a community that's mostly known for being really into anthropomorphic fantasy animals and dressing up in fursuits at conventions"* (Thomas, 2022, para. 5).

> *"Thousands of people dressed as 'humanized' animals, known as 'furries,' are in Pittsburgh for the annual Anthrocon convention"* (Buffitt, 2014, para. 2).

> *"furries—people who have an interest in or dress up as anthropomorphic animal characters"* (Petersen, 2022, para. 1).

---

[1] A kigurumi, or "kigu" for short, is a Japanese-style loose-fitting, one-piece, full-body outfit, somewhat akin to what a child might wear for pajamas. They're usually animal-themed.

"[Furries] dress up as animals (or other make-believe characters) that possess human personalities, like the ability to walk on two legs" (Laychuk, 2020, para. 3).

From these descriptions alone, you'd think that wearing a fursuit was an essential part of what it means to be furry. But remember, most furries don't mention fursuits at all in their definition of what makes a furry a furry (see Chapter 5 for more on this). So why is it that fursuits are so synonymous with furries and furry culture despite not being a necessary or common feature in most furries' definition of a furry?

There are at least two possible reasons. The first possibility is that fursuits are distinct and easily recognized, and are therefore an iconic representation of furries. Another possibility is that most furries own a fursuit, in which case the characterization of furries as people who wear fursuits would be accurate, whether or not furries spontaneously mention it in their definition of a furry.

Let's consider both of these possibilities.

Speaking of the first possibility, furries are far from the only fandom to be distilled down to its most visibly recognizable elements. If, at the start of the chapter, I had asked you to imagine a *Star Wars* fan instead of a furry, you would probably have pictured a person wearing white stormtrooper armor or swinging around a lightsaber. Likewise, *Star Trek* fans are often reduced to people wearing a black-and-red Starfleet uniform[2] and pointy Vulcan ears, *Harry Potter* fans are pictured waving around magic wands, and sports fans wear jerseys and paint their faces in their team's colors. It's unlikely that all or even most of the fans in these groups adorn themselves in these outfits most of the time—many of them probably don't have the accessories to do so even if they wanted to.

If we saw a more typical-looking fan of these interests—what might we expect to see? Well, they're probably a fairly unremarkable-looking person wearing average clothing, sitting on a couch, and consuming their favorite piece of media, be it listening to the game, watching a movie, or reading a book. The problem with this image is that it lacks any obvious indicators of what the person is a fan of.[3] While this is probably the most common way the fan consumes their preferred media, nothing about the scene activates the

[2] The colour does depend on whether the wearer is part of the command, engineering, or science and medical division of Starfleet!

[3] Except, of course, for whatever's on the screen or whatever book is in their hands at that moment.

stereotypes we think of when we imagine a fan. Just looking at the scene without any context, this could be a fan of pretty much anything—it might not even be a fan at all! For that reason, it's not an especially helpful image if you want to communicate to someone that this is a particular type of fan. Instead, we tend to imbue the image with symbols specific to the fan culture, with recognizable, iconic trappings of the interest.[4]

Let us now turn our attention to the other possible explanation: is it possible that we naturally think of fursuits when we think about furries because most furries wear fursuits?

Prevalence of Fursuiting

At first glance, it seems like it should be pretty simple to figure out how many furries own a fursuit: just get a sample of a bunch of furries and ask them if they're fursuiters or not. In fact, we did exactly that in four different samples of online and at-convention furries from 2016-2020! We asked participants to put a checkmark in a box if they were a fursuiter. The results were fairly comparable across the samples, with 28.1% of convention-attending respondents checking the box and 27.7-35.8% of online respondents checking the box. That, right there, should be enough to put this idea to rest: across samples, the data show that only about one-quarter to one-third of furries are fursuiters. Or, to put it another way, more furries are not fursuiters than are fursuiters, so it would be inaccurate to describe furries as people who fursuit—something that the majority of furries do not do.[5]

But if that settles the question, why does this section continue on for several more pages?

Critical readers might take issue with the way we asked the question in the above paragraph. Technically, we only asked whether respondents considered themselves to be a fursuiter. This isn't the same thing as asking whether they *owned* a fursuit. It's entirely possible, for example, that

---

[4] As an analogy, imagine you're a film director trying to establish that your movie takes place in San Francisco. If you just showed clips of a typical-looking suburb, it would be unlikely to be recognized by viewers as San Francisco—not without flashing the words "San Francisco" on the screen. If, instead, you started your film with a panning shot of the Golden Gate Bridge, the audience would immediately recognize that the city is San Francisco and would probably call to mind thoughts, feelings, and relevant information about San Francisco as they watched.

[5] Converging evidence for this point can be found in Chapter 5, in which we asked furries what furry means to them. While a small number of furries did spontaneously identify fursuits as part of their definition of a furry, the vast majority of furries did not.

someone might own a fursuit but not wear it enough to feel like the term "fursuiter" applies to them. Alternatively, someone might own a fursuit and used to wear it a lot, but they haven't done so in years, and so they no longer actively identify as a fursuiter. And while you could argue that most people who own a fursuit probably call themselves fursuiters, we should probably ask specifically about fursuit ownership, rather than just inferring it from a label someone applies to themselves. As the saying goes, anything worth doing is worth doing right.

In this spirit, we next turn to a set of four earlier studies from 2011-2016, in which we asked furries recruited online and in-person at a convention to specifically indicate, yes or no, whether they owned a full or a partial fursuit.[6] The results revealed that ownership of a full or partial suit ranged from 31.5-45.2% across samples, with the online samples being somewhat lower in ownership (33.9%) than the average of samples recruited at conventions (40.8%). These numbers are notably higher than the number of furries who labeled themselves as fursuiters, supporting the idea that at least some furries who own fursuits may not be calling themselves fursuiters. Of course, there is another possible interpretation of these data: perhaps identifying as a fursuiter and owning a fursuit is the same thing, and the differences in these results are based on the fact that the studies took place in different years, and perhaps rates of fursuiting have happened to decline in recent years. While this possibility exists, data from furry conventions would beg to differ and frequently show a growing proportion of attendees participating in their fursuit parade—an event where fursuiters at a convention all line up and march together through the convention space. As an illustrative example, in 2010, 16.8% of attendees took part in the fursuit parade, while in 2022 that number had increased to 26.4% ("Anthrocon 2010," 2023; "Anthrocon 2022," 2023).

But this study also introduced a new wrinkle into the question—the distinction between different types of fursuit ownership. A deeper look into

[6] Typically, a "full" fursuit refers to a suit that covers the wearer's entire body, and often includes, as separate or connected pieces, a head, torso, arms and hands, legs and feet, and a tail, wings, horns, or other accessories. In contrast, a "partial" fursuit typically refers to a fursuit that lacks one or more components to make it a full fursuit. Many partial suits, for example, do not have the torso (the wearer instead wears clothing, with the fursuit's arms and hands, head, and feet appearing to pop out of the clothing). There is no established definition of what constitutes a partial suit, however. In our studies, we left the term undefined, allowing furries to answer based on their own definition.

the results of our studies found that furries were about twice as likely to own a partial fursuit as they were to own a full fursuit. This could be for several plausible reasons. For one thing, it's generally cheaper to commission, and easier to make, a partial fursuit than a full fursuit, almost by definition (i.e., a full fursuit contains all of the parts of a partial fursuit, plus more). Speaking to this idea, an independent scholar named Abigail Torbatian shared data with us that she had collected from more than 100 different fursuit builders. The data revealed that the price of a partial fursuit in 2020 ranged from $550.00 to $3,875.00, with an average cost of $1,647.61.[7] In contrast, prices for full fursuits from the same fursuit builders depended on whether they were plantigrade or digitigrade,[8] but averaged, respectively, $2,676.15 and $3,107.92, with ranges of $994.00-5,750.00 and $1,056.00-6,650.00—significantly more than the cost of a partial suit. Given that partial suits are more affordable, they are also more accessible to people than full fursuits, which may be prohibitively expensive for some people.

In addition to partial fursuits being more affordable, more people may simply prefer to wear a partial fursuit to a full fursuit. For one thing, wearing a fursuit without the torso (i.e., wearing clothes instead of the bodysuit) is much cooler, temperature-wise, than wearing a full fursuit. For those who fursuit outside or in places lacking air conditioning, this can make partial fursuiting a far more appealing—and less dehydrating—prospect! Moreover, it's much easier to put on and take off a partial fursuit (e.g., a fursuit without the torso, or one that is not a single bodysuit) than it is to put on and take off a full fursuit. This might appeal to someone wanting the versatility of being able to switch in and out suit (e.g., to facilitate social interaction, to make photo opportunities easier) without having to find a change room and spend ten minutes changing. As such, even among furries who could potentially afford a full fursuit, some may opt instead for a partial fursuit simply for the comfort, ease of wearing, and type of fursuiting they want to do.

---

[7] All prices are in $USD.

[8] The terms "plantigrade" and "digitigrade" refer to the shape of the character's legs. Plantigrade legs refer to the type of legs that humans have, wherein the entire foot generally touches the ground. In contrast, digitigrade legs are sometimes (erroneously) described as appearing to have "backwards knees" like that of a horse: only the "toes" touch the ground, with the sole of an elongated "foot" remaining off the ground. The higher cost for a digitigrade suit is usually the result of additional padding and sculpting needed to create the illusion of a digitigrade leg on a suit being worn by a plantigrade wearer.

Data on fursuit ownership also raises an additional question: should all furries who own a fursuit be assumed to own just one fursuit? We assessed this idea across four additional studies from 2017-2019, where respondents at conventions and online were asked how many fursuits they owned. The convention studies, which did not distinguish between partial and full fursuits, found that 45.1-48.2% of furries recruited at a convention owned at least 1 fursuit, with 20.3-21.4% of furries saying that they owned more than one fursuit. These numbers are a few percentage points higher in some of the previous studies, further suggesting that fursuit ownership may be on the rise. In the online samples, 19.5-19.8% of respondents indicated that they owned one full fursuit and 23.3-26.4% indicated that they owned one partial fursuit, with 2.6-3.2% and 3.8-4.5% owning more than one full or partial fursuit, respectively. Put simply, the data show, especially among online furries, that those who own a fursuit are more likely than not to own a single fursuit. The findings also provide additional evidence that partial fursuit ownership is more prevalent than full fursuit ownership and that convention-going furries are more likely to own a fursuit than furries recruited online.[9]

To this point, we've seen that the number of furries who own a fursuit is consistently below the 50% mark, meaning that we have not encountered a sample in which more furries own a fursuit—partial or otherwise—than do not. This seems to drive a nail into the coffin of the claim that furries are defined as people who wear fursuits.

Nevertheless, if we're *very* charitable in our definition of what counts as a fursuit, there's still a chance of finding a kernel of truth in the claim. After all, we've only been looking at partial and full fursuits, but maybe some people imagine a furry as someone wearing cat ears, a tail, or a collar. With this in mind, we can broaden our line of questioning by asking how many furries own any sort of furry-themed clothes or accessories. We did exactly that in a 2014 study of convention-going furries, the results of which are shown in Table 8.1.

---

[9] This makes sense for at least two reasons. First, conventions can be expensive to attend, often costing hundreds or even thousands of dollars once you include the hotel, travel, and registration costs. Those who can afford to buy a fursuit may also be the same people who can afford to travel to conventions. Another possible reason, one we address later in this chapter, is that fursuits have a performative, social component to them. As such, those who do not attend furry conventions may have one fewer reason to own a fursuit (i.e., not able to wear it alongside other fursuiters and show it off to large groups of furries).

Table 8.1. Percentage of furry respondents who owned each of a number of different furry-themed items designed to display one's furry interest.

Display Item	% Ownership
Tail	48.1%
Clothing	34.3%
Ears	27.3%
Hand-Paws	16.7%
Head / Mask	16.7%
Foot-Paws	15.3%
Claws	9.7%
Wings	1.9%
Other Accessories	36.6%

The table reveals a couple of important facts. First, consistent with what we observed with fursuits, there is no single accessory or piece of furry clothing that is owned by a majority of furries. Second, the data suggest that while not all furries do so, many furries *do* enjoy expressing their fan interest through owning and wearing fan-related clothing or accessories. This is not unlike *Star Wars* fans, many of whom may not own a lightsaber, but it's undeniable that many also do own one because of its iconic nature in the series.

Before we wrap up this section, let's take a quick look at some additional findings to add some context and nuance to our discoveries. For instance, we've been talking about the number of furries who do or do not own fursuits, but we've yet to consider the extent to which furries are even interested in owning a fursuit in the first place. If more than half of furries do not currently own a fursuit, is it because that many furries have no interest in owning a fursuit, or are at least some of those people saving up to buy one in the future? To test this, we asked furries, both at a convention in 2016 and online in 2017, to indicate the extent to which they agreed with the statement "I want to own a fursuit" on a 7-point scale (1 = *strongly disagree*, 7 = *strongly agree*). The data for those who did not own a fursuit are shown in Figure 8.1.

The findings reveal that most furries without a fursuit nevertheless have a fairly strong desire to own a fursuit. This finding, coupled with earlier data showing the significant expense of a fursuit, suggests that many more furries would probably own a fursuit if they could afford to do so.[10] The data may also indicate that some furries may not currently own a fursuit, but are perhaps in the process of saving up for one, or have commissioned one but, due to long waiting lists and production times, may not yet have a suit.[11] Also, in line with the previously discussed findings, convention-attending furries have a greater interest in owning a fursuit than furries recruited online. This is not to say that furries recruited online had no interest in owning a fursuit, of course. After all, the most common response for both samples was maximum agreement with the statement. Nevertheless, convention-going furries scored higher, with an average score of 5.6, than furries recruited online, whose average score was 5.0.

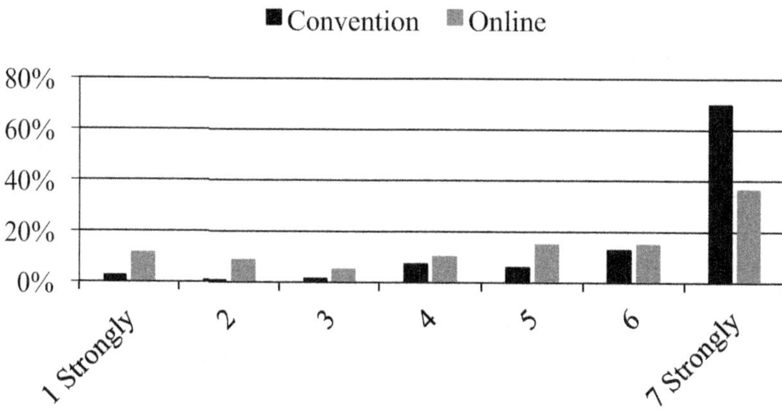

Figure 8.1. Extent to which furries in an online and convention study agree that they are interested in owning a fursuit.

---

[10] We can also find converging evidence from a 2011 convention study asking furries whether they currently had, wanted, or did not want to own a full or partial fursuit. While 37.6% of furries said they didn't have a partial fursuit yet, implying that they might in the future, only 2.7% said that they had no interest in ever owning a partial suit. Likewise, 49.3% of furries indicated that they did not yet have a full fursuit, while only 3.5% indicated that they had no interest in one.

[11] It is not uncommon, for example, for fursuits to take months to build, and for queues for popular fursuit builders to be one to two years long. It should also be noted that fursuit builders are somewhat uncommon in the furry fandom, and in fairly high demand. In our 2017 and 2020 studies we found that only 8.4-10.8% of furries considered themselves to be fursuit builders, although in a 2018 study we *did* find that about half of furries say they have customized or made at least *some* parts of their fursuit themselves.

We can also shift our focus away from fursuit ownership itself to instead ask furries who own a fursuit about the extent to which they actually wear it. After all, a furry who owns a fursuit but who has never worn it might consider their fursuit to be more of a collection piece, not unlike how a *Star Wars* fan might choose not to wear their stormtrooper armor but, instead, display it in a case. To test this, we asked fursuiters in an online 2019 study to indicate the frequency with which they fursuited, both in the past 12 months and at the point in their life when they fursuited the most. The results are shown in Figure 8.2.

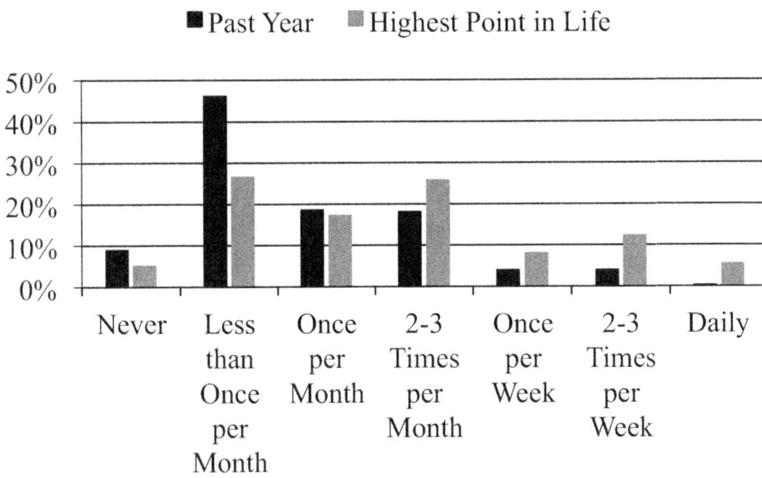

Figure 8.2. Frequency with which fursuit owners in an online study wore their fursuit in the past year and at the point in their life when they were most frequently wearing their fursuit.

The results reveal that most fursuit owners are not currently fursuiting as much as they had at their peak. In a finding that may be surprising to those who don't own a fursuit, a typical fursuit owner fursuits less than once per month, perhaps opting to do so only at a few conventions or local events each year. Even at the time in their lives when fursuiters did the most fursuiting, they did so perhaps once or twice per month. This is a far cry from popular representations of furries as people who love their fursuits and wear them around the house or at every opportunity when going out into the world. It's also worth noting that approximately 9.0% of fursuit owners said they hadn't suited a single time in the past year, something which, didn't stop them from continuing to identify as furries.

Which brings us back, one last time, to our original point: contrary to the way furry is commonly defined in popular culture as a group focused on wearing fursuits, there is little evidence that fursuiting is a defining feature of what it means to be a furry. Indeed, most furries do not currently own a fursuit, even if most find the idea of owning one someday appealing. And even among those who do own a fursuit, they tend to don the fursuit no more frequently than at a handful of get-togethers and conventions throughout the year. This is not unique to the furry fandom, as we would hardly expect anime fans to cosplay around their house or at their workplace, nor would we expect a typical sports fan to paint their face in their team's colors while watching the game from home. These activities, while eye-catching and distinct, are far rarer among fans—furries or otherwise—than are portrayed in media. This belief also overlooks the fact that most fans' interests manifest in other fascinating ways, a topic we discuss in greater depth in Chapter 5.

Fursuiter Motivation and Beliefs

We've seen that furries, as a group, are not defined by the wearing of fursuits. But we can hardly pretend that fursuits aren't a fascinating part of furry culture. Whether you consider the time and cost to create a fursuit or the physical toll that wearing a fursuit takes on the body[12], it's hard not to wonder what compels someone to go through all that effort when they could just watch a furry movie, admire furry artwork, or interact on a furry forum like so many other furries do.

We asked fursuiters this question in a 2016 study, specifically asking them to indicate how important eight different motivations were when it came to their interest in fursuiting.[13] Participants responded on a 7-point scale (1 = *not at all important*, 7 = *extremely important*). Each of the eight motivations studied was included based on our observations at furry conventions and on conversations we had with fursuiters. The results are shown in Table 8.2.

The results show that, of the motivations on the list, creative expression and entertaining others were the two most important motivators for

---

[12] Speaking from experience, I can attest to the fact that, having both done several 5k and 10k runs and fursuited for 3 hours in the summer heat, the latter is far more exhausting—although both require considerable amounts of hydration and recovery!

[13] Funnily enough, while we didn't ask participants to complete the survey in their fursuit, a few brave souls did exactly that, either by slipping off a fursuit paw, managing to hold a pen in their big, fuzzy paws, or by dictating their responses to a friend who read the questions to them. Whether this says something about the determination or sheer defiance of fursuiters is a subject for future studies!

fursuiters, followed closely by the ability to express some form of individuality or distinctiveness. To a somewhat lesser extent, fursuiters were also motivated by the ability to display a different or alternative identity and as a way to connect with the fandom. Among the least important motivations were to educate others (e.g., about the fandom) or to hide from some aspect of one's day-to-day self. There was considerable variability in the motivations of individual fursuiters, with no single motivation emerging as a clear and uniquely high motivator relative to the others. Likewise, follow-up analyses found that most fursuiters said that several of the motivators were fairly important to them, further complicating the picture of motivation: not only do motivations differ from person to person, but even within the same person there are usually multiple motivations to fursuit.[14]

Table 8.2. Average rating of importance on a 1-7 scale of eight different motivators for fursuiting as indicated by a sample of convention-going fursuiters.

Motivation	Importance
To Express Creativity	5.8
To Entertain Others	5.8
To Express Individuality	5.6
To Display a Different Identity	5.2
To Connect to the Fandom	5.1
To Create an Alternative Identity	4.9
To Educate Others	4.1
To Conceal My Day-to-Day Self	3.7

To better understand the experience of fursuiting, we've asked fursuiters over the years about their own experience with fursuiting. As a simple example, in two convention-based studies from 2017-2018, we asked fursuiters to indicate the extent to which they agreed or disagreed that they behave differently in their fursuit than they do outside of their fursuit. As Figure 8.3 illustrates, fursuiters largely agreed with this statement, that fursuiting brought out behaviors that they seldom engaged in during their day-to-day lives.[15] To see what sorts of behaviors we're talking about, we

---

[14] We also recognize that the list of possible motivations is incomplete. Instead, it illustrates how, even among just a subset of all the possible motivations to fursuit, there is considerable variability and no single motivation that drives all fursuiters.
[15] I'm often asked by my students and non-furry friends whether I do typical, day-to-day activities like lounging around the house or doing chores while in my fursuit.

asked a follow-up question in the 2018 study, which found that fursuiters tend to engage in behaviors that they would consider difficult or even impossible to do if they were outside of their fursuit (see Figure 8.4).

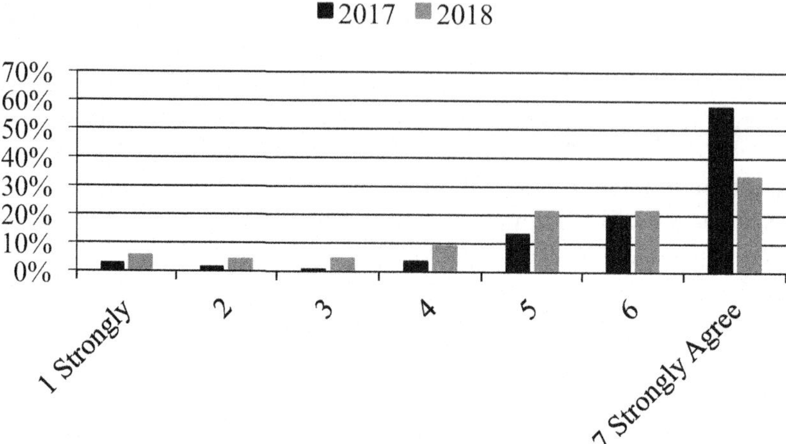

Figure 8.3. Extent to which fursuiters in two different convention studies agree that they behave differently in fursuit than they do out of fursuit.

Of course, this only raises a new question: what can you do in a fursuit that you can't do without a fursuit? Given that fursuits are typically heavy, cumbersome, and impair fine motor control, it's hard to imagine any physical activity that becomes easier to do in a fursuit![16] The answer lies not in the physical benefits provided by the fursuit, but rather in the psychological or social benefits fursuit can provide. To illustrate, fursuiters from the same pair of studies also strongly agreed that it was easier for them to meet and interact

---

They're often surprised to hear that my answer is "no," and the data here seem to suggest that I'm far from alone in saying so. It would be like dressing up in your finest three-piece suit to clean out the gutters or watching Netflix on the couch in your finest ball gown—you'd be overdressed for the occasion!

[16] One of the few examples that comes to mind is shoveling snow on a cold winter day, at least a few fursuiters have taken photos of themselves doing exactly that, with the overheating properties of fursuits proving to be an asset in sub-zero temperatures! This specific situation aside, fursuits usually make physical tasks more challenging. This is, in fact, the premise of fursuit talent shows, where fursuiters astound audiences with their ability to dance, juggle, or play an instrument passably well while wearing a fursuit!

with new people while in their fursuit than it was outside of a fursuit (see Figure 8.5). In other words, fursuiting allows them to overcome a psychological hurdle, be it social anxiety, feeling socially awkward, or worrying that the person with whom they're interacting might not like something about them. With these barriers lowered, the fursuiter may more confidently engage in social interactions that they would otherwise consider to be difficult or even impossible!

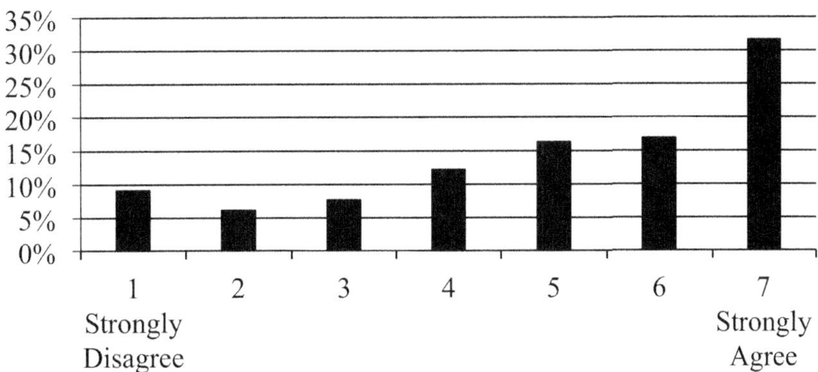

Figure 8.4. Extent to which fursuiters in a 2018 convention study agree that, when fursuiting, they do things that would normally be hard or impossible outside of their fursuit.

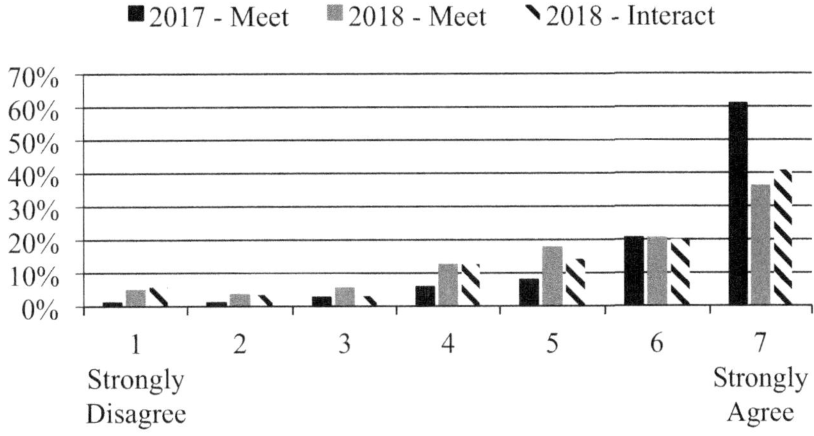

Figure 8.5. Extent to which fursuiters in two different convention studies agree that it's easier to meet and interact with strangers in a fursuit than it is to do out of a fursuit.

Additional questions from the 2018 study reinforce these findings. In one question, for example, fursuiters were far more likely to agree than they were to disagree that they felt more accepted by others when wearing their fursuit than when they were not (see Figure 8.6).

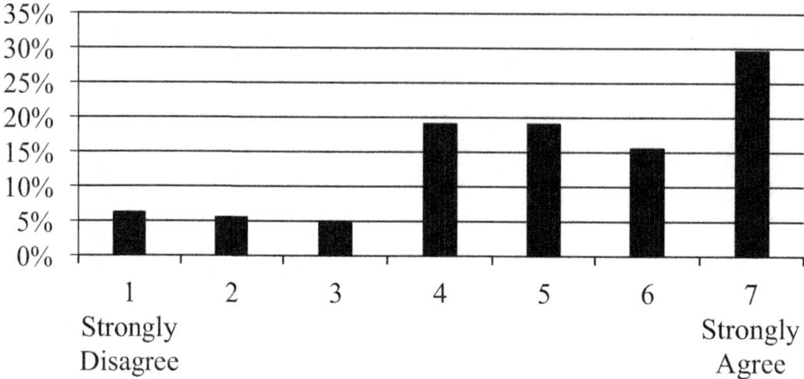

Figure 8.6. Extent to which fursuiters in a 2018 convention study agree that wearing a fursuit allows them to be more accepted by others than when they are out of fursuit.

When asked what facets of themselves furries felt were more accepted when in fursuit, they responded that a fursuit allowed them to overcome undesirable aspects of their personality and their age. To a lesser extent, some furries also felt that their sexual orientation was more accepted when they were in a fursuit, although with an average score of 4.3 on a 7-point scale, this was less clearly the case, and may depend on the furry's sexual orientation, to begin with.[17] A similar trend was observed with respect to fursuiters and feeling accepted concerning their gender identity; as a whole, fursuiters varied in the extent to which they felt a fursuit helped their gender identity to be better accepted, with an average score of 3.8, but this score was much higher for transgender fursuiters (5.8) than it was for cisgender fursuiters (3.2), suggesting that the stigma many trans people experience may

[17] Speaking to this point, gay, lesbian, bisexual, and asexual furries were more likely to agree that their sexual orientation was more accepted when they were in a fursuit than were straight furries, with average scores of 4.4 and 3.9 respectively. The stigma typically experienced for being part of a sexual minority may be overlooked or overcome entirely by their wearing the fursuit, which may conceal, distract, or simply put a more positive, friendly, fuzzy face to their sexual identity.

be overcome when they interact with other people through the use of a fursuit whose gender identity reflects how they wish to be seen.

In a similar vein, the two studies also revealed that fursuiters generally agree that their fursuits allow others to see the "real" them, with average scores across the two studies ranging from 4.3-4.9. Complicating the picture, however, fursuiters were somewhat more likely to agree that fursuiting allowed others to see another side of themselves, with average scores ranging from 5.2-5.5 across studies. While this would initially seem to be a contradiction, there are at least two possible explanations. The first is that fursuits have a different relationship to the self for different fursuiters; for some, a fursuit represents their most authentic selves, while for others, a fursuit is an attempt to embody something different from their day-to-day self. A second interpretation, however, one that is more consistent with evidence on fursonas more broadly (see Chapter 7), is that both of these things can be true: a fursuit can both represent who someone currently is and who they are striving to become. Insofar as both of these are facets of someone's true self (Higgins, 1987), it would make sense that a fursuiter could feel more accepted by someone who sees them through a character that represents an amalgam of who they are and who they are striving to become.

While our findings do not yet paint a complete picture of the motivations driving some furries to fursuit, they do, at the very least, illustrate how complex and multifaceted this drive can be. If nothing else, it provides a counterpoint to the belief that furries mindlessly spend thousands of dollars on a fursuit as a compulsive act of fan-related spending. Instead, furries fursuit for a combination of reasons ranging from the obvious (e.g., it's a fun and creative way to express oneself) to the nuanced and subtle (as a way to make social interactions easier by reducing social anxiety).[18]

Fursuiters versus Non-Fursuiting Furries

To this point, we've discussed the prevalence of fursuiters and delved a bit into what makes them tick. But given that most furries *don't* spend thousands of dollars on a fursuit, you may be wondering—as many laypersons do—whether there's something *different* about fursuiters. It's hard to imagine that there isn't some way we can predict *which* furries would make such an investment and which would not. Or, to ask it another way, are there measurable differences between those furries who do and do not own fursuits and, if so, can they provide us with additional information about what compels fursuiters to do what they do?

---

[18] The importance of fursuits as a way to break down barriers for social interaction is addressed again in the contexts of social anxiety and neurodivergence in Chapter 23.

The most obvious first candidate for a difference between fursuiters and non-fursuiting furries is in just *how* furry they are. It's unlikely, after all, that someone with only a passing interest in furry would spend hundreds of hours building a fursuit or thousands of dollars commissioning one. As an analogy, it's much more likely that a passionate, highly identified sports fan would spend thousands of dollars on season tickets to see all of their home team's games than a fan with only a passing interest would be to do the same. This doesn't mean, of course, that every highly-identified fan will necessarily have a fursuit/season tickets, nor does it mean that the only people who can call themselves "real fans" must have a fursuit/season tickets. But it does seem more likely that highly-identified fans will feel compelled to make such expensive fan-related purchases.

That's precisely what the data from our studies have shown: across nearly all of the studies where we've tested it, fursuiters have scored significantly higher than non-fursuiting furries on measures of fanship (how strongly one identifies as a fan) and fandom (how strongly someone identifies with other fans).[19,20] Providing converging evidence, our studies have also shown that, compared to non-fursuiting furries, fursuiters have also been furries for longer, consume more furry media (although they are no more likely to become *immersed* in furry media), and go to more furry conventions. Fursuiters also have a considerably higher average income than do non-fursuiting furries: $42,192.17 USD versus $25,501.54 USD, an unsurprising finding, given that a person with more expendable income is better able to afford furry-related content (e.g., art, movies, books), travel and hotel costs associated with furry conventions, and to be able to purchase a fursuit.[21]

---

[19] See Chapter 6 for more on fanship and fandom.

[20] On rare occasions, the scores of fursuiters and non-fursuiters on measures of fanship and fandom have been close enough that we cannot conclude that they are significantly different, but we have yet to find a sample where non-fursuiters score higher than fursuiters on measures of fanship or fandom.

[21] This gets into interesting questions about causality: is it the case that richer furries can afford to make more furry-related purchases which, in turn, makes them identify more strongly as furries, or is it the case that a person who is a more highly-identified furry with more expendable income simply more willing to spend it on fan-related purchases? There is no way to distinguish either of these possibilities with the data we currently have, although we'll point out that the two explanations are not mutually exclusive. We could be seeing a bidirectional link where the two pathways feed into one another in a positive feedback loop: being more furry = spending more on one's furry interest = becoming more furry.

In a related vein, our 2017 study of online furries found that fursuiters scored higher than non-fursuiting furries on the four dimensions of a scale known as the CAPE scale. Put simply, the CAPE scale measures different facets of one's fan interest, including their *Commitment* to the interest (e.g., amount of content owned/viewed, trivia known), seeing their fan interest as an *Asset* (e.g., gaining tangible benefits like friends or money from their involvement), experiencing a sense of *Presence* in the fan interest (e.g., using it for escapism, a distraction from the real world), and using the fan interest to *Express* some aspect of themselves (e.g., as an outlet for creativity, a muse; Plante et al., 2021). Higher scores across all of these dimensions would seem to suggest that fursuiting furries, on average, tend to be "more furry" than non-fursuiting furries in a holistic fashion, rather than on any single dimension, something that runs counter to the idea that a fursuiter is simply a furry with more expendable income.

We can also shoot down another misconception with evidence from the same 2017 online study: fursuiters are no more likely than non-fursuiting furries to have become furries because of an interest in furry-themed pornography. We'll explore the topic of porn as a motivator of furry interest in Chapter 19, but for now, we can say that there is little evidence to suggest that fursuiters are "just furries with a fursuit fetish." This is a point that runs counter to the way fursuiters are sometimes portrayed in popular media, which often focuses on fursuiters and portrays them as people with a single-minded drive to have sex in a fursuit. For example, in the television show *1000 Ways to Die*, furries are described as "people who like to put on animal costumes and get together for fun things like group sex" (McMahon et al., 2009).

With fursuiters seeming to identify more strongly as furries, one might wonder whether this leads to a sense of status or elitism among fursuiters. After all, with fursuits being one of the most recognizable elements of the furry fandom, and with many furries wishing they could have a fursuit—a point we established earlier in this chapter—it's possible that fursuiters might reside atop a hierarchy in the furry fandom.[22] Our 2017 online study

[22] Anecdotally speaking, this would seem to be the case. We've observed, in conversations with furries at conventions, that younger, newer furries often look up to fursuiters in the community. In fact, I was compelled to get a fursuit not long after I joined the fandom for precisely this reason: I believed that getting a fursuit would validate me as an undisputed member of the furry fandom. This idea has gained even more traction in recent years, with many fursuiters achieving celebrity status in the furry fandom, having their own YouTube channels and fan following. I recall talking

found a bit of evidence supporting this point, with fursuiters rating themselves significantly higher in felt status in the fandom than non-fursuiting furry participants. This might suggest that fursuiters recognize the coveted place they often hold in the furry fandom. Even so, subsequent studies have shown that fursuiters are no more likely than non-fursuiters to gatekeep new fans (e.g., look down upon them, fail to see them as "real furries"), nor were they more likely than non-fursuiters to call themselves "Popufur"—a tongue-in-cheek term used to describe a well-known, celebrity-like furry.[23]

Fursuiters versus Non-Fursuiting Furries: Fursonas

Beyond asking whether fursuiters identify as more furry or are held in higher regard by the fandom, we can also ask whether having a fursuit is a sign of feeling more connected to one's fursona. After all, if we assume that most fursuits are based on a person's fursona, and if one of the functions of a fursuit is to allow fursuiters to embody their fursona out in the real world, then it would seem to follow that fursuiters may feel a greater sense of connection to their fursonas.

The data suggest that this is the case, a finding we've observed across a number of different online and convention-based studies. All else being equal, fursuiters identify more strongly with their fursonas than non-fursuiting furries. Of course, this doesn't mean that fursuiters are the only furries who identify strongly with their fursonas, nor does it mean that all fursuiters necessarily create fursuits of their fursonas or identify strongly with their fursonas. However, one can imagine that a person who did not identify strongly with their fursona might not feel especially compelled to spend thousands of dollars to commission a fursuit of their fursona or another character—although this might not be the case for all fursuiters.

In addition to identifying more strongly as their fursonas, fursuiters are also more likely than non-fursuiters to say that their fursona represents an idealized version of themselves and were less likely than non-fursuiters to say that they have changed their fursona over time. This would seem to reinforce the idea that fursuiters create fursuits based on their fursonas, in part based on a desire to be like and experience the world as an idealized

---

to one new furry at a convention who was hoping to meet the fursuiter who got them into furry and who inspired them to make a fursuit of their own!

[23] For more on gatekeeping and elitism in the furry fandom, please see Chapter 12.

version of themselves.[24] This being said, one of our studies in 2017 showed that fursuiters do not conflate the experience of wearing a fursuit with the idea of being an animal: fursuiters are no more likely than non-fursuiting furries to feel less than 100% human—although they are more likely to say that they would become 0% human if the chance ever presented itself. This finding counters yet another popular misconception among laypersons, that people who fursuit think that they are non-human animals, a point erroneously made in numerous news articles and even in speeches by politicians speaking out against furries (e.g., The Guardian, 2022).

Other studies shed additional light on fursuiters and their fursonas. For example, a 2016 study of convention-going furries found that fursuiters tended to see their fursonas as being more unique (e.g., in terms of species, and characteristics) than did non-fursuiting furries, although, according to a 2017 study, fursuiters did not differ from non-fursuiters concerning the specific species they chose for their fursonas.

But what about the fursuiters themselves—are there any measurable differences between fursuiters and non-fursuiters beyond their interest in the fandom or how they relate to their fursonas? Can we point to personality or demographic differences to determine who is more likely to become a fursuiter? Speaking to the former point, the evidence would seem to suggest yes. On a measure of five important personality traits, our 2017 study of online furries found that fursuiters scored significantly higher than non-fursuiters on three personality traits in particular: *extraversion* (being energized by being around other people), *agreeableness* (getting along well with other people), and *conscientiousness* (tendency to plan, think before acting, and pay attention to detail), but did not differ with respect to emotional stability and openness to new experiences (see Figure 8.7). In other words, fursuiters are, on average, more detail-oriented, get along better with people, and are more likely to seek out and be excited by opportunities to be social—the latter point of which corresponds with fursuiters being motivated by a desire to have fun and improve their interactions with other people.

Fursuiters also seem to differ from non-fursuiters demographically. Specifically, according to a pair of online studies, fursuiters, relative to non-fursuiters, are significantly more likely to be female, more likely to be transgender, and more likely to be straight. They are also significantly more

---

[24] This may, in fact, at least partially explain why fursuits may help facilitate social interaction with others: giving furries the confidence to interact with others by putting their best (fuzzy) foot forward!

likely to currently be in a relationship than are non-fursuiters. While we talk about many of these points in other chapters throughout this book (e.g., Chapter 13), it is worth noting a few points. First, the fact that fursuiters are more likely to be female corresponds with findings from other fandoms, including the anime fandom, showing that cosplayers are more likely to be female (Reysen et al., 2018). Second, female and transgender furries are also more likely to be artists and content creators, which might also facilitate fursuit ownership (i.e., having the skills needed to build a fursuit yourself instead of having to pay to commission one). Finally, as we discuss in Chapter 15, transgender furries are especially likely to highly identify with their fursonas, and, as we've mentioned earlier in this chapter, are more likely to say that their fursuit allows them to feel that their gender is accepted by others, both of which may explain why transgender furries may feel particularly compelled to fursuit.

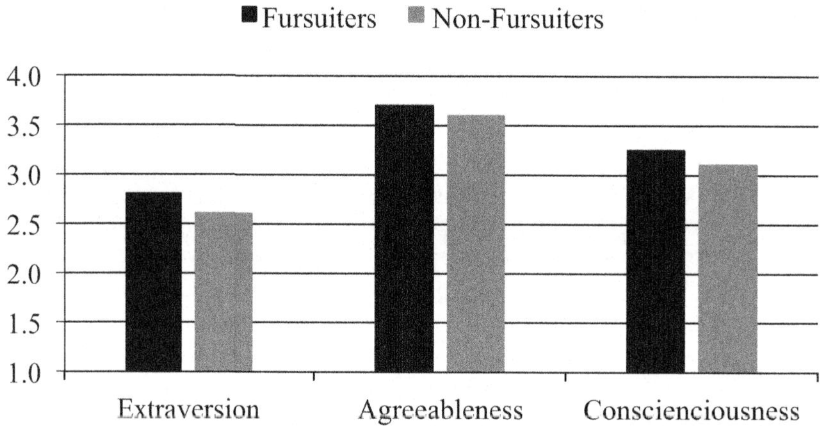

Figure 8.7. Fursuiters' and non-fursuiters' average scores on three personality traits assessed using a 1-5 scale. Differences between fursuiters and non-fursuiters shown are all statistically significant.

As we finish up this chapter, we'd like to consider one final misconception commonly held about fursuiters: that there must be something "wrong" with them. Fursuiting is a fairly unusual behavior, at least in the general population of non-furries. As such, when they see someone fursuiting, people—being amateur psychologists—may feel compelled to "explain" the behavior of fursuiters, doing so in an extreme way to account for what is seen as an extreme behavior. As such, they may turn to explanations that involve psychological dysfunction, suggesting that a person who would spend thousands of dollars on a fursuit must have poor planning or coping skills.

To the contrary, however, our 2020 study of online furries found that, while being especially passionate about their interest in furry, fursuiters are higher in healthy, "harmonious" passion than non-fursuiting furries, but they did not differ with respect to "obsessive" passion, the more reckless type of passion that predicts excess or dysfunctionality (Schellenberg et al., 2016). Likewise, fursuiters have generally been found to have higher self-esteem and overall psychological well-being than non-fursuiters across a multitude of studies, in no small part because, as found in a 2017 study of online furries, fursuiters are also more likely than non-fursuiters to have both given and received help from the furry fandom. For fursuiters, the furry fandom is especially likely to be an interest with a social component to it, increasing their likelihood of building a social support network. Such networks can prove vital as a source of resilience and a means to cope in difficult times (Roberts et al., 2015).

In fact, the only difference we've been able to find that might hint at maladaptation in fursuiters relative to non-fursuiters is a tendency for fursuiters to drink more than non-fursuiters do—alcoholic beverages, specifically. This was observed in a 2017 online study where the average fursuiter drank 3.3 alcoholic beverages per week as compared to the average non-fursuiter, who drank 2.2. Despite this difference, the levels of drinking are relatively low for both groups, and there is little evidence to suggest that this drinking behavior is frequently done to excess or causes any sort of problem in a systematic way for fursuiters.[25]

Conclusion

Despite being the most iconic and recognizable aspect of the furry fandom, arguably the most fascinating part of fursuiting is how unremarkable it is. Contextualized against other fan interests (e.g., cosplaying, wearing the jersey of one's favorite athlete), fursuiting is just another way for a fan's interest to manifest—neither necessary nor the most popular way for furries to express their interest, in part because it's prohibitively expensive for many!

Fursuiters have several motivations, not the least of which is for fun, as an outlet for their creativity and as a way to express themselves. There is also

---

[25] It goes without saying that it's important to stay hydrated while fursuiting! Alcoholic beverages have the opposite effect, and should generally be avoided while fursuiting.

evidence that having a fursuit may facilitate social interaction with others, allowing furries to be accepted for who they are, particularly if they're LGBTQ+ and struggle with stigma in day-to-day life.

While fursuiting may seem like a dramatically, categorically different way to engage with one's interest in furry content, evidence suggests that the differences between fursuiting and non-fursuiting furries tend to be a matter of degree rather than a matter of kind. Fursuiters do, on average, identify more strongly both as furries and with the furry fandom and are more involved in fan-related activities (e.g., going to conventions, consuming media), but this doesn't mean that someone without a fursuit cannot be equally passionate about being a furry. These differences may owe, at least in part, to fursuiters being in a better financial situation and being able to afford a fursuit, although there is also evidence suggesting that they may be motivated by being highly identified with their fursona. Fursuiters also differ somewhat from non-fursuiters demographically, being more likely to be female, transgender, and in a relationship than non-fursuiters, although this is a far cry from saying that all fursuiters are transgender or that all female furries are fursuiters.

Finally, and perhaps most importantly, we've seen how a little data can go a long way to dispelling misconceptions about fursuiting specifically and about furries in general. The studies in this chapter have shown that furries are not defined as people who wear fursuits (and, in fact, that most furries do not own a fursuit). Fursuiters are not motivated by a desire for sex in their fursuits or by a fetish-like interest in furry content, nor do they believe that they are non-human animals when they put on the fursuits. Fursuiters show no signs of maladaptation, which is perhaps one of the biggest surprises to non-furry laypersons, who might find themselves blaming dysfunction for the atypical, but otherwise harmless behavior of fursuiting.

As we continue our journey to better understand furries and the furry fandom, it will prove helpful to keep the lessons we've learned about fursuits in this chapter fresh in our minds. Just because an activity seems weird or unusual, that doesn't mean that it's evidence of seedy motivations or dysfunction. Sometimes a fursuit is just a fursuit.

References

Anthrocon 2010. (2023, May 13). In *Wikifur*. https://en.wikifur.com/wiki/Anthrocon_2010

Anthrocon 2022. (2023, May 13). In *Wikifur*. https://en.wikifur.com/wiki/Anthrocon_2022

Buffitt, K. (2014, July 3). Watch: Furries invade Pittsburgh. *Global News*. https://globalnews.ca/news/1430597/watch-furries-invade-pittsburgh/
Dickson, E. J. (2022, April 11). 'We're being bled dry': Furries aren't going to roll over for Etsy. *Rolling Stone*. https://www.rollingstone.com/culture/culture-news/furries-etsy-strike-1335805/
Higgins, E. T. (1987). Self-discrepancy: A theory relating self and affect. *Psychological Review, 94*(3), 319-340. https://doi.org/10.1037/0033-295X.94.3.319
Laychuk, R. (2020, January 29). Furry fandom: Westman furries break barriers and create smiles 1 sparkly dragon at a time. *CBC News*. https://www.cbc.ca/news/canada/manitoba/westman-furries-brandon-manitoba-1.5430922
McMahon, T. (Writer, Director), Arnarson, H. A. (Writer), & Miller, G. (Writer). (2009). Death over easy: Em-bear-assed [Television series episode]. In Original Productions (Producer), *1000 Ways to Die*. New York: Spike.
Petersen, K. S. (2022, April 8). Fact check: Wisconsin school district debunks claim that it has a 'furry protocol'. *USA Today*. https://www.usatoday.com/story/news/factcheck/2022/04/08/fact-check-wisconsin-school-district-doesnt-have-furry-protocol/9500305002/
Plante, C. N., Reysen, S., Brooks, T. R., & Chadborn, D. (2021). *CAPE: A multidimensional model of fan interest*. CAPE Model Research Team.
Reysen, S., Plante, C. N., Roberts, S. E., & Gerbasi, K. C. (2018). Motivations of cosplayers to participate in the anime fandom. *The Phoenix Papers, 4*(1), 29-40. https://doi.org/10.17605/OSF.IO/UT4FB
Roberts, S. E., Plante, C. N., Gerbasi, K. C., & Reysen. S. (2015). The anthrozoomorphic identity: Furry fandom members' connections to nonhuman animals. *Anthrozoös, 28*(4), 533-548. https://doi.org/10.1080/08927936.2015.1069993
Schellenberg, B. J. I., Bailis, D. S., & Mosewich, A. D. (2016). You have passion, but do you have self-compassion? Harmonious passion, obsessive passion, and responses to passion-related failure. *Personality and Individual Differences, 99*(5), 278-285. https://doi.org/10.1016/j.paid.2016.05.003
The Guardian. (2022, March 29). Republican retracts false claim schools placing litter boxes for 'furry' students. *The Guardian*. https://www.theguardian.com/us-news/2022/mar/29/nebraska-lawmaker-litter-boxes-claim-debunked

Thomas, D. (2022, February 2). Furries are leading the war against a book-banning Mississippi mayor. *Vice*. https://www.vice.com/en/article/wxdpen/mississippi-furry-book-banning

Torbatian, A. (2020). *Base fursuit prices* [Unpublished Raw Data]. Provided by Abigail Torbatian through private correspondence.

Walker, T. (2016, September 27). Killers and victims in California triple-murder were 'furries'. *Independent*. https://www.independent.co.uk/news/world/americas/killers-and-victims-in-california-triplemurder-were-furries-a7333956.html

Chapter 9
Makin' Stuff, Takin' Stuff: Furry Content

Stephen Reysen, Courtney "Nuka" Plante

According to an old saying, the best things in life are free. Whether this is true or not is a topic we'll leave to the philosophers because, as fan scholars, much of what we study is decidedly not free. Fan interests often involve the consumption of fan-related content or the creation of such content by fans to exchange or sell to other fans. We see this principle in action in the group of fans most studied by psychologists: sports fans. A sizable chunk of psychological research has been dedicated to understanding sports fan consumption habits, whether it's purchasing tickets to games or buying official merchandise (e.g., jerseys) to celebrate and display one's team affiliation. Meta-analyses compiling the results of numerous studies have found that the more strongly a person identifies as a fan of a particular team (i.e., fanship), the more likely they are to both purchase licensed merchandise (Kwon & Choi, 2018) and to attend games (Kim et al., 2019). Of course, Kim and colleagues (2019) found that other factors predict consumption beyond the extent to which one identifies as a fan (e.g., escapism, commitment to the team, the quality of the facility where the team plays, and even the physical attractiveness of the players), and certainly, there's more to being a sports fan than simply how much one consumes fan-related products and content. Nevertheless, fan consumption is big business, with sports, film, music, gaming, and other media franchises each representing multibillion-dollar industries—and so it's little wonder why there's so much demand for research into better understanding what drives fan consumption and what makes fans such reliable consumers.

Our work on the furry fandom hasn't been quite as focused on fan consumption, namely because we've aimed to understand the furry fandom from a multitude of perspectives (e.g., identity formation, well-being, social interaction). Nevertheless, we'd be remiss if we pretended to not be at least somewhat interested in furries' spending habits and the creation of content by the fandom for others in the fandom, if only because furries themselves (e.g., artists and other content creators) have frequently asked us questions about this topic.[1] In fact, in 2021 we released a book about fan cultures in

---

[1] It's not hard to imagine, for example, why a furry artist might have a vested interest in wanting to know about the size of the market for furry content, how much furries typically spend on different types of furry content, and what furries are looking for when it comes to furry merchandise.

general—but which prominently featured our work in the furry fandom that, among other things, developed a typology of fans and showed which types of fans were the most avid consumers of fan content (Plante et al., 2021).[2]

In the present chapter, we'll dive into some of this research to better understand both what furries consume (and how much of it they consume relative to other fan groups) and what predicts their fan-related consumption habits. First, we'll review the various fan activities that furries engage in—including consuming fan-related artifacts—to see how much particular types of consumption make up the bulk of furries' engagement with their interest in media featuring anthropomorphic characters. Next, we'll look at where furries seek out content and interaction with other furries in online spaces and how this is related to their felt connection to the furry fandom—do the same furries who go online to view furry content also go online to interact with other furries, or do they pursue furry as a solitary activity? This is followed by a look at what types of furry media furries tend to prefer. We'll then observe spending behaviors, looking at furry engagement in terms of actual dollars and cents, for those who are curious about the business of furry fanship. Lastly, we'll flip the script and look at furries not just as consumers of furry-themed content, but also as producers of it.

Consuming Fan Related Material

To begin our dive into fan-related consumption, we first wanted to get a brief overview of how common it was for furries to engage with various forms of fan-related content. Rather than looking at this data in isolation, we ran a parallel study in a sample of anime fans for comparison, allowing us to see which behaviors were distinct for furries and which were typical for comparable media-focused fandoms.

In this pair of studies, we asked both furries and anime fans to rate the frequency with which they engage in various fan-related behaviors (1 = *never* to 7 = *often*). As shown in Figure 9.1, the most frequent fan-related activities for furries was consuming furry media, both fan-made and official. While the predominance of consuming fan-related content was shared with anime fans, furries did differ significantly from anime fans in being significantly more likely to consume fan-made media. For furries, the consumption of fan-made media was just as important, if not more important, than the consumption of official media, whereas for anime fans there was a

---

[2] Just to be clear, however, we've never profited from our research, nor have we ever been paid by a company or organization to collect data on fans or for the purpose of market research.

significant preference for official media over fan-produced media.[3] As a potential downstream consequence of this, when it comes to the purchasing and collecting of fan-related merchandise, furries more frequently collect fan-made content, while anime fans are more likely to collect official content.

In contrast to the frequency with which furries consume fan-related media, the most infrequent of the activities involves attending in-person events (conventions, local meetups), something which was the case for both furries and anime fans. This is likely because fans are free to consume fan content whenever they want (e.g., streaming services, art distribution websites), but are limited in when they can attend real-world meetups to a handful of events in their region. For example, there may only be a single anime or furry convention in a year within driving distance of a given fan—if there's even one at all—while local gatherings and meet-ups may be limited to once-a-week or once-a-month gatherings. Even so, while furries and anime fans seem to attend conventions with about the same frequency, furries are significantly more likely to make it out to some kind of local meet-up.[4]

---

[3] This may stem from the fact that large studios and companies produce anime content specifically to be consumed by anime fans, meaning there is likely a larger market specifically for anime content. In contrast, very few major companies produce content specifically aimed at the furry fandom. Disney, for example, is a source of significant inspiration for many furries, but does not define itself as a producer of furry content. As a result, there may be a greater demand for unofficial, fan-made content tailored toward the furry fandom as a way to fill the void left by a lack of official producers of furry content.

[4] One possible explanation for this is that, as discussed in Chapter 13, furries tend to be a few years older than anime fans, on average. As such, it may be easier for them to make it out to local events (e.g., having a car, having the autonomy to go out to an event)—although this isn't a perfect explanation: It doesn't account for the fact that the two groups are nevertheless equally likely to make it out to a convention. An alternative explanation might be that there are simply more small-scale local furry meet-ups than anime meet-ups, although this explanation is also not without its drawbacks: The furry fandom is far smaller than the anime fandom, and so one would hypothesize that, if anything, there should be more anime meet-ups than furry meet-ups in a given locale. Despite being the smaller fandom, furries may simply be more likely than anime fans to host local meet-ups—for example, finding it more appealing to co-view content than anime fans, who might prefer to consume anime on their own.

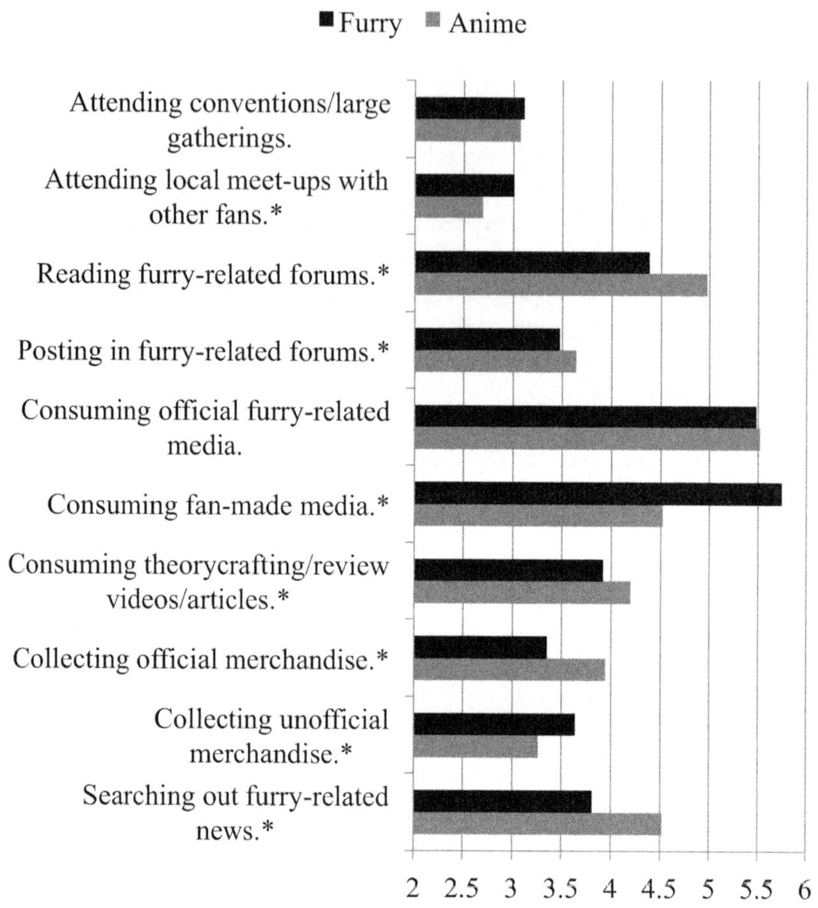

Figure 9.1. Mean ratings of the frequency with which furries and anime engage in various fan-related activities (7-point scale). * $p < .05$ significant difference.

Finally, the data also reveal other differences between furries and anime fans when it comes to interacting with other fans online. For instance, while furries seem to interact more in person than do anime fans (e.g., at local meet-ups), they are less likely to interact with anime fans on fan-related forums—both when it comes to posting and reading forums.[5] Perhaps related to this trend, furries are also less likely to actively seek out furry-related news than are anime fans.

Where do Furries Go Online?

In the previous section, we observed that media consumption and participating in furry forums were the fan-related activities that furries engaged in with the greatest frequency. Given that forums are obviously located online and given that furry content is frequently accessed by furries online,[6] we wondered whether there were common websites, repositories, or forums where furries most commonly congregated online.

To assess this, we constructed a list of furry-themed websites (some now defunct) based both on our the first-hand experience of one of our team's furry members, as well as from conversations with furries online and at conventions. After compiling this list, we asked furries in a survey to indicate whether they had visited or used any of the websites or programs in the past six months. As shown in Figure 9.2, the most popular site by far was FurAffinity, a website primarily used to share art and stories and which has built-in profile creation and forum features. Other popular websites and programs included Telegram, Twitter, Discord, and Facebook—all social media and communication websites developed for non-furries but prominently used by furries—and other art-sharing websites like e621, DeviantArt, InkBunny, SoFurry, and Weasyl. Furries also frequented forum-related websites like Reddit, specific convention websites, and F-List, a fetish-centered website that includes both forums and chat features that allow users to roleplay. Less common, but still somewhat frequented were furry

---

[5] This could be because there are simply more well-established or official forums in which anime fans can post relative to furry forums. Alternatively, it could be that furries may simply prefer other means of online communication, eschewing forums for other, more dynamic forms of online interaction like Telegram groups or VRChat.

[6] Many furries—especially those interest in the fandom formed in the 1990s and onward—cite the internet as a prominent source of inspiration. This is due, in no small part, to the ease with which furries are able to access furry-related content (e.g., art, stories) in a way that's been catalogued and organized by other furries. Given that there is no "official" furry fandom (as opposed to, say, the official Marvel or *Star Wars* fandom), it may be difficult to find furry content, with furry being a sort of meta-label loosely binding together a wide range of content that may, otherwise, have little else in common (e.g., Disney, science fiction stories, and anime stories that all share in common anthropomorphized animal characters).

news and information websites like Wikifur, our website (Furscience), and the news websites Dogpatch Press and Flayrah!

Taken together, these results highlight the focus of many furries' online activities as they seek out furry-themed media (e.g., FurAffinity) and communicate with other furries (e.g., Telegram), a finding consistent with the data we reviewed in the previous section. Next, we followed up this work by asking whether some online activities were more indicative of a furry's connection to the furry community. This question was inspired by the distinct, but related concepts of fanship and fandom (Chapter 6), which assess the extent to which someone identifies as a fan of something versus identifying with the fan community. It would make sense that those who frequent furry art websites with the intent of consuming furry media would be high in fanship, but this wouldn't necessarily speak to whether that furry was an active part of the furry fandom.[7] To test this, we conducted a type of statistical analysis called a *regression*, in which we were able to enter all of the different furry websites into the analysis simultaneously to see which ones predicted participant scores on fandom identification while statistically controlling for the fact that people who visit some websites might also visit other websites (e.g., users of FurAffinity—an art-sharing website—might also view other art-sharing websites like e621).

[7] This question is partly inspired by observations over the years that furries who claim to be furries "just for the porn" seem to avidly frequent furry content websites while having little interest in interacting with the broader furry community in-person or in online chatrooms or forums. This would be an example of someone high in fanship, but low in fandom.

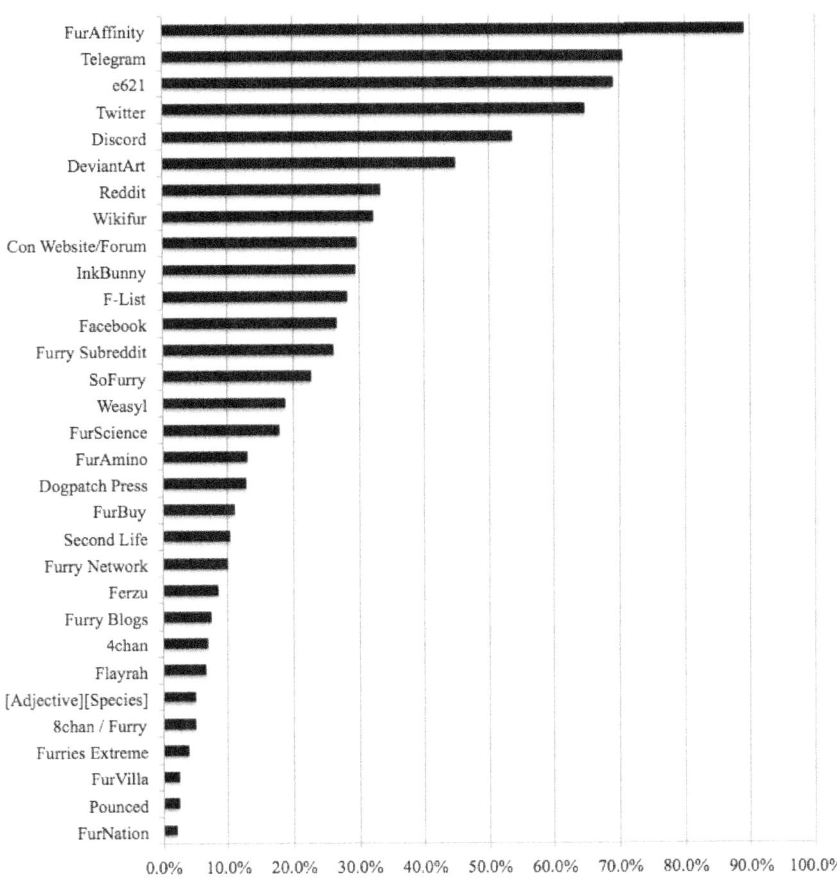

Figure 9.2. Websites visited by furries within the past six months.

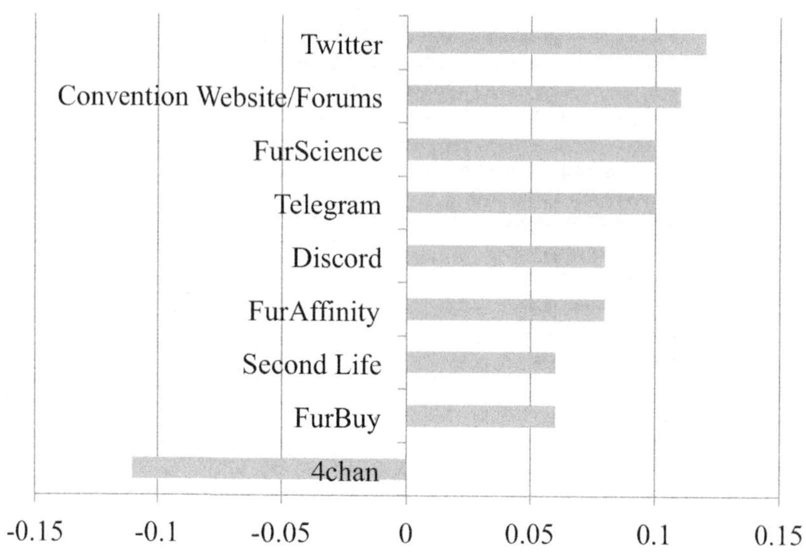

Figure 9.3. Websites frequented predicting furries' degree of fandom identification. All standardized betas are significant at $p < .05$.

In Figure 9.3 we illustrate the results of the analysis. First, for ease of presentation, we've removed all of the non-significant predictors—that is, all the websites that were unrelated to a person's fandom score. What we're left with are the websites that significantly predict the extent to which furries identify with the furry fandom: positive scores indicate that the more a furry uses that website, the higher their fandom scores tend to be, while negative scores indicate that the more a furry uses that website, the lower their fandom scores tend to be. As we can see, many of the communication and social media sites (Twitter, Telegram, Discord) emerged as significant predictors of fandom, which makes sense. Furries who are more involved in a fan community are more likely to rely on websites and programs like these to facilitate those social interactions.

Another significant predictor of fandom scores was the visiting of convention websites and forums. This, too, makes sense, given that those who are more connected to the furry fandom may be more inclined to attend a furry convention to be among other furries, which may require visiting a convention website to learn more about the convention (e.g., dates, hotel information, sign up to give a panel).

A few other websites emerged as predictors of fandom. Furscience was one such website, although it's not immediately clear what the link between this and fandom scores is. One possibility might be that furries learn about Furscience through friends within the furry community (they might be unlikely to stumble upon it spontaneously by themselves, or to seek it out if they are simply a lone furry perusing the internet for furry content). As for FurAffinity, it may emerge as the only art-themed site in the list because it is the single most popular website frequented by furries. As such, a member of the furry fandom may feel obligated to create a profile on FurAffinity simply because that's where most other furries can be located—and because it does have some forum features. Second Life—a site where furries can interact with other furries in a virtual world as a sort of precursor to more modern virtual reality programs (e.g., VRChat), represents another place where furries can interact with other furries (and is unlikely to be a solitary activity for most furries). As for FurBuy, a website focused on the auctioning of furry-themed items, it was a website where a furry could get an affordable fursuit (e.g., a used fursuit)—something which they would likely wear around other furries (e.g., at a furry convention), which might explain that connection with fandom scores.

Finally, we note that only one of the websites from the list emerged as a negative predictor of fandom scores: 4chan. The website 4chan is an imageboard that achieved a significant degree of infamy for, among other things, its "Random" board, wherein members could anonymously post images of anything that was not illegal. For years the website has had a mixed relationship with furries, both as a place where furry pornography is frequently posted and as a place where hatred toward furries is openly expressed. For this reason, a person who frequents 4chan may well epitomize someone who, despite liking furry content, may embrace a general disdain for the furry fandom as a whole and distance themselves from it.

Why Do Furries Like Furry Media?

So far we've established that furries are avid consumers of furry-themed media and that they frequently engage in behaviors (e.g., frequenting furry art websites) to access that content. Given the magnitude of this interest in furry media, it's worth asking what it is that furries like about furry media. After all, this is one of the questions we, as researchers, frequently find ourselves asked by laypersons and in media interviews: why do furries like furry media specifically and not something more *normal* and mainstream, like reality television, cooking shows, or sports? What do furries find so compelling about furry media that others simply don't resonate with?

To answer this question, we asked furries what it was about furry media that made it appealing to them. Specifically, in a survey study, we gave furries a list of reasons why a furry might be interested in media featuring anthropomorphized characters based on our observations of furries and conversations we've had with furries. For each of these reasons, furries listed the extent to which they agreed that it was a reason driving their interest in furry media using a 7-point scale.

As shown in Figure 9.4, the two biggest reasons why furries like media featuring furry characters are the same reasons why anyone might like any piece of media: they find the characters involved appealing and they enjoy the creativity involved. The same could almost certainly be expected of science-fiction fans who might appreciate the creativity of an alien world and a compelling alien species, or a fantasy world featuring creative settings and heroic protagonists.

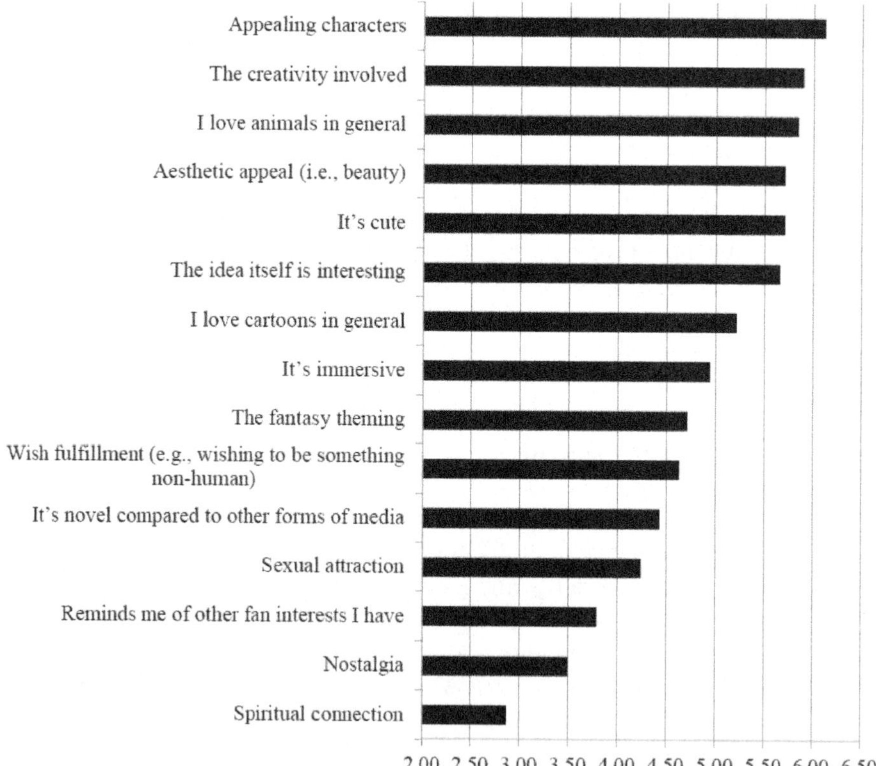

Figure 9.4. Mean ratings of factors that contribute to furries' interest in anthropomorphized animal characters (7-point scale).

It's not until you get to the third most common response that you find the first distinctly furry explanation: a general love of animals. It would make sense that a person with a particular fondness for animals (e.g., "cats and dogs are cute!") would be drawn to the aesthetics of a genre that prominently features characters with animal traits, and why someone who found animals generally unappealing might not find furry content to be all that endearing.[8]

As the list goes on, it becomes apparent that there is no singular reason why furries like furry content. Given that the midpoint of the scale is a 4, we can find that most of the items were agreed upon by most furries on average, but no one item single-handedly dominated the rest. Instead, it would seem that furries' interest is likely the interplay of a multitude of factors ranging from aesthetic appeal and fondness for animals to finding the creativity of the worlds in furry stories compelling and immersive.

It is worth making a couple of notes about this list before we move on. First, despite the popular misconception that furry is, first and foremost a fetish, the data in this table shows that, at best, sexual attraction to content featuring animals with human-like traits is a relatively weak driver of furry interest. We'll return to this point in more detail in Chapter 19, but for now, it's sufficient to say that sex doesn't seem to be what drives most furries to their interest in furry-themed media. Second, an overlap between furry and other interests (e.g., other fan interests, spirituality) doesn't seem to be what drives furries to their interest, nor does it appear to be residual nostalgia for something from furries' past.[9]

Spending Money

This chapter began by talking about fan spending as big business, given that fans are passionate about the things they love and, therefore, might be expected to enthusiastically spend money in the pursuit of that interest. With

---

[8] Notably, however, this doesn't seem to explain why *furry* media would be preferred specifically. If anything, this would seem to predict a person preferring shows that feature real animals (e.g., a movie about dogs or cats) over shows that feature anthropomorphized characters!

[9] This last point is especially surprising to the authors, both of whom would have hypothesized, in line with many furries' lay theories on this subject, that furries are interested in furry media as a side effect or leftover from most kids' interest in cartoons (many of which featured anthropomorphic characters like Bugs Bunny or Mickey Mouse). While many furries, like many non-furries, may have grown up with these cartoons, the interest as an adult seems to be something broader and perhaps more active than mere nostalgia.

that in mind, let's turn our attention to how furries spend money on their interest.

As with earlier sections, simply knowing the amount of money furries spend in isolation is not especially useful. Instead, we'll need context to be able to assess whether furries, compared to other fan groups, spend an inordinate amount or whether they are fairly frugal in their consumption spending. To this end, in this section we compare the extent to which anime fans and furries engage in six different types of purchases. Specifically, we asked participants how much money they have spent in the past 12 months (in U.S. dollars), and how much they would be willing to spend in that same period, if they had the disposable income to do so. The results are shown in Figures 9.5 and 9.6.

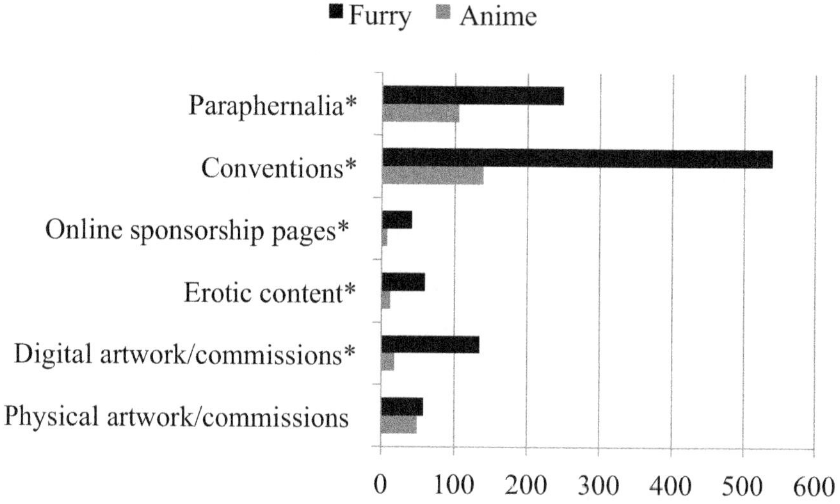

Figure 9.5. The amount of money that anime fans and furries have spent in the past 12 months. * $p < .05$.

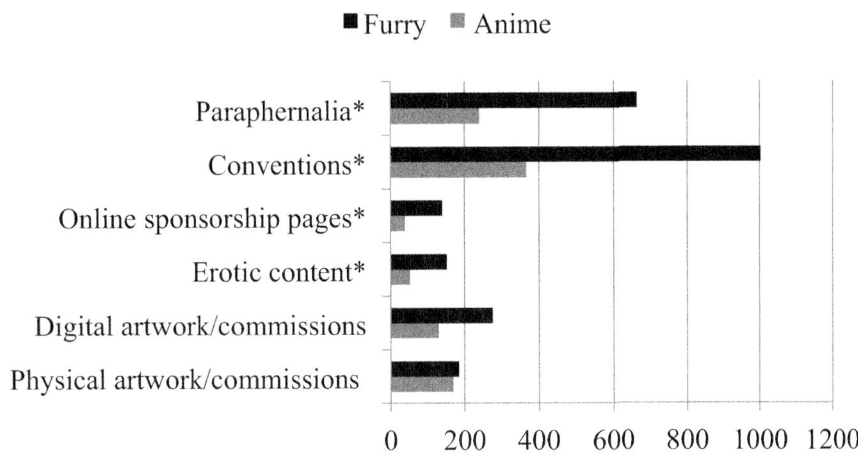

Figure 9.6. The amount of money anime fans and furries would be willing to spend. * $p < .05$.

The first thing to note is that the pattern of results is basically the same whether we're talking about actual spending or willingness to spend, with the only difference being a matter of scale—fans were willing to spend about twice as much as they currently spend. In other words, the data would seem to suggest that fans prioritize their spending in a way that matches their level of interest. For example, it doesn't seem like fans are reducing their spending on fan conventions simply to be able to buy proportionately more artwork or to support more content creators on websites like Patreon.

With that in mind, we can turn our attention to spending on specific categories of content. First, the data show that furries significantly outspend anime fans in all categories except for physical artwork or commissions.[10]

[10] One straightforward explanation may be that furries simply buy *more* stuff, attend more conventions, and support more artists online than anime fans. An alternative explanation is that furries and anime fans buy the same amount of stuff, but things are simply more expensive in the furry fandom (e.g., a furry convention might cost more than an anime convention to attend). Anecdotally speaking, in our research at both anime and furry conventions, we've overheard artists mention that they prefer to sell at furry conventions over anime conventions because of furries' looser spending habits. The claim is that anime fans complain or attempt to haggle prices while furries will simply slap down whatever the asking price is without question. The results would certainly support this anecdotal observation, although it's not a

Beyond this general tendency to spend more, however, furries do show a fairly similar pattern of spending as anime fans—namely, a tendency to spend the most on fan conventions and fan-related paraphernalia, such as t-shirts, stickers, badges, and other trinkets denoting one's membership in the fandom. This is likely because a single fan convention may cost hundreds of dollars while a single piece of artwork is more likely to cost somewhere from $10-100 on average. Given that fans could potentially get a dozen pieces of artwork or purchase numerous t-shirts or trinkets with the money spent on a single fan convention, it is telling that fans nevertheless seem to value being able to interact with other fans in person at fan conventions above simply collecting merchandise.

Curious readers may find that they have more questions than answers after reading the previous results. For instance, while the data refer to fans' spending habits in the previous year, there are other potentially interesting metrics. For example, a furry may save up for years to purchase a $3,000 fursuit, and unless the survey assessed their purchasing habits in the year they got the fursuit, it might miss this significant example of fan-related spending. Likewise, the above list of spending, in trying to be inclusive enough to be comparable between furries and anime fans, overlooks spending on items that may be unique to furries (e.g., fursuits, which lack an equivalent in the anime fandom). To this end, in a later study, we asked a sample of furries about a wider range of spending behaviors and asked specifically about lifetime rates of spending, rather than just the past 12 months (see Figure 9.7). However, this question is not without its problems: it has no way of distinguishing a furry who has made dozens of small art purchases that add up to a large amount over time and a furry who has made a single, large purchase. To account for this, in addition to asking participants how much amount they have spent on each category over their lifetime, we also asked them to indicate the amount of the single-largest purchase they've made in each category (see Figure 9.8).

---

perfect explanation for the findings. After all, this wouldn't necessarily explain why furries spend significantly more to sponsor/support artists online.

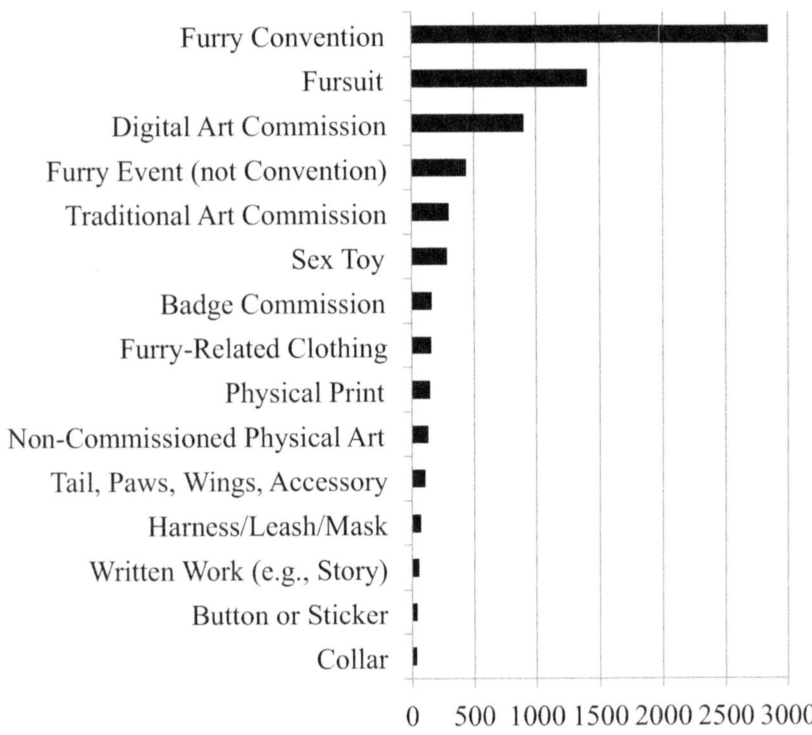

Figure 9.7. The amount of money furries spend in their lifetime.

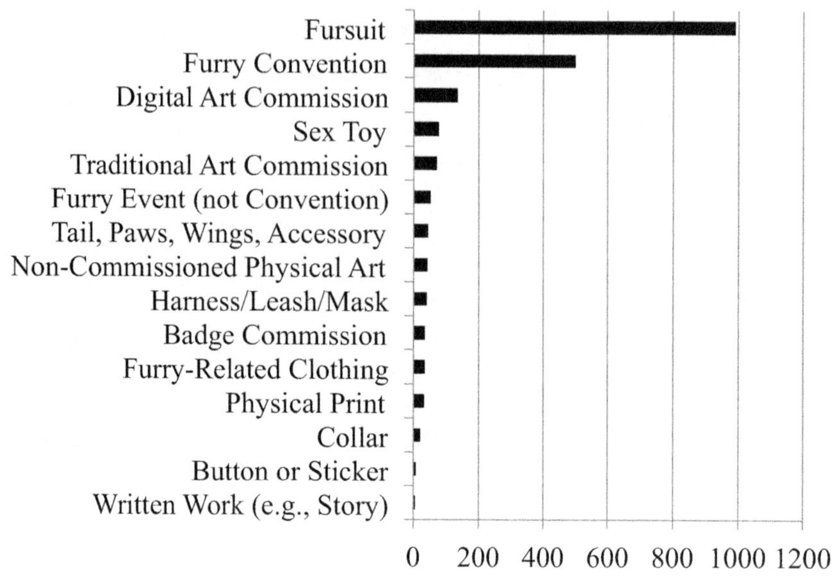

Figure 9.8. The single largest purchase made.

The distinction seems to be a telling one: looking just at lifetime purchases, it would seem that conventions represent the single-biggest expenditure for a furry—and, indeed, considered over a lifetime, this is the case. However, when it comes to individual purchases, there's no contest: fursuits represent the single-biggest purchase that many furries make.[11] And, in terms of the magnitude of single purchases, fursuits and convention attendance represent, by far, the single-largest purchases that furries make, with the next-biggest single purchase for many furries being a digital art commission, somewhere in the vicinity of about $150.[12] Nevertheless, the frequency with which furries commission artwork is revealed in the lifelong spending of furries, where spending on digital art commissions accumulates over time. Of course, the data also make it clear that conventions, unlike

[11] Keep in mind that, as we saw in Chapter 8, most furries do not own a fursuit. As such, the value shown for fursuits is an average calculated based on the fact that, for most furries, this value is "$0." A typical fursuit costs somewhere in the vicinity of $2,000-3,000—an amount that is prohibitively expensive for many furries who would like to own a fursuit.

[12] With a notable distinction between them being that while most furries do not own a fursuit, most furries do attend furry conventions (see Chapter 9).

fursuits, are seldom one-off purchases: most furries have attended at least a few of them, making the lifelong cost of conventions fairly high. It's a telling reminder that, despite attempts to trivialize fan hobbies as insignificant or silly, fans take them very seriously and invest a significant amount in them.

We'd be remiss if we didn't point out that several of the biggest expenditures for furries are for things that are, arguably, social in nature and thus indicative of fandom identification rather than fanship. For example, going to a furry convention, as we've found previously, is tied to fandom identification. Likewise, it would follow that a fursuit and other paraphernalia, which are often worn in social contexts as a display of one's fan identification, should similarly be tied to fandom identification. To this end, we ran an analysis comparing furries and anime fans, both with respect to the amount of money they've spent in the past year (which is predominantly spent on paraphernalia and convention attendance) and concerning their fanship and fandom scores. This specific type of analysis, called a *mediation analysis*, allows us to test specifically whether the difference in spending between furries and anime fans that we observed is accounted for, at least in part, by differences in fanship and, more importantly, fandom scores. The results are shown in Figure 9.9.

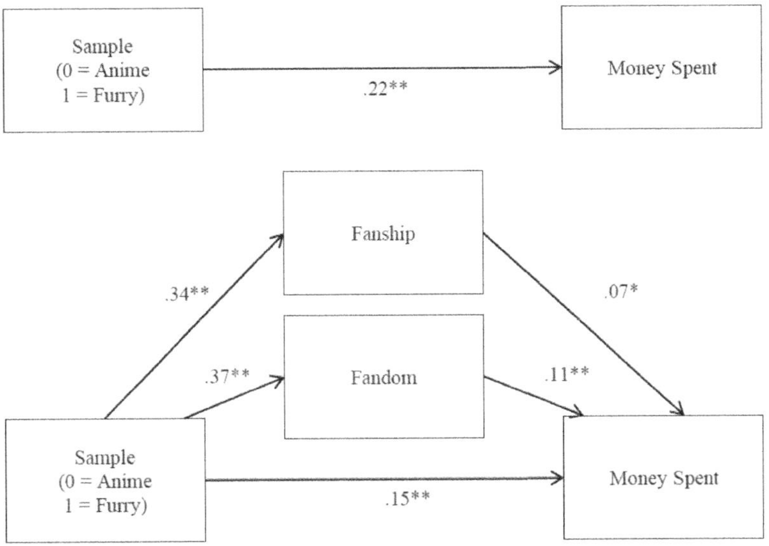

Figure 9.9. Mediation model of sample comparison predicting money spent through fanship and fandom. Standardized betas are presented. $N = 3136$, * $p < .05$, ** $p < .01$.

What this figure shows is that furries do, on average, score higher than anime fans on both money spent and on fanship and fandom scores. It also shows that both fandom and fanship are tied to spending habits, with higher fanship and fandom identification predicting greater spending. Most importantly, the analysis found that you can account for at least part of the difference in spending between furries and anime fans by taking into account differences in fanship and fandom scores—the fact that furries score higher in fanship and fandom is a possible explanation, albeit not a complete one, for why furries spend more.[13]

Motivations to Spend

Earlier we looked at a study testing what compels furries to be interested in furry-themed media in the first place. Similarly, we also ran a study asking furries what, specifically, compels them to make furry-related purchases. After all, watching a show or admiring a piece of artwork is a fairly passive experience, one that doesn't cost a person anything. Making a purchase, however, is active and costs a furry something. As such, we'll need to consider a different set of motivations to explain purchasing behavior—one can, after all, appreciate a piece of media without wanting to purchase it.

To delve into what motivates furries to make furry-related purchases, we asked them to rate several different motivations that may have affected their decision to spend, motivations that were drawn from a combination of prior work on consumer spending more generally and based on our prior observations as researchers who study various fan groups. The results are shown in Figure 9.10.

The most highly-rated motivation was, predictably enough, the extent to which furries wanted something. In other words, furries were making purchases that they wanted to make, rather than purchases they felt compelled to make based on peer pressure or obligation, as seen by these items being among the lowest motivations on the list. Other strong motivators included positive feelings associated with the purchase (e.g., going to a convention because it's fun), aesthetic appreciation (e.g., liking a

[13] These findings may shed light on our anecdotal evidence of the artists preferring to sell at furry conventions rather than anime conventions: perhaps furries are willing to spend more money unquestionably than anime fans because furries are simply bigger fans and may think about their purchases in the context of their fandom identification (e.g., being able to show this off and have it valued by other furries). We turn to this point in the next section.

piece of art and wanting to own it as such), wanting something to express a part of themselves (e.g., a fursuit to express a fursona, or commissioning art of one's fursona), and as a way to support another furry (e.g., commissioning a friend who is a content creator). In short, furries felt driven to make fan-related purchases for many different reasons, most of which are straightforward (e.g., people buy a new couch because they want it and because it would look good in their living room) and some of which are even laudable (e.g., to help out a furry content creator), with little evidence suggesting that furry spending is compulsive and, by extension, maladaptive (for more on this, see Chapter 22).[14]

[14] In a follow-up analysis, we tested whether these different motivations predict specific types of spending. The desire to have something specifically predicted spending on physical furry art. Peer pressure, showing off to other furries, and building a collection, on the other hand, were significant predictors of spending money on erotic art. Supporting another furry was the strongest predictor of money spent on sponsorship pages (e.g., Patreon), while "good feelings" predicted spending on conventions.

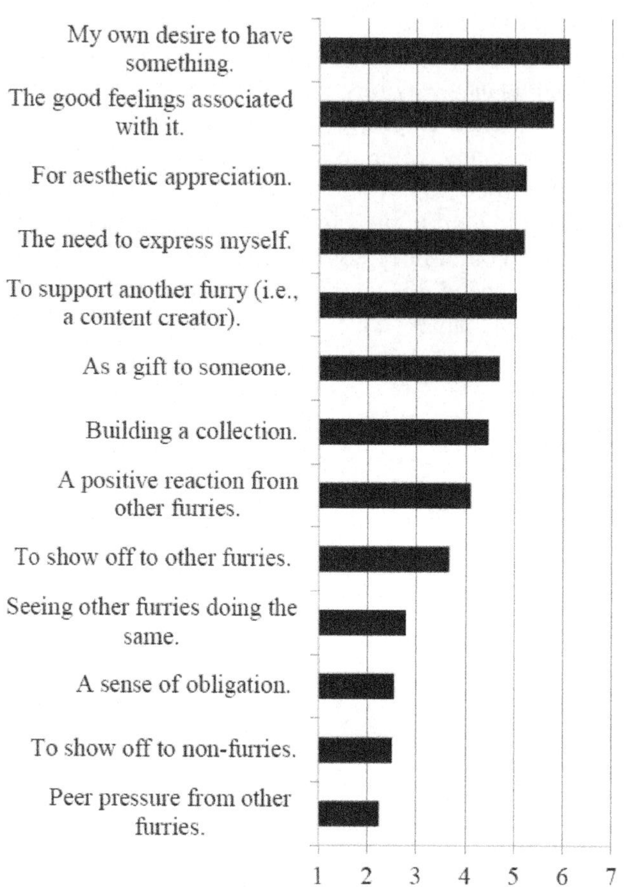

Figure 9.10. Mean ratings of motivations to spend money (7-point scale).

A few other noteworthy trends emerged when we looked at what compelled furries to spend and other measures of interest. For example, one analysis revealed that those who were motivated to spend due to peer pressure, because they saw other furries doing the same, and because they wanted to show off to other furries, also scored higher on a measure assessing the extent to which they wanted to conform with the furry fandom more broadly. Another analysis, looking at psychological needs and well-being (e.g., Rubin, 2017), found that those who purchase to show off tend to have lower self-control over their behavior in general, while those who made purchases to express themselves were people more likely to be searching for meaning in their lives and to have a greater need to be unique.

As a final, interesting look at this motivation data, we found that those who purchased to build a collection were also people who had a greater need to buffer or protect themselves against the existential anxiety of their own eventual death. This finding is in line with prior research on a subject known as *terror management theory* (TMT; Greenberg et al., 1986; Pyszczynski et al., 1997). TMT argues that humans are aware of their eventual death and act in ways to avoid the existential fear that comes with knowing there's nothing they can do to stop the inevitability of their death. According to the theory, people defend their cultural beliefs and seek meaning in life as a way to cope (or distract) from the fear of death. TMT researchers suggest that materialism may be one such defense mechanism, a distraction (Arndt et al., 2004). Speaking to this idea, Kasser and Sheldon (2000) found that after they put death on the minds of participants in a study, the participants expressed a greater expectation that they would soon spend money on things that made them feel good (e.g., clothing, entertainment, leisure). While we wouldn't go so far as to say that any furry looking to build a collection is consciously thinking about death and trying to distract themselves from it, it is worth noting that compiling a large and impressive collection of art to show off to others has at least superficial similarities to the great pharaohs of yore building pyramids and monuments that would exist to be admired long after they, themselves, had perished!

Commissions

As we've seen throughout this chapter, furries purchase a considerable amount of artwork. However, not all artwork purchasing is the same. For example, there is a difference between purchasing a print or acquiring a piece of art that was produced by an artist based on their inspiration and commissioning a one-of-a-kind piece from your favorite artist based on your specifications, interests, and characters.[15]

To assess the frequency with which furries commissioned artwork directly from artists, we asked them to indicate how many times they had commissioned art throughout their lives. As shown in Figure 9.11, the vast majority of furries have done so at least once, with only 18.9% stating that they had never commissioned an artist or writer to produce something specifically for them. While the single most common response to this question was to have commissioned art between one and five times in one's life, most furries have commissioned art more than five times. And while slightly less than 10% of furries have commissioned more than 50 pieces of

---

[15] For one thing, commissioned art is often an order of magnitude more expensive than simply purchasing a print!

work in their lifetime, they may well represent what some industries (e.g., the video game industry) call "whales"—reliable, repeat customers with fairly deep pockets who, if their loyalty can be earned, represent a lucrative client for any content creator.[16]

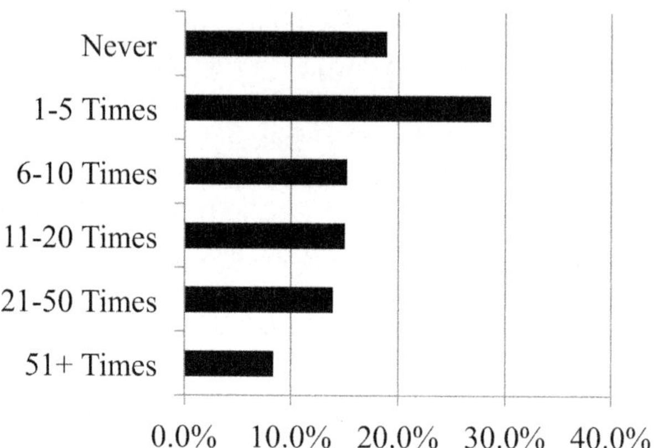

Figure 9.11. Frequency of commissioning a furry artist or writer.

[16] Anecdotally, based on conversations with furry artists, some of the most reliable customers are those who can have a very specific request fulfilled by a particular artist. For example, if one has a very particular or unusual interest—perhaps an uncommon fetish or a fascination with extreme violence and gore in art—they may struggle to find artists who are willing to accept their commissions. If they do find an artist who is willing to accept such requests (or even excel/specialize in that content), it's likely the commissioner may return to the artist for future commissions, knowing that they may be unable to find anyone else willing to accept the commission. On the flip side of this, some artists may find themselves typecast as being a particular type of artist; if it becomes known that an artist is able and willing to do the type of commission that most other artists would turn down, word of this may spread among enthusiasts of that type of commission, leading to the artist becoming renowned for that type of work. To avoid this sort of typecasting, some artists may accept such commissions under alternate accounts/pseudonyms.

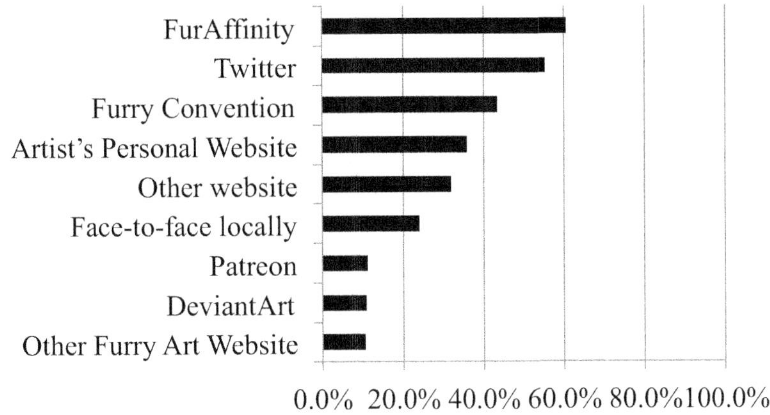

Figure 9.12. Places that furries commonly go to commission furry art.

In addition to asking furries about the frequency with which they commission art, we also asked them to list where they typically go when looking to commission an artist. The results, shown in Figure 9.12, reveal a familiar website when it comes to finding artists to commission: FurAffinity. Indeed, in addition to being the most popular site for furries to find and share artwork online, it is also where many furries discover artists they like, given that any piece that catches a viewer's eye will link back to the profile and gallery of its creator and, in turn, usually features the contact information of the creator. Other popular websites through which to commission artists include Twitter, personal websites built by artists, and websites like Patreon and DeviantArt. It's also worth noting that, despite the internet's ability to put clients in touch with artists, many commissioners still commission artists in person at conventions or through local meet-ups.

Fan Production

In the previous section, we began to transition our focus from fans as content consumers to fans as content producers. In this final section, we'll finish that transition by focusing our attention on those who create content for the furry fandom. Specifically, we looked at the extent to which furries considered themselves to be content creators. As we began alluding to earlier in this chapter, a distinguishing feature of the furry fandom is its decentralized nature. Unlike other fandoms, such as the *Star Wars*, Marvel, or *Harry Potter* fandoms, which are focused around a single franchise whose content is primarily produced by a single studio, artist, or corporation, the furry fandom is a conglomerate of different content producers ranging in size from the Disney corporation all the way down to small, independent artists, musicians, and writers. As such, while there is certainly fan-produced content in other fandoms, the focus of the fandom around a main, central pillar of content may steal the spotlight from small, independent content creators in a way that doesn't happen in the furry fandom.[17]

To test this possibility, we asked a sample of both furries and anime fans to indicate the extent to which they considered themselves to be writers and artists. As shown in Figure 9.13, furries scored significantly higher than anime fans on both being a writer and being an artist, consistent with what we've been suggesting. To put it another way, the average furry is more likely to see themselves as being an artist or a writer than the average anime fan is. To be sure, not every furry who considers themselves to be an artist or a writer is claiming to be independently employed and able to support themselves on their craft. It does, however, hint at the possibility that furries are more likely to create content themselves rather than being passive consumers of content.[18]

---

[17] We've already seen evidence for this possibility in the amount that furries and anime fans spend on official versus fan-made content, with furries consistently outspending anime fans with respect to fan-made content. This suggests that fan-made content may be more abundant in the furry fandom, or it may simply be valued more highly than it is in the anime fandom.

[18] Contributing further to this point is the fact that most furries create a fursona for themselves, usually early on their involvement with the furry fandom (see Chapter 7). This means that, for many furries, their first involvement in the furry fandom involves and act of creation (e.g., creating a character as part of a shared furry space).

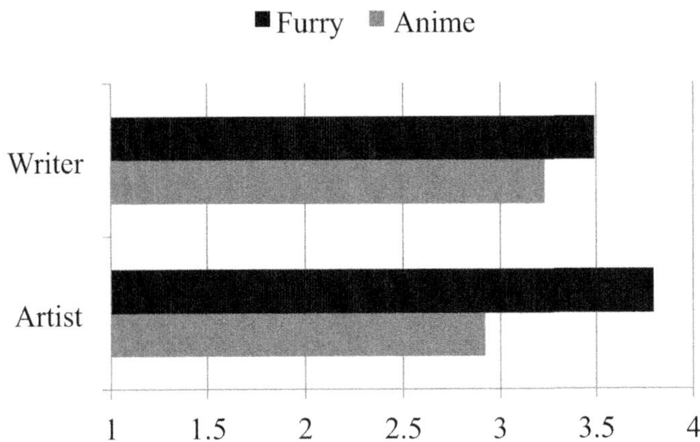

Figure 9.13. Mean ratings of furry and anime fans as writers/artists (7-point scale).

Let's finish with a last analysis that puts many of the things we've learned throughout this chapter together. First, the research discussed elsewhere in this chapter suggests that furries, despite lay misconceptions to the contrary, tend to do fairly well in terms of their well-being (see Chapter 22). Beyond this, we also know that furries tend to identify fairly highly with their fan communities (something which, in turn, is likely associated with well-being, since fan communities may provide a source of social support). We've also just seen that furries, in addition to identifying more strongly with their fandom than other fans (e.g., anime fans, see Chapter 6), are also more likely to produce content for their fandom than anime fans. These points in particular are important because prior research has shown that both fandom identification (Reysen et al., 2017; Reysen et al., 2021; Reysen et al., in press) and producing art (Fancourt & Finn, 2019) are associated positively with greater well-being.

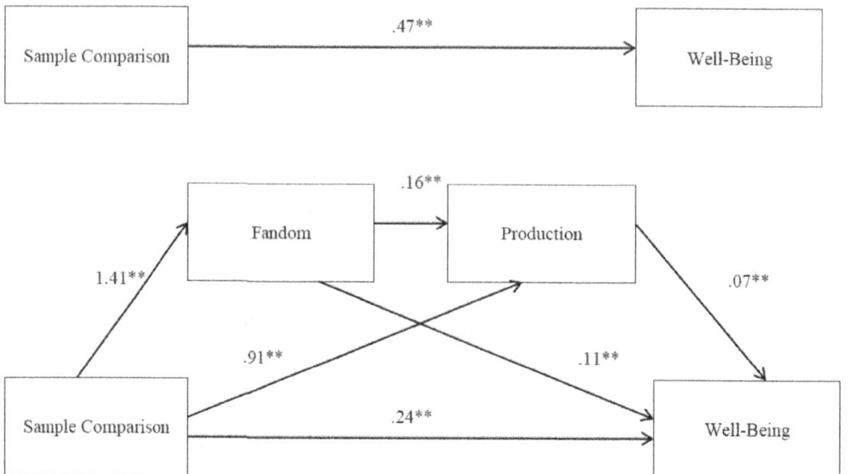

Figure 9.14. Serial mediation model with fandom identification and production as mediators of the relationship between sample comparison (0 = anime, 1 = furry) and psychological well-being. Unstandardized betas shown. ** $p < .01$.

So what if we tested a model that puts this all together? What if there are differences in the well-being of furries and anime fans—might these differences be accounted for by the fact that furries identify more strongly with their fandom and by the fact that furries produce more content themselves than anime fans? We tested the model—called a serial mediation model—and show it below in figure Figure 9.14. Put simply, we found evidence for every path predicted in this model: not only do furries score higher than anime fans in terms of well-being, but this effect seems to be driven, at least in part, by the fact that furries identify more strongly with their fandoms and, in turn, by the fact that furries are more active producers of fan content. In effect, being part of a community where producing fan content is normal and may foster connections between other furries and content creators could have beneficial downstream outcomes for furries' well-being.

Conclusion

We started this chapter with what some might consider to be a somewhat cynical, utilitarian view of fans, the way they might be seen by a corporation: fans, through their passionate interests, are ardent and reliable consumers of fan-related content. This has been shown in research on sports fans (e.g.,

Kim et al., 2019) and is the sort of research that a media franchise might draw upon when considering how to best extract profits from their fanbase.

It's been our goal, as we've moved through this chapter, to shift the focus away from mere dollars and cents to instead focus on the nuances and complexities of fan consumption and production. As it turns out, we can gain a much deeper understanding of fans through this work—a better understanding not only of how they consume, but, more importantly, why they consume and the significance of their consumption. Fan consumption, especially in the furry fandom, is far from a mindless, passive, obsessive endeavor where fans simply throw money at whatever has been churned out by a corporation's factories. Instead, fans purchase content for a wide range of purposes ranging from a desire to self-express to wanting to help struggling independent artists make ends meet. We've seen that many of the places where furries go to get their artwork, in turn, are places where furries congregate to network and interact. We've also seen that when it comes to their furry interest, many furries' biggest expenditures are not for the collection of stuff but rather to make it out to conventions where they can interact with other furries in person—the pursuit of shared positive experiences. And while most furries do commission art, their interest in the content itself is often a complex interplay of motivations that, in many cases, are no different than the motivations that drive everyone to whatever interests they may have. Despite the stigma furries often experience for having an unusual fan interest, at the end of the day the most telling finding has been how relatively unremarkable the underlying motivations for this interest are—a lesson that will repeat itself throughout this book.

As a take-away message from this chapter, we reiterate another point that we make throughout this book: just because a person's interest is unusual or seems silly, that doesn't mean that it's not deeply significant and beneficial to that person. One person's $3,000 fursuit or $1,000 furry convention is another person's self-expression or social support network, and may well be the thing that helps them to weather life's challenges and even an existential crisis or two.

References

Arndt, J., Solomon, S., Kasser, T., & Sheldon, K. M. (2004). The urge to splurge: A terror management account of materialism and consumer behavior. *Journal of Consumer Psychology, 14*(3), 198-212. https://doi.org/10.1207/s15327663jcp1403_2

Fancourt, D., & Finn, S. (2019). *What is the evidence on the role of the arts in improving health and well-being? A scoping review*. World Health Organization. https://apps.who.int/iris/handle/10665/329834

Greenberg, J., Pyszczynski, T., & Solomon, S. (1986). The causes and consequences of a need for self-esteem: A terror management theory. In R. F. Baumeister (Ed.), *Public self and private self* (pp. 189-212). Springer.

Kasser, T., & Sheldon, K. M. (2000). Of wealth and death: Materialism, mortality salience, and consumption behavior. *Psychological Science, 11*(4), 348-351. https://doi.org/10.1111/1467-9280.00269

Kim, Y., Magnusen, M., Kim, M., & Lee, H. W. (2019). Meta-analytic review of sport consumption: Factors affecting attendance to sporting events. *Sport Marketing Quarterly, 28*(3), 117-134. http://doi.org/10.32731/SMQ.283.092019.01

Kwon, H., & Choi, M. (2018). The relationship between team identification and consumption behaviors using a meta-analysis: Intention to attend sport events and to purchase sport team licensed merchandise. *Korean Journal of Sport Science, 29*(2), 315-327. https://doi.org/10.24985/kjss.2018.29.2.315

Plante, C. N., Reysen, S., Brooks, T. R., & Chadborn, D. (2021). *CAPE: A multidimensional model of fan interest*. CAPE Model Research Team.

Pyszczynski, T., Greenberg, J., & Solomon, S. (1997). Why do we need what we need? A terror management perspective on the roots of human social motivation. *Psychological Inquiry, 8*(1), 1-20. https://doi.org/10.1207/s15327965pli0801_1

Reysen, S., Plante, C., & Chadborn, D. (2017). Better together: Social connections mediate the relationship between fandom and well-being. *AASCIT Journal of Health, 4*(6), 68-73.

Reysen, S., Plante, C. N., Chadborn, D., Roberts, S. E., & Gerbasi, K. (2021). *Transported to another world: The psychology of anime fans*. International Anime Research Project.

Reysen, S., Plante, C. N., Roberts, S. E., & Gerbasi, K. C. (in press). Social activities mediate the relation between fandom identification and psychological well-being. *Leisure Sciences*. https://doi.org/10.1080/01490400.2021.2023714

Rubin, M. (2017). An exploratory measure of multiple motives. *Figshare*. 10.6084/m9.figshare.4502738

Chapter 10
OwO What's this? Sex and Pornography

Thomas R. Brooks, Frances H. I. Henry,
Anna R. Henry, Courtney "Nuka" Plante

My first furry convention was in 2017 at Texas Furry Fiesta in Dallas, Texas. This was my first year as a graduate student studying human sexuality under Dr. Stephen Reysen, and I, like many, was under the mistaken preconception that the furries were a fandom primarily motivated by sex. Through my subsequent experiences attending conventions, collecting data, and working closely with Furscience, I came to appreciate the complex nature of the furry fandom and the negotiations about sex and sexuality regularly discussed by furries both in-person and online. I learned that sexuality, while present, was not the primary reason for this collective of creatives to come together and support each other through shared interests and experiences. I learned about the openness and friendliness of the community and I was amazed by the willingness of the community to share their curiosity about themselves with Furscience.

Coming from a background of research in human sexuality, I am well aware of the problems that come with conducting sex research—it's a tough sell to ask people to share the most intimate details about themselves with a researcher. Working with furries has been a breath of fresh air, as they've proven themselves, time and time again, to be eager to share their experiences, beliefs, and preferences with me. In fact, our data show that the fandom may be distinct in this willingness to share information about their sexuality with researchers: in a 2017 online study furries, when compared to other fan groups (e.g., anime fans, bronies—adult fans of *My Little Pony*), furries were far more willing to discuss intimate details about their sex lives with researchers. Likewise, a 2013 convention sample of furries acknowledged that they were significantly more willing to discuss the topic of porn with others than were a sample of college students. Such openness provides a unique space for sex research, as it makes it easier to trust the information being shared with me by members of the furry fandom.[1]

[1] As an illustrative example: if a participant says that they seldom, if ever, look at pornography, should they be taken at their word? If pornography use is seen as something socially deviant or undesirable, a person who does look at pornography might feel compelled to downplay their porn use in a study, so as to avoid being judged negatively by researchers. But if someone is part of a community that speaks both frankly and positively about sex, then the person's claim that they don't look at

Of course, this distinct openness and willingness to talk about sex also leads to a conundrum: it is difficult to meaningfully compare rates of sexual motivation, kinks and fetishes, and pornography use between furries and other non-furry groups. Imagine, for example, we ran a study and found that furries report having more kinks than do non-furries. One interpretation of this data is that furries are simply more kinky than non-furries, an explanation that presumes the difference is in the sexual practices of the two groups. Alternatively, the difference could be a difference in willingness to disclose kinks to a researcher—perhaps furries and non-furries are equally kinky, but furries are more willing to talk about it. In this case, it's almost impossible to disentangle the two explanations for group-level differences in kinkiness.[2]

As we explore sexuality in the furry fandom in this chapter, please keep this in mind. We tend to consider the data from furries to be unusually sincere as far as typical sex research is concerned, and so it's worth remembering that if you wouldn't expect the sorts of responses noted here in a sample from the general population, that might say more about the honesty and openness of the average person than it says about the deviance of furries. In short, we should be cautious and resist the temptation to make one-to-one comparisons between this data on furry sexuality and data on sexuality from more mainstream samples.

Sexuality in the Furry Fandom

Before we explore sexual dynamics within the furry fandom, it's important to understand the complex meta-relation furries have with sexuality and pornography in the fandom. Mainstream views of furries typically portray furries as sexually motivated and deviant in their sexual behaviors (Brown, 2010; Castro & Barbato, 2001; Gert & Culver, 2009; Gurley, 2001; Rubin, 1984; Stewart, 2016; Weiss & Mylod, 2007; Zuiker et al., 2003; see Chapter 21 for more on this). According to social identity theory (Brown, 2020; see also Chapter 6), one result of this stigmatization from broader culture should be for furries to collectively reflect on the subject of sexuality and to work to reduce stigma by limiting potential sources of this stigma within their community—that is, ostracizing individual furries who engage in or promote the stigmatizing behavior. However,

---

porn can be taken at face value—they have far less reason to lie about it to researchers.

[2] That typically won't stop laypersons and the media alike from going with the interpretation that best feeds into the stereotypes and narratives they're looking to push about furries.

somewhat in defiance of what social psychological theory might predict, we typically see a more ambivalent or mixed attitude toward the discussion of sexuality and pornography within the furry fandom.

On the one hand, as previously mentioned, furries are frank and open in their discussion of sexuality within fandom spaces. A 2022 study found that convention-going furries were more open to discussing sex than were online furries, suggesting that many of these conversations were taking place face-to-face between furries. Some furries also believe that the fandom may be open to a fault; in a pair of convention and online studies in 2016 and 2017, furries were somewhat more likely to agree that the fandom is too open about sex than they were to agree that the fandom isn't open enough about sex (see Figure 10.1), although it should be noted that the majority of furries disagreed with both sentiments—meaning that most furries were okay with the current level of openness in the fandom when it comes to the openness with which sex comes up in the fandom.

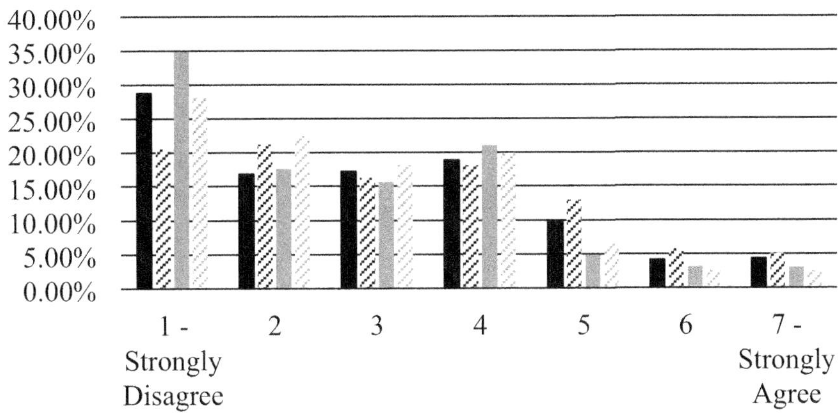

Figure 10.1. A 2016 (convention-going) and 2017 (online) sample of furries indicating their agreement that the furry fandom is too open or not open enough about sex.

Other studies have shown that the extent of fanship (i.e., identifying as a fan of furry content) is positively associated with how openly one discusses sexuality in fandom spaces, while fandom identification scores were not. This suggests that while furries who were "more furry" were more open in discussing sexuality in fandom spaces, one's tendency to do so was largely independent of the extent to which they identified as part of the furry fandom. Or, to put it another way, one's openness when talking about sex isn't an indicator of how closely tied one feels to the fandom as a whole (although it is more common among people who identify rather strongly as furries).

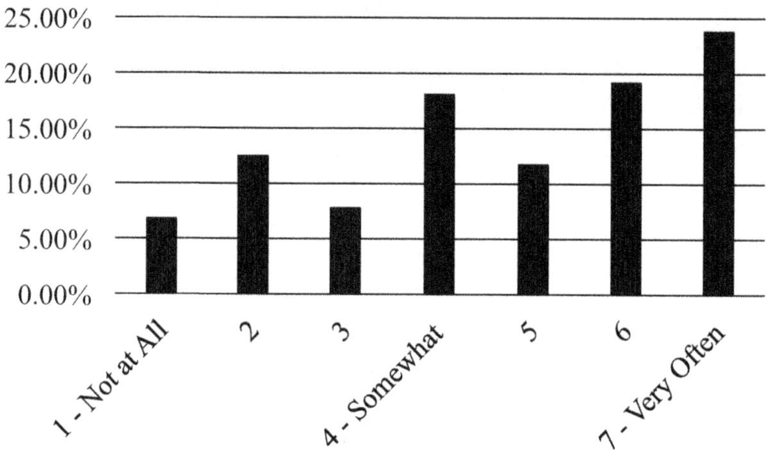

Figure 10.2. A sample of 2013 convention-going furries rating the frequency with which they discuss furry pornography in fandom spaces.

One reason why furries may not be on the same page when it comes to their perception of what's appropriate when it comes to discussing sex in the fandom may be that furries are not especially accurate when it comes to estimating the prevalence of various sex-related behaviors in their fandom. For example, in a 2013 convention study, we asked furries how frequently they discussed the topic of furry pornography with others in the fandom, and then asked them to estimate how frequently other furries discussed pornography in the fandom. The results revealed that furries significantly overestimated how frequently the average furry discussed pornography in fandom spaces. As shown in Figure 10.2, the average furry scored just slightly above the midpoint of the 1-7 scale, with a value of 4.7 on average, a number significantly lower than the average estimate of 5.2. The data suggest that furries typically discuss porn to some extent in fandom spaces, although most furries do not do so frequently, and many assume that the average furry does so more often than they do.

In a similar vein, we asked furries in a pair of convention studies from 2018 and 2019 to indicate the extent to which they considered furry to be a "fetish" for them, as well as to estimate the extent to which they think the average furry considers furry to be a fetish. As Figure 10.3 shows, furries tend to overestimate the extent to which other furries consider furry to be a fetish (average estimate of 3.8) compared to their own scores (average of 3.5), with much of this difference being driven by a tendency to underestimate the number of furries for whom furry is not at all a fetish and a tendency to overestimate how many furries consider furry to be at least somewhat a fetish.

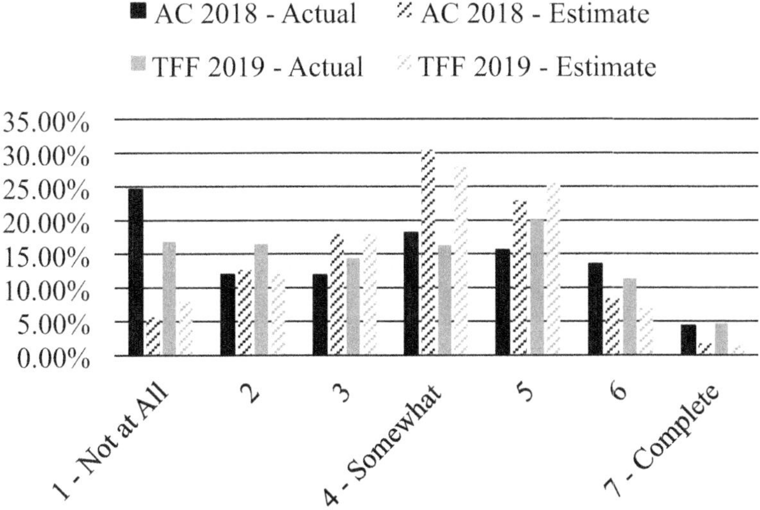

Figure 10.3. Samples of 2018 and 2019 convention-going furries rating the extent to which they consider furry a fetish and estimating the extent to which other furries consider furry to be a fetish.

Sexual Motivation

As mentioned previously, pervasive stereotypes of furries paint them not only as people who are open in talking about sexuality but also as being motivated in whole or in part by a sexual interest. This stereotype is reflected in popular culture depicting furries (Brown, 2010; Castro & Barbato, 2001;

Gert & Culver, 2009; Gurley, 2001; Rubin, 1984; Stewart, 2016; Weiss & Mylod, 2007; Zuiker et al., 2003), in academic research (e.g., Hsu & Bailey, 2019; Zidenberg, 2021), and even in the fandom itself, as we saw in Figure 10.3.

Nevertheless, the available evidence suggests that while furries, as a group, are not wholly devoid of any sexual motivation, sex is, relatively speaking, a fairly limited or minor motivator at best for most furries. Speaking to this, we ran a study in 2011 in which online and convention-going furries were asked to indicate how important, on a 1-7 scale, they felt each of the 14 different factors were to furry culture (see Figure 10.4). "Sex" was ranked 13th out of 14 in terms of importance, ahead only of drama. Countless other factors were considered more important to furry culture—and presumably to what drew participants to identify with the furry community in the first place, including the sense of community, the art, and norms of openness and acceptance—to name just a few.

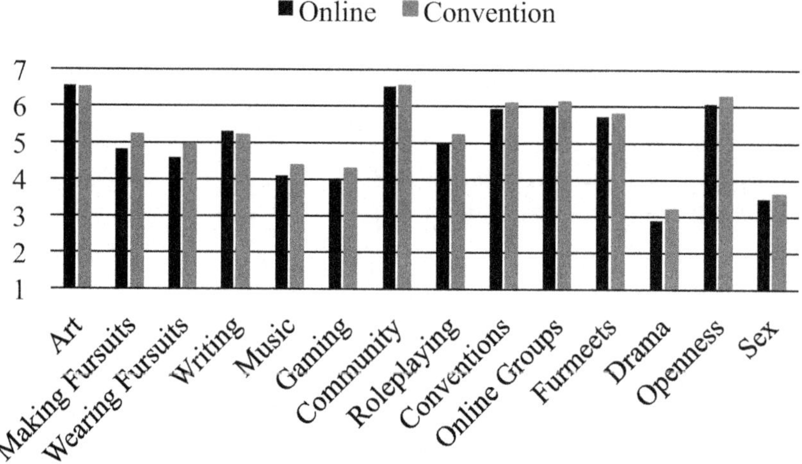

Figure 10.4. A 2011 sample of online and convention-going furries rating the importance of 14 different factors as part of furry culture on a 1-7 scale.

That said, simply stating that sex is not a prominent part of furry culture is not the same thing as saying that furries are not motivated by sex at all. To this end, in the same 2011 study, we also asked furries about their motivation to be in the furry fandom directly. Specifically, we presented furries with a list of different motivations drawn from existing fan research by Daniel

Wann (see Chapter 19 for more on this) and asked them to indicate, for each one, the extent to which it played a significant role in driving their interest in furry. As Figure 10.5 shows, sexual attraction to furry media consistently ranked lower than other, far more prominent motivators, including entertainment, escapism, positive stress, aesthetic appreciation, and a sense of belongingness. Figure 10.6 shows the breakdown of responses for just the sexual motivation score and reveals that while the highest level of agreement was the single most common response, it only made up about 20% of responses—furries were fairly ambivalent towards this item, showing a mixture of agreement and disagreement toward it, although furries were, on average, slightly more likely to agree than to disagree with the item. Taken together, these data suggest that sexual motivation, while present for some furries, is rarely the biggest motivator driving furries to their interest in furry.[3]

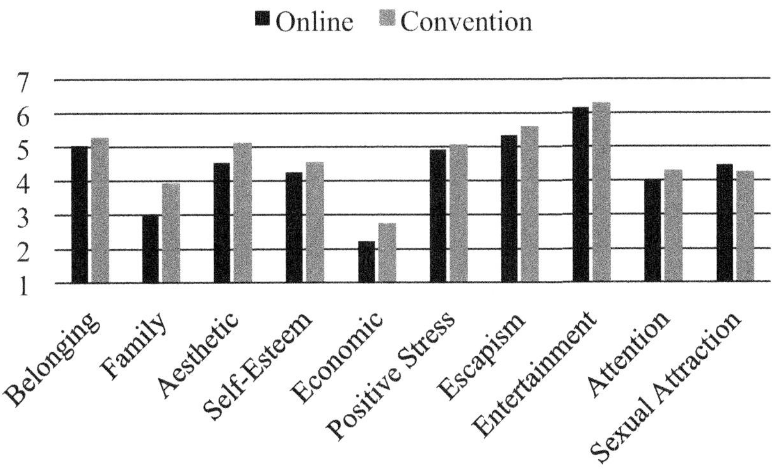

Figure 10.5. A 2011 sample of online and convention-going furries rating the extent to which 10 different motivations drove their interest in furry on a 1-7 scale.

[3] In fact, it's probably the case that those in Figure 10.3, who strongly agreed that furry was a fetish to them would likely make up many of the people who, in Figure 10.6, consider sex to be a very significant motivator of their interest in furry. In other words, it might be accurate to describe a small proportion of furries as being strongly or even primarily motivated by sexual interest, but this is hardly the case for most furries.

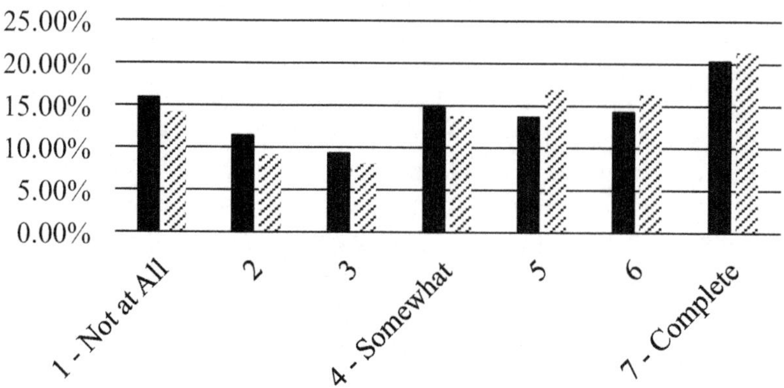

Figure 10.6. A 2011 sample of online and convention-going furries rating the extent to which sexual attraction to furry media drives their interest in furry on a 1-7 scale.

On the subject of sex being a motivator for some furries, we've noted, in some of our research, that furries recruited online and furries recruited in person at conventions seem to differ concerning the extent to which sex is a driver of their furry interest. In a pair of online and convention studies in 2016 and 2017, for example, we asked participants to indicate the extent to which they agreed, on a 1-7 scale, that one of the main reasons why they were a furry was specifically because they liked furry porn. Online furries more strongly agreed with the item than did convention-going furries (3.8/7 versus 3.1/7 respectively), although both samples, consistent with the above findings, scored below the scale's midpoint (see Figure 10.7). Given the earlier finding noting that fanship scores were more strongly tied to pornography use than were fandom scores, and given other findings suggesting that online furries are more likely than convention-going furries to identify as a furry than with the furry fandom, this may be evidence that furries whose interests in furry are predominantly driven by an interest in the content with less interest in the community may be those who are most likely to see furry as a fetish—or, at very least, are more likely to be motivated by sex.

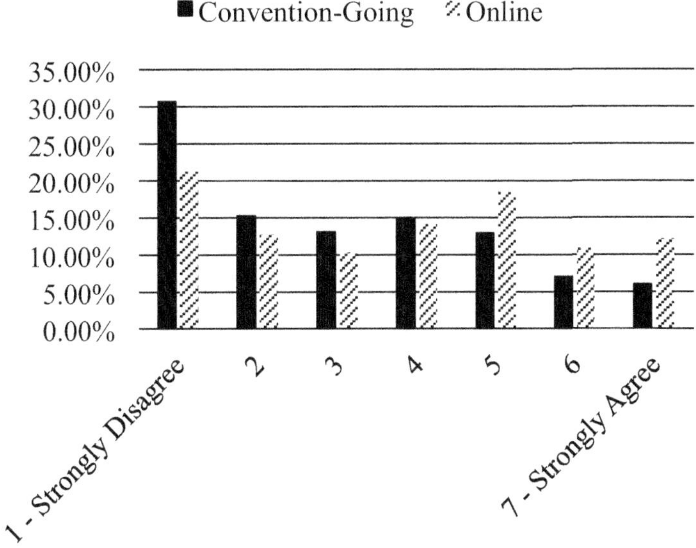

Figure 10.7. A 2016 and 2017 sample of online and convention-going furries rating the extent to which furry pornography was a main reason for their interest in furry on a 1-7 scale.

Speaking further to this idea, in a 2019 study we asked a sample of online furries questions assessing the extent to which they were drawn to various furry activities for sexual reasons and for social reasons using a pair of 1-5 scales. As Figure 10.8 reveals, across the various activities, most of which involve a degree of social interaction, it is unsurprising that social motivation was a stronger driver of engagement in the activity than sexual interest. There was only a single exception: producing or consuming furry art. In this case, sexual motivation was slightly more strongly tied to furry media consumption and production than was social motivation, a finding consistent with the idea that furries for whom the main way their interest manifests is through solitary consumption of furry media with little interest in social activities with the furry fandom, sex may play a more important role as a motivator of their interest.

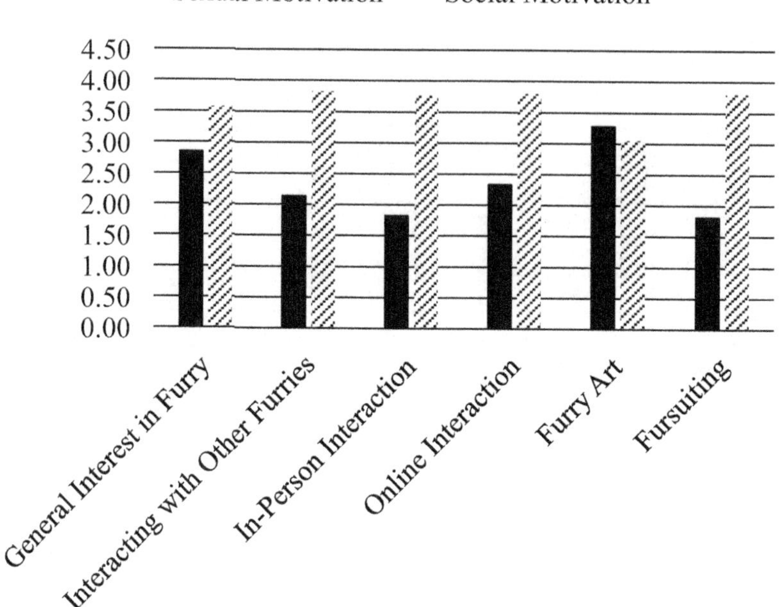

Figure 10.8. A 2019 sample of online furries indicating the extent to which their participation in various furry activities is typically motivated by sex or by social factors on a 1-5 scale.

The findings in Figure 10.8 also help to dispel a misconception that was raised in Chapter 8 on fursuiting—the idea that fursuiters are motivated to fursuit due to a desire to have sex in a fursuit. The present findings suggest that, quite to the contrary, social motivations seem to be a much stronger driver of interest in fursuiting than in sex. Or, looked at another way, 78.0% of fursuiters said they were largely uninterested in sexual motivations to fursuit, as compared to only 11.1% of furries who said they were strongly motivated by sex to fursuit.[4]

In sum, data on the sexual motivation of furries largely flies in the face of conceptualizations of furries as people driven solely by a fetish-like interest

[4] This does not mean that there aren't fursuiters for whom sex is their primary reason to fursuit; rather, it suggests that most fursuiters fursuit for social reasons, not for sexual ones (e.g., because fursuiting helps them to meet new people or to overcome social awkwardness).

in furry-themed media. And while it may be true that furries recruited in online samples may be somewhat more motivated by sex than are furries recruited in-person at conventions, across the board sexual motivation seems to be a rather minor motivation at best for most furries, except for those few for whom it is more accurately conceptualized as being primarily a fetish. For most furries, furry is far more likely to be motivated by social factors, including an interest in the sense of belongingness and community provided by the fandom, a point we return to in Chapter 19.

Fetishes and Fantasies

To this point, we've looked at the extent to which furries may be driven to their interest in furry by sexual attraction, but we've been somewhat vague concerning what, precisely, it is that furries might be attracted to. For example, we've seen, across various studies, that fanship—the extent to which one identifies as a fan of furry content (rather than with the community)—is associated with, among other things, being attracted to one's fursona, with thoughts of being one's fursona, with dressing up as a furry character for sexual reasons, and with an attraction to both anthropomorphic and non-anthropomorphic animals. In other words, it doesn't appear that it's a simple matter of "being more furry means being more attracted only to furry media", but, rather, that this attraction can manifest in a variety of ways.[5]

Let's take a closer look at some of the different facets of this attraction to furry. In that 2019 study described earlier, we asked furries to indicate the extent to which they were sexually attracted to different targets—specifically, attracted to humans, anthropomorphic animals, and non-anthropomorphic animals. The data, shown in Figure 10.9, make it abundantly clear, first and foremost, that furries are not people who are unattracted to humans; by far the single-biggest response for humans was the

[5] The picture is also complicated by the fact that this is only the association between fanship and these factors, with fanship being more associated with these variables than is fandom. In line with our earlier discussion about ambivalence toward sexuality in the furry fandom, it would make sense that those who may be more interested solely in the content rather than in the fandom itself may find it easier to break away from the group's social mores and aversions to sexual behaviors that may contribute to stigmatization of the furry fandom. An alternative explanation might be that those whose interest in furry is predominantly sexual may simply have less interest, relatively speaking, in more social aspects of the fandom, construing their furry interest as a solitary activity engaged in for sexual gratification and which doesn't require the inclusion or participation of others.

highest level of attraction, with participants averaging a score of 8.3/10. However, if furries are attracted to humans, they're even *more* attracted to animals with human traits (or, to put it another way, humans with animal features, like cat ears and a tail)—scoring an average of 9.0/10. Most furries find something appealing, both aesthetically and sexually, about anthropomorphized animal characters.[6]

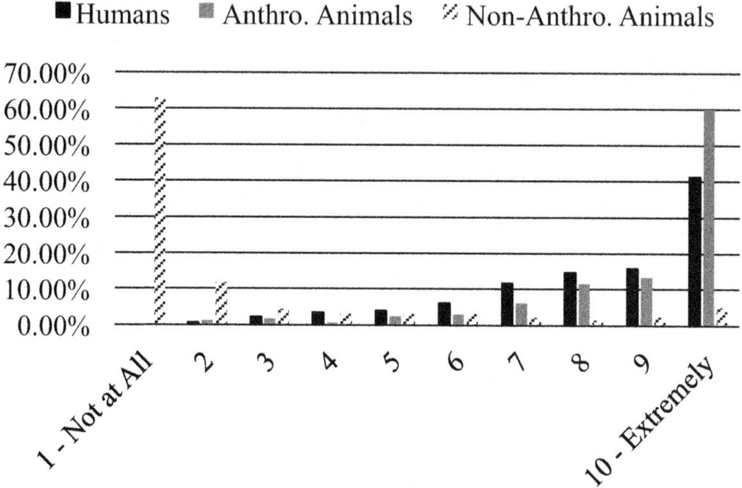

Figure 10.9. A 2019 sample of online furries rating the extent to which they are attracted to humans, anthropomorphized animals, and non-anthropomorphized animals on a 1-10 scale.

But what about non-anthropomorphized animals? One common way in which furries are stigmatized is through the assumption that furries are people harboring a secret sexual attraction to non-human animals. As the data in Figure 10.9 show, however, this couldn't be further from the truth; furries are about as *unattracted* to non-anthropomorphized animals as they are *attracted* to anthropomorphized animals. In hindsight, this response could have been anticipated simply by looking at how most furries define furry—as a shared interest in media featuring *anthropomorphized* animal characters

---

[6] That this is hardly unique to the furry fandom, of course: neko, or catgirls, are a popular trope in anime fandom, and frequently appear in hentai (anime-themed pornography), while one of the most iconic symbols of pornography is the Playboy bunny, with models for the company sometimes being referred to as Playboy bunnies and donning a pair of rabbit ears and a tail.

(see Chapter 5). This being the case, it would make little sense for furries to be attracted to non-anthropomorphized animal characters—this is not what the fan interest is organized around. It would be akin to expecting science-fiction fans to be attracted to elves, orcs, and heroes wielding swords and magic staves, or expecting fantasy fans to be attracted to robots and aliens from space!

Fetishes: Zoophilia

The question of whether furries are sexually attracted to animals is, in essence, a question about a specific fetish—zoophilia. It makes sense why, at least at first glance, a layperson might suspect that furries would be sexually attracted to non-human animals: seeing pin-ups of characters with animal ears, tails, muzzles, and genitals, coupled with the fact that furries are, as we've seen, fairly open about discussing their sexual interests, might lead some to assume that furries are more likely than the average person to show an interest in zoophilia. Indeed, even academics who study zoophilia, but who have relatively little expertise on the furry fandom, have suggested that furries may be connected to zoophilia (Zidenberg, 2021).

To contextualize these findings, let's first look at how common various kinks and fetishes are within the furry fandom. In the same 2019 study above, we also asked furries to indicate the extent to which they had more than "just a little" interest in various unusual sexual behaviors. The most common of these interests include attraction to non-human objects (e.g., shoes, panties; 42.7%), being watched by strangers (34.2%), non-sexual parts of the body (e.g., feet; 26.6%), exposing oneself to others (26.0%), and being insulted or humiliated by a partner (24.2%). And in a later, 2022 study of both online and convention-going furries, we asked furries to indicate, based on an open-ended list we gathered in an earlier study, the extent to which they had at least somewhat of an interest in various kinks and fetishes. Some of the most common results were: BDSM (65.6%), costumed sex (e.g., cosplay, outfits, fursuits; 54.2%), transformation (52.4%), impregnation (49.6%), hypnosis / mind control (44.2%), pet play (43.2%), specific materials / textures (e.g., leather; 40.1%), sizeplay (33.9%), humiliation (32.1%), feet / shoes (29.5%), watersports[7] (26.0%), vore[8] (25.4%), inflation / expansion (21.5%), ageplay (13.3%), and yes, zoophilia (13.3%).

---

[7] Watersports refer to a broad range of activities that involve, in one form or another, urination, and can range from urinating on/ being urinated on by one's partner to the act of drinking urine.

[8] "Vore" refers to vorarephilia, sexual attraction to the idea of eating or being eaten, in whole or in part, by one's partner. An interest in vore can range from fantasies

As the list above makes clear, zoophilia is far from the most common paraphilia endorsed by furries, and is, in fact, endorsed by a relatively small number of furries. For comparison, rates of zoophilia have been estimated, at various points, to be between 2% and 8% of the general population (Baltieri, 2017; Kinsey et al., 1948; Hunt, 1974), although at least two caveats are warranted in interpreting this data. First, it should be noted that in these studies (unlike our own), the authors were assessing the frequency with which people had actually engaged in sexual behaviors with animals, not the extent of their attraction to fantasies of doing so—as such, they are likely be underestimations, since many, if not most people who fantasize about doing so may not act on this urge. Second, such studies were conducted in the general public, a group who, as we've mentioned above, relative to furries, are less inclined to be as open and honest about their sexual proclivities as furries. For these reasons, it is difficult to draw any conclusions about whether or not rates of zoophilia are meaningfully higher in the furry fandom than they are in the general public.[9]

It's also worth noting that, despite furries' openness and acceptance toward sexuality in general and most kinks and fetishes specifically, there is a strong stigma directed toward zoophiles within the furry fandom.[10] Whether this is because furries, due to their tendency to anthropomorphize animals, may feel a greater sense of empathy toward animals and a greater felt need to protect them, or whether it's simply a matter of wanting to distance or gatekeep those who embody a common stereotype about furries remains to be seen in future research. However, we can, at present, see themes of this discrimination in the open-ended responses of participants in our studies who self-identify as zoophiles or as zoosexuals:[11]

---

about being inside the mouth of a creature (e.g., a dragon) to, on the more extreme end, tearing apart, eating, and digesting one's partner.

[9] We can state, at very least, that most furries are not zoophiles and that most zoophiles are not furries (Zidenberg, 2021). For one thing, zoophilia has been around since well before the furry fandom became a thing in the 1980s (see Chapter 2 for the history of the fandom).

[10] As a testament to this fact, zoophilia was more likely to be endorsed by online participants than it was by convention-going participants. This may point to the fact that zoophiles do not feel welcome in furry spaces like conventions as a result of this stigma.

[11] Some participants in our studies have used the term zoosexual to indicate that they feel their attraction to non-human animals is more akin to a sexual orientation than it is a fetish. They are quite rare in our studies, making up less than 1% of respondents.

"I'm also zoosexual and many young furries frown upon that."

"I'm also a non-practicing zoophile, and will remain so, unless the laws change. The feral artwork is an excellent outlet, and means of managing this deviancy. Unfortunately [,] the Fandom isn't so welcoming towards that, and in many cases, outright hostile."

"Pedophile, zoophile Furry art is a safe space to forever bury these under layers of fantasy and separation from anything remotely real. At the same time, ostracization from the discovery of my preferences is a constant background fear behind the otherwise freeing experience of interacting with a relatively open-minded community."

"Furries are pretty bigoted against zoos, especially the younger generations. Besides the general purity spiral already ongoing within the younger groups of the fandom, and the already not too uncommon [sic] negative human gut reflex against bestiality, there's also the fact that zoo and furry have a lot of overlap, and this causes zoos in denial about themselves as well as those who fear undue association to wish zoosexuals just stopped existing. They verbalize this misguided wish with hate speech, harassment, misinformation and just general cancel culture."

"Zoophile often leads to drama and controversy."

"Being a zoo in furry spaces either means complete demonization or complete acceptance based entirely on the people you surround yourself with. There's very little in-between these days."

"Yes, I am a zoophile. There are a number of furs who despise folks like me. This is likely influenced by the zoosadism leaks a while back as well as society's views in general. I am NOT a zoosadist. I am in love with my dog. Why would I hurt her? Zoosadist and rapist are labels applied to me without merit. So I have to keep this side of myself mostly hidden from furs. Otherwise [,] I would likely be banned and ostracized from the few furry spaces I do occupy."

The idea of zoosexuality as a distinct sexual orientation is contentious, but has been endorsed by at least some scholars (e.g., Miletski, 2017).

"I am a zoophile, & I am not afraid to be such. However [,] I [sic] get constant death threats & harrassment [sic] for it."

"Yes. I've had to hide my zoosexuality from the public fandom while being accepted in smaller spaces. I increasingly believe they furries, as a whole, are no longer as open and tolerant as they were."

"As a zoophile, which I would say is a minority, I feel an intense need to hide that identity for fear of (essentially) excommunication from furry spaces. I have never had intercourse with a non-human animal and would never harm a non-human animal, but am faced with the reality that - first, merely existing upsets people and - second, we define harm differently and - third, it's impossible to reason with people on the matter at all."

"I identify as a zoophile in the Fandom and because of that [,] I am ostracised, bullied & threatened basically daily. I do not feel accepted by the majority but I assure you that some furries do accept me and people like me, the hateful people are always the loudest but I know that not all hate me."

"I don't feel accepted. I have to hide my real feelings about being [a] zoo, otherwise[,] I'm subjected to an onslaught of hate online."

Taken together, the present data suggest that, despite the prevalence of a wide range of kinks and fetishes in the furry fandom, zoophilia is highly stigmatized by furries and, relatively speaking, comprises a fairly small minority of furries. To this end, it would be factually incorrect to characterize furries as people with a sexual attraction to non-human animals.

Autoanthropomorphozoophilia

A lesser-known fetish associated with the furry fandom by some academics (i.e., Hsu & Bailey, 2019) is *autoanthropomorphozoophilia*, a mouthful of a word meaning that a person is sexually aroused at the thought of becoming or being an anthropomorphic animal character. While the 2019 study by Hsu and Bailey tested and found evidence for this phenomenon, a conceptual replication and extension of their original study provided important context that the evidence for autoanthropomorphozoophilia is sparse at best (Brooks et al., 2022). Put simply, our data suggests that while pornography and sexual fantasies about anthropomorphic animals are common in the furry fandom, it occurs within a larger structure of social motivations and suggests, in contrast to the conclusions suggested by Hsu and Bailey, that most furries are motivated not by a sexual attraction to the thought of oneself as a furry character, but rather by social factors and a general interest in furry media.

Delving just a bit more into these two studies, we can look at the question of how common it is for furries to have sexual fantasies regarding themselves as anthropomorphic animals. The data from our follow-up study found that furries were more attracted to the idea of being an anthropomorphic animal in a sexual context than they were to the fantasy of just being an anthropomorphic animal. Moreover, they were more attracted to the idea of being a human with an idealized body type than they were to the idea of being an anthropomorphized animal and were more attracted to the idea of being a human and having sex than they were to the fantasy of themselves as an anthropomorphic animal in a non-sexual context. However, being able to dress up as or fantasize about being one's fursona was largely unimportant for a furry's masturbation or sexual fantasies, with furries scoring an average of 1.9/5 on this measure, well below the midpoint of the scale.

When looked at together, these findings generally run counter to the idea that furries are sexually attracted specifically to the fantasy of themselves as an anthropomorphic animal character. The presence of fursonas in furry erotica typically has less to do with a general attraction to oneself as an anthropomorphic animal and likely has more to do with their attraction to anthropomorphic characters and the sexual fantasy of being with that character (or even just with being in a sexual situation in the first place). Speaking to this idea, furries generally agreed in our study that anthropomorphic characters would be more attracted to their fursonas than they would be to themselves as humans. As such, when they imagined themselves interacting with anthropomorphic characters in sexual and non-sexual situations, they were more likely to do so as their fursona than they would as their non-fursona self.[12]

---

[12] To be clear, this doesn't mean that there *aren't* furries who are sexually attracted to thoughts of themselves as their fursona, nor is there anything inherently wrong if someone has those fantasies. However, it would be inaccurate to suggest that most, or even many furries' interest in furry is driven predominantly by such fantasies.

Pornography

Attitudes Toward Pornography

Throughout this chapter, we've spoken about furry sexuality and frequently referred to erotic furry content and furry-themed pornography. However, we have not yet focused our attention on furry pornography and furries' attitudes and behaviors regarding it. Given the central role that it plays in furry sexuality—as indicated by the frequency with which furries talk about furry porn and their stated attraction to anthropomorphized animal characters—it seems like a fitting place to end this chapter.

First, let us define what we mean by furry pornography and its scale within the furry fandom. Furry porn refers to a wide range of media, including 2D or 3D digitally composed pieces of still or animated artwork, as well as erotic stories, all of which feature anthropomorphized animal characters in erotic or sexual situations. This work is generally created by independent artists and writers and released to the fandom directly or through commissioned work (e.g., by furries commissioning pieces involving their fursonas or favorite characters). Despite its sometimes contentious nature in fandom discussions, it is undeniable that furry porn is pervasive, prevalent on popular art-sharing websites like FurAffinity and e621 as well as on social media sites (e.g., Twitter) and even on repositories for porn that are not specifically focused on furry porn, but rather on porn in general (e.g., Pornhub).

As mentioned earlier in this chapter, the furry fandom has a somewhat ambivalent attitude toward furry porn. While we've mentioned that this can stem from disagreements about its prevalence or furries' attitudes toward it, it may also stem from a simple disagreement about what even constitutes porn in the first place. Speaking to this idea, we conducted an experiment in a 2013 study in which convention-going furries and a control sample of college students viewed various images of nude characters, erotica (e.g., naked characters touching suggestively), and sexually explicit content (e.g., characters having sex). The images were either furry (i.e., artwork) or non-furry (i.e., photographs) and included both gay, lesbian, and straight scenes. For each image, participants were asked to rate how explicit the image was. The results revealed that furries and college students differed when it came to their ratings: furries tended to rate all of the furry images (nude, erotic, or sexually explicit) as being equally explicit to the human images, whereas college students tended to rate the human images as significantly more explicit than the furry images. Likewise, while furries rated the furry images as being more arousing than did the college students, furries were also more likely to rate the furry images as more erotic than the human images, consistent with findings we discussed earlier showing that furries tend to consider anthropomorphized animal characters more attractive than human characters. In short, the data suggest that furries do tend to consider furry content to be more explicit than non-furry college students, and even within furries there was considerable variability in what constituted explicit content. While we might think it's easy or obvious to decide what does and doesn't constitute pornography or explicit material, this study shows that, to some extent, explicit is in the eye of the beholder.[13]

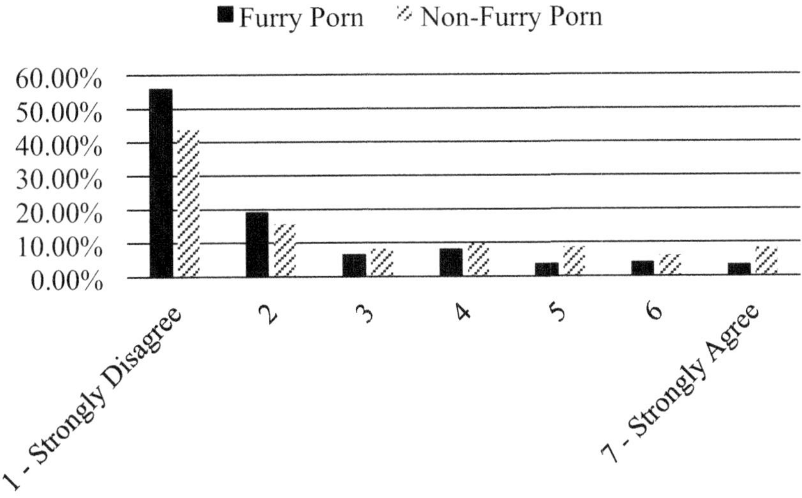

Figure 10.10. A 2015 study of convention-going furries rating the extent to which they felt uncomfortable while looking at furry and non-furry pornography on a 1-7 scale.

In addition to generally finding furry pornography to be more arousing than non-furry pornography, a 2015 study also found that furries were less uncomfortable looking at furry-themed pornography than they were at looking at non-furry pornography (see Figure 10.10). These findings again suggest that furries may have a preference for furry-themed porn over non-

[13] This is based on the fact that non-furry college students, who weren't attracted to anthropomorphized animal characters, did not consider the furry characters to be nearly as explicit as the furries did. One could imagine a line of thought going something like, "What's explicit about it? They're just cartoons."

furry porn and also mirror research from a 2019 online study in which furries showed a generally favorable attitude toward furry porn (5.1/7), with furries being 4 times more likely to score above the midpoint of the scale than below the midpoint of the scale.

Even though furries, on average, hold a fairly positive attitude toward furry pornography, results such as those seen in Figure 10.10 illustrate that not all furries are equally comfortable with pornography. One possible explanation for this variability in responses could be participant gender. After all, in a fandom whose single-biggest demographic is cis men, it's possible that the bulk of the pornographic content is targeted toward the preferences of cis men, which might be off-putting to others. Testing this idea, we asked participants in a 2022 online and convention study to indicate their attitude toward furry porn. Consistent with expectations, cis men had the most positive attitudes toward furry porn (6.0/7), followed by trans men (5.8/7) and trans women (5.8/7), with cis women having the most ambivalent attitude (4.5/7).

In short, while we can say that, in general, furries have a fairly positive attitude toward not only anthropomorphized animal characters, but also toward sexual content featuring those characters, one should be cautious to avoid overgeneralizing—not every furry is attracted to furry pornography, and there may be important systemic reasons for these different attitudes.

Pornography Use

Given the above tendency for most furries to have a positive attitude toward porn, we can also ask about the extent to which furries consume furry pornography itself. After all, a person may have a positive attitude toward expensive sports cars without ever driving or owning one themselves. To this end, we can look at data from a series of studies we ran between 2013 and 2022 on the subject of pornography use in the fandom. The results reveal that, when it comes to consuming furry content, the percentage that furries consume which is, by their own definition,[14] pornographic in nature ranges from an average of 47.6%-51.0% across samples, and did not differ

[14] As we've already seen this chapter, the definition of what constitutes explicit content varies from furry to furry. To avoid imposing a definition of pornography that furries might disagree with, we allowed furries to use their own definition of pornography.

significantly between online and con-going furries. In other words, about half of the furry-themed content that furries consume is sexual.[15]

As an interesting contrast, in this same series of studies, we also asked furries what percentage of art or furry content that furries own was pornographic in nature. Far from the approximately 50% of content noted above, only about 18.8%-27.6% of owned furry content was sexual in nature, with no difference between online and convention-going furries. This means that furries are more likely to look at explicit furry content than they are to purchase explicit furry content. There are several possible reasons for this. One may be that furries may feel uncomfortable or embarrassed at the prospect of commissioning explicit artwork from artists, or perhaps prefer to not include their fursonas—a representation of themselves in many cases (see Chapter 7), in sexualized art. Alternatively, practical considerations may prevent furries from purchasing or owning explicit furry content, such as living with roommates, a spouse, or family member who might disapprove of the owning or displaying of explicit furry art.[16]

A related question, one often asked to us by laypersons and scholars alike, is whether furries' use of furry-themed pornography precludes or is done to the exclusion of viewing non-furry pornography. We tested this in a 2019 study of online furries, finding that most furries (68.0%) indicated that most of the pornography they consume is furry-themed in nature, with 32.9% of furries indicating that 90-100% of the porn they consume is furry-themed. Even so, when asked in a 2022 study whether furries limit their pornography use to furry-themed porn, very few furries agreed with this idea (see Figure 10.11), meaning there is little reason to worry that furries might be completely replacing their interest in humans with an interest in anthropomorphic animal characters.

---

[15] In other studies comparing furries to other fan groups (e.g., anime fans, sports fans) we've found that, while other fans consume interest-themed erotic content, furries were more likely to do so.

[16] For one thing, neighbors are less likely to complain if you hang a piece of innocuous furry art in your window than if you hang a piece of explicit furry art in your window!

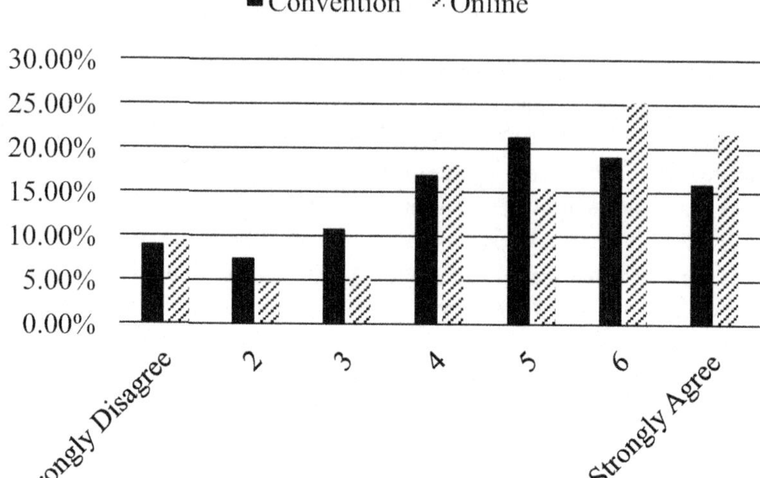

Figure 10.11. A 2022 study of convention-going and online furries rating the extent to which they agreed that their pornography use is limited only to furry pornography on a 1-7 scale.

Finally, in terms of frequency of use, we asked furries in an online 2019 study about the frequency with which they looked at furry-themed porn. The study found that 59.3% of participants looked at furry porn daily, in contrast to the 68.1% who say that they look at non-pornographic furry content at least daily. In other words, despite the prevalence of erotic furry art, furries do seem to consume more non-erotic furry artwork.

Looking at frequency another way, we asked furries in a 2013 convention study approximately how many times they looked at furry porn in the past month. The results found that 6.8% of furries have not viewed pornography at all in the past month. In contrast, 15.4% said they had viewed porn at least 1-4 times, 16.7% had done so 5-10 times, 18.5% said 11-20 times, 12.8% said 21-30 times, and 29.9%—the single-most common category, indicated that they viewed furry porn more than 30 times in the past month. Furries, it would seem, are prolific consumers of furry content—explicit or otherwise—with many doing so on a daily basis.[17]

Conclusion

I feel both optimism and excitement for the future of sex research in the furry community. The generosity and willingness of furries to be open and honest in our studies allows sex researchers to explore bigger, more interesting questions about human sexuality than we might otherwise be able to study in samples who are typically more reserved about discussing sex. There are plenty of fruitful avenues for future research, such as exploring the dynamics of partner selection and norms surrounding dating and sex within a fandom context. These dynamics may include questions about sexual scripts that form in fandom spaces and impact how members of a fandom negotiate online and offline connections. For example, according to a trio of convention and online studies from 2013 to 2022, the amount of online roleplaying furries do that's pornographic in nature is about 31.5-32.3%. This value is consistent across convention-going and online samples and has remained consistent over an approximately 10-year period. The single most common response is that "less than 10%" of the roleplaying furries do online is sexual. However, we can ask what social dynamics are at play in the 90% of online roleplaying that is non-sexual which enables the 10% of sexual roleplaying to occur.[18]

As I conclude this chapter, I can't help but reflect on the past five years I've spent working with Furscience and the chance I've had to explore the intersections of sexuality and fandom. From these experiences, I've learned that the fandom is largely ambivalent to sexuality—on the one hand, creating

---

[17] One possible explanation for this high frequency of viewing may stem from furries making viewing furry content (erotic or otherwise) a part of their daily routine. For example, websites like FurAffinity can be used to keep track of when one's favorite artist has uploaded new work. As such, a furry could easily spend a few minutes checking this site when they've got some downtime on their phone to see this new content. It's worth noting that the question only asked about frequency of viewing pornography—it did not ask about masturbation, which is an entirely different question—one which we've not yet asked about! It may well be the case that many of these participants viewed explicit furry content in brief while scrolling through updates on sites like FurAffinity without actively engaging in sexual fantasies or masturbating while viewing them.

[18] For example, perhaps non-sexual roleplays allow furries to hone their skills at roleplaying so they are more adept when the time comes for erotic roleplay. Alternatively, furries may forge relationships of trust and reciprocal sharing in non-sexual roleplay that facilitates more intimate forms of roleplay.

a space for diversity of sexual interests and for content creators to produce evocative erotic content and, on the other hand, the hypervigilance furries have shown through the fierce stigmatization of those who stray too far from what is considered "acceptable" within a group that, itself, is often considered deviant by society at large. And, as demonstrated through our research (e.g., Brooks et al., 2022), it's clear that the furry fandom is a place where sexuality, kinks and fetishes, and erotic self-expression can take place even though sex itself only plays a minor role in drawing furries to the fandom in the first place.

References

Baltieri, D. A. (2017). An exploratory study on psychosocial variables of people participating in zoophilic blogs / websites. *Sex Health Issues, 1.* https://doi.org/10.15761/SHI.1000107

Brooks, T. R., Bennett, T. N., Myhre, A., Plante, C. N., Reysen, S., Roberts, S. E., & Gerbasi, K. C. (2022). "Chasing tail": Testing the relative strength of sexual interest and social interaction as predictors of furry identity. *The Journal of Sex Research.* https://doi.org/10.1080/00224499.2022.2068180

Brown, R. (2020). The social identity approach: Appraising the Tajfellian legacy. *British Journal of Social Psychology, 59*(1), 5-25. https://doi.org/10.1111/bjso.12349

Brown, T. O. L. (2010). *"If someone finds out you're a perv": The experience and management of stigma in the BDSM subculture* [Master's thesis]. Athens, OH: Ohio University.

Castro, F. & Barbato, R. (2001). *Plushies and furries* [film]. World of Wonder Productions, Inc.

Gagnon, J. H., & Simon, W. (1973). *Sexual conduct: The social sources of human sexuality.* Aldine.

Gert, B., & Culver, C. M. (2009). Sex, immorality, and mental disorders. *The Journal of Medicine & Philosophy, 34*(5), 487-495.

Gurley, G. (2001). Pleasures of the fur. *Vanity Fair.* Retrieved from http://www.vanityfair.com/culture/2001/03/furries200103

Hsu, K. J., & Bailey, J. M. (2019). The "furry" phenomenon: Characterizing sexual orientation, sexual motivation, and erotic target identity inversions in male furries. *Archives of Sexual Behavior, 48*(5), 1349-1369. https://doi.org/10.1007/s10508-018-1303-7

Hunt, M. (1974). *Sexual Behavior in the 1970s.* Playboy Press.

Kinsey, A. C., Pomeroy, W. B., & Martin, C. E (1948). *Sexual Behavior in the human male.* W.B. Saunders Company.

Miletski, H. (2017). Zoophilia: Another sexual orientation? *Archives of Sexual Behavior, 46,* 39-42. https://doi.org/10.1007/s10508-016-0891-3

Rubin, G. S. (1984). Thinking sex: Notes for a radical theory of the politics of sexuality. In C. S. Vance (Ed.), *Pleasure and danger: Exploring female sexuality* (pp. 267-319). Routledge & Kegan Paul.

Stewart, S. (2016, May 6). What it's like to have sex as a "furry." *New York Post.* Retrieved from http://nypos t.com/2016/05/06/inside-the-life-of-a-furry

Weiss, R. & Mylod, M. (2007). The day fuckers [Television series episode]. In Ellin, D., Levinson, S., Wahlberg, M., & Weiss, R. (Executive Producers.), *Entourage*. Home Box Office (HBO) & Leverage Management.

Zidenberg, A. M. (2021). *Toward a greater understanding of the assessment, psychological correlates, and management of human perpetrated sexual behavior toward animals* [Doctoral dissertation, University of Saskatchewan]. Harvest. https://hdl.handle.net/10388/13537

Zuiker, A. E., Stahl, J., & Lewis, R. J. (2003). Fur and loathing [Television series episode]. In J. Bruckheimer (Executive Producer.), *CSI: Crime scene investigation*. Los Angeles: CBS Paramount Network Television.

Chapter 11
Fuzzy Lines: Subgroups and Furry-Adjacent Groups

Stephen Reysen, Courtney "Nuka" Plante

Way back in Chapter 5, we took a crack at trying to define what a furry was. While we didn't arrive at a universally agreed-upon definition or consensus, we saw that most furries generally agreed that furry, at a minimum, generally involves a fan-like interest in stories, art, media, and fantasies featuring anthropomorphized animal characters.

It would be easy to take that singular facet of the definition of furry and reduce the entirety of furries to just that. And, to some extent, this is what laypersons and the media alike do when they think about furries: they imagine furries as people who gather solely to wear fursuits, produce and consume furry media, and talk about where and when they're going to meet up next time to do this.

One can hardly be blamed for this way of thinking, given that, when we think about fan groups, we often imagine fans of a single, clearly-focused interest: Whovians like the TV show *Doctor Who*, Trekkers[1] like *Star Trek*, Cheeseheads like the Green Bay Packers American football team, Phisheads like the musical group Phish, and Parrotheads like the musician Jimmy Buffett. In each of these examples, we can point to a single object or interest that fans organize around, a single source of content (e.g., a studio, corporation, or organization), with gatherings of fans that often feel organized by a corporation or company (e.g., top-down programming) rather than coming from fans themselves (e.g., bottom-up programming; Booth, 2016). For example, Los Angeles Anime Expo, Los Angeles E3 Expo, and San Diego ComicCon are all put on by organizations with the aim of helping major studios and production companies announce new releases rather than representing gatherings of fans who produce and share content (e.g., panels) with other fans.[2]

In stark contrast to this, furry draws from no single canonical text, nor are any of its conventions, large or small, run by a major studio or corporation. Instead, furries congregate loosely around a diverse range of media that

---

[1] While outsiders often use the term "Trekkie" to refer to *Star Trek* fans, the term "Trekker" is generally preferred by the community, as the term "Trekkie" is often used as a derogatory term for an obsessive or out-of-touch fan.

[2] That's not to say that there aren't smaller conventions run by anime fans, gamers, and comic book aficionados, but the largest of their fan conventions are undoubtedly top-down enterprises.

includes but is not limited to, physical and digital artwork, comics, stories, TV shows, movies, video games, board games, music, books, and virtual reality. And although you could certainly find examples of furry content generated by major corporations (e.g., Disney), most of this content is not produced with the intent of being "furry content."[3] Content targeted specifically toward furry audiences is typically generated by furries themselves.

A consequence of this broad, decentralized, multimedia fandom being organized primarily around a large number of small, independent content creators is that, unlike other fan groups, which might be expected to be fairly homogeneous in their interests (i.e., we're all here for the same reason), we might expect the furry fandom to be comprised of many significant subgroups. In the present chapter, we'll explore this idea, starting with a brief overview of some of the different media genres that furries prefer. Next, we'll delve into some of the more unique aspects or idiosyncrasies of specific subgroups in the furry fandom to see how belonging to one subgroup or another might say a bit about who you are.[4] Lastly, we'll briefly talk about hierarchies and the perceived status of different subgroups within the furry fandom.

As a final note before we delve into the topic properly, we'd like to unequivocally state that while we do typically find small differences between these different subgroups and the broader furry community, the differences are relatively modest in size. At the end of the day, everyone discussed in these results are furries above all else and, as a result, have a lot more in common than they have differences. In other words, resist the urge to read too much into these differences and avoid making proverbial mountains out of empirical molehills![5]

---

[3] Even Disney's most arguably "furry" movie *Zootopia* was not released explicitly as a "furry movie." While there are suggestions that the marketing team may have reached out to furries for some extra publicity (Notopoulos, 2016) and certainly recognized the potential for furries to be ardent fans of the film, the film was almost certainly intended to cater to a much broader, general audience.

[4] We generally identify furry participants as being part of these different subgroups by giving participants in our studies a list of different subgroups and having them check off which of the subgroups they identify with (e.g., writer, artist, brony). Over the years, this list of subgroups has grown considerably as furries continue to suggest additional options that we've missed in previous studies.

[5] We feel it's important to make this point because, as we point out in Chapter 6, social identity theory suggests that people very naturally divide the world up into "us" versus "them," even on fairly mundane or meaningless characteristics. The last

Media Genre Preferences

As we mention throughout this book (e.g., Chapter 5, Chapter 19), there are a plethora of different routes into the furry fandom. As such, unlike with different fan groups, where we might expect fans to have fairly predictable preferences when it comes to media genres (e.g., sports fans like sports, science-fiction fans like science fiction), we might expect furries to have all manner of different media preferences. To test this, we asked furries, in a pair of open-ended questions, to indicate their favorite genres of film/television and their favorite genres of music. Their responses were organized and coded into categories, shown in Figure 11.1 and Figure 11.2.

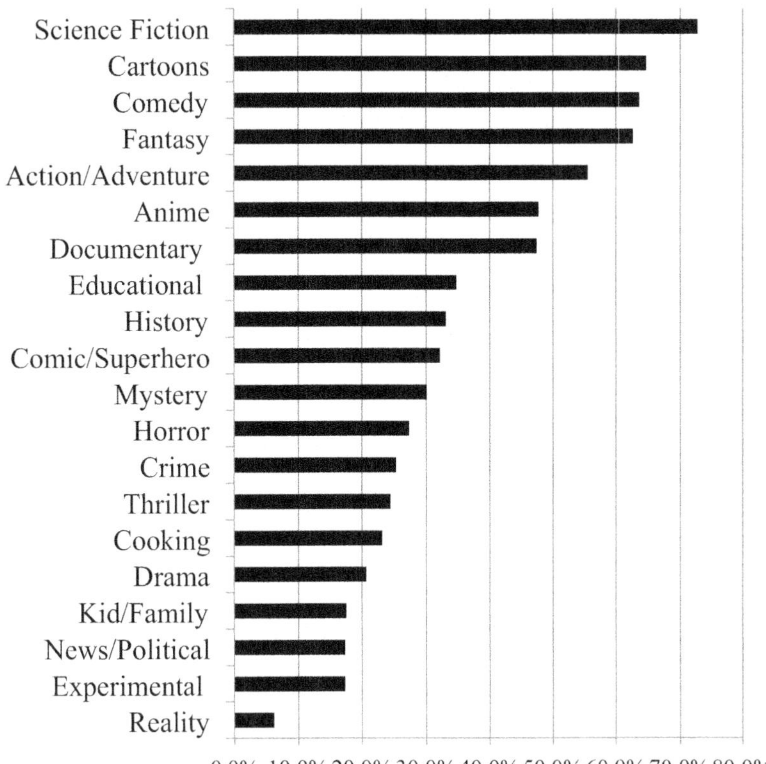

Figure 11.1. Furries' favorite genres of television / film.

---

thing we want to do is spark a furry civil war over tiny differences between furries who prefer one genre over another!

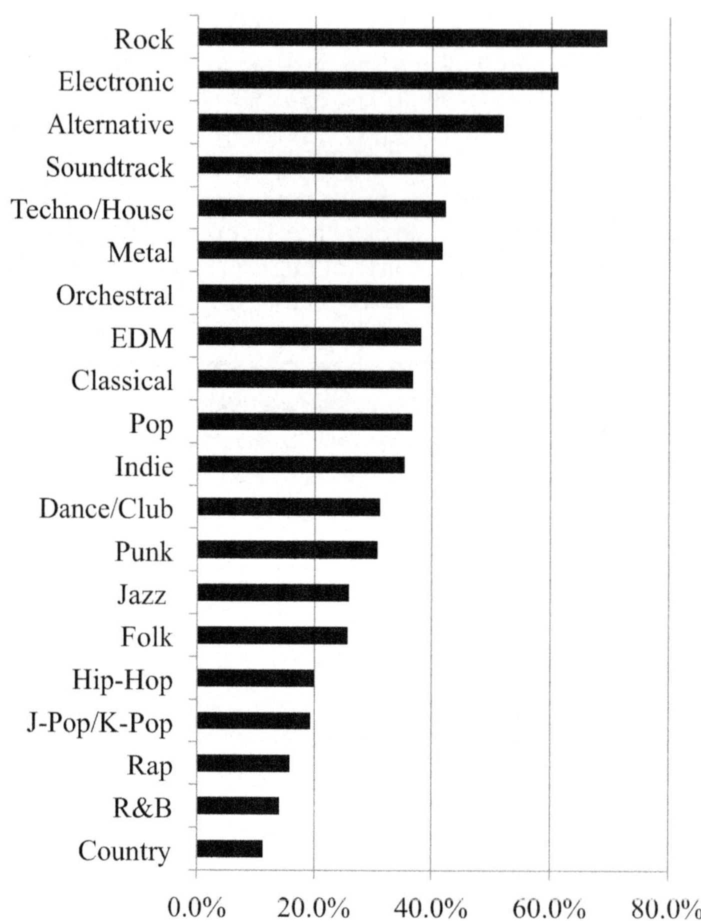

Figure 11.2. Furries' favorite genres of music.

The data on television and film preferences makes it clear, first and foremost, that while no genre of media is universally beloved by furries, some genres are more preferred than others. Science fiction emerged as the most frequently stated favorite genre among furries, followed closely by cartoons, comedy, and fantasy, respectively. These preferences make sense, given the furry fandom originated as an offshoot of the science-fiction fandom, along with having some deep roots in the cartoons and animation of yesteryear and in stories that prominently feature anthropomorphic animal characters in science fiction, fantasy, and action settings (see Chapter 2, as well as Strike, 2017, for more on the history of furries). Likewise, many of the first furries played an indispensable role in bringing anime to the awareness of popular culture in North America, which might explain the strong preference for anime as well. Finally, there have, in recent years, been several prominent documentaries about furries created by furries themselves (e.g., *The Fandom* by Ash Kreis and Eric Risher, and *Fursonas* by Dominic Rodriguez), hinting at furries' interest in both viewing and creating documentaries. And while other genres, such as cooking shows, dramas, children's programming, and news were far from being the most popular genres among furries, they nevertheless were represented among a non-trivial minority of furries.[6]

In a similar vein, there is no single genre of music that is universally liked among furries, although genres such as rock, electronic, and alternative music are fairly prominent, and represented among some of the best-known furry musicians (e.g., Pepper Coyote and Fox Amoore, who produce rock and electronica music). It should also be noted that genres such as electronic, techno/house, and EDM are fairly commonly represented at furry conventions, with furry DJs frequently performing live sets at dances and raves. Other genres, such as hop-hop, J-pop / K-pop, R&B, and country, while not as popular in the broader fandom, may nevertheless be popular with some furry subcultures and do have some notable furry content creators (e.g., Bucktown Tiger, a furry hip-hop artist).

Science-Fiction Fans

The data in the previous section revealed that, when it comes to furries' media preferences, science fiction is among the most popular. But does a preference for science fiction necessarily translate into identification as a science fiction fan? After all, a person can enjoy the aesthetics of science fiction as a genre or enjoy specific science fiction stories without necessarily considering it to be a part of their fan identity.

Data from several years of studies suggests that a sizable proportion of furries—nearly half—do, in fact, see themselves as science fiction fans (see Figure 11.3). This could mean that they see their interest in furry as a

---

[6] One possible explanation for the lower representation of these genres among furries may stem from the fact that, demographically, furries are primarily comprised of a group of men in their teens and 20s (see Chapter 13) and, as such, may not necessarily be the target audience of these genres. Likewise, while some genres are likely to have conceptual overlap with common themes of furry media (e.g., science fiction, fantasy), there may be a more tenuous connection between genres like news / politics or cooking and furry media.

manifestation of a broader interest in science fiction or that, in addition to their interest in furry, they have a fan-like interest in other popular science fiction work (e.g., *Doctor Who*, *Star Trek*, *Star Wars*).[7] Regardless of the nature of this interest, it continues to be a prominent part of many furries' interests, although trends over the past six years may hint at a slight downward trajectory in the popularity of science fiction—perhaps pointing to a gradual straying of the furry fandom from its science fiction roots.

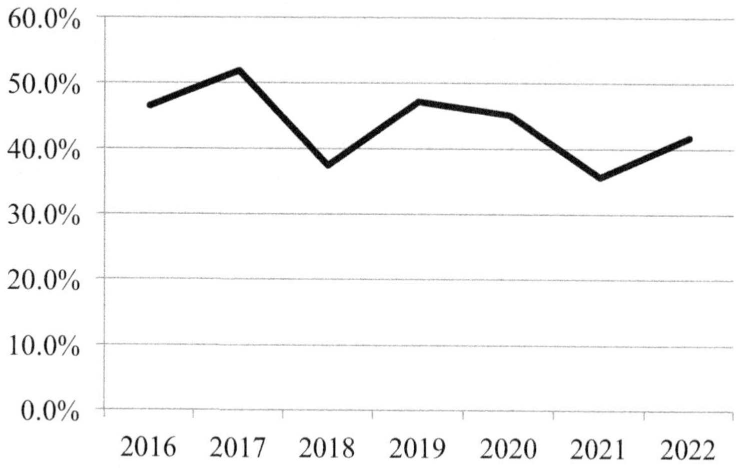

Figure 11.3. Percent of furries who identify as science-fiction fans by year.

In addition to assessing the prevalence of science-fiction fans among furries, we can also ask whether there are any observable differences between furries that are science-fiction fans and furries that are not. Some small differences observed across studies, summarized in Figure 11.4, include the fact that furries who are also science fiction fans tended to become more immersed in furry-themed media than furries who were not science-fiction fans. They were also less likely to show elitist attitudes toward other furries and were less likely to keep up with popular trends in the fandom. Personality-wise, they were fairly comparable to other furries, although furries who were science-fiction fans did score higher on measures of emotional stability and conscientiousness, perhaps suggesting that they are

[7] While a single datapoint is not a trend, the furry co-author of this chapter is, indeed, a lifelong *Star Trek* fan and a lover of science-fiction films (e.g., *The Matrix*, *The Terminator*), books (e.g., *Ender's Game*, *Jurassic Park*), and games (e.g., *Starcraft*, *FTL: Faster Than Light*, *XCom*, *Fallout*).

people who have a greater need to think things through and who are less prone to emotional outbursts. Finally, compared to other furries, science-fiction fans had a stronger need to use distractions to buffer themselves against the fear of death, had more pro-transgender attitudes, and were more likely to have been bullied when they were younger. Taken together, these data might fit the stereotype of a science-fiction fan as someone who was a bit strange, eccentric, or unusual as a child, someone who, as a result, may have sought refuge or escape in media as a result and who may have been especially drawn to science fiction over another genre (e.g., fantasy) because of an interest in science or other cold, analytical pursuits.[8]

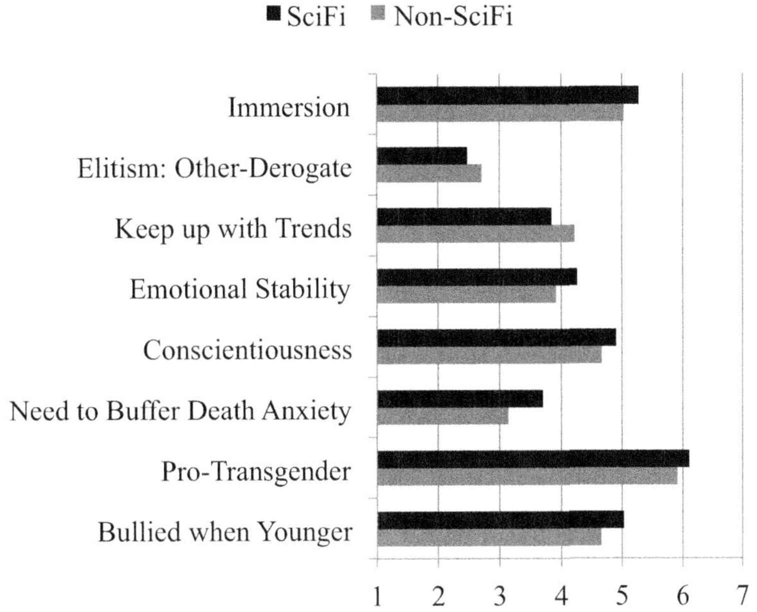

Figure 11.4. Comparisons between furries who are SciFi fans vs. non-SciFi fans (7-point scale).

[8] This profile is just an example that takes into account most of the findings seen here. In reality, it's rare to find someone who perfectly embodies every dimension or characteristic of a category or archetype, nor do we mean to suggest that most furries who are science-fiction fans would fit this profile! You can see for yourself that the differences observed in Figure 11.4 are relatively small differences of magnitude, rather than differences of kind.

Anime Fans

In the same way that most furries having an interest in science fiction hints at the presence of a large subpopulation of science-fiction fans within the furry fandom, we can also look for the presence of an anime fan subgroup within the furry fandom. Anime fans are enthusiastic and ardent supporters of Japanese animation (anime) and comics (manga). Our work on anime fans (at least, English-speaking, fans mostly from North America) shows that they tend to be, on average, young, college-age men who consume anime/manga to escape from daily life hassles and who tend to be introverted and identify as gamers (Reysen et al., 2021; Reysen et al., 2016). Most presently relevant, however, a significant amount of anime features anthropomorphized animal characters (e.g., *One Piece*, *Odd Taxi*, *Beastars*, *BNA: Brand New Animal*, *Aggretsuko*, *Fruits Basket*, *Dorohedoro*), or caters to many fans' penchant for catgirls (e.g., *Nekopara*, *Cat Planet Cuties*, *High School DxD*). As such, it's easy to see why furries, including Fred Patten, a prominent historical figure in the furry fandom (Horbinski, 2019), would be drawn to anime. To this end, our data show that just under half of furries are anime fans—only slightly less than the number of furries who are science-fiction fans (see Figure 11.5). And, like with science fiction fans, this number has remained fairly stable over time, although it seems to lack the slight downward trajectory observed in the science-fiction data.

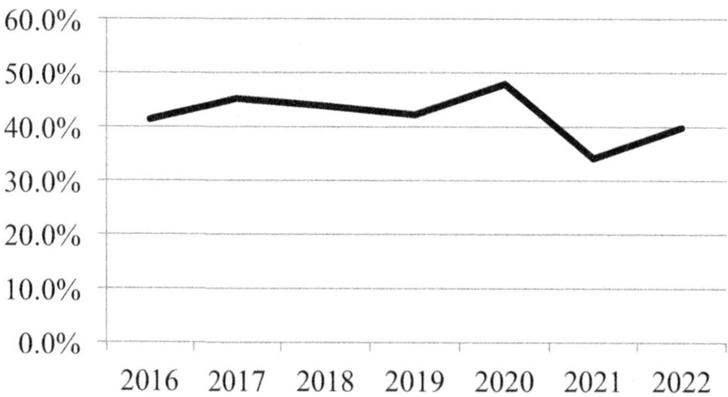

Figure 11.5. Percent of furries who identify as anime fans by year.

As we did with science-fiction fans, we ran a series of analyses testing whether there were any observable differences between furries who were anime fans and furries who were not. The results are shown in Figure 11.6. First, they reveal that furries who are anime fans tend to be more ardent and passionate consumers than non-anime fan furries, including collecting more merchandise, being more likely to overspend on merchandise, consuming more media in general, and becoming more immersed in media. They tend to identify more strongly as nerds, and while they are more prone to believing stereotypes about fursona species, they are less likely to dislike furs and less prone to think of themselves as better than others. They tend to feel a greater sense of solidarity with non-human animals, including a greater spiritual connection to animals. Personality-wise, they were more emotionally expressive—including both being more agreeable toward others, but also more aggressive, more anxious, more depressed, and more uncomfortable in social situations. They are also lower in conscientiousness—meaning they are more prone to acting without planning—and are prone both to unhealthy eating habits specifically and, more broadly, are prone to reduced well-being (physically, psychologically, and in terms of their social interactions).[9]

---

[9] Another possible explanation for the reduced well-being observed in furries who are anime fans comes from prior studies showing that furries are fairly stigmatized within the anime community (Reysen et al., 2017). It's not hard to imagine how being a furry who is a member of a group that dislikes furries might take its toll on someone's self-esteem or well-being, especially with research showing, in other contexts, that being a member of a stigmatized community is generally tied to lower well-being (Schmitt et al., 2014).

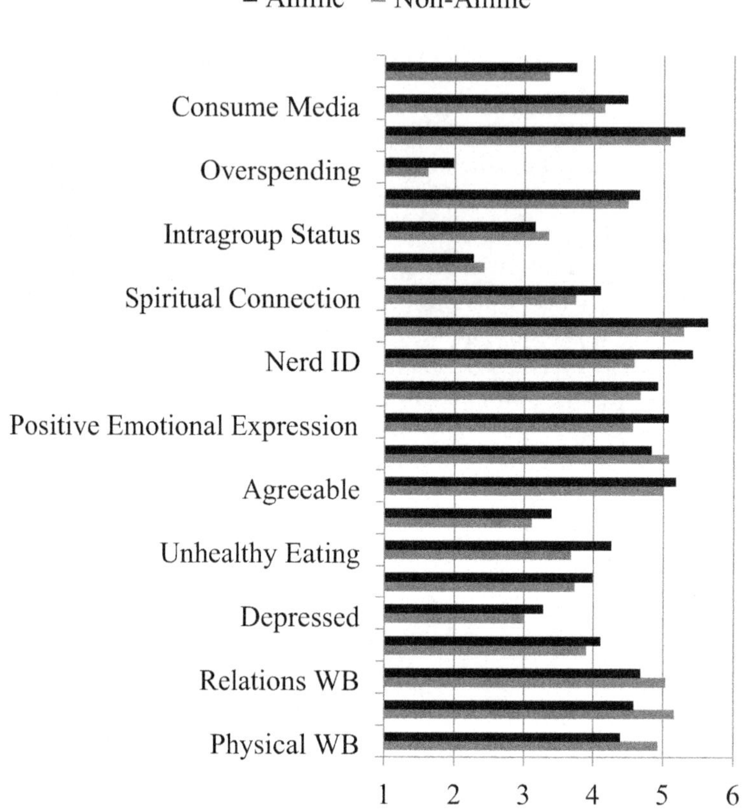

Figure 11.6. Comparisons between furries who are anime fans vs. non-anime fans (7-point scale).

Bronies

While we're on the subject of fans of specific genres, let's briefly look at fans of a very specific piece of media that overlaps considerably with the furry fandom while not necessarily being a piece of furry media.[10] A brony is

[10] The question of whether *My Little Pony* fans should be lumped in with furries has been hotly contested by furries and bronies alike. On the one hand, the show itself seems to fall into the category of "furry media," given that it is a show about anthropomorphized horses—and, indeed, for some furries, this was a draw to the show. On the other hand, some bronies distinguish their interest from furry, arguing that liking a specific instance of furry media does not, in and of itself, make them a

a (typically adult male) fan of the television show *My Little Pony: Friendship is Magic* (Edwards et al., 2019). The show debuted in October of 2010 and ran for nine seasons, until October, 2019. Starting shortly after the show's beginning, and continuing into more recent studies, we've been asking furries whether they consider themselves to be a brony. This interest predominantly stemmed from furries themselves asking us to study bronies, given that, at the time, the show's popularity had a significant impact on content in the furry fandom—many fandom artists were drawing *My Little Pony* fan art.[11]

As shown in Figure 11.7, the percentage of furries who were also bronies started at around 25%, when most people who had become *My Little Pony* fans were jumping onto the show.[12] Over time, the proportion of furries who were bronies gradually dropped to about 15% in 2019 when the show ended, and has continued to gradually trickle downward in the wake of the show, holding at around 10% of furries.[13] There are multiple possible reasons for this decline in furry bronies over time, with one possibility being that fans simply became uninterested in the show and left over time. Edwards et al.

---

furry and, by extension, arguing that not every show with anthropomorphized characters should be considered a "furry show." As another example, the television show *Bojack Horseman* prominently features anthropomorphic animal characters (including the show's titular character, Bojack), but most of its fans would neither consider the show a "furry show" nor consider themselves to be furries, despite the fact that furries may watch the show and construe it as a piece of furry media. Furry, it would seem, is in the eye of the beholder.

[11] Often to the chagrin of non-brony fans, who expressed their frustration with the common refrain that bronies were flooding or taking over the furry fandom. Despite these protests, however, which assume that non-furry bronies were "invading" the furry fandom and stealing away the attention of furry artists, our own data seem to suggest that, if anything, the "invasion" was coming from within: bronies tend to have been in the furry fandom for about a year longer than non-brony furries (9.4 years versus 8.4 years). In other words, bronies weren't coming into the furry fandom from the outside, but rather furries were becoming bronies!

[12] As is discussed in Edwards et al. (2019), many folks initially watched *My Little Pony* as a sort of joke or dare from their friends, never intending to watch more than one episode. The show's quality animation and writing surprised a lot of folks, including one of this chapter's authors who is, to this day, a self-identified brony.

[13] While *My Little Pony: Friendship is Magic* ended in 2019, its successor series, *My Little Pony: Make Your Mark*, began in 2021. As of the time of writing, indications seem to be that the show, while generally received positively by fans, has failed to capture lighting in a bottle the same way that *Friendship is Magic* did.

(2019) argue, however, that this may not be the full story, as most bronies who got into the show tended to remain with the show throughout its run. In contrast, as we see in Chapter 13, furries have a fairly considerable influx of new members from year to year, coupled with older fans generally drifting away over time. With this in mind, we're likely not seeing furries who've stopped being bronies, but rather new, non-brony furries entering the fandom.

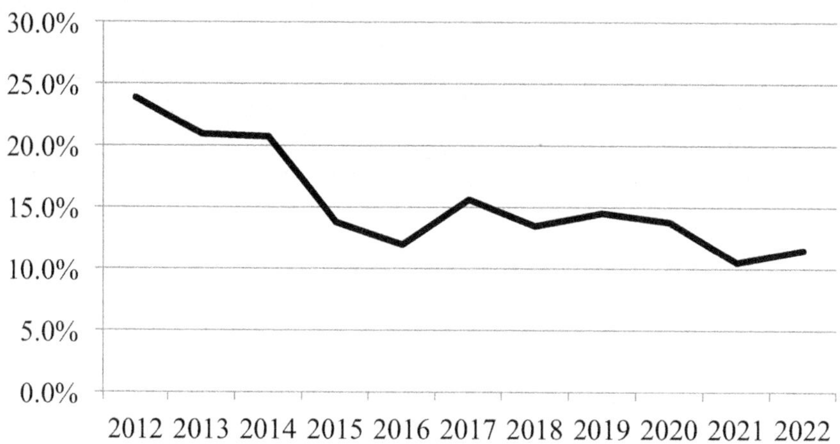

Figure 11.7. Percent of furries who identify as bronies by year.

Next, we tested whether there are any notable differences between furries that are bronies and non-brony furries. One difference we found was that bronies tend to have a smaller friendship network (an average of 9.2 friends they regularly interacted with) than non-brony furries (an average of 12.0 friends). Despite this smaller friendship network, however, brony furries do not differ significantly from non-brony furries concerning well-being, self-esteem, or diagnoses of mental illness.[14] We also find that, unlike anime fans, who are stigmatized for being furries, bronies are not typically stigmatized by the brony community for being a furry[15] and, indeed, tend to show better well-being for being part of both fandoms (Reysen et al., 2022).

A few other differences between brony furries and non-brony furries are shown in Figure 11.8. For one thing, bronies tend to value and be more

[14] This is noteworthy, given that having social support networks is generally tied to well-being, a point we return to in Chapter 22.

[15] In fact, according to Edward et al. (2019), approximately 10% of bronies are furries themselves.

active in the furry fandom than non-brony furries, as seen by their greater involvement in in-person events and a greater sense of belonging. Bronies are also more likely to be drawn to the furry fandom because of the entertainment it provides. Perhaps in support of their stereotype as being obsessed with a show intended for a different demographic, bronies are also more likely than non-brony furries to be more obsessive in their interest in furry, although they are also more likely to disclose their interest to others.[16] Despite studies showing that watching *My Little Pony* is associated positively with a sense of empathy, brony furries score lower than non-brony furries on a measure of perspective-taking, although they do feel a greater sense of solidarity with animals and feel a greater sense of spiritual connection to their fursona species (Plante et al., 2018). On the subject of spirituality, bronies are more likely than non-brony furries to both endorse new-age beliefs and identify as more spiritual. Finally, even though both furries and bronies would be considered stereotypically "nerd" fan groups, furries who were also bronies tended to score higher on a measure of nerd identity than non-brony furries.

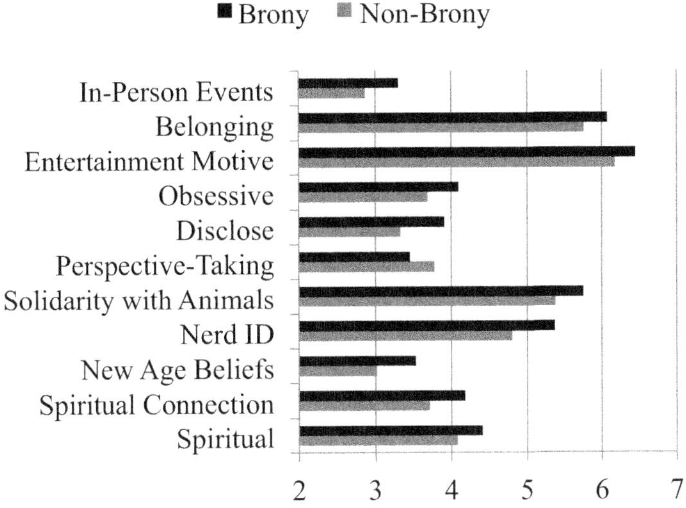

Figure 11.8. Comparisons between furries who are bronies vs. non-bronies (7-point scale).

---

[16] Indeed, many laypersons find it baffling that a brony would openly admit to watching a show intended for children, suggesting they may be especially likely, among furries, to be unabashed in discussing their interests with others.

Gamers

It will come as no surprise to anyone familiar with furry culture that many furries strongly identify as gamers—a term that can refer both to players of video/computer games but also to board games and tabletop games. After all, examples abound of board and tabletop games whose themes prominently feature anthropomorphized animal characters (e.g., Root, Mice and Mystics, Libertalia: Winds of Galecrest), while many video games allow players to play as, or interact with, furry characters (e.g., *Undertale*, *Dust: An Elysian Tail*, *Night in the Woods*). Likewise, most furry conventions can be expected to have a room dedicated to video and or computer gaming and a room dedicated to tabletop gaming. To this end, our studies show that more than half of furries self-identify as gamers, a number which has remained fairly consistent over time (see Figure 11.9).

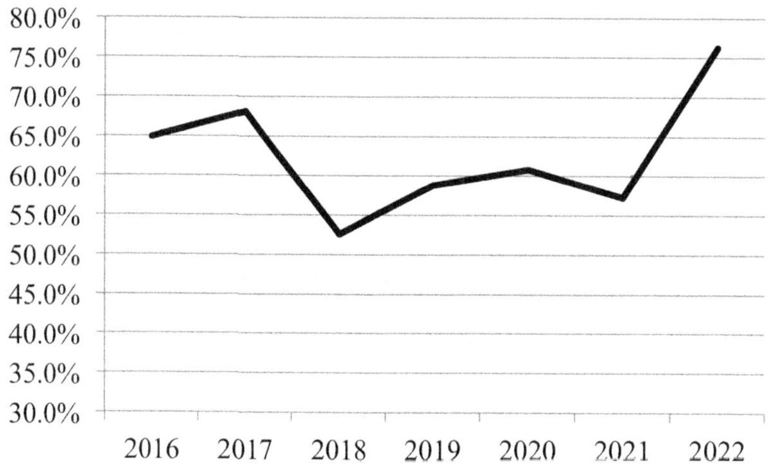

Figure 11.9. Percent of furries who identify as gamers by year.

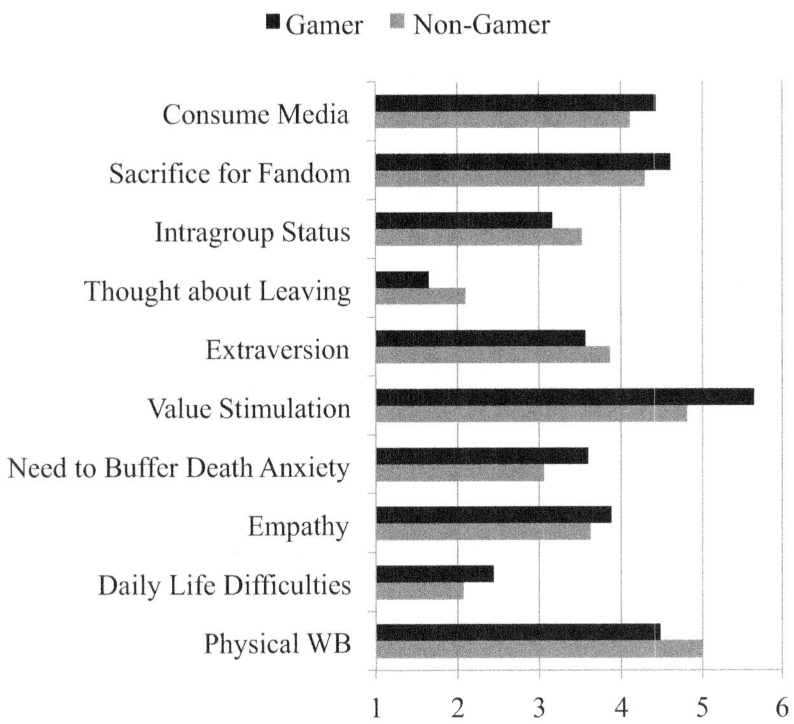

Figure 11.10. Comparisons between furries who are gamers vs. non-gamers (7-point scale).

As shown in Figure 11.10, gaming furries (vs. non-gaming furries) differ in several small ways. They tend to consume more furry-themed media than a typical furry and, perhaps in a related vein, sacrifice more for their fandom interest (e.g., spend more), although they tend to report feeling lower in status than other furries. Other studies suggest that those who identify as gamers may turn to gaming as a distraction from their own lives, valuing the stimulation provided by fandom activities more than a typical furry, having a greater need to buffer against the fear of death, experiencing more day-to-day difficulties, and suffering from worse physical health; perhaps related, they are also less likely to have thought about leaving the furry fandom than other furries, perhaps because they are especially likely to draw benefits from their involvement in the fandom. And while gamers may be more introverted than typical furries,[17] they are also higher in empathy, a finding not entirely inconsistent with some research suggesting that some games (e.g., games with prosocial messages) can foster greater perspective-taking and empathy in players (e.g., Greitemeyer et al., 2010).

Musicians

As previously mentioned, there are several notable examples of prominent musicians in the furry fandom. And while musicians may not be quite as central to the furry fandom as they are in other fandoms (e.g., the brony fandom), it is rather telling that, in one of our studies asking furries to list their favorite content creators, three of the top ten were furry musicians (Fox Amoore, Pepper Coyote, NIIC). Across studies, approximately 16% of furries consider themselves to be musicians (see Figure 11.11). As a group, these furries, compared to other furries, tend to feel a closer sense of connection to the furry fandom (e.g., a sense of shared fate with the fandom and greater solidarity; see Figure 11.12). They are also more likely to be outgoing and involved in fandom happenings—for better or for worse—are more open to new experiences and partying, and are more involved in fandom drama.

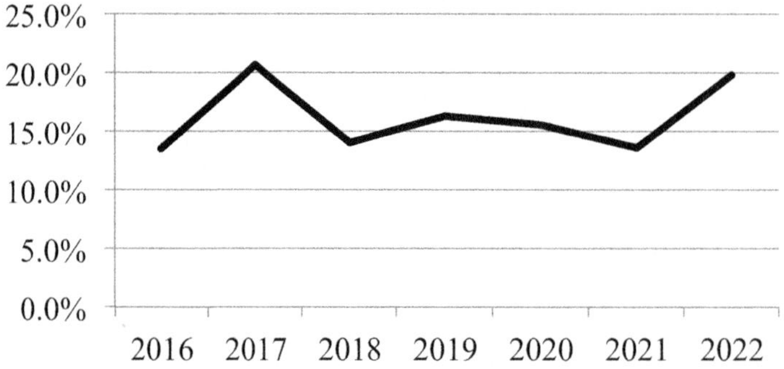

Figure 11.11. Percent of furries who identify as musicians by year.

[17] Which is saying something, given that furries are, as a group, fairly introverted (see Chapter 18).

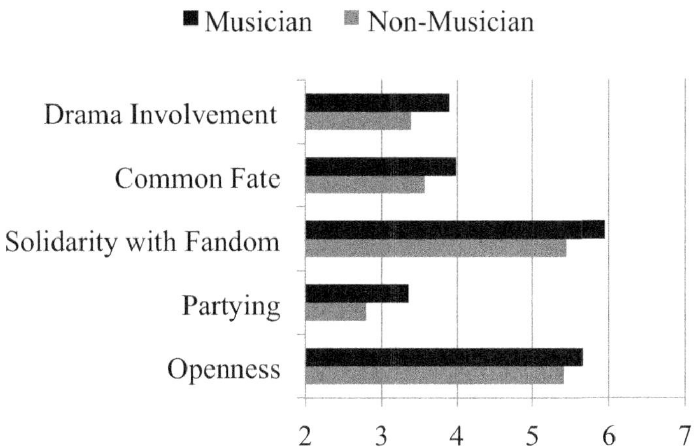

Figure 11.12. Comparisons between furries who are musicians vs. non-musicians (7-point scale).

Writers

Writers in the furry fandom have a lot in common with musicians. As with musicians, writers are represented among the top 10 most favorited furry content creators (e.g., Rukis Croax, Kyell Gold), although they are not held with the same degree of prestige as they are in other fandoms (e.g., fanfiction writers in the *My Little Pony*, *Sherlock*, *Doctor Who*, or *Supernatural* fandoms). When asked, writers were only somewhat more common than musicians in the fandom, with approximately 22% of furries identifying at least somewhat as a writer (see Figure 11.13). Writers are somewhat more distinct from typical furries in their own way (see Figure 11.14), including, like musicians, a tendency to feel a close sense of connection with the fandom—albeit one in which furry is an important part of who they are, with furry representing a source of help and support. Writers are more mature than other furries on average, showing a greater ability to perspective-take and more empathy, both with humans and with animals. They lead more active fantasy lives and generally believe that it's a positive thing for furry, as a fandom, to become more prominent and mainstream. They are also more open to new experiences and show a greater sense of new-age beliefs, including a spiritual connection to their fursona. Finally, there is evidence suggesting that writers are more likely to have a history of being bullied in their youth and to have lower physical and relationship well-being—although their psychological well-being is on par with other furries.

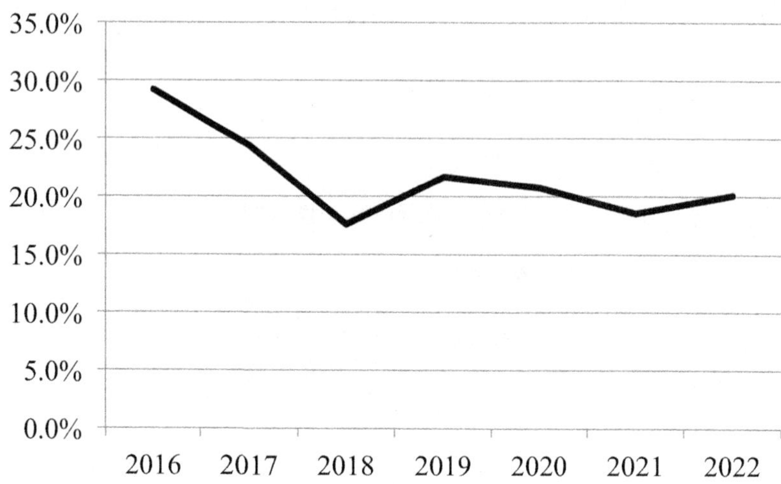

Figure 11.13. Percent of furries who identify as writers by year.

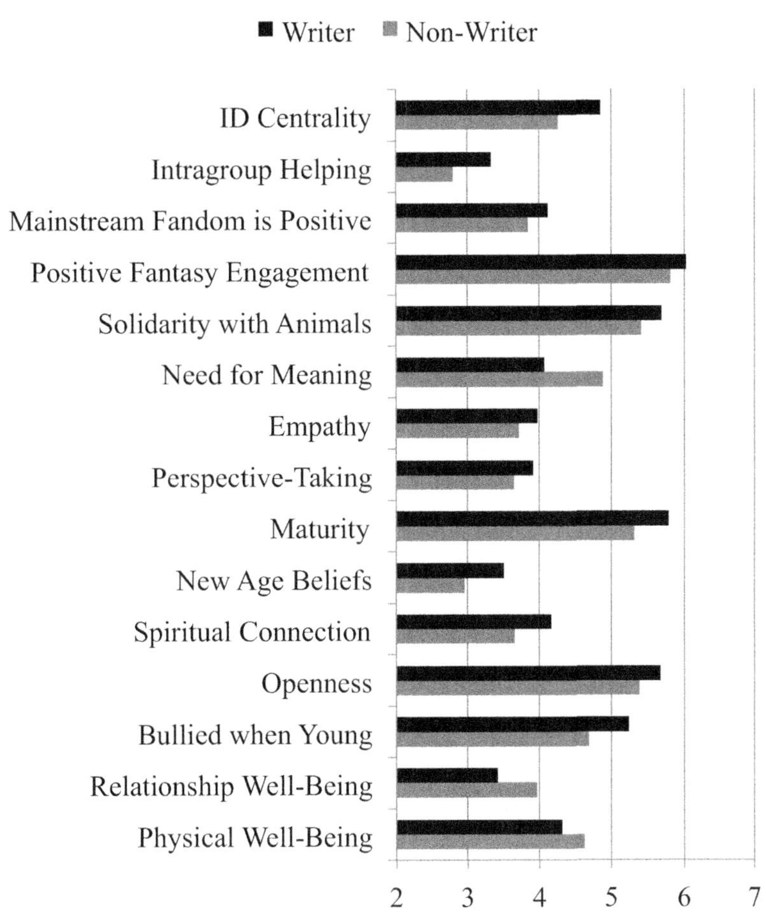

Figure 11.14. Comparisons between furries who are writers vs. non-writers (7-point scale).

Artists

Compared to the other content creators we've looked at, artists are among the most prominent and revered content creators in the furry fandom (a point we'll return to later in this chapter). Given the importance of art in the furry fandom, including being featured on convention badges, fursona profile pictures, and prominently displayed throughout many a dealer's den at furry conventions the world over, it makes sense that the vast majority of responses to our question about favorite content creators named artists.[18] Over the years our surveys have found that, on average, 34% of furries self-identify as artists (see Figure 11.15).

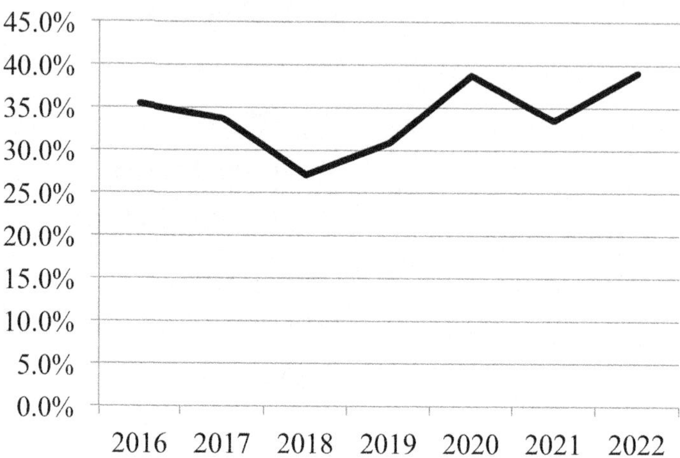

Figure 11.15. Percent of furries who identify as artists by year.

In many ways, furry artists share a similar profile with furry writers (see Figure 11.16). Like with writers, their furry identity is a fairly central part of who they are, something they openly express and do little to conceal from others. In addition to being producers of content, many artists also collect merchandise themselves. They lead fairly active fantasy lives and see their interest in furry as a means of self-expression and a potential source of benefits (e.g., revenue, helping them to develop and express aspects of themselves). Furry artists, on average, tend to score lower in emotional stability, the need for precision, and conscientiousness, and score higher in impulsive emotional expression, findings in line with stereotypes of artists as passionate and spontaneous. They are also fairly agreeable—a useful skill for interacting with clients— and are generally more positive toward transgender

[18] While artists only made up three of the top ten favorite content creators (Rukis, Dark Natasha, Kenket), this is likely because there are, comparatively, so many more artists than there are writers and musicians in the furry fandom. As such, one's choice for a favorite artist may involve a competition between dozens or even hundreds of artists, while only a handful of favorite musicians or writers may vie for the same title.

people than the rest of the furry fandom.[19] Artists, like musicians, also seem to struggle with greater difficulties in their lives, including more day-to-day problems as well as a history of being bullied. They are also more likely to have problems with both their physical health and the quality of their relationships.

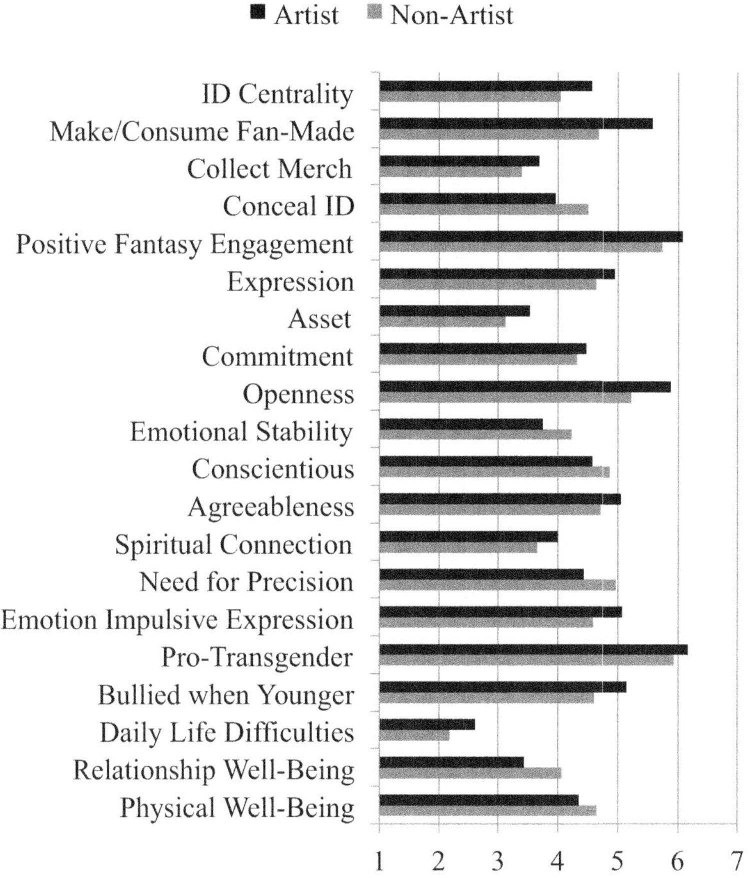

Figure 11.16. Comparisons between furries who are artists vs. non-artists (7-point scale).

[19] This is despite the furry fandom's already-progressive views on transgender people and may stem from the fact that, as some of our studies have shown, artists are significantly more likely to be transgender themselves.

Military Furs

Shifting our focus away from content creators, we can find a variety of other noteworthy subgroups in the furry fandom, groups organized around features other than a liking of particular content or one's role in the fandom. One such example are the military furs, also known as "MilFurs," furries who are either actively members of, or veterans of, their country's armed services (Plante et al., 2016). While the number of MilFurs in the fandom seems to be declining over time, they have, on average, made up about 6% of the furry fandom (see Figure 11.17). As a group, MilFurs (vs. non-MilFurs) differ in several ways from the trends observed above with artists (see Figure 11.18). As an example, while artists tended to be more emotionally tempestuous and less conscientious, Milfurs tended to be more emotionally stable and conscientious than a typical furry, as well as more extroverted. While they feel less entitled to special treatment than a typical furry, they do hold themselves in higher regard (self-inflation, elitism) and are more likely to gatekeep in the fandom (e.g., to push for the exclusion of some people from fandom spaces). MilFurs tend to be more extroverted and seek out novelty and excitement, which may be related to a greater tendency to drink alcohol. Politically, they are less liberal and more conservative, both in economic terms (e.g., a greater desire for economic liberty) and with respect to social policies (e.g., being more opposed to transgender rights). In terms of well-being, they tend to have a greater sense of self-esteem and show greater physical and relationship well-being than typical furries.

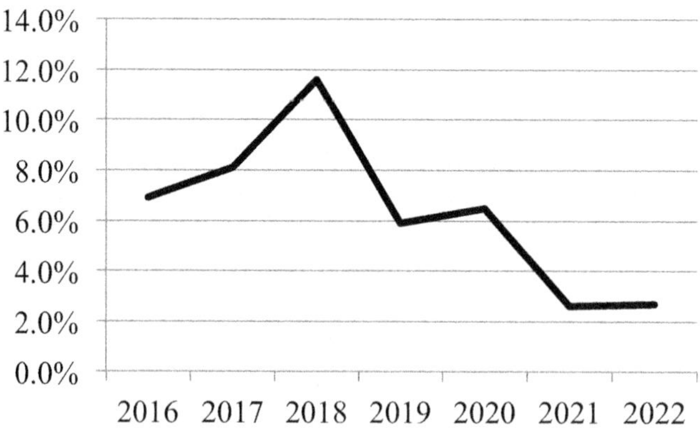

Figure 11.17. Percent of furries who identify as military furs by year.

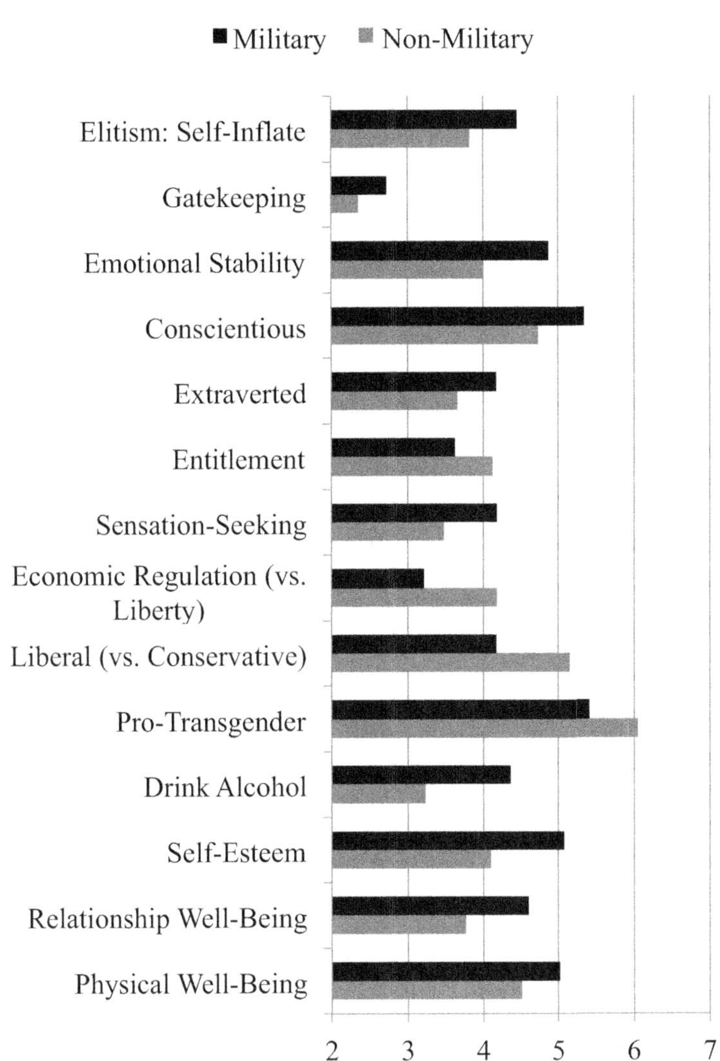

Figure 11.18. Comparisons between furries who are MilFurs vs. non-MilFurs (7-point scale).

Babyfurs

Babyfurs (and the related group, cubfurs) are a subgroup of furries defined by their interest in age play (e.g., an interest in stories and art featuring young, child-age anthropomorphic animal characters; Plante et al.,

2016).[20] The number of babyfurs in our studies has fluctuated over time, but, on average, represents about 7.6% of the fandom (see Figure 11.19). As a group, babyfurs (vs. non-babyfurs) tend to be characterized by a greater sense of passion for their interest in furry, scoring higher on measures of both fanship (e.g., collecting more merchandise) and fandom (e.g., feeling a greater sense of solidarity with furries), as well as identifying more strongly with their fursonas and scoring higher on measures of healthy and pathological passion and lower on self-control (see Figure 11.20). They are also more highly motivated furries across various measures of motivation (commitment, asset, presence, and expression), suggesting that babyfurs, as a group, identify in almost every way as being "more furry" than a typical furry, including being more likely to anthropomorphize non-human things in the world around them (i.e., not just animals, but also technology, furniture, and vehicles). In line with their higher level of involvement in all things furry, they tend to keep up more with trends in the fandom and to see themselves as being somewhat higher in status than other furries, perhaps because of their greater involvement with, and commitment to, furry. They are lower in avoidant attachment relative to other furries, suggesting a greater need to get closer to others, and feel a greater need for significance (meaning, belongingness) in their lives.

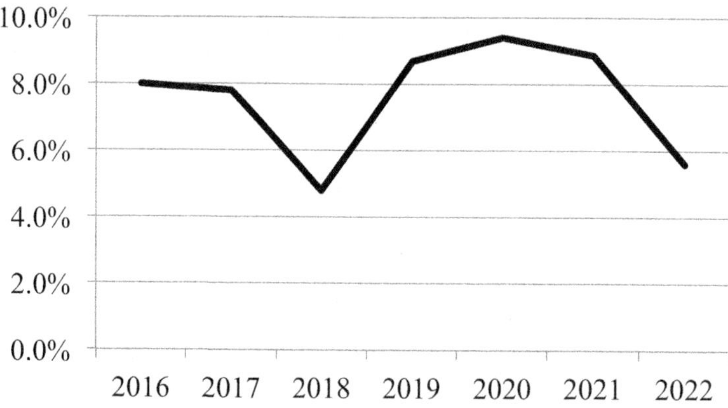

Figure 11.19. Percent of furries who identify as babyfurs by year.

[20] The concept was once explained to one of the authors of this chapter by a babyfur who said that, in the same way that most furries see the concept of species as malleable for the purpose of creating a fursona (e.g., being a human with a cat fursona), babyfurs see the concept of age as malleable (e.g., being an adult with a toddler-age fursona).

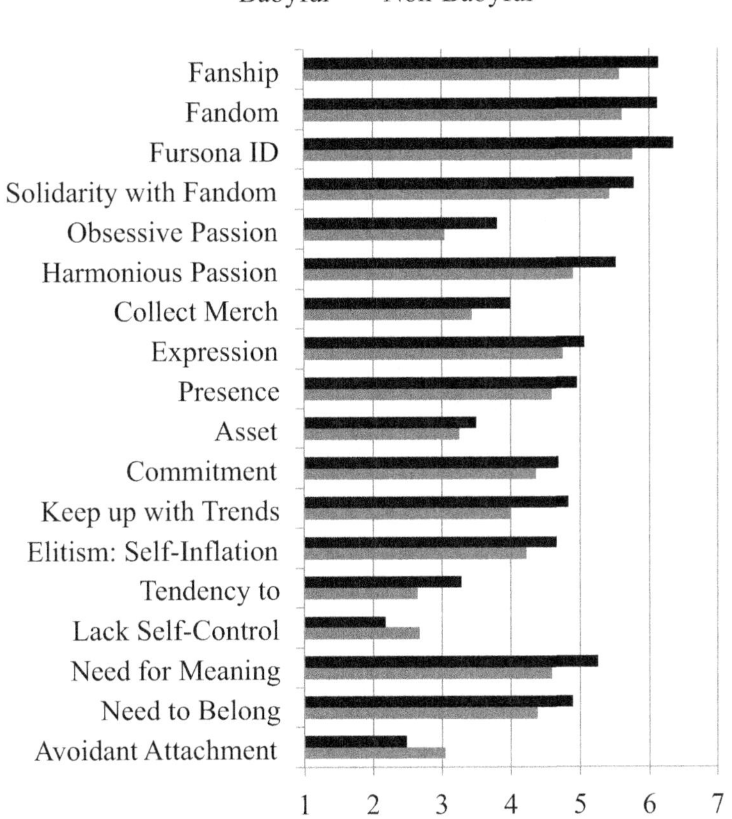

Figure 11.20. Comparisons between furries who are babyfurs vs. non-babyfurs (7-point scale).

Popufurs

The last subgroup we'll look at directly is popufurs. The term popufur is a somewhat tongue-in-cheek expression used to refer to a furry who is popular among other furries—regardless of the reason.[21] People referred to as

[21] The term itself is often used in a mocking or sarcastic manner. One possible reason for this is because the term itself is a bit of a forced pun on the term "popular," itself making fun of furries' tendency to awkwardly incorporate furry-themed puns into their vocabulary. Another reason is because it makes fun of the notion of being popular in a group that's generally characterized as being full of

popufur can vary, ranging from popular artists to well-known fursuiters to those who've achieved notoriety on social media to those who are known for planning and running furry-themed events. As with the other subgroups in this chapter, we make no prescriptive claims about the subgroup's labels, nor do we attempt to define them—choosing instead to let participants decide whether the term is one they would use to describe themselves. Keeping this in mind, approximately 5% of furries, in any given sample of furries, identify with the term popufur Figure 11.21.

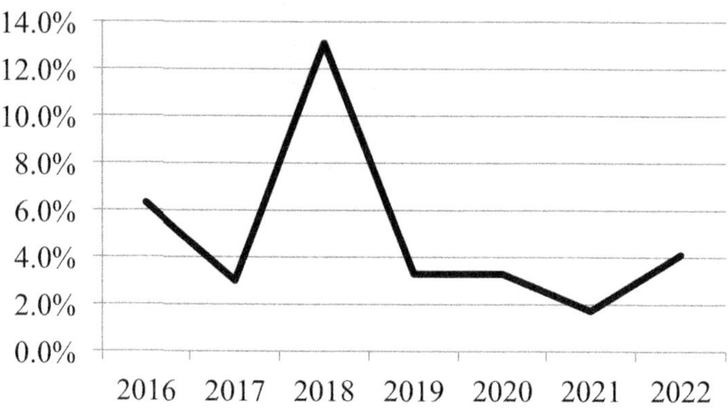

Figure 11.21. Percent of furries who identify as popufurs by year.

As shown in Figure 11.22, we found many differences between self-described popufurs and non-popufur furries. First, those who called themselves popufur tended to, like babyfurs, be more furry in almost every way: being a bigger fan of furry content (e.g., consuming and making more furry content), identifying more strongly with the fandom, identifying more with one's fursona, considering furry to be a more central part of their sense of self, and being significantly more passionate (in a pathological way) with furry in general. They were also significantly more likely to be motivated to be furry for a wide variety of reasons and tended to anthropomorphize the world around them more—also in line with babyfurs.

---

outcasts, deviants, and strange by the general public (see Chapter 21 for more on this). As such, being popular among furries is akin to being the tallest child in kindergarten—a fairly modest accomplishment in perspective.

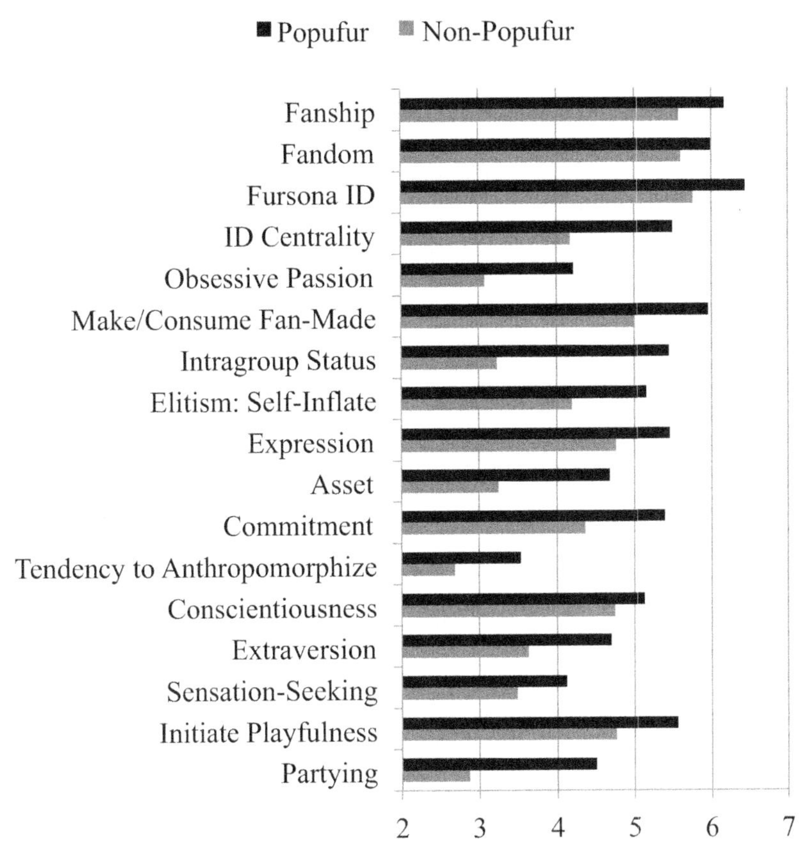

Figure 11.22. Comparisons between furries who are popufurs vs. non-popufurs (7-point scale).

As one might expect from a group who self-identifies as being popular, popufurs stated that they had a greater sense of status within the fandom, and tended to see themselves as being above typical furries. Personality-wise, they were far more extroverted than a typical furry, were more sensation-seeking, reported being more playful, and claimed to party more. They were also more conscientious, suggesting that they put more thought into planning and thinking things through before acting on them.

Taken together, it's hard to know exactly what to make of popufurs other than to take them at face value. While one might expect, given the tongue-in-cheek nature with which popufur is often used in the furry fandom, that someone who identifies as a popufur would do so ironically or as a joke, with a sense of self-deprecation. Instead, it would appear that furries who truly do see themselves as being "especially furry" and who are frequently involved in fandom activities are the ones most likely to use this term to describe themselves—perhaps doing so in a non-ironic way. Importantly, there seems to be little sign of maladaptation or problems when it comes to popufurs—as a group, they were no more likely than any other furry to be struggling with mental or physical health problems, something we might expect to see in a group defined by pathology or maladaptation.

Intragroup Hierarchy

Having discussed many different subgroups within the furry fandom,[22] we'd like to finish this chapter by focusing one last time on the differences between different subgroups. As we've seen, there are average differences between the members of different subgroups: some show small personality deviations from a typical furry, others are more involved or more passionate about furry as an interest, while some simply hold themselves in higher regard than other furries.

With this in mind, let's focus on one last difference between subgroups in the fandom: the extent to which they are generally held in higher or lower regard by the fandom. As with any group, over time natural hierarchies may form among its members. Given the human tendency to divide ourselves into groups and amplify the differences between those groups (see Chapter 6), it only makes sense that we would think about our groups and how they stack up against the groups around us. With time, some subgroups will emerge as being more revered or respected than others, while others are relegated to lower status than others. For example, in the field of psychology, some subdisciplines, like clinical psychology, are held in higher regard than others, like educational psychology. The reasons why this may be the case, or whether there's any merit to this perception, are beyond the focus of this last section. For now, we're simply interested in the question of whether there are some subgroups within the furry fandom that furries look down upon.

To this end, we asked furries in one of our earlier studies of convention-going furries to rate how positively or negatively they viewed 14 different subgroups within the furry fandom. Higher scores on the 7-point scale indicate greater status within the community, a group that furries look up to

---

[22] By no means are these the only subgroups within the furry fandom! There are dozens, even hundreds of significant subgroups that we could potentially study. These are, to date, the subgroups about which we have the most data, and about which we are most commonly asked by furries.

and would want to be a part of. In contrast, lower scores represent a group that is disliked or even despised, a group that some or even many furries may want to see excluded from the fandom.

As shown in Figure 11.23, most of the subgroups we measured were above the midpoint of the measure (i.e., 4), indicating that furries generally accepted and liked many of the more popular subgroups (e.g., artists, writers, fursuiters, musicians, and gamers). These groups may be held in high regard because of their perceived role in contributing to the content of the fandom (e.g., artists, writers), or simply because they represent something coveted by many in the fandom (e.g., a fursuit, see Chapter 8), or they may simply represent a group to which most furries belong (e.g., gamers).

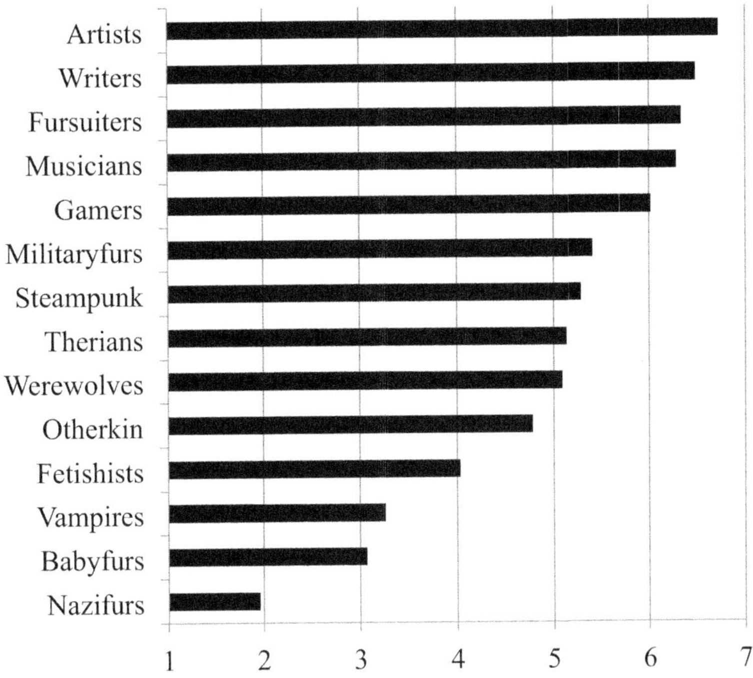

Figure 11.23. Subgroup ratings of how positively they are viewed within the furry culture (7-point scale).

Groups below the midpoint included vampires, babyfurs, and Nazifurs, with Nazifurs, in particular, falling well below the other groups by far. In the case of vampires, furries may see this as a subgroup only tangentially related to the furry fandom, as something not really furry and, as such, perceive it to be a sort of outsider or outgroup against which to compare the rest of the furry fandom (us vs. them).[23] As for babyfurs, one possible reason for their negative perception may stem from the association that some furries make between babyfurs and pedophilia. Put simply, it's fairly common for furries to commission artwork featuring their fursonas in erotic contexts. Insofar as furries presume that babyfurs do this (or to the extent that it actually happens), there is a belief among some furries that babyfurs support or are, themselves, pedophiles—one of the most strongly condemned groups in society. At the moment, we've got insufficient data to test these or other hypotheses about why babyfurs represent such a maligned group in the furry fandom, though it will almost certainly be a subject for future studies.

As for Nazifurs, opposition to them almost certainly stems from the fact that Nazi beliefs—and fascism more broadly—are at odds with both the progressive ideology of the furry fandom (see Chapter 17) and with the fact that most furries are, themselves, LGBTQ+ (see Chapter 15 and Chapter 16), something which would be targeted as "degenerate" within Nazi ideology. While some self-identified Nazifurs might counter that they, themselves, do not endorse Nazi ideology but, rather, admire the aesthetics or fashion of the regime, our findings suggest that most furries find such arguments, at best, to be a weak justification (e.g., why be enamored with the aesthetics of a hateful ideology) and, at worst, thinly-veiled deflection from one's truly-held convictions (e.g., a Nazi in denial). As we see in Chapter 17, self-identified Nazis are exceedingly rare in the furry fandom, and these results would seem to suggest why—they are decidedly unwelcome in the fandom.

Conclusion

In this chapter we took a deeper look at different subgroups within the furry fandom that spring up around, among other things, different types of preferred media consumption and production, other, related (and unrelated) group memberships, and subgroups which furries have strong feelings toward or a lot to say about (e.g., babyfurs, popufurs). We found that furries, as a group, have a lot of similarities (e.g., shared interest in science fiction, cartoons, comedy, and fantasy genres of media), although they are far from a homogeneous group. A more fine-grained look at furries revealed the multitude of subgroups into which they define themselves, subgroups that seem fairly stable over time in most cases. We found that most of these subgroups are viewed by the fandom in a mostly favorable light, although a

---

[23] The inclusion of this group in the study was a product of the ongoing popularity, at the time, of the *Twilight* series of books / films, and a broader cultural interest in vampires that has seemingly waned since.

few are fairly highly stigmatized and are generally seen as unwelcome in the fandom. Finally, we note that despite a plethora of small differences observed between members of these groups, the most telling story is the relatively small magnitude of most of these differences; furries usually have far more in common than they do differences. While individual furries are nuanced and varied, and these differences add spice and variety to this fandom, one should not overlook the fact that furries tend to see themselves as a big, inclusive fandom for a reason—the differences, in many ways, are skin-deep relative to the far more substantive similarities furries have in common with their fellow furries.

References

Booth, P. (2016). *Crossing fandoms: SuperWhoLock and the contemporary fan audience*. Palgrave Macmillan.

Edwards, P., Chadborn, D. P., Plante, C., Reysen, S., & Redden, M. H. (2019). *Meet the bronies: The psychology of adult* My Little Pony *fandom*. McFarland & Company.

Greitemeyer, T., Osswald, S., & Brauer, M. (2010). Playing prosocial video games increases empathy and decreases schadenfreude. *Emotion, 10*(6), 796-802. https://doi.org/10.1037/a0020194

Horbinski, A. (2019). What you watch is what you are? Early anime and manga fandom in the United States. *Mechademia, 12*(1), 11-30.

Notopoulos, K. (2016, March 2). Proof Disney is actually marketing "Zootopia" to furries. *Buzzfeed News*. https://www.buzzfeednews.com/article/katienotopoulos/proof-disney-is-actually-marketing-zootopia-to-furries

Plante, C. N., Reysen, S., Brooks, T. R., & Chadborn, D. (2021). *CAPE: A multidimensional model of fan interest*. CAPE Model Research Team.

Plante, C. N., Reysen, S., Roberts, S. E., & Gerbasi, K. C. (2016). *Furscience! A summary of five years of research from the International Anthropomorphic Research Project*. Furscience.

Plante, C. N., Chadborn, D., Groves, C., & Reysen, S. (2018). Letters from Equestria: Prosocial media, helping, and empathy in fans of *My Little Pony. Communication and Culture Online, 9*(1), 206-222. https://doi.org/10.18485/kkonline.2018.9.9.11

Reysen, S., Plante, C. N., & Chadborn, D. (2022). Perceived permeability of group boundaries as a mediator between belonging to multiple fandoms and loneliness. *Popular Culture Studies Journal, 10*(1), 315-333.

Reysen, S., Plante, C. N., Chadborn, D., Roberts, S. E., & Gerbasi, K. (2021). *Transported to another world: The psychology of anime fans*. International Anime Research Project.

Reysen, S., Plante, C. N., Roberts, S. E., & Gerbasi, K. C. (2017). Accuracy of perceived prejudice toward one's fan group. *The Phoenix Papers, 3*(1), 122-129.

Reysen, S., Plante, C. N., Roberts, S. E., Gerbasi, K. C., & Shaw, J. (2016). An examination of anime fan stereotypes. *The Phoenix Papers, 2*(2), 90-117.

Schmitt, M. T., Branscombe, N. R., Postmes, T., & Garcia, A. (2014). The consequences of perceived discrimination for psychological well-being: A meta-analytic review. *Psychological Bulletin, 140*(4), 921-948. https://doi.org/10.1037/a0035754

Strike, J. (2017). *Furry Nation: The true story of America's most misunderstood subculture*. CLEiS Press.

Chapter 12
The Drama Llama: Conflict in the Fandom

Courtney "Nuka" Plante

As we've discussed in other chapters (e.g., Chapter 5), what it means to be furry differs considerably from person to person. Oh sure, we can point to specific behaviors or beliefs that are fairly common among furries, like the fact that most furries have a fan-like interest in anthropomorphized animal characters, most consider the fan community to be a big draw to the interest, and most create a fursona to represent themselves in fan spaces. But beyond this handful of common traits, furries are required to have little else in common.

For example, it's true that furries, on average, tend to be in their teens or early adulthood (Chapter 13), are LGBTQ+ (Chapter 15 and Chapter 16), and are generally secular and hold progressive political beliefs (Chapter 17). But very little about what it means to be furry *requires* these features. There's no reason why a 70-year-old religious, conservative-leaning, straight, cisgender woman can't be just as "furry" as a 20-year-old liberal, atheist, gay, non-binary person. At the end of the day, as long as they both have a strong interest in furry-themed content and both use the term "furry" to describe themselves, most would probably agree that they're both furries. Nevertheless, they may have dramatically different political and religious beliefs and life experiences, and manifest their interest in dramatically different ways (e.g., watching cartoons and purchasing art versus fursuiting and attending furry conventions).

This leads us to ask: do the relatively simple requirements for being a furry and the resulting diversity of opinions ever lead to friction? As a simple example, imagine a furry for whom furry is a fun, light-hearted outlet for their creativity, an occasional romp into fantasy that adds spice to an otherwise comfortable, if somewhat routine life. Now imagine a second furry for whom the fandom is their found family: these aren't just their friends, they've become a valuable source of social support, allies against a world that's hostile toward them just for being who they are (e.g., LGBTQ+). Now, imagine how these two furries might clash when it comes to the question of what's appropriate in fandom spaces. The first furry might get annoyed at the second for dragging politics into their lighthearted artistic outlet. The second, in response, might see the first's behavior as trivializing their struggle and not recognizing the value of the fandom as a source of moral support and an arena for social change.

In this chapter, we document the potential for conflicts like these to arise among furries when differences in opinion, experience, and vision of the furry fandom arise. Conflicts like these range from the fairly trivial—disagreements about which art styles or popular trends are positive—to the fairly serious—arguments about the appropriateness of extreme attitudes and behaviors in fandom space and their potential to harm vulnerable members of the community. We'll begin by discussing some of the different types of conflict that arise in the fandom—from conflicts over content in the fandom to conflicts over specific attitudes and behaviors—before then defining and discussing the concept of drama, distinguishing it from other types of conflict. Finally, we'll talk about some of the most probable sources of conflict in the fandom, the proverbial tinderboxes waiting to go up in flames.

Conflict Over Art / Content

Since one of the most unifying features of furry is a shared interest in furry-themed content, this seems as good a place as any to start looking for disagreements. If nothing else, furry content is something we'd expect most furries to have an opinion about—even if that opinion is just an aesthetic preference for one style or medium over another.

One way we've assessed conflicts over content is by asking a sample of furries recruited at a 2020 convention to indicate, in an open-ended fashion, what trends in furry media they'd like to see more or less of. These responses were coded and organized into common themes, allowing us to see what percentage of furries spontaneously asked for more of something or less of it (presumably because they liked or disliked it). We'll discuss these findings throughout this chapter, but we'll begin with one of the most common sentiments expressed: 10.3% of furries indicated that they wanted more of a specific type of content. This included wanting to see more 3D modeling, animation, comics, dancing, educational videos, games, music, music videos, puppetry, sculpture, streams, tutorials, virtual reality content, written work, and YouTube videos. Put simply, while visual artwork is often the focus of furry media, there's demand for a much broader range of media content.

That being said, let's delve into furries' feelings about visual art specifically, given its prominence in fandom spaces. To start, in the same 2020 convention study, we found that 11.4% of furries wanted more of a specific type of art, including more references to popular memes, specific formats (e.g., traditional, physical artwork instead of digital), artwork with specific themes (e.g., transformation), or different types of commissions (e.g., "your character here"[1] pieces). In another category, respondents were very specific about the content they wanted to see more of, with 1.9% wanting to see more artwork featuring specific body styles or body parts (e.g., eyes, paws, bellies). Others (9.1%) referred to a particular aesthetic they wanted more of (e.g., cute, dark, realistic, stylized, cartoonish).

A smaller proportion of participants, however, responded by listing what they wanted to see *less* of. For example, 2.9% indicated that they wanted to see fewer "your character here" or "adoptable"[2] pieces. Another 1.4% pointed to general themes in artwork that they wanted to see less of (e.g., gore, death, violence), while 1.7% pointed to very specific characters they wanted to see less of in furry artwork (e.g., police officers and figures of authority, human characters).

Another way to gauge the fandom's attitude toward furry content is through a measure called a feeling thermometer, where respondents indicate how negatively or positively they feel about something on a 0-100 scale (0 = *very negative*, 50 = *neutral*, 100 = *very positive*). In the same 2020 study,

---

[1] "Your character here," or "YCH" pieces are commissioned pieces in which the artist creates a scene or sketches out a specific pose in advance without a particular character. The piece is then bought or auctioned off, where it is then completed by the artist using the buyer's character of choice (e.g., their fursona). Some artists like this format because it allows them the freedom to start with a pose or scene that inspires them rather than relying on commissioners to dictate the framing of a scene. Buyers may be drawn to the fact that they can get a pretty good idea how the piece will look before buying. Detractors may dislike YCH pieces because they feel it gives them little control over the scene or its framing, making the piece feel less like it was custom-made for them. Others may simply be annoyed at frequency with which YCH pieces (which are, by nature, unfinished) are advertised on furry art websites.

[2] Adoptable characters are original characters created by an artist with the intent of selling ownership of the character to a buyer. Depending on the character, this could include selling just a reference sheet of a character or it could include selling a gallery full of artwork featuring the character, transferring ownership of the art and the right to the character to the buyer. Artists may also use a template to create a set of characters, each of whom can be auctioned off or bought. Proponents of adoptable characters may prefer this as a way of acquiring an appealing fursona rather than developing one themselves. Alternatively, they may simply enjoy collecting characters they can use in future commissions. Opponents may decry purchasing adoptable characters as promoting laziness in those who don't develop their own fursonas, or they may see adoptables as a low-effort way for artists to make money by relying on recolored templates.

convention-going furries completed a number of these feeling thermometers, the results of which are shown in Figure 12.1.

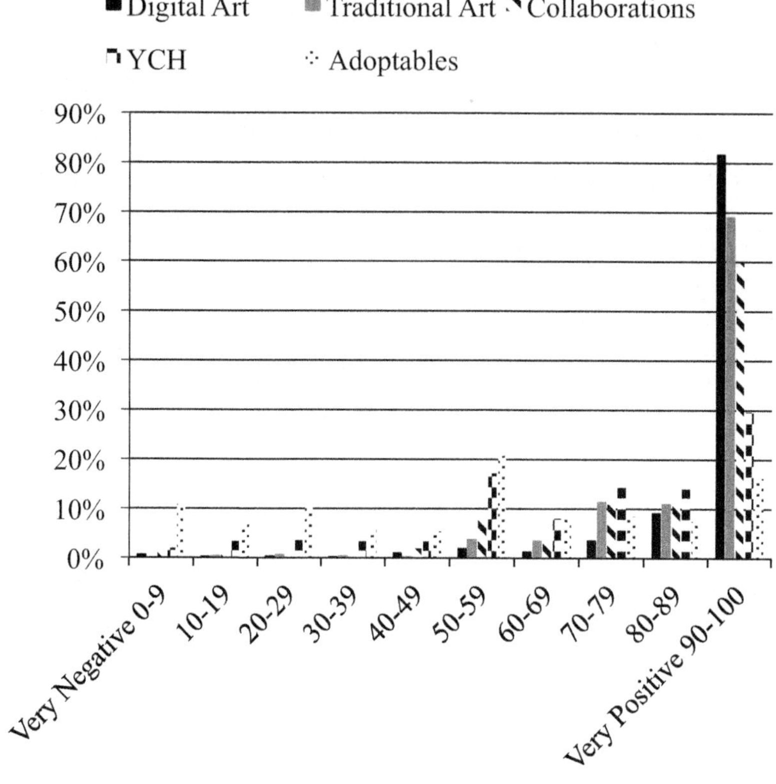

Figure 12.1. Feeling thermometers assessing the feelings of furries recruited at a furry convention toward various trends and content in furry-themed artwork.

The figure demonstrates, first and foremost, that furries are overwhelmingly positive about art in general, both digital and traditional, with only a slight preference for digital art over traditional art.[3] Furries were

[3] Follow-up analyses suggest that age may affect this tendency. While older and younger furries both appreciate traditional forms of artwork, younger furries express more positive feelings toward digital artwork than do older furries who, while still positive toward it, are somewhat less positive. This may be a product of differences in the artists, technology, and trends that were popular for different generations of

also fairly positive about collaborations between artists. On the other hand, furries were far more mixed when it came to "Your Character Here" pieces and adoptables. While generally more positive than not toward "Your Character Here" pieces, less than half of furries were exceedingly enthusiastic about them. And when it comes to adoptable characters? Furries are fairly divided on the subject. The average response to adoptables was fairly neutral, but only 20% of furries expressed a neutral position. This means that a fairly equal amount of furries expressed positive and negative views about adoptables, revealing them to be a fairly polarized issue. Taken as a whole, these results suggest that while furries are generally in agreement about certain aspects of art (e.g., digital and traditional art are a good thing), they disagree considerably about specific types of content, such as adoptable characters.[4]

Another potential point of conflict when it comes to furry artwork is the issue of diversity of content. As an abstract concept, furries seem to be fairly open to the idea of having a broad range of content: 8.2% of respondents to the 2020 convention study spontaneously mentioned that they liked seeing diversity, novelty, and creativity in content, be it new artists, new species, or new styles that keep the medium fresh. However, some disagreement emerged concerning LGBTQ+ content and characters. While 1.9% of respondents indicated that they wanted to see more LGBTQ+ characters in furry content, 1.4% of respondents said just the opposite, that they wanted to see fewer LGBTQ+ characters. One possible explanation for the desire to see fewer LGBTQ+ characters may be that straight, cisgender furries feel that there are fewer characters "like them" than they're accustomed to seeing in mainstream media contexts.[5] Another possibility is that some furries hold

---

furries (e.g., digital art is more common today than it was in the 1990s or early 2000s). We discuss other generational differences later in this chapter.

[4] While furries may have such disagreements about furry content, the same study found that furries were also fairly supportive of artist livestreams and online art auctions as ways to interact with artists.

[5] This concept, known as heteronormativity or cisnormativity, is based on a culture's tendency to treat straight, cisgender people as the "default" or norm, due to their being proportionally more common than LGBTQ+ people. As a result, LGBTQ+ characters are generally underrepresented in popular culture or, when they are portrayed, the character being LGBTQ+ is often their sole defining feature. The fact that a straight, cisgender person can find themselves represented in most popular media characters is something that's easy to take for granted until they find themselves in a context in which LGBTQ+ characters may be just as prevalent, or

negative attitudes toward LGBTQ+ people (see Chapter 15 and Chapter 16 for more on this). These, as well as other possible explanations, remain to be tested in future studies. For now, however, they illustrate a point of contention between furries when it comes to the content they want to see.

We can also look at furries' attitudes toward mainstream furry content—that is, media featuring anthropomorphized animal characters that became popular in mainstream culture and which may be a cultural representation of, or gateway into, furry. As an illustrative example, the Disney film *Zootopia* received mainstream acclaim (Metacritic – Movie Reviews, 2016) while also being a hit among furries (Josephs, 2016). For 4.7% of respondents in the 2020 furry convention study, they would like to see more positively-received furry content in mainstream media—if for no other reason than to counteract some of the stigma directed toward the furry fandom (see Chapter 21 for more on this). In contrast, 2.6% of furries want to see less mainstream furry content. These respondents were generally trying to prevent large corporations like Disney from taking over furry spaces and elbowing out thousands of small, independent content creators.

Evidence for this disagreement goes beyond the 2020 study, with at least one 2017 online study showing that furries were fairly mixed in their opinions about whether furry should "remain underground" or "become mainstream." Specifically, the study found that 46.0% of furries preferred the idea of furry remaining underground while 13.9% would prefer furries become more mainstream (the remaining 40.1% expressed mixed feelings or had no strong preference either way). In short, furries are far from reaching a consensus on the matter.

We can also look beyond furry media itself to see whether furries are divided about other facets of their furry interest. For instance, a look at furries' feelings about fursonas, fursona species, and fursuits reveals that furries are also seldom united on these matters. When it comes to fursona species, there are some species that furries want to see more of: 8.6% of furries pointed to a specific species that they hoped to see more of in the future, including new, creative, custom fursona species (e.g., monsters, protogens[6]). In contrast, 1.2% of respondents expressed a desire to see fewer instances of specific fursona species. Some of the mentioned species were

even more prevalent, such as in the furry fandom. As the saying goes, when you're accustomed to privilege, equality feels like oppression.

[6] If you don't know what a protogen is, do yourself a favor and look up some pictures of them right now—they're a really cool fusion of cute/fuzzy critter and technology!

among the most common species in the fandom (e.g., canines), and may represent furries' desire to see more variety in fursonas.[7] Others mentioned specific novel or new species (e.g., sergals, Dutch Angel Dragons), possibly expressing disapproval over what may be seen as people picking fursona species based on what was "trendy" or opposition to species that could be considered by some to be promoting gatekeeping or stifling creativity.[8] Providing additional context for these findings, Figure 12.2 summarizes feeling thermometer responses from the same study, showing that furries, while largely positive toward original or unique fursona species, were far from unanimous in doing so.

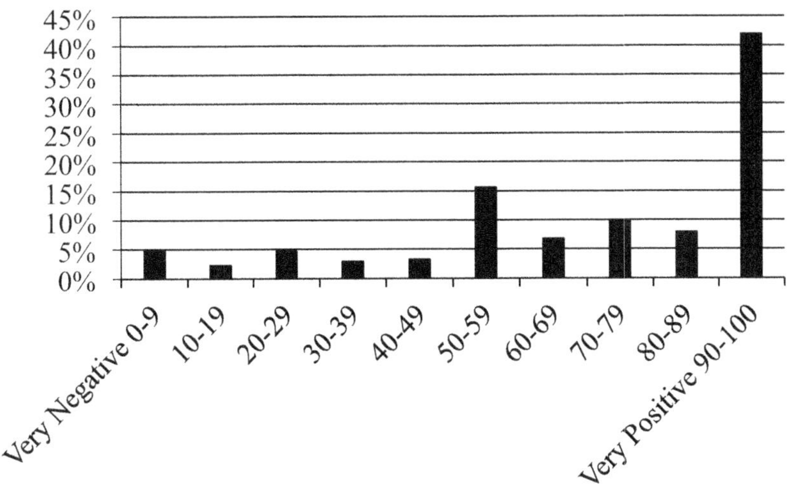

Figure 12.2. Feeling thermometer assessing the feelings of furries recruited at a furry convention toward original fursona species.

[7] This may also tap into a social psychological concept known as optimal distinctiveness, where people are motivated to stand out from the crowd and be distinct, albeit not too much (Leonardelli et al., 2010). One can imagine how a furry with a wolf or husky fursona may feel somewhat indistinct, like they've been "lost in the crowd" when they see that so many other furries have chosen the same species for their fursona. Trying to steer furries away from choosing the same species may well be a way to preserve the sense that one's fursona is special, unique, or distinct.

[8] Dutch Angel Dragons are an example of a "regulated species," a species whose characteristics or use is limited by the original creator. In the case of Dutch Angel Dragons, for example, the creator states explicitly that "hybrids, taurs, and shapeshifters of Dutch Angel Dragons are not allowed" and that "The species is entirely sexless and genderless" (DutchAngelDragons.com, 2019).

When it comes to fursuits, furries have even more nuanced and complex feelings. As we saw in Chapter 8, wearing a fursuit is an iconic way to express one's furry interest that many—though fewer than half—of furries engage in. Illustrating that fursuits are beloved by many, 4.4% of furries in the open-ended responses said that they would like to see more fursuits in furry spaces. Others showed more ambivalence or outright opposition to fursuits: 2.1% said that, while not wholly opposed to fursuits, they would like to see less of an emphasis on fursuits at furry conventions. Such sentiments may reflect opposition to newer generations of furries' growing focus on fursuiting.[9] Alternatively, more than half of furries who do not have a fursuit (see Chapter 8 for more on this) may feel "left out" of programming at furry conventions that highlights or emphasizes fursuiters (e.g., fursuit parades,[10] fursuit dance competitions).

Other fursuit discourse focuses less on the prevalence of fursuits and more on fursuit design. A sizable proportion of the open-ended responses (8.2%) spontaneously stated that they wanted to see more types of fursuits, although which kind varied from person to person (e.g., partial fursuits, digitigrade fursuits).[11] Others (2.1%) wanted to see advances in fursuit technology and greater incorporation of this technology into fursuits, including animated heads, the use of LED lighting, and 3D printed features.[12] These findings may coincide with the fact that furries, as a group, tend to be fairly tech-savvy and drawn to traditionally "geeky" fields such as computers, technology, and science.

Not everyone is as enthusiastic about these features in fursuits, however. For instance, 1.2% of furries wanted to see fewer designer fursuits—expensive fursuits created by highly popular, renowned fursuit builders. Whether this opposition is due to perceptions of elitism toward such suits, or

---

[9] Speaking to this point, individual fursuiters are increasingly becoming famous in a way that they generally weren't in the 1990s or 2000s. In previous generations, artists and content creators were generally the most iconic or recognizable "celebrities" in the furry fandom.

[10] Most furry conventions shut down part of, or even the entire convention's programming to focus entirely on the parading of fursuiters through the convention space. Few events receive this much attention at a furry convention, though it could be argued that few events could compete with the spectacle of a thousand fursuiters parading through a lobby!

[11] For a full explanation of partial and digitigrade fursuits, see Chapter 8.

[12] Many such features are incorporated into protogen fursuits—yes, my mind is still on protogens. Seriously, go check out some videos to see how much technology they weave into their fursuits!

simply out of a desire to support smaller, independent creators remains to be seen.[13] Regardless of the specific reason, the feeling thermometer data shown in Figure 12.3 makes it clear that furries are fairly mixed when it comes to their feelings about high-end or designer fursuits. While furries, as a group, are more likely to support designer fursuits than to oppose them, there are three fairly clear schools of thought on the matter: strong proponents, strong opponents, and those who are neutral or undecided on the matter.

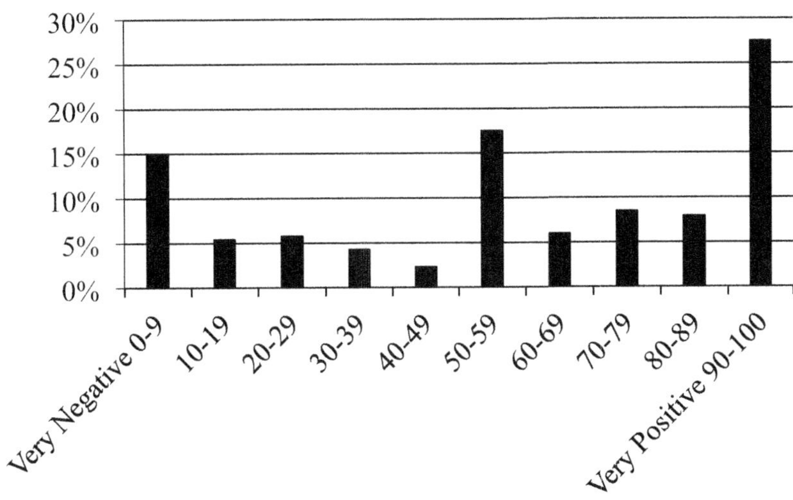

Figure 12.3. Feeling thermometer assessing the feelings of furries recruited at a furry convention toward designer fursuits.

Taking one last look at fursuits, let's look at divisiveness when it comes to how furries *wear* their fursuits. "Poodling" refers to someone wearing a partial fursuit (for a discussion of full and partial fursuits, see Chapter 8) in a way that leaves the wearer's skin visible.[14] For instance, if a person were to wear a fursuit head and hand paws along with a short-sleeved t-shirt, their bare forearms would be visible and would constitute poodling. The issue rose

[13] The issue made its way into popular discourse after a company known as Zweitesich promoted itself as a maker of luxury fursuits. Furry backlash to the company was reported in a number of pop culture outlets (e.g., Lal, 2019; Weill, 2019).

[14] To the best of our ability to discern, the term poodling is an allusion to French poodles and the style of grooming most commonly associated with them that includes poofs of fur contrasted against bare skin.

to prominence in the late 2010s, peaking with a discussion surrounding the Swedish furry convention NordicFuzzCon, where the con's purported policy of kicking fursuiters off of the convention floor if they were found to be poodling sparked an online debate about the appropriateness of poodling.

The reasons to support or be opposed to the practice of poodling vary considerably. Proponents of poodling argue that a person who purchases a fursuit is entitled to wear that fursuit in whatever manner they so choose. They also argue that anti-poodling is a form of elitism, discriminating against fursuiters who are unable to afford a full fursuit. The decision to poodle may also be a practical one, allowing the wearer to keep cool and avoid overheating or dehydration, something which happens often enough to fursuiters that furry conventions have one or more "headless lounges," complete with fans and water, to allow fursuiters to rapidly cool off.

Opponents of poodling counter by arguing that fursuiting is a performance art and that, by showing skin, the fursuiter has broken the illusion and cheapened the artistic integrity of fursuiting. This is reflected in the taboo, often referred to by furries as "breaking the magic," of taking one's fursuit head off in public or convention spaces.[15] This taboo is part of the reason for headless lounges, which are off-limits to non-fursuiters, in part to preserve the distinction between fursuiters and the characters they perform. Being anti-poodling may also be part of a broader opposition to changing trends in the furry fandom's conceptualization of fursuiting. Whereas fursuiting may once have been seen as a performance, something to be taken seriously, there has been a shift among younger furries toward a more casual approach to fursuiting, including being okay with taking one's fursuit head off and on in public spaces as preference and practicality warrants.[16]

Regardless of the specific reasons to be supportive of, or opposed to, poodling, the available evidence does suggest that furries are somewhat divided on the issue, as seen in Figure 12.4. To be sure, the difference is more a matter of strong support for poodling versus ambivalence to it, rather than full-throated opposition to poodling. Nevertheless, follow-up analyses

---

[15] "Breaking the magic" is likely a reference to the costumed characters at theme parks such as Disneyland who are taught to never take off their heads in public to avoid shattering a child's illusion that they are meeting the *real* Mickey Mouse.

[16] It should be noted that, as of the writing of this chapter, these reasons to be pro-poodling or anti-poodling are based on first-hand observations at conventions and anecdotal evidence. Future research is needed to more fully explain the multitude of reasons underlying furries' feelings toward poodling.

do offer at least some support for the idea that opposition to poodling is a product of reluctance toward changing norms about fursuiting: older furries are significantly more likely than younger furries to be opposed to poodling as a practice. Also adding a layer of complication to the data, those who identify more strongly as a furry (fanship, see Chapter 6) tend to be more opposed to poodling, while those who identify more strongly with the furry fandom are far more supportive of poodling as a practice. In conjunction with the above finding, this may suggest that people who take furry seriously may be the ones who see poodling as a violation of performance art, while those most inclined to see furry and fursuiting as a social activity may be less bothered by poodling and more inclined to see fursuiting as something casual they do with their friends at a furry convention.

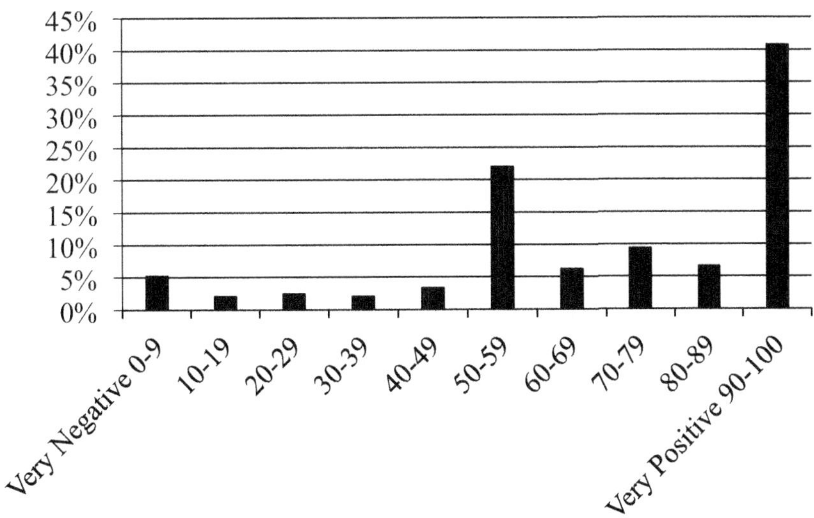

Figure 12.4. Feeling thermometer assessing the feelings of furries recruited at a furry convention toward fursuiters engaging in "poodling."

As we finish up this section on furries disagreeing about furry content, we'd be remiss if we didn't talk about one final observation from our 2020 convention study. Given that many of these discussions and debates occur between furries on social media, it comes as little surprise that 2.6% of respondents spontaneously stated that they would like to see a stronger social media component to the furry fandom. As we address in other chapters (e.g., Chapter 9), the primary way furries interact with one another is online. With younger people being increasingly likely to use social media as part of their daily experience (Metallo & Agrifoglio, 2015), and with the fandom being predominantly comprised of younger furries (see Chapter 13), this desire to see a greater social media presence in the furry fandom makes a lot of sense.

Conflict over Beliefs / Attitudes

As we discuss at length in Chapters 13-17, furries come in all shapes and sizes and from very different walks of life, given that the only thing they all have in common is a shared interest in media featuring anthropomorphized characters. As such, on occasions where we've measured various attitudes and beliefs across the fandom, we tend to find some disagreements, some fairly trivial, others fairly divisive and substantial.

One of the easiest ways to see a vast array of different positions was shown in a 2022 study of online and convention-going furries who were asked, among other things, about their vision of what the furry fandom ought to be. Specifically, participants were presented with eleven different functions that the furry fandom might fulfill for a person and were asked to indicate, on a 7-point scale (1 = *strongly disagree*, 7 = *strongly agree*), the extent to which they felt that the furry fandom ought to fulfill that function. The results are shown in Table 12.1 in order from the most agreed-upon function to the least agreed-upon.

Table 12.1. Average agreement scores (1-7 scale) of furry respondents recruited online and at a convention with respect to whether they felt the furry fandom ought to fulfill eleven different functions. Online scores were statistically significantly higher than con-going scores for every category.

Function	Avg Score (Con)	Avg Score (Online)
A Source of Inspiration and Creativity	6.6	6.8
A Place to Be Yourself	6.6	6.8
A Place to Find and Consume Furry Content	6.5	6.7
A Place to Discuss Furry-Related Subjects	6.5	6.8
A Place to Socialize with Friends	6.4	6.8
A Source of Social Support	6.2	6.6
A Space Free from Judgment	5.8	6.2
A Source of Entertainment	6.2	5.7
An Escape from the Real World	5.5	6.1
A Space to Organize Real-World Events	5.5	6.0
A Space for Free Speech	5.4	5.9

For at least some functions, furries reached a general consensus. For example, furries overwhelmingly agreed that the furry fandom should be a space of inspiration and creativity, a place where someone can be themselves and where one can consume furry content and discuss furry-related topics with friends while also drawing upon those friends as a source of social support. Division begins to creep into some of the other items, however, such as whether furry ought to be a form of escapism from the real world, whether it should be a space for real-world event organization, and whether the fandom should function as a haven for free speech. While furries still generally agreed with these functions, as we can see in Figure 12.5, they did so to varying degrees. We'll spend the rest of this section diving deeper into the nuances behind some of these differences.

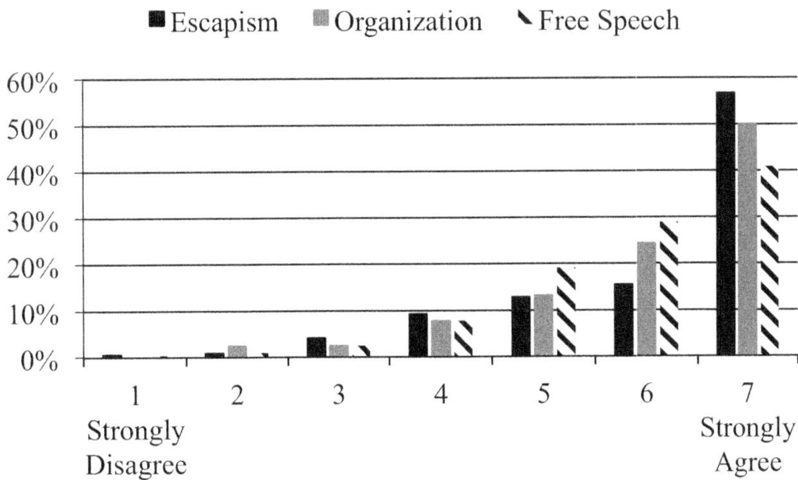

Figure 12.5. Extent to which convention-going furries agree that the furry fandom ought to fulfill three different functions.

Let's start with the idea that furry should be a place to escape from the real world. People who experience a great deal of stigma and anxiety in their day-to-day lives may see the fandom as a safe space in which to seek refuge. For LGBTQ+ people in particular, who often find themselves targeted by societal stigma (Barnes & Meyer, 2012), fandoms may be an especially useful retreat from bullying and harassment (Meyer, 2003). The open-ended questions from our 2020 convention study speak to this: 2.8% of furries stated that they wanted to see more acceptance in the fandom in general, with 1.2% specifically saying that they wanted to see greater LGBTQ+

acceptance. In the same vein, 4.1% of furries also indicated that they wanted to see less bigotry and hate in fandom spaces, including less racism, sexism, and judgment based on a person's sexual orientation or gender. In a later 2021 study of online furries, furries were generally in agreement that the furry fandom should be a judgment-free space, as seen in Figure 12.6.

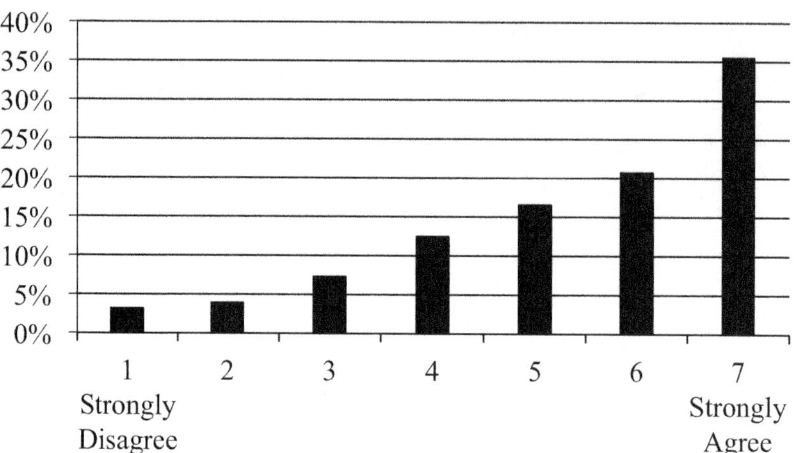

Figure 12.6. Extent to which a 2021 sample of online furries agree that the furry fandom should be a judgment-free space.

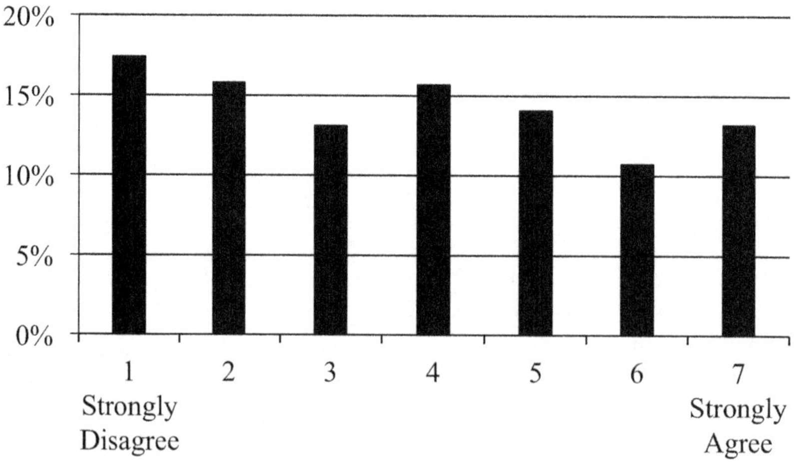

Figure 12.7. Extent to which a 2021 sample of online furries agree that the furry fandom should be accepting of all people, no matter what.

While most furries agreed with the sentiment that the fandom should be a judgment-free space, there were some—approximately 15%—who disagreed with this sentiment. We might be able to understand where this disagreement is coming from with another item from the same 2021 study. We asked furries whether they agreed or disagreed that the fandom should be accepting of all people, no matter what. As Figure 12.7 reveals, furries were exceedingly divided on this subject.

At first glance, it seems like a contradiction: how can furries claim to want a space free from bigotry and judgment on the one hand, yet be completely divided about whether or not to accept everyone? Some additional context might help to shed some light on the matter. In the 2010s and 2020s, the proliferation of extreme right-wing ideologies, including the rise of Nazi organizations, brought the issue of groups defined by their intolerance into focus for furries (Conti, 2017).[17] Because of the strong wording of the original question, which asked about accepting all people *no matter what*, it's conceivable that many furries would have generally agreed with the statement except insofar as it would necessitate accepting those with hateful ideologies.[18] Speaking somewhat to this idea, in a 2011 sample of online and convention-going furries, the most negatively viewed group by far was Nazifurs, supporting the idea furries, while generally tolerant of most people, may have reservations about a select few, particularly those who espouse intolerance.

Further attesting to this point, results from a 2015 study of convention-going furries found that furries are more likely to disagree than to agree with the sentiment that they feel the need to hide some facet of themselves from the furry fandom (see Figure 12.8). This suggests that, for the most part, furries feel like they can be themselves in the fandom. If nothing else, these data, taken together, seem to suggest that furries strive to—and generally

[17] Speaking to this idea, 1.2% of furries from our 2020 study spontaneously said that they wanted to see fewer extreme positions in the furry fandom, with many explicitly citing Nazis as an example.

[18] In fact, on several occasions when we've presented this data to furries at conventions, they've been quick to point this very fact out to us. They would be willing to accept anyone in the fandom *except* for those who would not similarly accept everyone. If nothing else, these data and anecdotes seem to suggest that furries are unlikely to fall prey to the "paradox of intolerance," where organizations who show unlimited tolerance undermine themselves by admitting those who are intolerant (Popper, 1971).

do—create inclusive, accepting spaces for those who may be escaping stigma and intolerance in their day-to-day lives, though how specific items are worded may lead to disagreement about who should or should not be allowed into furry spaces in accordance with the goal of acceptance and tolerance.

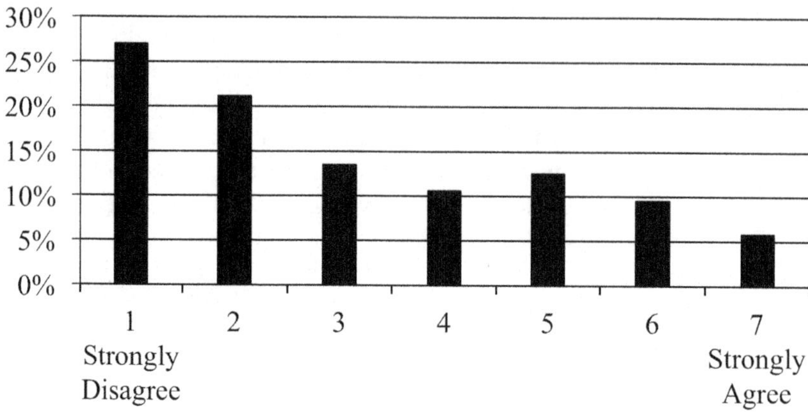

Figure 12.8. Extent to which a 2015 sample of convention-going furries agree that they sometimes have to hide some facet of themselves from the furry fandom.

Returning to the point raised in Figure 12.5, we can also try to contextualize furries' disagreements about the utility of furry spaces as places for organizing real-world political activities.[19] For instance, in our 2020 convention study, 1.4% of furries who completed the open-ended question spontaneously said that they wanted to see less politics in the furry fandom.[20] We more directly tested this notion by asking furries, in a 2021 online study, whether they agreed that the fandom should be a place for having fun and nothing more, whether the fandom should be a politics-free

[19] Of course, we also acknowledge that the original question's wording was vague, and it's likely that at least some furries were simply referring to organizing furry-focused gatherings and meet-ups!

[20] In Chapter 17, we illustrate that this sentiment is primarily expressed by those with more centrist or conservative beliefs who feel that their views are at odds with the beliefs of most in the fandom. As such, many of these folks would likely prefer to treat the fandom solely as a hobby, if only to avoid being dogpiled by the majority of furries who would likely disagree with their political views. That being said, a desire to keep the fandom politics-free is also espoused by some with progressive beliefs, particularly those who see the fandom as becoming *too* political.

space, and whether they felt the fandom ought to be a place for political expression and advocacy. The results for all three items are shown in Figure 12.9.

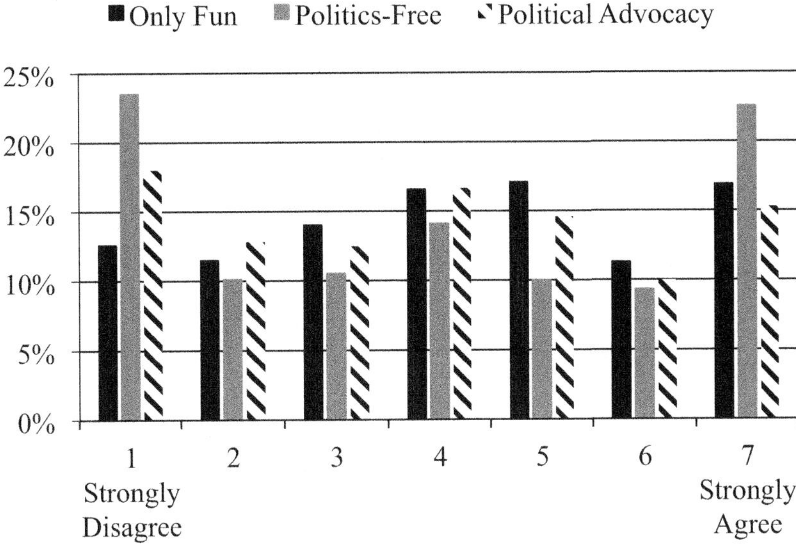

Figure 12.9. Extent to which convention-going furries agree with items pertaining to the role of politics in the furry fandom.

The figure shows general disagreement among furries about the role of the fandom. The statement about whether furry ought to be a politics-free space was the most polarizing of the three items, with nearly half of furries taking one of the two most extreme positions (*strongly disagree* or *strongly agree*), with an equal proportion of furries on either side of this position. When it comes to the fandom as a place only for fun or the appropriateness of political advocacy, furries were slightly less polarized in their positions, being somewhat more likely to adopt middle-ground positions. Even so, the overall trend across the three questions shows that furries, as a group, disagree considerably about the role that politics ought to play in the furry fandom.

What about the third divisive issue from Figure 12.5, how do furries feel about the issue of free speech? To start, responses to our open-ended question in the 2020 convention study found that 1.4% of furries spontaneously stated that they liked and wanted to see more freedom of self-expression in the furry fandom. Furries echoed this point in a 2021 online study, strongly agreeing that the fandom ought to be a place where people can express themselves freely (see Figure 12.10).

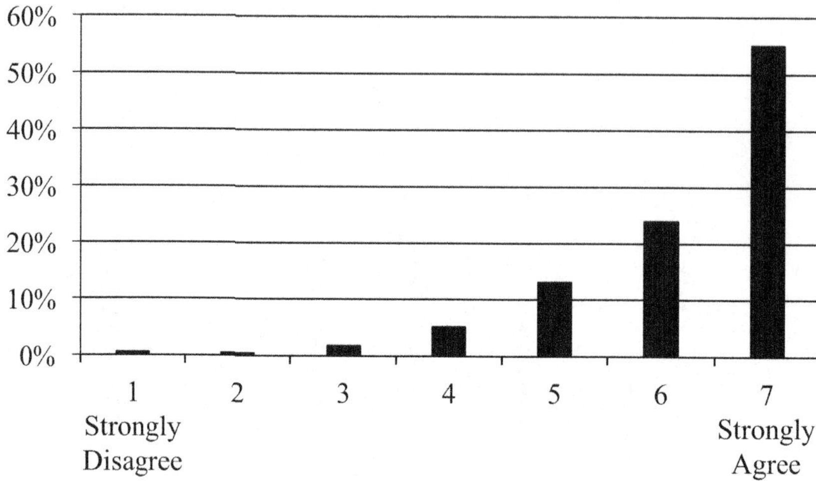

Figure 12.10. Extent to which a 2021 sample of online furries agree that the furry fandom ought to be a place where people can freely express themselves.

Of course, one can ask what, precisely, is meant by the freedom of self-expression. Does it mean, for example, the freedom to go by one's preferred name, wear their preferred clothing, and draw the art that they want to draw? Or does it mean the freedom to express one's political views regardless of the position's popularity or how heinous it may be? The above question doesn't delve into these nuances, and so we need to rely on other questions for context. For example, in the same study, we also asked furries whether they agreed or disagreed that some opinions do not belong in the furry fandom. We also asked respondents to consider the relative importance of free speech, both in the face of concerns raised by other furries about the possible consequences of allowing certain opinions to be expressed and, more directly, about the importance of free speech relative to the safety of others in the fandom. The distribution of participants' responses to these three questions is shown in Figure 12.11.

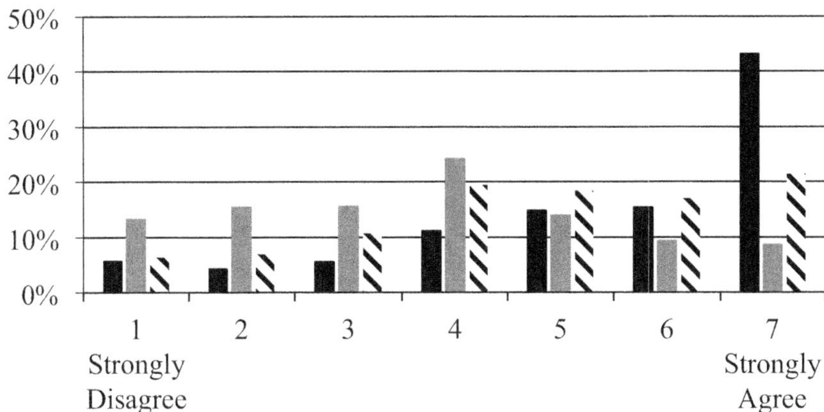

Figure 12.11. Extent to which convention-going furries agree with items pertaining to free speech in the furry fandom.

First and foremost, these data show that furries generally agree that there should be limitations on the opinions expressed in the furry fandom. This position is largely in-line with the findings we discussed earlier showing that furries generally agree with inclusion except in the case of intolerant groups like Nazis. Furries are somewhat more divided, however, about the relative importance of free speech: some seem to support the idea that others' concerns supersede free speech, while others argue that free speech trumps the concerns of others, while a plurality of furries falls somewhere in-between these two positions. Even so, furries were more likely to agree than to disagree with the principle that other furries' felt safety was more important than free speech. The discrepancy may stem from differences in what is considered a viable or credible concern,[21] although this remains to be

[21] As an example: if a furry were to espouse the position that trans people should not be permitted to use the bathroom of their choice, trans furries would see this position as one that inevitably leads to violence against trans people. The person espousing the view might perceive the trans person's position as hyperbolic, invalidating it as a credible safety threat. As such, they might not consider the trans furry's concerns as

tested in future studies. Regardless, furries overwhelmingly agree that it's important for furries to feel safe in the fandom, as shown in Figure 12.12.

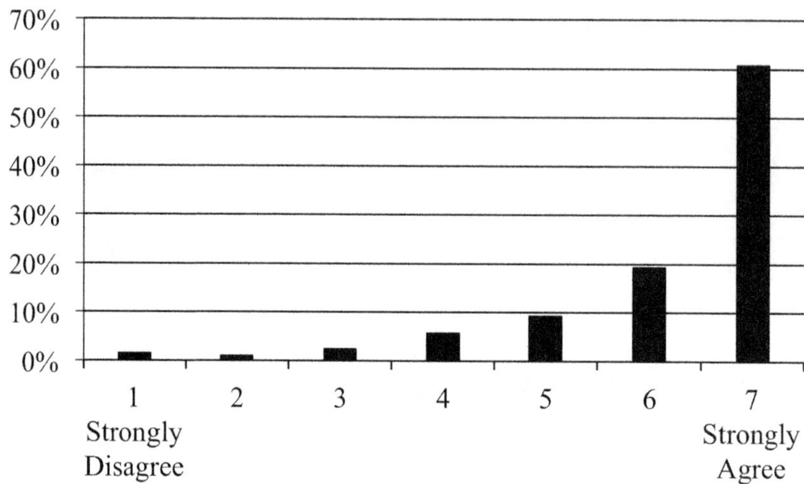

Figure 12.12. Extent to which a 2021 sample of online furries agree that the furry fandom ought to be a place where furries can feel safe.

In sum, our studies suggest that furries, while generally agreeing on some fundamental principles about what the fandom is or ought to be (e.g., safe, a place to gather around a shared interest in furry content), do disagree when it comes to the implementation of some of these principles. A deeper dive into some of these issues reveals that some of the divisiveness boils down to the interpretation of nuances and subtleties rather than to fundamental disagreements (e.g., whether the exclusion of Nazis is taken as a given, or to what extent free speech ought to be limited rather than whether free speech should be limited at all).

In the next section, we'll shift gears from disagreements about attitudes and beliefs to look at specific behaviors that furries may find contentious or disagreeable.

---

sufficient to warrant stifling their position. Of course, it goes without saying that those with privilege are the ones least likely to recognize the downstream harm of their espoused positions given that they are unlikely to be personally affected by them—studies show that those with status and power are the least likely to see things from another person's perspective (Galinsky et al., 2006).

Conflict Over Behavior

We'll once again begin a section by returning to the results of our open-ended question from the 2020 convention study. Some furries spontaneously stated that there were certain behaviors that they considered to be troublesome or undesirable and, as such, they wanted to see less of it. Some of these behaviors reference issues we discuss elsewhere in this book. For example, 1.2% of furries stated that they want to see less art and character theft, referring to incidents where furries acquire art through bypassing of paywalls (e.g., piracy), embellishing or taking credit for other artists' work, or copying another fursona or character for their own use (see Chapter 7). Others spoke more generally about how furries handle disputes in the fandom, including 2.6% of furries who stated that they wanted to see less callout culture (e.g., publicly shaming, ostracizing, and creating negative consequences for someone in response to undesirable behavior, usually amplified or directed through social media campaigns).[22]

In this section, however, we'll focus on behaviors that are largely unrelated to the previous topics we've covered, behaviors that may be contentious or lead to disagreement among furries because of how common they are or how big of a problem they may represent.

One example of such behavior comes from furries' responses to a 2015 convention study. In the study, furries were asked to indicate the extent to which they agreed that they sometimes felt uncomfortable during interactions with other furries. The question was worded in a fairly general way to capture a wide range of behaviors that could be construed as social awkwardness or the violation of social boundaries, behaviors that are often part of the negative stereotypes people attribute to stigmatized fan groups (e.g., Reysen et al., 2016). The results, shown in Figure 12.13, reveal that while furries generally disagree with this sentiment, a non-trivial number of furries (about 22.4%) agree at least somewhat, that interacting with other furries can sometimes make them feel uncomfortable.[23]

---

[22] Criticisms of "callout culture" generally go hand-in-hand with concerns about "cancelling," wherein a person is deplatformed or otherwise has their voice silenced as a result of a concerted effort by critics, typically in response to behavior deemed to be egregious or inappropriate and which has generally gone unaddressed or led to little negative consequence for the person engaging in the behavior.

[23] There are, of course, numerous ways to interpret this question that have nothing to do with social awkwardness. For example, a furry respondent who's not yet disclosed their furry identity to others might feel uncomfortable interacting with other furries for fear of being "outed" as a furry. Despite this and other alternative

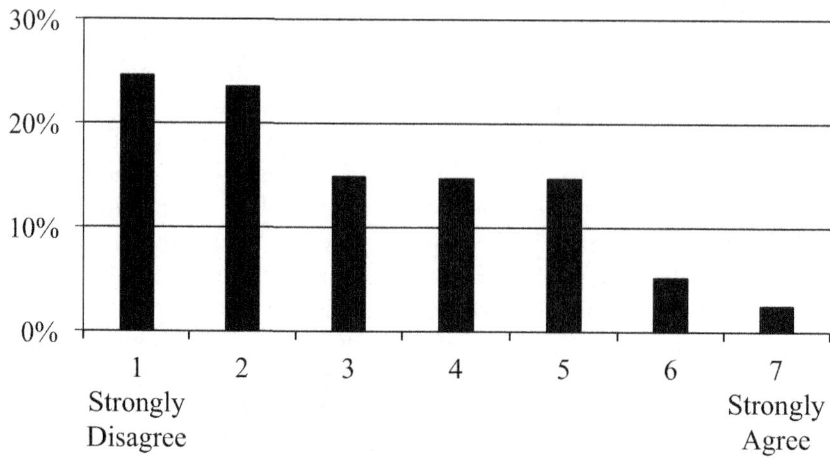

Figure 12.13. Extent to which a 2015 sample of convention-going furries agree that they sometimes feel uncomfortable interacting with other furries.

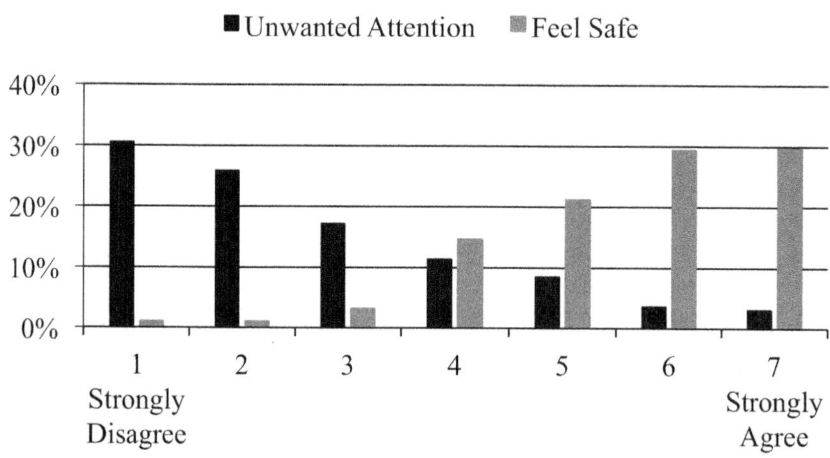

Figure 12.14. Extent to which convention-going furries agree with items pertaining to experiencing unwanted attention and feeling safe around other furries.

explanations, the general stigmatization of non-mainstream fan groups as socially awkward leads us to assume that social awkwardness or "cringe" is the most common way this question is interpreted, although it is certainly a topic which could be studied in the future.

Moving beyond mere awkwardness, we also asked furries, in the same study, whether they regularly received unwanted attention from other furries. Importantly, this item is asking about more than just the violation of social norms and starts to veer into the category of harassment. We again found that furries are significantly more likely to disagree with this item than they are to agree with it—a generally positive finding, although we shouldn't gloss over the approximately one-quarter of furries who indicated at least moderate agreement with this item (see Figure 12.14). This finding hints at the possibility that more serious or concerning behavior among furries may be at least somewhat common. Having said that, when asked whether they felt safe being around other furries, participants strongly agreed that they felt safe around other furries. Taken together, these findings suggest that while a minority of furries may experience some troublesome attention from others in the fandom, in most cases this may be more of a nuisance than a threat to one's safety, and that furries generally feel safe being around other furries.[24]

We should also look at furries' tendency to engage in behaviors that, themselves, are divisive or controversial, as well as how common furries believe those behaviors to be. A good example of such a behavior is alcohol consumption. In our 2017 study of online furries, the average furry reported consuming 2-3 drinks per week, with considerable variation around this central tendency: 59.4% of furries hadn't had a drink in the past week, while 12.5% of furries had consumed more than 5 drinks in the past 7 days. In other words, there was tremendous variability in furries' drinking habits. This may, in and of itself, reflect the divisiveness of alcohol use as an issue, especially given that attitudes toward drug and alcohol use have, both historically and contemporarily, proven to be divisive (e.g., prohibition, debates about which drugs should be legalized).

With this potential for conflict in mind, let's take a moment to consider a potential catalyst for this divisiveness: *pluralistic ignorance*. Put in simple terms, pluralistic ignorance is when a person erroneously believes that the attitudes, beliefs, or behavior of a group of people differ from their own (e.g.,

---

[24] Of course, even fairly rare occurrences of harassing or stalking behavior should be taken seriously and not swept under the rug. Providing additional context for this topic, another item asked whether furries sometimes felt pressured by other furries to be in romantic relationships that they, themselves, were not interested in. Approximately 16.5% of furries agreed at least somewhat with this statement, and scores on this question correlated significantly with responses to the statement about unwanted attention. This suggests that at least some of the unwanted attention may take the form of unwanted advances or statements of attraction from other furries.

Miller & McFarland, 1991). As an illustrative example, a college freshman attending a party may not feel comfortable with drinking. However, looking around them, they see others drinking, and so they decide to have a drink themselves, if only to fit in. Even as they drink, they think to themselves "I'm not like these other people, I'm only drinking to fit in. I don't even really like drinking, unlike them." In stating this, however, the freshman overlooks the possibility that many of the other college students in the room may feel the same way that they do and may, themselves, be looking at the freshman's behavior as an illustration of the fact that college freshmen ostensibly like to drink.

So what does this have to do with furries and potentially divisive behavior? Well, we can imagine asking furries about many potentially contentious or undesirable behaviors, like drinking, smoking, partying, using drugs, or risky sex. It's possible that furries may look at their engagement in some of these behaviors and think "I don't do this to a troublesome degree—I keep it under control, do it only recreationally, and don't have a problem." If they see other furries engaging in the same behaviors, however, they might not be as charitable, and may be prone to overestimating the prevalence of the behavior and the extent to which it's a problem for other furries—those furries do it to a problematic extent and have no control over it.[25] In other words, pluralistic ignorance may be causing furries to see these sorts of behaviors as a bigger or more common problem than it actually is in the fandom.

We studied this possibility in a 2017 study, recruiting furries in person at a furry convention. We asked them to indicate the frequency with which they engaged in a number of potentially controversial or troublesome behaviors on a 7-point scale (1 = *never*, 7 = *very frequently*) and then asked them to estimate how often the average furry did the same. The results, shown in Figure 12.15, are striking: furries' estimates of how frequently the average furry did each of the activities were significantly higher than how frequently the average furry reported actually engaging in the activities.

[25] Indeed, one of the reasons we studied this subject is precisely because, over the years, we've had numerous furries suggest to us that we should study partying, drug use, drinking, and risky sexual behavior because they believed there was an epidemic of such behavior in the fandom.

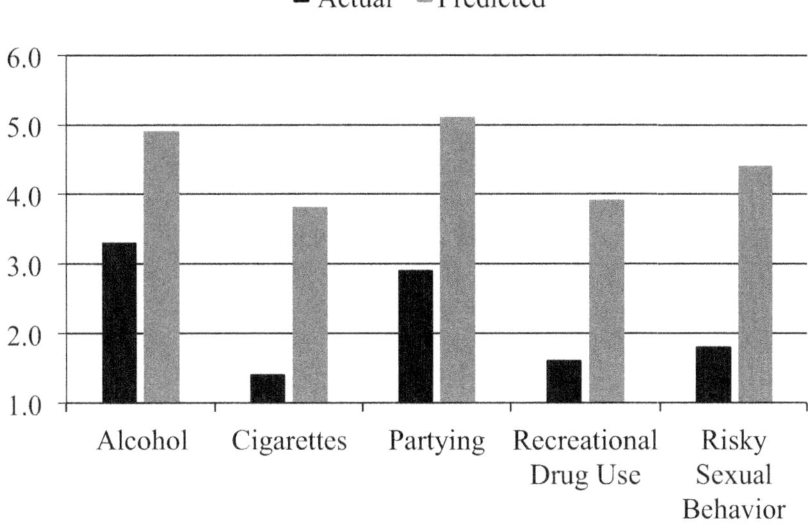

Figure 12.15. Convention-going furries' estimates of how much the average furry engages in five different potentially troublesome behaviors, alongside the actual average of furries' self-reported engagement in each of the behaviors.

Of course, we need to consider several caveats. For one thing, furries may be accurately assessing the frequency with which the average furry engages in these activities, and are simply downplaying their engagement in these behaviors to present themselves in a desirable light to researchers. Alternatively, furries may simply not be aware of the frequency with which they engage in these activities, or may be in denial about having problems with these activities.[26] While these possibilities do exist, and may explain at least some of the difference between furries' self-reported behavior and the perceived behavior of the average furry, it seems unlikely, given what we know about pluralistic ignorance. For instance, the surveys themselves are

[26] Another possibility might be that we've somehow introduced a bias into our sample by only recruiting furries who don't drink, party, or engage in risky sexual behavior. While it's true that we might be less likely to get a survey into the hands of a furry who does nothing but drink and party all weekend at a convention, we typically recruit furries who are standing in the registration line at the convention—well before any drinking, partying, or risky sex has begun!

anonymous, meaning there would be little incentive for furries to downplay their concerning behavior for a researcher who will never be able to match their responses to them. What's more, high-profile or memorable examples of furries engaging in troublesome behaviors (e.g., struggling with drug or alcohol abuse, experiencing the detrimental consequences of unsafe sexual practices, partying to a reckless extent) would likely cause furries to selectively remember these behaviors when trying to assess how common such behaviors are, leading them to overestimate the prevalence of such troublesome behaviors which, in turn, might lead them to adopt harsh or strict stances on these issues that are unwarranted or unsupported by reality.[27]

Conflict Over Sex

In the previous section, we briefly mentioned risky sex as a potentially controversial or divisive behavior. It's worth taking a closer this and other sex-related topics in a bit more depth, given that sex, as a subject, is fairly emotionally charged and can lead to all manner of debates. As an illustrative example, contemporary debates about sex in popular culture include but are not limited to, the age at which a person can consent to have sex, the need to censor sex in television, film, and art, the legality of selling sex and its impact on the safety and well-being of sex workers, and the debate over whether pornography is a net positive or a net negative for society.

The furry fandom itself has grappled with, and continues to deliberate over, sex-related issues. As just one example, the "Burned Furs" and "Improved Anthropomorphics" movements of the late 1990s and early 2000s sought to improve the furry fandom's public image by downplaying and, in many cases, outright opposing any show of kinks, fetishes, and sexual content in furry culture, encouraging furries to keep such matters private ("Burned Furs," 2021). We discuss many of the nuances when it comes to sex in the furry fandom in greater detail in Chapter 10, including some of the topics that concerned organizations like the Burned Fur movement. For now, however, we'll focus our attention on some of the more contentious issues,

---

[27] For example, a furry who knows one or two furries who struggle with drug addiction may erroneously believe that it is a more common problem than it actually is in the fandom, projecting the behaviors of a small minority of furries onto the fandom as a whole. If this leads them to believe, as a result, that most furries have a drug addiction, it could lead them to believe that there is something about being a furry that *causes* furries to develop drug addictions. Alternatively, it could lead them to push for fandom-wide policies to address a problem that is far less common and smaller in scope than they might believe (e.g., mandatory drug testing at conventions).

including debates about the appropriateness of creating, wearing, or displaying fursuits used for sexual purposes (i.e., "murrsuiting"), zoophilia, bestiality, artwork featuring feral characters, and the sexualization of underage furry characters in artwork.

Looking once again at open-ended data from the 2020 convention study, 3.3% of participants indicated that they wanted to see furries engaging in less sexually charged behavior in public spaces. Examples of such behavior include the discussion or display of erotic material in public spaces (e.g., showing off furry erotica while at a furry meet-up in a family restaurant), engaging in sexual behavior in public spaces (e.g., groping or other sexual behaviors on a convention floor or while fursuiting in public), or the display of paraphernalia that some would consider to be sexual in public contexts (e.g., wearing harnesses, hoods, leashes, or bondage gear during a public fursuit walk). Debate over such topics generally stems less from disagreements over the broader principles (e.g., whether it is or is not appropriate to display sexual content in public spaces, where minors may be present) and more from disagreement on the finer points and details of these matters, such as whether harnesses, leashes, or leather pup hoods should be considered sexual in nature.

Starting broadly, when it comes to sexual content in furry media, the divisiveness of the topic begins to show through. In the 2020 open-ended data, 2.6% of furries spontaneously said that they wanted to see more safe for work (i.e., non-sexual) content and 3.6% said that they wanted to see less not safe for work (i.e., sexual) content. In contrast, 3.0% of furries said just the opposite, that they wanted to see more sexually explicit content.

We can once again drill down deeper into the topic by looking at what facets of sexual content furries want to see more or less of. Of particular note, while approximately 3.0% of furries listed specific fetishes that they wanted to see more represented in furry artwork, 4.1% said that they wanted to see less fetish content in general. Feeling thermometer data from the same study shows that furries, while certainly far more positive than negative when it comes to fetish-themed content in general, nevertheless expressed a variety of views, with fewer than 50% of furries scoring "very positive" on the matter (see Figure 12.16).

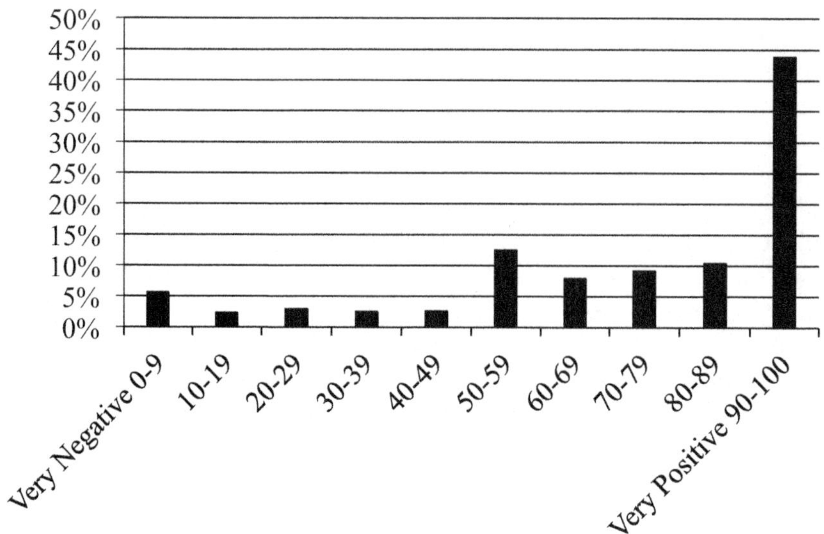

Figure 12.16. Feeling thermometer assessing the feelings of furries recruited at a furry convention toward fetish-themed art.

One possible explanation for the somewhat mixed feelings toward fetish-themed content may have less to do with furries' overall feelings toward fetishes and more to do with furries' feelings toward specific fetishes. For example, a furry who is okay with fetishes in general, but who happens to be thinking about a particularly extreme, illegal, or aversive fetish while answering the question, may adopt a more negative overall impression of fetishes as a result—the proverbial bad apple spoiling the barrel. Speaking to this possibility, the open-ended data from our 2020 study reveals that numerous furries spontaneously listed the specific fetishes that they were opposed to and wanted to see less of. These include but are not limited to, fetishized/sexualized artwork of cubs / underage characters, vorarephilia, fetishes involving specific body parts, hyper fetishes (i.e., sexual attraction to body parts that are extremely, disproportionately large), pup play (e.g., wearing leather "pup hoods" or full-body outfits, roleplaying as someone else's pet), scat or watersports (i.e., sexual activities involving feces or urine), artwork featuring feral characters or acts of zoophilia, and numerous other specific fetishes.

For a fuller discussion of furries' mixed attitudes toward other sex-related attitudes and behaviors (e.g., pornography use), please see Chapter 10. For now, it's sufficient to state that sex is just one of many examples of the specific attitudes, beliefs, and behaviors around which conflict and controversy can form. In the rest of this chapter, we'll explore several other examples of specific topics that are, to varying degrees, controversial among furries.

Conflict Over Drama

Spend enough time in any fandom and you're bound to hear the term "drama" used to describe—often in a trivializing manner—conflicts within the fandom, usually between two or more members of the fandom. Drama is certainly present in the furry fandom: in our 2020 open-ended dataset, 3.1% of respondents spontaneously stated that they wanted to see less drama in the furry fandom.

But what, exactly, is drama? If we want to measure furries' attitudes toward drama, we should first make sure we've got a definition we can work with. This is a tricky prospect, given that the term's day-to-day use differs somewhat from that of a dictionary, which might characterize drama as a theatrical performance or as an emotionally charged incident (e.g., the drama of The Titanic sinking). Indeed, it's unlikely that furries are using the term "drama" in the same way when arguing about poodling at conventions or debating online about whether it's appropriate for an artist to heavily reference someone else's work in their art.

We decided to use data to help us come up with a definition for "drama." Specifically, we asked furries to give us their definition of the term "furry drama" in a 2017 convention study. After looking through hundreds of responses, we extracted the most common themes. The result was a three-part definition of furry drama, along with several examples and an important caveat. Beginning with the definition, furry drama:

1. Involves a conflict between two or more people.
2. Takes place in public spaces, on social media, or otherwise involves additional attention from third parties.
3. As a result of the additional attention, the conflict gets blown out of proportion; trivial disagreements escalate into insurmountable rifts.

The first component of this definition, that furry drama involves a conflict between two or more people, was reflected by many participants who pointed out that, if nothing else, furry drama is, at its core, an interpersonal conflict.

> *"Unresolved conflicts in the fandom between 2 or more people that spills [sic] over into the rest of the fandom."*

"Interpersonal conflict and social woes between people within/involved with the fandom."

"A conflict, usually personal in nature, between two furries and/or on or at a furry meeting place."

"Furry drama is when 2 popular furs who are fighting and their fans help. Some who does not agree with someone and make [sic] a huge deal out of it."

The second component emphasizes how the conflict occurs in places where additional participants or witnesses who otherwise were not involved in the initial conflict can be drawn into it. Typically this involves disagreements in public spaces (e.g., furry meet-ups, conventions) or on social media (e.g., Twitter).

"When personal conflict between two or more people becomes public knowledge or otherwise expands to involve people unrelated to the conflict, you get drama."

"Furry Drama" is when a social conflict among furries gets aired an/or integrated into the presence of third parties."

"When members of the fandom spread their disputes and disagreements with others publicly."

"When a disagreement between two or more furries becomes public and polarized."

"Facebook/Twitter wars."

"People airing out their personal business for attention and shock value at the detriment of others."

"When two or more furries argue in public."

"It's what occurs when a fur/furries have a disagreement and call each other out usually online."

The final component in our definition of drama involves disproportionate response or attention being given to the issue, given its original scope. Often, furry drama is characterized as trivial or silly, emphasizing how the magnitude of the response is unwarranted given how mundane or small the original conflict was.

"Furry drama is when individuals on groups of individuals cause or get involved with conflicts that arises[sic]. Usually over stupid shit."

"Conflict between members of the furry community aired publicly, usually on the interent[sic]. Usually used to imply that the dispute is petty or not relevant to others, i.e. a serious crime would not be drama."

"Over sensationalizaiton [sic] of issues in the fandom. Generally between individuals but sometimes about group issues."

"Generaly [sic] something [is] blown out of proportion for the incident. Makes me think of mob mentality."

"Drama is an elongated drawn out, overblown problem or disagreement where on [sic] or both parties over exaggerate the issues."

"When someone takes a minor slight against them and blows it out of proportion so ridiculously that it seems like a desperate grab for attention or sympathy."

"Furry drama is making a big deal out of a little offense or disagreement and holding it longer than is healthy."

Many furries responded to the question not by defining drama, but rather by providing examples of the sorts of conflicts, disagreements, or issues that are prone to sparking drama. Some of these may be furry-themed, but other times they may stem from broader disagreements about politics or involve relationship problems.

"Drama being associated with but not limited to feelings on various topics, thoughts [,] and emotions on various things, political opinions, art theft/tracing, deviating from the furry social norm."

"More often than not; created from relationship issues."

"Probably arguments over payment for commissions or how to act in a fursuit?"

"Relationship problems between fans, Fandom's relationship with those outside of the fandom, different political beliefs within the fandom."

Finally, we note that several participants were quick to point out that drama was far from a uniquely furry phenomenon, although some speculated that furries may be more prone to drama by (ostensibly) being especially open, vocal, or vulnerable. Many emphasized that furry drama was essentially no different from interpersonal drama observed in other contexts (e.g., other fan groups), and was simply made "furry" by the presence of furry participants or having a furry-related subject as the catalyst for the conflict.

"Just normal drama but the people are also furries."

"It's the same as normal drama but within the context of furry related [sic] stuff."

"Furry drama is no different than drama in other communities and life."

"Human drama in the furry fandom."

"The same as drama in any fandom, we just seem to have more of it."

"To me, it is just a human condition. It is nothing special to our fandom, but we do tend to have more people who may feel 'wronged' by society. This could lead to easier/more frequent feelings of victimization."

"It's to be found in any group, but I suspect furries are, by nature, more sensitive and vulnerable."

"I don't think furry drama is any different than drama found in other groups. We're just often more vocal about it so issues carry on longer."

"'Furry drama' is like drama, except because furries have a tendency to be more open about things, they also may tend to share such conflicts more readily and thus seem to create more drama, often about matters the general population considers trivial."

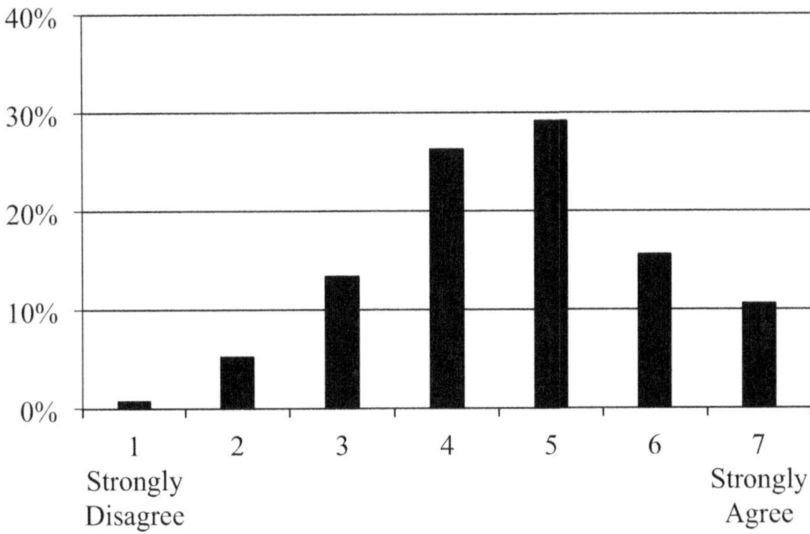

Figure 12.17. Extent to which a 2017 sample of convention-going furries agree that drama in the furry fandom is undesirable.

Having now defined what furries generally mean when talking about furry drama, we can delve into their attitudes and beliefs when it comes to drama to see whether drama itself is a point of contention for furries. To start, we turn to data from one of our 2017 convention studies in which furries were asked to indicate whether they agree that drama in the furry fandom is undesirable. As shown in Figure 12.17, furries adopted a moderate stance on this position: while they were more likely to agree with the position than they were to disagree with it, most furries' stance on whether drama was a bad thing or not was fairly moderate. One possible explanation is that furries may see at least some value in drama (e.g., insofar as the conflict allows furries to see how other furries feel about an issue, or if drama brings a previously unknown issue into broader awareness) and take the good with the bad, so to speak, when it comes to the potential downsides of drama (e.g., creating rifts or schisms in the fandom). As for why furries' responses are moderate, this may stem from furries being somewhat unsure about what does and does not constitute drama and wanting to avoid taking a strong stance without having a better sense of what they are or are not condemning.[28] We may be able to counteract this possibility in future studies by providing furries with our empirically derived definition of drama to see whether, having that definition, furries respond differently to this question. Until then, the best data available would seem to suggest that furries are of a somewhat mixed mind when it comes to whether or not furry drama is undesirable or not.

We also asked furries about whether drama was an inherent element of the furry fandom, whether drama is a product of the fandom itself (rather than being created by a handful of individual furries), and whether they believed that drama was more common in the furry fandom than in other fandoms. We asked these questions to furries recruited online or in-person at conventions in 2017. The data, shown in Figure 12.18, reveal that, as with the question of whether drama was considered a bad thing, furries were generally fairly moderate, albeit a bit divided in their opinions. Specifically, furries moderately agreed that drama was inherent to the furry fandom, though they were undecided and divided about whether drama comes from the fandom as a whole or whether it came from specific furries. Furries were fairly torn on the issue of whether drama was more prevalent in the furry fandom than in other fandoms, with an almost equal number of furries strongly disagreeing with the statement as had no opinion one way or another.[29]

---

[28] For example, if furries subscribed to the belief that drama involved *any* conflict, regardless of how significant or trivial it was, they may be of mixed opinion about its utility because they see *some* conflict (e.g., conflict over crucial bellwether issues) as necessary to help determine the fandom's position.

[29] In a somewhat-related finding, we also asked furries from the same pair of 2017 studies whether they agreed or disagreed with the statement "Furries ruin everything," a tongue-in-cheek statement commonly made within the furry community to imply that furries—including furry-related drama—necessarily wrecks whatever it comes into contact with. Furries were united in condemning this assertion, despite its popularity, further speaking to the idea that it may be tongue-in-cheek. This raises additional questions about whether some furries' beliefs about the inherence of drama to the furry fandom is similarly satirical.

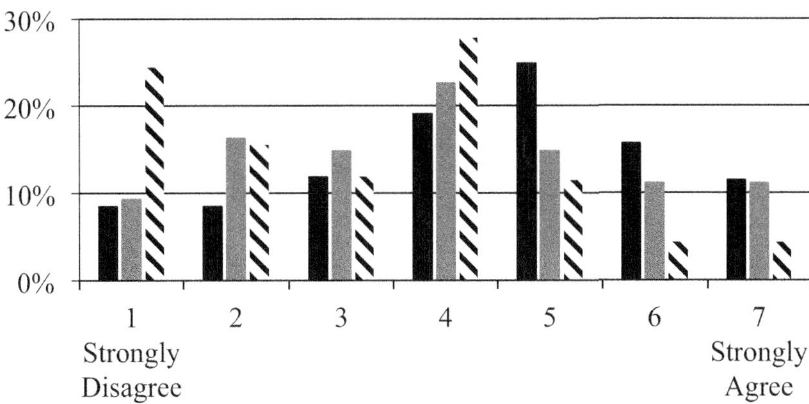

Figure 12.18. Extent to which furries recruited across a pair of 2017 online and convention studies agree with items pertaining to drama as part of the furry fandom.

In addition to asking about drama in the abstract, we also asked respondents in the same studies about their own experience with drama. Specifically, we asked furries whether they had personally been involved in furry drama, whether they tended to watch drama unfold when it did occur, and whether drama had ever made them consider leaving the furry fandom. As shown in Figure 12.19, the results reveal that most furries have generally avoided becoming personally involved in drama, although furries are fairly divided over whether they tend to personally watch drama unfold.[30] The data also strongly suggest that, for most furries, drama does little to motivate them to want to leave the fandom. This finding, however, should be taken with a fairly significant grain of salt, as it comes from a sample of currently

[30] In the case of both of these items, it is worth once again keeping the concept of socially desirable responding in mind: respondents may want to present themselves in ways that make them look better. If respondents consider being involved in drama or watching it unfold to be unflattering, they might downplay their involvement. As such, these should be considered conservative estimates of respondents' actual tendency to be personally involved in drama or to watch drama when it unfolds.

active furries who have not left the fandom. It would be useful, albeit practically difficult, to conduct a study on furries who have left the furry fandom—or at very least considered it—to ask them the same thing. In some preliminary data from an online study, we did look, in an open-ended fashion, at furries who had left or considered leaving the furry fandom in the past and found evidence that drama may be one of the more substantial reasons why furries leave the fandom.[31]

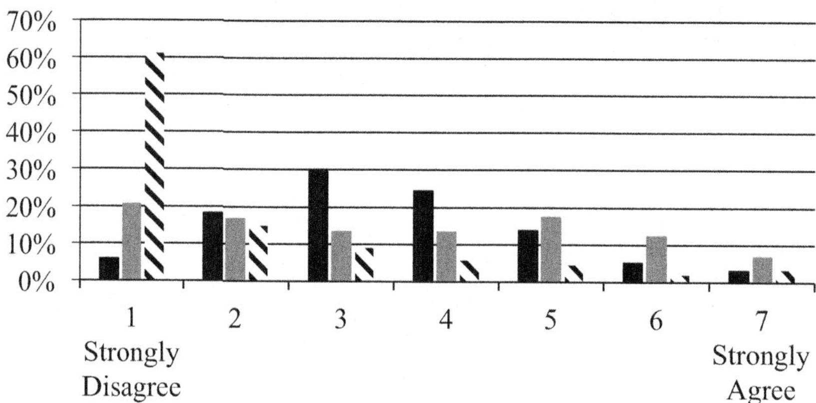

Figure 12.19. Extent to which furries recruited across a pair of 2017 online and convention-studies agree with items pertaining to personal involvement in furry-related drama.

In sum, the available evidence shows us that while drama is a thing, it's not unique to furries. While furries have a general sense of what drama is, they remain fairly ambivalent and somewhat divided about its impact on the fandom or where it comes from. Furries also tend to report not being especially likely to be directly involved, or even to simply watch furry drama

[31] The discrepancy between these findings and the findings in Figure 12.19 suggest that drama doesn't drive furries out of the fandom…until it does. Furries may find themselves unfazed by specific instances of fandom drama until they encounter fandom drama relevant to them, at which point they may find themselves motivated leave the fandom.

when it unfolds, although it is worth noting that the very existence of furry drama, by definition, implies that *someone* is engaging in conflict with other furries and *someone* is watching it unfold on places like social media. Whether this apparent discrepancy is because only a small number of furries create and spread most of the fandom's drama or because furries are motivated to downplay their responsibility for creating and perpetuating fandom drama remains to be seen.

Source of Conflict: Ageism / Generation Gap

In Chapter 13, we present evidence that, demographically speaking, the furry fandom is fairly young, with most furries in their late teens and early 20s. Nevertheless, there are quite a number of furries who are well into their 30s, 40s, 50s, and above. And, as we hinted at earlier in this chapter, differences between older and younger furries may be more than just a number on a birth certificate: older and younger furries may differ considerably in terms of their political ideology and religious beliefs. Even if we imagine two furries, one in their 20s and one in their 50s, who share identical political leanings and religious beliefs (or lack thereof), there's still ample room for misunderstandings or disagreements between the two of them. After all, if they both became interested in furry at the usual time for most furries—sometime in their teenage years—then the younger furry and the older furry would have gotten into the furry fandom at very different times.

For one thing, the older furry would likely have gotten into the furry fandom at a time when there were only a small handful of furry conventions, when sharing furry artwork involved contributing to or knowing someone who had access to, small, independent fandom publications. It was a time when fursuits were fairly rare and created by the suiter themselves, a time when furries were limited in their ability to interact with other furries unless they had the internet and a working knowledge about Usenet newsgroups, MUCKs,[32] and chatrooms.

In contrast, the younger furry would have come into the fandom at a time when there were dozens of different furry conventions taking place every year and when they could access furry content easily through one of many different furry-themed art repositories and art-sharing websites. The younger furry could commission a fursuit from one of the hundreds of builders—if

---

[32] MUCK stands for "multi-user created kingdom" and refers to a text-based online role-playing game; it could be considered the spiritual precursor to Second Life, VRChat, and other programs that allow multiple users to interact with one another in constructed virtual spaces.

they had the money to do so—and would be able to easily interact with thousands of furries worldwide through social media websites like Twitter, instant messaging programs like Telegram, or through videos and responses on YouTube.

These differences are just the tip of the iceberg, saying nothing about differences between the older and younger furry in terms of the specific media that got them into the furry fandom (e.g., comics vs. YouTube videos), differences in which artists and styles were popular when they joined the fandom, and differences in the norms and values of the average furry they encountered as they interact with the furry fandom.

What's more, we're only talking about the differences between the older and younger furry that pertain to the furry fandom! The older and younger furry also likely differ with respect to their lived experiences. The older furry is far more likely to have a career, to have become married or had children, to own their own home, to have traveled, to have lived through more significant world events, and to have a better sense of themselves and their place in the world. In contrast, the younger furry is more likely to be a digital native, born and raised in an era of new technology with a greater sense of proficiency and comfort with this new technology. The younger furry is more likely to be thinking about college, working toward moving out of their parent's home, and thinking about their first anniversary with their current partner than they are to be thinking about career advancement, a mortgage, marriage, or raising kids.

For these reasons, it's easy to imagine what would happen if we were to plunk the 20-year-old furry and the 50-year-old furry down in a room together. They might well struggle to hold down a conversation, given their different perspectives on the furry fandom, differences in their lived experience, and the relatively little common ground upon which to converse. Social norms might also interfere with the interaction: would it be considered "creepy" or "childish" for a 50-year-old to even be talking to a 20-year-old? Would a 20-year-old be seen as "weird" for spending time with someone so much older than them, or worry about being perceived as immature?

In short, as this example illustrates, there's plenty of reason to believe that age and generation differences may lead to divisiveness, rifts, and conflict in the furry fandom.[33]

---

[33] The idea of studying generation differences was first brought to our attention by several different older furries who contacted us at conventions. They had noted some similarities, as well as a multitude of differences, between older and younger furries, as well as some of the issues that would sometimes arise when older furries and

One way to study this potential conflict is to assess whether there is evidence of ageism in the fandom. At present, we're defining ageism as the differential treatment of other people based on their age. So if, for example, without knowing anything else about a person, one were to decide that they would not want to interact with them because that person was 20 years older than them, this would be considered a form of ageism.[34]

Okay, so how do we measure ageism? We took a crack at it in a 2017 convention study by asking furry participants from different age groups to imagine interacting with hypothetical furries of various ages in different contexts: talking at a furry meet-up, getting a ride to a furry convention from them, sharing a room at a furry convention with them, chatting online with them, becoming good friends with them, seeking advice from them, and simply wanting to interact with them. For each of these items, respondents answered on a 4-point scale (0 = *not at all*, 3 = *would for certain*), doing so for a hypothetical 18-year-old, 25-year-old, 35-year-old, and 55-year-old furry. We averaged scores across the 7 different types of interaction, meaning that, for each respondent, we had a single score indicating their average willingness to interact with a furry of four different ages across contexts. Next, we divided respondents up by age: respondents 24 and younger, respondents aged 25-34, and respondents 35 and older. The results are shown in Figure 12.20.

The data show that, in general, furries generally show a preference for interacting with furries that are around their age group: 18-24-year-old furries wanted to hang out with an 18-year-old furry more than 25-34-year-old or 35+-year-old furries did. Likewise, 18-24-year-old and 25-34-year-old furries wanted to hang out with a 25-year-old furry more than 35+-year-old furries did. 25-34-year-old and 35+-year-old furries wanted to hang out with a 35-year-old furry more than 18-24-year-old furries did. Finally, 35+-year-old furries wanted to hang out with a 55-year-old furry more than 25-34-year-old furries who, in turn, wanted to hang out with the 55-year-old furry more than 18-24-year-old furries did. These findings are precisely what we

---

younger furries would be thrown into the mix together online or at a furry convention. We are grateful to those furries for jump-starting our interest in this topic!

[34] To be clear, for now we're not saying whether or not there are valid or defensible reasons why a person may or may not want to interact with someone who was older or younger than them. We're simply considering whether, all else being equal, someone would be more or less willing to interact with someone on the basis of their age. We delve into some of the reasons why this may be the case later in this section.

would have predicted based on the premise that younger furries simply have more in common with younger furries than they do with older furries, and vice-versa. These findings also suggest that ageism is a two-way street: just as younger furries were generally less interested in interacting with older furries, older furries were generally less interested in interacting with younger furries.[35] Such findings are also consistent with social psychological research suggesting that people generally prefer to interact with and show positive biases toward those with whom they share something in common (Tajfel, 1970; Tajfel et al., 1971, 1979, 1987).[36]

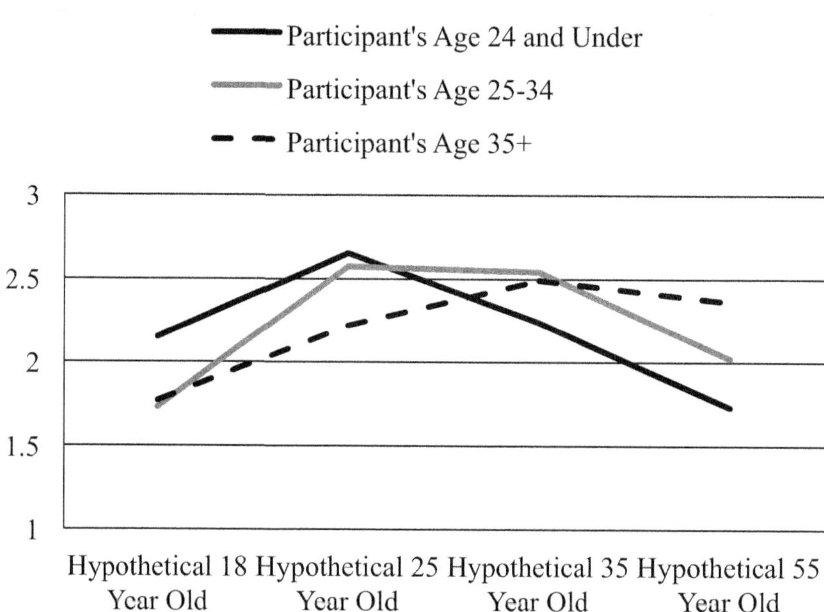

Figure 12.20. Extent to which furries of different ages, recruited at a 2017 convention, would interact with a hypothetical furry of different ages on a composite measure of 7 different types of interaction.

---

[35] These data would also seem to suggest that the best age to be a furry is between 25-35 years old if you're looking to interact with *everyone* in the fandom!

[36] We'll also note that by "ageism" we're not meaning to imply hostile or malicious intent. While it's true that furries tend to prefer interacting with furries of their own age group, we don't think this is because they hold any sort of hostility or ill will toward other furries. Ageism, just like other forms of discrimination, can happen without active intent or a desire to adversely impact anyone else. Or, to put it another way, you can get a discriminatory outcome without prejudice.

One could argue, however, that merely showing that furries prefer to interact with furries their own age is not the same thing as showing that conflicts and generational divides exist. To more directly test this possibility, we turn to an additional pair of studies we ran online in 2020 and 2021. In the 2020 study, we asked respondents in an open-ended fashion to describe whether they had ever had the experience of feeling out-of-touch with younger or older furries in the fandom and, if so, to describe what this experience was like. We then compiled the responses, categorized them, and ranked them in terms of the frequency with which different themes arose.

When it comes to feeling out of touch with older furries, the most commonly-mentioned experiences involved:

1. Feeling that an older furry was intimidating or condescending toward them
2. Seeing older furries as being overly ostracizing or cliquish
3. Believing that older furries were too openly sexual or accepting of kink-related groups in the furry fandom
4. Being put off by bigotry or prejudice from older furs (e.g., toward racial groups or sexual minorities)
5. Not knowing something about an older technology (e.g., MUCKs)
6. Being put off by the immaturity or negative behavior of an older furry
7. Seeing older furries espousing conservative opinions or being reluctant to change
8. Seeing older furries engaging in "creepy" behavior
9. Seeing older furries who were excessively interested in furry
10. Feeling out of touch with the norms or values of older furries

For comparison, when it comes to furries feeling out of touch with younger furries, a different set of experiences emerged:

1. Seeing them use different programs or technology (e.g., TikTok, Furry Amino)
2. Being put off by younger furries' promotion of "cancel culture" or being overly judgmental, political, or concerned with political correctness
3. Not understanding specific memes, trends, or slang
4. Seeing younger furries behaving in immature ways
5. Seeing younger furries being new to, or ignorant about, the furry fandom and its norms, or being put off by their desire to change the fandom in a negative way
6. Seeing younger furries as overly sexual, excessively kinky, or too focused on LGBTQ+ issues

7. Seeing younger furries engaging in specific negative behaviors (e.g., drug use, annoying online behavior, stealing content)
8. Being put off by a younger furry's rudeness, entitlement, lack of empathy, or know-it-all attitude
9. Being unable to relate to "younger" experiences personally (e.g., going off to college)
10. Seeing younger furries participate in, or spread, drama and conflict

The differences in the list hint at the very real possibility of generational differences at play, many of which could reasonably be expected to contribute to conflict in the fandom. For example, perceiving older furries as being condescending or cliquish, or younger furries as overly political or judgmental, could almost certainly spark disagreements between older and younger furries.

As a follow-up to this study, in our 2021 online study, we asked respondents to rate furries who were older than themselves and furries who were younger than themselves on a list of traits derived from these open-ended findings. In general, both older (age 24 and above) and younger (less than age 24)[37] furs rated older furs as more intimidating and more awkward with technology. In contrast, both old and young furs rated younger furs as more cliquish, more bigoted or unaccepting of differences, behaving more inappropriately in fandom spaces, being more overly judgmental, being harder to interact with, being more responsible for making the fandom worse, being overconfident in thinking they know more than they do, having a greater sense of entitlement, being uncomfortable to be around, causing more drama, being too open toward sex in the fandom, and having made fandom spaces more political.[38]

---

[37] The age of 24 was chosen not because we think that 24 is an especially old age, but rather because it represented the approximate median ("middle") age of a furry in the study. Doing so allowed us to compare two groups of approximately equal size. If we had made the split at an older age—say 40 years old—we would end up comparing one very large group (young furries) to one fairly small group (older furries).

[38] One might wonder why it is that *both* old and young furs seem to be united in their willingness to go after older and younger furs. After all, one might expect older furries to "pick on" the younger furries while younger furries do the same to older furries. While we have not yet tested the reason for this, we strongly suspect that it has to do with the wording of the question in terms of furries who are older and younger than the participant. In other words, a 20-year old furry disparaging younger furries may not be speaking ill of their *own* age group, but rather be thinking about furries *younger* than themselves. This would allow them to escape the criticism that

Continuing on, we also asked respondents to the 2020 and 2021 online studies to complete a number of measures asking about the source of possible generation gaps in the fandom. Rather than comparing the responses of furries who were older and younger, which overlooks the possibility that a 50-year-old could be brand new to the fandom and that a 25-year-old could have 15 years of fandom experience, this time we divided respondents based on the number of years they had been in the fandom: those who had been in the fandom for 10 or more years and those who had been in the fandom for less than 10 years.

Across both studies, we noted several potential sources or symptoms of generation gaps. For one thing, older furries[39] were more likely than younger furries to agree that the fandom was different from when they first joined it. Older furries were also more likely to agree that they feel they have less in common with other furries than they did when they first joined. In line with what we suggested earlier, this may highlight older furries' recognition that the artists, websites, shows, and norms that were present when they first joined the fandom have changed and that these feelings may get stronger the longer one has been in the furry fandom. Speaking to this idea, newer furries were more likely than older furries to agree that the fandom is pretty much the same as it was when they first joined. Newer furries were also more likely to agree that they have as much in common with the average furry as they did when they first joined. For newer furries, the fandom has had far less time to change and become unfamiliar to them, and so they feel they have more in common with furry content and with other furries.

Notably, older and newer furries didn't differ from one another with respect to feeling like the fandom has improved or worsened; specifically, both were inclined to agree that the fandom had improved since they first joined and to disagree that the fandom had worsened since they had first

---

might be levelled at them as a fairly young furry themselves. The same would be true for older furries: a 40-year-old furry may have no problem speaking ill of older furries, as they are technically speaking about furries older than them, despite the fact that, to most furries, they would be considered an older furry! In both cases, participants are free to acknowledge and take shots at old and young furries while distancing themselves enough from the groups to plausibly deny that the criticisms might also apply to them.

[39] In this paragraph, "older" refers to furries who have been in the fandom for longer, not necessarily furries who are higher in chronological age—although it's likely that most furries who have been in the fandom for longer will also be higher in chronological age.

joined. Moreover, older and newer furries didn't strongly disagree that they had thought about leaving the fandom in the past year.

Taken together, these data suggest that while the fandom may become less and less familiar to furries as they spend more time in it, they don't necessarily see these changes as a negative thing—even if it may cause them to feel a bit out of touch with younger furries as a result.[40]

Source of Conflict: Gatekeeping & Elitism

In this final section, we'll consider one last, specific point of conflict that may arise among furries, one that overlaps with many of the topics discussed throughout this chapter: gatekeeping and elitism. Put simply, elitism is the idea that someone or some group of people are better than others. Gatekeeping is the idea that some privileged people or groups ought to be permitted access to a group (i.e., the furry fandom) while others should be kept out. In theory, it's possible to gatekeep others from the furry fandom for most of the reasons discussed in this chapter: disapproving of their political views or beliefs, seeing them as a source of drama, or the perception that newer furries are changing the fandom for the worst.

On the subject of gatekeeping, open-ended data from our 2020 convention study reveals that 4.1% of furries spontaneously identified gatekeeping as something they wanted to see less of in the furry fandom, suggesting that gatekeeping is far from a trivial or minor concern for furries. In general, it would seem that furries are far more opposed to the principle of gatekeeping overall than they are in support of it, at least as indicated by the relative dearth of furries wanting to see more gatekeeping as a general principle. That said, earlier in this chapter, we noted several examples of furries wanting to keep very specific groups out of the furry fandom (e.g., Nazis). Rather than adopting an "all-or-nothing" approach to gatekeeping, findings such as these suggest that gatekeeping should be considered on a sliding scale, rather than an all-or-nothing fashion. We should be asking furries who they would gatekeep, how much they would prefer to gatekeep, and under what conditions they would exclude others from the fandom, rather than asking whether they were entirely opposed to, or supportive of, gatekeeping as a concept.

To better understand the conditions under which someone might support gatekeeping, we first turn to data from a large 2011 study of furries recruited

---

[40] This may also be why we see some furries congregate at conventions based on their age. "Greymuzzle meetups" for example, are a common feature at many conventions—see Chapter 12 for more on greymuzzles (a label sometimes used to describe an older furry).

online. We asked participants a series of five questions about gatekeeping. Without explicitly asking about gatekeeping, the questions asked furries to indicate their agreement on a 7-point scale (1 = *strongly disagree*, 7 = *strongly agree*) with the following:

1. The definition of furry should be limited because, otherwise, it's too easy for anyone to call themselves a furry.
2. There are many people who call themselves a furry that really are not furries.
3. The fandom should be accepting of anyone who calls themselves a furry.
4. People who invest a lot of time in the furry fandom are the "real" furries.
5. People cannot consider themselves to be a furry unless they've been to a furry convention.

The first three items tap into the extent to which respondents believe in restricting the definition of furry to exclude people whom the respondents do not consider to be furries. As the data in Figure 12.21 shows, furries generally disagreed with this idea—although approximately 20% of furries did agree with these sentiments at least somewhat. On the flip side, most furries agreed that the fandom should, in principle, accept anyone who identifies as a furry.

Concerning the fourth and fifth items, which try to make furry identification contingent upon the degree of interest or engagement in a fairly common furry activity (e.g., attending a furry convention), the data in Figure 12.22 suggests that furries, while somewhat divided on the first point, largely disagree with this notion of tying furry identity to whether one engages in specific activities or meets a pre-determined threshold of interest. To be fair, there's at least *some* agreement from furries that someone who engages in a lot of furry-themed activities can almost certainly call themselves a furry. But there seems to be little desire for furries to check for furry credentials, so to speak, when it comes to specific types of involvement.[41] In short, some of

---

[41] One could argue that this study only looked at one specific criterion, convention attendance, and that other criteria might be seen as more diagnostic (e.g., having a fursona, buying / producing furry content). While this may be true, we note that most furries have been to at least one furry convention (see Chapter 9 for more on this), and that furry conventions do typically require a significant expenditure of time and money to attend. One could argue that this might be more of a candidate for a diagnostic criterion than, say, consuming furry artwork, which anyone with access to the internet could do, and which might be seen as too lenient a criterion for

our earliest data suggests that, at least in principle, furries are open to the idea of anyone being a furry if they want to be.

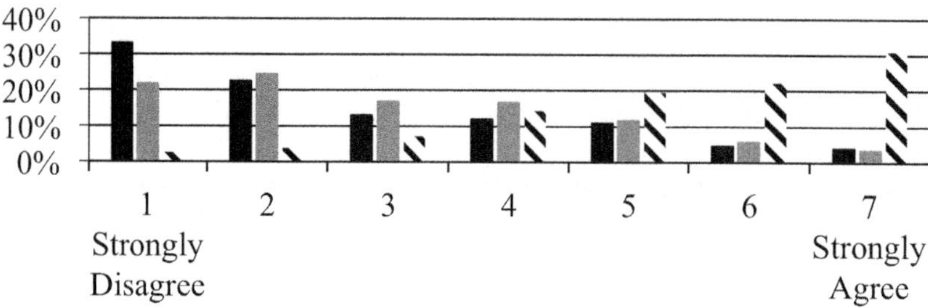

Figure 12.21. Extent to which furries recruited in a 2011 online study agree with items pertaining to gatekeeping in the furry fandom.

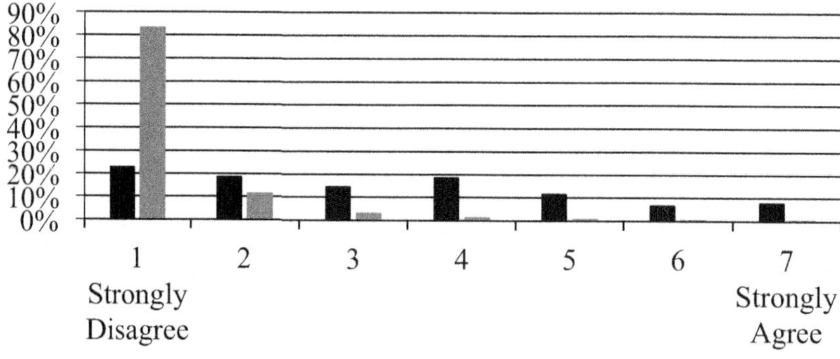

Figure 12.22. Extent to which furries recruited in a 2011 online study agree with items pertaining to gatekeeping in the furry fandom.

---

inclusion. Regardless, it would seem, from the other data in this section, that furries are largely uninterested in these sorts of checks to validate one's claimed furry identity, preferring instead to take furries at their word if they call themselves furries and recognizing furry as a label one ascribes to themselves.

To provide a more direct test of furries' support (or lack thereof) for gatekeeping, we tested three different measures of gatekeeping that we developed in a 2017 online study and at two different convention studies in 2018 and 2020. These measures were composites of 8, 10, and 12 items, respectively, that asked furries to indicate their agreement or disagreement on the same 7-point scale with various statements about gatekeeping behavior. As Figure 12.23 shows, whether we're looking at online samples or convention samples, and regardless of the specific measure used to assess gatekeeping, the results are fairly consistent with what we found in the above study: furries are generally opposed to the principle of gatekeeping in the furry fandom.

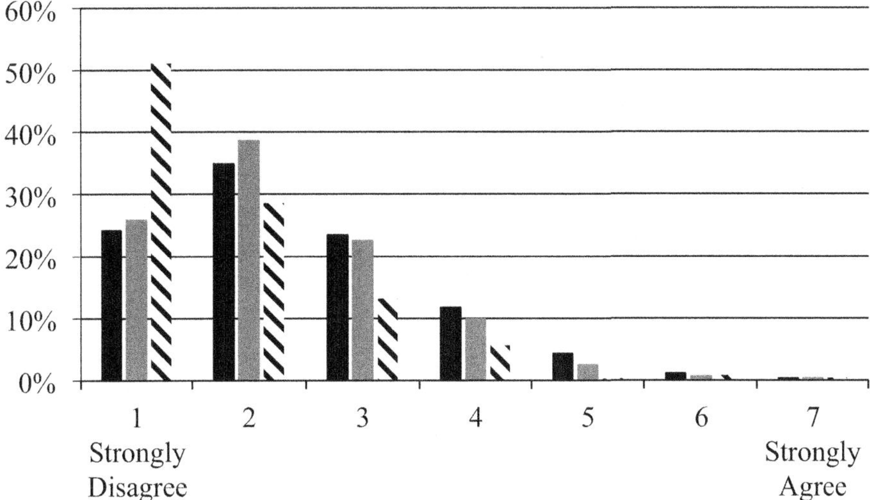

Figure 12.23. Average scores of furries across three studies on composite measures assessing support for gatekeeping.

While furries may be opposed to gatekeeping in general, what about the possibility we introduced earlier in this chapter, that furries may nevertheless support gatekeeping in specific circumstances, such as when it comes to excluding particularly worrisome or extreme subgroups? We've assessed this possibility in two different studies. The first, a 2016 convention study, asked furries to indicate their agreement (on the same 7-point scale mentioned above) with a set of five items assessing their willingness to exclude or ostracize some groups of furries (e.g., "Some groups in the furry fandom should be discouraged from participating," "Some groups in the furry fandom should be made to feel they're not welcome"). The other study was a 2017 online study that asked furries to rate their agreement with a single item asking whether they wished the fandom did more to exclude specific furries from events. Responses to both of these measures are shown in Figure 12.24.

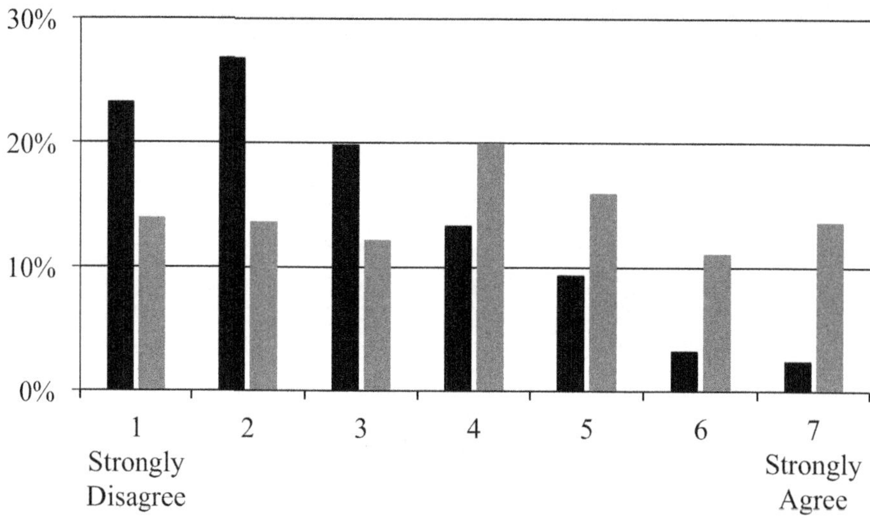

Figure 12.24. Responses of furries across two studies on measures assessing support for gatekeeping of subgroups or specific furries.

As the figure indicates, furries are generally opposed to the idea of excluding entire subgroups from the furry fandom, although 15% or so of furries showed at least some agreement with the idea. More divisive, however, was the notion of excluding individual furries: respondents were largely undecided on this issue, with about the same number of people agreeing with the item as disagreeing with it. This would seem to support the idea that while furries are generally opposed to the notion of gatekeeping, many furries can probably think of examples of individual furries or perhaps some very specific subgroups that they think the fandom would be better off without.[42]

As a counterpoint to gatekeeping, we can also look at data collected from furry samples regarding whether furries, as a group, believe that the fandom should be open to anyone, no matter who they are. We asked furries to indicate their agreement with this item in a convention study and an online study in 2016 and 2017, respectively, the results of which are shown in Figure 12.25. Across both studies (but especially in the convention study), furries were clearly in support of the idea that the furry fandom should be open to anyone. As of yet, we have no explanation for why online furries were less likely to agree and more likely to disagree with this item.

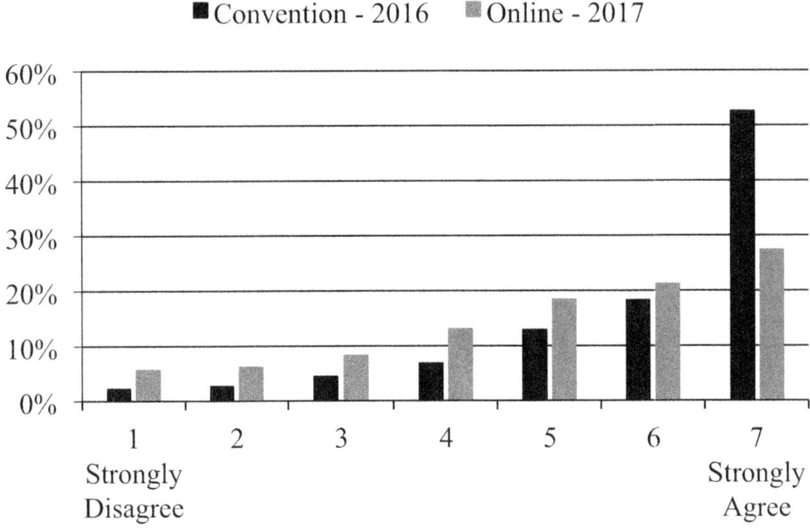

Figure 12.25. Agreement of furries across two studies with the idea that the furry fandom should be open to anyone, no matter who they are.

[42] We would like to emphasize that we are not imposing a value judgment on this belief. We don't think that this belief, in and of itself, is inherently good or bad. It is perfectly defensible, for example, to argue that a group would be better off if it had fewer Nazis in it. It is also defensible to argue that, as a principle, people should not be excluded from a group based on their membership in other groups, but rather should be considered as individuals, or to argue that, in principle, no one should be in a position to dictate what or who is allowed in the furry fandom. We are simply reporting how furries feel in response to these specific questions—whether you think they represent the right or wrong direction for the fandom is up to you.

Diving a little deeper into the subject of specific subgroups, we return to our earlier suggestion that some furries may gatekeep specifically against newer furries as a potentially undesirable subgroup.[43] To this end, we asked respondents recruited at two different conventions in 2017 and 2018 whether they agreed with 8 items measuring their felt negativity towards new fans (e.g., "You can't call yourself a furry unless you've been in the fandom for a while," "The furry fandom would be better if it were less accepting of new members," "I dislike when there is a wave of new furries following a fad"). As Table 12.26 shows fairly conclusively, furries are fairly united in disagreeing with hostility toward new fans. Or, to put it another way, for furries who do gatekeep, their animosity is likely not directed at new members of the fandom.[44]

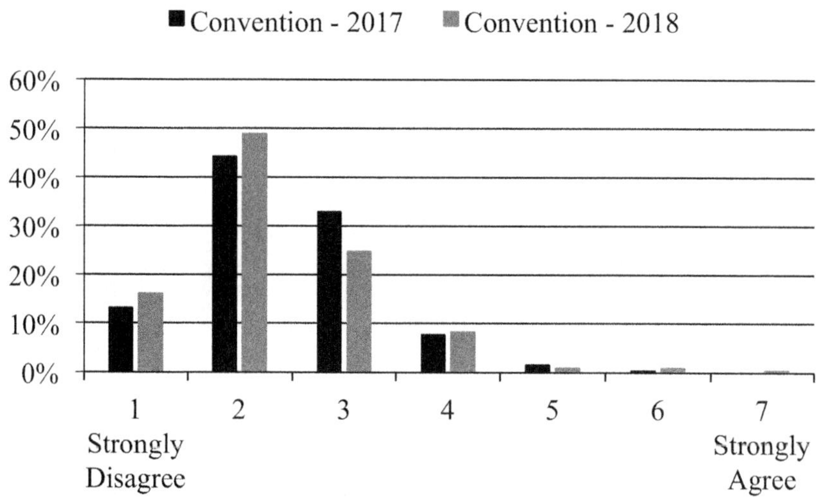

Figure 12.26. Agreement of furries across two studies with items espousing negative attitudes toward new fans.

---

[43] The idea that new fans may be disliked by older fans is not our own idea: prior studies suggest that bandwagon fans, fair-weather fans, and new fans are often seen as lacking loyalty (e.g., Zhang et al., 2018), something that people generally dislike when they see it in members of their own group (e.g., Travaglino et al., 2014).

[44] It remains for future studies to delve further into what specific subgroups or individuals furries are the most keen to keep out of the fandom and to see whether furries, as a group, are united in the desire to gatekeep these groups/individuals out or whether the targets of gatekeeping differ between furries in a predicable way.

Beyond questions of how furries feel about gatekeeping in general and which groups they would like to target with their gatekeeping, we can also ask which furries are the most likely to engage in gatekeeping. Within the studies discussed thus far, we've run several follow-up analyses to see whether furries who score high on certain measures are more likely to endorse gatekeeping. For example, we've found that those who identify more strongly as furries (fanship, see Chapter 6) are more likely to endorse gatekeeping, while those who identify more strongly with the furry fandom are less likely to do so. Surprisingly, fursuiters and self-described popufurs (see Chapter 11 for more on popufurs) were no more likely to support gatekeeping than other furries were, despite generally scoring higher on measures of fanship. Gatekeeping was also found to be more common among those who believe that drama is an inherent part of the furry fandom. Finally, one analysis found that those who felt a sense of entitlement and status—that is, furries who see themselves as better than other furries—were the most likely to endorse gatekeeping, specifically towards new fans.

This last finding in particular raises an important point about gatekeeping: how is it related to a furry's felt status and elitism? Before we more fully test the idea that status and elitism contribute to gatekeeping, we should first ask to what extent furries are inclined to see themselves as being high-status or among the elite of the fandom. One way to do this is to ask furries to what extent they agree with statements about being higher in status or admired by other furries. This is precisely what we did in a 2017 online study and a 2018 study at a furry convention. Across the two studies, we used two different scales, which featured items such as "Status-wise, I would say that I am probably in a higher standing in the fandom than the average furry," "I think a fair number of furries would want to be in my position in the fandom if they could," "Other furries look up to me as an example of what a furry should be," and "I have a lot of status in the furry community." The results are shown in Figure 12.27.

Despite using different scales, the pattern of results is largely the same: furries slightly disagreed with items suggesting that they were high in status—but only somewhat. Only a few furries strongly disagreed with the items, and only a few furries strongly agreed with the items. One possible interpretation of this finding is that most furries consider themselves to be somewhat in the middle of the fandom when it comes to status—neither at the bottom nor at the top—while a small number of furs saw themselves on the extreme ends when it comes to status.

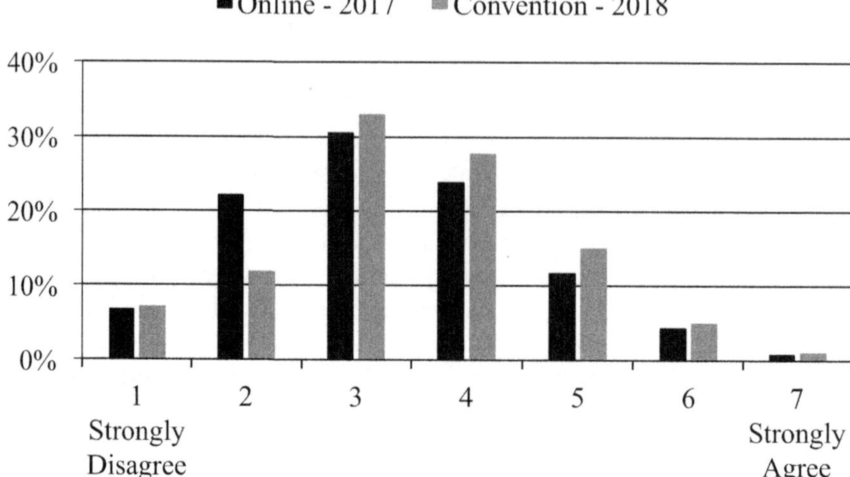

Figure 12.27. Agreement of furries across two studies with scales assessing their perceived status in the furry fandom.

Having said this, we should note that it may be considered bragging or egotistical to imply that one is high in status, even if one truly feels that way. As such, furries may be once again presenting a socially desirable image of themselves to researchers, wanting to come across as fairly modest (which might explain the relative dearth of furries who strongly agreed). In other words, this might represent a somewhat conservative estimate of how furries actually see their status in the fandom. Nevertheless, even with furries' scores hovering around the indecisive middle of the scales on average, there is evidence of variability: some furries do see themselves as "below average" in status, while others almost certainly see themselves as "above average"—even if only slightly so.

But is recognizing one's status in the fandom the same thing as elitism? After all, one can imagine a well-known, well-respected content creator in the fandom being honest and accurate about the fact that they are held in high regard by the fandom while nevertheless insisting that they are no better than anyone else. As such, we need to distinguish the concept of status from elitism in our measures. To assess elitism, we developed a scale over the course of several convention studies from 2018-2020, which ended up being published in a peer-reviewed journal (Plante et al., 2020). This "fan elitism scale" breaks elitism down into two components. The first component is called self-inflation, a person's tendency to see themselves in an overly positive manner. It's measured with items such as "I know more about furries than most fans" and "My opinion regarding furries is usually correct."[45] The second component of elitism is called other-derogation, a fan's tendency to put down other fans. It's measured with items such as "I avoid the new fans in most discussions of furries" and "I don't take the opinions of most furries seriously." Furries at a 2018 and a 2020 convention completed the scale (see Figure 12.28).

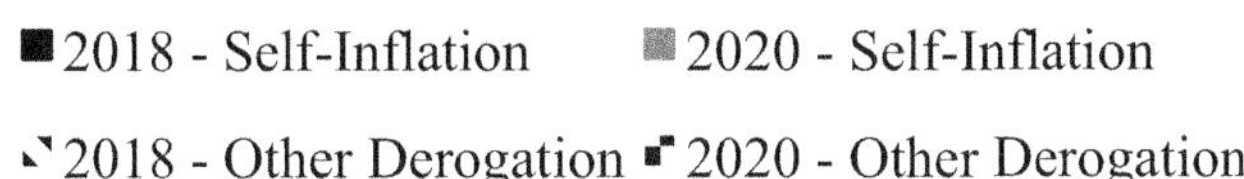

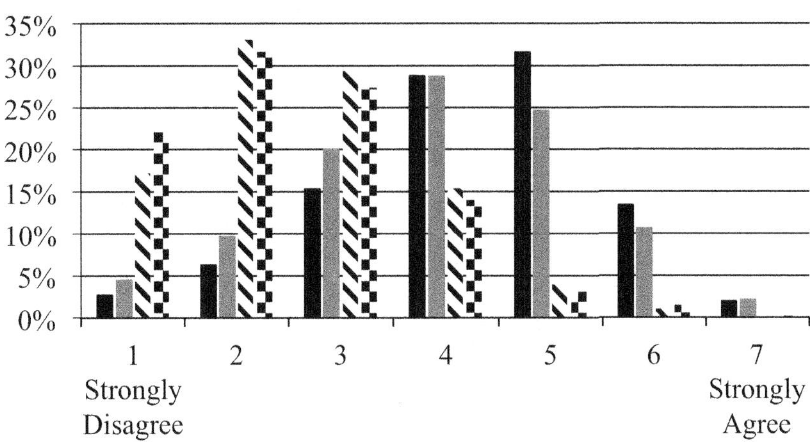

Figure 12.28. Average scores of two samples of furries recruited at conventions on the two subscales of the fan elitism scale.

Looking at the solid-color bars, it's clear that furries show considerable variability when it comes to their self-inflation scores. While many furries tended toward the middle of the scale, showing a lack of strong feelings one way or another, a lot of furries did agree with the items more than they disagreed with them. In contrast, the patterned bars present paint a different picture: furries are far more likely to disagree with the derogation of other

[45] These items represent the scale as it was adapted for use with furries. It has also been tested and used with other fan groups (e.g., bronies, anime fans, *Star Wars* fans). Of course, the specific wording of the question is changed to reflect the fandom being studied.

furries. Even so, there was still considerable variability concerning *how strongly* furries were opposed to the derogation of other furries.[46]

So why does this matter for gatekeeping? Well, in that published article, we went on to show that those who self-inflated and derogated others were more likely to gatekeep new fans, with derogating others being the stronger predictor of the two. In other words, a fairly good indicator of a person's willingness to gatekeep fans may be the extent to which they think of themselves as an especially big fan and, even more importantly, the extent to which they look down upon other fans. One can imagine how a person in this position might take it upon themselves to decide that they know what's best for the fandom and to decide which people do and do not belong in it. One can also imagine how furries who differ in the extent to which they have elitist beliefs about themselves might end up differing when it comes to whether they want to, or even feel comfortable, making such claims about who should or should not be allowed in.

Conclusion

Throughout this chapter, we've looked at many of the different ways conflicts and disagreements can and do arise among furries. We've demonstrated how furries may differ with respect to their specific beliefs about fandom content, their attitudes and behaviors related to the fandom, their vision for what the fandom ought to be, and their beliefs about who to gatekeep (or whether gatekeeping is acceptable in the first place). We've also discussed some of the potential catalysts for these disagreements, including the role of drama, generation gaps, and feelings of status and elitism as factors that may amplify these conflicts.

While it may be tempting to walk away from this chapter with the feeling that furries, as a group, are fairly divided, we'd suggest a different interpretation based on the demographic composition of the fandom as a whole. We started this chapter by pointing out that furries are a fairly diverse group, encompassing people from all walks of life. As a result, furries with different political and religious views, from different countries, and with different levels of life experience often find themselves thrown into the mix together. In such circumstances, one can expect a fair amount of elbow-bumping and even some minor scuffles. What stands out to us as remarkable is the fact that, despite these differences, the furry fandom remains unified.

---

[46] Follow-up studies found that the more one identifies as a furry (fanship), the higher they tend to score on both self-inflation and other derogation. In contrast, fandom scores were negatively associated with these scores. In other words, fanship is a stronger predictor of elitism than is fandom.

Despite how seemingly frivolous or trivial the thing they have in common seems to be to outsiders (e.g., liking a particular type of media), this is often enough to allow furries to see themselves as a cohesive group with shared norms and values. Even when disagreements do arise, the community generally remains coherent, with little evidence to suggest that it's on the verge of tearing itself apart or suffering an insurmountable schism.

And, as furries are often quick to point out to us, much of the conflict, whether drama or far more significant in nature, is far from unique to furry, nor is it a defining feature of what it means to be furry. Instead, it's a fairly predictable outcome when you bring together any group of people, let alone a group of people as varied as furries. What distinguishes furries from other groups we've studied is the strength of this community and the benefits it confers to its members, a point we'll return to in Chapter 19 and Chapter 22.

References

Barnes, D. M., & Meyer, I. H. (2012). Religious affiliation, internalized homophobia, and mental health in lesbians, gay men, and bisexuals. *American Journal of Orthopsychiatry, 82*(4), 505-515. https://doi.org/10.1111/j.1939-0025.2012.01185.x

Burned Furs. (2021, October 8). Retrieved June 7, 2022, from https://en.wikifur.com/wiki/Burned_Furs

Conti, A. (2010, February 9). Even furries are fighting fascists. *Vice.* https://www.vice.com/en/article/78we5z/even-furries-are-fighting-fascists [Accessed 2022, June 7].

DutchAngelDragons.com. (2019, March 7). *Guidelines for creating characters*. https://www.dutchangeldragons.com/design-guidelines [Accessed 2022, June 6].

Galinsky, A. D., Magee, J. C., Inesi, M. E., & Gruenfeld, D. H. (2006). Power and perspectives not taken. *Psychological Science, 17*(12), 1068-1074. https://doi.org/10.1111/j.1467-9280.2006.01824.x

Josephs, B. (2016, March 17). Furries love 'Zootopia'. *Vice.com: Entertainment*. https://www.vice.com/en/article/8gkjep/the-long-love-affair-between-furries-and-disney

Lal, K. (2019, June 3). Why furries are fighting over 'designer' fursuits. *Dazed Digital*. https://www.dazeddigital.com/fashion/article/44690/1/furries-furry-community-designer-fursuit-costume-controversy-backlash-zweitesich [Accessed 2022, June 6].

Leonardelli, G. J., Pickett, C. L., & Brewer, M. B. (2010). Optimal distinctiveness theory: A framework for social identity, social cognition and intergroup relations. In M. Zanna & J. Olson (Eds.), *Advances in Experimental Social Psychology, 43*, 65-115. New York: Elsevier.

Metacritic.com. (2016). *Metacritic – movie reviews:* Zootopia. [Online]. https://www.citethisforme.com/topic-ideas/other/References-20313938 [Accessed 2022, June 6].

Metallo, C. & Agrifoglio, R. (2015). The effects of generational differences on use continuance of Twitter: An investigation of digital natives and digital immigrants. *Behavior & Information Technology, 34*(9), 869-881. https://doi.org/10.1080/0144929X.2015.1046928

Meyer, I. H. (2003). Prejudice, social stress, and mental health in lesbian, gay and bisexual populations: Conceptual issues and research evidence. *Psychological Bulletin, 129,* 674-697. https://doi.org/10.1037/0033-2909.129.5.674

Miller, D. T. & McFarland, C. (1991). When social comparison goes awry: The case of pluralistic ignorance. In J. Suls & T. A. Wills (Eds.), *Social comparison: Contemporary theory and research* (pp. 287-313). Lawrence Erlbaum.

Plante, C. N., Reysen, S., Chadborn, D., Roberts, S. E., & Gerbasi, K. C. (2020). 'Get out of my fandom, newbie': A cross-fandom study of elitism and gatekeeping in fans. *The Journal of Fandom Studies, 8*(2), 123-146. https://doi.org/10.1386/jfs_00013_1

Popper, K. R. (1971). *The open society and its enemies*. Princeton University Press.

Reysen, S., Plante, C. N., Roberts, S. E., Gerbasi, K. C., Mohebpour, I., & Gamboa, A. (2016). Pale and geeky: Prevailing stereotypes of anime fans. *The Phoenix Papers, 2*(1), 78-103.

Tajfel, H. (1970). Experiments in intergroup discrimination. *Scientific American, 223*(5), 96-103. https://www.jstor.org/stable/24927662

Tajfel, H., Billig, M., Bundy, R., & Flament, C. (1971). Social categorization and intergroup behavior. *European Journal of Social Psychology, 1,* 149-178. https://doi.org/10.1002/ejsp.2420010202

Tajfel, H., & Turner, J. C. (1979). An integrative theory of intergroup conflict. In W. Austin & S. Worchel (Eds.), *The social psychology of intergroup relations* (pp. 33-47). Brooks/Cole.

Travaglino, G. A., Abrams, D., Randsley de Moura, G., Marques, J. M., & Pinto, I. R. (2014). How groups react to disloyalty in the context of intergroup competition: Evaluations of group deserters and defectors. *Journal of Experimental Social Psychology, 54,* 178-187. https://doi.org/10.1016/j.jesp.2014.05.006

Turner, J. C., Hogg, M. A., Oakes, P. J., Reicher, S. D., & Wetherell, M. S. (1987). *Rediscovering the social group: A self-categorization theory.* Blackwell.

Weill, K. (2019, May 4). Luxury brand started selling $6,000 animal costumes. Furries are furious. *The Daily Beast.* https://www.thedailybeast.com/furries-furious-at-luxury-brand-zweitesich-trying-to-sell-dollar6000-fur-suits [Accessed 2022, June 6].

Zhang, J. S., Tan, C., & Lv, Q. (2018). "This is why we play": Characterizing online fan communities of the NBA teams. *Proceedings of the ACM on Human-Computer Interaction, 2,* 1-25. https://doi.org/10.1145/3274466

Part 3
By the Numbers: Furry Demographics

Chapter 13
Generation Furry: Age, Socioeconomic Status, and Relationships

Courtney "Nuka" Plante

The main goal of this book is to better understand furries. Throughout this book, we approach the subject from various perspectives: defining what the term "furry" means, comparing an interest in furry content to an interest in the furry fandom, looking at popular furry-related behaviors, and even delving into the history of furry. While none of these approaches is, by itself, a complete picture of what it means to be furry, each adds a layer of complexity to our developing picture.

The present chapter, as well as the next few, will add yet another layer, one which focuses less on distinctly "furry" features and, instead, gives us a look at the demographic composition of the fandom. Of course, it would be silly to describe furries as "a group of young adults" or "a mostly college-educated group"—we recognize that furries have features that make them distinct from others in the same demographic category. Nevertheless, knowing some of the demographic features of the furry community can help us to contextualize and explain some of its nuances. In the process, we'll also compare furries to other fan groups we've studied to see which of the furry fandom's many idiosyncrasies cannot simply be chalked up to demographic characteristics—as well as which similarities between furries and other fan groups *can* be understood through a demographic lens.

In this chapter, we'll start with some of the most basic demographic features of furries as a group. We'll begin by considering age-related variables, including how old furries are, the age at which they become involved in furry, and two different furry subgroups based on furries' actual and subjective age. Next, we'll look at socioeconomic status, including furries' level of education, income level, and living arrangements, as well as the impact these variables have on furry behavior. Finally, we'll delve into the topic of relationships in the fandom, including family composition, intimate and romantic relationships, friendships, and some furries' use of the furry fandom as a source of social support.

Age

A typical Furscience survey includes anywhere from 150-300 questions. Most of the time, the survey includes all manner of variables testing a constantly changing array of different hypotheses. But across dozens of studies over more than a decade, nearly every survey has had one thing in common: we almost always begin the survey by asking participants their age.

Part of our interest in measuring age is purely pragmatic: we simply have to. Our research—like almost all research conducted through a university—is supervised by one or more ethics review boards. These boards set rules for what researchers can and can't do to protect the well-being and safety of participants.[1] Among the many considerations of these reviews is the ability of participants to give informed and voluntary consent to participate in the study[2] and the need to protect potentially vulnerable populations. In both matters, the participant's age is relevant.

To see why, let's imagine that a 15-year-old furry wants to participate in one of our studies. An ethics board might be concerned by this, arguing that a minor might not legally be able to give informed consent to participate. After all, in many societies minors are not permitted to drink or smoke, to sign up for military service, to have certain medical procedures done, or to enter into legally binding contracts. While minors may be interested or enthusiastic about these activities, the law has decided that they are not yet capable of fully considering the implications and long-term consequences of such actions and, as such, cannot give informed consent.[3]

For similar reasons, minors are also considered to be a vulnerable population, that is, a group of people who could be easily coerced or taken advantage of or for whom negative consequences could be especially harmful. One can imagine, for example, that offering a $20 reward in exchange for the risk of suffering some potential harm might not be especially incentivizing for an adult with a good-paying job. For a teenager

---

[1] The last thing you'd want as a participant in a study is to have your private information leaked or to be traumatized or physically injured by an insidious manipulation. Believe it or not, this was a real possibility in the days before ethics review boards!

[2] One of the many rules of conducting ethical research is that the rights, dignity, and humanity of participants be respected. This means they typically have to be made aware that they're being studied and agree to be studied, although there are rare occasions when this can be waived (e.g., when there's minimal risk of harm and no other way the study could be conducted, and, even in such circumstances, participants must be informed about the study as soon as possible and be given the opportunity to withdraw their consent now that they've been made aware of the study).

[3] This position is certainly not without its critics, of course. Numerous advocates argue, for example, that teenagers should have the right to make decisions about their own bodies (e.g., taking birth control, access to hormones and other gender-affirming treatments) without necessitating parental consent, especially in cases where trying to obtain parental consent might put the teenager at risk.

who might not be working or who might be making minimum wage, however, the same amount of money might be exceedingly coercive, causing them to agree to a risk that they would otherwise be unwilling to consider were they not in such need for money.[4] Moreover, even if a minor and an adult were both equally willing to agree to a certain level of risk, it's possible that younger people may be especially prone to negative side effects or long-term consequences due to a possible lack of experience, coping mechanisms, or having a still-maturing brain and body.

Having said all of this, you could argue fairly convincingly that the level of risk to respondents in our surveys is pretty minor. After all, being asked questions about their opinions or their hobby-related behaviors is unlikely to lead to any foreseeable long-term harm. Even so, ethics boards don't like to take chances when it comes to participant safety and often require additional restrictions and safety procedures as soon as a study involves minors.[5] For these reasons, we're generally unable to study minors, something readers will note in the following data summary. Asking participants their age is one way to enforce the rules imposed by our ethics boards, allowing us to stick to studying adults.[6]

But there are other reasons to measure a person's age beyond adhering to the rules of our ethics boards. For one thing, it allows us to get a general idea of the furry fandom's composition, including the presence of furries from different generations, their relative prevalence in the fandom, the rate of growth of the furry fandom, where changes in fandom composition are coming from (e.g., younger furs coming into the fandom, older furs leaving the fandom), and how the composition of the furry fandom differs from other

---

[4] For similar reasons, many other populations are also considered vulnerable, including people living in poverty and incarcerated individuals.

[5] One such procedure is the requirement that we get consent from the participant's parents if they are a minor. In some cases (e.g., online studies) this is impractical, as there's no easy way to obtain parental consent. In other cases, it's possible, but undesirable. If, for example, a furry wants to participate in our study but is looking to keep the fact that they're furry away from their parents, it would probably be a bad idea for us to ask their parents to consent to their child participating in our study about furries. We would prefer to avoid accidentally "outing" someone as a furry, however unlikely they may be.

[6] One could argue, of course, that a determined respondent might simply lie about their age to participate in our study. Unfortunately, there's little we can do besides taking participants at their word, as we have no ability to verify their age and identity—nor would we want to, as doing so would undermine the anonymity of our studies. As we said throughout Chapter 4, there are no perfect studies.

fandoms. Age is also an important variable for predicting other variables we're studying (e.g., political opinions, fandom-related attitudes, consumption behavior).

With all the preamble out of the way, let's get to the data! We can start with the most basic age-related question: how old is the average adult furry? When we look at aggregated data from more than 30 studies of online and convention-going furries, we find that, across samples, the average adult furry is between 23.1 and 30.1 years old (see Table 13.1), with only small differences from sample to sample.

Table 13.1. Average age of furry respondents recruited online and at conventions in studies from 2011-2022. Study names indicate the year of the study (e.g., 2021) and, when there was more than one study of a type (online, convention-going) per year, the chronological order in which case the studies occurred.

Study (Online)	Avg. Age	Study (Con)	Avg. Age
2011-1	23.1	2011	25.8
2011-2	24.2		
2012	24.0	2012-1	27.4
		2012-2	26.1
		2013-1	25.1
		2013-2	26.0
		2014-1	27.0
		2014-2	26.8
		2015-1	27.8
		2015-2	26.4
		2016-1	27.0
		2016-2	26.5
2017	26.4	2017-1	28.3
		2017-2	27.4
		2018-1	28.3
		2018-2	27.9
2019-1	27.4	2019-1	28.0
		2019-2	28.2
2020	28.4	2020	28.3
2021-1	30.1		
2021-2	25.8		
2022	27.3	2022	26.9

Of course, by itself, the average age of the fandom tells us very little. Without more information about the distribution of ages, it's impossible to know whether a sample with an average age of 24 years was made up entirely of 24-year-old furries or a bunch of 18 and 30-year-olds. As Figure 13.1 shows, furries in both our online and convention-going samples tend to be in their late teens and early 20s, with a gradual decline in prevalence starting with furries in their 30s and older.[7] One notable difference between online and convention-going studies is that, in online samples, the single most common age group is the 18-21-year-old range whereas, in convention-going samples, this was only sometimes the case; in more recent convention studies, furries in their mid-20s were more prevalent than furries in their early 20s. This tendency may be due, at least in part, to the fact that the cost of attending a furry convention (e.g., travel, hotel, registration) may make it a more feasible activity for furries who have more income. As we'll see later in this chapter, older furries tend to make more money, in part because they're more likely to be more advanced in a career and no longer be in college.

As mentioned, the data shown in Figure 13.1 do not account for furries who were under the age of 18 at the time of our study. In other words, if we were allowed to study furries aged 12-17 and include them in our dataset, our estimate for the average furry's age would be lower, meaning that our estimates are an overestimation of the average furry's age. While this is unavoidable, we can try to circumvent this problem at least a bit by asking furries in our studies to indicate the age at which they first considered themselves to be furries and the age at which they first became part of the furry fandom. This is precisely what we did in a series of online and convention studies from 2012 to 2019. For example, results from a 2019 study of online furries revealed that about 7.6% of furries considered themselves to be furries for the first time before the age of 12, 29.3% did so between the ages of 12-14, 30.3% did so between the ages of 15-17, 15.5% between the ages of 18-21, and 18.3% at the age of 21 or older. To put it

[7] While the present data can only look at adult furries, we have reason to believe that a sizable proportion of furries are also in their mid-to-late teens. For one thing, data shown later in this section reveal that many furries say that their interest in furry and first involvement in the fandom began during their mid-to-late teenage years. For another thing, other datasets, like the "Furry Survey" conducted by Alex Osaki from 2003-2015, were unaffiliated with a university and, thus, were not restricted to studying adults. Such datasets have shown that a sizable proportion of furries are in their mid-to-late teens.

another way, nearly two-thirds of furries indicated that they already had considered themselves a furry before the age of 18. In several of our other studies, the average furry first considered themselves to be a furry at around the age of 16.5-17.9 years old. Taken together, these findings make it clear that our studies overlook many, if not most people, who self-identify as furries.[8]

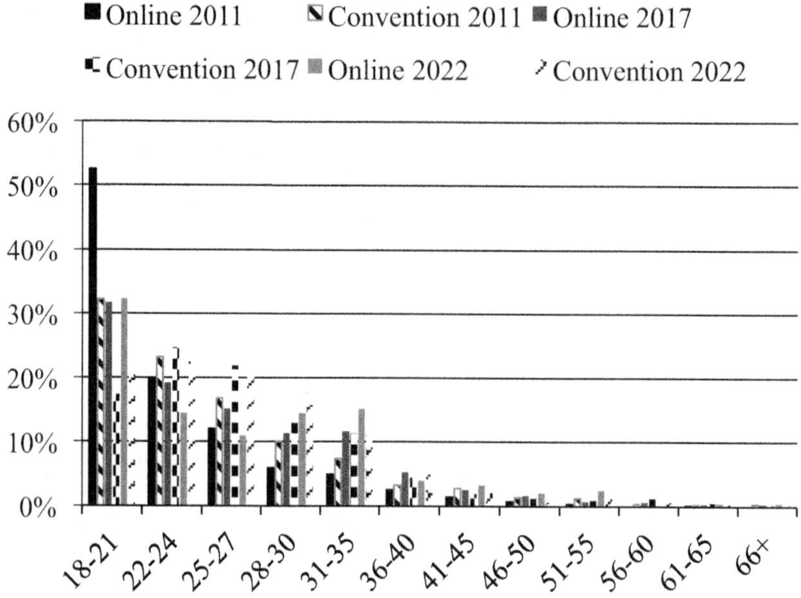

Figure 13.1. Age distribution of furries recruited in several large online and convention studies. Solid bars represent online studies and pattered bars represent convention studies.

Even so, it's worth noting a particularly important caveat: while most people may first consider themselves to be furries in their mid-to-late teens, it's possible that we would still be unable to study them even if we were permitted to study minors. In a series of eight online and convention studies

[8] Of course, as we continue to study furries and as these underage furries turn 18, they do eventually have the opportunity to participate in our studies. For example, a furry who was 14 in 2012 would have been eligible to participate in our study in 2016. Nevertheless, we cannot escape the fact that our methodology does leave a fairly sizable blind spot in our data, as furries in junior high and high school may well think, feel, and act drastically differently from adult furries.

from 2011-2014, we asked furries an additional question: at what age did they first interact with the furry fandom? Responses averaged between 17.5-20.3 years old across samples. This is an important distinction: while most furries said they had an interest in furry content at around the age of 16-18, they generally didn't become involved in the fandom (i.e., join forums, attend conventions) until about the age of 18-20, almost two years later. As such, we can surmise that many of the furries in this "gap" between calling themselves a furry and being active in furry spaces would have also fallen through the cracks and been missed by our studies, if only because they might not be active on the furry websites and forums or attending the conventions where we recruit. These data also highlight an all-too-common experience for many furries: furries often have an interest in media featuring anthropomorphized animal characters for months or years before they even discover that there is a word for their interest (furry) and for others who share it.[9] We discuss this in greater detail in Chapter 19.

Another question we can ask with this data is whether or not furries, as a group, are getting older over time. We recognize, of course, that individual furries are subject to the laws of entropy and age just like anyone else. But given that the data in Figure 13.1 shows us that there are considerably more younger furries than older furries in the fandom, we can ask whether the fandom, as a whole, gets older on average or whether an influx of new furries and an outflux of older furries keeps the fandom's average age approximately the same over time. Of course, because of the variability in age between online and convention-going furries, as well as differences between conventions in terms of average age, our best effort to detect changes in the average furry's age would be to compare the average age of furries drawn from the same convention in the same region at the same approximate time of year over time. With this in mind, Figure 13.2 plots the average age of furry samples drawn from the Texas Furry Fiesta convention from 2012 until 2022.[10] For comparison, we also plot corresponding data from studies we conducted on the brony (*My Little Pony*) fandom and the

---

[9] This was certainly the case for me! I spent nearly six years keeping my interest in anthropomorphized animal characters largely to myself before having the term "furry" explained to me by a friend I met in college, who coincidentally happened to be a furry. Before then, I had assumed I was fairly alone in my weird little hobby.

[10] This represents the most consistent, uninterrupted gathering of data from 2012-2022 available to us. Only the year 2021 is missing, as there was no Texas Furry Fiesta 2021 due to the COVID-19 pandemic.

anime fandom over about the same period (Edwards et al., 2019; Reysen et al., 2021).

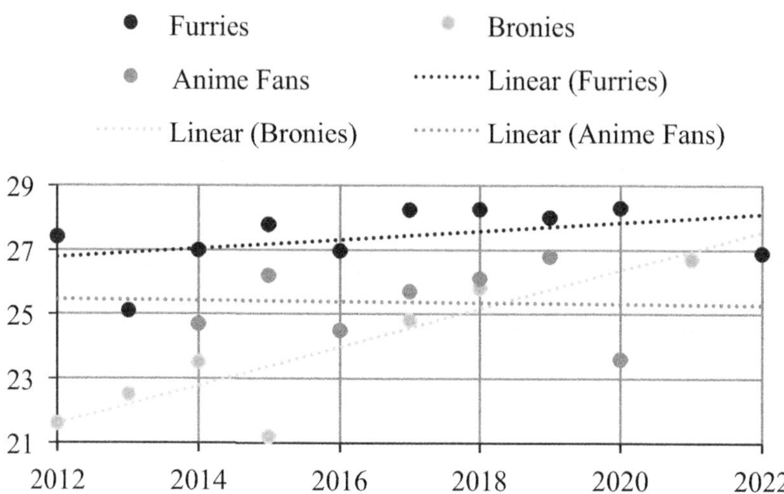

Figure 13.2. Change in the average age of furries, bronies, and anime fans from 2012-2022.

First, let's consider data from the brony fandom. The show *My Little Pony: Friendship is Magic* debuted in 2010, with most fans of the show joining the fandom within the following couple of years. From that point onward, there was only a fairly small influx of new fans into the fandom, meaning relatively few younger fans coming in to lower the fandom's average age. Or, to put it another way, the fans of the show in 2012 were roughly the same group of fans being measured nearly a decade later. As a result, the fandom aged along with the show. We can see this in the data: in the 10 years between 2012 and 2021, the average brony's age went up by approximately five years.[11] This is what we would expect from a fandom that

[11] The fact that the increase in average age is less than 10 years suggests that there were some factors keeping the average fan's age low. This may include older fans leaving the fandom and younger fans entering the fandom. Most likely, however, is the possibility that fans who were too young to be in our study in the early years (e.g., 16 years old in 2012) were becoming old enough to enter our study over time (e.g., 18 years old in 2014), making it seem like younger fans were suddenly "appearing." Anecdotally speaking, numerous fans told us that this was the case in

grew up around a single piece of media with relatively little migration into or out of it over time.

In contrast, look at the data for anime fans, a group we began studying in 2014. Over seven years from 2014-2020, the average anime fan's age remained largely unchanged. Since anime is a much broader media interest (comprised of hundreds or even thousands of separate series, all starting and ending at various points throughout the past few decades), we don't see the same phenomenon of everyone coming on board at the same time. Instead, there is likely a fairly steady flow of fans into and out of the anime fandom as some series end and new series begin. As a result, the average anime fan's age remains largely unchanged over time.

With these two different fandom models for comparison, we can see that furries look more like anime fans than they do the bronies. Over a 12-year period, the average furry's age has increased by about 1.5 years. This suggests that there is likely a net influx of furries into the fandom, as well as a possible emigration of older furries out of the fandom over time. This conclusion is reinforced by the data in Figure 13.1, which shows far more younger furries in the fandom than older furries. It is also consistent with the fact that furry conventions have fairly consistently grown in size at the same time (Furry Fiesta, 2022).

Another piece of evidence that there is a consistent influx of new furries into the fandom is the fact that newer, younger generations of furries consistently point to newer shows and series as the reason for their being furry. Illustrating this point in a slightly different way, we asked furries across four different online and convention studies to indicate the year in which they first became involved with the furry fandom. In theory, if furries joined the fandom at around the same time and were simply "aging into" being able to participate in our study, then we should expect to find a large number of furries who joined the fandom at one point in time, with a relatively low number of new furries after that point. Instead, as the data in Figure 13.3 shows, furries are much more likely to have joined the fandom in recent years than in past years.[12] This, coupled with the fact that the fandom

---

conversations at brony conventions, where they told us, while accepting a survey, that they had been waiting to be old enough to participate in our studies.

[12] A year-by-year analysis shows a spike in furry influx in the years 2012 and 2016. This largely corresponds to the release of two fairly influential pieces of (arguably) furry media: *My Little Pony: Friendship is Magic* (and the delayed growth of the brony fandom) and the release of the popular furry-themed film *Zootopia*. This also suggests that the continuous influx of new furries may be punctuated by periods of

hasn't been getting much older on average,[13] is strong evidence for a consistent influx of newer furries, possibly occurring alongside some older furries gradually leaving the fandom or being simply overwhelmed numerically by newer furries.

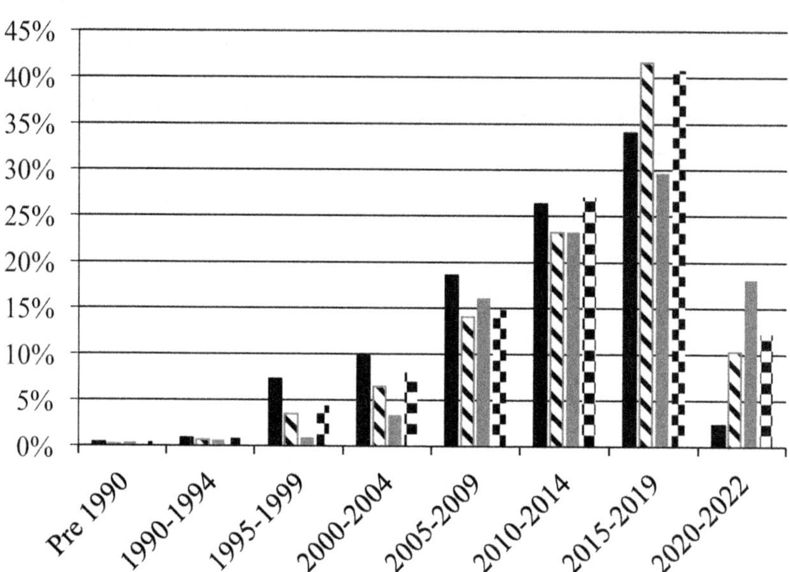

Figure 13.3. Distribution of the year furries joined the furry fandom for furries recruited online and at conventions.

As the data above suggest, the age composition of furries is generally comparable to other media-based fan groups popular with younger audiences. Specifically, furries are slightly older than anime fans and bronies (by about two to three years, respectively) and about four to five years younger than *Star Wars* and fantasy sports fans, respectively, as shown in

---

rapid increase in the wake of highly popular media. Anecdotally, furries observed similar growth in the wake of *The Lion King*, *Sonic the Hedgehog*, and *Pokémon*.

[13] Another finding supporting this position is the fact that, across 29 online and convention studies from 2011 to 2022, the average furry has been a furry for 7-12 years, a number which has only slightly increased across 12 years. If there were no consistent influx of furries over time, we would expect this number to increase significantly over time.

Table 13.2.[14] In this and many other regards, as we've indicated throughout this book, while furries differ from other fan groups in terms of aesthetic preference (e.g., for furry-themed content more than anime content), they are far more alike in more substantive ways (e.g., demographically, underlying motivation).

Table 13.2. Average age of furries compared to other fan groups.

Fandom	Avg. Age
Furries (Con – 2014)	26.8
Furries (Online – 2012)	24.0
Anime Fans (Con – 2014)	24.8
Anime Fans (Online – 2014)	22.7
Fantasy Sports Fans (Online – 2014)	31.7
Bronies (Con – 2014)	23.6
Star Wars Fans (Online – 2021)	30.1

Moving beyond the question of how old furries are, we can also look at the question of how old furries *feel*, a phenomenon known as subjective age. Anecdotally speaking, we've encountered numerous furries, particularly older furries, who say that their experience in the fandom has had a rejuvenating effect, helping them to feel young and vibrant at heart. That said, there is an old adage that youth is wasted on the young, with younger people (e.g., teenagers) wanting to be, and often tending to feel, older than they actually are (Johnson & Mollborn, 2009). In a 2016 convention study, we found evidence for both trends: on average, older furries tend to feel younger than they actually are, while younger furries tend to feel older than they actually are. Across four different online and convention studies, we find that, when it comes to subjective age, 30.6-55.1% of furries felt younger than their actual age, 24.8-44.8% felt about the same age as their current age, and 20.1-24.6% felt older than their current age. Importantly, furries over the age of 28 were nearly twice as likely as furries under the age of 28 to say that they felt younger than their current selves. Given that a fursona often represents an opportunity for a furry to embody an idealized self (see Chapter 7), one's fursona may allow furries to feel the age they want to feel, although more studies specifically testing this hypothesis are needed.

---

[14] Follow-up analyses show that, on average, furries tended to become fans at an older age than online and con-going anime fans, but at a younger age than fantasy sports fans and *Star Wars* fans.

While we're on the subject of subjective age, let's take a look at one final age-related phenomenon: age-related subgroups in the fandom. Specifically, we've studied greymuzzles—a term used by some older furries to describe themselves—and babyfurs/cubfurs—terms used to describe a furry whose fursona is an infant or child. Across a dozen online and convention-based studies we've found that 8.8-14.4% of furries self-identify as greymuzzles, while about 7.3-9.8% of furries self-identify as babyfurs or cubfurs. We consistently find that greymuzzles are, on average, around 10 years older than non-greymuzzle furries, with average ages ranging from 36.3-43.0 and 24.3-26.9 years old, respectively.[15] In contrast, those who identified as babyfurs or cubfurs were only rarely younger than those who were not; in only two of the studies did we find any evidence suggesting that babyfurs or cubfurs were younger than the average furry. These findings nicely illustrate the difference between a group that distinguishes itself based on actual age (greymuzzles)[16] and a group that distinguishes itself based on the age of one's fursona, but not their actual age (cubfurs/babyfurs).

Socioeconomic Status

Shifting our focus away from age, let's focus on another important demographic variable: socioeconomic status (SES). Broadly speaking, SES refers to a person's societal standing or status and is often indicated by the amount of education they have and their level of wealth. Those who are better-educated, live in a higher income bracket, work at better-paying, professional careers, and who own more capital and property are said to be higher in SES than those who are less-educated, paid less, work low-paying,

---

[15] It should be noted that while the term "greymuzzle" is often be used to describe older furries in the fandom, there is no agreed-upon age in which a person becomes a greymuzzle. In our own data we've found examples of 18-year old furries who describe themselves as greymuzzles and furries in their 50s who do not use the term to describe themselves.

[16] One could argue that the term "greymuzzle" may refer not to a person's actual age, but rather to how long they've identified as a furry. As such, a 50-year old who's only been a furry for two years might not consider themselves to be a greymuzzle, but a 30-year old who has been a furry for 15 years and who considers themselves to be a "veteran" of the furry fandom might use the term as a sort of badge of honor. Having said that, we've run analyses and found that a person's actual age is a stronger predictor of greymuzzle identification than is their years as a furry, although both were significant predictors. In other words, there may be truth to both of these conceptualizations of a greymuzzle.

entry-level jobs, and who own little to no property.[17] There is no single way to measure SES, just as there is no single way to measure a broad concept like "physical fitness." Instead, we have, over the years, considered a range of different SES-relevant indicators.

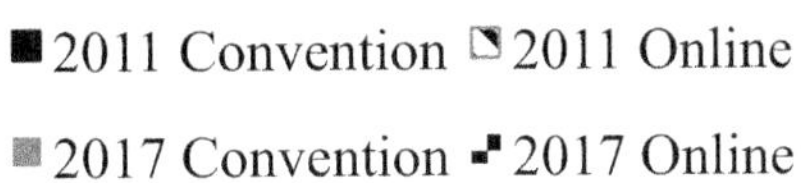

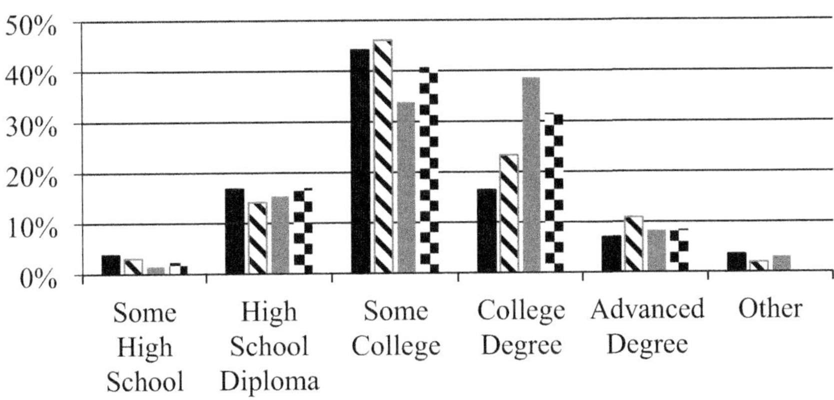

Figure 13.4. Level of education across several representative studies of online and convention-going furries.

Our most commonly assessed measure of SES is furries' level of education, a variable we've measured across 19 different studies from 2011 to 2019, both online and at conventions. Across these studies, the data show that most furries are either currently in college or have completed a college degree, a point illustrated by several representative studies in Figure 13.4. If we assume that many college students begin post-secondary education in their late teens or early 20s, and with a typical degree taking between three and five years to complete, then it comes as no surprise that many furries, being in their late teens and early twenties (see previous section) would be

[17] It's important to note that SES should not be seen as a value judgment: a person's SES says nothing about their character, nor does everyone strive to be high in SES. Likewise, we make no prescriptive claims about whether it *ought* to be the case that education and wealth determine status in society. We are studying SES only as a predictor of other useful or relevant variables, such as a person's ability to make fan-related purchases (e.g., fursuits) or their likelihood of facing practical difficulties, such as struggling to pay rent or afford food.

currently in the process of completing a college degree rather than having already completed their degree. These findings are somewhat consistent with research suggesting that approximately 40% of employed American millennials in the year 2016 have completed a bachelor's degree or higher (Graf, 2017) and, if anything, may even suggest that furries are somewhat more educated than the average person their age (if we assume that half or more of furries currently enrolled in college will continue on to complete their degree, an assumption in-line with current findings from the general population; Schaeffer, 2022).[18]

As a quick aside, while not specifically related to SES, we've also measured how well furries tend to do in school. To do this, we asked furries recruited at a 2016 convention to describe their average grade from their most recent schooling. As shown in Figure 13.5, the average furry scored somewhere in the mid-to-high "B" range, with 42.7% of furries indicating that their average grade was somewhere in the "A" range. This finding is consistent with the stereotype that geeks and those in subcultures labeled as "geeky" are well-educated (e.g., Reysen et al., 2016).

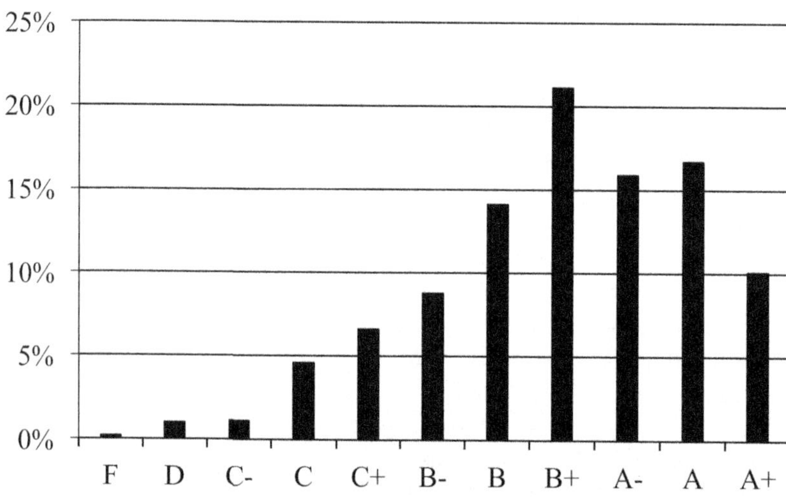

Figure 13.5. Self-reported average grade (from most recent educational experience) of furries recruited at a 2016 convention.

---

[18] These numbers are also fairly consistent with educational data we've collected from other "geek" fan cultures, such as the anime fandom and the brony fandom (Edwards et al., 2019; Reysen et al., 2021), after taking into account age differences between the fandoms.

Measurements of SES often also include the educational attainment of the respondent's parents. After all, those who are better-educated tend to work in better-paying careers (U.S. Bureau of Labor Statistics, 2021) which, in turn, increases the likelihood that their children will complete post-secondary education (e.g., paying for tutors, private schooling, paying for college tuition). We've measured the educational attainment of furries' parents across a pair of studies at two different conventions in 2012 and 2013, the results of which are shown in Figure 13.6. The data show a trend similar to that of furries, with the exception that parents, being older than their furry children, were more likely to have completed their college degree instead of currently being in progress. For both mothers and fathers, across both studies, the most prevalent response was having a basic college degree (e.g., bachelor's degree, associate's degree), with having an advanced degree being almost as common as having a high school diploma. In short: as a group, furries tend to excel at school and are well-educated, often being children of well-educated parents.

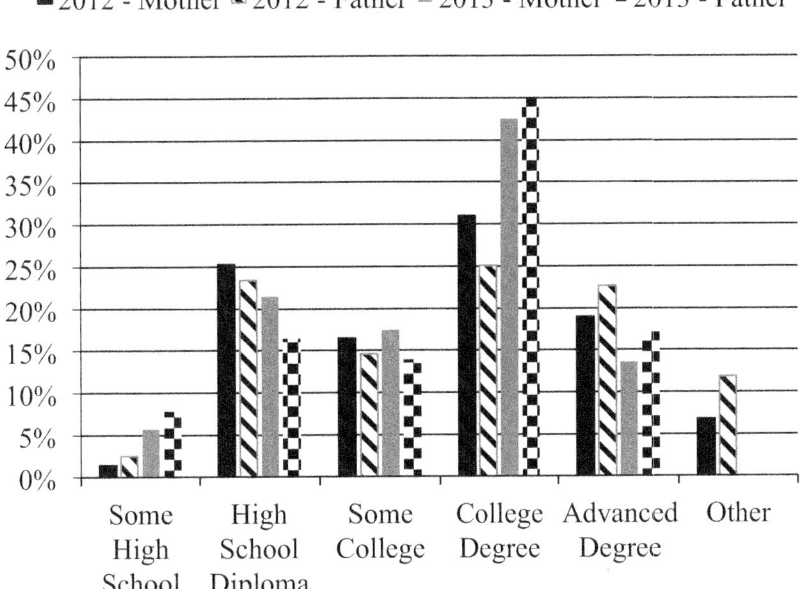

Figure 13.6. Level of parental education across two studies of convention-going furries in 2012-2013, separated by parent. "I don't know" responses were put in the "other" category, which was not available in the 2013 study.

One of the simplest and most common sense measures of a person's SES is their income. To assess this, we asked furries in six different online and convention-going studies from 2012 to 2017 to indicate their annual income in $USD. The data are shown in Figure 13.7. Across studies, furries' average annual income ranges from $29,448.90-$31,942.54, with 5.2%-12.7% of furries across samples indicating that they had no income in the past year. It's worth noting that our samples of convention-going furries may represent an overestimation of the average furry's income given that, almost by definition, they include furries who can afford to attend a furry convention. That said, the average income of the online furry sample ($30,256.54) fell in the middle of the range of the online samples obtained. For comparison, we also compared the average income of our furry samples to the average income of a control sample of approximately 800 typical Americans: the result found that furries did not differ statistically significantly. As the distribution shows, the most common annual income for furries tends to be $30k or less, with a fairly long "tail" representing 12-20% of furries who earn $60k or more pulling the average upward.

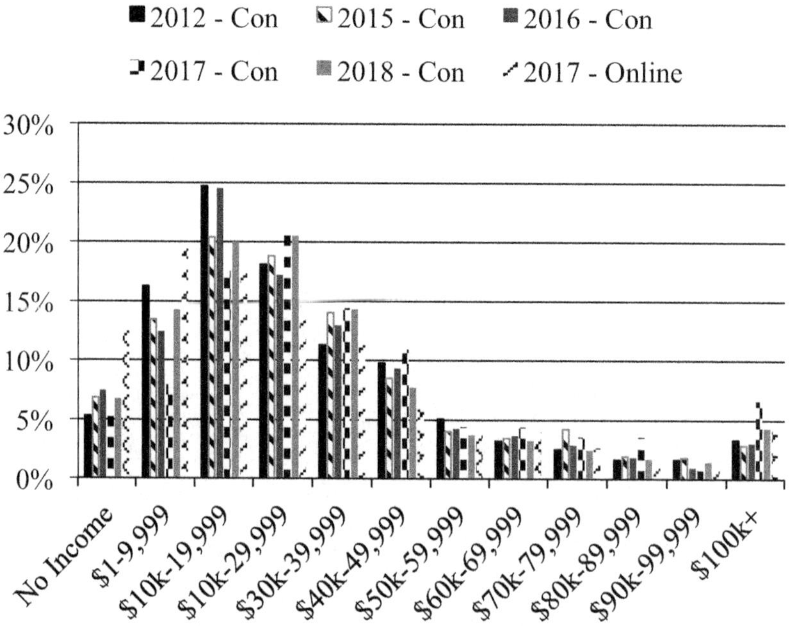

Figure 13.7. Self-reported annual income of furries recruited in online and convention studies from 2012 to 2017.

It is worth keeping in mind, as we interpret this income data in conjunction with the data above, that the relatively modest earnings of many furries are likely a product of both the young age of the typical furry and the fact that many furries are, themselves, currently enrolled in post-secondary education, something which is both expensive and which makes it more difficult to work. Follow-up analyses of these and other studies support this interpretation. For example, in a 2013 convention study looking at the combined self-and-partner income of furries, 71.6% of furries under the age of 23 reported a combined annual income of less than $15k, while only 32.7% of furries aged 23 or older fell into the same income range.[19] Likewise, the same 2013 study found that the most common working situation of furries under the age of 23 was "full-time student" (56.7%), while the most common working situation of furries over the age of 23 was "working full-time" (47.6%).

On the subject of furries and their work, we've also looked at the sorts of jobs that furries work. Specifically, in a 2014 study of convention-going furries, we asked participants to briefly describe, in an open-ended fashion, what their job description was. From this, responses were organized into themes, from which seven different categories emerged. The most common category, consistent with what we've mentioned above, was "student," which made up 24.0% of all responses. The next two categories were tied for prevalence, with 18.1% of responses falling into the "skilled work" category and 18.1% falling into the theme of "office work." The remaining categories were "unskilled" (14.2%), "computer-related" (12.6%), "professional work" (7.1%) and "not working" (5.9%). Taken together, these findings are consistent with a picture of the furry fandom as being primarily comprised of college students or recent graduates working skilled, white-collar, or professional jobs. It's also worth noting that a significant number of furries work in fields related to computers and technology, also consistent with stereotypes of geek culture (Reysen et al., 2016).[20]

Another indicator of SES is one's housing situation. Given what we've already read about furries as a group—they're mostly young, current, or

---

[19] It should also be noted, as we'll report later in this chapter, that younger furries are also more likely to be single, which may also explain lower combined annual income scores (i.e., being based on only one income instead of two).

[20] Even among geeky subcultures, however, furries may be especially associated with careers involving computers and technology: a follow-up analysis comparing furries to anime fans and fantasy sports fans found that furries were the group most likely to describe their work as involving computers or skilled work.

recent college students who make $30k or less per year—we might surmise that furries—younger furries, especially—are unlikely to be living on their own. Instead, we might expect them to make ends meet by living with roommates or romantic partners to make rent or with their parents to avoid having to pay a landlord. As a test of this, we asked furries at two different furry conventions in 2013 and 2014 to choose which of several options best described their current living accommodations. As Figure 13.8 reveals, the data are pretty much in line with our expectations. Across age groups and studies, living with one's parents was the single most common category chosen. However, furries were half as likely to be living with their parents after the age of 23 as they were to be living with their parents before the age of 23. We also unexpectedly found that rates of living with roommates were virtually unchanged for older and younger furries, with most of the change between younger and older furries coming from an increased tendency to live alone or live with a spouse or romantic partner over time.[21]

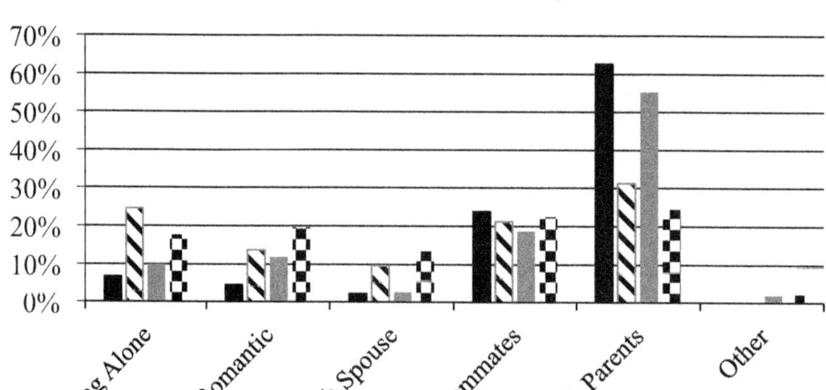

Figure 13.8. Living accommodations across two studies of convention-going furries in 2013-2014, separated by older and younger respondents.

[21] Also in-line with earlier findings, this is likely due to furries being more likely to be in a serious relationship or married as they move into their mid-20s.

As a brief aside, let's take a moment to place the above findings in a historical context. At first glance, you might think that a 21-year-old who's still living with their parents, making less than $10k per year, and who doesn't have a career might seem uncommonly "behind", given the common societal prescription that young people are "supposed to" move out, get an entry-level job, transition into a career, get married, and purchase a home. Our findings, however, suggest that furries are not an anomaly, but rather are on par with findings from anime fans and bronies (Edwards et al., 2019, Reysen et al., 2021). In other words, this "delayed adulthood" is not unique to furries, but is, instead, common among "geek" fandoms and may even be an indication of broad generational differences. In the general population, for example, 36% of 18- to 34-year-olds have never moved away from their parents or have been forced to move back in due to difficult financial circumstances (Fry, 2016). In the wake of a major economic recession and ongoing market instability, reduced availability of affordable housing, stagnant wages, an increased cost of living, and changing social norms about when people are expected to get married (or even whether they should get married at all), it's little wonder that the millennial and zoomer generations are opting (or, in many cases, forced) to delay what older generations would typically consider to be "typical adulthood"—at least until they're better-prepared (Levenson, 2010).[22]

To finish up this section on SES, we'd like to look at one last measure, one that's broader and more abstract than the measures we've mentioned above, called the MacArthur Scale of Subjective Social Status (Adler et al., 2000). Respondents are shown a figure of a ladder with numbered rungs going from "1" to "10," from bottom to top. They're asked to imagine that the ladder represents the socioeconomic status of people in their country, with the people who are worst off represented at the bottom of the ladder and the people who are doing best off at the top of the ladder. Respondents are then asked to indicate which of the rungs represents where they see themselves relative to others in their country. It's about as straightforward a measure of subjective SES as one can get, with people who feel as though they're better off choosing higher rungs and people who feel worse off choosing lower rungs.

We gave this measure to nine different samples of furries recruited from 2016-2020 in both online and convention studies. The results were fairly

---

[22] For more on this delayed transition into adulthood, see Chapter 24.

consistent across studies, with some representative studies' results shown in Figure 13.9. In general, relatively few furries described themselves as being on the lowest or highest rungs. Instead, most furries described themselves as being on the middle of the ladder, with the most common scores occurring somewhere between rungs 4 and 7.

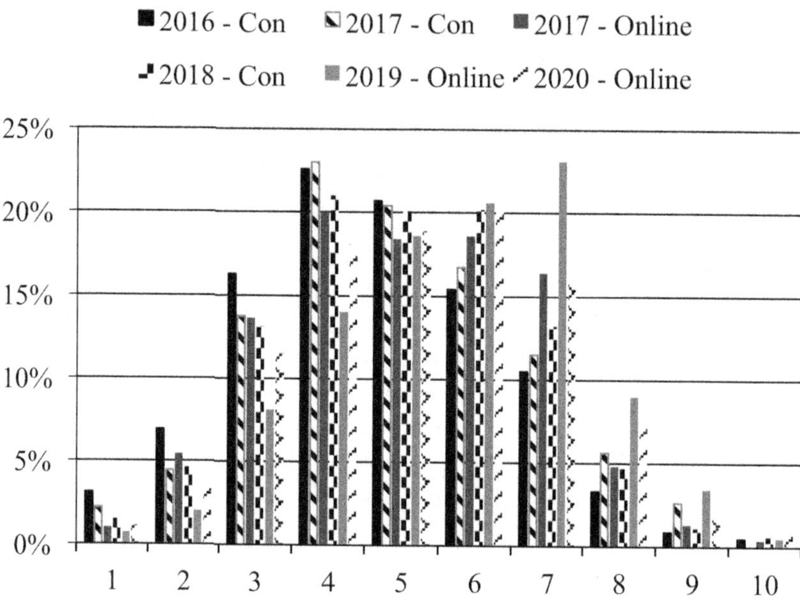

Figure 13.9. Self-reported relative socioeconomic status as measured by rung choice across multiple samples of online and convention-going furries from 2016-2020.

One could argue that the ladder measure of SES is a bit abstract, and maybe some furries, while considering themselves to be generally middle class, might not know what constitutes "middle class" on a ladder with ten different options.[23] To avoid this complication, we also ran a study of online

[23] This is far from the measure's only problem. For example, social scientists recognize the concept of "relative deprivation," the tendency for people to feel that they are not especially well off in comparison to others they see frequently (e.g., neighbors, in the media) who have more than they do (Smith et al., 2011). Because of this, a person who, objectively speaking, is fairly well off (e.g., able to consistently and comfortably pay for their necessities and a few luxuries) may nevertheless feel that they are doing worse than average if they routinely compare

and convention-going furries in 2019 where we asked furries specifically which of six different labels they identified with: "lower class," "working class," "lower middle class," "middle middle class," "upper middle class," and "upper class." Across the two samples, furries showed the same tendency: the single most common response category was middle middle class (27.5-31.5%), followed by upper middle class (22.2-23.8%) and lower middle class (19.9-21.9%). And, just as with the ladder measure, relatively few furries chose the lowest (3.7-4.7%) or highest options (0.7-1.7%).

Taken together, the data reviewed in this section paint a picture of furries as being a somewhat variable group when it comes to SES, one centered around a fairly typical, middle-class experience. Some furries—likely furries in their mid-twenties and above—tend toward the upper-middle class side of the scale, being more likely to live on their own, complete college, and be working full-time. In contrast, younger furries, like many young adults in the 21st century, may fall on the lower end of middle-class, in that they are currently in college and have aspirations of one day having a good-paying, professional career, but for now find themselves paying off student loans, working as a full-time student, and living with their parents as a necessity. None of these features are uniquely furry, although they are a fairly common experience among many furries (and among other geek cultures more broadly).

Relationships

As the saying goes, no one person is an island. Throughout this book we've seen how identifying as a furry and identifying with the furry fandom frequently go hand-in-hand, to the point that it's often difficult to get a complete picture of an individual furry's experience without considering the furries around them. Broadening this idea just a bit, we'll finish this chapter by taking a look at the family, friends, and romantic partners that furries surround themselves with. As we'll see, an understanding of furries' social networks is essential to forming complete pictures of a furry, including their motivations and behavior both inside and outside the fandom.

To start, let's consider furries' family lives, a topic suggested to us by furries and non-furries alike wanting to know whether something about a person's family life might compel them to become a furry. In a 2011 study, we asked participants questions about their family composition, choosing

---

themselves to others doing far better than they are (e.g., watching millionaires or billionaires in the media). In other words, a "5" on the ladder might mean two entirely different things to two different people, depending on who they're comparing themselves to.

questions that had been suggested to us as potential catalysts for someone becoming a furry.[24]

First, we found that, across samples, approximately one-third of furries (33.4-35.0%) say that their parents were divorced. This number is actually below the approximate 50% divorce rate of marriages in the United States (CDC/National Center for Health Statistics, 2022),[25] meaning that, if anything, having parents who *did not* get divorced might be a better predictor of becoming a furry than coming from a home where one's parents were divorced.

As a second question, we asked respondents whether they had siblings and, if so, whether the respondent was the oldest, youngest, or somewhere in the middle in terms of birth order. The data revealed that, across studies, 12.8-17.7% of furries did not have a sibling, meaning that most furries have at least one sibling. Specifically, 38.5-40.6% of furries have exactly one sibling, 23.2-26.5% have two siblings, and 19.9-20.6% have three or more siblings. While having siblings isn't a distinct feature of being furry, one factor that *did* stand out was data on birth order: among furries who had at least one sibling, furries were about 1.5 times more likely to be the oldest sibling than they were to be the youngest sibling (47.3-47.4% vs. 33.5-34.3%, respectively).[26] Given that there should be an equal number of oldest children as there are youngest children if it were due purely to random chance, this suggests a fairly strong tendency for furries to be the older child. Future research is needed as to why this is the case, although I (as both a furry and an oldest sibling myself) offer this hypothesis from my own experience: perhaps oldest children are exposed to cartoons and other media intended for children for longer than is typical because they live with

---

[24] People who suggest family structure as a possible "cause" of furries are often vague about the mechanisms involved. Trying to fill in this theoretical gap, we might speculate that a furry whose family life was in turmoil (e.g., parents getting divorced) might retreat into fantasy-themed activities. However, as we'll see, there is no empirical evidence to support this pathway. This doesn't rule out the possibility that *some* furries may have found their way into the furry fandom this way, but there is little reason to believe that it's common.

[25] This estimate is called the "crude divorce rate," based on dividing rates of divorce per capita by rates of marriage per capita. As the name indicates, it's a fairly crude approximation, and so interpretations using it should be taken with a grain of salt.

[26] Don't worry, frequently-overlooked middle children, we didn't forget about you! Approximately 18.4-19.1% of furries were neither the oldest nor the youngest child in their family.

younger siblings who watch these shows and, more often than not, won the battle for the TV remote.[27,28]

Taken together, the data do not compellingly make the case that furry is a byproduct of familial structure. Moving on from considering furries' family lives, let's now consider furries' social lives—specifically, their friends. After all, stereotypes of geeks often portray them as socially awkward, lonely, and isolated from others (Reysen et al., 2016), so it's worth asking whether furries reflect this stereotype or, if they don't, whether they surround themselves with fellow furries.

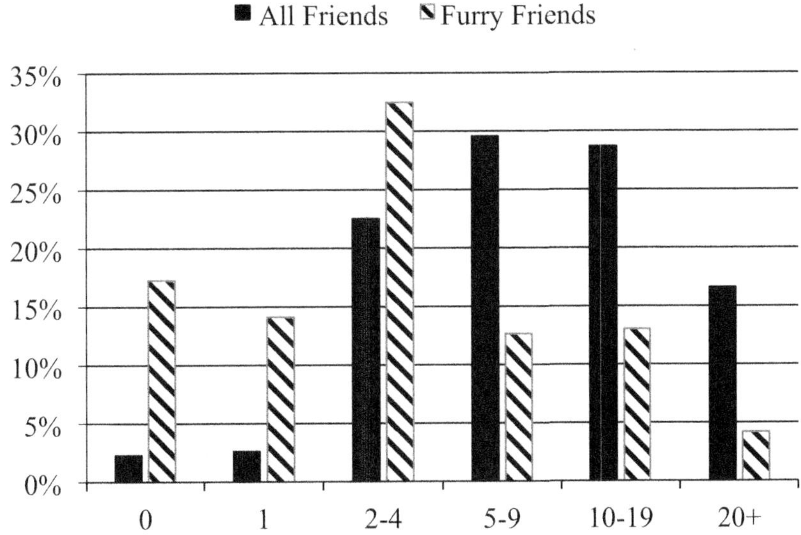

Figure 13.10. Number of friends, total and furry, interacted with in a typical week as reported by furries in a 2014 convention study.

---

[27] For those who are curious, my younger siblings were avid fans of *Pokémon*, a show I would not have watched on my own. As luck would have it, one of the characters in the show, Mewtwo, unexpectedly sparked a lifelong interest in anthropomorphized animal characters.

[28] Following this same logic, one could argue that those who take care of kids—like parents—should also be more likely to become furries themselves. This seems unlikely, given that, from what we can tell, parents' usual response to their child's television-viewing is annoyance and a desire to avoid it. Moreover, this same study found that only 4.7-5.7% of furries have children themselves, likely due to their younger age and, as we'll see later in this section, are generally unmarried and not in a serious long-term relationship.

One way we tested these questions was to ask furries in a 2014 convention study to indicate how many friends they see or speak to (online or in-person) in a typical week. They were also asked to indicate how many of these friends were, themselves furries. The data, summarized in Figure 13.10, found that the average furry interacts with about 11-12 friends per week on average, about half (48.2%) of whom were furries themselves. Only about 17.3% of furries say that they don't interact with other furries in a given week. In other words, the data suggest that the stereotype of furries as loners is wrong: Furries typically do have friends, many of whom—but certainly not all—are furry.

Follow-up studies allow us to further contextualize these findings. For example, when we directly compared furries to other fan groups (e.g., anime fans, fantasy sports fans) in other studies, we found that furries tended to have a smaller percentage of friends who shared their interest than did anime fans, although furries did not differ from fantasy sports fans in this regard. In other words, anime fans were more likely to surround themselves with other anime fans than were furries or fantasy sports fans, who had a higher proportion of friends who were not fans of their respective interests. One possible explanation for this boils down to the much larger size of the anime fandom. While we don't have precise estimates of the size of each fandom, it's a safe bet that the anime fandom is far larger and more mainstream than both the furry fandom and the fantasy sports fandom, both of which are smaller and more niche. For this reason, it may simply be harder for furries to find other furries to interact with than it is for anime fans to find other anime fans to interact with.[29]

Skeptical readers might push back against our findings, arguing that the quantity of friends is less important than quality of friends. After all, a person who interacts with hundreds of people online in a forum but forms no deep and meaningful bonds with those people may feel more lonely than a person with a single friend with whom they share a deep and significant connection. To account for this possibility, we asked about friendships in a different way in a 2019 online study. Rather than asking furries to indicate the number of friends with whom they interacted weekly, we instead asked them to indicate on a 7-point scale (1 = *not at all*, 7 = *completely*) to what extent they agreed with the statement "I have a close set of friends." As the data in Figure 13.11 show, on average, furries strongly agreed with this item, scoring an average

---

[29] Speaking to this point, it is not uncommon for high schools to have an anime club. In contrast, the author is unaware of any schools with a furry club.

of 5.3 on the scale, with a strong majority of furries choosing the highest two options on the scale.

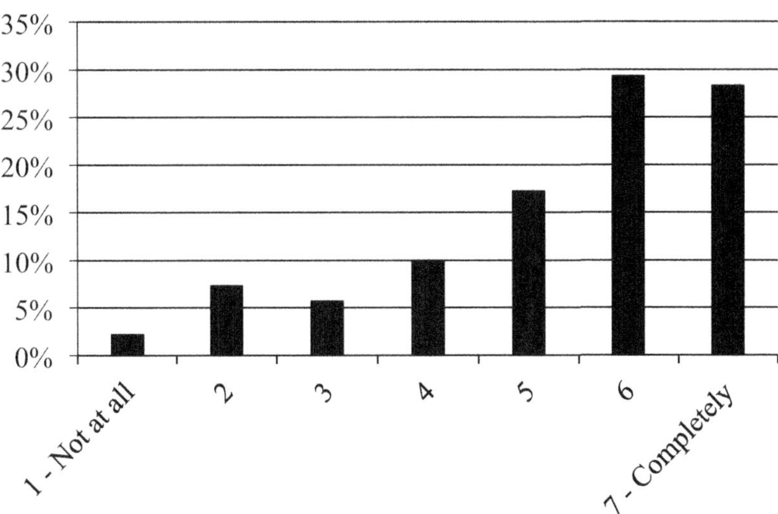

Figure 13.11. Extent to which furries recruited online agree with the statement "I have a close set of friends."

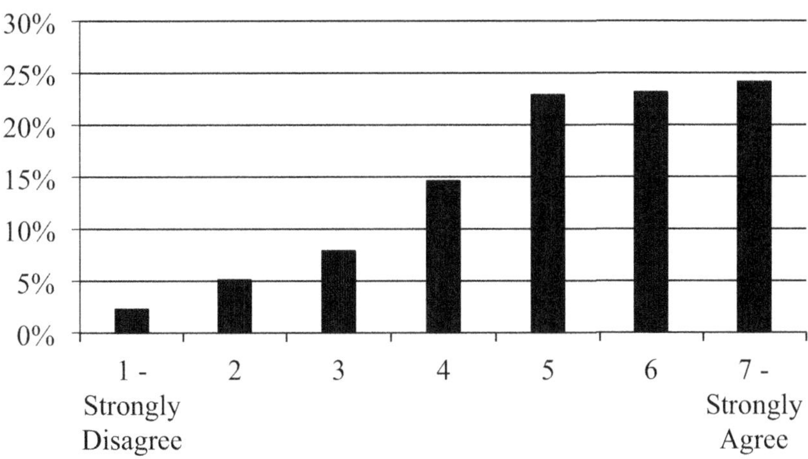

Figure 13.12. Extent to which furries recruited online agree with statements related to the furry fandom providing them with social support (measure adapted from Zimet et al., 1988).

While these data, by themselves, don't necessarily point to furries' furry friends as being the ones with whom furries feel a close connection, other analyses from the same study shed further light on this possibility. For example, one analysis found that furries who scored higher on measures of fandom (i.e., identifying as part of the broader furry fandom) were also more likely to agree that they had a close set of friends.[30] Another analysis from a 2021 study of online furries found that furries generally agree that the fandom provides them with the social support they're looking for (see Figure 13.12). While furries might not surround themselves exclusively with other furries as the sole source of their social interaction, many furries do have a fair number of furries within their friendship networks and seem to rely upon those friends for support in difficult times.[31]

It's one thing to look at friendships and their ability to satisfy broader, more abstract needs for social support. But what about the ability of furries to satisfy more fundamental needs for physical affection and touch? After all, humans are an inescapably social species, and physical contact with one another—everything from a mother's touch to a hug from a friend to the embrace of a lover—has been shown to be important for our psychological health and development (e.g., Carlson & Earls, 1997; McNichols, 2021). Is there evidence that furries have these same basic needs and that they rely, at least in part, on the furry fandom to satiate some of those needs?

The answer is yes, with data coming from a 2016 study of furries attending a convention. We asked furries questions about the amount of touch they were receiving in their lives. Furries were fairly mixed in their responses to questions asking whether physical touch was absent in their lives or the extent to which they longed for touch (measures adapted from Punyanunt-Carter & Wrench, 2009). They did, however, strongly indicate that they liked physical touch, including hugs (see Figure 13.13). Follow-up questions found that 51.4% of furries felt like they were getting less physical interaction than they would want outside of furry settings (i.e., when not at a

---

[30] In contrast, fanship scores (identifying as a furry, but not necessarily with other furries; see Chapter 6 for more on this distinction) were, if anything, negatively associated with having close friends. This may reflect the stigma associated with being a furry, a point we address in Chapter 21.

[31] We can find further evidence of this from online and convention studies in 2016, 2019, and 2020. The studies found that furries, like anyone, feel lonely from time to time (measure adapted from Russell et al., 1980). However, furries who identified more strongly with the furry fandom scored lower on a measure of loneliness than furries who only weakly identified with the furry fandom.

furry convention). In contrast, only 28.0% of furries said they experienced less physical interaction than they would want while at a furry convention.[32] Taken together, these data suggest that furries enjoy touch, but may vary in whether they are currently getting enough of it in their lives, a need that at least some furries can address at a furry convention. And, far from trivial, the same study found that furries who report not getting as much physical touch as they would like also score worse on measures of psychological well-being.

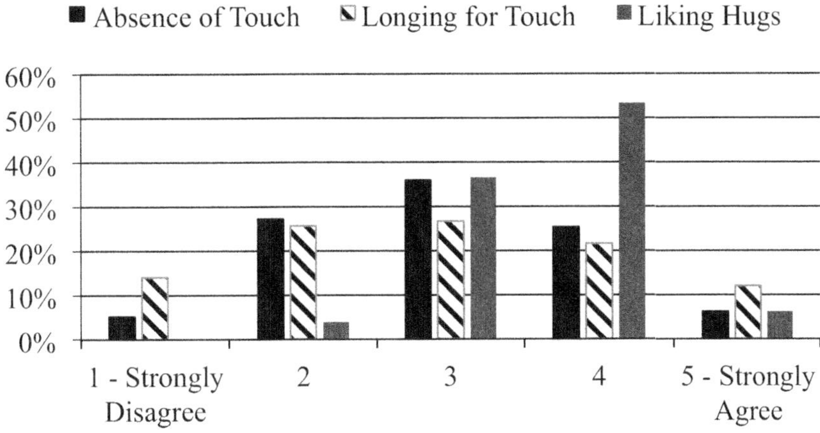

Figure 13.13. Agreement with items pertaining to physical touch as assessed in a 2016 sample of furries recruited at a furry convention. Items adapted from Punyanunt-Carter and Wrench (2009).

Having shown the importance of friendship and physical interaction for furries, let's finish up this section on relationships by considering what are, for many, the most important relationships of all: close, intimate, romantic relationships. To start, we asked furries across 18 different online and convention studies to indicate their relationship status. Over the years, how

[32] Speaking further to the idea that furries can satisfy the need for basic physical interaction in convention settings, we asked furries about the number of hugs they'd like to get, both in their day-to-day life and at a convention. While 40.1% of furries said they'd like 5 or more hugs per day in their day-to-day life, 74.9% of furries said they'd like 5 or more hugs per day while at a convention. This suggests, in line with our anecdotal observations at conventions, that furries often feel far more comfortable physically expressing affection in fandom settings than they do in other contexts.

we've asked the question has changed, evolving from a "choose one of the options below" style question to a "choose all that apply" approach. Moreover, the number of options available to respondents has increased over time, with some of the labels changing. For example, in recent years we've begun to include "common law," "polyamorous," and "open relationship" as categories that, in early years, were overlooked as options.[33] Likewise, the category of "single" has changed in recent years to become "not dating," to more accurately reflect how people in this category would describe themselves. Because of this changing terminology, the prevalence rates of each category have varied over time. Nevertheless, we can give some rough estimates of each category in Table 13.3.

Table 13.3. Prevalence of relationship status across 18 online and convention-going studies of furries from 2012-2022.

Category	Prevalence
Single / Not Dating	38.5-54.8%
Dating	20.6-39.6%
Engaged / Married / Common-Law	12.1-25.3%
Widowed	0-4.1%
Divorced	0.4-2.3%
Open Relationship[34]	7.5-9.8%
Polyamorous	0.8-13.4%
Other	1.8-6.6%

Despite the variability of estimates across studies, some general trends have emerged. For starters, across every study, the most common category selected is single/not dating, followed by dating. Indicators of more serious involvement, including engagement, marriage, and common-law arrangements tend to be less common, owing, at least in part, to the fact that furries, as a group, tend to be relatively young. We also note a fair number of furries who are polyamorous and who have open relationships, numbers which are higher than what is found in studies of the general population (Levine et al., 2018).

---

[33] As is the case with all of our studies, we are eternally grateful for the constructive feedback we've received from furries who've helped us shape and improve the questions to better capture the whole range of responses from respondents.
[34] While we use the terms "polyamory" and "open relationships" in our studies because most respondents understand these terms, we recognize that terms such as "consensual nonmonogamy" are more commonly used in the research literature.

Individual studies also allow us to compare furries to other fan groups when it comes to relationship status. For example, in a set of 2014 studies, we found that furries were less likely to be dating than members of some fan groups (i.e., fantasy sports fans), but more likely to be dating than other fan groups (i.e., anime fans). Furries were also more likely than fantasy sports fans and anime fans to self-identify as polyamorous. In a 2020 study, we also found that furries were more likely to be in a current romantic relationship than were *Star Wars* fans, although *Star Wars* fans, who were older on average, tended to have been in their current romantic relationship for longer.

Given that many furries report having friends who are, themselves, furries, we can ask whether furries in romantic relationships tend to date other furries. In a 2020 study of online furries, we found that 76.7% of furries who were currently in a relationship also had a partner who was also furry.[35] Elaborating further, among those furries who were in a relationship, 62.3% said that both they and their partner were already furries when they met, compared to 7.2% who said that neither of them were furries when they first met. Furthermore, 11.7% of respondents said that one member of the relationship got the other one into the furry fandom. Finally, 17.5% of furries in a relationship said that they were furry, but their partner was not. Taken together, these findings suggest that while most furries are not currently in a romantic relationship; among those who are, they are more likely than not to be dating a furry, and to have met their partner while both of them were furries.[36]

We can add an additional level of nuance to the story by considering sexual orientation. A 2019 study of online furries found that furries who were attracted predominantly to men were more than twice as likely than furries who were attracted predominantly to women to have met their current relationship partner through the furry fandom (70.4% vs. 42.2%). In contrast, furries who were predominantly attracted to women were about twice as likely as furries who were predominantly attracted to men to have a partner

---

[35] Follow-up analyses revealed that furries share a lot in common with their furry partners: their level of fanship, identification with the fandom, and amount of engagement with furry convent were significantly correlated, meaning the "most furry" furs tend to be dating one another, while more "casual furs" also tend to be dating one another.

[36] We assume that some, although not all, of these circumstances involve meeting their partner in furry contexts, such as on furry websites or at a furry convention, rather than coincidentally happening to date a person only to find out, after-the-fact, that they're a furry!

who is not a furry (31.7% vs. 15.9%) and were twice as likely to say that they introduced their partner to the furry fandom (18.0% vs. 8.4%). In other words, whether or not a furry is likely to be dating another furry, and whether or not they met that partner through the furry fandom or had to bring them into the fandom, may depend on the type of partner one is interested in and how prevalent they are in the furry fandom.[37]

Table 13.4. Most common themes extracted from open-ended responses of furries in a 2020 online study regarding the positive and negative ways in which furry has influenced their romantic relationship.

Theme	Prevalence
Positives	
It's how we met (e.g., online, at a con)	29.7%
We have activities we can do together (e.g., cons, fursuiting)	26.4%
I like having a shared interest with my partner	21.7%
It helps us express aspects of ourselves (e.g., emotions)	18.4%
The fandom is accepting of our orientation/gender/sexuality	16.0%
It gives us a way to meet other friends	14.2%
It allows us to improve ourselves/our relationship (e.g., improved confidence)	12.7%
Allows us to explore facets of ourselves/new things (e.g., roleplay)	9.4%
Provides us with social support	7.1%
It's part of our business (e.g., working as an artist/vendor)	5.7%
Negatives	
Jealousy (e.g., toward others in the fandom, taking up a partner's attention)	6.1%
Concerns about stigma (e.g., what if the partner's family found out)	6.1%
Problematic people in the fandom are hard to get away from	4.7%
Fandom is too open to things that make me/us uncomfortable	3.8%
Partner not as interested in furry as I am	3.3%
Fighting over money (e.g., fandom-related spending)	2.4%
Drama and fandom-related conflict	2.4%
Disagreements about fandom-related content (e.g., favorite artists)	2.4%
Conflict about fandom-related activities (e.g., going to cons)	2.4%
Immaturity of other members of the fandom	1.9%

Regardless of how, precisely, furries ended up in their relationships, we can ask whether, once in those relationships, there are benefits and drawbacks to a furry being in a relationship with another furry. One way we've assessed this is by asking furries in a 2020 online study who were in a

[37] We know, for example, that men are significantly more prevalent in the furry fandom than are women (see Chapter 15). As such, a person with a strong preference for men as their romantic partner has a much wider available potential dating pool in the furry fandom than a person with a strong preference for women as their romantic partner.

relationship with one or more furries to describe some of the ways being a furry has influenced their relationship—for better or for worse—in an open-ended fashion. Their responses were organized and coded into common themes, allowing us to list the most common themes to emerge. We summarize these themes in Table 13.4.

Perhaps the most apparent trend in the data is that furries were far more likely to see furry as a benefit to their relationship rather than a negative: even the most prevalent negative theme barely matched the 10th most prominent positive theme in terms of prevalence and was dwarfed by some of the most commonly-cited themes (e.g., the way we met, shared activities and interests). And while this data was collected in an open-ended fashion, we've also observed similar trends in closed-ended questions. For example, in a 2020 study, we compared a sample of furries to a sample of *Star Wars* fans on questions asking about how the fandom impacted their relationship. As Figure 13.14 illustrates, while furries were slightly more likely than *Star Wars* fans to say that their fandom involvement had the potential to cause problems in their relationship, furries were also far more likely to characterize their involvement in furry as beneficial to their relationship. In contrast, for *Star Wars* fans, their fan interest, while not harmful to their relationship, was also not especially beneficial for it.

As a final piece of evidence converging with the above findings, we asked furries to rate the quality of their romantic relationships overall. In a 2021 online study, we asked furries specifically whether they agreed with items in a scale asking them whether they were satisfied with their current romantic relationship (adapted from Hendrick et al., 1998). As Figure 13.15 reveals, furries were overwhelmingly positive about their relationships, suggesting, much in line with our data about furries and their friends, furries, counter to stereotypes, were fairly content with their current relationships, even if just over half of furries were not presently involved in a romantic relationship.[38]

---

[38] Somewhat unexpectedly, follow-up analyses revealed that furries in relationship with a non-furry were just as satisfied with their relationships as furries in a relationship with another furry. This could mean that, while dating a non-furry may introduce a potential source of friction into the relationship, it's likely not enough to significantly alter furries' overall happiness with the relationship.

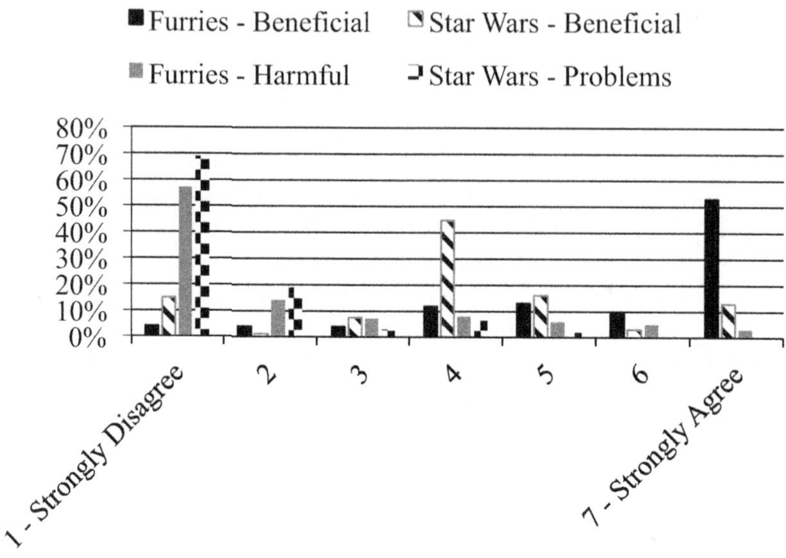

Figure 13.14. Agreement with items about the role of fan involvement on relationship quality in a sample of furries and *Star Wars* fans recruited online.

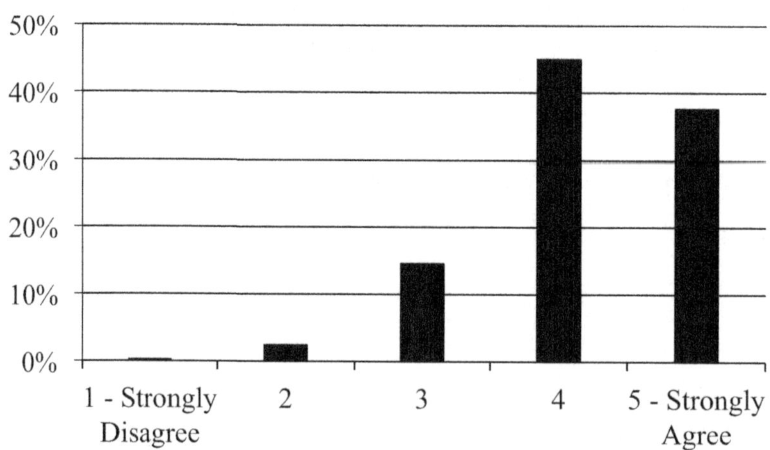

Figure 13.15. Extent to which furries recruited online agree with statements related to their relationship quality being high (measure adapted from Hendrick et al., 1988).

Conclusion

In isolation, it's easy to fall into the trap of thinking that the demographic data in this chapter are little more than tidbits of information—trivia to make readers go "Oh, interesting" and nothing more. This couldn't be further from the truth, however. We can point to dozens of findings throughout this book that can be contextualized—and really only make sense—if you understand the demographic composition of the furry fandom. Questions about the political leanings of the fandom, furries' consumption habits, intra-fandom conflict, well-being, and much, much more are all inexorably tied to furries' age, socioeconomic status, and the structure of their social networks and relationships. By understanding that furries, as a group, are fairly young with a continuing influx of new members, by knowing that they're comprised primarily of past, current, or future college students struggling financially throughout their 20s, and by seeing how important furries' relationships are to them and the value of the fandom in helping them form and maintain these relationships, the puzzle of the furry fandom starts to put itself together.

References

Adler, N. E., Epel, E. S., Castellazzo, G., & Ickovics, J. R. (2000). Relationship of subjective and objective social status with psychological and physiological functioning: Preliminary data in healthy, white women. *Healthy Psychology, 19*(6), 586-592. https://doi.org/10.1037//0278-6133.19.6.586

Carlson, M., & Earls, F. (1997). Psychological and neuroendocrinological sequelae of early social deprivation in institutionalized children in Romania. *Annals of the New York Academy of Sciences, 807,* 419-428.

CDC/National Center for Health Statistics. (2022). Marriage and divorce. Accessed June 15, 2022, https://www.cdc.gov/nchs/fastats/marriage-divorce.htm

Edwards, P., Chadborn, D. P., Plance, C., Reysen, S., & Redden, M. H. (2019). *Meet the bronies: The psychology of adult* My Little Pony *fandom.* McFarland & Company.

Fry, R. (2016, May 24). For the first time in modern era, living with parents edges out other living arrangements for 18-to-34-year-olds: Share living with spouse or partner continues to fall. *Pew Research Center: Social & Demographic Trends*. Retrieved from http://www.pewsocialtrends.org/2016/05/24/for-first-time-in-modern-era-living-with-parents-edges-out-other-living-arrangements-for-18-to-34-year-olds/

Furry Fiesta. (2022). Retrieved June 13, 2022, from https://en.wikifur.com/wiki/Furry_Fiesta

Graf, N. (2017, May 16). Today's young workers are more likely than ever to have a bachelor's degree. *Pew Research Center*. Accessed June 14, 2022, https://www.pewresearch.org/fact-tank/2017/05/16/todays-young-workers-are-more-likely-than-ever-to-have-a-bachelors-degree/

Hendrick, S. S., Dicke, A., & Hendrick, C. (1998). The relationship assessment scale. *Journal of Social and Personal Relationships, 15*(1), 137-142. https://doi.org/10.1177/0265407598151009

Johnson, M. K., & Mollborn, S. (2009). Growing up faster, feeling older: Hardship in childhood and adolescence. *Social Psychology Quarterly, 72*(1), 39-60. https://doi.org/10.1177/019027250907200105

Levenson, A. R. (2010). Millennials and the world of work: An economist's perspective. *Journal of Business and Psychology, 25,* 257-264. https://doi.org/10.1007/s10869-010-9170-9

Levine, E. C., Herbenick, D., Martinez, O., Fu, T.-C., & Dodge, B. (2018). Open relationships, nonconsensual nonmonogamy, and monogamy among U.S. adults: Findings from the 2012 national survey of sexual health and behavior. *Archives of Sexual Behavior, 47,* 1439-1450. https://doi.org/10.1007/s10508-018-1178-7

McNichols, N. K. (2021). The vital importance of human touch. *Psychology Today. https://www.psychologytoday.com/ca/blog/everyone-top/202108/the-vital-importance-human-touch*

Punyanunt-Carter, N. M., & Wrench, J. S. (2009). Development and validity testing of a measure of touch deprivation. *Human Communication, 12*(1), 67-76.

Reysen, S., Plante, C., Roberts, S. E., Gerbasi, K. C., Mohebpour, I., & Gamboa, A. (2016). Pale and geeky: Prevailing stereotypes of anime fans. *The Phoenix Papers, 2*(1), 78-103.

Reysen, S., Plante, C., Chadborn, D., Roberts, S. E., & Gerbasi, K. (2021). *Transported to another world: The psychology of anime fans.* International Anime Research Project.

Russell, D., Peplau, L. A., & Cutrona, C. E. (1980). The revised UCLA loneliness scale: Concurrent and discriminant validity evidence. *Journal of Personality and Social Psychology, 39*(3), 472-480. https://doi.org/10.1037//0022-3514.39.3.472

Schaeffer, K. (2022, April 12). 10 facts about today's college graduates. *Pew Research Center*. Accessed June 14, 2022, https://www.pewresearch.org/fact-tank/2022/04/12/10-facts-about-todays-college-graduates/

Smith, H. J., Pettigrew, T. F., Pippin, G. M., & Bialosiewicz, S. (2011). Relative deprivation: A theoretical meta-analytic review. *Personality and Social Psychological Review, 16*(3), 203-232. https://doi.org/10.1177/1088868311430825

U.S. Bureau of Labor Statistics. (2021). Education pays: Earnings and unemployment rates by educational attainment, 2021. https://www.bls.gov/emp/chart-unemployment-earnings-education.htm

Zimet, G. D., Dahlem, N. W., Zimet, S. G., & Farley, G. K. (1988). The multidimensional scale of perceived social support. *Journal of Personality Assessment, 52*(1), 30-41. https://doi.org/10.1207/s15327752jpa5201_2

Chapter 14
Racialized Identity Groups and Ethnicity in the Furry Fandom

Sharon E. Roberts, Camielle Adams, Courtney "Nuka" Plante

In our earliest studies, we often included demographic questions about racialized identity groups[1] in the furry fandom. We would summarize the data in a table and generally left it at that. More recently, thanks in no small part to feedback from BIMPOC[2] furries—both in the public and academia—we've begun the process of contextualizing these statistics and supplementing them with the words and lived experiences of racialized furries through more qualitative explorations of these topics. From a methodological perspective, this additional detail allows us to seek out more nuanced and impactful research questions that might otherwise be overlooked, develop and test theories, and forge new understandings of an important are of research that cannot be adequately captured by demographic information alone.

However, a more pragmatic purpose of this deeper exploration of race is to highlight BIMPOC experiences in the furry fandom that are sometimes obscured by data. For example, imagine if a survey found that approximately 85% of furries identified exclusively as White, while 15% of furries identified as BIMPOC (e.g., Black, Asian, Latino, Indigenous, Multiracial). Were we to simply aggregate this data, we might summarize our findings by claiming that "the average furry is White" or "a typical furry is White." While this statement is technically true, it may have the unfortunate—albeit

---

[1] It's important to recognize that, while often used interchangeably by laypersons, the terms "race" and "ethnicity" are not the same. Race is usually used to refer specifically to physical attributes such as skin color that society has defined as meaningful, while ethnicity is a broader category that includes physical traits, but also considers cultural heritage, language, nation of origin, and religion. Importantly, we recognize that both of these concepts are social constructs—that is, they are systems of classification used to differentiate people, often in a violent or oppressive fashion—and, as such, are politically charged terms. Our goal at present is to discuss the labels people apply to themselves and their meaning in furry spaces and not make essentialist or divisive claims about groups of furries.

[2] The acronym BIMPOC stands for "Black, Indigenous, Multiracial People(s) of Color" and is a term used instead of a term like "non-White," which frames discussions of race around whiteness as a sort of "default" against which other racial groups are compared. It should be noted that while BIPOC is more typically used, we used BIMPOC to make it clear that those of multi-racial backgrounds are also included in this definition.

unintentional—side effect of making racialized furries feel "atypical" as furries, even if they are otherwise indistinguishable from other furries (e.g., having a fursona, consuming furry-themed media, feeling a sense of kinship or shared identity with the fandom). Even at their most innocuous, demographic findings alone could put BIMPOC furries on the back foot, making them feel as though they need to do extra work that other furries don't have to do just to establish their "furry credentials" and prove that they do, in fact, belong in the fandom.[3] This might feel especially necessary if the commonly salient image of a furry is that of a White person, meaning that a BIMPOC furry might not be seen as a furry at all simply because they don't "look the part."

This brings us to our third and most important reason to include a qualitative exploration of race in the furry fandom: it gives a voice to those who have often found themselves spoken over or simply ignored. If we only discuss aggregate data or the most common experiences in the furry fandom, we may fail to capture important variability in the experience of furries. In doing so, important issues, points of consideration, and insights offered by BIMPOC furries would be missed. For this reason, while this chapter begins with a brief overview of aggregated statistics regarding the racial composition of the furry fandom, the bulk of this chapter will be dedicated to exploring some of the nuances and experiences of race in the furry fandom from a variety of perspectives.

Race and Ethnic Composition

As we begin this section looking at the prevalence of different racialized groups in the furry fandom, it's worth making an important point: there is nothing about furry content specifically, or fan interests more broadly, that should make them any more or less attractive to one racial or ethnic group over another. As we cover in Chapter 20, people around the world and at all points in human history have shown an interest in the concept of anthropomorphic animals. Likewise, fans of various interests can be found all over the world, from football to K-pop music. As such, there is little reason to suspect that the racial composition of the furry fandom should differ dramatically from the racial composition of the general population in the region where the sample is drawn.

---

[3] This phenomenon has been noted in other contexts, such as in classroom settings, where stereotypes can threaten a person's feeling that they belong in a university class (Steele, 1997). These concerns weigh heavily on the minds of those experiencing the threat, even when it goes unspoken or is seemingly non-existent to those who aren't the target of the stereotype.

To this end, it's essential to keep in mind that most of our samples of furries are collected from conventions across North America and Western Europe and, when collected online, are conducted in English and largely advertise to English-speaking websites.[4] As an illustrative example of the result, a 2017 online study revealed that the majority of our participants came from the United States (64.7%) and other predominantly White countries such as Canada (9.1%), the United Kingdom (5.6%), Germany (3.3%), and Australia (1.6%). For this reason, estimates of the racial composition of the furry fandom are more likely to reflect the demographic composition of these populations than the true racial composition of the global furry fandom. If, on the other hand, we were fluent in Portuguese and were able to recruit a sizable number of furry participants from Brazil, we would almost certainly find a much higher proportion of BIMPOC furries than in a predominantly American sample simply by there being a higher proportion of racialized individuals in Brazil.

We can find examples of regional differences in racial and ethnic composition even within the United States via studies conducted at different furry conventions. For example, we conducted two convention-based studies less than a year apart, one in Pennsylvania and the other in Texas. At the convention in Pennsylvania, 89.2% of participants self-identified as White and 5.5% self-identified as Hispanic. In contrast, fewer participants, 82.7%, identified as White and 11.9% identified as Hispanic in the Texas sample.[5] This sort of variability even within the same country makes it clear how tricky the question of estimating the racial and ethnic composition of the furry fandom is.

The problem becomes even trickier when it comes to figuring out an appropriate way to measure the race and ethnicity of a group of people. One possibility is to simply give people an empty box and allow them to describe,

---

[4] There have been exceptions to this over the years. For example, in a set of 2019 studies, we recruited participants from an American furry convention and a European furry convention, the latter of which translated our survey into German to increase its accessibility for convention attendees.

[5] As pointed out earlier, it is important to note that race and ethnicity are not the same. In this example, White—a term commonly used to describe a person's race—is being compared alongside Hispanic—a term used to describe ethnicity (and which, itself, needs to be contrasted against other terms associated with being Latin American). We are not meaning to suggest that these are both racial terms or both terms indicating ethnicity but, rather, that they are labels that people commonly identify with.

at length, their race and ethnicity. While this approach has the benefit of allowing every person to describe themselves as they see fit, it has the drawback of making it difficult to aggregate (i.e., add up) data or organize people into categories, especially if different people use different labels to describe what might otherwise be similar ethnic or racial categories.[6]

Another approach is to provide people with a handful of common racial and ethnic labels and let them indicate which of those labels they identify with. The upside of this approach is that it allows for easy organization and counting of data. However, it, too, carries with it several drawbacks. For one thing, some people may not identify with *any* of the labels we provide, and thus feel pressured into choosing a label that only somewhat applies to them. We could potentially get around this problem by adding an "other" category, which, unsurprisingly, can be exclusionary in and of itself. Those problems aside, we also need to address other questions, such as which terms we should use: should we stick only to terms relating to race (in which case people might be frustrated at the inability to describe their ethnicity, which may be more important to them), or only to terms relating to ethnicity (in which case we might be omitting categories that are essential to answering questions about prejudice and racism)?

And even if we were to nail down the perfect set of labels to use in our study—something which, as it should be apparent, is next to impossible to do—we need to consider yet another important question: should we allow people to choose only one label (i.e., the one they most strongly identify with), or as many as they see fit?[7]

In the end, there is no one "right" way to measure these concepts, only a number of flawed and imperfect ways to approximately measure the variables we're interested in. Throughout the years, we've asked this question on our surveys in a myriad of ways, sometimes including more categories, sometimes including fewer, sometimes forcing people to choose the single option which they most strongly identify with, but more often allowing them to choose as many as they wish. The results of these various approaches, aggregated across 23 separate samples from 2011 to 2021,

---

[6] You could argue that this is reason enough to do away with the whole endeavor of pigeonholing people into boxes based on such labels in the first place!

[7] To conduct statistical analyses of group differences, each participant should fit into at *least* one category but also *only* one category (mutually exclusive and exhaustive options). It is also optimal to have reasonably equivalent sample sizes and/or variances in the analysis.

including online and convention-going samples, are summarized in Table 14.1.

Table 14.1. Furry participant self-identification with different race and ethnicity labels across 23 studies from 2011-2021. Results are separated based on whether participants were forced to make a single choice or were permitted to choose multiple categories.

Label	Single Choice	Multiple Choice
White	72.6-89.6%	67.5-91.8%
Hispanic	1.4-7.4%	3.5-15.9%
Black	1.0-3.2%	1.1-5.2%
Asian	1.0-3.8%	2.1-24.3%
Native American / First Nations / Indigenous	0.4-4.6%	1.5-6.3%
Middle Eastern	0.0-0.8%	0.0-1.4%
South Asian	0.0-0.5%	0.0-1.6%
Other	0.3-14.8%	1.6-5.1%

Table 14.2. Fan self-identification with different race and ethnicity labels across online studies from 2014 (Fantasy Sport, Anime) and 2021 (Furry, *Star Wars*).

Label	Furry	*Star Wars*	Anime	Fantasy Sport
White	89.2%	89.4%	72.9%	77.4%
Hispanic	5.9%	5.9%	8.5%	8.6%
Black	1.1%	1.1%	3.5%	10.2%
Asian	4.3%	3.2%	19.5%	6.2%
First Nations / Indigenous	4.3%	1.6%	2.4%	1.0%
Middle Eastern	1.1%	0.5%	1.6%	0.2%
South Asian	1.1%	1.1%	1.1%	0.5%
Other	3.8%	4.3%	1.8%	0.0%

Across studies employing common methodologies, it was found that the category most frequently identified across samples was White—hardly a surprising finding given that the countries from which most participants were recruited are, themselves, predominantly White (e.g., United States Census Bureau, 2019). As seen in Table 14.2, furries were comparable in this regard to other fan groups we've studied in online studies of predominantly

American fans, including anime fans, fantasy sports fans, and *Star Wars* fans. Of particular note, while participants most commonly identified as White, the number was far from being 100% White, and there was a significant prevalence of other racial and ethnic groups in these fandoms. As we'll see in the next sections, however, the predominance of White people in fandom spaces can nevertheless create the impression that the fandoms themselves are "White" spaces, with implications for racialized groups in these spaces.

Differences in Thoughts about Race and Ethnicity

In this section, we consider the responses of furries who were recruited for a 2021 online survey. In addition to being asked to indicate which racial/ethnic labels the participants themselves identified with, they were also asked a series of open-ended questions about the issue of race and ethnicity in the furry fandom. These questions were designed to tap into whether they thought about these facets of their identity in fandom spaces and, if so, whether it was generally in a positive or a negative way. We also asked respondents to describe the sorts of experiences they had in general in fandom spaces regarding these topics. These responses were coded and organized, with some of the most common or recurring themes extracted.

Perhaps most importantly, however, we wanted to explore the lived experiences of those who frequently find themselves overshadowed, silenced, or forgotten about in the fandom. For this reason, in each of the following sections, we compare the responses of people who self-identified as White with people who did not (e.g., Black or African American furries). Given the limited nature of our sample size, we cannot make more nuanced distinctions between racialized groups (e.g., contrasting the experiences of Black furries against the experience of Asian or Indigenous furries). Instead, our focus is to draw attention to differences in how the fandom is experienced by people who are in the numerical majority (i.e., White furries) and people who do not identify as such.

Frequency of Thoughts about Race or Ethnicity

We start with the most basic of considerations when it comes to thoughts about racialized identity groups in fandom spaces: the frequency with which these thoughts occur. When we consider the 158 participants who did not identify as White, 41.8%—fewer than half—said that their race or ethnicity was not something they thought about in fandom spaces. In contrast, 61.7%—a majority—of the 660 respondents who identified as White said the same thing. Or, to put it another way, BIMPOC furs were only two-thirds as likely as White furs to say that their race or ethnicity wasn't something they thought about or that came to mind in fandom spaces.

The other end of the continuum is even more illustrative: 14.6% of BIMPOC furs said that they thought about their race or ethnicity in fandom spaces all the time, as compared to 3.9% of White furs. This means that BIMPOC furs were 3-4 times more likely than White furs to say that their race or ethnicity was something that they thought about fairly commonly in fandom spaces.

These findings are consistent with prior research showing that the same pattern of results occurs in other contexts (e.g., classrooms) and for variables other than race or ethnicity (e.g., gender; McGuire et al., 1978). Put simply, when a person is in a situation where they differ from others around them, they will be especially likely to notice and be aware of that difference and to think of themselves in terms of that difference. As such, a racialized furry who attends a furry convention and finds themselves surrounded by mostly White furries will be *far* more likely to be aware of their race—a feature that distinguishes them from the furries around them—than a White furry, whose race isn't something they're likely to notice because they look like the other furries around them.[8]

Importantly, the operation of this mechanism is a product of our mind's tendency to seek out novelty and distinctiveness. In other words, it operates even if nothing is explicitly done by the people involved to draw attention to such differences. As such, for a BIMPOC furry attending a panel surrounded by White furries, even if no one mentions race or consciously does anything to make the BIMPOC furry feel different, they are nevertheless more likely to be aware of their race simply by virtue of being a numerical minority in the room than are the other White furries in the room.[9]

We can look to representative quotes from the respondents in our studies to see whether there's evidence for these differences. First, we turn to quotes from racialized furries, many of whom say that issues of race and ethnicity are salient to them to varying degrees:

---

[8] This same mechanism operates for women and non-binary people in a fandom comprised predominantly of men, a point we address in Chapter 15.

[9] This point should be emphasized, as a skeptic may argue that there should be no reason for a BIMPOC person to think of their race in a perfect accepting space. Even if furry spaces were *perfectly* accepting and tolerant spaces with absolutely no implicit or explicit prejudice among *any* of their members, BIMPOC furries will still be more likely to be aware of their race as a function of our brains being natural pattern-recognizing machines.

"In the particular space I'm in it doesn't come up much but ever since 2020, I do think about my race and how [I] fit in the fandom a lot more."

"Not really often... My race only comes up once I feel It's crucial in getting to know new people."

"It rarely is mentioned or brought up."

"I sometimes think about my race in fandom spaces."

"My race is part of my identity; I'm always aware of it. That said, it is rarely at the forefront of my attention."

"Often, as there's a lot of unchecked white supremacists running around. I keep my ethnicity in my bios to repel their interaction."

"Often, especially when meeting people face to face [sic] for the first time."

"Pretty often."

"I think a lot about my race in fandom space."

"Always... In all of my fandoms [,] I think about it all the time."

"Like it's always come up when I talk in Discord or I hang up with white furry friends. I don't know why but there [sic] always make a racist remark about me being Black."

"All the time, because it is a big part of my experience of the world in a general sense."

"Every hour and moment."

Following what psychological theory would predict (e.g., McGuire et al., 1978), several racialized furries specifically pointed to the fact that their awareness of their race or ethnicity stemmed from recognizing the ways in which they were distinct from the other furries around them.

"A lot... Getting bored of being the only POC at local furmeets."

"I don't think about it a lot but I do notice I'm quite the minority in furry spaces."

"Often... If it comes up at all: 'Oh, look. An Asian.'"

That said, while racialized furries, as a group, are generally aware of their race or ethnicity in fandom spaces, many also indicated that this was not unique to the furry fandom, and that, if anything, aspects of the furry fandom made it a place where their race was *less* of an issue than it was in other spaces:

"Usually [I] don't think about it too much (one of the perks of navigation in a community where everyone wears a mask of sorts)."

"I don't think about it very much in furry fandoms, but I know in human-driven fandoms, like anime ones, mixed race or non-white cosplayers can be subject to bullying... I have had no personal experience with racist bullying or harassment in the furry fandom."

"I rarely do since even these racist groups don't lash out on me at all which is probably due to the valiant efforts of the rest of the community keeping hate like this at a minimum."

"Only occasionally and it's mostly in a cultural setting. I've never faced any discrimination, thankfully - that said, I've only ever really existed in small, predominately left-wing furry environments where (I would like to hope!) such behavior would be minimal anyway..."

There were, of course, also some BIMPOC furries for whom race isn't especially salient:

"I don't think about my race."

"Basically[,] I would completely forget about races when thinking about furry fandom."

"I haven't thought about it. Possibly because it hasn't bothered me at any point in my life."

"[I] really don't think about it, its [sic] simply something not that important for me."

"Race usually never comes to mind most of the time, though I'm happy to share if anyone asks."

We can contrast the findings of BIMPOC furries against White furries who, while not completely unaware of their race, most often indicated that it is a fairly minor or trivial concern for them.

"never [sic]. [I] dont think about it"

"It is never brought up in any context."

"It never really has come up."

"Literally never. It has no bearing whatsoever on fandom stuff."

"I don't think about it most of the time."

"I don't, until other people make it a factor."

"I don't think about my race often in fandom spaces at all."

Some White respondents noted the distinction between thinking about the idea of race or racial issues more broadly and being made aware of their *own* race:

"I think about important race (equality) issues most of the time, but I don't [sic] usually think about -my- race."

"I try to follow a variety of people so race tends to come up a lot, unfortunately, it's typically people experiencing racism."

Several of the respondents even recognized the role that being in the racial majority played in making race a fairly non-salient issue for them:

"Since the majority of the fandom here is white [sic], I don't think it comes up at all, and is just part of the 'background'."

"Almost never, most of the events I've been to were overwhelmingly white [sic]. I've never witnessed anyone being racist or uncool toward the very few black [sic], asian [sic] or hispanic [sic] furries I've seen at conventions, so race was almost never on my mind."

"I don't think about it often at all, but that is likely because I am white [sic] and have the privilege not to have my race brought up a lot."

Other respondents appealed to a shared common identity between people of all races or a desire to ignore race and, instead, see all people as being equal:[10]

"I don't think about it, we are all humans."

"Race in general doesn't carry any value whatsoever for me, mine or another's. The only race that matters to me is the human race."

"I don't think about it at all. I've never felt I needed to acknowledge my own race, since I always see everyone as equal."

Finally, some respondents found the idea of discussions of race themselves to be aversive or counterproductive:

"I don't think about it, but injecting race issues into things for the sake of virtue signaling, I view negativity"

---

[10] While the notion of not judging people on the basis of their race or ethnicity is laudable, it is worth keeping two things in mind. First, it is possible to hold prejudicial attitudes that one is not aware of (implicit), since these have been shown to be only modestly correlated with prejudicial attitudes that one is aware of (explicit; Akrami & Ekehammar, 2005; Dovidio et al., 2002). Second, "color-blind" strategies that involve ignoring the reality of race have been shown to reduce peoples' ability to recognize prejudice when they see it (Apfelbaum et al., 2010).

"I try not to think of race ever. I think that people who try to include it in parts of the Fandom end up segregating people instead of including them. I do not like people that bring it up in the Fandom."

Taken together, the results of our open-ended questions shed some light on some of the different experiences people have in the furry fandom based on their race or ethnicity. Specifically, the data suggest that there is considerable variability in the salience of race and ethnicity for BIMPOC furries. While some say that these issues never come to mind in fandom spaces, many others say that their race or ethnicity is something they are mindful of in fandom spaces—sometimes only a bit but, at other times, frequently so. In contrast, White furries generally spend less time thinking about, or being aware of, their racial identity in the fandom. This may be, in part, because they can typically expect to see others who are like them, making their race or ethnicity indistinct from others and, thus, not something they dwell upon. Overall, the data suggest that being part of a majority can cause some White furries to be generally unaware of how the experience of BIMPOC furries may differ from their own. However, it may be easier to declare that race and ethnicity are unimportant issues when one doesn't regularly have to think about them.

Valence of Thoughts about Race or Ethnicity

Moving beyond the fairly simple question of how frequently furries think about race and ethnicity in fandom spaces, we can also consider the valence of those thoughts—are they generally positive, neutral, or negative in nature?

Prior research suggests that preoccupying thoughts about one's race or ethnicity in the context of being a member of a minoritized group are seldomly positive, especially if there are cultural stigmas directed toward the group. For example, decades of research have shown that such preoccupying thoughts can lead to self-doubt, negative expectations, and anxiety, and they generally distract people from the experience they're trying to have (Pennington et al., 2016).[11]

We can again turn to our open-ended data to see whether the experience of BIMPOC furries differs from the experience of White furries with respect to their response to having their race and ethnicity brought to mind. We've already seen that this is more likely to happen in the first place for BIMPOC furries than for White furries. But we can go one step further and ask, when

---

[11] These findings also pertain to other heavily-stereotyped or stigmatized identities (e.g., some gender identities), a point relevant to an analogous discussion we have in Chapter 15.

it does happen, are the experiences of BIMPOC and White furries comparable or do they differ? Is having one's race or ethnicity brought to mind when one is part of a minoritized group generally more negative than when one is part of the majority?

When it comes to numbers based on the coded valence of responses, we find that BIMPOC furries are less likely to have a neutral response to being aware of their race (41.9%) than White furries (58.2%). White and BIMPOC furries are fairly comparable, however, when it comes to the frequency of negative responses, with rates of 20.3% and 20.2%, respectively, as well as when it comes to mixed responses, with rates of 8.9% and 8.1%, respectively. Finally, the data show that BIMPOC furries are more likely (29.8%) than White furries (12.6%) to have a positive response to their race or ethnicity being made salient.

The numerical data suggest that thinking about one's race or ethnicity is a far more neutral prospect for White furries than it is for BIMPOC furries. When it comes to the valence of non-neutral responses, the story is more nuanced: we could describe thinking about one's race to be a more polarizing experience for BIMPOC furries than it is for White furries.

With this in mind, we can turn to the words of the respondents themselves to compare and contrast these experiences. Beginning with BIMPOC furries, many espoused fairly neutral feelings when it comes to thinking about one's race in fandom spaces:

> *"I sometimes think about my race in fandom spaces. It is typically in a neutral manner."*

> *"I'd say in a normal circumstance ie I am a furry at a furmeet it's pretty neutral. Despite the fact [sic] I'm usually the only person of color attending."*

> *"I seldom think abt [sic] my race in fandom spaces. It is in usually a neutral manner."*

> *"Sometimes I will state where I come from when introducing myself to people I meet on discord [sic] for the first time. Their reaction is always neutral or positive because the fandom space I am in is multicultural, where people are usually nice."*

"I support movements like Black Lives Matter, but my own experiences have always been fairly neutral."

"I think of it neutrally."

"It's usually neutral, but in the usual minority 'well, the central conversation will be from a white perspective' kind of way."

While negativity was less commonly experienced than neutrality among BIMPOC furries, many participants did indicate unambiguously that the contexts in which race or ethnicity come up are typically negative:

"A lot. In the negative."

"To be quiet [sic] honest I don't think it's ever came up in a positive manner beyond someone saying 'wow [sic] were [sic] diverse!'"

"When the topic of my race does come up it's usually in a negative manner."

"At best it is neutral, but most commonly it is negative."

"Race rarely comes up. When it does, it's usually negative."

For racialized furries, negative feelings were typically a direct response to incidents that personally affected them and were described in fairly strong terms (e.g., traumatizing, dogpiled, jaded):

"In the events it would come up, it was always negative, traumatizing, and frustrating."

"I always have to be cognizant of that when engaging in online spaces, but it's especially necessary in furry. Since joining the fandom, I've noticed that many spaces allow and even encourage outright racism, and I was the target of a racist fur who harassed me off the internet for a period of nearly 2 years."

"I have had personal experiences of learning how close friends and artists I respect really felt about African Americans when the curtains are

closed that has left me jaded, cautious, and more negative about personal fandom involvement."

"I've managed to cultivate my friend group well enough that I can usually avoid the worst of it, but yes. I'm so tired of vaguely native-coded fursonas made by white [sic] people. If I or my friends speak up about it, we're usually dogpiled by hundreds of white [sic] furries with death threats."

"Whenever Asians are mentioned in fandom spaces, it is mostly manifested as racist jokes and cultural appropriation rather than any sort of 'racism', hate or attack, or even in any particularly positive manner or context. I thus perceive any mention of Asians in the community with some weary skepticism, since many of these instances are in negative contexts and manners."

That said, almost one third of BIMPOC also reported positive feelings associated with thoughts of their race or ethnicity—a number even higher than the number who reported negative feelings.

"Its [sic] always positive for me."

"More recently It [sic] has become a lot more positive, and this is mostly due to various recent trends online."

"Frequent positive when I communicate with other Furries [sic]."

"I don't like mentioning my race, but whenever I do, it's been a positive experience overall."

For some BIMPOC furries, the positive response had less to do with their race or ethnicity in fandom spaces and more to do with a general sense of pride or positivity associated with their identity.

"I am positive, proud of my race."

"Almost exclusively positive. I have a few friends who make OCs based off Native tribes and the spirits they worshipped. Seeing the designs and

the research that was done to make the OCs accurate makes me feel as though my culture is not dying out."

"I am proud of who I am as a person, I am proud of being a Hispanic, I always see myself and my race in a positive light, if others don't like me simply because I am Hispanic? That is an ignorant person I am going to walk past and only wish they better themselves [sic], because ignorance isn't healthy."

However, one of the strongest sources of positivity related to thoughts about one's race and ethnicity came from the feeling of kinship or shared group identity with others in the fandom like themselves:

"I don't really think about it, except when I start seeing other black [sic] creatives in the fandom speaking up. Then I feel mighty proud!"

"Positive way. I find it peaceful to know I am not alone in liking this hobby."

"I think of my race a few times when I'm in fandom spaces. It's mostly positive as the people I tend to surround myself with share a background or upbringing so we have a mutual understanding of what we see."

"In the fandom space, for me [sic] it is more on the positive side because my furry friends are happy to know that I am a Filipino, one friend of mine said that Filipinos speak really good in English, and my other friend said to me that he as a Hispanic furry felt closely related to me because of our similarities in culture."

"Mostly positive, when I meet fellow hispanic [sic] furs and we chat and joke around in Spanish or make jokes that only Latin Americans would understand, I feel proud of my roots and culture, and my sense of belonging is better because of it."

We can contrast these experiences against the experiences of White furries, for whom the most common response was to indicate that thinking about their race or ethnicity was neither a good nor a bad thing, usually because of how rarely and inconsequentially the issues arose for them:

"I think of it once in a while and usually in a neutral manner."

"Don't think about it too offen [sic], usually in a neutral manner when I think about it."

"Fairly frequently, in a neutral manner."

"I think the only times I do think about my own race is when I think about how overwhelming [sic] white and male the fandom is. I'd say if anything that is a neutral, observational point of view."

"It's usually neutral all things considered."

Some White furries did experience negativity when discussions about race or ethnicity arose, albeit for a variety of reasons. One of the most common reasons was due to the negative association of "White" with racist movements (e.g., Nazis, ethnonationalism) and a desire to distance oneself from such movements:

"I would say it often comes up in a neutral/negative manner attributed to white nationalism/[neo]nazism. And I think it's important for that to be talked about because the furry fandom is so diverse and a lot of us have been and continue to be negatively impacted by racism, antisemitism & such."

"It comes up less, and when it does I see it in a negative light, as most people who bring up "white" [sic] as a race, are acting in negative ways such as neo-nazis or other like minded [sic] hate groups."

Other respondents indicated that the negative feelings stem from the discomfort or guilt that comes with confronting systems that have disproportionately favored White people:

"Currently a lot of hate [is] being tossed around for Cis white [sic] males in the fandom and how we are the majority issue with the fandom. I fully agree that POC, women, and our transgender community have suffered more, and the fandom is currently pushing for more POC, first nations [sic], womens [sic] involvemt [sic] / recognition in the community."

"Due to general white-washing of many media (which has luckily changed in recent times) and myself being white, I sometimes find myself surprised when I learn that the human behind a furry character is e.g. a person of color. I dislike this feeling [sic], because of course [sic] PoC are furries too! I wish this involuntary surprise reaction would go away."

"Usually negative, as in I [sic] don't have to deal with all of that because I am lucky to be white and the unfairness make [sic] me rage ..."

For others, the feelings of negativity are driven by the feeling that they are being targeted and adversely affected for being White:

"A lot of times it can be negative. If I bring up my race I'm often ostracized...it doesn't feel like much has changed since the 60's. I'm sick of race being a deciding factor if a person is trustworthy or not, their own actions and personality should speak louder, but it seems nothing changes."

"I worry people would judge me for just being another white [sic] furry, so I tend to avoid sharing my race."

"Somewhat negative. The overwhelming negativity towards people who are white, especially in regards to privilege, combined with attitudes in [an] industry towards racial diversity, has made me question whether me [sic] being white has given me fewer career opportunities in an already very scarce market with my qualifications."

Several participants also made points that illustrate the importance of not conflating race and ethnicity. While White, they also identified as members of stigmatized ethnicities themselves, adding nuance to the discussion:

*"Neutral or negative. It comes up when people use ["g***y"] (slur) themes and language to design characters and make caricatures of us (an example would be the species called yinglets)."*

Finally, several respondents indicated that the negativity came not from being targeted for their race or ethnicity, but rather because they found discussions of race or ethnicity to be aversive in and of themselves (e.g., "drama"):

"Almost never. If the subject comes up it's almost always because of racism and dramas (so negative manner)."

"Negative, because people are too sensitive and misunderstanding happen [sic]."

"You cannot have a discussion in the fandom without race, gender, politics, or some other very polarizing thing thrown in. Furries need to let go. Just let go. Politics divides the soul. Race divides physical. Identity divides the human. Why do furries like to divide themselves into neat little boxes that the world will READILY judge you on.[sic] You did this to yourself. I HATE it. So yeah. Negative af."

Among White participants, when awareness of race or ethnicity was associated with positivity, it was almost never because of one's labels—they were not feeling positive about being White. Instead, the positivity was almost exclusively directed toward appreciating diversity as a concept, appreciating the fandom's espoused values of diversity, or enjoying jokes and banter about race in general.

"To me, any time I am aware of diversity in fandom spaces it is a positive thing. I have not personally witnessed or encountered issues of racism but I know it remains an active concern in the fandom."

"Frequently. I view it as a positive, seeing people from all races getting together to enjoy their hobby makes me happy and I would like to see more of it."

"I typically see race in a positive manner within the fandom. The fandom may have issues with small groups of racists or white supremacist individuals, but overall I'm proud of the community for standing up for and supporting racial minorities."

The data in this section suggest that if one takes a fairly superficial look at the valence of race or ethnicity-related thoughts, BIMPOC and White furries may seem somewhat alike, given that many report neutral feelings, with a smaller number of respondents reporting positive or negative feelings. A deeper, more nuanced look suggests several important differences between the groups, however. For BIMPOC in the furry fandom, issues of race and ethnicity are personal and polarizing. Whether positive or negative in valence, their feelings are likely to be driven by lived experiences, such as being personally targeted by prejudice or interacting with other furries like them. For White furries, in contrast, both positive and negative responses to race and ethnicity-based thoughts seem less grounded in one's own identity and more grounded in a broader discussion of these topics as abstract concepts.

This difference may uncover and explain an important source of conflict between White and BIMPOC furries. For White furries, it may be easy to discuss issues of prejudice in abstract, seemingly sanitized terms, or to downplay or trivialize the significance of race and ethnicity in fandom spaces since these issues are ones that they, themselves, have relatively little first-hand experience with. For many BIMPOC furries, however, first-hand experience—for better and for worse—has driven home the importance of these topics, making them impossible to sweep under the rug or to ignore.

Themes and Experiences Regarding Race and Ethnicity in the Furry Fandom

To this point, we've considered both the frequency and the valence of thoughts related to race and ethnicity when it comes to the furry fandom. In this final section, we delve more into the specific content of these thoughts, extracting some of the more common themes and experiences. Many of these themes have already been alluded to in the previous sections, but it is nevertheless informative to look more directly at the themes and experiences to see which ones are the most common and to compare whether these common experiences differ between BIMPOC and White furries.

Among BIMPOC furries, the most common theme involved feelings of isolation or marginalization—that is, feeling overlooked, unseen, alone, or ignored by the fandom:

> *"I believed I'm the only one on [sic] this small fandom in my city but as a Black person, my race affected a lot my interaction with furry fandom who are dominated by white [sic] people...They either realized last years [sic] Black furry [sic] exist in the furry fandom or still closed their eyes about the racism issue to not deal with it... I only feel welcome by BIPOC's [sic] and Black furry [sic] in other country [sic]."*

"As an African American, my identity has been disregarded in regards to global events (ex. Black Lives Matter movement and how it affects my people)."

"For the most part [sic] I haven't met a lot of black [sic] furs and [sic] my local community. There's been multiple times where I've been the only black person, or one of two at a meet. While there's usually a small handful of BIPOC fur[sic] It's [sic] still primarily white [sic]."

"I find out it was much harder to find others like me within the fandom."

"I think it does, the fandom has generally been accepting but there are times i [sic] still sort of feel out of place."

"The fandom is mainly white [sic] people. People don't really think black [sic] people are here but we are."

"Art wise [sic] it's difficult to find an artist to properly represent my characters because none of them know how to, and some refuse to, draw afrocentric [sic] hairstyles."

"POC furries are routinely ignored in favor of whiter flavors."

"Not that many Hispanic Furry Creators out there, that I know of."

"When I became more active in the fandom around 2015-2016 and joined this app called telegram [sic]. I joined local groups and at first[sic] I felt alone and uncomfortable being the only fur of color... I'll also add, it is a major struggle we face in this fandom to this day still[,] as sometimes we are not given chances to be heard about the concerns we have in some spaces in the fandom, which would include for example local group chats, or some certain cons."

"I've been shut down and ignored by people for asking them to boost and listen to other BIPOC voices, especially in tender times. The more time I spend in the fandom, the more I grow to hate it. Not because of the community, but because of the people within it and their attitude."

"Being Asian, I tend to feel like I'm going to stand out a lot because[,] in many areas, you don't see a lot of east [sic] Asian furs."

"I find white [sic] furries to for the most part be very dismissive of non-white [sic] furries and their concerns. Even those that are our 'allies' seem to be very eager to talk over us and virtue signal for clout."

The second-most common theme involves what some would call "microaggressions"—actions and situations that, while not intentionally malicious or hostile, are nevertheless uncomfortable manifestations of broader societal problems when it comes to issues of race and ethnicity. In and of themselves, these issues could be trivialized or dismissed as harmless or minor, but as part of a consistent pattern and as a signal of broader societal problems, they take a toll on the mental and physical health of those who experience them.[12] As BIMPOC participants state, these experiences are not uncommon in fandom spaces:

"Now I haven't experienced any capital P problems, there's been a number of comments, conversations, and situations that really that [sic] really [sic] put into question how people feel about such topics. Often it puts me in this weird dilemma of what do I do at that point. I tend to be a minority of [sic] these situations what does this off color [sic] comment mean about this person and how should I respond.[sic] Oftentimes[,] that easiest answer is to pass of least resistance."[13]

"Knowing that people hide behind their fursona to make racist remarks is really shitty. Nobody's said anything to my face, but I'm hoping that people are a little less bold of doing crazy stuff in the future."

---

[12] Despite frequently being trivialized or mocked by pundits and critics in mainstream media, there is a considerable body of research demonstrating the prevalence of microaggressions (e.g., Smith et al., 2007) and their impact on self-esteem (Nadal et al., 2014), anxiety (Blume et al., 2012), psychological health (Farber et al., 2021), and school performance (Keels et al., 2017). For a review of this literature, see Ogunyemi et al. (2020) or Yosso et al. (2009).

[13] The participant illustrates another particularly insidious aspect of microaggressions—the fact that those who experience them often find themselves questioning how to respond to them, lest they be perceived as overreacting, irrational, or, worst of all, playing into some of the stereotypes themselves.

"The amount of people who keep trying to touch my hair and getting upset when I tell them not to it's also baffling."

"Most of the time were[sic] sexualized by these people and then thrown away once we stand up for ourselves."

"Being lusted after solely because I'm a minority by white[sic] peers."

The third-most common theme expressed by BIMPOC participants is being keenly aware of both the presence and behavior of bigoted individuals and hate groups in the fandom as well as being aware of the inaction of administrators, staff members, and other members of the fandom to put a stop to their actions, which is often seen as tacit support for the views being espoused:

"Being black [sic] has had it's [sic] fair share of expericences [sic] while in the fandom. Mostly[sic] it being limited to the events that transpire on the furry corner of twitter [sic]. Notably when someone in the fandom is outed as being a racist but no person truly listens to the black [sic] person."

"Despite this [sic] fellow people of color in the fandom have voiced concerns and discomfort with some goings on that I completely understand, and it hurts whenever a bigoted, racist in our fandom does pop up and get revealed to be scummy. Like even in an accepting fandom we cannot escape people who hate us."

"The white [sic] supremacy furries give me pause."

"My race has been literally pointed as the blame for my local scene 'degrading' in quality by a moderator and owner of a local state fur group, in particular [sic] my being around along with many others who are also Black furs. I've on numerous times felt extremely uncomfortable being in certain spaces because of outward racists, or racists through their actions and had 0 action taken by moderation to curb racism within their spaces with public outcry by multiple people."

"There's a lot of negative and really racist people in the fandom; While I haven't faced any open racist attitudes towards me thus far, I definitely

feel the pain other BIPOC furs feel from any attitudes they get. My race shouldn't be an influence in this, but I am extremely frustrated and angry at the fandom for allowing racists and Nazis into the fandom and not doing anything about them and just letting their transgressions slide for the sake of 'uwu pawsitivity.'"

"The furry fandom [sic] especially in my city doesn't have any idea how to interact with Black people. They make a racist joke, microaggression, macroaggression, exotification, pretending to be BIPOC when it's convenient and profitable to them, sexualised my skin color, make a [sic] issue of me being black [sic], use the N-word, bad cultural appropriation, part of the BLM but don't care about us ect... To be honest it's hurt for me to have only having [sic] bad experiences by this community."

*"I help run a state group so I often get called a [n****r] (slur) by those who don't like how we operate."*

Many BIMPOC furries also feel distanced from issues of race or ethnicity by a fursona or the primarily online nature of their interaction with the fandom:

"I know there's not many furry minorities but the great thing about being a furry is many people see you for your fursona, what you wish to be seen as sometimes, rather than race."

"People are more likely to talk to me in fursuit but slowly back away after I [sic] take off my fursuit head."

"Before meeting or seeing me, many assume I'm a white [sic] male based on the appearance of my sona."

"Some in the fandom expressed their surprised [sic] when I either revealed or gotten [sic] artwork that identified my race."

"Considering my low and mostly online involvement so far, no."

"I don't really get personally involved with the fandom (going to furmeets or cons), so no."

"Not heavily as most of the experience I [sic] have is from behind [a] screen normally."

"Not really, as I experience it primarily online. So any racial tints on [sic] the fandom I experience are everybody's general experiences too, so they're harder for me to notice. On the internet, nobody knows you're a cat :3"

As a final theme, we return to a point introduced earlier in this chapter, that some BIMPOC furries derive positive experiences in response to the awareness of their race or ethnicity-based labels. This can be through pride in one's own identity or through interactions with other BIMPOC furs:

"I have even created an OC based on my tribe and my middle name which is native to my tribe. I enjoy bringing my culture into the fandom, it is great to also see representation of my culture even from others who are outside of it."

"I only feel welcome by BIPOC's [sic] and Black furry [sic] in other country [sic]."

"Yes, for a long I had thought that most furry communities were majority white [sic]. But I have found BIPOC furry communities that I am comfortable in."

"Finding PoC at FWA[14] years ago fully connected me to the fandom."

We can compare the thoughts of BIMPOC furries against those of White furries, for whom the single most common theme to emerge was an acknowledgment of a sense of privilege or comfort that comes from being in the majority, alongside a feeling of gratitude or appreciation for this fact:

"As a white [sic] person I know I don't have to deal with a lot of the prejudice inherent with being a minority with largely white fandoms."

"I feel like i [sic] could say more about the things I don't face in fandom because I am white (and therefore, impacting my experience by making

---

[14] An initialism for the furry convention Furry Weekend Atlanta.

me not have to deal with those things) than I could point to how I am affected."

"Being in the majority probably led to [a] simpler and easier road to acceptance."

"My people are seen as kinda the default, so im [sic] both kinda "basic", and don't face any adversity for my race."

"I don't interact in-person as much but I certainly feel like I have experienced, and will continue to experience, much less hostility, pushback, and outcasting from the rest of the community because I am white [sic]."

"There's just as much racism in the fandom as there is in American society at large. Being white [sic] shields me from experiencing that."

In a related vein, it was almost as common for White participants to explicitly state that others in the fandom may have worse experiences than they do when it comes to issues of race and ethnicity. Sometimes this was acknowledged in a collective, abstract way, while other times it was through a specific example of someone they know personally:

"I do not experience the hardships POC fandom members experience."

"I think as a white [sic] person I have had a much smoother experience of the fandom than a POC fur might, having to deal with bigots and the white [sic] desire to "escape" racial issues through furry."

"I am privileged as a white [sic] person, and I have seen how people of color are treated by certain people in the fandom. I definitely think I would have it harder (and possibly wouldn't be able to interact with the fandom) if I were a POC."

"I hear most often from furs of colour that they've at one point or another experienced some form of prejudice."

The next most common theme expressed among White respondents is the idea that they have been largely shielded from or had little need to encounter, issues of race and ethnicity. For some, the use of fursonas, fursuits, and the anonymity afforded by online interactions, which allow them to selectively reveal or hide information about themselves, was the cause:

> *"No, with the furry fandom[,] you kinda leave your race at the gate in trade of a species."*

> *"I think furry has created a kind of interesting race blindness in me, where when I see people talking about, for example, BIPOC furry creators on my Twitter timeline, I have to double take and think 'oh [sic] right, that's a thing, that person isn't just a tiger.'"*

> *"It can but only out of suit. Hard to determine race while someone is suiting."*

> *"Race really isn't [an] issue in fandom as I see it. Plus the costumes themselves cover human underneath as well so no one knows [the] race or sex of suitor [sic]."*

> *"I wouldn't say I gained any privlege [sic] from being a white [sic] furry. In fact, I never make my whiteness [sic] apparent so I very rarely have racial issues in furry."*

For others, race and ethnicity were non-issues for them simply because of the infrequency with which they interacted with other furries in person:

> *"As a mostly online person, nope."*

> *"Being strictly online and not showing myself or those details I believe not."*

> *"Considering that my experience mostly consists of lurking on furry Reddit subs, probably not. I expect it could in the future, though.;[sic] I don't think so. Most interactions are online."*

> *"I think that I have revealed little enough of myself online (and I haven't interacted with the furry fandom in person at all) that it has not, positively or negatively."*

Some White participants also pointed to their own experiences with racially or ethnically diverse groups of friends to explain why these were non-issues for them:

"Hardly. My friend group is diverse and race never plays a factor in my friendships."

"I have friends of all races and honestly we are too busy being furry to notice."

"Not really, since I have many friends of various races in the fandom, my race doesn't affect my experience cause it doesn't matter what race we are, we're family."

"Yes, the fandom has actually introduced me to more diversity and acceptance, and I am very appreciative of it! Otherwise, I might still have a biased mindset brought from my "White" upbringing."

A final common theme to emerge among White participants involves minimizing or denying that race and ethnicity are, or should be, issues in the first place. Distinct from stating that they have not been adversely affected by these issues themselves, this theme instead insists that they are, or should be, non-issues. For some, this includes insisting that one is or should strive to be, "color-blind" on issues of race, or instead see beyond race:

"I hold no racial bias as far as I can tell, and I do not care about anyone's skin colour as long as they are friendly people."

"Personally[sic] I'm color-blind to race. It just doesn't matter."

"I live in solidarity for just about every color, race, lifestyle. Just don't push your agendas."

For others, they insist that the furry fandom itself is a space where race and ethnicity are non-issues:

"Race has no bearing on fandom but what counts is who you are inside and how you interact with others. You may be [a] minority but who cares

if your [sic] nice and you could be white [sic] and a jerk so shunned. Race really isn't [an] issue in fandom as I see it."

"I'd like to think that the furry fandom goes beyond race."

"I've personally never seen anybody from the furry fandom even pay much attention to somebody else's race, I've always seen the fandom be very welcoming to people of all races, orientations, etc."

"For the most part, I haven't seen that race much matters inside the fandom itself."

"Race is typically not a feature of a person that matters in interactions, especially with how generally removed it is from the furry community."

Future Directions

This chapter represents an exploratory step towards understanding issues of race and ethnicity in the furry fandom. Our early focus on quantitative studies and our scholarly expertise meant that our understanding of race and ethnicity in the furry fandom was largely limited to demographic information. Furries checked off boxes in surveys to indicate which out of a list of labels best described them—a process that missed important labels, sometimes used outdated terminology, and occasionally limited people to identifying with no more than one label. The approach yielded demographic data that was limited. Little else was said on the matter until relatively recently, when other scholars and critics suggested that we explore the subject more thoroughly and with more diverse methodology.

As a result, we're now just starting to gain a more nuanced understanding of how race and ethnicity are experienced in the furry fandom and, more importantly, how they are experienced differently by members of the fandom. We're moving beyond an exclusive focus on aggregate data and

taking the time to listen to the voices of those who too often find themselves shouted over, marginalized, or simply drowned out by the masses. In doing so, it becomes apparent that race and ethnicity can be experienced with great variability in fandom spaces. For BIMPOC furries, issues of race and ethnicity are far more frequently on their mind, with responses being far more likely to be polarizing than neutral. Their words reveal that they experience prejudice in the fandom despite its espoused norms of tolerance and acceptance—both in terms of explicit, in-your-face prejudice as well as the day-to-day microaggressions that often fly under the radar or otherwise go unnoticed by those who aren't the target of them. It's also clear that while many White furs are aware of the problems experienced by BIMPOC furs—both in broader society and in the furry fandom specifically—more could be done to translate this awareness into action, including becoming better at recognizing, speaking out against, and taking actions to stop prejudice.

There is also a greater need to listen more attentively to the experiences of BIMPOC furs and to be aware that their experiences do often differ from the lived experiences of White furries. It's well and good to label the fandom as a safe and inclusive space for everyone and to believe that complex issues are negated by the fandom's online nature and the presence of fursonas that hide one's race. This is little comfort or utility, however, to those who frequently find themselves on the receiving end of prejudice and who need allies to understand their experience, listen to their needs, and stand with them in ways that make a difference.

While the research discussed in this chapter is just a first step, Furscience is already planning future studies on these topics, which includes designing studies with more targeted recruiting of BIMPOC furries. Moreover, future research questions should move beyond initial questions of one's thoughts about race and ethnicity to ask more sophisticated research questions—projects that will include diverse research partnerships and overseen by BIMPOC furs. These may include questions about the importance of BIMPOC-exclusive spaces at conventions, representation in furry media (art, music, fursuits), the role of race and ethnicity in fursona creation and self-expression, and experiences with the furry fandom in-person and in online spaces.

References

Akrami, N., & Ekehammar, B. (2005). The association between implicit and explicit prejudice: The moderating role of motivation to control prejudiced reactions. *Scandinavian Journal of Psychology, 46*(4), 361-366. https://doi.org/10.1111/j.1467-9450.2005.00466.x

Apfelbaum, E. P., Pauker, K., Sommers, S. R., & Ambady, N. (2010). In blind pursuit of racial equality? *Psychological Science, 21*(11), 1587-1592. https://doi.org/10.1177/0956797610384741

Blume, A. W., Lovato, L. V., Thyken, B. N., & Denny, N. (2012). The relationship of microaggressions with alcohol use and anxiety among ethnic minority college students in a historically White institution.

Cultural Diversity and Ethnic Minority Psychology, 18(1), 45-54. https://doi.org/10.1037/a0025457

Dovidio, J. F., Kawakami, K., & Gaertner, S. L. (2002). Implicit and explicit prejudice and interracial interaction. *Journal of Personality and Social Psychology, 82*(1), 62-68. https://doi.org/10.1037//0022-3514.82.1.62

Farber, R., Wedell, E., Herchenroeder, L., Dickter, C. L., Pearson, M. R., & Bravo, A. J. (2021). Microaggressions and psychological health among college students: A moderated mediation model of rumination and social structure beliefs. *Journal of Racial and Ethnic Health Disparities, 8*(1), 245-255. https://doi.org/10.1007/s40615-020-00778-8

Keels, M., Durkee, M., & Hope, E. (2017). The psychological and academic costs of school-based racial and ethnic microaggressions. *American Educational Research Journal, 54*(6), 1316-1344. https://doi.org/10.3102/0002831217722120

McGuire, W. J., McGuire, C. V., Child, P., & Fujioka, T. (1978). Salience of ethnicity in the spontaneous self-concept as a function of one's ethnic distinctiveness in the social environment. *Journal of Personality and Social Psychology, 36*(5), 511-520. https://doi.org/10.1037//0022-3514.36.5.511

Nadal, K. L., Wong, Y., Griffin, K. E., Davidoff, K., & Sriken, J. (2014). The adverse impact of racial microaggressions on college students' self-esteem. *Journal of College Student Development, 55*(5), 461-474. https://doi.org/10.1353/csd.2014.0051

Ogunyemi, D., Clare, C., Astudillo, Y. M., Marseille, M., Manu, E., & Kim, S. (2020). Microaggressions in the learning environment: A systematic review. *Journal of Diversity in Higher Education, 13*(2), 67-119. https://doi.org/10.1037/dhe0000107

Pennington, C. R., Heim, D., Levy, A. R., & Larkin, D. T. (2016). Twenty years of stereotype threat research: A review of psychological mediators. *PLoS One, 11*(1): e0146487. https://doi.org/10.1371/journal.pone.0146487

Smith, W. A., Allen, W. R., & Danley, L. L. (2007). "Assume the position... You fit the description": Psychosocial experiences and racial battle fatigue among African American male college students. *American Behavioral Scientist, 51*(4), 551-578. https://doi.org/10.1177/0002764207307742

Steele, C. M. (1997). A threat in the air: How stereotypes shape intellectual identity and performance. *American Psychologist, 52*(6), 613-629. https://doi.org/10.1037//0003-066x.52.6.613

United States Census Bureau. (2019). *A More Diverse Nation: Distribution of Race and Hispanic Origin by Age Groups.* https://www.census.gov/library/visualizations/2019/comm/age-race-distribution.html

Yosso, T., Smith, W. Ceja, M., & Solorzano, D. (2009). Critical race theory, racial microaggressions, and campus racial climate for Latina/o undergraduates. *Harvard Educational Review, 79*(4), 659-691. https://doi.org/10.17763/haer.79.4.m6867014157m7071

Chapter 15
Sex and Gender in the Furry Fandom

Anna Renee Henry, Frances H. I. Henry,
Sharon E. Roberts, Courtney "Nuka" Plante

Almost anyone who's spent time in the furry fandom will tell you that it's a space dominated primarily by men. Even so, one thing that became abundantly clear to us as we studied furries is the fact that it's far more diverse in terms of gender than we had initially expected based on these common presumptions! Before we get to our data on gender, however, we'll begin with a brief overview of the current discourse on gender and how a scientific understanding of gender is constantly evolving. Then, we'll look at how these sex and gender categories relate to furries by looking at their prevalence in the furry fandom across a multitude of studies. Next, we'll look at some open-ended data regarding participants' thoughts about gender in fandom spaces: the frequency with which they come up, their valence (e.g., positive or negative thoughts) when they arise, and the content of such thoughts. We'll then finish the chapter by looking at furries' gender-related attitudes and their implications for how we, as researchers, can study gender in the future and how the fandom broadly thinks about gender.

Sex and Gender—A Brief Primer

Before we dive into the data on sex and gender, let's take a moment to clarify the meaning of these terms as they're understood.[1] More than any other modern identity (except perhaps sexual orientation), these terms have undergone a revolution in the past several decades. Historically[2], the terms "sex" and "gender" have just been two different words that mean the same thing. Indeed, one of the authors of this chapter recalls being taught that "gender" was the term you used instead of "sex" when you wanted to be polite and avoid using an emotionally-charged word like "sex" in polite company. He was taught that these two words meant the exact same thing, and it wasn't until years later that the distinction between the two was explained to him.

So just what is this distinction? A simple, albeit still wanting, distinction is that sex refers to a cluster of biological characteristics that, taken together, define a person as being either male or female, while gender refers to the

[1] At the time of writing, of course. As we'll see, thinking on the subject evolves quickly, and by the time you're reading this, it's possible, or even likely, that our terminology or way of thinking about gender are already out of date!

[2] And still today, at least for some people.

socially constructed behavior, social roles, and interests assumed to accompany this biology. Despite being fairly easy and clear to understand, some folks will already find the distinction between biology and social construction to be too complex (it *is* far simpler to just treat sex and gender as interchangeable), but the reality is, as is often the case in the sciences, that even this fairly simple distinction is an oversimplification. Distinguishing sex and gender is, in some ways, like a mirage—it disappears the nearer we come to it. Reality is frequently far more complicated than the language which tries to describe it!

To illustrate this complexity, let's look briefly at the history of thinking about sex and gender. For much of human history, qualities that we now see as separate issues, like gender and sexual orientation, were considered an integral part of biological sex. Social roles, such as taking care of children or protecting the family, were thought to be an essential product of reproductive biology—your body determined your role in the family.[3] Societies generally divided sex into two categories: male and female, although some cultures and societies recognized the existence of intersex people (those with characteristics of "both" sexes). One result of this categorization, coupled with the belief that certain behaviors or social roles were tied to one's sex, is that, in the 19th century, early psychological and scientific theories on the origins of homosexuality assumed that sexual attraction was tied to a person's biological sex, meaning that attraction to women was thought to be part of what made men "men," while an attraction to men was seen as an essential characteristic of womanhood (Kennedy, 1981).

Examples like the above illustrate how even the "hard science" of human biology exists within a society and has an evolving history—one that is far younger than we might think. For example, historian Thomas Laqueur has shown that the idea of two different and opposite sexes only emerged only in the late 18th century (Laqueur, 1990). Moreover, the Western concept of sex is far from the only one. Intersex people (those with biological characteristics of "both" sexes) have been recognized as distinct sexes in sources such as the Talmud (Gross, 1999), while in some Indigenous societies, transgender people were recognized as a distinct sex, as well as frequently being seen as a third or even fourth gender (Williams, 1992).

Even if we try to simplify the issue by ignoring gender roles and gender-coded behavior and just focusing on biology, the issue is far more nuanced

---

[3] This idea prevailed despite the fact that these roles and what they entailed differed from culture to culture, despite the fact that reproductive biology is largely a constant in humans!

and complex than we might think. For example, if you want to tie sex to biology, which biological indicators should we use? Genitals? Chromosomes? Hormones? Secondary sex characteristics (beards, breasts, etc.)? A close look at each of these indicators reveals that sex is far more complicated than a simple biological dichotomy!

Take genitals, for instance—most of us don't go around asking to see each other's genitals before deciding for ourselves whether they're male or female! Anyone who did so would rightly be charged with sexual harassment! Those who insist that genitals determine a person's sex overlook the fact that they, themselves, do not actually use their genitals for this purpose, but rather base their decisions on a combination of social cues (e.g., what's the person wearing, what does their hair look like?) Even if you did staunchly tie a person's sex to their genitals, you'd have to acknowledge that genitals, like other body parts, aren't set in stone: for more than 70 years, people have been able to undergo surgery to alter their genitals. Likewise, this dichotomy overlooks intersex people who may possess ambiguous genitalia or have a variety of hormonal or developmental conditions that make it so that their bodies don't fall neatly into one category or another. And while a common retort is to sweep intersex people under the rug as an anomaly, data suggests that they could make up as much as 1.7% of the population (Fausto-Sterling, 2000)—around the same prevalence rate as people who have red hair (Barry, 2010). Hopefully, you recognize the futility of trying to pretend that red-haired people don't exist just so we can cling to an overly simplistic model of hair color as having only two options, brown or blonde—and yet, people try to erase the existence of intersex people every day using the same logic.

Okay, so if basing sex on genitals is a problem, why not just base it on chromosomes or hormones? After all, you can't change your genetic code with surgery![4] Even so, it's not long before we see many of the same problems that we saw with genital-based distinctions. For example, unless you happen to walk around with a genetics lab in your pocket, it's unlikely you've ever used a person's chromosomes to determine the sex of another person. And even if you could get a hold of the genetic information of every person you met, things would still be far more complicated than a simple male/female dichotomy. You might assume, in line with what you learned in middle school biology, that it's a simple matter of looking at whether they have an XY ("male") or XX ("female") pairing of their 23rd chromosome.

---

[4] … yet!

But what about people who have other genetic combinations (e.g., XXY, XO)? Or what if someone *did* present with a typical "XY" chromosome, but their body is insensitive to the androgens (male hormones) that they produce? Such a person may have most of the physical traits one would associate with being female despite being "genetically male." In fact, unless you've been karyotyped yourself, you can't know, just based on your body's appearance, what your chromosomes look like![5]

Despite the frequency with which people try to ground their distinctions in genitals or genetics, the reality is that most people determine a stranger's sex based on secondary sex characteristics—ironically, the most mutable of all of these biological features! People can, after all, enlarge or reduce their breasts, alter the shape of their face, or even just shave their beards, not to mention the fact that most of these characteristics are the result of hormones which, themselves, can be changed. Entire industries revolve around shaping these features to fall in line with societal expectations, such as procedures and surgeries that try to eliminate facial hair. And if, despite all this, you still wanted to argue that secondary sex characteristics are a sound way to determine a person's sex, you'd have to account for the fact that children do not show these secondary sex characteristics before puberty—nevertheless, we still make judgments about their sex based on other features (e.g., hairstyles, clothes, toy preferences), features which, you'll note, are decidedly non-biological and which are, instead, rooted in cultural assumptions and can differ radically across time and culture.

In short, "biology" is far more nuanced and complex than most people would care to admit. It's not only incorrect to insist on their only being "two" sexes, but doing so ignores the fact that the basis of such determinations (hormones, genitalia, secondary sex characteristics) can change, either as the result of age, weight gain, cosmetic, chemical, or surgical procedures. Instead, we need to recognize that what we call sex is a combination of mostly mutable biological factors, that, while tending to fall into two general categories, still have a great deal of variability. When people are claiming to make distinctions about a person's "biological sex," what they're typically doing is basing their determination on a mixture of secondary sexual characteristics and gender cues (mannerisms, clothing, speech patterns) while making assumptions about that person's genetics, genitalia, and hormones.

---

[5] And this is to say nothing about the hormones which drive the association between genotype and body development and which are, themselves, alterable through hormone replacement therapy.

The fact that so much of what we use to determine sex is actually gender means that, while they are by no means the same thing, gender must be considered alongside sex. To do that, let's delve into what we mean by gender. At the start of this section, we defined gender as being "socially constructed." What does this mean? Some people, on first hearing the term, assume that this means that gender isn't real, that being a social construct means being imaginary. This couldn't be further from the truth! When social scientists describe something as a "social construct," they're describing it as a concept or system developed by a culture to serve a social function. Just because something was developed by a society (rather than occurring "naturally"), doesn't mean it doesn't have a very real existence and impact on that culture. While gender is a key example of this, it is far from the only one. Money is a social construct, for example, but we'll still work long hours to get our hands on some of it so we can put a roof over our heads and put food on our tables. Likewise, numbers are a social construct—abstract and intangible,[6] but nevertheless essential to our understanding of the world!

When we describe gender as a social construct, we mean that it's a system developed by a culture that helps its members create meaningful labels for people. For example, many cultures use the labels "man" and "woman"[7] to categorize people, although how different cultures' conceptualize "men" and "women" differs. In some cultures, for example, certain hairstyles, clothes, jobs, and personality traits are thought to be more feminine, whereas in other cultures, those same features may be considered more masculine. Heck, even within the *same* culture we can find examples of how what is considered masculine and feminine has changed: in early 20th Century America, pink was more likely to be worn by boys than by girls, who tended to be dressed in blue; dresses were also not coded as either masculine or feminine, and so it was common for little boys and girls to both wear dresses (Maglaty, 2011).[8]

Even the number of genders recognized varies considerably from culture to culture. While it's fairly common for most cultures to recognize

---

[6] You can't smell or touch or see the concept of the number 3!

[7] The terms "male" and "female" are generally used to refer to sex, while the terms "man" and "woman" are typically used to refer to gender.

[8] For a simple example of this, a quick image search through the childhood portraits of Franklin Delano Roosevelt—the 32nd president of the United States—will reveal images of him with long hair wearing a dress, something considered fashionable for young boys at the time. And on the subject of long hair in men, need we say more than 1970s and 1980s hair metal bands and mullets?

something akin to a masculine and feminine gender, many cultures also recognize other genders, including genders that prominently feature both masculine and feminine traits and genders that are completely tangential to masculinity and femininity. For example, the Inuit in the Canadian Arctic recognize a third gender category called sipiniq or kipijuituq which is distinct from what we would call "man" and "woman" (Issenman, 1997).

Part of the reason why people conflate the terms "sex" and "gender" is because there tends to be a high correlation between the two concepts. However, a high correlation is not the same thing as a "perfect" correlation: just because two concepts are highly related does not mean there isn't significant and meaningful variability. There are, for example, plenty of "males" who dislike the hobbies, clothes, roles, and stereotypical behaviors of men and who identify more strongly with features we typically ascribe to women, and vice-versa. Moreover, there are people who don't identify with either label, since their behaviors, feelings, and preferences don't line up well with either of these categories. To put it simply, there's nothing about one's sex that *requires* that a person adopt a particular gender identity.

There's been growing cultural awareness about the fact that some people simply don't line up with cultural prescriptions of gender. More and more we're starting to recognize that some "males" don't identify as men, and some "females" don't identify as women. Likewise, some people are intersex, making it difficult for them to find a gender role for themselves and creating friction when their preferences, feelings, and behavior don't align with how others see them. Some people eschew the traditional dichotomy of "men" and "women" altogether, instead identifying with a bit of both or with neither (e.g., non-binary). In general, all of these folks would tend to identify with the umbrella term "transgender," although they may also identify with additional, more precise labels.

Transgender people have always existed, even if some cultures have been slow or reluctant to acknowledge this fact. The apparent growth in their prevalence in recent decades is likely the product of growing cultural awareness, research, and validation of trans identities, rather than simply being a fad or trend. Prior to recent awareness and cultural acceptance of trans people, many trans people were shoehorned into a gender identity that didn't match their self-conceptualization, often being forced to "fake it" or suffer ostracism and social backlash. As a fairly timid example, terms like "sissy" and "tomboy" are commonly used—typically in a derogatory way—to describe males and females whose behavior is inconsistent with the prescribed behaviors for men and women.[9] Being called insulting names is one of many ways trans people may have been bullied into "falling in line" with societal gender roles and, as a result, their existence went largely unnoticed and underestimated.[10]

The term "cisgender" is used alongside the term transgender and refers to those whose gender identity matches the sex that they were assigned at birth. The term comes from the Latin preposition "cis" meaning "on this side of." It was coined in the 1990s as a way to identify non-transgender people in a way that did not treat them as "normal" or the default, which, by extension, would treat transgender people as deviation or abnormal, contributing to their stigmatization and devaluation. The creation of the term also encourages cisgender people to be more aware of the ways that having a gender identity that conforms to cultural expectations is normalized and privileged in our society.

Now that we're armed with a more nuanced understanding of the distinction between the concepts of sex and gender, as well as how these concepts are constantly evolving and growing, we're now ready to look at the research on sex and gender in the furry fandom, beginning with data looking at their prevalence.

Sex and Gender Composition

As we mentioned in Chapter 4, there is no single "right" way to measure a variable, be it something as simple as an object's height or as complex as a person's identity. Every means of measurement necessarily involves trade-offs—simplicity for a loss of nuance, focus on one facet for neglect of another, precision for breadth.

With this in mind, let's consider the way Furscience has approached the measurement of sex and gender prevalence in the furry fandom over the

---

[9] That these terms are also used to stigmatize gay, lesbian, and bisexual (GLB) people shows that there is still a very high perceived correlation between sexual orientation and gender presentation.

[10] A similar trend occurred for left-handedness which, up until recent decades, was often considered to be maladaptive or something needing to be corrected. Even the term for left-handedness, sinistral, shares an etymological root with the term sinister, a fairly unflattering thing to be called. Being left-handed was considered fairly rare up until recently, in part because left-handed children were forced by teachers and parents to learn to write with their right hands despite their natural proclivity to do otherwise. When the social stigma towards left-handedness began to dissipate, rates of left-handedness in the population appeared to increase. This wasn't because it was suddenly cool or trendy to be left-handed; rather, it was an illusory effect caused by left-handed people no longer needing to hide the fact that they were left-handed.

years. Early in the research—in the project's first few years—we approached the topic the way many social psychologists did: with a simple, single, fairly cursory measure of sex. Participants were given one of two boxes to check: "male" or "female." As was common at the time,[11] we didn't consider adding an option for intersex people, nor did we consider assessing gender independent of sex. We were interested only in the participant's sex because, well, that's what most social scientists assume they're interested in. In many regards, sex was used as a stand-in or proxy for gender, and was treated as a dichotomous variable (i.e., people were expected to fall into one category or another). When assessed this way in a pair of 2011 studies, we found that most furries (80.2-83.3%) were male and that a significant minority of furries (16.7-19.8%) were female. The results were simple to present and were consistent with stereotypes of furries and with the general beliefs of the fandom: furry is a predominantly male space. As far as we knew, there was no reason to look beyond these initial results.

However, not long after our original results, furries began to critique the measure as deeply flawed. For one thing, it didn't give an option for intersex people, who would be forced, as intersex people often are, to categorize themselves into a box that doesn't accurately describe them.[12] For another thing, it overlooked the concept of gender entirely. And while this was likely not an issue for most people, for whom their sex assigned at birth aligned with the gender society typically associates with that sex (e.g., the assumption that males identify as men and females identify as women), for trans people, the question presented them with a dilemma. If, for example, a person was assigned the sex of male at birth, but their gender identity is that of a woman, they would be forced to check the "male" box if they answered as assigned sex at birth or "female" if they identified as a woman. Without any sort of option to indicate otherwise, trans participants were left with the unenviable choice of skipping the question entirely—meaning that this facet of their identity would be effectively erased or ignored—or choosing an option that did not accurately reflect who they were, just another instance of a problem all-too-frequently faced by trans people every time they fill out a

[11] And, unfortunately, is still all-too-common in many social scientific studies today.
[12] To refer back to an earlier analogy, imagine being a person with red hair being forced to choose whether their hair colour was "brown" or "blonde." The dichotomy seems to suggest that red hair isn't a valid alternative and could understandably be upsetting to a person with red hair to suggest that their hair color isn't a real option, or so suggest that they were "basically just a brown-haired person" (especially if their red hair was an important part of their self-concept!).

government form, sign up for a gym membership, or join a dating website. What's more, if they underwent gender-affirming surgery, the sex they were assigned at birth would no longer reflect either their sex or their gender! Regardless, answering the question meant erasing a part of their identity.

To correct this oversight, we next rolled out a revised version of the question, one that attempted to address both of these concerns, albeit in a fairly ham-handed manner. Rather than assessing sex and gender separately, we simply added two additional options to the question. In addition to the "male" and "female" options, we now had the options "trans" and "other." This revised version of the question was used in 10 studies over the next 3 or so years, yielding the following prevalence estimates: male (72.4-83.5%), female (14.2-24.9%), trans (0.9-3.6%), and other (0.0-1.6%).

It's worth noting a few points about these findings and about the question itself. First, the inclusion of this change, far from being trivial, has a notable impact on the data. For example, 1-5% of the sample was suddenly able to choose an option to represent themselves in a way that would not have been possible in the first version of the question. These are people who would have either ignored the first question or been forced to choose an option that didn't accurately describe them—in both cases silencing their identity and erasing it from the data. In this respect, the question is a notable improvement over the original.

In many other respects, however, the question still suffers from many of the limitations of the original. The question still conflates the concepts of sex and gender: a person assigned the sex of male at birth might be a trans woman, but which box would they select? Technically speaking, one could argue that both "male" (because of sex assigned at birth, chromosomes) and "trans" (their lived experience) could be correct options for this person, but so could "female," depending on their circumstances (hormones, genitalia, secondary sex characteristics, gender presentation)! By trying to measure sex and gender in the same question and allowing only a single possible response, trans participants were limited to being able to either discuss their gender or were forced into an inadequate definition of sex that did not recognize the mutability of this category.

Another problem with this question is that it engages in what's called "othering." In essence, othering involves sweeping up any group that doesn't fall into one of several pre-determined categories into a non-descript, catch-all category. To be sure, having an "other" category is better than having no option at all, as it means that people who might otherwise find themselves ignored by the question have at least some way of being represented.

Nevertheless, othering can have the undesirable effect of making people who fall into this category feel invalid or unseen. In the case of intersex people, who frequently struggle to be recognized and seen as valid in society, not having an "intersex" option certainly doesn't help this feeling of being invalid. In both cases, the question, while an improvement over the original, was wholly inadequate.[13] It is also imprecise, as it does not identify why, and which groups were identifying themselves as "other."

Taking into account these critiques, which primarily came from furries themselves,[14] we next sought to improve our measure by asking about gender identity in a separate question. Specifically, in a series of 6 studies from 2012 to 2015, we added an additional question assessing furries' gender identity along a single dimension ranging from "completely masculine" to "completely feminine"—with an option of "other" for those who didn't feel they fell within this continuum (e.g., non-binary people). These data, summarized in Table 15.1, provide an informative supplement to our above findings.

Table 15.1. Furry participant self-identification along a gender continuum across 6 studies from 2012-2015.

Label	Prevalence
Completely Masculine	26.7-31.7%
Mostly Masculine	26.6-36.0%
Equal Masc. and Fem.	14.9-21.0%
Mostly Feminine	9.8-12.0%
Completely Feminine	6.5-10.7%
Other	0.0-4.2%

The data clearly illustrate how much nuance you lose when participants are forced to choose "male" or "female" and when these terms are used as a

---

[13] Granted, it could be argued that, at the time, we were not equipped, nor were we interested specifically in deeper questions about sex and gender in the fandom beyond simply calculating aggregated prevalence data for demographic purposes. Nevertheless, this raises the valid critique of why bother assessing something at all if you're only going to do a clumsy and ultimately inadequate job of it? As the saying goes, if it's worth doing, it's worth doing right.

[14] The fact that furries were the ones to push us to do better rather than other academics (e.g., journal reviewers, ethics review boards) is both a testament to furries' progressive and informed thinking on this subject and a sign of how slow scientific practice can be to keep up with current advancements.

proxy for gender. As these data suggest, there is considerably more "middle ground" than is suggested by the statement "furries are 4-5 times more likely to be males than females." The 15-21% of furries who identify as equally masculine and feminine are completely lost if one only considers participant sex, and this only further illustrates the need to look beyond sex. Having said that, the question is *still* significantly flawed in that it only conceptualizes gender along a single dimension while othering those whose gender identity does not fall along this continuum. While it is an improvement, it's still far from ideal.

From 2015 onward, heeding the advice of several furries, we sought suggestions from LGBTQ+ organizations and experts in the field of sex and gender studies. This was part of what was now a committed effort to studying the topic of gender in the furry fandom more seriously, rather than just collecting the data so we could list off the demographic properties of our sample. To this end, we incorporated several different ways to assess both sex and gender that didn't conflate participant sex and gender and aimed to be more inclusive and respectful of people of all gender identities.

In a series of seven online and convention studies from 2015 to 2019, we assessed sex as its own question (alongside other, separate questions about gender). In these measures we included intersex as its own category, avoiding the need for intersex people to identify as "other" (while also providing an "other" category for those whose sex doesn't fall neatly into any of the three provided categories). These results revealed numbers that were comparable to our previous findings about sex, with the following proportions: male (71.2-84.4%), female (14.4-26.3%), intersex (0.0-1.2%), and other (0.0-0.4%).

In several of these same studies from 2015 to 2017, we assessed gender with its own separate question. We did away with the masculine-feminine dimension question in favor of a question that more simply asked participants to indicate which of several labels most accurately described them. The options provided in this question were "man" (68.6-74.8%), "woman" (15.9-21.7%), "non-binary" (5.6-10.2%), and "other" (4.2-5.4%). Importantly, these findings reveal a point that was alluded to earlier in this chapter: while sex and gender are highly correlated concepts, they are far from perfectly correlated. If, for instance, sex and gender were one and the same, we would expect a virtually identical proportion of males and men across these studies. Instead, we find, across studies, that there are consistently more males than there are men. Possible explanations for this are that some of the participants who were assigned the sex of male at birth are non-binary or women, a distinction that is completely overlooked if one were only to look at participant sex.

Looking at sex and gender as separate constructs in separate questions, while affording several benefits, does have its own set of drawbacks. For one thing, it can make it somewhat difficult to accurately assess the number of trans furries in the fandom. While one could try to identify trans furries by looking at the number of male furries who also selected the label of woman or non-binary and the number of female furries who also selected the label of man or non-binary, it would be presumptuous to infer a person's identity as a trans person indirectly. Instead, it seems far more preferable to simply ask them. Another added challenge included the "check all" nature of some of these questions. While it allows people to indicate the many ways they identify, it also becomes difficult when it comes time to explore differences of experience based on gender. For example, many statistical analyses require that participants be included in only one category. We needed to find a way to limit people to one gender category for the purpose of doing statistical analyses while still being respectful and mindful of the wide range of experiences they may have.

Our best approach, to date, is reflected in some of our most recent studies as of writing this book, in 2021 and 2022. Across three studies, we presented participants with a forced choice from a set of six options that attempt to capture a range of gender identities while also differentiating cisgender from transgender furries and allowing for people who fall outside of these categories to use the options "genderqueer"[15] and "other." The results are shown in Table 15.2 below.

The data reveal some pretty striking findings, not the least of which is that upwards of one-quarter to one-third of furries do not identify as cisgender. This is worth drawing attention to, given that our initial investigation into sex and gender began with a fairly cis-normative assumption—that sex and gender were essentially the same concept. Moreover, the data illustrate the complexity of trying to adequately capture the variability of gender as a concept relative to sex. As we saw earlier, once the labels of "male," "female," and "intersex" were accounted for, there remained less than half of a percent of furries whose sex fell outside of those categories. Sex, it would seem, is a far simpler construct to label and describe than gender, as

[15] While there's no universally agreed-upon definition of genderqueer, it most commonly refers to people for whom their gender identity falls outside of conventional attempts to describe or define it, including concepts such as genderfluidity and non-binary.

indicated by the 4.2-7.9% of furries shown in Table 15.2 whose gender identity is inadequately described using five different labels, including the fairly broad label of "genderqueer." This further reinforces the fallacy of only focusing on participant sex or a limited range of gender identities: you end up missing entirely the rich and varied landscape of gender identity.

Table 15.2. Furry identification with different gender labels across three online and convention-based studies from 2021-2022.

Label	Furry
Cis Woman	5.6-10.7%
Cis Man	60.9-62.8%
Trans Woman	2.5-5.6%
Trans Man	3.5-3.6%
Genderqueer	12.6-18.5%
Other	4.2-7.9%

Another point worth mentioning is that while our more recent measures represent a marked improvement over our initial measures of these topics, they remain far from perfect. In every one of our studies—including studies using our most refined measures informed by transgender scholars on our team with lived experience—we still receive feedback from furries who feel that the options we provide or our conceptualization of gender leaves them without an appropriate way to indicate their gender. It is unlikely that we, nor anyone else, will ever be able to construct a measure of these constructs that perfectly addresses everyone's concerns, especially given that different people may hold contradictory views of gender and how to best conceptualize it. Another part of the challenge is that the language used to describe these phenomena is perpetually evolving, as is scientific understanding of it. Nevertheless, it's a goal worth striving for, especially given the importance of gender for many people's identities and the historical and broader cultural tendency to oversimplify these constructs and silence those whose gender identity falls outside what is deemed conventional.

We would also like to draw the reader's attention to our more recent tendency to move away from measures of sex to focus on measures of gender instead. This is due, in part, to feedback given to us by several critics and LGBTQ+ organizations who asked us a deceptively simple, but very important question: what are you *actually* interested in? At the end of the day, as a team comprised primarily of social psychologists and other social scientists whose work focuses on identity and self-concept, we are more interested in the way people see and express themselves than we are in their sex—more interested in how they dress, think, behave, and see themselves fitting into social roles than in their physical or biological characteristics.[16]

Before we wrap up this section on the prevalence of different sex and gender categories in the furry fandom, we thought it would be worth looking at a few specific questions about these topics which can be assessed quantitatively, before we look at more open-ended questions. The quantitative questions represent aggregated data that can be further contextualized when participants discuss their gender in their own words, as we'll see in the next sections.

In a 2022 study, we assessed the relative prevalence of different genders in a sample of convention-going furries and a sample of furries recruited online. The results revealed that the convention-going sample had about twice as many cis women (10.7% vs. 5.6%), a comparable proportion of cis men (62.8% vs. 61.4%), half as many trans women (2.5% vs. 4.8%), about as many trans men (3.5% vs. 3.6%), and somewhat fewer people identifying as genderqueer (19.6% vs. 24.5%). To date, we have little explanation for why these differences may occur or how consistent and replicable they will be over time.

We also have comparisons of sex and gender data between fandoms. For instance, evidence from some of our earlier studies from 2014 suggests that, compared to anime fans, a group with which furries share a reasonable overlap (see Chapter 11), furries tend to have a higher proportion of males (72.4% vs. 52.9%) and, in terms of gender identity as assessed along a continuum, tend to identify as more masculine and less feminine than do anime fans. To date, there is little explanation for why this distinction exists, as there doesn't seem to be anything intrinsic to an interest in anthropomorphized animal characters that makes it any more likely to be proportionately favored by males than anime.[17]

---

[16] This is not to say, of course, that there are no circumstances in which questions about a person's sex matters. However, the most relevant questions to the issue of sex tend to be about biology (e.g., a person's risk of ovarian cancer or their relative level of androgens), topics which are largely outside the purview of the studies we typically conduct as social scientists.

[17] One possible explanation may stem from the fact that furry may have historically been seen as a male-dominated space, which could create norms that make female furries keenly aware of their gender and ultimately feel out-of-place or like they don't belong as a result (e.g., McGuire et al., 1978; Steele, 1997). Of course, this

A more recent 2021 study of gender in the furry and *Star Wars* fandoms revealed that transgender people were upwards of 15 times more prevalent in the furry fandom than in the *Star Wars* fandom (7.5% vs. 0.5%). Moreover, furries were 4 times more likely to identify as gender non-conforming, 4 times more likely to identify as non-binary, 5 times more likely to identify as genderqueer, 2.5 times more likely to identify as genderfluid, and 1.5 times more likely to identify as agender. Findings such as these reveal a point that will be reiterated in the open-ended responses of transgender people in later sections: the furry fandom is a place that is not only receptive to transgender people but is also comprised predominantly of LGBTQ+[18] furries.

In accordance with ideas that we'll address later in this chapter, we have also, at various times, measured the flexibility of gender expression in furry spaces. For example, across a series of five online and convention-going studies from 2011 to 2012, we asked furries to indicate whether they expressed their gender differently in the furry fandom than they did in their day-to-day lives. Across samples, approximately 55.0-61.8% of furries said that they did not and would not do so. A further 19.8-24.7% said that they did not, but they might be willing to do so. In contrast, 10.1-13.9% of furries said that they occasionally do so, 2.5-4.2% said that they regularly do so, and 2.9-5.2% said that their primary fursona fit this description (i.e., being a different gender identity than their day-to-day gender identity). While cosplaying as an identity does not necessarily mean that one shares that identity, it may suggest that for at least some furries, the fandom may represent a space where they feel safe expressing different facets of their gender identity (e.g., showing a "softer" side not traditionally associated with masculinity) or where they may be able to try out or express a gender identity that they otherwise suppress in day-to-day life (e.g., a transgender person whose fursona represents the gender identity they would prefer to be able to express in their day-to-day life).[19]

---

wouldn't explain *why* furry started out being a predominantly male space, a question perhaps best left to fandom historians to answer.

[18] For more on the predominant LGBTQ+ presence in the furry fandom, see Chapter 15 and Chapter 16.

[19] Other findings suggest that the furry fandom may not be unique in this respect—or even the best outlet for this sort of gender expression. For example, a 2014 study found that furries, compared to anime fans, were about half as likely to say that they might or do express their gender differently in fandom spaces than in their day-to-day life. There are significant sex and gender differences in the composition of the two fandoms, however, which could partly explain these findings. For example, cis

In a final set of findings, we turn to the results of a 2019 study looking specifically at furries' gender identity and the gender identity of their fursonas. The findings suggest that cis women were almost four times more likely to have a fursona whose gender identity differs from their own than were cis men (10.9% vs. 2.7%). The same study also found that approximately half (53.1%) of transgender furries had a fursona who was, themselves, also transgender. This is generally in line with some of our other research showing that furries often imbue their fursonas with elements of their own identity and that many furries consider their fursonas to be fairly similar to themselves (see Chapter 7 for more on this).[20]

To summarize: given the complexity of the concepts of sex and gender, it comes as little surprise that the task of trying to assess the prevalence of sex and gender categories in the furry fandom is equally complex and riddled with nuance. In its early years, Furscience was guilty of many of the common oversimplifications of these topics, including treating the concepts of sex and gender as one and the same, overly focusing on sex to the exclusion of gender, excluding important identity labels (e.g., intersex, transgender), and assessing these concepts in a ham-handed and uninformed manner. Through the generous feedback of furries and LGBTQ+ organizations alike, the quality of our assessment tools greatly improved, as did our understanding of the need for research more precisely targeting the nuances and complexities of this topic. In doing so, we've both gained a more accurate picture of the gender landscape of the fandom and acknowledged and given voice to those who frequently find themselves ignored or erased by cis-normativity and the presumption that furry is a space exclusively for cis men.

Differences in Thoughts About Gender

In this section, we consider the open-ended responses of furries in a 2021 online survey to questions assessing their thoughts about gender in the fandom. The questions themselves asked furries whether they've ever

---

women may be more flexible (or find it more acceptable) to experiment with the expression of their gender identity than cis men, a point also suggested in the next paragraph's findings.

[20] Findings from a 2022 study found that trans furries tended to identify even more strongly with their fursonas than did cis furries, lending further credibility to the idea that furries—especially trans furries—are especially likely to use their fursonas as a means of exploring or expressing elements of their gender identity that they might otherwise struggle to express in day-to-day life, a point made directly by some participants in the open-ended data later in this chapter.

thought about their gender in fandom spaces and, if so, to describe the content of those thoughts, including the frequency with which they happened and what emotions the thoughts provoked. Their responses were coded and organized, with some of the most common or recurring themes extracted. We present these themes alongside representative quotes from participants to minimize the amount of interpretation or bias that we, as researchers, may inadvertently introduce when presenting our findings.[21]

Frequency of Thoughts about Gender

We begin our look at the open-ended data with a fairly simple question about gender-related thoughts: how frequently do thoughts about one's gender arise? Consistent with our findings on race and ethnicity in the fandom (see Chapter 14), as well as with broader psychological research (McGuire et al., 1978), we would hypothesize that, in a fandom predominantly comprised of cis men, cis men should be less likely to think about their gender and gender issues in fandom spaces than cis women or transgender furries. This isn't likely the result of malice or any sort of social or political agenda on the part of cis men, of course. Rather, it's a product of how the human mind works: we tend to be fairly self-focused and our attention is drawn to differences, unique cases, and exemplars that stand out from the crowd. As such, if we differ somehow from the majority of people around us, we'll be keenly aware of this fact, even if it's something that others around us pay little attention to.

The tendency to see your own identity as normal, and thus to be able to avoid thinking about it and how it impacts your life, is one of the key markers of privilege. White people seldom have to think about race, cis men seldom think about gender, straight people seldom think about sexual orientation, and right-handed people rarely have trouble finding scissors and can openers that work for them! It's only when this privilege is pointed out that we're made to question these facets of our identity, to recognize the ways our identity shapes our experiences. This can sometimes lead to defensiveness or feeling threatened as we lose the privilege of ignoring and assuming that our own experience is "normal."

Our open-ended data are generally in agreement with these principles. Among the 425 open-ended responses from cis men who mentioned frequency in their response, 76.7% indicated that they never, or only rarely

[21] It's especially important, as we point out in Chapter 14 on race and ethnicity, to ensure that participants belonging to marginalized groups have their words and experiences expressed as directly as possible, rather than merely being paraphrased, summarized, interpreted, or glossed over.

thought about their gender in fandom spaces, with only 11.1% indicating that they thought fairly often about their gender. In contrast, among the 54 open-ended responses from cis women who mentioned frequency in their responses, far fewer—53.7%—indicated that they never, or only rarely thought about their gender in fandom spaces, while far more—29.6%—indicated that they thought about their gender fairly often. Finally, the 219 transgender and genderqueer participants were the least likely (10.5%) to say that they never or only rarely thought about their gender in fandom spaces and were the most likely (51.1%) to say that they thought about their gender fairly often. In other words, cis men were the least likely to have thoughts about their gender in a fandom where they made up the majority of participants, while cis women, transgender people, and genderqueer people were more frequently aware of their gender in fandom spaces.

We can look beyond count data to see these themes expressed in the words of participants themselves. The group most likely to think about gender were transgender and genderqueer participants, who lack the privilege of considering themselves to be "normal." They also had the greatest variability in their responses. Many transgender and genderqueer furries indicated that their gender was a topic that came up to varying degrees in the fandom:

> *"It comes up less often now that more people are outwardly identifying as some form of nonbinary than before. Before, it came up awkwardly because I could be the sole "woman" at a furry event, except I didn't identify that way and others would still peg me as such."*

> *"Fairly often as I have both a male and female fursona, so I am able to RP through both."*

> *"I usually notice how the men vastly outnumber the women."*

> *"Being trans means gender is always in the back of my mind. Will I get clocked as trans in the restroom? Will my mom deadname me? Do I pass? Will I get misgendered? Its [sic] not just a fandom thing, it's a neutral, anxiety filled [sic] everywhere thing."*

However, there were some transgender and genderqueer folks for whom their gender is largely a non-issue,

"There's never really any discussion about my gender, so there aren't really any contexts I can think of when it comes up."

"Had it come up very occasionally."

or for whom the times when they thought about gender owed more to non-fandom causes than to something about the furry fandom itself:

"Doesn't come up with any furry topics, only stuff outside the fandom."

"It doesn't have any significance and [the] only reason it ever comes up is because English has grammatic [sic] gender, which my native language does not, so it complicates things with written language, and one must know what to write in order to accommodate whoever is being written about. Lack of grammatical gender would make life a lot easier."

Speaking to the psychological research we discussed earlier, it's rather notable that, for some, the fact that gender is a non-issue is because the participants actively surround themselves with others whose gender identity is comparable to their own, effectively making them like the majority cis men who rarely think about their gender. After all, they are frequently surrounded by other cis men:

"I don't often think about it because I try to surround myself with other gender-variant people."

"I find myself surrounded by other femme nonbinary people, so I don't think about it much."

In other cases, surrounding themselves with other transgender and genderqueer furries had the opposite effect, leading to frequent thoughts and discussions of gender, as the quotes below suggest:

"All of the time! The furry fandom is a queer space and I'm forever grateful to it for that. I have never felt more love and support about my gender identity than within this community."

"Extremely often. I, and almost all of my social circle, aren't cisgender and are at various stages of transition[,] so it's a topic that comes up a lot."

"Frequently. I have a lot of trans furry friends so gender is a common topic."

Finally, some transgender and genderqueer furries indicate that the frequency with which their gender arises is a product of their own exploration of gender and the fandom's encouragement of this self-discovery:

"Fairly often. For the past few years[,] I've tried a bunch of gender labels, and may continue to change them. I realize I'm likely to be considered a cis man even though that doesn't truly describe my relationship with gender, and that does make me self-conscious."

"I am always thinking about it because the fandom encourages discovery in my own experiences."

As might be expected, cis women were more likely to think about gender than cis men, though not nearly as often as transgender and genderqueer furries. Among cis women, there was considerable variability. Many indicated that they did not often think about their gender in fandom spaces, although some indicated that being a woman was something that they at least occasionally thought about, or that they were aware of why a woman's gender might be something a person might think about. Others indicated specific experiences that made their gender identity salient:

"I don't think much about my gender ever, much less in fandom spaces... since a fursona can be any gender we like, our genders as humans become irrelevant as a result."

"I don't think much about my gender, because there's no gender discrimination in our circle, okay."

"This does not come up for me. Many furries are cis women. But I know other individuals have it much harder."

"I had a few clients and such who thought I was male and didn't even bother correcting them."

"I get ignored for being a cis woman a lot."

Cis men, however, commonly expressed the idea that gender was simply a non-issue for them, something unimportant that they simply never had to think about in fandom spaces, or, if it did come up, only did so in very specific circumstances.

"I typically do not think about my gender. I don't consider it a good use of my time or mental energy."

"Don't think about it. Sometimes people ask me if I'm a man when they only can see my fursona name."

Other cis men spontaneously brought up their sexual orientation, despite it not being asked about in the question, lending further credibility to the idea that other facets of their identity (i.e., their sexual orientation) are more salient to them in the fandom than their gender is:[22]

"I don't think about my gender much in fandom spaces... I think about my sexuality more maybe."

"I really don't think about my gender. I'm a gay man and that's how I express myself. There's not usually a question about it."

Finally, those cis men who more commonly thought about gender indicated that they did so in a more abstract fashion (e.g., thinking about gender issues more broadly, rather than focusing solely on their own gender):

"Not specifically about my gender, but the topic of gender is usually around in a furry space."

---

[22] This may be due to the fact that, as we discuss in Chapter 16, there is considerable variability when it comes to sexual orientation in the furry fandom, such that no single category of sexual orientation is a dominant majority in the furry fandom.

"Almost daily and usually in a positive manner about my own. There are furries I interact with who struggle with their gender identity. I appreciate the confidence I have with my own gender."

Taken together, the pattern of responses is consistent with the idea that gender is generally not seen as being an overwhelmingly salient topic of thought for people in the furry fandom. That said, issues of gender seem to be the least salient for cis men, more salient for cis women, and particularly on the minds of transgender and genderqueer people in the furry fandom.

With this in mind, we next turn our attention to the valence of these gender-related thoughts—how people felt about these thoughts.

Valence of Thoughts About Gender

Consistent both with existing psychological research and with findings from our chapter on race and ethnicity (Chapter 14), we can ask whether the frequency-related findings noted above can foreshadow our findings pertaining to the valence of gender-related thoughts for furries. After all, if cis think relatively rarely about their gender in fandom spaces, it would seem to follow that gender is a fairly neutral topic for them. In contrast, among cis women, transgender, and genderqueer furries, who thought more frequently about gender in fandom spaces, it seems likely that these thoughts are more likely to be emotionally charged—for better or for worse.

Turning once again to count data extracted from the open-ended responses, the evidence suggests that, consistent with the frequency data, thoughts about gender tend to be fairly neutral (51.4%) or positive (38.4%) for cis men, with relatively few (10.1%) indicating that gender-related thoughts were generally negative.[23] In contrast, while a comparable number of cis women consider gender-related thoughts to be neutral (47.8%), they were equally likely to experience these thoughts as either positive or negative (26.1% for both categories). Finally, transgender and genderqueer furries

---

[23] It's also worth noting that only two-thirds as many cis men indicated anything about the valence of their feelings in their responses as said something about the frequency of their responses. Given that the most common response for cis men regarding frequency was to say that gender never came up, we could consider this to be an underestimation of the number of cis men who would consider gender-related thoughts to be neutral. In contrast, for cis women and transgender / genderqueer participants, participants were actually *more* likely to indicate the valence of their thoughts than they were to indicate their frequency, further contributing to the idea that gender-related thoughts are far more emotionally-charged for them than they are for cis men.

were by far the least likely to experience gender-related thoughts in a neutral fashion (18.9%); they were about equally likely as cis women to experience negative gender-related thoughts (22.9%) but were *especially* likely to experience positive gender-related thoughts (58.2%).

Once again, it's informative to substantiate these numbers with participants' own words. Let's take a closer look at the valence of responses from transgender and genderqueer furries. As mentioned earlier, they were the least likely of the groups to experience gender-related thoughts in a fairly neutral fashion, although some still did so, often pointing out that gender-related thoughts only arose in specific, rare contexts:

> *"It's fairly neutral as I'm masculine presenting."*

> *"Gender also does not come up often but when it does, it's usually positive or neutral. It's usually either people clarifying their identity if somebody makes a mistake or people supporting their friends in their experience or exploration of their gender identity."*

> *"Gender is usually in a neutral space. It's [sic] feels similar to knowing someone's name. It usually comes up when introducing others or when I inevitably trip up on pronouns. One refresher later and everyone's back on the same page."*

> *"Normally[,] it's a neutral manner. I think about it when I have to introduce myself of [sic] make a bio for a social media. Sometimes[,] I think about it in regards to characters as well."*

Several transgender and genderqueer furries also indicated that thoughts about gender were neutral not because of a lack of emotionally-charged feelings, but rather due to a complex interplay of positive and negative events:

> *"Being trans in the furry fandom is a multifaceted experience, especially presenting as a woman."*

> *"My own experiences with my gender have been positive. But I have seen transphobia in online spaces and speak out against it and let others in the community know about bigots."*

"Seeing NB people come up is usually neutral. Seeing men is a mix of neutral and negative. It comes up in far too many contexts to list out."

"All the friggin' time. At least on a daily basis. Whether it's positive, neutral, or negative depends a lot on who in the fandom I'm around."

"All three. Positive because we have a lot of representation, neutral because most people don't give me crap about it but also negative because right leaning [sic] furs will be abusive about it."

"I find that because of my gender[,] I tend to be more wary of making new friends, in case they aren't accepting of it, but I also love using my experience with gender to make a ton of fun OCs!"

"Mix of both, Mix of positive and negative, most of the fandom is super open to it until you upset them, in my experience."

"The Fandom helped me explore my gender through my characters. However[,] I've also faced my fare [sic] share of gatekeepers, and ignorance, due to how big the community is."

Genderqueer and transgender participants reported about as many negative thoughts as neutral thoughts. Many of these negative thoughts were tied to concerns about prejudice from within the furry fandom:

"Negative. It seems like people hate that I'm not born a woman and still play a female character, like somehow that's offensive to them."

"I do think that generally though there is still a lot of homophobia and misogyny in fandom spaces though, and if I did interact more with fandom spaces I feel like I would receive some amount of hate/pushback for being not only biologically female but also Non-binary."

"I am aware at all times that I am perceived [as] male and will be reacted to by unfamiliar women with a degree of uncertainty. As such I try to take that into account when meeting new people."

"Again negative, they don't respect trans/queers people in this fandom."

For other transgender and genderqueer participants, the negative thoughts were tied to specific experiences they had gone through:

> *"Creepy men and chasers are the only people who bring it up as anything but a social glue thing. I try to ignore them. Around them, I feel greasy and unclean just by their questions."*

> *"As someone born female, gender comes up often. There is a large amount of white homosexual men (especially in a con space) who are willing to ignore or deflect you, especially if you haven't come with a costume. This is often negative. At my last [convention name], one of my roommates was a white gay man. He didn't acknowledge me for THREE DAYS until we both ended up in our hotel room together for a few hours and he said a few words to me."*

> *"I have experienced significant harassment and sexual assault in furry spaces related to my sex and gender expression. It is usually negative."*

Despite these negative responses, however, the most common emotional responses of transgender and genderqueer furries to gender-related thoughts in the fandom were positive. This was usually due to the fandom's positivity and acceptance as well as the much higher proportion of transgender and genderqueer people in fandom spaces:

> *"Positively, for it seems to be widely accepted as a gender expression and identity."*

> *"Everyone is open and accepting to each other about it, generally very positive."*

> *"Fandom spaces are the one place where I can let out my feminine side."*

> *"My groupchats [sic] and the fandom as a whole are very trans positive [sic], so I still feel positive about my gender."*

> *"It's nice to have a character that represents my actual gender because it's cheaper than surgery let's be real, so overall it's a positive experience in that regard."*

"It is generally a positive and affirming experience, def compared to 'irl'"

"Very positive. Noticing much more non-male people and so many trans people."

"Almost always positive, other trans people sharing their experiences (usually positive) and bonding over the joy of being the people we have become."

When it comes to cis women in the fandom, as with the frequency of their gender-related thoughts, there is considerable variability in the valence of their responses. Some thought about their gender only infrequently and therefore considered these thoughts to be neutral. These thoughts were often related to the experiences of others in the fandom:

"I do not think about my gender often in fandom spaces. When I do, it is usually in a neutral manner."

"I rarely think of my own gender, but I certainly think of others since trans furs seem to be common, at least in my own circles. I'd say it's NORMALLY positive or neutral, though these furs are often attacked and I see a lot of their responses in my circles."

Much more common to the responses of cis women, however, was an emotional response to being a relative minority compared to cis men—although the valence of these thoughts differed from person to person:

"Most of the times [sic] in a positive or neutral manner, related to being confronted with a lot of gay or bisexual males, which makes me feel kinda special. I never felt as [sic] a minority, which excites me."

"Not super often, though furry did give me the space to analyze my gender enough to know definitively that I am comfortable identifying as a cis woman. I would say that I think about my gender positively, but it can be discouraging when some folks seek to exclude those who are not cis men."

"A bit more often than I like to since (cis-)woman [sic] are kind of a minority in the furry fandom and especially at furcons [sic] just 15% of

all visitors at best. This is really saddening. I would feel more comfortable with more [women] around. I often read how others have been harassed or made uncomfortable in other ways by men. Both in real life and online."

As we saw with cis women, cis men tended to consider the category of "neutral" as generally synonymous with the idea that gender infrequently comes up or is largely irrelevant to them:

"I do sometimes think of my gender, but never for long, so it's mostly just neutral."

"It's more of a background thing that's more neutral to me. Honestly what's in my pants or how my brain is wired is for me and me alone unless I [sic] want to share it."

"Neutral because it's not a part of who I am, it's simply what I am biologically."

"Neutral, Im [sic] a dude, a party loving [sic], beer chugging [sic], weed smoking [sic] dude. I never really deal with that in any context."

Even among cis men indicating that their gender-related thoughts were positive, it was often (though not always) in a fairly non-distinct or general sense, often characterizing neutrality or the non-existence of a problem as positivity:

"Fairly positively, since the fandom has helped me make more male friends than at any point in my life."

"Rarely, has no impact so I suppose that's also positive."

"Gender is neutral, or perhaps positive if the stance of 'You do you, I'll support you because YOU are nice' is considered positive."

On the relatively rare instances when cis men reported negative feelings related to the topic of gender, it was usually characterized by disliking difficult or complex conversations about gender or due to perceived attacks against cis men, masculinity, or males:

"I try not to, its [sic] a complicated nebulous thing I avoid dealing with."

"Negative sometimes. This happened [sic] every time I see radical feminist comments, hatred of men and the hate speech against male gay furry on furry fandom, in social media. These make me feel upset of [sic] my sexuality sometimes."

"Negatively[,] usually. There's a lot of animosity against men, because of a large problem of harassment in the fandom."

It's also worth noting that the gender-related thoughts of some cis men were grounded less in thoughts about their gender and more in the observations or broader notions of gender as experienced by others struggling with their gender identity in the fandom:

"The topic of gender isn't too common, except for my friend complaining that they want to be female."

"I find that with the increasing level of non-binary and trans furries that are within the fandom as people discover themselves, that you find your gender to matter a bit. I find it's both had positive and negative responses, as in [the] context of life experiences."

"I usually don't think much about it, but when I do it's either in a neutral or negative manner. It's neutral when I think of how the furry fandom allows for [the] exploration of gender identity and sexuality with fewer limitations than other spaces. It's negative when I hear about the harsh discrimination some artists face based on their gender or the dismissals they receive from the community."

To summarize: the open-ended data on the valence of gender-related thoughts is largely consistent with our findings concerning the frequency of gender-related thoughts. Cis men in the fandom tend to think the least about gender and, when it does arise, tend to think about it in a largely neutral fashion, except when they think about the gender-related struggles of others in the fandom or perceive hostility toward men. Cis women tend to be somewhat comparable to cis men, sharing many of the same sentiments (e.g., gender not coming up often), although they are more likely than cis men to experience negative thoughts, often driven by the awareness of their status as a numerical minority in the fandom. Finally, the thoughts of transgender and genderqueer furries are by far the most emotionally charged. For them, positive thoughts are by far the most common, often related to the presence of similar others in the fandom as well as feelings of acceptance in the fandom that contrast against their day-to-day lives. Many transgender and genderqueer furries also have negative gender-related thoughts, often driven by concerns about prejudice in the fandom or informed by specific negative experiences. Perhaps most telling, even the "neutral" gender-related thoughts of many transgender and genderqueer furries are less about apathy or lack of relevant experience and more about the averaging of positively- and negatively-charged thoughts.

Themes and Experiences Regarding Gender in the Furry Fandom

Having now looked at both the frequency and valence of gender-related thoughts among furries, let's take a closer look at some of the most common themes and experiences described by participants. Doing so may help to illuminate the most pressing issues, common concerns, blind spots, and problems pertaining to gender in furry spaces that might otherwise go unspoken or unheard when we look at aggregate, statistical data.

Let's start by considering the most common themes to emerge in the gender-related thoughts of transgender and genderqueer participants, as they are the groups most likely to think about gender. Coinciding with our earlier finding that these thoughts are more likely to be positive than negative or neutral, the single most common theme to emerge by far was an appreciation for the furry fandom as an LGBTQ+ supportive space, especially as many transgender and genderqueer furries find others like them in the fandom:

> *"I definitely notice that furries tend to be far more aware and respectful of transgender people's pronouns than non-furries, who frequently misgender me despite my having come out to them, and despite my obviously male name... Furries tend to call others they/them if they're unsure, which is really considerate."*

> *"I feel I'm able to express my gender most comfortably in the fandom[;] if it wasn't for the fandom I'd probably still be very lost, confused and uncomfortable about my gender but the fandom has allowed me to see how others can experience gender differently [and] it has really helped me discover myself and be able to be me."*

"I tend to think about it more in fandom spaces since it is a talking point among other trans friends I have in the fandom... the majority of the time it's overwhelmingly positive and I've made plenty of friends who are also trans men and trans women, it often comes up as we compare our progress in transition and share advice."

"Most of my friends are trans people in the furry fandom, so we feel comfortable talking with one another about gender. This is a community where it just feels normal to be openly queer."

"I have found a group of others like me (queer people of color) and we've made a safe spot for others who also have the same racial and LGBT problems as us. That's one positive that this has granted me. Others come to us for advice or even help with related and unrelated problems."

Despite this overwhelming positivity, however, the second-most common theme when it comes to the gender-related thoughts of transgender and genderqueer participants involves stigma directed toward transgender and genderqueer people. This manifests in a variety of ways. For example, many furries described a general sense of transphobia in the fandom:

"I feel negatively about my gender because I am unable to start transitioning right now, so I am frequently perceived as a woman even though I am a trans man. I experience misogyny when people think I'm a woman and transphobia when I correct people and tell them I'm a man. Discrimination against trans men is often downplayed or even encouraged in the queer community, so I often don't feel welcome in these spaces."

"My gender expression is a large way that I interact with the fandom, and to be honest[,] there are many people in the fandom who are transphobic or unkind towards trans people. I deal with especially the type of problems trans men face, which are their own unique problems on top of generalized transphobia."

"I've dealt with transmisogyny, being ignored by cis guys, talked over, treated as lesser and had any concerns hand waved away."

"I have estrogen-coded hardware and fit a feminine sexual stereotype, and on feminine days seeing 'women' in general get harassed, talked over, objectified, and belittled makes me feel unwelcome in some fandom spaces where that's happening."

"I don't describe myself as agender for fear of being called 'transtrender'. I try to never bring it up, unless it's with my closest friends."

Some participants indicated that transphobia wasn't necessarily part of the broader furry fandom, but, rather, it was a product of specific groups or specific individuals in the fandom:

"While this Fandom is very lgbtq+ friendly, I have seen some transphobic and homophobic furries so I do worry from time to time about being disrespected."

"I generally do not think of gender in fandom spaces at all, except in places where NB or female people have obviously been made to feel unwelcome."

"Unfortunately, there is transphobia in the furry community! There's so many accepting people, and granted, way more than nonfurry communities, but there's still some bad apples out there."

When it comes to how transphobia manifests, respondents indicated numerous different ways. For example, one common way was through being treated differently once people learned about the participants' gender identity:

"While I'm relatively accepted these days, transphobia remains common in the fandom and I lost a stunning number of people I thought to be friends upon coming out seven years ago."

"I am always worried about telling people [about the participant's gender identity] in fear of being judged for it."

"Being trans is a significant part of all my life so it makes its way into fandom spaces. I am not often met with direct hostility but sometimes feel my being trans does drive certain groups of people away."

"Thanks to the misogyny in the fandom I can walk through an LGBT furry club night and everyone will part out of the way because they don't like breasts. People avoided me up until the [sic] found out I wasn't a woman and then suddenly they get very buddy buddy[.] Straights would try to message me but once they found out I was trans they would stop talking to me."

Another common observation was the fetishization of trans people, reducing them to little more than a sexual object:

"Sometimes theres [sic] transphobia and misongy [sic] within the fandom presenting as fetishistion [sic] of trans masc folks and a distaste for afab[24] people."

"Being seen as female in the furry fandom is annoying, because you'll either be seen as a sex object, or be seen as faking if you're trans."

"No matter how enlightened we try to think we are, societies [sic] bigotry still exists. People are people, even in furry spaces, and the objectification of certain genders does persist, sometimes even in ways that doesn't [sic] happen in mundane society. Primarily it comes up in artwork, where it's a fine line to walk between appreciation and objectification, especially when it comes to female and female-adjacent genders."

Other participants pointed to derogatory language as an example of transphobia, including the use of transphobic slurs and other incendiary language:

"In the fandom, I had no problem with it. Except [for] the couple of toxic classic straight people that are bad, or people that still think cunt-boys are a thing."

---

[24] AFAB is an initialism meaning "assigned female at birth."

"It's often a theme that I get called a futa, trap or shemale because I am transgender but I refer to myself as female."

"The intersex community has had a hard fight pushing back against how comfortable the furry fandom has been with using the word 'hermaphrodite'."

"Some people tag art with transphobic (typically also interphobic) slurs, and that just sucks."

Another common theme among genderqueer and transgender furries, when it came to thoughts about gender, was the spontaneous mentioning of gender in online spaces, sometimes for better, other times for worse:

"In online situations, I prefer to present and be viewed as 'male' or 'neutral', as this feels safer and puts space between my online and 'irl' lives."

"People often put their pronouns or gender identity in their profile I hate to out myself to anyone, because everyone would subconsciously try to figure out my biological sex. I usually just say that I'm cis and that's it."

"I came out as 'it' and almost got banned from the game Furcadia because everybody hated me. That's negative to not be able to be yourself."

"Sometimes people may misgender me and call me a "she" when my pronouns are they/them but everyone corrects themselves. There was a time where [sic] a fur said "no you're a girl you have breasts..." he got banned from a lit [sic] of chats for being rude to lots of people who are trans or gender fluid. Thankfully the admins saw his behavior and did something about it."

"Women, both trans and cis, are frequently harassed when interacting online and this is only a little better in furry spaces."

"When I was in the closet and had to perform as female, I felt like I stuck out like a sore thumb and just wanted to be "one of the guys". Now that I'm one year into HRT, I feel as if I'm in a weird no man's land. I keenly

want to pass as male, but I often don't. It hasn't been a huge issue recently - I'm not going to any conventions/meetups right now until covid [sic] has been dealt with, and in online furry spaces it's very easy to pass as male. Time will tell when I feel comfortable enough to go back to conventions and meetups if I pass."

"Physical spaces- often negatively, as passing and presenting myself as a woman is a constant challenge and reminder of how I'm 'different' and the risks that come with this, plus being seen as an openly trans person and how everything I do and say reflects people's direct association with trans folks as a whole. Online spaces- varies greatly depending on the interactions and spaces. It's easier to safely find and interact with other non-cis folks and express myself as myself."

As a final theme worth mentioning, transgender and genderqueer furries also indicated that having a fursona can prove beneficial with respect to exploring and validating one's gender identity:

"It is also nice to only use my furry name and to never have to use my legal name (deadname) or a name that might not fit the perceived gender, my furry name is neutral."

"I do think about it since my character represent [sic] me in my gender. And being genderfluid, or trans, is not easy in real life in workplaces and such at times."

"When I was first exploring my gender, I used my fursona to do so. I take that as a positive, as it did help a lot."

"It's nice because I can use my fursona to represent what I wanna be and how I wanna look."

"Also, because of my male fursona, people in the fandom often correctly assume my pronouns are he/him, which is something I rarely get to experience otherwise."

It should be noted that while some cisgender and transgender furries indicate that a fursona may be an important part of their gender identity, evidence from at least one of our other studies indicates that fursonas might be an especially important part of transgender furries' sense of self. In a 2022 study of online furries, participants were asked to indicate, on a 7-point scale, how strongly they identified with their fursonas. While both cisgender and transgender furries scored high on this scale on average, transgender furries scored significantly higher as a group (6.3) than cisgender furries (5.7). This suggests that while a fursona is often a particularly important part of a furry's identity (e.g., imbued with facets of one's personality, appearance, and other attributes—see Chapter 7 on fursonas), for transgender furries its function as a means of expressing or validating their gender identity may make it especially important.

Next, we turn our attention to cis women and some of the predominant themes in their gender-related thoughts. The most prevalent of these themes is a topic already hinted at earlier in this chapter by cis men and cis women alike—being keenly aware of the fact that cis women are a numerical minority in the fandom relative to cis men. The impact of this awareness varies considerably from positive to neutral to negative, depending on the participant:

> *"Ever since I discovered that the fandom is almost entirely composed of men, I found myself thinking about gender a bit more."*

> *"[I] sometimes get singled out as an anomaly in the fandom."*

> *"Even though I'm a cis woman with long hair, large breasts, big hips, a high pitched [sic] voice, etc., I still get called a man if these signifiers are not visibly apparent (e.g. posing lying on my belly, or if I have my hair pulled back, or in text-based online chats where people can't hear my voice)."*

> *"Men are still assumed to be the default. This is reflected in a lot of furry slang terms, like 'good boi' or even just general usage of dude, bro, guy, etc. Almost all of the major furry clothing/underwear brands are run by men and cater exclusively to men, specifically with underwear like jockstraps and boxers."*

> *"My gender, female, seems to be less valued than males, this is due to seeing MANY more popular people being gay and male."*

"A bit more often than I like to since (cis-)woman [sic] are kind of a minority in the furry fandom and especially at furcons just 15% of all visitors at best. This is really saddening. I would feel more comfortable with more [women] around."

The second-most common theme expressed by cis women in their responses is conceptually linked to the first theme, pertaining to feelings of discomfort in the furry fandom and a sense of insecurity about whether or not the participant belongs in the furry fandom. This finding is again consistent with research on prejudice and stereotypes suggesting that even without outward hostility and explicit endorsement of stereotypes by others, simply being aware of one's status as a numerical minority can instill feelings of doubt and concern that one doesn't belong. For cis women in the study, this often manifests as feeling overlooked and ignored, but also includes having their belongingness in fandom spaces challenged by others:

"I notice that the fandom is overwhelmingly male dominated [sic], and admittedly it does make me feel a bit left out."

"A lot of furry artists only draw men or are only practiced at drawing male characters."

"Sometimes I wonder if I receive positive or negative treatment just because I'm a girl... People often make jokes or bring up the fact I'm a woman and that I'm 'rare' and it feels weird. Sometimes I'm the only woman in a group and I feel like the odd one out."

"I often get ostracised because of my gender, to the point that I am made to feel unwelcome in certain spaces."

"I don't feel it effects [sic] anything most of the time, but I have felt disrespected and excluded for being a woman in a predominantly male and gay fandom. Female friends of mine have had much worse experiences than me though."

The third-most common theme for cis women has to do with attracting negative or unwanted sexual attention and being harassed for not being considered attractive (e.g., to a gay man):

"Mostly neutral but online discussions about gender in the fandom have put it in a negative light a bit. Between women who are either harassed or sexualized for their gender in a fandom that claims inclusivity while treating them like intruders in a [sic] Lgbtq+ space."

"Being female brings a lot of unwanted creepy attention, but it's manageable."

"I do remember that, when my presence in the furry fandom was online, it was expected that there weren't any female furs. As conventions became more accessible to public attendees, female-presenting attendees were often made to feel unwelcome in some areas of con space like gaming and artist alley [sic]. As time went on, and attendee rates increased, this view became antiquated. These days I usually only deal with sexual harassment or gender bullying when people are incredibly intoxicated."

"I haven't experienced this myself, but I have heard of experiences of females being discriminated against in the furry fandom because most of the community isn't attracted to females."

"With all the assaults happening at cons[,] it's scary to think what could happen to me if I'm not always surrounded with friends and people I trust."

"I've never had any negative experience, but it restrains me from leaving open forms of contact besides of [sic] work because of any freak that might be around."

Again, in a related vein to the previous themes, another common theme expressed by cis women involves sexism, misogyny, and outright hostility towards women in the fandom:

"The fandom is very male heavy [sic], and women are often overlooked, disliked, [and] discriminated against. Being a female furry can be difficult."

"I think about it a lot, and it often comes up in a negative context because as a cis-woman in a fandom dominated by gay men, furry is rampant with misogyny."

"My gender is an integral part of who I am as a person, so of course it influences my experience in furry. I'm glad to see a larger representation of women in furry these days. It was much harder to find positivity directed at women even just a decade ago. I still notice a great deal of misogyny in the furry community, both overt and unintentional."

"Women are hugely marginalized in the NSFW sector of furry, including art and fursuiting. It's common to see comments like 'ew vagina' or 'if only you were a guy.' Friends of mine who are fursuiters have been rebuked when the person they were interacting with discovered the person in the costume was a woman."

"Recently I've been thinking about it more as more and more women are coming forward about the misogyny they face."

Several participants also indicated that sexism, misogyny, and hostility tend to be especially bad, or unique, to online contexts:

"Sometimes on Twitter etc., you see women being talked about negatively in the fandom, although for the most part[,] it's meta discourse [sic] / second hand [sic]. That's the only time I think about my gender in a negative manner in regards to the fandom."

"Again, one of the perks is that I usually don't unless I come across some misogynistic rhetoric online."

"I think about it sometimes cause just like how there aren't a whole lot of POC in the fandom, there aren't a huge amount of women either. I see this come up a [sic] mainly on social media sometimes when other (male) furries talk about how the fandom is a "male space" or other misogynistic comments. This doesn't really bother me as much as the racial comments do but hey it's still messed up."

"A more negative context is mainly via social media, in where [sic] women in the fandom are often harassed by straight men within the fandom."

Finally, though to a lesser degree than transgender and genderqueer furries, cis women also recognized the potential for exploration of one's gender identity in fandom spaces, including through the ability for a person to express a different gender identity through their fursona:

"Every so often I wonder if I truly identify as female while in a fandom space. This is a positive feeling as I feel comfortable exploring different aspects of my identity. Someone may make a post about how some days they feel more masculine, some days more feminine, and I wonder if that is similar to what I feel."

"I explore my gender through my fursona and like to keep my gender private in the fandom outside of locals."

"It's another character/actor situation. Most of the time, I only see the suits/sonas (I only have a couple of friends in the fandom), so I don't have any kind of preconceived notions about who they are."

Finally, let us consider the responses of cis men and the most common contexts in which gender-related thoughts arise, and the themes that emerge within them. The single most common theme by a significant margin is a recognition that cis men comprise the majority of the fandom and acknowledging that a certain amount of privilege follows from this fact:

"The Furry fandom is quite male-dominated anyway, so I'm comfortable being a cis-gender male."

"The community seems fairly male-focused and I enjoy being a part of that."

"The fandom is highly made up of men, with little to no women in sight. Unless it's somebody identifying as a woman if they're transgender."

"Honestly not a lot and mostly just when talking to other people who seem to have issues with their gender (e.g. transgender). It made me realize how little importance I place on this particular subject for my own life and I guess I'm just glad I got dealt a hand that I'm content with playing."

"Cis male privilege is very much a thing."

"I don't feel an issue with being a cis-male myself. I enjoy discussing the experience of people who aren't cis because it is an interesting topic, while my gender is kind of the most boring and usually associated with the worst kind of people. Aside from that baggage, which is extremely rarely brought up, it still feels like easy mode."

The next-most common gender-related theme expressed by cis men pertains broadly to issues of sexual orientation and sexuality. Speaking to sexual orientation first, many cis men spontaneously brought up their sexual orientation or the preferred gender of their sexual partners when asked about their gender, despite there being no mention of sexual orientation in the original question, suggesting that for at least some cis men, their sexual orientation may be an inextricable part of their gender identity:

"I definitely identify as male on [sic] fandom spaces. That comes up a lot because I interact with mostly other gay furries."

"I never think of my gender as an issue. It might be worth noting that as a male homosexual my focus lies solely on male anthropomorphic characters."

"I would say I think about my gender semi-regularly, maybe once or twice a week...It typically comes up when talking about sex or sexual partners."

"Usually I only think about my gender in the context of dating, I am straight and I will only accept one gender, traditional woman [sic]."

"I'm not straight so I don't care much about females in the Fandom, I don't find interest in female fursuiters. Its [sic] nothing like I don't like them, I just like males, and they interest me more."

"Very often. There aren't a lot of straight males, so it feels I have to put on my fursona in order to better fit in."

"Well since I'm gay it's a positive experience, I'm not an incel either so there's not much to say other than, nice cock."

Speaking about the theme of sexuality more specifically, many cis men indicated that thoughts of gender were often associated specifically with erotic thoughts or pornography:

"Gender is usually talked about positively, often alongside sexuality."

"I sometimes think about my gender in fandom spaces. It comes up often when relating to adult topics."

"Never unless it's related to a particular search I want to do on e621."[25]

"Not super often. Usually, the babyfur scenes can get pretty teasing, so gender teases arise sometimes (you're a girl, oh what a sissy etc). Generally positive and erotic. Doesn't come up exceedingly often though."

"It's usually neutral. In one hand, males are more tolerated by the [sic] society. On the other hand, I always admire females as they have [a] stronger orgasm."

Adding further to the link between thoughts about gender and sexuality, a small number of cis men also indicated that thoughts about gender reminded them of times when they had been the target of unwanted sexual advances (e.g., a straight man being hit on by a gay man):

"As a particularly large (tall, well built [sic]) guy in the fandom, it has made me a target for unwanted sexual advances."

"Rarely, but when I do it's because I'm thinking about how to avoid getting flirted with."

A third common theme expressed by cis men on the subject of gender coincides with the earlier theme of recognizing a sense of privilege or advantage that comes from comprising the majority of the fandom—recognizing that, by extension, there are others in the fandom who are less

---

[25] e621 is a website where furry-themed art is displayed. It is often associated with pornographic artwork specifically, with a tagging system that allows users to easily search for fetish-specific content.

fortunate and the responsibility of being a good ally to those people, especially if they are friends:

> *"18 years ago, jokes about sexual orientation or transgender were a lot more common. I am well aware of that so nowadays I try hard to be respectful of people's choices (gender, pronouns) and not get into fights about it."*

> *"A significant portion of my friends are trans in some capacity so it's generally a lot of supporting each other."*

> *"I would understand someone who is still struggling to find themselves, so I try to avoid possibilities of discomfort among others. Treating someone the way I wanted to be treated is always a thing for me."*

> *"I don't think it's really ever come up much in fandom spaces at all. I do keep really positive in gender expression with others though, and I try to be more inclusive myself. Like working my brain that was raised used to gender to be better about using they/them and not gender my non-binary friends or to not misgender my trans friends because my dumb brain will hear a certain gender to a voice and assume that one. It's been a process of pretty much re-learning that stuff, but I strive to be better[,] especially for my friends."*

> *"Many others identify differently, so I have to be especially conscious of what I say or create, lest I carelessly offend or hurt someone that I have no intention of offending or hurting."*

A fourth common theme expressed in the gender-related thoughts of cis men pertains to participants' exploration of their own gender identity, sometimes aided by their fursona:

> *"I nearly never think about my gender. Furthermore, I never considered any gender to my fursona. Once someone asked me while I was in Fursuit which gender that character represents. I could not instantly answer because I never thought about that. So, there is a gap between my human gender identification and my fursona gender identification. For my fursona[,] I feel more gender-less/-neutral. but if I had to decide male/female it would also be male."*

"The fantasy elements of the fandom have allowed me to explore my gender in a safe environment, in which I feel more in control of how I present myself.; [sic] I think about my gender sometimes, usually by exploring my fursona as a woman. While fun, those explorations have reaffirmed my identity as a cis man."

"People don't always have their fursona stick to their gender in real life like I did. Some people even practiced cross-voicing to have better experience role playing [sic]."

"I'm positive with my own gender, but often explore what it would be like as another gender because it's fun."

A final common theme to emerge among the gender-related thoughts of cis men pertains to broader discussions about the politics of gender and sexism, both in fandom spaces and more broadly. For some, these thoughts tend to be fairly progressive, emphasizing opposition to traditional gender norms and aversion to bigotry and sexism directed toward women and trans people:

"I'm personally comfortable with my gender assigned at birth, but I have a strong distaste for many of the gender roles and conventions that society forces on people and would be happy to see them moved on from."

"I find it invaluable to question the imposed roles of gender and find inspiration in people who question and defy them."

"I feel more comfortable identifying as male in the furry fandom than outside of it. I don't feel like the common expectations of men are included in the fandom (liking sports, beer, cars, etc.)"

"The negative I experience basically strictly in relation to others. As an example, the most common source of shame from my gender comes from gay misogyny- by this, I mean things such as that women or vaginas are disgusting, or that men are superior. This complete lack of acknowledgement [sic] of the presence of female voices makes me extremely uncomfortable and even shame that I share my gender and community with someone who thinks that."

"Concerns about misogyny come up in several furry sites--particularly in the past 4 years or so."

"Mostly Cis people come up in a negative manner. It's almost always justified as Cis people usually throw up in arms whenever gender non Conforming [sic] people or anyone else make light of their treatment by Cis people."

For other cis men, their thoughts reveal feelings of defensiveness and the perception of being targeted for being cis men:

"Tend to think about it too often. Tend to feel I'm in a minority amongst furries, and that being cisgender and straight is in cases considered a bad thing."

*"Being male is a *HUGE* detriment these days, particularly in liberal minded [sic] social groups who have chosen to denigrate anyone who is male for no other reason than their gender."*

"Frequently. Negative sometimes. This happened [sic] every time I see radical feminist comments, hatred of men and the hate speech against male gay furry on furry fandom, in social media. These make me feels [sic] upset of my [sic] sexuality sometimes."

"I am sometimes disappointed in the community, and I feel as though there are some spaces where I may not be welcomed because I am cis-gender. However, this is not at all exclusive to the fandom."

"I get a little concerned sometimes when there is pushback against males by certain gender activists present at events, or pushback when I misidentify somebody's gender since it can be a very touchy subject for some based on their experiences, but otherwise, it's not usually an issue."

Cis men in the furry fandom rarely think about gender-related issues, and when they do, it's often in a neutral fashion. Theme-wise, the most common themes are frequently less about their gender and more outward-focused, including recognizing (and often standing up to protect) women and trans people in the fandom, although it was also common for cis men to think about gender as a component of their sexual orientation or erotic interests. Finally, while some cis men saw the fandom's flexible and atypical gender norms as an opportunity to express and explore new aspects of their gender and to challenge existing societal gender norms, some saw the fandom as hostile toward cis men—although the prevalence of this latter theme was relatively rare.

The themes most commonly expressed by cis men and cis women in the fandom reveal a significant amount of complementarity. For one thing, many cis men recognize the privilege afforded by being the majority in the fandom while many cis women are keenly aware of their minority status and often express feeling unwelcome in the fandom. As another example, it was common for cis men to bring up erotic interests and sexuality in response to thoughts of gender, while for cis women the experience of being sexualized or receiving undesirable sexual attention often arose.[26] Finally, some cis men reported feeling attacked for being cis men because of the presumption that they were misogynist or would harass women; in contrast, it was a fairly common theme for cis women to describe experiences (first-hand or those of others they were aware of) of misogyny and harassment in fandom spaces.

In summary, the open-ended responses to our question about gender-related thoughts in fandom spaces reveal how important it is to listen to voices that are often downplayed, talked over, or simply drowned out when data are aggregated. The findings make it clear that cis men, cis women, and transgender/genderqueer furries do not think about gender in the same way, nor are their experiences related to gender issues in the fandom the same—both between these groups and even within these groups. Cis men are in a position where they rarely have to consider issues of gender beyond being occasionally mindful that others in the fandom have experiences that differ from their own. As a testament to this privileged position, gender is often a sexualized subject for cis men, tied to questions about sexual partners or erotic content. Cis women often struggle with feeling non-existent or like they don't belong in the fandom, as well as having to often deal with being the target of misogyny, sexism, and unwanted sexual attention. Finally, the experiences of transgender and genderqueer furries illustrate the double-edged sword that characterizes the furry fandom on gender issues. On the one hand, the furry fandom provides them with the opportunity to meet and forge highly positive communities of similar others who provide social

---

[26] As we pointed out above, a few cis men also reported experiencing unwanted sexual advances, typically as straight men receiving unwanted advances from gay men.

support and companionship in a world that's frequently hostile toward them. On the other hand, many transgender and genderqueer furries experience transphobia from within the fandom itself, either due to the actions of specific individuals or simply due to the fandom's predominantly online nature, which can both provide a way of distancing themselves from the harassment and make them more susceptible to it, as people are more willing to behave in ways online that they otherwise wouldn't in person.

In the following section, we'll finish up discussing our research on sex and gender in the furry fandom by looking at quantitative data regarding the fandom's attitudes and beliefs about some of the topics (e.g., misogyny, traditional gender roles, transphobia) introduced in this section.

Gender-Related Attitudes

Common sense dictates that if you want to measure sexist attitudes in a group of people, the easiest way would be to give a group of people a bunch of blatantly sexist statements to read (e.g., "women are inferior to men in every way") and ask them how much they agree with those statements. Then, you just need to look at their scores, with the people who scored highest on your scale being the most sexist and the people who scored the lowest being the least sexist. You could even figure out the average sexism score of the group and draw conclusions about how sexist the average group member is based on this.

Unfortunately, there's a flaw with this plan, something you may, by now, recognize as *socially desirable responding*. In a nutshell, people in a study know that they're in a study, and so they might think about why the researchers are asking these questions. They know that their responses will be scrutinized and that, depending on how they respond, it may not reflect well on them. As such, a group of participants that hold highly sexist or racist beliefs might nevertheless score low on a measure of sexism or racism that makes it clear what it's assessing—not because they don't agree with the items, but because they're not responding truthfully to avoid coming across as holding sexist or racist views.

Of course, researchers have devised use tricks to get around this problem, such as by making surveys anonymous. After all, people are more likely to admit to undesirable things when their responses can't be directly tied to them. Even so, when it comes to measuring attitudes and beliefs that don't reflect well on a person, participants may still feel compelled to downplay their true beliefs or respond in desirable ways—perhaps to avoid confronting these undesirable parts of themselves, or because they don't realize that these are their true feelings.

So how do we, as researchers, get around this problem of measuring some of the less savory beliefs that people may have?

A fairly common way is to accept that people may hesitate to outwardly support the most extreme of these beliefs and, instead, ask about more tepid or moderate versions of the same beliefs. This was the rationale behind the development of scales like the Modern Racism Scale (McConahay, 1986; McConahay et al., 1980), which asks participants to indicate their agreement with items that are relatively moderate (e.g., "Discrimination against Blacks is no longer a problem in the United States")[27] than more blatant racism-related items (e.g., "Immigrants are generally not very intelligent;" Akrami et al., 2000).

These reasons underpin our use of measures like the Ambivalent Sexism Inventory (Glick & Fiske, 1996), a measure of sexism that contains two subscales. The first subscale, hostile sexism, looks at more blatant, in-your-face sexism, the sorts of beliefs that are pretty blatantly sexist and which people might be unlikely to admit to having (e.g., "Women seek to gain power by getting control over men"). In contrast, the second subscale, benevolent sexism, comes across as far milder, and even contains items which, despite being sexist, might actually sound somewhat positive on their surface to some people (e.g., "Women should be cherished and protected by men").[28]

In a 2017 study of convention-going furries, we gave participants the benevolent sexism subscale of the ambivalent sexism inventory as a way of measuring sexist attitudes. Despite seeming to represent fairly "moderate" beliefs, one of the main reasons for our use of the scale was because research has shown that people who endorse benevolent sexist beliefs are also more likely to endorse more hostile sexist beliefs (Glick & Fiske, 1996). In other words, to skirt issues of socially desirable responding, it's possible to use the benevolent sexism inventory as a sort of "proxy" measure for more intense

---

[27] It should be noted that even "moderate" items like this are still fairly blatant by today's standards, with some suggesting that even these measures need to be replaced with subtler measures because of concerns about socially desirable responding in today's modern political climate (Migetz, 2004).

[28] If you're wondering how the second item counts as sexist, it's because the item taps into traditional gender norms of men as strong protectors and women as objects that should be valued and protected from being stolen or damaged by others—it contributes to the objectification of women and the placing of them on a pedestal, as something to be admired rather than as a person.

sexist beliefs. The questions were asked on a 7-point scale, the results of which are shown in Figure 15.1 below.

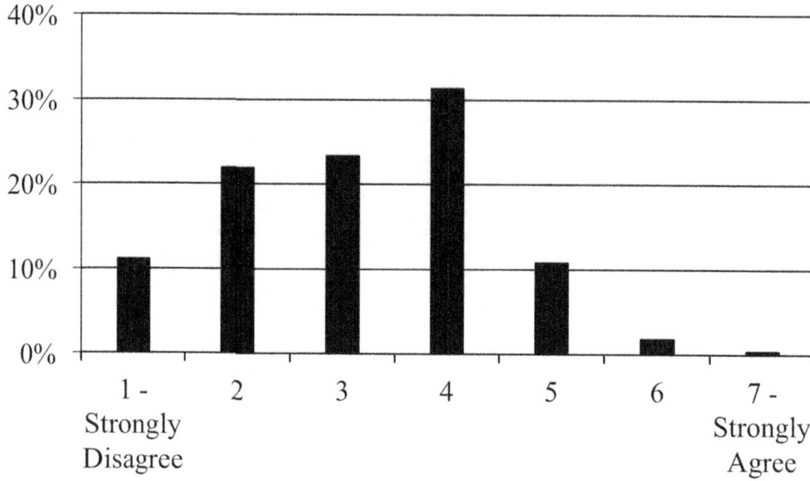

Figure 15.1. Average scores on a scale assessing benevolent sexism in a 2017 study of convention-going furries.

The aggregated data reveal that, as a group, relatively few furries scored extremely high on the scale. That said, approximately one-third of furries did score at the scale's midpoint, indicating that furries, as a group, were not entirely strangers to the sorts of beliefs that give way to more hostile forms of sexism. In follow-up analyses, it was found that furries' age was not associated with sexism (i.e., older furries were no more likely to endorse sexist beliefs than were younger furries). However, there were gender differences: cis men, as a group, were the most likely to endorse benevolent sexism (average score of 3.3) relative to cis women (2.9) or transgender/genderqueer participants (2.9). In other words, cis men were the group most likely to believe it was desirable to put women on a pedestal and engage in protective behaviors akin to those endorsed by traditional gender roles.

In fact, in the same study, we also included a measure of traditional gender roles, which asked participants the extent to which they felt that specific words, associated with stereotypes of men and women (e.g., "gentle," "dominant;" Bem, 1981; Hoffman & Borders, 2001), were better descriptors of men or women. While the overall results found no differences in the endorsement of these sex roles between cis men, cis women, and transgender/genderqueer participants in general,[29] we *did* find a significant positive correlation between endorsing benevolent sexist beliefs and traditional gender norms. While most furries, as a group, did not endorse traditional norms about gender, those who were more likely to do so were also more likely to endorse modestly sexist beliefs which, themselves, have been shown to predict more insidious and hostile sexist beliefs (Glick & Fiske, 1996).

Taken together, the above findings coincide with and substantiate many of the open-ended statements provided by participants in our studies. The available evidence seems to suggest that misogynistic, highly sexist furries are far from the norm in the fandom, something that was largely endorsed by the generally progressive—if somewhat occasionally blind to gender issues—statements of many cis men. Nevertheless, also consistent with what was reported by cis women and transgender/genderqueer respondents, there are those in the fandom who endorse more traditional gender roles and this may be a red flag for more insidious, blatantly sexist beliefs and misogyny, the type which manifests as stories of misogyny, harassment, and sexist behavior.

Let's end this section with a look at one last set of beliefs about gender in the fandom: the fandom's overall acceptance of transgender and genderqueer people. This research was conducted across a series of studies from 2018 to 2022, both convention-going and online, as part of a broader effort to better understand the experience of transgender people in the fandom and whether their experience coincided with, or differed from, reports from cisgender people.

To start, we look at data collected from four different studies in which participants were asked to estimate the level of acceptance of transgender, gay/lesbian, bisexual, asexual, and straight people in the fandom and then to indicate their own acceptance of each of these categories. Responses were provided on a 7-point scale indicating how strongly they agreed with the idea that each of these groups were accepted within the fandom. As shown in Figure 15.2, the data are quite promising across all studies, revealing that all of these groups, including transgender furries, were held in significantly high

---

[29] We also observed that older furries were more likely to endorse traditional women's roles (but not traditional roles for men), suggesting somewhat of a double-standard whereby older furries were more okay with the idea of men branching out and expressing non-stereotypical behavior, but still somewhat expected women to act in gender-stereotypical ways. In a later, 2019 study, we found, in line with these results, that older furries are less likely to identify as feminists than younger furries.

regard by furries on average, consistently scoring well above 6 out of 7 on the scale.

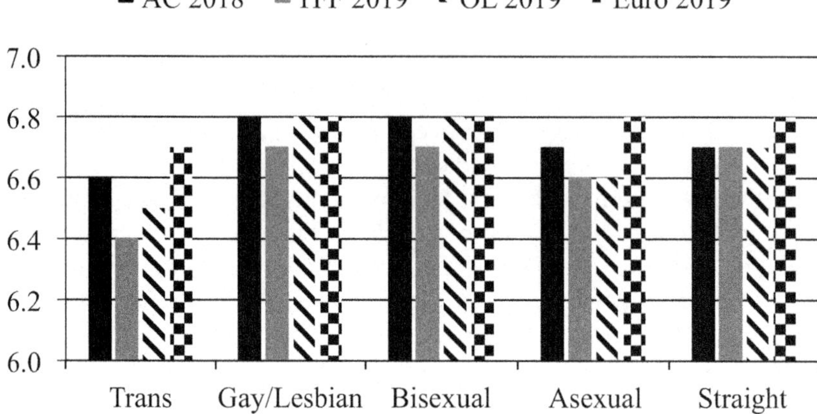

Figure 15.2. Average acceptance of different groups in the furry fandom across four different studies on a 7-point scale.

Follow-up analyses of these data revealed a few caveats for interpreting these findings. First, participants' actual regard for each of these groups was well in excess of what they estimated for the fandom as a whole. While furries estimated that the average furry would score approximately 6.0 in acceptance, the average furry scored significantly higher than that across all four studies. Or, to put it another way, furries may somewhat underestimate the rates of acceptance of transgender furries by the rest of the fandom.

Having said that, follow-up analyses also revealed a second finding: While transgender furries were generally held in rather high regard and highly accepted by the fandom as a whole, in every single sample transgender furries scored significantly lower in acceptance than the other groups. This suggests that while the fandom as a whole is generally quite accepting of people from all walks of life, they are less accepting of transgender furries than they are of gay/lesbian, bisexual, asexual, or straight furries.

There are at least two possible ways to interpret this difference. One possibility is that there isn't dislike of transgender furries relative to other groups, but rather less strong liking, with fewer people scoring "7" and, instead, scoring 5 or 6. Another possibility is that most people *did* score 7, but a handful of people expressed a strong dislike (e.g., a "1"), dragging down all of the 7s.

As it turns out, the answer is a little of both. Speaking to the former possibility, significantly fewer people chose the "7" option for transgender furries (86.5%) than they did for the other groups (gay / lesbian: 94.6%, bisexual: 93.9%, asexual: 90.0%, straight: 93.5%). Moreover, significantly more people chose the "1" option for transgender furries (2.2%) than did for the other categories (gay / lesbian: 0.5%, bisexual: 0.9%, asexual: 1.7%, straight: 1.3%). As the higher number of people choosing "1" for transgender people does not fully account for the reduced number of people choosing the "7" option, this suggests that there were not only more people choosing "1," but also more people choosing options like "5" and "6." In other words, there were more people openly opposed to transgender people than there were to any of the other categories, but also fewer people who were strongly in support of transgender people. Such findings are consistent with the open-ended reports of transgender participants discussed earlier who indicated that, while generally positive toward transgender people, is it not uncommon to encounter the occasional bigoted or transphobic person in furry spaces.[30]

Another noteworthy analysis came out of the 2019 studies, in which we compared prejudice toward transgender furries on another measure: a desire to maintain distance from them, including not wanting to live or work next to them. Specifically, we were able to compare the prejudice of convention-going furries—who were presumably more likely to interact with transgender furries face-to-face—and furries recruited online—who may be less likely to interact with other furries face-to-face. Analyses found that convention-going furries were less prejudiced toward transgender furries than were online furries, a finding again consistent with statements from transgender furries who often pointed out that they were more likely to encounter harassment and bigotry in online spaces.[31]

---

[30] Lest the presence of bigotry and transphobia in the fandom be disheartening, another analysis from the same dataset found that those who most strongly accepted transgender people in the fandom were also the ones who most strongly identified with the furry fandom. In other words, one could argue that those who are openly hostile toward transgender furries—and thus out of accordance with the fandom's overall norm of acceptance—are also the least-highly identified members of the furry fandom.

[31] It should be noted, however, that despite being more likely to be prejudiced toward transgender furries than convention-going furries were, online furries were

We would do well to remember the lesson we learned from our examination of the open-ended data: important nuances are often lost when minority voices are overwhelmed or erased in the aggregation of data. Keeping this in mind, we can also ask whether beliefs about the acceptance of transgender people in the fandom are perceived the same way by cisgender and transgender furries. Data from a 2017 online study reveal why this distinction is important: compared to cisgender furries (average score = 5.9/7.0), transgender furries were significantly less likely to say that transgender and gender-diverse people were accepted in the furry fandom (5.4/7.0). To be sure, the difference is a fairly modest one, suggesting that transgender furries still largely see themselves as accepted by the fandom as a whole. However, as we saw in the open-ended responses, people often have blind spots to issues that have little to no impact on their own lives. As such, cisgender furries may be somewhat unaware of the relatively rare instances of bigotry and transphobia that do occur in the fandom, or they may simply not appreciate how impactful such incidents can be in making someone feel unwelcome or unaccepted by the fandom as a whole.

As a final point, it's worth keeping in mind that the experience of minority groups in the furry fandom, be it based on race, ethnicity, or gender is often a double-edged blade. On the one hand, as we saw in Chapter 14 and the present chapter, many minority groups experience occasional harassment and prejudice from others in the fandom, something that might be made worse when contrasted against the fandom's espoused norms of acceptance and inclusivity. Despite the pain that such incidents create, however, many nevertheless find solidarity, comfort, and support in the fandom, especially when they're able to find like-minded others. For many in the fandom, especially those struggling against broader societal stigma, the fandom becomes a source of social support for them. Speaking to this point, data from our 2017 online study found that while most furries turn at least sometimes to other furries for help (and, in turn, help other furries), transgender furries were *especially* likely to do so. For these furs, it might be accurate to say that the fandom is far more than just a place to have fun and talk about their favorite furry content—it becomes a source of comfort, security, social support, and resilience.

Conclusion

As mentioned in our chapter on race and ethnicity (Chapter 14), this is not intended to be the final word on issues related to gender in the furry fandom.

---

still, as a group, overwhelmingly likely to be positive and accepting toward transgender furries.

As has been clear through the discussion of our many early attempts to study sex and gender in the furry fandom, Furscience has only just begun to delve into the complexities of these topics. In the future, we'd like to follow the threads of our current lines of inquiry. For example, we would like to better understand the potential blind spots and misunderstandings that contribute to apathy and inaction when it comes to pushing back against sexism and transphobia in fandom spaces (e.g., conventions and forums). Focus groups and other open-ended questions can also be targeted more precisely toward understanding the struggles (and benefits) that come with being a cis woman or a transgender / genderqueer person in the furry fandom. Finally, future studies should include questions about the barriers that sometimes prevent open discussion of gender-relevant issues in fandom spaces, including the belief that the furry fandom shouldn't be a politicized space (see Chapter 17 for more on this) or the belief that some grievances are not being heard (e.g., cis men who perceive hostility toward cis men in the fandom).

In addition to pursuing questions like these, we also hope to benefit from the continued feedback of furries and scholars alike, who generously give their time and energy to help us improve our methods and better understand the most pressing research questions waiting to be explored. As we continue to reach out and seek out further collaboration, we've no doubt that our approaches to, and understanding of, this topic will only get better.

References

Akrami, N., & Ekehammar, B., & Araya, T. (2000). Classical and modern racial prejudice: A study of attitudes toward immigrants in Sweden. *European Journal of Social Psychology, 30*(4), 521-532. https://doi.org/10.1002/1099-0992(200007/08)30:4<521::AID-EJSP5>3.0.CO;2-N

Barry, J. D. (2010). Red for danger? The effects of red hair in surgical practice. *BMJ: British Medical Journal, 341*(7786), 1304-1305. https://doi.org/10.1136/bmj.c6931

Bem, S. L. (1981). Gender schema theory: A cognitive account of sex typing. *Psychological Review, 88*(4), 354-364. https://doi.org/10.1037/0033-295X.88.4.354

Fausto-Sterling, A. (2000). *Sexing the body: Gender politics and the construction of sexuality*. Basic Books.

Glick, P., & Fiske, S. T. (1996). The ambivalent sexism inventory: Differentiating hostile and benevolent sexism. *Journal of Personality and Social Psychology, 70*(3), 491-512. https://doi.org/10.1037/0022-3514.70.3.491

Gross, S. (1999). Intersexuality and scripture. *Theology and Sexuality, 1999*(11), 65-74. https://doi.org/10.1177/135583589900601105

Hoffman, R. M., & Borders, L. D. (2001). Twenty-five years after the Bem Sex-Role Inventory: A reassessment and new issues regarding classification variability. *Measurement and Evaluation in Counseling and Development, 34*(1), 39-55. https://doi.org/10.1080/07481756.2001.12069021

Issenman, B. K. (1997). *Sinews of survival: The living legacy of inuit clothing.* UBC Press.

Kennedy, H. C. (1981). The “third sex” theory of Karl Heinrich Ulrichs. In S. J. Licata & R. P. Peterson (Eds.), *Historical perspectives on homosexuality* (pp. 103-113). Haworth Press.

Laqueur, T. (1990). *Making sex: Body and gender from the Greeks to Freud.* Harvard University Press.

Maglaty, J. (2011). When did girls start wearing pink?: A *Smithsonian Magazine* special report. *Smithsonian Magazine.* https://www.smithsonianmag.com/arts-culture/when-did-girls-start-wearing-pink-1370097/

McConahay, J. B. (1986). Modern racism, ambivalence, and the Modern Racism Scale. In J. F. Dovidio & S. L. Gaertner (Eds.), *Prejudice, discrimination, and racism* (pp. 91-125). Academic Press.

McConahay, J. B., Hardee, B. B., & Batts, V. (1980). *Modern Racism Scale (MRS).* [Database record]. APA PsycTests. https://doi.org/10.1037/t03873-000

McGuire, W. J., McGuire, C. V., Child, P., & Fujioka, T. (1978). Salience of ethnicity in the spontaneous self-concept as a function of one’s ethnic distinctiveness in the social environment. *Journal of Personality and Social Psychology, 36*(5), 511-520. https://doi.org/10.1037//0022-3514.36.5.511

Migetz, D. Z. (2004). *Reassessing the Modern Racism Scale in modern times.* [Unpublished doctoral dissertation]. The University of Tennessee, Knoxville.

Pickover, C. A. (2011). *The physics book: From big bang to quantum resurrection, 250 milestones in the history of physics.* Sterling Publishing.

Steele, C. M. (1997). A threat in the air: How stereotypes shape intellectual identity and performance. *American Psychologist, 52*(6), 613-629. https://doi.org/10.1037//0003-066x.52.6.613

Williams, W. L. (1992). *The spirit and the flesh: Sexual diversity in American Indian culture.* Beacon Press.

Chapter 16
Sexual Orientation in the Furry Fandom

Frances H. I. Henry, Anna Renee Henry

One of the most common observations about the furry fandom from those who've spent time in it is its openness and diversity concerning sexuality and sexual orientation. This chapter will take on a similar format to previous chapters (e.g., Chapter 14, Chapter 15) in discussing this diversity and inclusivity. As with the previous chapter on gender, we'll begin with a brief overview of academic work on sexual orientation, including recognizing that these concepts are in constant flux. Next, we'll look at the statistics when it comes to the prevalence of various sexual orientations in the furry fandom, followed by a deep dive into some open-ended responses from participants about how their interactions with the furry community have been impacted by (and impacted) their sexuality. Finally, we'll consider opportunities for further research on sexual orientation within the furry community.

Sexual Orientation—A Brief Primer

Just as we saw with gender, social understanding of sexual diversity and sexual orientation have undergone considerable change over the last century. Recognition of sexual diversity as natural and normal has become commonplace over the last 50 years, at least in the West. The internet has allowed members of sexual minorities (such as the asexual community) to share experiences, find words to express their feelings and desires, and advocate for more nuanced and complex understandings of sexual diversity.[1] Meanwhile, the modern scientific consensus is that same-sex behaviors are not only natural but common among both animals and human cultures (Roughgarden, 2009). In this section, we'll briefly review how we arrived at this point, taking a look at the diversity of sexuality in both the animal kingdom and throughout human history across cultures.

For centuries, homophobic discourse condemned same-sex sexuality as both bestial and unnatural (McFarlane, 1997). Some, like the Earl of Shaftesbury, saw same-sex sexual appetites as something uniquely human (Henry, 2019). Animals, in his view, are driven by "Nature," and would not

[1] Regardless of what your grandfather might say, sexual diversity is not a new phenomenon. While he may be more aware of different sexual orientations now than when he was a child, this reflects the increased awareness and tolerance for sexual diversity. Unsurprisingly, it's far easier for people to "come out" when they don't have to fear rejection, arrest, and institutionalization (with lobotomies and shock therapy)!

behave in any way that did not lead to reproduction. For others, illicit sexual behavior (particularly homosexuality, but also incest or bestiality), was deemed to be the result of a lack of human reason and restraint. Contrary to such condemnations of homosexuality as unnatural, however, same-sex behavior has been observed in three hundred vertebrate species, including over a hundred different mammalian species and at least 94 avian species (Roughgarden, 2009). Some species, such as geese, form same-sex pair bonds that can last more than a decade. Among swans, male-male pairs not only last for many years but frequently raise offspring together.[2] In other animal societies, same-sex coupling is common enough that it is the most common behavior, with male-female couplings being in the minority. Among bighorn sheep, for example, almost all males court and copulate with other males. Those who do not are labeled as "effeminate" and are considered aberrant by scientists. These same-sex pairs don't just take place among males, either: in some species (e.g., red deer and kobs), same-sex mating is more common among females than among males (Roughgarden, 2009). Unlike male-female couples, female red squirrels form pair bonds that include both sexual and affectionate behaviors and raise a single litter together. In short, despite the protestations of those who decry same-sex sexuality as unnatural or uniquely human, ample evidence from the animal kingdom suggests otherwise.

Another common argument in homophobic discourse is the logical fallacy of appealing to extremes: homosexuality cannot be tolerated because, if it were, everyone would partake in it, eliminating heterosexual couplings and dooming humanity to extinction. This is, of course, ridiculous.[3] Homosexual couplings among primates have been studied extensively since the 1970s and have led some investigators to question the assumption that all sexual behavior is tied to evolution and the propagation of species (Roughgarden, 2009). Studies among Japanese macaques and domestic sheep, for example, have shown that homosexual couplings are not the result of a lack of heterosexual options.

---

[2] Interestingly, male-male swan pairs are much more successful at parenting than male-female pairs: 80 percent of these pairs successfully fledge their young, compared to only 30 percent for male-female pairs! These pairs, while making up a minority of couples, nevertheless make up a sizable minority: 15% of geese and 18% of swans.

[3] For one thing, it either speaks very highly about the quality of same-sex coupling or about the dismal quality of heterosexual coupling to suggest that *everyone* would abandon heterosexual coupling if given the chance to engage in same-sex coupling!

So, what purpose does same-sex sexual behavior serve, if not for reproduction?[4] It's an oft-debated question (Roughgarden, 2009). From an evolutionary perspective, maladaptive behavior (e.g., squandering time and resources) phases out through evolution due to competition with competitors who are more streamlined and efficient. A corollary to this point is that if a behavior hangs around in an evolutionary context, it must, at the very least, not be maladaptive, but could also confer some sort of evolutionary advantage to the person engaging in the behavior or to their kin. This possibility has kept evolutionary psychologists speculating for decades.

The neutralist position argues that homosexuality exists as a harmless, neutral by-product of the evolution of other traits. According to this perspective, homosexuality serves no evolutionary purpose, but it also doesn't hinder evolution. Instead, it's seen as a by-product resulting from the evolutionary development of sexual pleasure: sexual pleasure evolved to encourage organisms to have sex, and this increased desire to have sex increased the likelihood of having offspring and the proliferation of an organism's genes.[5] Ultimately, the benefits of finding sex pleasurable were a net gain to the propagation of the species and, thus, hung around, even if its non-specificity meant that some people would find same-sex behavior to be equally (or more) pleasurable. From this perspective, same-sex behavior came along for the ride, as part of a different adaptation that improved the survivability of our evolutionary ancestors.

Another position, the adaptationist perspective, argues that homosexuality is not merely a neutral hitchhiker, but might, itself, be a beneficial adaptation. According to this perspective, behavior doesn't need to improve reproduction specifically to improve the species' adaptability and success: benefits may include improving social interactions and the building of communities, something that same-sex pairings may do. Same-sex behavior may increase social bonds among unrelated members of a group, improving the sharing of resources, reducing intra-species conflict, aiding in the integration of newcomers, and helping forge alliances and coalitions. Part of the reason why pairs of mated male swans are so successful in parenting is

---

[4] As a quick caveat before delving into this topic: it should go without saying that no one has to justify their existence. The reality is that asexual people and people who engage in same-sex behavior exist, regardless of how they fit into someone else's models or theories. We'd do well to keep this in mind to avoid invalidating everyone who does not engage exclusively in heterosexual behavior.

[5] With the assumption being that organisms who find sex to be pleasurable engage in more of it and have more offspring than organisms who don't find sex pleasurable.

because they use their collective size and strength to get the best territory and disproportionately more resources.[6]

To this point, we've largely discussed sexual orientation solely in the context of sexual behavior.[7] Humans, however, are an extremely complex and sophisticated species. Our behavior is inextricably intertwined with our identity and our culture, with its written language, art, and artifacts, all of which provide additional context for how people in the past have understood sexual behavior and how this understanding has shaped our current views and attitudes. Human societies have always displayed sexual diversity, although the nature of this diversity has varied greatly between cultures and over time (Bullough, 1976). But just as there have always been people romantically and sexually attracted to the opposite sex, there have always been people who were attracted to the same sex, to "both" sexes, and to no one at all. What differs between societies and cultures is how these people are understood and how they understand themselves.

Social institutions like religion and family, as well as socially constructed identities such as class and gender, play a huge role in how human sexual diversity is understood and treated within a society. Anthropologist Stephen O. Murray (2000) explored how various human cultures and societies throughout the world, both historically and in the present, understood homosexual relationships. He found broad trends, including relationships based on age (older / younger), gender roles (masculine / effeminate; butch / feminine), status or hierarchy (master/servant, teacher/student), and between equal adults. He considers how, in various cultures, same-sex sexual behavior has been understood as a sign of divinity, a rite of passage, an important social ritual, a sin, a crime, and an unmentionable act.

Traditionally, the narrative shaped by historians (in the West) was one of increasing persecution (Halperin, 2002). According to this thesis, past societies (especially the Greeks and Romans) recognized homosexuality and bisexuality as natural, and indeed, even as noble or praiseworthy. Even the

---

[6] Adaptionist scholars also point out that sexual diversity is often a mark of a species with a complex and sophisticated social system, and may well play a contributing role in the development of such a system!

[7] It's informative to distinguish sexual behavior, which refers to specific sexual acts a person engages in, from sexual orientation, which refers to desire or attraction. Sexual behavior, while largely correlated with sexual orientation (all else being equal, you are more likely to engage in sexual behavior with people whom you are attracted to than people whom you're not attracted to), is not perfectly correlated with it.

early church recognized that same-sex relationships based on love and commitment were blessed. However, beginning in the high Middle Ages and increasing particularly during the Enlightenment, there was a certified effort to suppress and eradicate any discussion or mention of sexual diversity. Many laws and homophobic accounts reveal a concerted effort to combat sexual diversity and establish sex as nothing more than a necessity for the purpose of reproduction. As a result of colonialism and religious evangelism, these repressive laws were spread throughout the globe, as demonstrated by the fact that many of the countries whose laws are most hostile to queer people forged their legal code from those of Europe.

Despite the prevalence of this narrative, sociologist/historian Michel Foucault threw a spanner into the works with the first volume of his *History of Sexuality* (Foucault, 1978, as cited in Henry, 2019). He argued that rather than a history of repression, the history of sexuality is a story of increasing awareness and discussion of sexuality. The emergence of communities and societies around sexual behavior in the 18th century led to an increasing tendency for people to see their behavior as an identity (Henry, 2019). According to Foucault, 19th-century scientists and scholars, with their need to label and understand everything, transformed human sexuality from a collection of acts (licit and illicit) that could be done by anybody, to an identity. As a result, binary labels such as "heterosexual" and "homosexual" emerged in the late 19th century and replaced the labels people had previously used to describe behavior.

Of course, societies don't *completely* abandon old prejudices based on new models or information (Bullough, 1976). Much of the old language of sin and crime associated with sexual diversity during the medieval and early modern period was then attached, no longer to the act, but to the category of the person believed to be singularly capable of them: the homosexual. The Victorian and early 20th-century scientists trying to understand and "help" homosexuals only worsened stereotypes. They popularized the notion of sexuality as a psychological drive rather than a moral choice, leading many societies to remove the death penalty for (consensual) homosexual behavior and replace it with institutionalization. However, since early scientists were drawing their conclusions from studying those who came to them to be "cured" of their homosexuality or by interviewing criminals in prisons, homophobic stereotypes were reinforced and baked into new laws, all while reinforcing the idea there were only two options for sexual orientation: heterosexual (seen as "normal") and homosexual (who was deviant).

One of the most important scholars to revolutionize the concept of sexual orientation was Alfred Kinsey. He keenly believed that sexuality was a spectrum, not a binary, and he and his colleagues demonstrated this in a series of ground-breaking studies of human sexual behavior (1948, 1953). They interviewed tens of thousands of men and women from puberty to old age about their sexual behavior and psychosexual responses. Based on the accounts of their sexual history, Kinsey then placed them on a scale, where 0 represented completely heterosexual and 6 represented completely homosexual. He had an additional category, X, of people who experienced "no socio-sexual contacts or reactions" (Kinsey et al., 1948/1998, p. 656). Unfortunately, Kinsey's work still showed the tendency to conflate sexual behavior with sexual orientation (Bullough, 1976), but it was nevertheless the model used for much of the scholarship on sexual orientation in the 50s, 60s, and 70s. Being based on behavior and not attraction, however, it didn't measure sexual orientation as we understand it today. Instead, under Kinsey's system, a man attracted to women who exclusively had sex with men, either for financial (prostitution) or situational reasons (same-sex schools, prison), would still be classed as a Kinsey 6 (completely homosexual). Conversely, a deeply closeted gay man who only had sex with his wife would be classed as a Kinsey 0 (completely heterosexual). Despite these flaws, Kinsey's work went a long way to combat the homophobic discourse on homosexuality (Halperin, 2002). By interviewing healthy, ordinary Americans, Kinsey's studies challenged the suggestion that homosexuality was predatory, unnatural, and associated with mental illness and despair.

Since the 1970s, the history of sexuality has become an established sub-discipline within history and related disciplines. As the LGBT movement began to gain widespread acceptance and legal protections, the discipline became more academically established and was able to divorce research from the political needs of the community. This, combined with a similar movement within the social sciences more broadly in the 1990s, focused on the ways that identity (gender, race, age, sexual orientation) is socially constructed. Rather than being an unchanging universal, this new focus recognized that social meaning and understanding are variable. This led to far more diversity in research topics, including the recognition that heterosexuality itself is socially constructed and reinforced (Blank, 2012). Just as the concept of homosexuality as an identity was born in the 19th century, so too was the concept of heterosexuality established as the "norm" against which sexual diversity was measured. While much of the research continued to focus on heterosexuality and homosexuality (expanded to include female homosexuality), bisexuality also began to be considered, rather than merely being lumped into the history of homosexuality.

However, the increased number of rights and the establishment of mainstream recognition of sexual diversity had another effect. Given the space and the freedom to explore and express themselves, queer people have greatly expanded their understanding of sexual orientation. This increased sense of community and connection allowed for more specific and accurate labels and descriptions. The internet allowed small populations to connect with each other and to organize, catalyzing this process. In the rest of this section, we will explore some of the new sexual orientations to arise from this work to get a better understanding of how the concept of sexual orientation is understood today.

We've already considered the early establishment of categories for heterosexuals and homosexuals (both male (gay) and female (lesbians)). We also saw how Kinsey's research proposed sexuality as a spectrum rather than a binary. In fact, Kinsey and his colleagues argued not only for the existence of bisexuality but that it was the most common sexual orientation. Another shift that influenced the establishment of new sexual orientations was a decoupling of sexual attraction from sexual behavior (Bogaert, 2012). In 1980, Michael Storms argued that sexual attraction was a far more reliable measure than sexual behavior. He argued for a model that ignored behavior altogether and instead argued for two 7-point scales. The first measured homoeroticism (sexual attraction to those of the same sex) on a scale from low (1) to moderate (4) to high (7). The second measured heteroeroticism (sexual attraction to the opposite sex), again from low to high. His system could thus account for homosexuality (high on the first scale, low on the second), heterosexuality (low on the first scale, high on the second), bisexuality (high on both scales), and asexuality (low on both scales).

The problem with these categories was the underlying assumption that there were only two sexes and that sex and gender were interchangeable concepts. As the transgender movement began to gain steam in the 1990s and 2000s, some people who identified as bisexual began to point out limitations inherent in the label. They argued for a new term, one that recognized genderfluidity, and proposed the name pansexual, suggesting that the prefix *pan-* (meaning all) was preferable to the more limited *bi-* (meaning both). The conflict was intense and bitter: pansexuals accused bisexuals of being transphobic, while many bisexuals complained that pansexuals were being unnecessarily divisive. They argued that they were not transphobic, and that bisexual could include sexual attraction to trans people. While this conflict between the two groups has not entirely gone away, many people simply sidestep the issue by using the two labels interchangeably. One of the authors of this chapter identifies as pan (preferring the more inclusive term) but will use bi as a label in situations and places where she expects the first term will not be recognized and wishes to avoid having to explain and justify her labels.

The issue of genderfluidity has also required the creation of new labels for sexual orientations. The current construction of homosexual and heterosexual assumes a cisgender individual. But what if the individual is trans or genderfluid? In recent years, other terms have emerged to describe the targets of sexual attraction for someone who identifies as trans or genderfluid. For example, a genderfluid person who is attracted to men would be neither gay nor straight. Instead, terms such as androsexual (or gynosexual) have been suggested to communicate a desire for men or women by gender-diverse individuals.

In the early 2000s, an American named David Jay started a website called the Asexual Visibility and Education Network (AVEN). Asexuals experience sexual attraction or their sexuality on a spectrum that ranges from little to no interest in sexual activity or sexual relationships. This is not a physical or hormonal limitation, but one based on a lack of attraction rather than on their sexual behavior. Many asexuals still masturbate and may even choose to engage in sex as an activity.[8] Knowing how transformative it was to find a label that described the experience of not being sexually attracted to anyone, David hoped to share the term and help others like him who were looking for a community.

Through discussions in this community and others like it, many asexuals pointed out how crucial it is to identify and categorize different types of attraction. Romantic and sexual attraction had always been assumed to be part of the same emotion, romantic love. However, the fact that romantic love needs to be distinguished from love for one's friends and family based on its inclusion of sexual attraction highlights the problem of conceptualizing romantic and sexual attraction as two aspects of romantic love. Asexuals, who often do not desire sex, still often fall in love, with their romantic desire (excluding sex) feeling different than the feelings they have for friends or family. This continues to be one of the elements that allosexuals (people who experience sexual attraction, opposite of asexual) find most difficult to

---

[8] There are many reasons other than sexual attraction to engage in sex, such as to experience closeness and intimacy with someone or to explore a fetish.

understand. Given the widespread desire for casual or anonymous sex or for "friends with benefits" agreements, it's surprising that people should struggle with the idea that sexual attraction and romantic attraction are distinct concepts: if there can be sexual attraction without romantic desire, then there can be romantic desire without sexual attraction.

The existence of romantic attraction as a distinct dimension allows for the concept of romantic orientation. As with sexual orientation, romantic orientation is a spectrum: homoromantics desire to have romantic relationships with people of the same gender, heteroromantics with the opposite gender, bi/panromantics with varied genders, and aromantics do not desire any romantic relationships. It's important to recognize that people of all sexual orientations also have a romantic orientation, and one's romantic orientation doesn't need to correspond with their sexual orientation. This helps to explain the experience of some gay men who nevertheless fall in love with their wives or straight women who have intense, romantic relationships with other women. It can help people who desire casual sex but have no desire for romantic relationships to understand themselves as existing within a known spectrum rather than feeling deviant, immoral, or abusive.

Of course, as awareness of asexuality became more widespread, some members of the community felt that the term asexual did not fully describe their experience—they needed a term for someone who only occasionally experiences sexual attraction, or who does so only in specific contexts and situations. While several terms were suggested, the community eventually settled on gray asexual for the first group, and demisexual for the second. Demisexuals tend to experience sexual attraction with people they already know and have a relationship with. Experiencing sexual attraction to strangers or casual acquaintances is a rare occurrence for them. As a part of the asexuality spectrum, demisexuals and gray asexuals usually include both their romantic and sexual orientations as part of their identity.

Some (particularly older) members of the community find the proliferation of these new identities overwhelming. Just as some members of the early bisexual community did when confronted with the identity of pansexual, there is a sense that this is unnecessary and divisive. However, labels are not only useful for creating community but can help provide a sense of normalcy and reassurance. Many younger members who identify on the asexuality spectrum continue to search for words to describe their experience of sexual attraction, including describing situations in which they occur, or its specific attributes and qualities.[9]

As the internet allows individuals to connect with others and share their diverse experiences and feelings, the psycho-sexual categories created by psychologists are becoming increasingly replaced by the categories people create for themselves. This allows for more nuanced and flexible terms that adapt to new understandings and allow for greater precision. The result is a proliferation of identities, roles, and expectations as complex as human sexual behavior, sexual and romantic orientation, and human culture itself.

Composition—Sexual Orientation

The furry community has the reputation of being an exceptionally welcoming place, one where being queer is the norm and where straight people are a minority. This impression didn't occur in a vacuum, it would seem, as our research supports this characterization. In survey after survey, people who identify as something other than straight make up the vast majority of the furry community. In our three most current studies from 2021 and 2022, furries were asked about their sexual orientation, indicating which of several labels from a list best described them. Wishing to include as many types of sexual orientations as possible, we included many common labels (lesbian/gay/homosexual, straight/heterosexual, bisexual, pansexual, asexual, and demisexual). For those who were still exploring their sexual orientation, or who felt that these common categories did not accurately reflect them, we also included "I don't know" and "something else" as options. Those who selected "something else" were encouraged to include their preferred labels as additional responses.

The results from this survey reveal tremendous diversity in sexual orientation. Over a quarter of furries identified as lesbian/gay/homosexual (25.2%), compared to only 10% of respondents who identified as straight/heterosexual. Nearly a quarter of furries identified as bisexual (22.4%), with another 13.2% identifying as pansexual. Unlike the general population, where being straight is typically a significant majority, straight participants make up just 10% of the sample. Asexuals and demisexuals were, in comparison, far more prevalent in the furry community than in the broader population, making up 7.9% and 4.8% of furries, respectively.

Unfortunately, since the categories only allowed respondents to select a single option, many of our respondents were forced to use the 'something

---

[9] Examples of such words include labels such as sapiosexual (sexual attraction towards smart people), or aegosexual (people who experience a disconnect between self and the object of sexual attraction).

else' category or used open-ended questions later in the survey to express the fluidity of their sexual orientation. Several respondents used bisexual and pansexual interchangeably, and so identified as both. The existence of romantic orientations further complicated the issue. For example, one of the respondents selected "straight," but in their open-ended responses clarified that they were asexual with a hetero-romantic orientation. Others who selected "asexual" later identified themselves as bi / pan, lesbian, or gay. Still others selected "something else," and used the open-ended responses to clarify the ways they identified as multiple sexual orientations.

As a result, despite showing the furry fandom to be an incredibly diverse place with respect to sexual orientation, the aggregate data likely *underestimates* the full degree of this diversity. The question itself will need to be redesigned for future studies, including being designed to allow people to identify with a multitude of labels and to recognize the fluidity of sexual orientation.[10] Fortunately, the open-ended responses, analyzed below, provide additional context and evidence of greater diversity than is captured in the aggregate data.

Differences in Thoughts About Sexual Orientation

As in previous chapters, this section is a deep dive into the open-ended responses of furries collected in our 2021-2022 studies. While we didn't ask furries an open-ended question specifically about their sexual orientation, many participants discussed their sexual orientation while responding to two broad questions: (1) how do their "labels" (left deliberately vague to allow for the widest possible range of responses) influence their experience with the furry fandom, and (2) their experience of acceptance or marginalization in the fandom in light of those identities. While not all responses were related to sexual orientation (many involved race or gender), those involving sexuality revealed interesting details about how sexual orientation shapes and influences furries' experience in the fandom. Many also revealed ways in which fandom shaped their understanding of, and relationship to, their sexuality.

The following subsections identify some of the most common themes emerging from these responses. As much as possible, these will be described using participants' own words and phrasing.

---

[10] As we mention in the previous chapter on sex and gender, we should never expect to design a perfect measure of these complex and dynamic concepts, but rather strive to constantly improve our survey questions toward the unreachable goal of a perfect question.

Fursona and Sexual Orientation as Facets of Identity

As we saw in Chapter 7, most furries create a fursona as part of their involvement in the furry fandom. Many imbue their fursonas with elements of their own identity and, as we saw in Chapter 15, some (predominantly cis women and trans furries) use their fursonas to explore other identities. Open-ended responses about labels impacting furries' experience in the fandom revealed a similar tension between those who see their fursona as a reflection of themselves and those who see it as a way of exploring (or even ignoring) other aspects of their identity.

When it comes to straight furries, most did not express a connection between their sexual orientation and their fursona. In fact, only one straight furry explicitly mentioned the relationship between their sexual orientation and that of their fursona.

> *"I don't go by many labels where I'm from. So[,] perhaps this does not affect me much to [sic] whatever I'm doing. In terms of orientation of my characters, some male and also female, but they are all straight."*

As we explored in Chapter 14, people whose identity is considered normative often think little about that aspect of themselves until it is brought to mind directly: White people seldom think about their race, while cis men rarely spend time thinking about gender issues. And while straight people are a minority in the context of the furry fandom, they're arguably accustomed to being in the majority in the broader culture. As such, it's possible they have little reason to think about the sexual orientation of their fursona, and may simply take it as a given that their fursona would be straight, like them, by default.[11]

In contrast to straight furries, LGBQA furries were far more likely to mention their fursona while discussing their sexual orientation. Several broad trends emerged in these discussions. For example, many indicated that their fursona was an extension of themselves, one that shared many of their aspects of identity, including their sexual orientation.

> *"As my fursona really is an avatar for me to use in online/furry spaces, he embodies most of my own labels: male, gay, doctor, Iranian-British, Marxist. None of these labels really affect my experience in furry spaces*

---

[11] Of course, it's hard to interpret and raw conclusions based on behavior that people *don't* engage in. We'll be testing this hypothesis more directly in future studies.

(as furry is full of gay men and I only really interact with people who are left-leaning/left-wing within furry)."

"Yes, specially [sic] my bisexuality, but also my interest in science and mathematics (i'm [sic] a physics student). Both of these are personals [sic] traits that i [sic] apply to my fursona, and to how i [sic] show myself within the fandom."

"... I would identify with mainly Asexual, Non-binary, Student, and Canadian. I can say for sure my gender and sexuality have affected me as a Furry as my fursona has no biological sex, no sex organs, and used they/them pronouns. Though I feel like that correlation is more because of my gender and sexuality and not labels."

For other LBGQA furries, their fursona was not only an extension of their identity but a way to explore their identity meaningfully in a safe space.

"I first came out using my furry avatar and the response was overwhelmingly positive"

"... Furry is about self expression [sic], and we often use labels to describe ourselves. I often use characters to express and explore these labels"

"A couple of labels have caused a change in my name and fursona over the years."

Others indicated a desire to have a fursona that did not share any facets of their identity.

"no, furry or fursona is a mask for me."

"I have a lot of labels for myself irl as a musician, banker, polyglot, bisexual, etc., but in the fandom, I really try not to have many labels. Just a plain old snow leopard. Every species does have some stereotypes (whether accurate or not) so sometimes jokes about those will come up"

"... To me, it starts from my identity, and labels are just shorthands to designate this or that aspect of my identity. If the question is about how

RL labels affect my furry identity, uh. I don't actually know. :) Probably not a lot: IRL I'm demi; my dragon persona online is very pan. I'm white; my dragon is blue-grey (though probably encodes whiteness in ways I'm not aware of, okay). I'm on the autism spectrum and (as those things are measured) smart; my dragon persona is sociable, friendly and[,] a bit dumb. I'm soft-cis male; my dragon persona is soft-cis male."

Others found that having their fursona share their sexual orientation could either facilitate their experience by making it easier to find others,

"Yes my [fursona name] *is also a gay and it did bring me a lot of my kind"*

"If anything my labels (gay/transgender) have just helped me connect with others like me in the fandom. It doesn't affect me much as a furry aside from my fursonas and other furry characters I've made often sharing those labels."

or complicate their interactions within the broader community.

"Having a dragon persona, people tend to think I'm also a dominant gay man, but I'm much more submissive. This tends to result in people seeking me out for things I cannot provide easily."

"I think people are quick to develop romantic feelings towards people's fursonas, and being a bisexual/aromantic person, it can get a little uncomfortable having to deal with people who don't quite understand that I'm not looking to get into some kind of relationship."

"My fursona/character is asexual like me. And so it is hard to exist in a fandom space where so much of it is sexualized..."

Another trend that came across regarding the relationship between fursona and sexual identity was those who preferred to focus on the animality of their fursona. While their sexual orientation was still relevant, it was subsumed by the animal.

"I'm too busy being a gay deer to notice. And your garden is very tasty."

"Ridiculously Handsome Pansexual Lion"

As we've seen in this section, open-ended responses revealed several trends when it comes to how a furry's sexual orientation intersects with their fursona. While most straight furries did not mention an association between their sexual orientation and their fursona, LGBQA+ furries often saw their fursona as an extension of themselves, a place to explore aspects of themselves in a safe space or to play with identities different from their own, although some used their fursona to avoid these labels altogether. For furries whose fursona shared their sexual orientation, this could either smooth over interactions with others by making it easier to find other queer people, or (particularly for asexual, demisexual, or aromantic people) they could also make interactions more difficult. These responses show the need for more research directly studying how furries' sexual orientation manifests in, or impacts, the development of their fursona.

Intersection of Sexual Orientation with Other Facets of Identity

Because of the broad phrasing of the open-ended questions, many responses considered how various facets of one's identity—not just sexual orientation—impacted their experience in the fandom. Some respondents highlighted how aspects of their identity, particularly issues such as race, gender, and (dis)ability, intersected with their sexual orientation in furry spaces, with many revealing an awareness of the fact that some aspects of their identity were more easily welcomed than others.

One of the recurring themes that emerged was a celebration of the fact that multiple aspects of respondents' identities were welcomed and accepted within the furry community. While a general discussion of the degree of acceptance of LGBQA will be left to another section, some of the responses deliberately focused on how the furry fandom was welcoming to the respondents' entire identity.

"I feel as though I belong here as a gay person with a non-binary gender identity. I think here in furry, I'm not seen as weird or different at all for it"

"I feel very accepted within the fandom. I've never felt the need to hide that I'm gay, non-binary, autistic, or any other aspect of myself"

"I'm non-binary, bisexual, therian, and an artist. I feel the furry fandom is the only place that my identity, in full, is accepted and celebrated."

"No, I haven't [felt marginalized]. *I don't think being half Asian or gay has been something I've ever needed to hide."*

"I think because the fandom is largely LGBTQ+, being pansexual helps being accepted into it a little more. Also being neurodivergent (I have autism) like a majority of the fandom also helps me fit in a bit."

Other respondents reported differing levels of acceptance depending on a particular facet of their identity. While sexual orientation was frequently welcomed, other aspects of their identity were not as universally accepted. Race was often mentioned as an issue.

"Well[,] I already explained how being a black woman can be pretty difficult in this fandom. I'm not really concerned about my sexuality in terms of the furry fandom because a majority of the fandom isn't straight anyways."

"Being a [L]atino, I know there's fewer spaces for me to explore my experiences in the fandom in my own language. Most of the easily available content is in English and with North american [sic] or European connections. Some other labels like my nationality or sexual orientation also affect some of the content I like to see, which in turn makes me focus on certain areas of the fandom over others."

"For the most part, yes, I do feel accepted especially now that there are more groups, events, and opportunities being offered to BIPOC+queer furries within the fandom space. It is still a gamble though and you can run into people who do not accept you and will try to run you out of the fandom. But it is mostly positive and there is more support and more people willing to defend/stand up for BIPOC+queer furs."

"Actually, There are many homosexuals in furry fandom... nine out of ten furry are gay. It's obvious. Furry fandom is extremely tolerant of minority groups. But because of China's traditional culture, many people cannot accept homosexuality. So many people choose to hide[.]"

"As somebody who's biracial, gay, trans, & disabled, I do feel safe and accepted within the fandom, however[,] I do understand and am well

aware of the issues the community has with several of my identities (especially with race)."

"I identify as androsexal, though I mostly present myself as gay for simplicity's sake. On that ground[,] I have felt little need to repress or hide my status. When it comes to my nationality and race, I do tend to hide both of them because they tend to create pity or make some people patronize me. Besides those two, I usually feel accepted in the fandom."

Ironically, some straight furries found that other facets of their identity were more broadly respected than their sexual orientation.

"I am black. I've never been given any crap for it, at conventions or online. I am tired of being made fun of for being straight though."

Other respondents highlighted how the intersection between gender and sexual orientation frequently caused them issues.

"Yes, I feel like I'm treated differently and not as included in the general community because I'm female, but much more accepted by fellow furry artists. Most furry artists are female. I also feel I can connect with other furry friends through my bisexual/lgbt identity."

"I feel my lable [sic] as non binary [sic] and lesbian effect [sic] it, as [I] dont [sic] feel as respected because of it. Theres [sic] a lot [sic] of misogyny with furries like everywhere."

"I think it affects me to a point. Lesbian furries are not often represented and are less "attractive" to the popular gay men public in the fandom. I am lucky to have good friends who do not treat me any different [sic] because I am gay and a woman. The only times i [sic] get reminded that some people actually do not like me because of these two things is in furry conventions. Do [sic] not happens [sic] that much luckily"

"Oh[,] it completely does. I got treated far different [sic] in furry spaces when I was presenting as just a bi cis [sic] guy. It's been far different since realizing I'm trans fem, non-binary, pan lesbian, and asexual."

Some furries felt that they were relatively welcome in the fandom, even to the point of being a part of the majority for being both queer and neurodivergent.

"I generally feel accepted, as queer identity, transgender identity, and mental health-related disability are some of the more common marginalized identities in the fandom (from my anecdotal experience). I make a point to not hide these parts of myself when they are relevant."

"Autistic, queer, bigendered [sic], poly, kinky, writer... I have a lot of labels. I feel like the furry community accepts them all"

"I am LGBT and I have a few disabilities. I feel very accepted and never felt the need to hide these things."

"... I do not hide that I am trans, gay, and disabled when I am in the furry fandom."

However, this was not a universal experience. Other furries reported that disability was not always as accepted within fandom as their sexual orientation or gender.

"I identify as a disabled, trans gender [sic], MLM furry who's interested in abdl [sic] and stoner stuff. Because of this[,] my experience is a bit different than others, as someone who's queer I'm ethier [sic] loved or rejected, as someone who's into abdl [sic] and smoking again I'm ethier [sic] loved or rejected and as someone who's disabled I find myself unable to really connect with the able-bodied in spaces generally made for them. In the furry fandom[,] most people are really welcoming but there's always the shame of who I am and what I enjoy holding me back[,] and its [sic] like that for lots of us."

"I identify most as lesbian, trans, and disabled. Of the three, the third affects my interactions the most. We get very little attention, and a substantial amount of it is not positive. I feel that it makes me and others like me more likely to be ignored or pushed to the sidelines."

"Gender and sexuality I feel as safe as I could really expect. Good use of block tools helps. I rarely reach out to anyone because of my autism. I

don't hide my autism, but worry over miscommunication leads to me rarely speaking. I don't hide my marginalised status, I just hide."

Other aspects of identity that intersect with sexual orientation include body image and appearance, age, or atypical social roles.

"I feel accetped [sic] when it comes to my sexuality and race, but not when it comes to my body and appearance. I feel like I [sic] need to hide the latter from the people i [sic] interact with."

"In terms of the fandom, being an older fur has sometimes been marginalizing but I have never hid this when online. I spent too much time in the closet when young to do that again. I am who I am."

"Yes. I have been told that I am not gay enough, too old, and too conservative to belong to the fandom"

"Parent. Homoromantic sex-positive asexual. Both inform my interactions with others in the fandom."

Members of the furry community who identify as non-human (therian, otherkin, alterhuman) report that the intersection of this identity with their queerness leads to a disjointed relationship with the furry community.

"Depends on the form of marginalization. I'm very openly trans and ace, but. Far less openly plural, otherkin, and a few other parts of myself I fear judgement [sic] for."

"I've been quite happy that a broad variety of sexualities are accepted in furry, but I definitely feel reluctant to share that I'm a therian. I think it's frequently seen as "furry, but taken too far",[sic] when it's not actually that. Really, I'm a therian first and a furry only as a coping mechanism, regardless of what benefits I've experienced since joining the fandom."

"i [sic] consider my furrydom to massively intersect with alterhumanity and queerness. i [sic] also consider my position as an anarchist to be influenced by my alterhuman/furry identity and vice versa, and there's a gap i'm [sic] hoping to narrow between the two groups in general."

*"I find that my queer identity is the most prominent identity that affects my furry experience, followed very closely by my identity as otherkin. Those things color every aspect of my life; I don't *stop* being nonhuman or being queer, and furry culture is the perfect way to express those feelings of being othered or different, in a way that still feels inclusive on the whole."*

Straight furries were much less likely than LGBQA+ furries to mention their sexual orientation as impacting their interaction with the furry community. Those who did tend to recognize that, while their sexual orientation made them a minority within the fandom, they were still operating from a place of privilege due to the heteronormative nature of broader society. This was particularly the case with furries who were also white and cisgender.

"Not that I've noticed, although since I'm a white straight cis woman and also older (and therefore reasonably confident), I'm playing on easy mode here."

"Yes, being Cis & straight means I'm actually in the minority for once, and understanding the experiences of those who aren't is always a learning experience for me. There are plenty of other labels that could be given to me that set me apart from the majority of furries, but I won't get into all of them."

"Within the fandom, the only minority that I appear to be a part of is "heterosexual". No demographic that I am a member of has any standing to complain about marginalization."

Some LGBQA furries also recognized that not being visibly queer also gave them some degree of privilege in the broader community, while others recognize that being the majority within the furry fandom grants them privilege in furry spaces. Occasionally, awareness of this majority status brought with it a sense of responsibility to bring awareness to the needs of marginalized furries.

"I think, being white, reasonably financially stable, and not visibly queer has insulated me significantly from any kind of marginalization, so I'm not sure I would ever have found myself in that position even if the furry

Fandom were not accepting. Still, I have no doubt that it is an accepting space, and one in which none of my qualities has ever or would ever stand out or draw negative attention."

"I am only marginalized in the way that I am gay, and that is nothing compared to the trials and tribulations of other minorities or otherwise marginalized people. Especially in the very gay accepting place such as the fur fandom, I have had no issues."

"Somewhat. Being nonbinary and gay is comforting when I see many other LGBTQ people. Being a white male makes me try to evaluate my privilege and understand how my life is different — and often easier — than other people's."

"I am a white, middle aged [sic] cis man. None of these attributes socially, economically[,] or culturally marginalise me in Australia. I am also bi/pansexual and identify as queer. This is a complete non-issue in the fandom[.]"

"Being white and male — despite being gay and not exactly cis — I still feel within the relative majority of most people. Within a purely fandom context, I absolutely feel within the majority given the fandom is predominantly white, male, and LGBTQ. I do not feel a need to hide my identity in the fandom."

"i'm [sic] white and queer -- both majorities within the fandom. however, i [sic] often take the side of nonwhite furries when it comes to fandom issues and have done so from the start thanks to twitter [sic] voices like sean [sic] chiplock [sic] (i [sic] don't think i [sic]would've found out about HMHF if it wasn't for him), so i find it hard to vibe with anyone in "regular" furry spaces where it's uwu escapism all the time, and that energy is present even more so in the local groups and chats where i'm [sic] from. but i [sic] have double privilege, so no -- i've [sic] never had the experience of being "checked" like BIPOC and trans furries have at times[.]"

The responses in this section reveal that the experience of sexual orientation in the furry fandom is often influenced by other facets of identity. While sexual diversity was accepted (for the most part), other identities such as race, gender, or (dis)ability influence the degree to which queer furries felt safe and welcome in furry spaces, especially for queer furries who also identify as non-human. Finally, many furries saw themselves as being part of the majority, whether because they were part of the broader cultural majority or part of a majority specifically within the fandom.

Friendliness of a Sexually Diverse Fandom

Most of the responses to the open-ended questions highlighted a sense of overwhelming openness and acceptance toward sexual diversity within the furry fandom. Many respondents reported feeling accepted and welcomed by the community. In the words of one respondent, they were made to feel,

> *"Completely accepted, unabashedly embraced, unconditionally loved. Like how cults perform "love bombing", but without the malicious intentions,"*

while another insisted that the community was

> *"REALLY REALLY accepting."*

Most reported feeling welcome and included by the community when it came to their sexual orientation. However, those with particular sexual orientations sometimes found that they felt marginalized or excluded as a result of their sexual orientation. This section will focus on the duality of these different experiences within the fandom, as well as on who is most likely to have which experience.

People identifying as gay were the most likely to describe the furry fandom as friendly and accepting toward sexual diversity.

> *"I feel like the fandom is an extremely accepting place of gay men, amongst others."*

> *"The only part that can be marginalized is me being gay, but the fandom as a whole is very open and accepting so I've never had any problems"*

> *"Not remotely, since I am primarily marginalized in terms of my sexuality, and the furry fandom is overwhelmingly accepting in that regard."*

"As a gay man[,] I felt particularly welcomed in the fandom back in 2003."

"No, furry is very lgbt friendly and that is one of its high advantages compared to other fandom spaces."

"Homosexuality is generally viewed positively in fandom spaces."

Some respondents felt that this friendliness comes at the expense of not being able to fully discuss their experiences within fandom spaces. Others found that the unwillingness of (some) furry communities to censor homophobia, transphobia, misogyny, and racism left them feeling as if the acceptance was shallow and superficial.

"Considering the high density of LGBT+ people in this community, I feel fairly welcome as a gay person. There's still some degree of overt "don't talk about identity, it's shrill and annoying" here that limits my willingness to publicly opine about certain things, but generally, I'm not uncomfortable being open about it."

"I suppose, on a broad level furry is accepting of queer people, but on an intracommunity level furries are very quick to criticize queer people for their "flaws". However, I never hide who I am as I want to be seen for who I am."

"I generally feel accepted, but often in a shallow way (gender and orientation recognized but spaces not protected from those that threaten people like me). Despite this, I have never hid my status online in the fandom."

"Outside of the loud Nazi minority, i [sic] feel comfortable being myself in fandom spaces"

For lesbians, who are part of the majority in terms of their sexual orientation ("homosexual"), but who are a minority in terms of their gender, many reported feeling (mostly) accepted while also feeling somewhat erased by the community's focus on gay men. Others expressed a fear that publicly identifying as lesbian would lead to unwelcome sexualization.

"I do not identify as a minority or marginalised person, no. The most I can think of is being Lesbian, but the fandom is very LGBTQ+ positive."

"I feel like the fandom accepts my identity as a lesbian, and I do not feel the need to hide it, though I do also feel that there should be more community events to show support and promote the work of WLW creators."

"I do feel like I need to hide as I feel as if I reveal that I am a lesbian people will take that as a reason to sexualise me[.]"

As for participants who identified as something other than gay or lesbian, responses revealed tension between feelings of acceptance and feelings of marginalization. Respondents identifying as bisexual often reported feeling welcome, on the one hand,

"I have only been a minority in terms of sexual preference. (Im not straight, idk much more) it has never been an issue to me in or out of the fandom. The fandom does feel very open and accepting from what i [sic] can tell[.]"

"If being bisexual and a woman counts as marginalized, I actually feel very accepted in the fandom and share these facts freely."

"Very accepted. It's been quite easy to be out as bi and trans in furry spaces and I've never needed to hide[.]"

"I feel accepted. The furry fandom is very LGBTQ+ friendly, so I have not felt the need to hide it."

"I think the most "out of bounds" part of me is being bi(ish).. so i [sic] think i [sic] just don't feel even slightly marginalised. It's all cool for me."

"The only thing that has changed regarding my identity is the amount of bi pride [sic] furry pins I have collected. The furry fandom seems very LGBTQ+ friendly so I feel quite welcome."

while feeling marginalized (e.g., being told to pick a side) or erased (e.g., the presumption that they were gay) on the other hand.

"As a bisexsual [sic] male, I am more attracted by females than male[sic]. This my [sic] surprise people since they usually assume you are gay."

"My identity as a bisexual man in the fandom has affected me negatively. I'm seen as a lesser person at times since I'm expected to take a side when it comes to sexual orientation. Gay people see me as a straight man, while straight people see me as a closeted gay man, and I don't receive any kind of acceptance for it."

"Sometimes, beeing [sic] bi still causes some disbelive [sic] with the typical "you have to choose one" phrase. Most of the time, furs are really including and welcomming [sic] any experience[.]"

The responses of pansexual furries reflect a similar tension to those experienced by bisexual furries, feeling welcomed on the one hand,

"I am pansexual and genderqueer, which is fairly well accepted in the small subsection of furry culture I choose to interact with. I feel accepted and do not need to hide my sexual or gender orientation. However, it should be noted that I don't interact with the vast majority of the furry community, so my experiences may be atypical."

"I do not identify as a minority or a marginalized person, but if I do fit that description, I do feel accepted. Most don't really care about me being trans or pansexual, though."

"As a pansexual person, I've felt mostly positive feedback."

and erased or marginalized on the other hand.

"It can, definitely. I typically keep my gender identity and orientation a secret. If I tell people, even in some LGBTQ spaces that I'm pansexual, they will tell me to choose a side."

"Yes. Especially being male and pansexual, I am frequently assumed to be gay. However, despite this, I do lean more towards cis-straight than

anything else and I find this frustrating to explain sometimes, and feel I am looked down on if I speak up about it[.]"

Furries who were still questioning and exploring their sexual orientation report that it's often a very welcoming and encouraging place to do so. This was also expressed by some who identified as "something else."

"LGBT, I feel furry is an inclusive space where I can be "myself" without judgment[.]"

"I am queer as in sexual orientation, but I couldn't hope for a better space than the furry fandom. I feel absolutely accepted[.]"

"The fandom is quite the safe space for lgbtq-people [sic]."

Asexual furries expressed a more complicated relationship with the furry community than did many others with non-heterosexual orientations. Many asexual furries did find the community to be incredibly welcoming and inclusive of sexual diversity.

"As an ace[,] i [sic] felt very welcomed in the furry Community, here everyone metters [sic] and i [sic] feel very happy about that."

"Being asexual makes furry a particularly welcoming community. It is 'sex positive', in that people who like sex are encouraged to have it. But much more than mainstream American culture, emotional openness and intimacy exist in contexts outside a sexual relationship."

"Yes, I was openly bi/ace within the fandom. They are supportive to [sic] sexuality and mental illness so it felt safe. I didn't need to really hide anything from the fandom specifically"

For others, the openly sexual or sex-positive nature of the fandom, including a significant portion of the media being erotic or pornographic in nature, results in a sense of alienation from the community. For those who are not interested in the sexual aspects of fandom, this can lead to feeling isolated, ignored, or excluded.

"Yes, as an Asexual i [sic] often feel left out and ignored, because so much of the fandom is just about sexuality"

"As an asexual person, I often feel extremely alienated and left out from the general furry community because of how hypersexual every aspect of it it has become[.]"

"My asexuality definitely affects my experience with furry. Many furries are used to interacting with each other in a highly flirtatious or sexual way and/or engaging in romantic PDA like [sic] full-on cuddling, and it can make me really uncomfortable to be around things like that. It's easier to sidestep online, which may be part of why I've always preferred the online furry community to the offline one."

"My asexuality tends to make people avoid me because there is no expectation for sex."

"Being asexual raises eyebrows with disappointing reliability. It often negatively affects my experience when talking to other fandom members as they naturally expect a "fellow furry" to be sex-positive, which leads to disappointment when that proves to not be the case."

"As an asexual cis woman[,] I feel largely accepted within the spaces I've found myself in. It can be kind of discouraging when people don't want to interact with me because I'm ace and/or a woman but I also recognize that many of those folks who do so are seeking sexual experiences with men and that's not a space I belong in or want to inhabit."

"Being asexual I have found that there is a lot of misinformation and assumptions made about asexual people online and in real life. I feel as though if I were to participate more in fandom spaces I would be warry [sic] of how I told that I was asexual because of the amount of annoying comments I might get about asexuality and also even possibly intrusive and rude questions/comments. I feel similar about being non-binary but I feel like non-binary is more understood generally than asexuality, but I still feel like the same kinds of comments might come to me because of that as well."

Aromantic furries expressed similar discomfort with the emphasis on relationships within the community.

> *"i [sic]dont feel the need to hide my identity but i [sic] don't [sic] feel like i [sic] fit in either as [the] fandom is so saturated with romance and i [sic] don't [sic] experience romantic feelings"*

One participant, who identified as an aromantic bisexual ("bordering on asexual") expressed a wish that,

> *"...furries didn't act weird that I don't want to be in a realtionship [sic], sexual or otherwise."*

Some asexual furries specifically reported experiences of discrimination and exclusion, leading some to hide their asexuality in furry spaces for fear of bias.

> *"The fandom can be overly populated by gay males and I have experienced bullying and exclusion for not being gay."*

> *"I have often been excluded from furry spaces because especially earlier on in my fandom involvement people thought that I would be sex repulsed or uncomfortable since I am extremely asexual"*

> *"As an ace person, I feel I have to hide that side of my identity a lot."*

> *"Being asexual in the fandom can be fairly interesting. People who meet me as asexual first and a furry later think that's an oxymoron -- "how can an ace person be in such a horny fandom"? In the fandom itself[,] I don't mention my asexuality too much. There are certain people who equate asexuality with prudishness, or anti-sexuality. I don't want people to think I'm trying to nay-say their NSFW[12] art."*

Some asexual people are interested in engaging in sexual role-play, but report experiencing erasure of their identity as a result.

---

[12] An initialism meaning "not safe for work," usually used to describe content that is explicitly sexual, crude, or graphic in nature.

"I am Panromantic Asexual. I find this awkward when roleplaying, as my fursona is also Asexual. There are many people who do not respect this and see it as a Gay or Bisexual faking being less interested to control situations and steer them in a direction of their choosing. I have been called a fake, liar, confused, delusional etc[,]. It has really made things difficult for me, and has lead [sic] me to understand the importance of blocking and ghosting individuals that do not want to accept me as I am. Unfortunately, as with any fandom or group, there are always going to be assholes and jerks that are bigots and think the world revolves around them."

Furries who identified as demisexual (or as on the demisexual spectrum) responded with many of the same experiences as asexual furries, both positive and negative.

"... the furrys [sic] community is welcoming of all backgrounds and a lot [sic] of the community is LGBT+"

"... As a demisexual, I also prefer not to be physical with strangers, which can be a disappointment to more outgoing furs."

"Though I am demisexual, very heavily leaning on the side of asexuality, I still associate with areas of the fandom that are nsfw [sic], at least in forms of conversation. I value furry chatrooms as a chill way of facilitating social interaction in my freetime [sic], and I generally prefer to stay in spaces without minors, but I digress. My asexuality definitely affects my experience in the fandom, in that though I am very much sex positive, seeing some extremely horny and lustful people definitely makes me feel uncomfortable."

"Specifically in furry spaces? Usually being ... openly Omnisexual-Demisexual, as most people either don't understand it or call it some form of phobic."

"No. I don't feel really accepted. I tend to hide it because I've had people avoid talking to me because of it, or they would want to be inappropriate towards me."

"I am demisexual in terms of my actual sexual attraction and interactions with people, but in terms of what I find attractive in furry art, I am gay. Being gay is not really a problem in furry. Demisexual is often misunderstood and thought to be a choice. They seem to confuse sexual attraction with sex and say that they are demisexual because they choose to wait to have sex until they know someone better."

Perhaps the sexual orientation that had the most complicated relationship between sexual orientation and the furry community was heterosexuality. Used to being the majority in broader society, heterosexual furries expressed some sense of discomfort at being a minority within the furry community. They reported a range of responses when it came to whether or not they felt accepted within furry spaces.

Some felt some pressure to identify as gay or bi, or experienced the weight of homonormative expectations.

"Sometimes it's frustrating being straight in a space where everyone seems to be gay, bi, etc. It can feel like being the only sober person at a party. I'm sure gays probably feel this way often, though."

"I don't identify as a minority. That being said, being straight in a predominantly LGBT community has meant I'm usually assumed a different sexuality from what I am."

"Sometimes, I felt pushed by some members identified as homosexual to give up my identity as hetero. But aside frome [sic] that, which was unusual for me, I've never received any particular feedbacks [sic] for my identity in furry interactions compared to non-furry related interactions."

"I have had to hide the fact I'm straight in plenty of social circles within the furry fandom because people treat you like you're a homophobe unless you're actually gay. There are furmeets in the [area] I simply cannot go to because I was told I should just accept inappropriate touching as a compliment because it's okay for people to assume I'm gay because I'm at a furmeet. The people who think that are idiots that I have no desire to interact with anyway so it's no skin off my back, but I fear I'll be left with no social circle at all if I let it bother me."

Heteroromantic asexual and demisexual people similarly reported frustration about their "straightness" not being acknowledged within the furry community. A heteroromantic demisexual furry observed that,

> *"... many find it difficult to believe I am straight, because I am soft spoken [sic] and not an aggressive personality type."*

while a heteroromantic asexual furry admitted that,

> *"I don't tell people I am straight to avoid bullying."*

Some heterosexual furries experienced other negative consequences related to being a minority. This includes having their membership in the community invalidated or being expected to date other heterosexual furries simply due to the small number of furries like them.

> *"People often say that "straight furries are rare" or sometimes something along the lines of "if you're straight you're not a real furry", but that doesn't really bother me. I sometimes feel that since straight furries make up a smaller portion of the fandom that [sic] there's an expectation that you should date another straight furry, but I have no interest in that being in a committed relationship already. Most of the time people don't mind what your sexuality is it seems, it rarely comes up for me!"*

Being straight in a primarily queer fandom can feel strange to some and alienating to others, who felt lonely due to feeling like it was difficult to build relationships with other furries.

> *"But it's hard for me to build relationships, both platonic and romantic. If it comes to romantic relationships, the problem is, that there are not that many straight women that I share interests in the fandom. The furry fandom is very queer, which I don't have a problem with[.]"*

> *"In Chinese furry fandom, straight people may find it is [sic] hard to get into the atmosphere in [a] certain place several years ago. i [sic] don't need to hide it, but it is still a little lonely. things are better nowadays."*

> *"It's *hard* being a straight female in the fandom, I'll tell you that much."*

"As a female minority, I can't hide that so if I had to experience the furry fandom in more depth it wouldn't be something to hide. I'm kind of scared to interact with others in the furry community as a cis, straight female."

While the furry community has a well-earned reputation for being welcoming of sexual diversity, not all sexual orientations within the community find it equally welcoming. Gay furry men seem to have the easiest time feeling welcome and accepted in the furry community—although, even for them, the reluctance of many furry groups to discuss real-world discrimination or to censor groups expressing violent or homophobic ideology can lessen this feeling of inclusion. Among other queer identities, while the feeling of being welcome and accepted remains, it is measured against experiences of erasure, ignorance, bigotry, sexual harassment, isolation, and exclusion. Straight and heteroromantic furries also report experiences with discrimination, isolation, and marginalization as a result of their sexual orientation, in line with the experiences of LGBQA+ people in broader society.

Influence of Sexuality on Fandom Experiences

Given the varying degrees of acceptance and inclusion experienced by furries as a result of their sexual orientation, it's not surprising that furries chose to discuss their thoughts on how their sexual orientation has influenced how they, themselves, engage with the furry fandom. For example, one of the themes that emerged for many LGBQA+ furries was the recognition and celebration of their majority status within the community. Given their marginalization in the real world, queer furries often revel in the feeling of normalcy, recognition, and validation that comes from being a part of a majority.

"Like every furry is gay[.]"

"I am not in any clearly definable minority from the perspective of the furry fandom. Me being gay makes me feel like I am part of the majority in the fandom, even if this label makes me a minority in everyday life. I never felt marginalized in furry spaces."

"Since LGBT+ people are so common in the fandom, I find that being a furry gives me an opportunity to feel "normal" and confident."

"My only claim to minority status is my sexuality [demisexual], *and to be frank, I am not a minority here"*

"Being gay affects my identity in the sense that it makes me feel welcomed / normal given how many queer people are in the community."

"Many furries are gay, so being gay usually feels to be part of the identity of furries. This helps promote a feeling of inclusion and acceptance."

Most LGBQA+ furries contrasted the freedom they felt in furry spaces to their experience in non-furry spaces. Even among those who didn't always feel completely accepted in furry spaces, they reported nevertheless feeling more accepted and welcome in furry spaces than in broader society.

"Being gay, I feel more accepted within the furry fandom than I do in the general public. I have never felt the need to hide that fact about myself when interacting with other furries."

"Yes, I feel accepted within furry, I've never had to hide my sexuality or gender identity within the fandom. I was even given a warm welcome and have more furry friends than non furry [sic] friends."

"In furry spaces[,] it always feels like a little island of happiness where I can be as casual about mentioning what I am in terms of sexual identity, as I wish we all could in the "normie world" too."

"I've never really felt the need to hide the fact I'm LGBT from the furry fandom. The only times I do is due to real world [sic] influences."

"Mine don't seem to be the sort of labels the [sic] really impact my experience or identity as a furry. I mean, there's still going to be jackasses out there because of the "pan" thing, but that feels less common in furry spaces than anywhere else."

"I have never felt the need to hide my gender or sexual orientation [asexual], on the contrary, im [sic] more open about it in fandom than out[.]"

Other queer furries remarked on the ease of finding other furries who shared their experiences and interests.

"I think being trans and gay have almost helped me fit in more with other furries, since so many other furries have the same or similar labels. And even the ones who don't are often very accepting of those who do have these labels."

"I feel that being gay helps me fit in with the others, since a huge amount of the furries I know are gay or bisexual."

"If anything my labels (gay/transgender) have just helped me connect with others like me in the fandom."

"I find the furry community very queer-friendly in general. I don't think I would be a furry if it wasn't as queer as it is. I started off as a brony,[13] *but a big part of why i [sic] became a furry instead was because of the queerness."*

Many furries recognize that these positive experiences are a result of homonormativity. The assumption that most furries were gay cis males was often seen as having a negative side effect of marginalizing others within the community who did not share this label.

"Being gay definitely makes my experience in furry spaces more comfortable, but I do feel like there is some homonormality in the fandom. People who are straight (particularly women) a lot of times have a more difficult time feeling comfortable in furry spaces, at least from what I've seen[.]"

"I certainly feel like gays might overepresent [sic] the fandom to a degree, but since the community is overall accepting, I've never had any negative effects with my "labels" [sic][.]"

"As a gay white cis male, it feels like the part of the fandom that I experience is the most central one - from my perspective, it seems like I'm

---

[13] For more on bronies and their overlap with the furry fandom, see Chapter 11.

part of the demographic that a lot of furry content and events that I see cater to, sometimes at the expense of others non in that demographic."

"It is easy for me to assume that other men in the fandom are gay like me."

Queer cis-male furries reported enjoying the fact that the high proportion of queer men in the fandom facilitates both physical and emotional intimacy, which eases communication and a sense of fellowship, a finding consistent with data discussed in Chapter 13 showing that gay cis men are especially likely to find a significant other through the fandom.

"Being a gay male and being surrounded by many other males in the fandom who are gay/bi/pan, my friendships quite often involve some level of platonic intimacy"

"Sure, being gay means that I sometimes like to have physical / emotional closeness to some other males."

"I think being a gay furry has a definitive impact on my experience in furry spaces. ... For many gay furries, the fandom is very closely woven in with sexual experience and experimentation, though that is not always the case."

As we saw in the previous section, the easy intimacy between queer cis-men can have the unintended side effect of alienating (or even sexually harassing) straight and heteroromantic men, as well as some asexual and demisexual people. In addition to those groups, queer trans-males can feel excluded or unwelcome in this space, and miss the connections and intimacy shared by queer cis males.

"I very much feel like the furry community (and the male gay community) makes me feel inferior at times because I have no penis/am afab [sic] despite presenting and identifying as masculine. There is a concerning amount of cis gay men that insist on treating anything "feminine" related as "disgusting". I don't think this represents most of the community and this has not been the bulk of my experiences with it but it is extremely disheartening to see. I have found my own group of friends of various agabs [sic] and genders that do not tolerate this behavior, however."

Some asexual and demisexual people interested in sexual roleplay also reported that the assumption of sexual attraction and a general lack of knowledge and awareness of how asexuality works caused difficulty in their sexual relationships.

"In terms of interactions, it makes roleplay more difficult sometimes being Asexual. I (and my fursona) do have a libido and can become aroused, but it must be via different means. For me and my fursona, a fetish must be involved in the roleplay. Just having sex or sexual acts for the sake of having them results in poor interactions, abandoned roleplays, and creating a gap in making a social connection. I find that because of this, it takes more effort on my part to find people I can interact with successfully."

"A few decades ago, I used to allow people to assume I was a gay male to be accepted in to [sic] online role playing [sic] spaces, but I would not do that now. If they don't like it, I don't need to hang out with them. It was just part of having to learn and grow up and find my paws."

Furries with less common sexual orientations also sometimes reported using more common sexualities to feel included in the community. This could sometimes cause them to stay silent about experiences with discrimination to hide their minority sexual orientation.

"Since the fandom around me are [sic] being dominated by gay male [sic], I feel like I need to conceal myself when talking about potentially [sic] misogyny contents [sic] among these people, not showing myself can be attracted and attract woman [sic]."

"Since the broad public doesn't know what androsexual is, but do [sic] know what gay is, I'll use that as my marginalized category. I don't feel like I need to hide that at all, which is really nice."

"i [sic] am not very open w/ my asexuality - usually ID as gay when meeting new people"

However, not all asexual furries found that their sexual orientation was misunderstood. Generally, asexual and demisexual furries found the furry community to be much more aware of, or at least open to, their sexuality and identity than outside the furry community.

"I feel accepted usually. Though asexuality is way much rarer than gay/lesbian, the furries are often more familiar with this concept and are more friendly."

"I'm queer in many ways, but to be honest, I don't think that even counts as a minority within the fandom. My particular identities may be unusual, but the overall vibe is so strongly in favor of queer identities in general that I've always found everyone to be very accepting."

"I don't see a lot of Asexual people here, but that's something I deal with inside and outside of the fandom. The few who are here tend to be accepted for the most part[.]"

"I have found my asexuality is not only accepted but represented in the community."

"In regular life being queer [demisexual] *and neurodivergent put me in a minority, but within the fandom those are both very mainstream things so I kind of feel like I get to leave my minority status at the door, so to speak."*

"Aegosexual/Agender? No, if anything[,] more are curious about it that [sic] any real rejection."

This broader level of awareness of queer identities was also helpful to others with less common identities.

"In the furry fandom[,] I can be openly pansexual and not feel like I have to explain myself every time, as I do in other spaces in the rare times it comes up. I cannot think of a more welcoming group for that particular aspect of my identity."

"I've noticed I'm much more inclined to interact with people whose labels more closely mirror mine; that they've gone through what I have, or even more. It makes discussions with other furries much less awkward in that I don't have to worry as much if I have to "explain" myself, or worry that

they're some flavour of bigot later on. This applies mostly to labels of cultural background, gender, orientation [pansexual] and support for social movements. I don't get much feedback from other furries about my labels other than positively/neutral about my pronouns or orientation."

Despite this positivity, LGBQA+ furries recognized the need to sometimes filter aspects of themselves in the community, especially online.

"As someone who's queer and disabled[,] I don't hide who I am online in the fandom, I mean there's not much to say about people being dicks about it other than they're bigots and blocking them. Sometimes it's hard to feel accepted in the fandom but I try not to let it get to me and just try and enjoy this little safe space."

"Being lesbian and gendefluid [sic], I feel accepted in the fandom for the majority of [sic] time. Many people are showing publicly their colors, so you know where to go and avoid. But sometimes you need to fight for your rights even online. Being online is being anonymous, anonymous means being able to harrass [sic] and bully people[.]"

"It's definitely helped shape the specific spaces I'm in within the furry community. Nearly every fellow furry i [sic] follow on twitter [sic] is LGBTQAI+ in some way, though there are a few who aren't. I know that trans people get a lot of shit so i [sic] feel best keeping company who I know won't do that kinda crap. Because of that, I've had mostly positive experiences all round [sic] with regards to that."

"At conventions and meets I've always felt accepted and supported, sooner than I did in my life outside the fandom. Online there is more hostility both from a few individual furs and people outside the fandom but that doesn't make me feel the need to hide it."

"Generally feel accepted but there's still going to be heavy friction points[,] especially in online spaces. Having a sexuality label mashup like pan lesbian [sic] causes problems. Being asexual causes problems. Being trans causes problems. The community is not at all devoid of transmisogyny, misogyny, queerphobia, acephobia, going after more niche labels, the list goes on."

Whether by curating which furry groups and spaces they joined, by being careful with who they shared information, or by organizing groups and creating safe spaces, queer furries try to ensure that their sexuality is supported within their fandom experiences.

> *"I feel included for the most part--a lot of people here are like me, and if there's one thing that's embraced more than anything in the furry fandom, it's gender and sexual orientation. There's tons of diversity. In fact, it seems like 99% of who i [sic] interact with are LGBT+ in some sense. i [sic] have like... only one cishet furry friend. i [sic] don't really hide much of myself in the furry community?[sic] outside of gender/sexuality... i [sic] dont [sic] know how much of a minority i [sic] really am, tbh."*

> *"I have hidden what I am* [asexual] *a few times in certain spaces, but for the most part[,] I feel like I have a good, close community that I try to curate as much as possible. I am accepted in that space, and if I branch out into other spaces, the vaguely left-leaning nature of furries mean [sic] I'll fare better in a furry space than I would in, say, the workplace. It could always use improvement, but it's better than irl sometimes.*

> *"It would make me avoid contacts [sic] with other furries that state them as homofobia [sic], and I believe it is vicr [sic] versa."*

> *"...My queerness has affected how I interact in furry spaces, and leads to being discerning about who I associate with; I don't want queerphobes in spaces. Political identify [sic] comes into play, as again, I don't want bigoted and hateful people in spaces with marginalized people."*

However, some queer furries recognize that these safe spaces can contribute to the sense of marginalization and exclusion experienced by heterosexuals.

> *"I have never personally had any problems with the only minority identity I have (homosexual), however in the spaces I interact with, the gay presence tends to outweigh the straight, and I often see unfavorable behavior towards the straight members of the community."*

> *"Truthfully I almost see gay and straight furries as a different community altogether."*

This marginalization of straight men in a majority gay fandom is not a unique feature of the furry fandom. For example, research has shown that straight and bisexual men in the majority gay Eurovision fandom state that they have to hide or minimize their sexuality in order to feel part of the community (Halliwell, 2023). Our data similarly show that some heterosexual furries avoid discussions about sexuality for this reason and others, avoiding directly disclosing these elements of their identity unless asked.

> *"Oddly as a non marginalized [sic] person, I fell [sic] needing not to disclose to make others feel comfortable."*

> *"I don't hide it, but I don't go telling everyone my entire identity and life story asap. I mention it if asked about, but rarely have reason to feel like I have to explain who I am[.]"*

> *"Hilariously, I've often felt that I need to hide my status as a majority among society as a whole in order to fit in with the fandom."*

> *"Anymore the straight christian [sic] is a rarity in the fandom, and it's starting to be in The Wider world. I often feel like I must hide this information due to past experiences within the fandom."*

In one furry's response, they explained that there's no single furry fandom, but rather an interconnected collection of spaces and people. While the overall environment is friendly to multiple identities, they point out that there's a need to be aware of the diversity of spaces within the community.

> *"i [sic] feel... normal in the fandom, or at least the spaces i [sic] run in, because most of the people in those spaces are also trans or far left or whatever. i [sic] think it's hazardous to concieve [sic] of the furry fandom as one monolithic entity, and i [sic] try not to treat 'furry' as an automatic guarantee that we'll be sympatico (bizarrely, some furries are transphobes! Some [sic] furries are straight up fucking fascists!) but statistically speaking i feel safer and more open with furries than the average person."*

Taken together, this section shows that furries of all sexual orientations can find their experience in the fandom and their fandom-related behavior shaped by their sexuality. Whether it was through finding a space where they felt 'normal' and a part of a majority or having the freedom to engage openly in physical and emotional intimacy, many queer furry cis men felt free and comfortable in the fandom. Though this led to some issues for others, there was a general consensus among LGBQA+ furries that the fandom was a much safer and more welcoming place for them than other fandoms or broader society. However, the easy expression of sexuality for cis queer men did cause some feelings of alienation and exclusion among gay trans furries, as well as complicating the experience of asexual furries interested in sexual encounters. Finally, many LGBQA+ furries indicated that they deliberately created safe spaces in the fandom by curating their friendships and communities. While this helps to create a greater sense of comfort and safety, it did contribute to the sense of disunity and marginalization felt by some straight furries.

Influence of Fandom on the Experience of Sexuality

In addition to pointing out how their sexuality impacted their experience in the furry fandom, some LGBQA+ furries also reported that the opposite was true as well: that their experiences within and as a part of the furry fandom influenced how they understood and expressed their sexuality. The sense of belonging and camaraderie described in earlier sections as a result of feeling a part of a majority also encouraged exploration and inspired confidence in those who were unsure, closeted, or timid in expressing their sexuality.

> *"I feel like im [sic] able to be open easily with my gender and sexuality since the furry community is largely lgbt+."*

> *"The furry fandom has always been very accepting of me technically being a minority in terms of sexual orientation and identity, and in fact it has been sorta encouraging and reassuring me to simply be myself, due to a higher mix of sexual orientations/gender identities/etc. in the fandom."*

> *"The furry fandom was the first space ever where I could just freely and openly be gay and it's been good to just wear that label and feel safe there."*

"On the contrary, I feel most open about my identity while interacting with members of the furry fandom, especially online. I feel a great deal of acceptance within the fandom as a gender, sexual, and racial minority."

"I guess as a Pansexual, being able to interact with other non-hetero furries has helped me feel more comfortable with myself. Never had I felt the need to hide myself from other furries."

"I guess I would consider myself a minority (gender and sexuality-wise). I feel pretty accepted. There's always a few people who aren't accepting, but that's everywhere. I've never felt a reason to hide in the furry fandom. It actually gives me an outlet to be myself."

Several queer furries explained that it was being part of the fandom that allowed them to accept their sexuality, particularly those who were closeted or felt unsafe in other parts of their lives.

"... the fandom is what allowed me to shed my homophobic ideals that I had growing up and accept not only myself but a vast number of others."

"The fandom was very welcoming to me as a young gay man just starting to accept his sexuality when I was 17 & 18 years old. It helped me to accept that part of me that I'd been raised to despise."

"I would say as a queer person, I can relate more closely with the majority of the fandom that is also queer. The stereotypical flamboyance of queer people fits well with the flamboyance of the fandom, and I think this atop the very accepting nature of the fandom contributes to the very high percentage of queers in the fandom. I see this as a positive, and as a person coming from an extremely homophobic household, it is and was an extremely helpful avenue for being able to be myself without any limitations on sexuality - almost an epiphany if you will, as it is for many."

"As a bisexual white cis-man[,] I feel accepted within the fandom, because the fandom is very open regarding sexual orientations. I never felt the need to hide my sexuality within the fandom, quite the contrary the fandom helped myself [sic] with my inner coming-out."

"Never had to hide as a bisexual in the fandom. (I hide here from the rest of my reality)."

Of course, not all queer people can be open and honest about their sexuality in their families, work, and community. For some queer furries, the safety of the community gave them a space to be "out," that is separate from their lives in the wider world. The relative anonymity of the furry community (online spaces/ fursonas) offers a great deal of protection and security, giving them the freedom to explore and express their true selves.

"It is a place to me where I can be myself without judgement, and be able to state things about myself that I would be terrified to say to my family or people in real life but matter very much to me with no fear. It nurtures a true acceptance and appreciation of yourself in a way that no other place can, truly[.]"

"Being bisexual, I actually feel more welcome online than in real life. I live in a conservative area, but the overall acceptance of LGBT+ people and the mask of semi-anonymity the fandom provides is quite appealing to me."

"I only feel part of a minority in terms of my sexuality (pansexual, polyamorous) and in the fandom[,] I feel largely free and safe being open about this, while in my 'day to day' life outside of the furry community I feel these are things I must hide, especially the polyamory."

"I do identify myself as trans and queer, with some unsureness on non-binary. I feel rather accepted and do not struggle interacting with a variety of people - with an exception of avoiding spaces where people are regarded as sexual relief through text chats, as those tend to, too often, discard my fursona as part of me. I never really felt I need [sic] to hide any of the potentially marginalized labels or identities in furry circles. In fact, furry fandom is the place that allowed me to strengthen my identity in regards [sic] to worries of how others might perceive and react to it. Without [the] furry fandom[,] I would not feel as strong as I do about it, and I would struggle to accept it as a part of me. Especially I would, without the furry fandom, struggle to show any of it to others in public spaces (Twitter, Discord, etc). I am still not open about it in real life or in any spaces that directly connect to my real life [sic] name/identity, but

otherwise[,] I am rather blatant and open about my identity thanks to [the] positive reception and experiences I have had within [the] furry fandom."

"I felt accepted within said community but I am not open about it in public for reasons being of fear for [sic] discrimination."

"In normal life, I am closeted in my sexual orientation. However, within my interactions with furries, I always have felt free and extremely welcome to call myself gay. This has helped me accept my orientation more because I have met my furry friends in real life and have dated male furries."

"Identities help us feel more secure in finding people we relate to! Honestly[,] I feel more comfortable when I see BLM in a profile or that the person is Lgbt or BIPOC like me. I don't always feel safe IRL and I live in a very white conservative southern area so finding people like me online is comforting[.]"

For queer furries who are only beginning to explore their sexual orientation, the furry community offers a safe, understanding, and welcoming space in which to do so. This allows them to have time to explore, to question, and to understand themselves.

"It's giving me more of an avenue to feel open about it, but still have personal hesitance."

"I'd say the fandom has helped me explore having a gay identity in a safe and controlled manner, to the point where I am now comfortable adopting it generally in other situations.

"Of course: my queer identity is v important to who I am as a person. In fact[,] I'd say that having the ability to explore my appearance/presentation had helped me come to terms with my identity thanks to the fandom"

*"**...** The openness about gender and sexuality in the fandom has been invaluable in exploring my own."*

"Personally Im [sic] still at a point where talking about it still feels a bit weird. I havent [sic] felt the need to hide it, but bringing it up is still difficult most of the time."

"the [sic] fandom is overwhelmingly queer, and has been unfailingly supportive in my continuing understanding of myself."

Unfortunately, despite the general perception of the fandom as encouraging, safe, and positive, not every corner of the fandom is as welcoming to queer identities and experiences. Some furries report experiencing harassment and discrimination which made them feel unwelcome and marginalized as a result of their sexuality.

"I have [experienced marginalization], *though it was in a tiny overly Christian religious space. At that point[,] I had not been fully accepting of my sexuality and their toxic rethorics [sic] had pushed me deeper into the closet[.]"*

"As part of LGBT, I do feel that there is [sic] occasional issues with more religious members of the fandom, though it is VERY few and far between in my personal experience."

"We feel accepted in leftwing/explicity [sic] queer spaces but the broader centrist spaces are often mixed or hostile"

The general degree of acceptance and the largely queer nature of the furry community can play a significant role in helping some queer furries who are confused, questioning, or closeted to have a safe space to experiment with their sexuality, to learn to understand themselves. For many furries, the safety and anonymity of the fandom gave them the safety and encouragement they needed to discover and understand themselves. However, not all corners of the fandom are welcoming, and not all sexual orientations experience whole-hearted acceptance. For these furries, curating their content, avoiding places where they feel unsafe, and finding a community where they can be themselves are paramount to finding their place in the furry community.

Conclusion

As is often the case in research more broadly, our findings concerning sexual orientation and LGBQA+ identity in the furry fandom have led us to a few answers, but even more questions about the interplay between sexual orientation and experiences within the furry fandom.

The present study represents a flawed and limited, but nevertheless illuminating first step into the study of this subject. One problem with the study is that the open-ended questions were far too broad and not specific to sexual orientation. Numerous respondents were unsure about what "affect your identity as a furry" meant, with long strings of question marks being a common response. Many others declined to answer simply because they didn't understand what the question was asking. The lack of specificity also meant that we received a wide range of answers, only some of which were related to sexual orientation. Many furries discussed other aspects of their identity, including social roles (parent, friend, daughter, son) and professions (student, tradesperson, scientist), although many did, as we'd hoped, discuss the intersection of their gender, race, and sexual orientation. The deliberate broadness of the question did allow for a nuanced understanding of some of the intersections between multiple identities and the furry fandom but ultimately prevented a deeper analysis of specific issues relating to sexual orientation.

Even so, the fact that we were able to find so much in the responses to this flawed question illustrates how fruitful future research on this subject is likely to be. The experiences of straight furries navigating the minority experience—possibly for the first time—is one such avenue, as is directly assessing and comparing the nature of straight and LGBQA+ furries' relationships to their fursonas. The experiences of asexual furries in a sex-positive and openly sexual fandom space is another potential question, as is the need to better understand the association between sexual and romantic orientation and how these facets of one's identity manifest in and interact with fursonas and the broader furry fandom.

We look forward to seeing where a more targeted and focused approach to this subject will lead us in the future—both finding answers to the questions we've raised here and discovering new questions that haven't even crossed our minds yet!

References

Blank, H. (2012). *Straight: The surprisingly short history of heterosexuality.* Beacon Press.

Bogaert, A. F. (2012). *Understanding asexuality.* Rowman & Littlefield Publishers.

Bullough, V. L. (1976). *Sexual Variance in Society and History.* John Wiley and Sons.

Halliwell, J. (2023). 'Are you sure you're not gay?': Straight and bisexual male experiences of Eurovision Song Contest fandom. *Social & Cultural Geography, 24*(6), 1024-1041. https://doi.org/10.1080/14649365.2021.2000016

Halperin, D. M. (2002). *How to do the history of homosexuality.* University of Chicago Press.

Henry, F. H. I. (2019). *Love, sex, and the noose: The emotions of sodomy in 18th-century England.* (Publication no. 29247116) [Doctoral dissertation, Western University]. ProQuest Dissertations Publishing.

Kinsey, A. C., Pomeroy, W. B., & Martin, C. E. (1998). *Sexual behavior of the human male.* Indiana University Press. (Original work published 1948)

McFarlane, C. (1997). *The sodomite in fiction and satire, 1660-1750.* Columbia University Press.

Murray, S. O. (2000). *Homosexualities.* University of Chicago Press.

Roughgarden, J. (2009). *Evolution's rainbow: Diversity, gender, and sexuality in nature and people.* University of California Press.

Chapter 17
Furry Beliefs: Religion and Politics

Courtney "Nuka" Plante, Camielle Adams

An old adage states that there are three things you should avoid talking about in polite company: politics, religion, and money. By following this advice, you'll steer clear of some awkward conversations at your next office party or family dinner. Scientists, on the other hand, are under no obligation to avoid the awkward or uncomfortable and, if anything, occasionally enjoy a good feather-ruffling. In this spirit, the present chapter focuses on furries' religious beliefs and political ideology—we'll leave the money talk to another chapter (Chapter 13), if only to avoid violating all *three* taboos in a single chapter!

Religion and Spirituality

It's hard to hypothesize whether there should be an association between being a furry and holding a particular religious or spiritual belief. One reason is the fact that furries come in all shapes and sizes and approach the fandom from all walks of life. As other chapters in this book illustrate, furries can be in their early-to-mid teens or their seventies and beyond; they can be cisgender and heterosexual or they can be genderqueer and pansexual; they can be starving students or well-off entrepreneurs and professionals, and they can come from any continent on the planet.

Prior research shows that, when it comes to religious beliefs, these are "differences that make a difference." For example, studies show that younger generations (e.g., millennials, zoomers) tend to be less intrinsically and extrinsically religious[1] than older generations (e.g., boomers, Gen X), although they are much more comparable concerning how spiritual[2] they

---

[1] Without going into too much detail, intrinsic religiosity can be thought of as "genuine belief"—that is, adherence to religious tenets regardless of external influences; in contrast, extrinsic religiosity refers to religion motivated by external pressures or rewards (e.g., social groups, peer pressure; Bergin, 1991).

[2] While there is no universally agreed-upon definition for these terms, loosely-speaking, spirituality refers to the seeking of significance or meaning in one's life, whereas religiosity refers to one's adherence to the rituals and practices of an institution or organization, often in service of some kind of spiritual end (Arrey et al., 2016). It's entirely possible for a person to be spiritual (e.g., seeking meaning and significance in the world) without belonging to a religious organization or identifying as religious. An atheistic scientist could describe their pursuit of knowledge and meaning as a spiritual pursuit, as Carl Sagan expressed when he

tend to be (McMurray & Simmers, 2020). Other studies have shown that lesbian, gay, and bisexual people are less likely to be religious, but not less likely to be spiritual, than straight people (Schwadel & Sandstrom, 2019), a fact owing, in whole or in part, to the condemnation of LGBTQ+ people by many religious organizations (Barnes & Meyer, 2012). Socioeconomic status is similarly associated with religious involvement, such that people with more wealth and status are less likely to go to church, pray, or read religious scripture (Schieman, 2010), while those who attend post-secondary education tend to score lower on measures of religiosity (Schwadel, 2016). Finally, it should come as no surprise to readers that some religious beliefs are more prominent in some countries over others, with Christianity being fairly evenly distributed around the world while other religions, such as Buddhism and Hinduism, are distributed predominantly in Asian-Pacific countries (Pew Research Center, 2012).

Taking all of this into account, the demographic variability of the furry fandom might lead some readers to speculate that religious and spiritual beliefs should be unrelated to one's furry identity. After all, few furries include spiritual or religious elements in their conceptualization of what it means to be furry (a topic we address in Chapter 5). Having said that, the fandom's demographic composition might lead us to a different hypothesis. We know, based on data reviewed in Chapter 13, that most furries are in their teens or early-to-mid 20s, are fairly likely to be LGBTQ+, have some college education, and that the largest concentration of furries is in the United States (9 out of 10 of the largest furry conventions in the world occur in the United States; Wikifur, n.d.).[3] These factors should predict trends toward atheism, agnosticism, and a generally low degree of religiosity (but not necessarily spirituality), even against the background of Christianity that predominates the American religious landscape (Pew Research Center, n.d.).

Keeping this in mind, let's turn our attention to some data from our studies to see whether they're in line with our demographic-based expectations. Our first look comes from data collected across six different studies from 2011-2015 which recruited furries either online or in-person at

---

wrote "Science is not only compatible with spirituality; it is a profound source of spirituality" (Sagan, 2011, p. 54).

[3] The only non-American furry convention in the top 10 would be Eurofurence, which takes place in Berlin, Germany. That said, there has been considerable growth in the size and number of non-Western furry conventions, including prominent furry conventions arising in The Philippines, Taiwan, Brazil, and Japan.

conventions.[4] Respondents were asked, across studies, to indicate in either an open-ended fashion or to choose from a list of options, what their religious affiliation was. In the case of open-ended responses, respondents' responses were coded and organized into categories. The range of average responses is shown in Table 17.1.

Table 17.1. Percentage of furry respondents across convention-going and online samples who identified as belonging to different religious affiliations. * Wasn't an option in the specific study.

Religious Affiliation	% of Sample (Online)	% of Sample (Pennsylvania)	% of Sample (Texas)
Christian	25.2	11.1-24.5	19.6-36.3
Agnostic	23.9	8.8-44.3	17.3-24.9
Atheist	25.7	3.7-4.4	14.0-24.9
Pagan / Wiccan	5.3	5.9-8.5	7.8-12.8
Buddhist	1.3	1.1-2.1	0.4
Shinto	0.8	0.0	1.7
Jewish	0.6	1.3-1.9	0.6-1.4
Satanist	*	0.0-0.9	1.1
Muslim	0.4	0.0-0.2	0.0-0.7
Hindu	0.2	0.0-0.4	0.4-0.6
None / Not Applicable	*	0.0-50.6	*
Other	16.8	3.4-14.3	16.8-18.9

The first thing worth noting in the table is the sizable variability in the agnosticism/none categories in the Pennsylvania sample. This stems from differences across studies in how atheism and agnosticism were assessed and scored across samples: in some studies, an atheism option was not provided (participants were asked to choose "none," indicating no religious affiliation,

[4] Of note, the conventions took place in the United States, either in Dallas, Texas or in Pittsburgh, Pennsylvania, meaning the convention results in particular are largely skewed toward American furries from these regions.

or were sometimes rolled into a combined "atheist / agnostic" category). Keeping this in mind, a few trends emerge across the samples. First, despite coming from largely American samples, in which the majority of the population identifies as Christian (Pew Research Center, n.d.), only about one-fifth to one-quarter of furries identify as Christian. In contrast, a sizable proportion of furries—approximately one-third to one-half—identify as atheist or agnostic, numbers that again significantly exceed those found in the general American population (Pew Research Center, n.d.). Both of these trends are consistent with what we would expect to see based on the demographic composition of the furry fandom and what prior research has shown us about demographics and religious beliefs.[5]

To better illustrate whether the result obtained speaks to something unique about furries or whether it would be expected in any group with comparable demographics, we can compare data from two different studies we ran in 2013 and 2014. These studies involved a sample of convention-going anime fans and a sample of convention-going furries, both of which were drawn within a year of one another in Dallas, Texas. The results, shown in Table 17.2, reveal that a comparable number of participants identified as Christian across both samples. While furries were more likely to identify as agnostic/atheist, this likely has to do with the addition of a "none / not applicable" option in the anime sample that wasn't available in the furry sample. This aside, the trend toward being less religious and more secular than the general population observed in furries[6] is probably not unique to furries, but rather is a product of demographic trends (e.g., being a younger, college-educated group of people),[7] although it is notable that the tendency for furries to have significantly more Pagan / Wiccan participants even

[5] We should also note that while rates of Buddhism, Muslim, Jewish, and Hindu participants were pretty much on-par with rates in the general American population (Pew Research Center, n.d.), prevalence rates of Pagan / Wiccan respondents were significantly higher than what we would have expected, and are far more prevalent than what is found in the general population. To date, we have no explanation for these particular findings.

[6] Further supporting this idea, in one of our 2013 studies, furries at a convention in Dallas, Texas were less religious and spiritual than a sample of liberal arts college students recruited from a Texas college.

[7] Speaking further to the idea that it's a matter of demographics and not simply a matter of fan groups as a whole being non-religious, one of our 2019 online studies found that, compared to *Star Wars* fans, who were, as a demographic, older and less LGBTQ+, furries were significantly less religious.

compared to a demographically comparable sample is, perhaps, an idiosyncrasy of the furry fandom.

Table 17.2. Percentage of anime fan and furry respondents at two Texas-based fan conventions in 2013 / 2014 who identified as belonging to different religious affiliations. * Wasn't an option in the specific study.

Religious Affiliation	% of Sample (Anime)	% of Sample (Furry)
Christian	21.6	19.6
Agnostic	5.7	24.9
Atheist	3.1	24.9
Pagan / Wiccan	3.6	7.8
Buddhist	2.5	0.4
Jewish	1.8	1.4
Muslim	0.0	0.7
Hindu	0.1	0.4
None / Not Applicable	39.2	*
Other	23.4	18.9

As we've seen, religious affiliation data are a fairly messy affair,[8] one that risks diverting us from the more pointed question of whether furries, as a group, are any more or less likely to be religious or spiritual, regardless of what their particular affiliations or beliefs happen to be. To more directly address this question, we can measure the extent to which furries consider themselves to be religious or spiritual. By asking about the two concepts separately, we can better distinguish between adherence to the tenets of a religion (religiousness) and those actively journeying toward a sense of greater meaning or purpose in their life, regardless of whether they do so through a religious institution or on their own terms (spirituality).

Across a set of five different studies from 2012-2021, we asked furries, sometimes recruited at conventions and sometimes recruited online, to indicate the extent to which they would consider themselves to be spiritual and, separately, the extent to which they considered themselves to be religious. These were asked in slightly different ways across each study, but

[8] This isn't even considering all of the nuances in the data, such as distinguishing between different denominations of Christianity or different types or degrees of agnosticism!

the pattern of results was always the same: on average, furries reported being more spiritual than religious. For an illustrative example from a 2012 study at a Pennsylvania furry convention, see Figure 17.1. As the figure shows, most furries consider themselves to be fairly non-religious. In contrast, while many furries also did not consider themselves to be spiritual, a comparable number of furries also consider themselves to be fairly, or even extremely spiritual. In short, the available evidence suggests, in line with our hypotheses, that furries, as a group, are not especially interested in formalized religion, even if they are somewhat interested in independently pursuing questions about significance, purpose, and meaning.

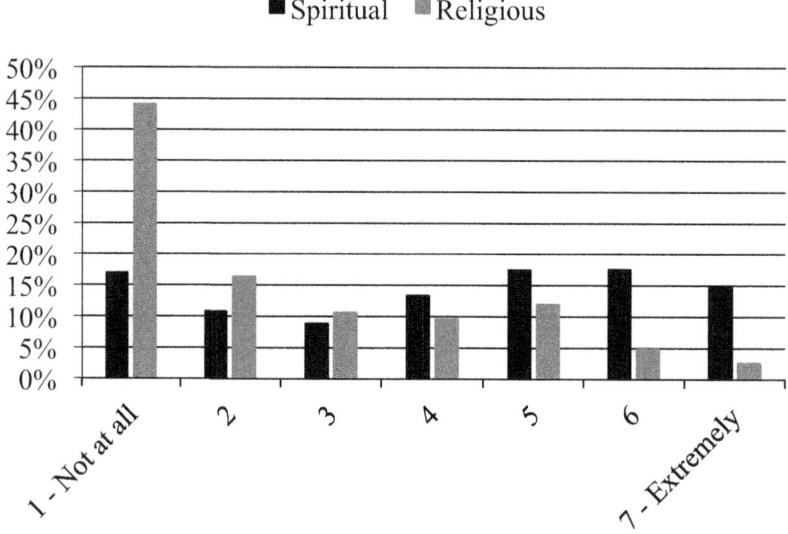

Figure 17.1. Extent to which furries recruited at a Pennsylvania furry convention considered themselves to be religious or spiritual.

Follow-up studies shed additional light and context on these findings. For example, a pair of 2017 and 2018 studies of furries again recruited from a Pennsylvania furry convention found that furries, while somewhat interested in spiritual matters (if not religious ones), were less interested in specific new-age beliefs (e.g., “spiritual energy”), suggesting that they may be more interested in self-directed spiritual pursuits rather than simply adopting non-mainstream beliefs. In other studies, identifying more strongly with the furry fandom (and, to some extent, identifying more strongly as a furry in general—fanship) was associated with higher spirituality scores, but not with higher religiosity scores. While this doesn't necessarily mean that being "more furry" *causes* a person to become more spiritual, it does, at the very least, suggest that those who identify more strongly as furries are, on average, the same people who consider themselves more spiritual. One possible explanation for this is that some furries use the furry fandom, furry content, fursonas, and other facets of their furry interest as a source of guidance or significance in their lives, something that we've observed in at least some highly identified *My Little Pony* fans (e.g., Edwards et al., 2019).

To wrap up this section on the religious beliefs of furries, the picture is complex, as it is with so many aspects of the furry fandom. No single category, affiliation, or term unilaterally describes the religious or spiritual beliefs of furries as a group—they are neither defined by a particular religious affiliation nor are they defined by a resounding lack of religious beliefs. We can say that, as a group, furries tend to be somewhat more spiritual than they are religious, suggesting that many have moved away from formal, organized religious institutions in place of the individual pursuit of significance, purpose, and meaning in life—though this is part of a larger trend we see in demographically similar groups. Religion, spirituality, and a lack thereof are not inherently furry, and the demographic variety observed among furries leads to considerable variety in the manifestation of their religious and spiritual beliefs. Even the tendency for some highly identified furries to rely on the fandom as a source of significance, purpose, and meaning is probably not unique to the furry fandom, having been observed in similar fandoms. If there is a feature that's fairly unique or idiosyncratic to furries, it's the significant number of Pagan / Wiccan furries whose prevalence is much higher than what has been observed in other fan groups—although the reason for this is currently unknown.

Political Beliefs

In the same way we did for religious beliefs, we can form hypotheses about furries' political beliefs based on their demographic composition. Specifically, based on the features we mentioned in the previous section, we can hypothesize that furries, as a group, ought to be fairly progressive, liberal, or left-leaning in their political views.[9] For example, the general

[9] We should note that we're discussing politics here in an American-centric system, where "left-leaning" refers to more liberal/progressive political ideology and "right-leaning" refers to political conservatism with an emphasis on individual freedoms. We should also note that by "progressive" political beliefs we're referring to political beliefs that espouse policies aimed at increasing egalitarianism including, but not limited to, income redistribution, affirmative action, protective legislation for

belief that younger people are more progressive in their political leanings than older people has been shown to hold empirical water (e.g., Truett, 1993). Likewise, there is evidence that post-secondary education is generally associated with an increase in political liberalism (Hastie, 2007).[10] LGBTQ+ people have also been found to hold significantly more liberal beliefs than non-LGBTQ+ people (Worthen, 2020). In short, the fairly young, largely college-educated, predominantly LGBTQ+ demographic composition of the furry fandom ought to predispose it to be fairly liberal-leaning in its political views.

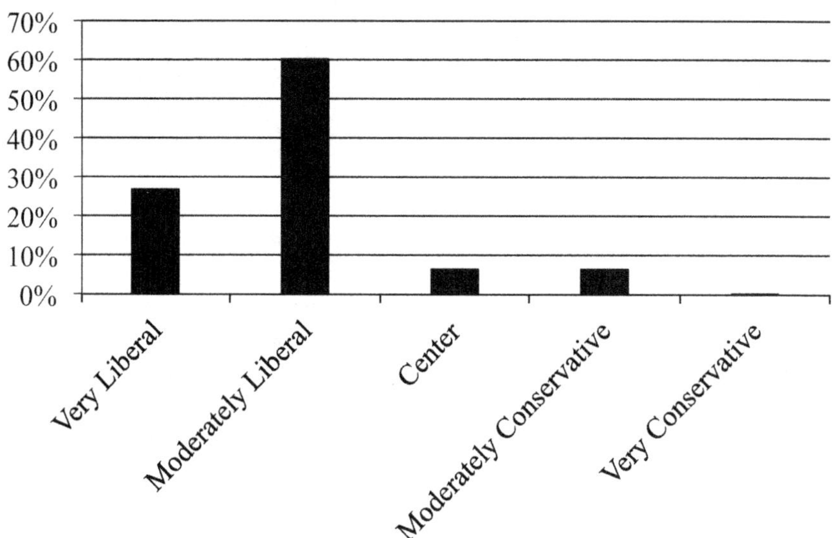

Figure 17.2. Percentage of a sample of online furries recruited in 2021 who identified with various political leanings, coded based on open-ended responses to a question asking them to describe their political identification.

---

minority groups, and strengthening of workers rights (e.g., unions). This is contrasted against more conservative policies aimed at maximizing personal liberty (e.g., free markets, minimizing taxation, minimizing government interference).

[10] There are some important qualifiers to this, including the fact that the effect differs considerably depending on the academic discipline one is in and the fact that there is still considerable debate over the mechanisms driving the effect (e.g., do more liberal people choose to pursue specific academic fields or does learning more about liberal ideas and spending time around people espousing more liberal ideas change a person's own political orientation?).

Table 17.3. Examples of furry respondents' open-ended responses to a question about political identity and how they were coded.

Category	Examples
Very Liberal	"Extreme-left anarchism Marxist Communism Anti-Capitalism" "Definitely lean strongly left, to the point where both major parties in the U.S. are farther right than me." "Far left, socially and fiscally"
Moderately Liberal	"Australian Labor Party (center-left/left)" "Center-left Democrat" "Center-left Canadian NDP" "Democrat" "Progressive centrist" "Left leaning, but not fixed on a specific party"
Center	"According to political compass literally center center" "Centrist, I guess? Idk what they call it when you like to listen to both sides (or more) of a debate before deciding" "Moderate/Center with leanings towards both political parties"
Moderately Conservative	"Center, right leaning" "Central with Right views" "Center-right" "Centrist-Republican" "Conservative"
Very Conservative	"Paleoconservative"

Table 17.4. Prevalence of specific political labels in furry respondents' open-ended responses to a question about political identity.

Label	% of Responses
Socialist / Communist	30.3
Anarchist	8.3
Libertarian	6.5
Environmentalist	5.1
Humanism	2.4
Antifa / Antifascist	1.4
Anti-Capitalist	1.1
Syndicalism	1.1
Capitalist	0.8
Nationalist	0.6
Authoritarian	0.3
Nazi	0.2
Anti-Socialist	0.2
Neutral / No Affiliation / Independent	19.6
I don't care / Apathy / I don't know	17.5
Mixed	3.5
I don't want to discuss my politics	1.5

Hypotheses aside, what do the data show? We've tested our hypotheses across a number of different studies, measuring political orientation in a myriad of different ways with varying degrees of complexity. The first, and perhaps the most straightforward way we've done so is to simply ask furries to describe, in an open-ended fashion, how they identify politically. This was the approach we took in a 2021 online study. Looking through the different responses, participants were categorized in two different ways. First, where possible, their beliefs were categorized on a five-point, single-dimension scale ranging from "very liberal" to "very conservative." The prevalence rate of these different categories is shown in Figure 17.2.[11] We also illustrate how respondents were coded into each of the different categories with some representative responses for each category in Table 17.3.

[11] Note that this table does not include the approximately 20% of participants who indicated no political beliefs, political apathy, or who indicated that they did not want to provide their political beliefs.

In addition to the single dimension above, we also tallied noteworthy political identifiers and their frequency in Table 17.4.

Taken together, these results are in accordance with our hypotheses based on the demographic composition of the furry fandom: in open-ended responses, furries tend to be moderately liberal-leaning, with a fair number of furries identifying as very far to the left. This is reflected both in terms of their categorization on a continuum and in terms of some of the most prevalent specific labels used (e.g., socialist, communist). In contrast, centrist and conservative views tended to be far less prevalent, both as assessed using a continuum and in terms of the prevalence of specific conservative-based labels (e.g., libertarian, capitalist). It should also be noted that amidst this "variability around a general tendency toward liberalism," approximately one-quarter to one-third of furries consider themselves to be uninterested in politics or to have no particular political affiliation.

One could argue that the open-ended nature of these results lends itself to a great deal of interpretation from us researchers, who choose how to best interpret a participant's specific response (e.g., as "very liberal" or only "moderately liberal"). What's needed is converging evidence from other, more objective measures to see whether this general tendency toward liberalism is consistent and reliable. To that end, we turn to results from additional studies.

As a fairly analogous point of comparison, we can look at the results of two different studies from 2012 and 2014, both of which recruited participants from a furry convention in Pennsylvania. Relevant to the previous findings, respondents were asked to indicate where their political orientation fell on a single, 7-point dimension ranging from "very liberal" to "very conservative." While the scale lacks the nuance of the open-ended measure, including not allowing participants to indicate "I don't care", it does eliminate any potential bias we may have when categorizing participants along the continuum since participants categorized themselves. The results, shown in Figure 17.3, reveal a fairly similar pattern of responses, with furries being far more on the liberal side of the dimension than on the conservative side, as well as being more moderately liberal than very liberal. We should also note that the higher prevalence of people in the middle of the scale may be the result of respondents who were apathetic or undecided choosing to pick the most "neutral" response available. If nothing else, this possibility merits caution when interpreting the meaning of a centrist response to this measure.

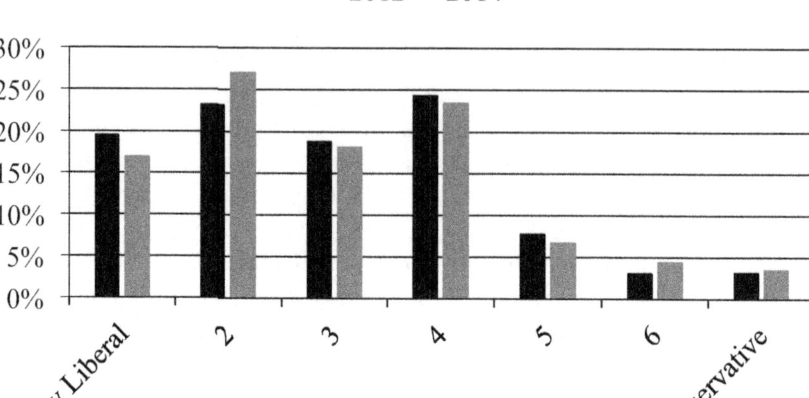

Figure 17.3. Responses of furries recruited at two Pennsylvania furry conventions to a unidimensional measure of political orientation.

Readers who are well-versed in political discourse might, by this point, find themselves exasperated by the fairly simplistic approach we've taken to political orientation. After all, peoples' political beliefs can be multifaceted and nuanced: someone could be fairly progressive when it comes to laws protecting the rights of LGBTQ+ people while also taking a more conservative stance regarding taxation and social welfare projects. To this end, we ran a study in 2013 in which furries recruited at a Texas furry convention were asked to indicate their political orientation on the same 7-point scale ranging from "very liberal" to "very conservative," but to do so three separate times: once with respect to their views regarding social policies (e.g., affirmative action, gay marriage, trans rights), once concerning their fiscal views (e.g., universal healthcare, lower taxes), and once for their overall political identity.[12] The results are shown in Figure 17.4.

[12] Another importance difference with the measure in this study is that it allowed participants to indicate "I don't know" as an option, which approximately 20% of furries chose. By taking this into account, we can more confidently say that respondents choosing the neutral or center option are probably genuinely indicating a centrist position rather than not knowing how else to indicate apathy or a lack of political understanding.

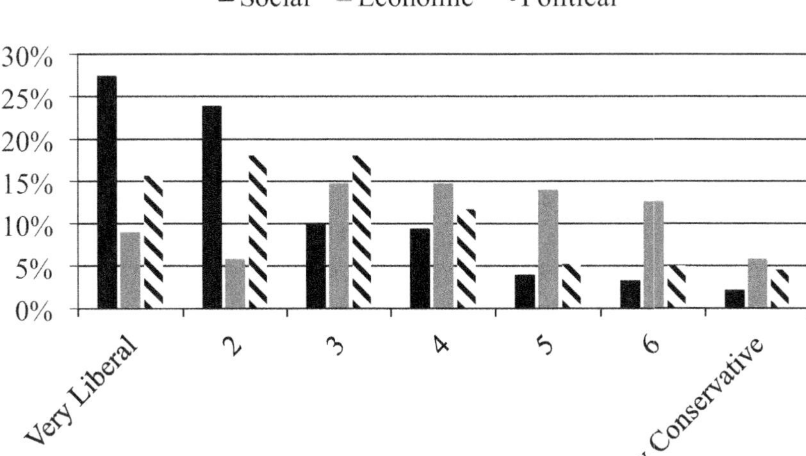

Figure 17.4. Responses of furries recruited at a Texas furry convention to three unidimensional measures of social, economic, and political orientation.

Our first observation concerning the "political" dimension is that furries, again, tend to identify far more on the liberal side of the scale than on the conservative side. This consistency was observed even though this sample was recruited from a convention in Texas, a more conservative state than Pennsylvania based on both presidential and congressional elections since the 1990s. Despite coming from the Deep South, as opposed to the North, we nevertheless observed the same trend toward liberal beliefs, with a stronger preference for moderate beliefs over very liberal beliefs, once again indicating the consistency of this general finding.

Offering more nuance to the findings, we also found a dramatic difference between responses about social and fiscal policy. Specifically, furries showed a very strong preference toward socially liberal policies but held deeper centrist, almost conservative positions with respect to economic policies. That said, this measure is not without its own set of problems, one of which is whether furries can be taken at their word when they call themselves liberal- or conservative-leaning in their political views. Studies have shown that people—especially younger people—are prone to adopting political labels that don't necessarily reflect their actual positions (Zell & Bernstein, 2013). For example, a person raised in a liberal household may identify as a liberal, the label of their ingroup identification (e.g., coming from a "liberal family"), despite holding predominantly conservative fiscal and social positions.

We assessed this possibility in a 2019 study at a Texas furry convention. There, we gave furries a 42-item political scale designed to assess their opinions regarding specific political positions. The scale's original designer created the scale to assess three dimensions of political belief: economic socialism (e.g., "In order to protect the rights of workers, labor unions should have more power"), contemporary populism (e.g., "Borders should be closed for asylum seekers") and social conservatism (e.g., "Minimum wages should be abolished;" Laméris, 2015). As Figure 17.5 reveals, when it comes to furries' actual responses to specific political issues, they tend to lean toward more liberal positions, both in terms of social and economic policies. Furries also scored fairly low on a measure of contemporary populism, which also speaks to a general adherence to a more liberal ideology.

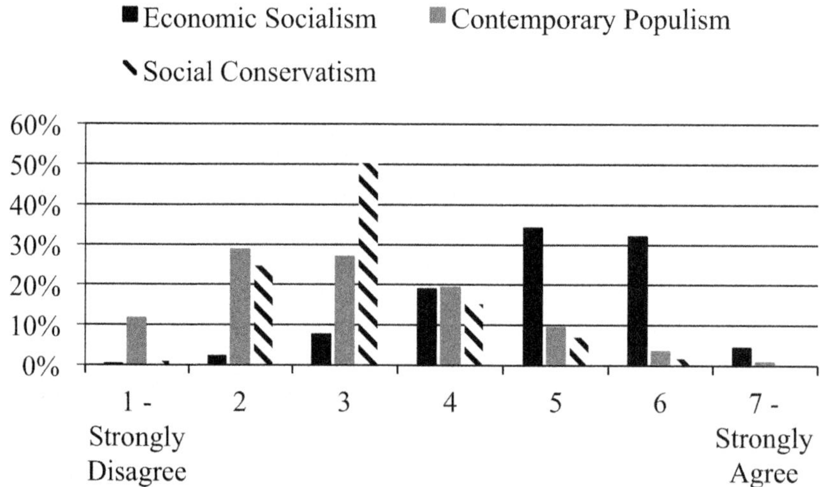

Figure 17.5. Average agreement of furries recruited at a Texas furry convention along three different scales measuring different facets of political orientation.

As a final look at some of the nuances in furries' political beliefs, as part of the same 2019 study of Texas furries, we presented respondents with a set of six different dimensions that referred to different political beliefs. For each one, furries indicated, on a 7-point scale, where their own political beliefs fell. Table 17.5. The results reveal, in line with prior findings, that furries are far more likely to identify as liberal than to identify as conservative. They also tend to be more liberal-leaning concerning economic issues, at least when it comes to imposing economic regulations and supporting egalitarianism over elitism.[13] In line with their tendency toward more moderate liberalism, however, furries were more opposed to, than supportive of, collectivism. Furries also showed a generally moderate view on the role of state power and generally leaned toward absolute free speech over imposing limitations to free speech.

Table 17.5. Prevalence of responses by furries recruited at a Texas-based fan convention to six different political dimensions.

Anchor 1	% Leaning to Anchor 1	% Neutral on Issue	% Leaning to Anchor 2	Anchor 2
Conservative	16.0	20.1	63.9	Liberal
Economic Liberty	31.1	28.9	40.1	Economic Regulation
Individualism	50.7	26.1	23.9	Collectivism
No State Power	27.5	48.5	24.0	Complete State Power
Elitism	10.5	31.0	58.5	Egalitarianism
Absolute Free Speech	67.8	16.8	15.3	Limited Free Speech

In short, the data we've reviewed generally support the idea that furries, as a group, are fairly liberal-leaning, a finding consistent with what we would hypothesize based on the demographic composition[14] of the furry fandom as a whole.[15] Nevertheless, there is variability around this central

[13] In hindsight, "elitism" was a poor choice of anchor wording, and would have been better represented with an anchor like "hierarchies."

[14] For further evidence that demographics contribute to furries' beliefs, we've also witnessed age differences *within* samples of furries. Specifically, across several of our studies from 2012-2019, older furries were, more often than not, more conservative and more spiritual than younger furries.

[15] Available evidence suggests that the liberal positioning of the furry fandom is far from unique to furries as far as fandoms go. Studies in 2013 and 2014 found that

tendency, with about 20-25% of furries being fairly apathetic, uninterested, or not knowing enough about politics to weigh in with their position, and a few furries who identify as conservative.

Perception of Political Beliefs in the Fandom

Before wrapping up this chapter, we'd like to briefly return to the 2021 study where we looked at furries' open-ended responses about their political affiliation. The question itself was part of a series of questions, two of which in particular shed light on how furries perceive politics in the fandom.

The first question has to do with whether furries feel comfortable expressing their political views in fandom spaces. It's a question we've often been asked to study by furries wondering whether there is a clash between some furries' desire to use the fandom as a means of escapism and other furries' desire to use the fandom to meet people who share their political views.[16] To gather relevant data on the issue, we asked furries to indicate, in an open-ended fashion, whether they generally felt comfortable expressing their political views in fandom spaces.

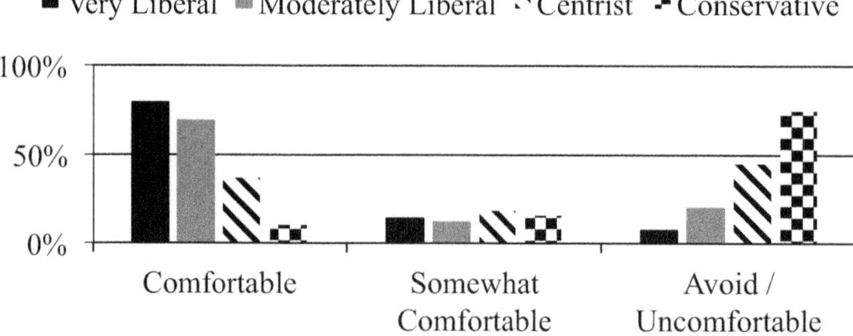

Figure 17.6. Percentage of very liberal, moderately liberal, centrist, and conservative furries recruited in an online study who feel varying degrees of comfort expressing their political views in the furry fandom. Moderately conservative and very conservative respondents have been combined due to their being relatively uncommon.

---

while furries, as a group, tended to be more liberal than the average liberal arts college student, they were no more liberal than samples of anime fans or fantasy sports fans.

[16] The point has become even more poignant in recent years as highly-charged political issues such as the acceptability of allowing alt-right and neo-Nazi furries into furry spaces have risen to prominence on furry social media.

The results, shown in Figure 17.6, make it clear that there are two very distinct perspectives on this matter. In general, liberal-minded furries feel quite comfortable expressing their political views in furry spaces, while centrists (to some degree) and conservatives especially feel uncomfortable expressing their political views in furry spaces. The most likely reason for this tendency stems from the fandom being comprised predominantly of furries who hold fairly liberal political positions. Centrist and conservative furries have likely picked up on the unpopularity of their positions in furry spaces and, as such, likely feel intimidated about expressing their positions in furry spaces, knowing that doing so runs the risk of getting them dogpiled[17] by others around them.

Speaking to this idea, it's illustrative to compare some of the responses of liberal and conservative furries to see whether they felt comfortable sharing their political views in furry spaces. Regarding liberal furries, most indicated significant comfort at the prospect of expressing their views, usually knowing that their position was likely to be a majority position in fandom spaces as compared to other places in their lives.

"Yes, for the most part, most of my friends are left leaning [sic]."

"Yes, most in the fandom that I've interacted with on the subject are either of similar ideals, or are open to civil discussion."

"Yes, most share similar views as myself in terms of human rights for people of all races/gender/sexual orientation, etc."

"Yeah, pretty much. a lot of the furry fandom members are leftists."

"Much more than anywhere else. Save maybe a star [sic] trek [sic] convention, but never tried that."

"Usually. Probably more so than outside the fandom."

"Yes. As with anything political, there will always be disagreements but in general, I feel that the majority of the fandom either shares similar beliefs or do not feel strongly either way."

[17] Pun only somewhat intended!

"Yes, I have no qualms about backlash since it's expected everywhere, though the furry fandom is naturally an easy place to be progressive."

That said, even being in a sizable numerical majority, some liberal furries nevertheless expressed hesitation at bringing up politics in fandom spaces, or, at the very least, limit topics of discussion to important ones, often as a means of keeping the peace or avoiding conflict.

"Yes, however[,] it's not something I like to do, I feel that although political [sic] are important[,] that [sic] they ruin relationships and burn bridges, so I tend to keep to myself on such things unless theres [sic] a good reason to speak up."

"Sure, but I choose not to because I draw furry art as my career and I feel like no business should be expressing political beliefs. My politics and how I vote are not something I want to discuss with the furry fandom, even if I know my beliefs are in line with the majority of the fandom."

"Yeah, my political leanings are fairly common. But I don't really think it's the place for politics."

"I try to keep my political opinions mostly to myself. There is a time and a place. Sometimes it is acceptable and beneficial to talk about politics, but most of the time it is unnecessary."

"I feel that expressing certain topics (ex. LGBTQ rights) should be expressed, while other topics should not."

"To most degrees[,] yes. I openly have BLM in my Twitter handle. I would put other things like ACAB[18] in there too, but some of these are still a little too "hot" for some furs, and aren't quite discussions we can have just yet."

"I do only if it is necessary to the discussion at hand. We should try to limit politics unless absolutely necessary, like in the case of BLM, LGBTQ rights, or Stop Asian Hate."

---

[18] ACAB stands for "all cops are bastards" and is generally used to express hostility or criticism toward police, usually in the context of abusing power or corruption.

In contrast, the majority of centrists and conservatives felt uneasy about expressing their political views openly in furry spaces, often out of fear of repercussions or backlash from the broader fandom. Most were very keenly aware of the unpopularity of their positions in fan spaces.

"No, people tend to take offence [sic] very quickly."

"Not at all. I have been banned from a local meet before for expressing that I was voting for a Conservative candidate. This has proved to me that furries aren't open to hearing other perspectives."

"Absolutely not, if you dare say any thing [sic] even that's not and [sic] extremely leftist view point [sic], you will get cancled [sic]."

"No. I would be burned at the stake."

"No, having any 'right-wing' ideals makes you the devil."

"Absolutely not. I'd rather only discuss politics with my very close friends. Discussing it in furry spaces will just lead to me being harassed/bullied, ostracized at IRL events, and shunned. It would destroy my business. The most marginalized group in the fandom are furries who aren't 100% left leaning [sic]."

"Given today's climate and how much online hatred towards Conservatives that [sic] there is, I would not be comfortable. Most of the online furries that I follow are very left-wing with things such as BLM and ACAB, and I often find myself feeling like I'm alienated when it comes towards [sic] politically socializing with other members of the fandom. Hell, given the January 6th Capitol visit, Furaffinity (one of my favorite online furry websites) went all political and left-wing worshipping that I felt sick of that website for a very long while afterwards. There are even some furries who had posted in their journal entries...that if anyone of their watchers or followers supported Trump, then would they please fuck off and unfollow them. While I do know that there will be at least some level of political divide in the furry fandom, the amount of left-wing worshipping and hatred towards anybody who has a right-wing opinion (even towards moderates like myself) feels like it goes against what the furry fandom stands for as a welcoming community. Given today's

political climate and how it has appeared to shove the furry fandom into the far-left political views (and I have seen a lot of that recently on websites such as Furaffinity, Twitter, YouTube, and several other sites for furries), I feel like I would be treated as the worst person in existence just because I dare have an opinion that differs from most furries I have seen online."

The last respondent mentions another topic that we've been asked to study with respect to perspectives on politics in the furry fandom: the idea that the fandom is becoming an increasingly political space. To address this question, we also asked participants in the same study to answer a final open-ended question about whether they felt the fandom was becoming more or less political, and whether this was generally a better or a worse thing. After coding the responses, the results were pretty one-sided: 72.2% of furries said that the fandom was becoming more politicized, while only 25.6% said it was no more or less political than it had ever been and 2.2% said it was less political than it had been in the past. That said, 58.1% of furries suggested that this change was largely for the better, a viewpoint much more likely to be espoused by liberal furries than centrist or conservative ones. In the case of liberal furries, it's often discussed as a catalyst for broader social change.

"Everything feels more political these days, but maybe that's just because I'm tuning in and noticing it more. At least in the fandom, it feels like things are always moving towards a better place." [Democratic socialist][19]

"More political, and that's a good thing as deplatforming [sic] conservatives and the far right is a neccesary [sic] part of a healthy society." [Progressive]

"I think it has become 'more political' in that discussions of how the fandom treats minority groups and what the fandom tolerates has become far more widespread, which I believe to be a good thing that will lead to a more accepting, safe, community for minority groups that are often excluded." [Quite left-leaning]

---

[19] Brackets indicate labels used by participants to describe their own political leanings.

"Fandom has become more political. Which is a good thing, we try to hide less of the shit in our midst." [Socialist]

"I think more folks are standard up to the rampant bigotry in the fandom, and that's not a bad thing. So, yes, I do. Folks ain't comfy sitting around while messed up stuff happens now, and I like that." [Progressive]

"From what i [sic] can tell, significant discussions have arisen surrounding the way the fandom treats black [sic] and indigenous [sic] furs in the wake of George Floyd... i'm [sic] hoping that this radicalises the fandom into a legitimate arm of change in the endgame, cos we have the power to do it like no other fandom has done before." [Anarchist / Leftist]

In contrast, more centrist or conservative furries tend to see the increased presence of politics as undesirable.

"It has become more political than is acceptable." [Independent]

"Absolutely more political, too much[,] and for the worse." [Libertarian I suppose]

"Much, much more political, and in a very negative and decisive way." [Libertarian, Independent]

"Leftist furries have made the fandom political to the point of gatekeeping." [Center Left]

"People[,] in general[,] have been hyper politicized [sic] to the point where I think they truly believe [sic] that there is A. Everything can be twisted into politics and that B. It's the most important thing. It's all rather depressing." [Conservative]

"More political. It feels like radical left-wing politics has invaded the furry fandom, and everyone must have the same views that Trump and the Republicans are evil even though the Republicans and Trump are working for their voter base. It feels to me like furries are more in support of communism, far-left ideology, and wanting to freely censor conservatives

and conservative furs rather than building the furry fandom together to be a strong welcoming community." [Moderate / Centrist]

"Compared to when i [sic] joined the community[,] it not only became more politcal [sic] but also way more radicalized. Instead of trying to understand why people one [sic] disagrees with (be it on an emotinal [sic], political or fundamental level) think that way, those get demonized and attemps [sic] are made to try to get those excluded from the fandom... if this continues in the following years, i [sic] have the felling [sic], the fandom will die for a lot of people because of the internal conflict. I have the feeling the vast majority hasn't any interest of [sic] understanding anyone who's outside their bubble. Investing time(!! not money) to try to understand/figure out/ change someone is very rare - not only that, but people who try to change others to [sic] the better often get put into the demoninzed [sic] places, instead of getting supported [sic] in their efforts." [Center center]

Centrists and conservatives were not the only ones who expressed negativity about the furry fandom becoming more political; some liberals saw it in an undesirable light, often referring to a perceived increase in extreme or violent political groups in the fandom or out of fear of reprisals or backlash by more extreme left-wing elements in the fandom.

"Recent years people with extreme views have been given too much of a voice." [Liberal Socialist]

"The fandom was always political, just some rotten apples from the Far right managed to found a safe space into it and this led us to the political drama of the recent years." [Apolitical / Liberal]

"With the rise of the alt-right and neo-nazis invading online spaces, it is definitely more political than it was in the 90s." [Left]

"The fandom is more political and more tense." [Communist]

"It has become incredibly political over the past five years. It is to the point that it is a problem, and that you can have your entire reputation ruined over anything that is taken negatively by either side." [Anarchist]

*"I feel like - with Twitter politics coming into play, it makes political conversations happen **way way** more than they used to, and it makes certain conversations incredibly hard - causing a kind of us vs them. I am left leaning [sic] myself, but seeing friends kicked out due to opinions they hold, is upsetting."* [Labour / Left leaning]

Conclusion

It would be foolhardy to try and condense the beliefs of a group as diverse as the furry fandom into a single category, be they religious beliefs or political beliefs. Furries do have a demographic central tendency toward being fairly young, college-educated, and LGBTQ+, which almost certainly explains at least some of the broad tendencies when it comes to furries' beliefs: being more secular in general relative to the general population and being more liberal-leaning or progressive relative to what one finds in the general population. This is not to say, of course, that all furries fall within these central tendencies, both demographically and in their beliefs: there are furries in their 30s, 40s, and 50s who are secular and progressive-minded and there are furries in their late teens who are deeply religious and who identify as politically conservative. While it would be a mistake to overlook this variability, however, it would also be a mistake to pretend that there aren't general trends either, trends which have been shown across a variety of studies employing various measures to ensure that the findings are unlikely to be a "fluke" or a quirk of any one study's methodology.

These trends certainly seem to be noticed by furries: open-ended data revealed that furries are keenly aware of the fandom's progressive attitudes as a whole. In general, progressive furries tend to see this as a positive, empowering them to express their positions and representing a catalyst for political action. In contrast, centrist and conservative furries may see this as stifling their free expression—a concern also shared by at least some progressive furries as well.

Finally, it should be noted that the pattern of beliefs observed in the furry fandom is likely a product of the demographic composition of the fandom rather than a unique feature of being a furry: similar patterns have been noted in other fan groups including anime fans and bronies. Likewise, our studies suggest that the extent to which a person identifies as a furry or with the furry fandom is largely unrelated to their political or religious beliefs, suggesting that there's likely nothing inherent in furry content itself that "makes" people secular or liberal. If nothing else, this chapter serves as an important reminder that while it's worth studying the quirks and characteristics of the furry fandom, we should never forget that furries are more than their interest in anthropomorphic animal characters. Demographic differences within the furry fandom itself and compared to other fandoms can and do affect furries' thoughts, feelings, and behaviors both in fandom spaces and in the broader world outside of the fandom.

References

Arrey, A. E., Bilsen, J., Lacor, P., & Deschepper, R. (2016). Spirituality/religiosity: A cultural and psychological resource among Sub-Saharan African migrant women with HIV/AIDS in Belgium. *PLoS One, 11*(7), e0159488. https://doi.org/10.1371/journal.pone.0159488

Barnes, D. M., & Meyer, I. H. (2012). Religious affiliation, internalized homophobia, and mental health in lesbians, gay men, and bisexuals. *American Journal of Orthopsychiatry, 82*(4), 505-515. https://doi.org/10.1111/j.1939-0025.2012.01185.x

Bergin, A. E. (1991). Values and religious issues in psychotherapy and mental health. *American Psychologist, 46*(4), 394-403. https://doi.org/10.1037/0003-066X.46.4.394

Edwards, P., Chadborn, D. P., Plante, C. N., Reysen, S., & Redden, M. H. (2019). *Meet the bronies: The psychology of adult* My Little Pony *fandom*. McFarland & Company.

Hastie, B. (2007). Higher education and sociopolitical orientation: The role of social influence in the liberalisation of students. *European Journal of Psychology of Education, 22*(3), 259-274. https://doi.org/10.1007/BF03173425

Laméris, M. (2015). *On the measurement and validation of political ideology* (Unpublished master's thesis). University of Groningen, The Netherlands.

McMurray, A. J., & Simmers, C. A. (2020). The impact of generational diversity on spirituality and religion in the workplace. *Vision: The Journal of Business Perspective, 24*(1), 70-80. https://doi.org/10.1177/0972262919884841

Pew Research Center (n.d.). *Religious landscape study. https://www.pewresearch.org/religion/religious-landscape-study/*

Pew Research Center (2012, December 18). *The global religious landscape.* https://www.pewresearch.org/religion/2012/12/18/global-religious-landscape-exec/

Sagan, C. (2011). *The demon-haunted world: Science as a candle in the dark*. Ballantine Books.

Schieman, S. (2010). Socioeconomic status and beliefs about God's influence in everyday life. *Sociology of Religion, 71*(1), 25-51. https://doi.org/10.1093/socrel/srq004
Schwadel, P. (2016). Does higher education cause religious decline: A longitudinal analysis of the within- and between-person effects of higher education on religiosity. *The Sociological Quarterly, 57*(4), 759-786. https://doi.org/10.1111/tsq.12153
Schwadel, P. & Sandstrom, A. (2019, May 24). Lesbian, gay and bisexual Americans are less religious than straight adults by traditional measures. *Pew Research Center*. https://www.pewresearch.org/fact-tank/2019/05/24/lesbian-gay-and-bisexual-americans-are-less-religious-than-straight-adults-by-traditional-measures/
Truett, K. R. (1993). Age differences in conservatism. *Personality and Individual Differences, 14*(3), 405-411. https://doi.org/10.1016/0191-8896(93)90309-Q
Wikifur. (n.d.). *List of conventions by attendance.* Accessed May 31, 2020 from https://en.wikifur.com/wiki/List_of_conventions_by_attendance
Worthen, M. G. F. (2020). A rainbow wave? LGBTQ liberal political perspectives during Trump's presidency: An exploration of sexual, gender, and queer identity gaps. *Sexuality Research and Social Policy, 17*(1), 1-22. https://doi.org/10.1007/s13178-019-00393-1
Zell, E., & Bernstein, M. J. (2014). You may think you're right… Young adults are more liberal than they realize. *Social Psychological and Personality Science, 5*(3), 326-333. https://doi.org/10.1177/1948550613492825

Part 4
It's All in Your Head: Furry Psychology

Chapter 18
From All Walks: Individual Differences

Stephen Reysen, Courtney "Nuka" Plante

Psychology is the study of behavior and the mind that drives it. In other words, it's the job of a psychologist to understand and explain why people behave the way they do. We understand that the answer to this question is usually incredibly complex: most behaviors are multidetermined, a product of dozens or even hundreds of separate variables, many of which aren't always apparent or equal in magnitude.

So how might we set about explaining a given piece of behavior? One way is to distinguish between internal and external causes. For example, if we imagine that Jenny has punched her classmate, Phil, we can ask whether this behavior is the product of something happening inside Jenny or whether it's a product of something external to Jenny—like the temperature or noise of the room or whether Phil was provoking Jenny. Social psychologists tend to study the external drivers of behavior, focusing on who's around us and what immediate and long-term factors may have driven this behavior; their work is based on the idea that most people in that situation would respond similarly. In contrast, personality psychologists focus their attention on the individual: what *type* of person would act in this way, and would they act in a similar fashion in a different situation?

In this chapter, we're going to put on our personality psychologist hats and look at individual differences: what is it that makes one person different from another, that makes them react differently from another person in the same situation?[1] This typically includes using a specially designed measure to assess a person's score on some dimension and then compare that score to others or measures of other scores. They can also be used to assess changes in a person over time, like whether someone has become more mature or less aggressive over time.

This chapter is generally framed as a chapter about individual differences since it's a review of research we've conducted over the years that uses a variety of individual differences measures. But we'll also note, from the start, that some of the variables we'll be looking at aren't necessarily variables that a personality psychologist would typically look at. Indeed, this chapter is also a bit of a catch-all chapter for interesting results that didn't fit

[1] Another way to think about individual differences is to ask "what do we carry around with us from situation to situation in terms of our personality, mindset, biases, and other quirks of our thinking?"

into other chapters or weren't substantive enough to make it into their own chapters.[2]

Personality

Personality is defined as "an individual's characteristic patterns of thought, emotion, and behavior" (Funder & Fast, 2010, p. 669). In other words, personality is the traits that people consistently display across time and situations that distinguish one person from another. Personality research has a long history, going all the way back to the ancient Greeks, and researchers since then have come up with hundreds of different variables along which to differentiate people.[3] However, today most researchers use the "Big Five" model of personality (Goldberg, 1990; Gosling et al., 2003; John, 1990). The five traits, or dimensions, are spectrums along which everyone falls. It's rare for people to fall on the highest or lowest extremes on the continuum; instead, people fall somewhere in-between when it comes to:

(1) Extraversion versus Introversion
(2) Agreeableness versus Antagonism
(3) Conscientiousness versus Impulsive
(4) Neuroticism versus Emotional Stability
(5) Openness to New Experiences versus Closed to New Experiences

In the following sections, we'll review what each of these dimensions are and why they're important to psychologists. After that, we'll look specifically at how furries, as a group, score on these dimensions and what these scores can tell us about their thoughts, feelings, and behavior.

Extraversion

Extraversion is "the degree to which an individual is outgoing, is energetic, and experiences positive emotion" (Funder & Fast, 2010, p. 679).[4]

---

[2] If it helps, you can think of this chapter as having the alternate title of "Miscellaneous Findings." That being said, just because the findings are a bit miscellaneous doesn't mean they're not still interesting. Indeed, if they were uninteresting we would have just cut them from the book!

[3] It's helpful to think about personality traits like elements in chemistry: everything in the universe is made up of some combination of the same fundamental elements. The tremendous variety in different materials is a product of these different combinations. Likewise, personality traits represent fundamental elements, different combinations and amounts of which lead to billions of different people—all of whom can be meaningfully compared based on how much of each personality trait they've got.

[4] Let's briefly correct a common misconception people have about extraversion: extraversion *does not* mean "someone who likes people." It's fairly common for

As you would expect, people higher on extraversion have more friends than introverted individuals (Feiler & Kleinbaum, 2015), are more drawn to social media (Azucar et al., 2018), have higher relationship satisfaction (see Ozer & Benet-Martínez, 2006) and report fewer symptoms of sexual dysfunction (e.g., trouble maintaining an erection, reaching orgasm; Allen & Walter, 2018). Extraversion is also related to higher psychological well-being (Sun et al., 2018), lower levels of loneliness (Buecker et al., 2020), and being more physically active (Rhodes & Smith, 2006; Wilson & Dishman, 2015). People who score higher on measures of extraversion tend to tackle problems head-on (Connor-Smith & Flachsbart, 2007), consider themselves to be more creative (Karwowski & Lebuda, 2016), value stimulation and achievement (Fischer & Boer, 2015), are more satisfied with their jobs (Judge et al., 2002), and prefer energetic and rhythmic music (Rentfrow & Gosling, 2003).

We generally live in a society that rewards extraversion—people are encouraged to network at their jobs and, despite gradual changes in the workforce, most people are still required to work jobs that require face-to-face interaction with others (e.g., customer service, meetings). Nevertheless, there are instances where extraversion has its drawbacks. For example, people who score higher on extraversion are also more likely to believe false rumors (Lai et al., 2020), to bully others (Mitsopoulou & Giovazolias, 2015), to engage in risky sexual behavior (Allen & Walter, 2018), and to consume more alcohol (Hakulinen et al., 2015). Specific to fan behavior, extraversion is associated with compulsive consumption in sports fans (Aiken et al., 2018) and with being a more entitled fan among furry, anime, and fantasy sports fans (Shaw et al., 2016).

Agreeableness

Agreeableness is "the degree to which an individual is cooperative, warm, and gets along well with others" (Funder & Fast, 2010, p. 679). As such, it should not be surprising that people who score higher in agreeableness

---

laypersons who enjoy quiet time at home to say "I hate people, so I must be an introvert" or "you're good with people, you must be an extravert!" Extraversion is more about preferred level of stimulation and response to high-energy situations. One way we conceptualize it for our students is this: what effect does being around a group of your friends have on you? If it charges your proverbial batteries, then you probably score higher on a measure of extraversion. If it's more likely to leave you feeling drained, then you probably score lower on extraversion. And if you find yourself thinking "well, sometimes it's one, other times it's the other," then you, like most people, probably fall somewhere in the middle, rather than at one extreme end of the scale or the other!

engage in more prosocial behavior (Thielmann et al., 2020), have stronger religious beliefs and behaviors (e.g., volunteering; see Ozer & Benet-Martínez, 2006), and value benevolence more (Fischer & Boer, 2015) while also engaging in fewer negative behaviors, like sexual infidelity (Allen & Walter, 2018). For this reason, agreeable people are also generally well-liked by others, which might explain why they tend to be less lonely than less agreeable people (Buecker et al., 2020). Highly agreeable people tend to be fairly mindful and considerate (Giluk, 2009) and put the future ahead of the present (Kooij et al., 2018), which may explain why they're less likely to become addicted to their smartphones (Erdem & Uzun, 2022) and more likely to satisfied with their jobs (Judge et al., 2002).

Conscientiousness

Conscientiousness is "the degree to which an individual is dependable, organized, and punctual" (Funder & Fast, 2010, p. 679). This includes a greater likelihood to take into account the feelings and wishes of others before acting. As such, like agreeableness, conscientiousness is related to less sexual infidelity (Allen & Walter, 2018), less loneliness (Buecker et al., 2020), less bullying behavior (Mitsopoulou & Giovazolias, 2015), and less antisocial and criminal behavior (see Ozer & Benet-Martínez, 2006). Conscientiousness is generally associated with mindfulness (Giluk, 2009) and thinking about the future impact of one's behaviors (Kooij et al., 2018). Highly conscientious people prefer to tackle problems head-on rather than avoid them (Connor-Smith & Flachsbart, 2007) and often strive for perfection in doing so (Stricker et al., 2019). The results generally show in their achievements: they're better at learning a second language (Chen et al., 2021), perform better in school (Noftle & Robins, 2007), are more satisfied with their jobs (Judge et al., 2002), and are more physically active (Rhodes & Smith, 2006), even preferring more upbeat, if conventional, styles of music (Rentfrow & Gosling, 2003). Of course, planning things out and thinking ahead does make highly conscientious people more likely to value the security that comes from conforming and playing it safe (Fischer & Boer, 2015), but they are also less likely to consume alcohol to excess (Hakulinen et al., 2015) and to become addicted to smartphones (Erdem & Uzun, 2022; Marengo et al., 2020) or the internet (Kayiş et al., 2016).

Neuroticism (Emotional Instability)

Neuroticism describes "the degree to which an individual worries, is reactive to stress, and experiences negative emotion" (Funder & Fast, 2010, p. 679). Highly neurotic people tend to experience intense, unpredictable, and highly reactive emotions in response to what's happening around them—

they experience high highs and low lows. For this reason, those who score high on neuroticism are often more prone to anxiety and depression (see Ozer & Benet-Martínez, 2006) and lower subjective and psychological well-being (Sun et al., 2018). Neuroticism is also associated with disordered eating (Farstad et al., 2016), problematic coping strategies (e.g., withdrawal) (Connor-Smith & Flachsbart, 2007), and less resilience after traumatic events (Oshio et al., 2018), often as a result of this strong tendency to struggle to maintain control over negative emotions. Neuroticism can lead to problems with others (see Ozer & Benet-Martínez, 2006), including sexual dysfunction (e.g., trouble maintaining an erection or orgasm; Allen & Walter, 2018), less marital satisfaction (Sayehmiri et al., 2020), greater loneliness (Buecker et al., 2020), aggression (Hyatt et al., 2019), bullying (Mitsopoulou & Giovazolias, 2015), and being more likely to believe false rumors (Lai et al., 2020). Finally, illustrating the excesses associated with neuroticism, highly neurotic people are more likely to be addicted to smartphones (Erdem & Uzun, 2022) and to the internet (Kayiş et al., 2016), are less mindful (Giluk, 2009), and, despite showing perfectionist tendencies (Stricker et al., 2019), engage in more counterproductive work behavior (Grijalva & Newman, 2015) and are generally less satisfied with their jobs (Judge et al., 2002).

Openness to New Experiences

The last of the Big Five personality traits, openness to experience is "the degree to which an individual is creative, open-minded, and aesthetic" (Funder & Fast, 2010, p. 679). Openness to new experiences is related to more liberal political attitudes and lower right-wing authoritarianism (see Ozer & Benet-Martínez, 2006), reflected in their open-mindedness toward issues such as sex (Allen & Walter, 2018), such as a great desire to engage in consensual nonmonogamy (Moors et al., 2017). Openness is also associated with placing a greater value on universalism (Fischer & Boer, 2015), which includes more prosocial behavior (Thielmann et al., 2020) directed toward others outside one's ingroup (Tidikis & Dunbar, 2019) and greater identification with the world community (Jenkins et al., 2012), something which also tends to make people open to experience feel less lonely (Buecker et al., 2020). Being high in openness is generally associated with creativity (Karwowski & Lebuda, 2016), as seen reflected in findings such as being better able to pick up a second language (Chen et al., 2021), a greater frequency of lucid dreaming (Hess et al., 2017), and preferring more reflective and complex music (Rentfrow & Gosling, 2003).

Big Five Personality Traits in Furries

Now that we've introduced you to the Big Five measures, we can ask how furries, as a group, generally score on the measures. We've included the Big Five dimensions in many of the studies we've conducted over the years, usually doing so using the short, 10-item measure from Gosling et al. (2003) because of space limitations in the surveys.

As shown in Figure 18.1, the average rating of furries along each of the dimensions has been relatively stable across studies, hinting at the consistency of our results.[5] Furries, as a group, tend to score the highest on openness to experience, followed by agreeableness, conscientiousness, and emotional stability (the other end of the continuum of neuroticism), with extraversion at the end, being the only dimension along which furries tend to fall near or below the midpoint of the 7-point scale. Taken together, the findings would seem to track with many lay conceptions of what furries are like. For one thing, the fantasy theme of the furry fandom and its highly creative nature would seem to draw in people who are highly open to new experiences. Likewise, the acceptance and tolerance valued by the fandom (see Chapter 19) is consistent with furries' fairly high scores on agreeableness and openness. On the other extreme, furries' fairly low extraversion scores are consistent with the idea that furries represent a group of people who were largely accustomed to being wallflowers or outsiders looking in, who may have spent a great deal of time engaged in solitary hobby-related pursuits (e.g., reading, writing, drawing).

---

[5] This is important, given that the measure used is a small one, and thus prone to fluctuation or "random noise."

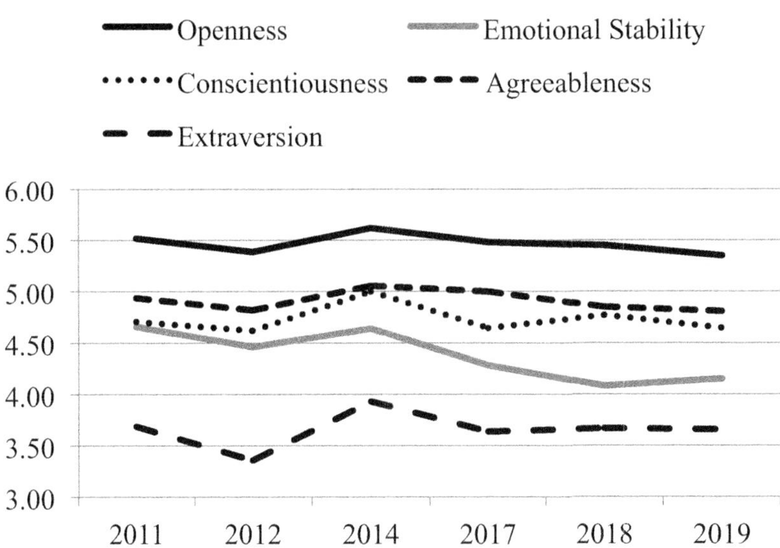

Figure 18.1. Average ratings of personality dimensions over time (7-point scale).

Big Five Personality Traits: Furries versus Other Samples

While it's informative to look at how furries score on the Big Five personality traits, these averages, by themselves, might not be especially useful. For example, while we've characterized furries as being fairly open to experience, this may be a mischaracterization if we were to find that most people score higher than furries on openness to experience.

To test for such possibilities, we've compared furries' scores on the Big Five personality traits with the scores of anime fans, fantasy sports fans, and undergraduate college students (Reysen et al., 2016). As shown in Figure 18.2, furries were generally comparable to fantasy sports fans and undergraduate students when it came to extraversion, agreeableness, and emotional stability scores. When it comes to conscientiousness, however, furries scored lower than college students—perhaps unsurprising, given that college students might be expected to be good at planning and organization, for having made it into college.[6] Relative to another media-based fan group,

[6] Of course, as we saw in Chapter 13, most furries are, themselves, college students or former college students, which might mean that, even among college students,

anime fans, furries scored significantly higher on extraversion, agreeableness, and conscientiousness, meaning that furries are less in line with conventional "geek" stereotypes (e.g., shut-ins, obsessed, argumentative online) than are anime fans.

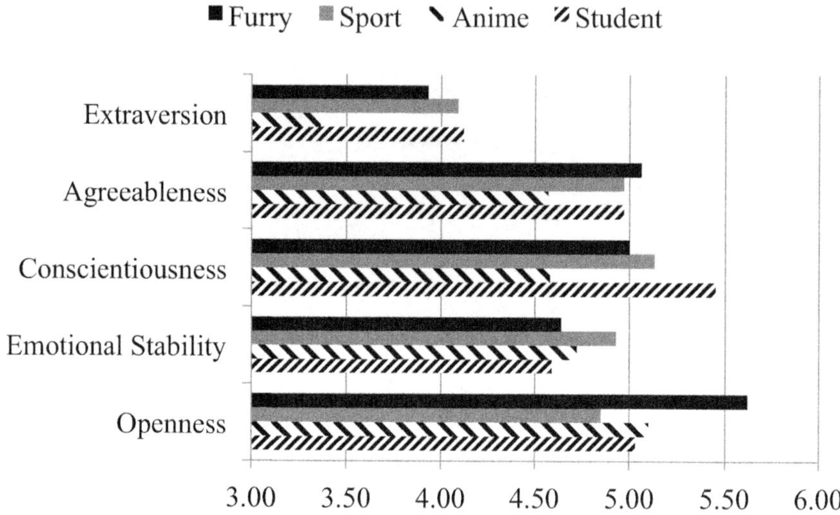

Figure 18.2. Mean comparisons between samples (7-point scale).

Finally, we'll note, in line with Figure 18.1, that furries were quite distinct among the studied groups with respect to their openness to experience, scoring higher than the other groups by a considerable margin. This may suggest that, even among other fan groups and others who are demographically comparable (e.g., college students), furries stand out as being particularly creative and willing to embrace the novel and unconventional.

Correlations with Other Measures

As we go through these different personality variables, it's easy to fall prey to the nominal fallacy—the belief that naming something means understanding something. If one isn't careful, measuring and labeling personality traits can lead us into this trap. For example, imagine that you were the first person to observe that iron filings organize themselves in a pattern around a magnet. You decide to label this phenomenon "magnetism."

---

furries may be a bit lower in conscientiousness—something which might explain their reduced felt need to conform and follow rules and conventions.

Great—now we know that it's called magnetism. But what does calling it magnetism get us? Does it help us understand *why* the filings organize themselves the way that they do? Does the label help us understand the conditions under which this doesn't happen? The label itself is not an explanation, nor do we come away with any more information about the phenomenon just by having named it.

The same holds true for our measuring personality traits in furries. We can point to furries that are very creative and say "Look, those furries are highly open to experience," and, when pressed, if someone asked how we knew this, we could say "Well, just look at them—they do creative things!" But this is all rather circular: furries are open to experience because they are creative, and they are creative because they are high in this personality trait of openness to new experiences.

To break out of this circle, we need to add a second stage to our exploration of personality traits: beyond just measuring the personality traits in furries, we also have to see whether these traits meaningfully predict *other* interesting thoughts, feelings, or behaviors. To return to our magnet example, it's not all that helpful to label the iron filings organized around the magnet as magnetism, but it *is* helpful to say "things that are magnetic will tend to attract other magnetic things," and to show that the magnet that attracted the iron filings will do the same thing to cobalt or nickel filings, but not to plastic filings.

And so, over the years, we've examined the extent to which the Big Five dimensions of personality predict fan-relevant variables in furries. A summarized version of these findings can be found in Table 18.1. The results show that the Big Five personality traits are far from the only predictors of furry-relevant variables, nor are they likely to be the biggest predictors. Nevertheless, they provide a useful piece to the complex puzzle of understanding furry behavior.

For example, when it comes to meeting other furries in person, extraversion was by far the strongest predictor of which furries go out to meetups and conventions and which stay home. In contrast, extraversion was far less of a predictor of interacting with other furries online (e.g., on forums and Telegram groups). This may suggest that it's easier for people who are less extroverted to interact with other furries online than it is for them to interact with other furries in person. And, in a related vein, extraversion was also the strongest predictor of being openly furry—that is, disclosing your furry identity to others. As we show in Chapter 21, not every furry feels comfortable disclosing their furry identity to those around them due to stigma, but extroverted furries seem better able to do so—whether it's because they're more confident and less bothered by the stigma or simply because they have a larger circle of friends and better social support network to draw upon.

Table 18.1. Correlations between Big Five personality dimensions and fandom-related variables.

Variable	E	A	C	ES	O
Freq. Meetups	.21**	.04	.09**	.04	.05
Freq. Conventions	.20**	.08**	.06*	.06*	.07**
Freq. Online Forums	.06*	.05	.02	.01	.06*
Disclose Furry ID	.17**	.03	.02	.02	.10**
Fursona Identification	.07*	.11**	.07*	-.01	.19**
Species Identification	-.05	.10**	-.01	-.11**	.09**
Species Liking	-.03	.03	-.05	-.04	.09**
Species Spiritual	.003	.12**	.05	-.04	.07*
Freq. Change Fursona	.02	-.05	-.09*	-.12**	.02
Solidarity with Animals	.04	.20**	.06	-.06	.22**
Neg. View of New Furs	-.10**	-.20**	.01	-.06	-.23**
Elitism Self-Inflate	.07*	.01	.03	.08**	.04
Elitism Other-Derogate	-.04	-.16**	-.04	-.04	-.11**

Note. * $p < .05$, ** $p < .01$.

When it comes to furries and their association with their fursonas, personality traits can again shed a bit of light. For example, when it comes to the extent to which a person likes their fursona species, openness to experience was the only one of the personality traits that predicted liking. In contrast, agreeableness was the trait most strongly associated with feeling a spiritual connection to one's fursona. As for identifying *as* one's fursona species (i.e., being a therian, see Chapter 20), a combination of agreeableness, openness to experience, and lower emotional stability (i.e., higher neuroticism) predicted this tendency,[7] although agreeableness and

[7] It's also rather amusing to see that the frequency with which one changes their fursonas is negatively associated with conscientiousness—the tendency to think ahead, be thoughtful, and plan. In Chapter 7, we mentioned that most furries only have one fursona, with furries who have more than one typically changing over time, often after discovering that their initial choice of fursona is not longer a good fit. Perhaps furries who are mindful and who think ahead are better able to choose a fursona that's most likely to "fit" who they are in the future. Alternatively, it may be

openness to experience were the variables most strongly associated with feeling a sense of solidarity with animals more broadly.

Finally, when it comes to gatekeeping and elitism in the fandom, personality traits can help us to understand who is the most likely to engage in this behavior. Specifically, people low in agreeableness and low in openness to experience (and, to a lesser extent, low in extraversion) are the most likely to hold a negative view of new furries coming into the fandom. As for feelings of elitism, extraversion and a lack of neuroticism are most strongly associated with a tendency to hold an inflated sense of self, while those who are lowest in agreeableness and those low in openness to experience were the most likely to look down at other furries.

Personality Change

There's been a longstanding debate among personality researchers about whether personality is consistent across situations and over one's lifespan, or whether personality is something that changes over time, or depends on the situation a person finds themselves in (e.g., Graham et al., 2020). Social psychologists[8] argue that the groups we belong to have stereotypical behaviors and beliefs associated with them and, as such, when a person is thinking about themselves as a member of this group, their personality, at that moment, will tend to look more in-line with the stereotypes of that group. Jenkins et al. (2012) took this approach and proposed that personality is just another one of the prototypical features of a group. As such, one's personality may change depending on what identity is on their mind at a given time (see also Turner & Onorato, 1999).[9]

We tested this notion in a series of studies with furries (Reysen et al., 2015). Specifically, we asked furries to complete a personality scale while thinking of their everyday self (e.g., when going to the grocery store) and to do it again while thinking of their furry identity (i.e., fursona).[10] Across the

---

that furies high in conscientiousness may simply be averse to change and prefer not to seek out a new fursona after having established one and had it for a number of years—sticking to the plan, so to speak!

[8] Like the authors of this chapter!

[9] As an example: Canadians are largely thought to be open-minded and accepting. If I were to think about myself as a Canadian, I should be a bit more likely to describe myself as being open-minded and accepting than if I were to think about myself in terms of another one of my identities (e.g., being a gamer, a man, or an atheist).

[10] To control for the possibility that the order in which people were asked these questions might matter, we randomized the order in which furries were asked on different versions of the survey—sometimes people were asked about their furry

studies, we found that furries rated their personality differently depending on which identity was on their mind. The results of one of the three studies are shown in Figure 18.3 alongside similar results from a sample of sports fans (think of everyday self and sport fan identity), to assess whether the findings were unique to furries. For both furries and sports fans, the results were the same: scores on each of the five personality traits differed depending on which identity was on the person's mind. For furries, their scores on all five of the dimensions increased in their furry identity relative to their non-furry identity—they saw themselves as more extroverted, agreeable, conscientious (albeit barely), emotionally stable (lower in neuroticism) and more open to experience as a furry.

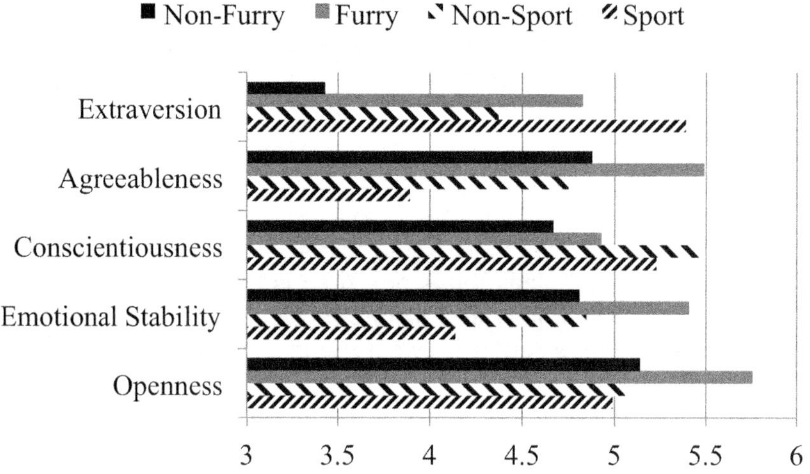

Figure 18.3. Mean comparisons for furry and sports fans rating personality for fan identity and non-fan, everyday self-identity (7-point scale).

To this point, we've focused our attention exclusively on the Big Five personality traits, the most commonly studied dimensions along which people are compared by psychologists. These are far from the only individual differences that psychologists study, however! For the rest of this chapter,

identity first and sometimes they were asked about it second! We also made a point of spacing the two measures apart, so participants weren't doing them one right after the other, in order to minimize the chance that participants were actively trying to directly compare and contrast their responses.

we'll consider some other individual differences and their ability to tell us more about the thoughts, feelings, and behaviors of individual furries.

Passion

Vallerand et al. (2003) developed a scale to measure the concept of "passion" among fans. Their concept recognized two different dimensions of passion: harmonious and obsessive. Harmonious passion is the effortless incorporation of one's interest into their sense of self (e.g., "Furry activities are in harmony with the other activities in my life"). Or, to put it another way, harmonious passion is the extent to which a fan naturally engages in fan-related activities without any influence from, or impact on, outside factors. In contrast, obsessive passion involves a more forced incorporation of one's fan interest into their identity: internal and external forces or pressures compel them to engage in fan activities (e.g., need for self-esteem or social approval). Obsessive passion is also characterized by the lack of ability to control one's excitement or enthusiasm for the topic—it's not a matter of doing it because you like it, but doing it because you feel compelled to do it by something else.

In their research, Vallerand and their colleagues found that harmonious passion was associated with a strong sense of being immersed in fan activities with a sense of positive emotions; in contrast, obsessive passion was associated with feelings of shame. In a study of UK soccer fans, Vallerand et al. (2008) found harmonious passion was associated with life satisfaction, while obsessive passion was associated with having a difficult recovery after a loss, engaging in superstitious activities to aid the team, skipping work to see a game, rumination about the team, and engaging in arguments about the team. A later study of soccer fans also found that harmonious passion was related to self-esteem and fanship, while obsessive passion was associated with hating the other team's fans and mocking fans of the opposing team. In short: harmonious passion seems to predict healthier fan behavior, while obsessive passion seems to predict more maladaptive fan behavior.

Curious to see whether the results would be similar in furries, we included the measure of passion in one of our 2020 studies. As shown in Figure 18.4, furries scored above the midpoint of the harmonious passion scale while scoring below the midpoint on the obsessive passion scale. We also found that fursuiters (vs. non-fursuiters) scored significantly higher on both measures, suggesting, in line with our findings from Chapter 8, that fursuiters are more passionate than the average furry, which would make sense, given their demonstrated willingness to spend thousands of dollars on a fursuit!

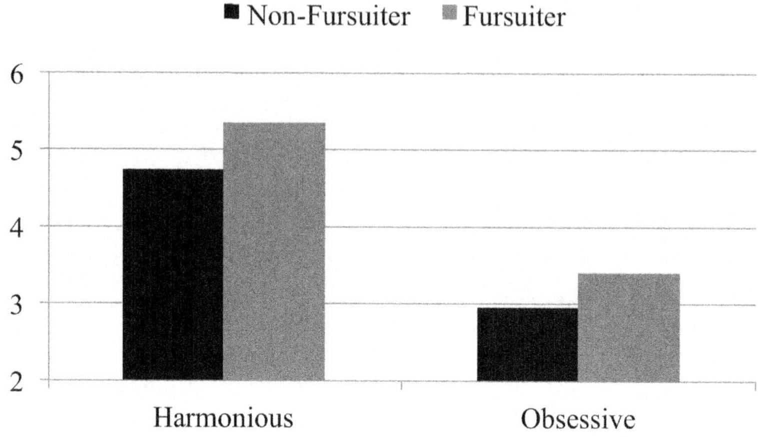

Figure 18.4. Mean comparison between non-fursuiters and fursuiters on dimensions of passion (7-point scale).

We also examined the relationships between passion and other furry-relevant variables. As shown in Table 18.2, harmonious passion was more strongly associated with watching furry-related content and with spending money on their furry interest and was negatively associated with post-purchase regret. Obsessive passion, on the other hand, was associated specifically with purchasing more commissions and with making purchases that harmed their financial situation. Harmonious passion was, relative to obsessive passion, more positively associated with keeping up with fandom trends, the perception that the fandom was getting better over time, and was negatively associated with a desire to leave the fandom—perhaps owing to the fact that harmonious passion was also associated with a greater sense of commonality and connectedness felt with other furries. And while obsessive passion was unrelated to furries' general sense of well-being, harmonious passion predicted less loneliness and greater well-being and life satisfaction. In short, the available evidence suggests that, at least when it comes to furries, obsessive passion might not be as strongly tied to negative outcomes as in other fandoms (e.g., sports fans), but harmonious passion is particularly tied to positive outcomes for furries.

Table 18.2. Correlations between harmonious and obsessive passion and fandom-related variables.

Variable	H	O
Watch/Read Furry-Materials/News	.42**	.28**
Spending	.14*	.09
Post-Purchase Regret	-.14**	.03
Purchases Harmed Finances	.09	.23**
Number Commissions	.09	.15**
Keep up with Trends	.30**	.15**
Leave Fandom	-.22**	-.09
Fandom Improved	.25**	.07
Increased Commonality	.32**	.11*
Increased Connectedness	.39**	.17**
Loneliness	-.12*	.06
Psychological Well-Being	.24**	.06
Satisfaction with Life	.12**	.02

Note. * $p < .05$, ** $p < .01$.

Fantasy

One of the most distinguishing features of furry content is its fantastical nature. The very premise of furry media—animals that can walk, talk, and do human things—requires a flight of fancy to buy into, and so it should follow that furries may be particularly high in their willingness to engage in fantasy.

Trying to study this interest in fantasy is a tricky prospect, however—there's no single, agreed-upon definition of what, precisely, fantasy is. Over the years, we've used a variety of measures based on different conceptualizations of fantasy. For example, we've assessed *transliminality*—a hypersensitivity to psychological experiences (e.g., senses, thoughts, feelings, ideas; Lange et al., 2000)—which has been associated with religiosity, lucid dreaming, paranormal beliefs, intuitive (vs. analytical) thinking, and trance states (see Lange et al., 2019). We've also looked at fantasy proneness—the tendency to engage in fantasies so intensely that one loses the ability to distinguish fantasy from reality (e.g., hallucinations, dissociative experiences; Merckelbach et al., 2001)—which has been linked to anxiety, depression, magical ideation, daydreaming, and acceptance of strange phenomena (see Merkelbach et al., 2021). A third variable we've looked at is interpersonal reactivity (Davis, 1983; Jordan et al., 2016), a person's tendency to identify with characters and become deeply immersed in stories, something which has been linked with lower emotional intelligence (Fernández-Abascal & Martín-Díaz, 2019), feeling (but not actually being) more rational (Martingano & Konrath, 2022), reading fictional narratives (Mumper & Gerrig, 2017), and becoming absorbed in stories (Rivers et al., 2016).

As shown in Table 18.3, all three of these fantasy-related measures were, for the most part, positively related to furry fanship and fandom, identification with one's fursona species, the belief that a fursona provides information about another person, and the belief that furry was a generally positive force in one's life.

Table 18.3. Correlations between transliminity (TL), fantasy proneness (FP), and interpersonal reactivity index's fantasy dimension (IRI) and related variables.

Variable	TL	FP	IRI
Fanship	.15**	.25**	.14**
Fandom	.17**	.22**	.09
Identification with Fursona Species	.25**	.28**	.22**
Fursona Tells You About Others	.24**	.17**	.24**
Being a Furry is Positive	.09	.23**	.22**

Note. * $p < .05$, ** $p < .01$.

While these findings were generally associated with interesting furry-related variables, we didn't like the fact that these scales generally tended to view fantasizing in adults as something abnormal or pathological. Fantasy proneness, for example, is almost, by definition, a measure of pathological fantasy engagement, the extent to which a person struggles to maintain the boundary between fantasy and reality. Despite this tendency to see fantasy in a largely pathological light, examples abound of adults engaging in positive acts of fantasy: people enjoying books and movies featuring fictional characters and settings, being motivated or inspired by daydreams (e.g., someday, I'm going to be a scientist!), and expressing themselves through fantasy-themed art and writing. There wasn't a lot in terms of scales that were designed specifically to assess this more healthy, normal, day-to-day type of fantasy that people engaged in, at least nothing flexible enough to be used in samples ranging from furries to college students.

To address this problem, we created our own measure, the Fantasy Engagement Scale (Plante et al., 2017), which acknowledges that fantasy, regardless of the form it may take, can have both positive and negative components. The measure measures both of these components, with some questions assessing positive aspects of the interest (e.g., "Fantasizing about this has helped me to become a better person") and negative aspects of the interest (e.g., "My fantasies about this have been the source of a lot of problems in my life"). As Table 18.4 shows, the two dimensions predict a number of important variables for furries.

Table 18.4. Correlations between positive (PF) and negative (NF) fantasy engagement with related measures.

Variable	PF	NF
Years Furry	.09*	-.04
Fanship	.53**	.13**
Fandom	.57**	.06
Fursona Identification	.50**	.10**
Species Identification	.18**	.14**
Species Liking	.31**	.09**
Species Spiritual	.21**	.08*
Number of Fursuits Owned	.14**	.05
Psychologically Similar to Fursona	.11**	-.10**
Frequency of Furry Activities	.31**	-.004
Immersion in Furry Activities	.38**	.14**
Frequency of Furry Dreams	.18**	.08*
Felt Belongingness in Fandom	.41**	-.19**
Difficulty Distinguish Reality	.07	.34**
Positive Emotions	.30**	-.16**
Negative Emotions	-.07	.24**
Satisfaction with Life	.14**	-.11**
Flourishing	.26**	-.20**
Depression	-.13**	.39**
Anxiety	.09*	.24**
Physical Well-Being	.11**	-.08*
Psychological Well-Being	.19**	-.13**
Relationship Well-Being	-.04	-.11**

Note. * $p < .05$, ** $p < .01$.

One common trend to emerge from the data is that engagement in the positive facets of furry fantasy is a stronger predictor of furry-related variables, including how strongly one identifies as a furry, with the furry fandom, or with their fursona, their likelihood of owning a fursuit, or their tendency to engage in furry-related activities. In contrast, negative fantasy engagement seems to be associated more negatively with measures of well-being (e.g., lower flourishing, more negative emotions, less physical and psychological well-being). Importantly, these data show that, contrary to popular misconceptions about furries as dysfunctional (see Chapter 21), it's not enough to simply look at a person engaging in an unusual flight of fantasy and deem it pathological or maladaptive; you need to know how and why the person is engaging in the behavior. The simple act of wearing a fursuit, despite being a bit weird, cannot, in and of itself, tell you whether the wearer is dysfunctional or not; if they're doing it for fun, if they do it with other friends, and if it helps them to express some aspect of themselves, the activity is likely to be beneficial for them. If, on the other hand, the person is wearing the fursuit excessively, is losing touch with reality, or is doing so in a way that's causing them legal or interpersonal problems, then we can say that the activity is harmful. But the act of wearing the fursuit is not inherently maladaptive, a point worth keeping in mind the next time you hear about someone who's had a bizarre dream or who has a hobby that, on the surface, seems peculiar: "weird" is not a diagnosis!

Magical Thinking

Conceptually related to fantasy—more precisely, to fantasy proneness—magical thinking is when a person relies on causal explanations that are impossible under the laws of nature (Brashier & Multhaup, 2017). Magical thinking is something people typically engage in most during childhood when their grasp of physics and the natural world are still being developed. With age, magical thinking tends to decrease, although some adults still exhibit this style of thinking. For example, beliefs about superstition (e.g., holding a charm will help you on a test) and contagion (e.g., using your grandmother's favorite cooking pot will improve the taste) persist in many people. Taylor and Acic (2020) found that magical thinking predicts fanship and fan behaviors in a sample of fans interested in fictional narratives. The researchers constructed a short, four-item (e.g., "There is something special about an item that a famous person has touched") measure that assessed beliefs that an item could become charged with an essence if touched by another person. The researchers explained this link by suggesting that fans may believe that some essence of the object of fan interest is conferred on the fans themselves, a belief which may be especially prominent in those who are more likely to enjoy the breaks from reality found in fictional narratives.

Curious to see whether we'd observe similar trends in the furry fandom, we included this measure in a 2020 study. As shown in Table 18.5, magical thinking was positively associated with fanship, fandom, and most of our measures of fan engagement (e.g., attending conventions). This was consistent with past findings showing that magical thinking was associated with greater fan interest in media featuring fictional content.

Table 18.5. Correlations between magical thinking and fan-related variables.

Variable	Magical Thinking
Fanship	.22**
Fandom	.26**
Attending furry conventions.	.17*
Attending local meet-ups with other furries.	.22**
Reading furry forums.	.23**
Posting in furry forums.	.28**
Consuming official furry media (e.g., films, books, art).	.27**
Consuming fan-made furry media (e.g., fan fiction, fan films, art).	.15*
Consuming furry theory-crafting / review videos/articles.	.28**
Cosplaying as furry characters.	.31**
Collecting official furry merchandise.	.26**
Collecting unofficial furry merchandise.	.24**
Chatting online with other furries (e.g., IM programs, Skype).	.03
Searching out furry-related news.	.22**
Playing furry-themed games (video games, board games, tabletop games).	.06

Note. * $p < .05$, ** $p < .01$.

We went one step further, testing whether the link between magical thinking and being a more involved furry (based on an average of the engagement behaviors shown in Table 18.5) was driven by the fact that greater magical thinking was tied to being a bigger fan which, in turn, was tied to more engagement in fan activities. As shown in Figure 18.5, we found evidence for this model: both fanship and fandom seemed to be driving the relationship between magical thinking and fan engagement, suggesting that those who engage in more magical thinking may identify more strongly as furries and with the furry fandom which, in turn, would compel them to engage in more furry-related activities.

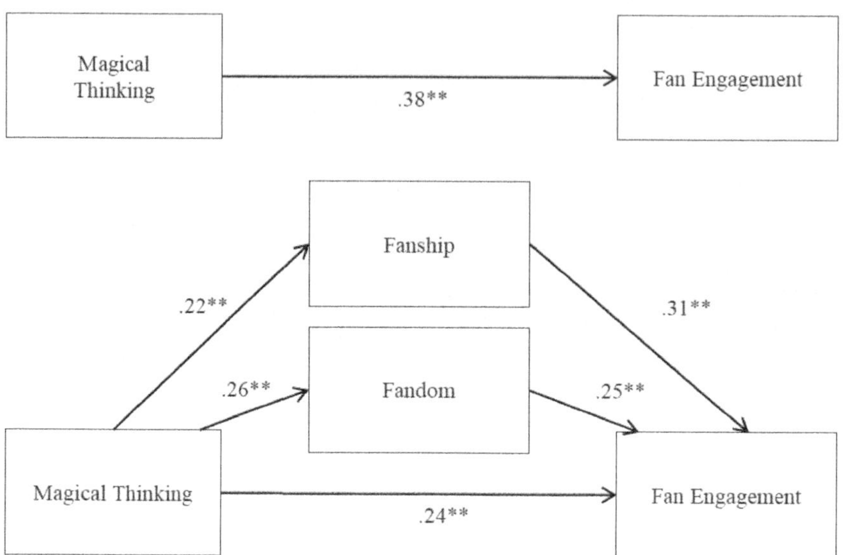

Figure 18.5. Mediation model of magical thinking predicting fan engagement through fanship and fandom. Standardized betas are presented. $N = 186$, ** $p < .01$.

Dreaming

To date, researchers have not yet agreed on one single reason for why people dream, although a multitude of theories abound (Cappadona et al., 2021). Researchers *do* know that dreaming has many functions, including aiding with long-term memory storage (e.g., organizing and strengthening pathways as we sleep) and with emotion regulation (Scarpelli et al., 2022). But regardless of why we dream, researchers do know a bit about what we tend to dream about. We know, for example, that the things we experience in our waking life often make their way into our dreams (e.g., if something upsetting or surprising recently happened, or if you're concerned or stressed about an upcoming event). Thus, the more you think about something in day-to-day life, the more likely you are to dream about it. For example, McCutcheon et al. (2021) found that those who had a stronger connection with a particular celebrity were significantly more likely to have dreams about that celebrity.

By extension, we wondered whether furries—especially those who were thinking a lot about furries, perhaps because they were at a furry convention—had furry-themed dreams. Gerbasi et al. (2020) asked convention-going furries to write about their most recent dream. Their responses were coded for furry-related content and showed that 36% of furries attending a furry convention had furry-related content in their dreams. In a follow-up question, we asked furries to rate the frequency with which they regularly have furry-relevant dreams. As shown in Figure 18.6, a majority of furries have had furry-related dreams, with just under half of furries doing so at least once a month.

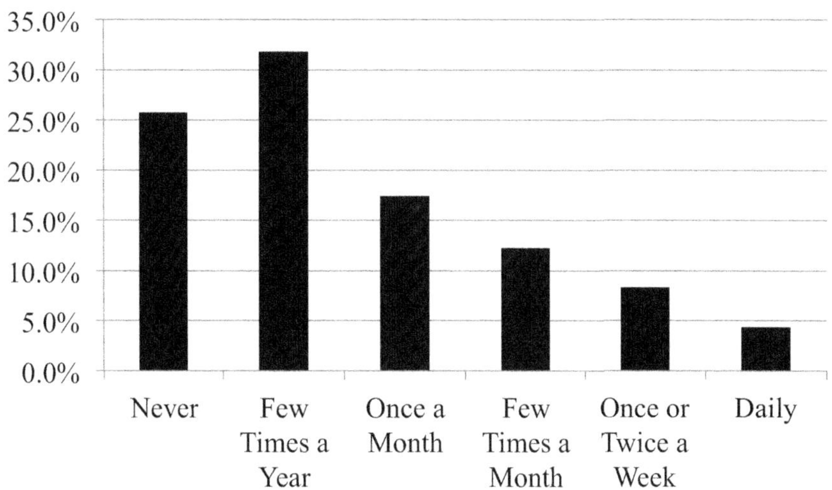

Figure 18.6. Percentage of responses for frequency of furry-related dreams.

Even more interesting than the frequency with which furries dream about furries is the question of whether this tells us anything interesting about the furry themselves. To examine that, we tested whether the frequency of having dreams predicted furry-related variables of interest. The results, shown in Table 18.6, reveal that furries who've been furries for longer, who identify more strongly as furry, and who identify more strongly with their fursona have more frequent furry-themed dreams. Likewise, furry dreams are related to spending habits and with fantasy engagement more broadly—especially positive fantasy engagement. Dreaming was also found to predict stronger connections to one's fursona species.

Table 18.6. Correlations of frequency of furry-related dreams with fandom-relevant variables.

Variable	Dreams
Years Furry	.12**
Fanship	.32**
Fandom	.28**
Fursona Identification	.31**
Money Spent	.12**
Negative Fantasy Engagement	.08*
Positive Fantasy Engagement	.18**
Species Identification	.32**
Species Liking	.29**
Species Spiritual	.30**

Note. * $p < .05$, ** $p < .01$.

Global Citizenship

Global citizenship is defined as "global awareness, caring, embracing cultural diversity, promoting social justice and sustainability, and a sense of responsibility to act" (Reysen et al., 2012, p. 29). In other words, it's the extent to which a person thinks about themselves as part of a global community, showing interest in, and concern for, others, including those from other parts of the globe. Reysen and Katzarska-Miller (2013, 2018) were interested both in what predicts who identifies as a global citizen and what effects global citizenship may have on the way a person thinks, feels, and behaves. In their work, they found that the extent to which you think that others around you are global citizens and the extent to which you are aware of others around the world both contribute to one's identity as a global citizen. They also predicted that global citizens should, as a result of being high in global citizenship identification, show greater empathy for individuals outside their group, should value diversity, should be concerned about social justice (e.g., human rights and equity), should care about the environment, should want to help others, and should feel a responsibility to act to make the world a better place.

This issue is presently relevant because many of the values and outcomes associated with global citizenship are espoused by the furry fandom, a global fan community with progressive values that include acceptance and inclusivity. For this reason, we examined whether furries and a comparison sample of non-furries would differ with respect to global citizenship and whether the groups they belong to were linked to their global citizenship and related behavior. Plante et al. (2014) tested the model in the two samples and found that furries (vs. non-furries) identified more strongly as global citizens. In addition, furries were more likely to say that those around them (i.e., the furry fandom) also supported global citizenship. The model ultimately showed that the higher rate of global citizenship in furries relative to non-furries was a product, at least in part, of the fandom's global citizenship norms, and that this led to higher scores on each of the prosocial values (e.g., greater caring for diversity, greater felt responsibility to act). In effect, being among furries seems to have downstream effects on furries' endorsement of prosocial values.

Empathy

Empathy, the ability to take the perspective of another person, is often associated with prosocial beliefs and behaviors which are, in turn, linked to cooperating and helping others (Jordan et al., 2016). Given the link between furries, global citizenship, and concern for helping others, we wondered whether empathy would be related to furry identification and relevant beliefs and behavior. We included a seven-item measure of empathetic concern that was developed in prior research (Davis, 1983; Jordan et al., 2016) in two of our furry studies. As shown in Table 18.7, empathy was positively correlated with fanship, fandom, and identification with one's fursona species, as well as with the belief that one's fursona is an ideal self and that it can help guide a person's behavior. This may suggest that empathy may contribute to furries' ability to take on the perspective of a hypothetical other (a fursona), or even imbue their fursonas with empathy as a desired trait

Table 18.7. Correlations between empathetic concern and related variables.

Variable	Empathy
Fanship	.20**
Fandom	.24**
Identification with Fursona Species	.28**
Fursona is the Ideal Self	.18**
Fursona Helps in Life	.20**
Derogate others' Fursonas	-.13*
Intragroup Helping	.27**
Furry Share Common Fate	.16**
Identity Centrality	.27**
Disliking New Furries	-.31**
Solidarity with Animals	.28**

Note. * $p < .05$, ** $p < .01$.

Empathy was also associated with many other important variables. For example, furries higher in empathy were less likely to make fun of other furries' fursonas and were more likely to help them. In part, this may be because furries high in empathy also consider being furry a central part of who they are and feel a sense of shared fate with other furries—they may want to help because they feel that what happens to one furry impacts all furries. This may also explain why high-empathy furries are less likely to dislike new furries—perhaps being able to recognize that they, too, were once a new member of the fandom. Finally, this ability to empathize with other furries may also reflect a tendency to empathize more broadly, given that they were also able to feel a sense of solidary with non-human animals.

Need to Belong

Psychologists have long suggested that, having evolved as a social species, humans have an innate, hardwired need to form stable and supportive connections with others (Baumeister & Leary, 1995). In other words, we all have a need to belong, an instinct that compels us to want to be part of a group,[11] especially when we've been rejected or ostracized (Leary et al., 2013).[12] This need to belong encourages social connection in a variety of ways, including having a better memory for social events or being more sensitive to social cues when the need is high (Garner et al, 2000; Pickett et al., 2004). In a recent study, Reysen et al. (2020) found that anime fans' need to belong was associated with being more involved with fandom-related drama. In effect, people high in the need to belong may be starting or jumping into fandom-related drama just to feel like part of the group (for more on fandom drama, see Chapter 12).

To test the need to belong in furries, we included a 10-item measure of it in a study (Leary et al., 2013). As shown in Table 18.8, furries' felt need to belong predicted a number of fan-related variables, including the same tendency to get involved in fandom drama. In addition, the need to belong was also associated with overspending—perhaps as a way of compensating for feelings of loneliness, wanting to increase one's felt status in the fandom, or simply valuing symbols of the fandom more highly. Need to belong was

[11] Of course, we don't all have this need to the same extent: the need may be stronger for some people over others, and we may satisfy this need in different ways. For some people, this need may be satisfied by having a small circle of friends, while others may need to belong to a large organization to scratch this proverbial itch.

[12] This being said, rejection also has other side effects, such as anger and aggression (Leary et al., 2006; Richman & Leary, 2009).

also associated with concerns about being accepted in the fandom and with a history of being bullied.

Table 18.8. Correlations between the need to belong and related variables.

Variable	Belong
Overspending on Furry Merchandise	.16**
Overspending at Conventions	.24**
Fandom Drama Involvement	.18**
Acceptance Concerns	.29**
Bullied by Non-Furs	.20**
Bullied by Furs	.18**

Note. ** $p < .01$.

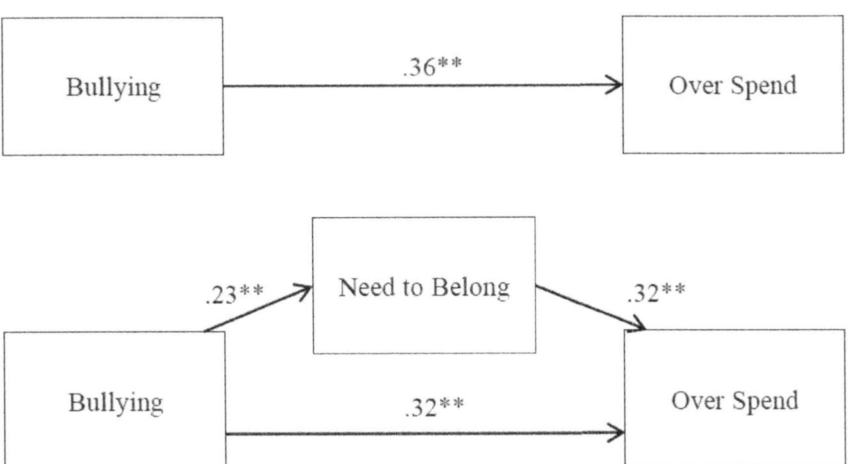

Figure 18.7. Mediation model of magical thinking predicting fan engagement through fanship and fandom. Standardized betas are presented. $N = 270$, ** $p < .01$.

Table 18.9. Regressions with dimensions of playfulness dimensions predicting fan-related variables. FS = fun-seeking motivation, UI = uninhibitedness, SP = spontaneity. Standardized betas are presented.

Variable	FS	UI	SP
Fanship	.23**	.03	.06
Fandom	.31**	.02	.02
Attending furry conventions.	.09*	.11*	.001
Attending science fiction conventions as a furry.	-.12*	.23**	.10
Attending other conventions as a furry.	.10*	.19**	.01
Attending local meet-ups with other furries.	.11*	.10*	.07
Reading furry-related forums.	.13**	.01	.12*
Posting in furry-related forums.	.08	.06	.09
Consuming official furry-related media.	.18**	-.04	.01
Consuming fan-made furry-related media.	.21**	-.08	.05
Creating fan-made furry-related media.	.07	-.01	.07
Consuming furry-related theory-crafting / review videos/articles.	.04	.12*	.10*
Producing furry-related theory-crafting / review videos/articles.	-.04	.13**	.13*
Cosplaying as furry-related characters.	.13**	.06	.13**
Collecting official furry-related merchandise.	.22**	.07	.05
Collecting unofficial furry-related merchandise.	.21**	.06	.09
Chatting online with other furries.	.20**	-.11*	.09
Searching out furry-related news.	.15**	.08	.13*
Playing furry-related themed games.	.18**	-.08	.12*

Note. * $p < .05$, ** $p < .01$.

Building on all of these findings, we next tested a model based on the fact that furries who had a history of being bullied were more likely to overspend. One possible interpretation of this finding is that furries that overspend are especially visible as targets for stigma (see Chapter 21 for more on this). Another explanation, one that we've alluded to already, is that furries who feel a strong need to belong may overspend as a way to temporarily satisfy this need, either by replacing fan interaction with consumption or perhaps by increasing their status as a fan (being "more furry" by having more furry merchandise), which might increase their potential to fit into the fandom. Regardless of the specific reason, we tested a model wherein bullying was associated with a greater felt need to belong and that furries, dealing with this increase in need, might turn to greater spending. We tested this model, shown in Figure 18.7, finding that the data largely supported our findings. Of course, this still doesn't directly test whether furries are overspending specifically as a substitute for social interaction or whether this is being done to increase one's likelihood of being able to fit into the fandom in the future, but the model at the very least suggests that there's value in further pursuing this research in future studies.

Playfulness

In this final section, we'll consider an individual difference that seems especially relevant to the furry fandom's lighthearted, fantasy-themed nature: playfulness. Shen et al. (2014) proposed a measure of adult playfulness that included three dimensions: fun-seeking (e.g., "I try to have fun no matter what I am doing"), uninhibitedness (e.g., "I understand social rules but most of the time I am not restricted by them"), and spontaneity (e.g., "I often act upon my impulses"). We measured these three dimensions in a study of furries and allowed them to predict various furry-related variables. As shown in Table 18.9, fun-seeking motivation was a rather consistent predictor of identification and engagement in furry-related activities. Uninhibitedness, on the other hand, was mainly associated with attending social gatherings, especially going as a furry to non-furry conventions. Spontaneity was mainly associated with reading articles (e.g., just happening to look up what is going on in furry news). In short, of the three elements of playfulness studied, the seeking of fun was the most strongly and consistently tied to engaging in furry activities.

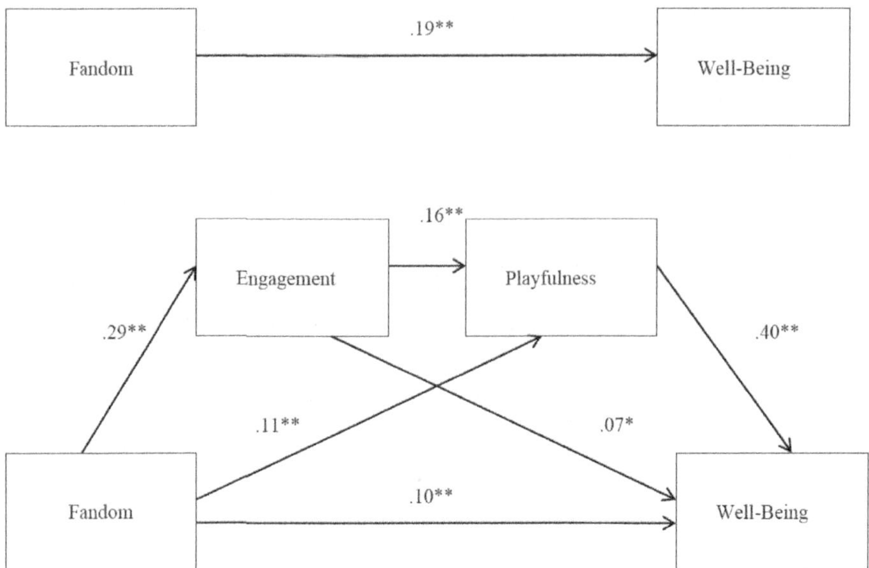

Figure 18.8. Serial mediation model with engagement and playfulness as mediators of the relationship between fandom identification and psychological well-being. Unstandardized betas shown. * $p < .05$, ** $p < .01$.

In some of our other work, we've seen that fandom identification is associated with both engagement with fan activities and with psychological well-being (Reysen et al., in press; see Chapter 22). Other studies have shown that engaging in fan activities (e.g., social activities) is a strong predictor of well-being (Reysen et al., 2017; Reysen et al., in press), since it may foster beneficial social connections. Combining these ideas, as well as with the finding above showing that playfulness is related to engaging in fan activities, we proposed the model shown in Figure 18.8, allowing fandom, engaging in furry-related activities, and playfulness to all predict a single-item measure of well-being (Reysen, Plante, Lam, et al., 2020). The results supported our model, showing that part of the link between fandom and well-being is the fact that fandom provides furries with opportunities to engage in social activities, activities which are, themselves, beneficial, but which also foster and reinforce a sense of playfulness that may be beneficial for well-being (e.g., helping to counteract anxiety or stress). Ultimately, more research will be needed to test the nature of the link between fan activities, playfulness, and well-being, but the data provide a tantalizing hint at some of the mechanisms driving the benefits we've seen coming from the furry fandom (see Chapter 22) and hint at a way that playfulness, despite being easily overlooked as trivial, foolish, or childish, may actually be an indicator of health and well-being in adults!

Conclusion

Although we've used this chapter as a catch-all for findings that didn't fit into other chapters, taken together, the findings cover a significant amount of theoretical ground and have hopefully illustrated the importance of considering some of the individual differences within the furry fandom, but also differences between furries and members of other fandoms. From the Big Five personality traits to magical thinking, from dreaming to playfulness, the results here illustrate that furries are not a homogeneous entity, but rather a diverse mix of people, each with a unique psychological makeup that makes everyone's experience in the furry fandom just a little different from everyone else's. If nothing else, this chapter should make it clear that every finding throughout this book should be taken with the caveat that results may vary depending on which furry we're talking about and what sort of person they are!

References

Aiken, K. D., Bee, C., & Walker, N. (2018). From passion to obsession: Development and validation of a scale to measure compulsive sport consumption. *Journal of Business Research, 87,* 69-79. https://doi.org/10.1016/j.jbusres.2018.02.019

Allen, M. S., & Walter, E. E. (2018). Linking big five personality traits to sexuality and sexual health: A meta-analytic review. *Psychological Bulletin, 144*(10), 1081-1110. https://doi.org/10.1037/bul0000157

Azucar, D., Marengo, D., & Settanni, M. (2018). Predicting the Big 5 personality traits from digital footprints on social media: A meta-analysis. *Personality and Individual Differences, 124,* 150-159. https://doi.org/10.1016/j.paid.2017.12.018

Baumeister, R. F., & Leary, M. R. (1995). The need to belong: Desire for interpersonal attachments as a fundamental human motivation. *Psychological Bulletin, 117*(3), 497-529. https://doi.org/10.1037/0033-2909.117.3.497

Brashier, N. M., & Multhaup, K. S. (2017). Magical thinking decreases across adulthood. *Psychology and Aging, 32*(8), 681-688. https://doi.org/10.1037/pag0000208

Buecker, S., Maes, M., Denissen, J. J., & Luhmann, M. (2020). Loneliness and the Big Five personality traits: A meta-analysis. *European Journal of Personality, 34*(1), 8-28. https://doi.org/10.1002/per.2229

Cappadona, R., De Giorgi, A., Di Simone, E., Zucchi, B., Rodriguez-Borrego, M. A., Lopez-Soto, P. J., Fabbian, F., & Manfredini, R. (2021). Sleep, dreams, nightmares, and sex-related differences: a narrative review. *European Review for Medical and Pharmacological Sciences, 25*(7), 3054-3065. https://doi.org/10.26355/eurrev_202104_25559

Chen, X., He, J., Swanson, E., Cai, Z., & Fan, X. (2021). Big five personality traits and second language learning: A Meta-analysis of 40 years' research. *Educational Psychology Review, 34,* 851-887. https://doi.org/10.1007/s10648-021-09641-6

Connor-Smith, J. K., & Flachsbart, C. (2007). Relations between personality and coping: A meta-analysis. *Journal of Personality and Social Psychology, 93*(6), 1080-1107. https://doi.org/10.1037/0022-3514.93.6.1080

Davis, M. H. (1983). Measuring individual differences in empathy: Evidence for a multidimensional approach. *Journal of Personality and Social Psychology, 44*(1), 113-126. https://doi.org/10.1037/0022-3514.44.1.113

Erdem, C., & Uzun, A. M. (2022). Smartphone addiction among undergraduates: Roles of personality traits and demographic factors. *Technology, Knowledge and Learning, 27,* 579-597. https://doi.org/10.1007/s10758-020-09467-1

Farstad, S. M., McGeown, L. M., & von Ranson, K. M. (2016). Eating disorders and personality, 2004-2016: A systematic review and meta-analysis. *Clinical Psychology Review, 46,* 91-105. https://doi.org/10.1016/j.cpr.2016.04.005

Feiler, D. C., & Kleinbaum, A. M. (2015). Popularity, similarity, and the network extraversion bias. *Psychological Science, 26*(5), 593-603. https://doi.org/10.1177/0956797615569580

Fernández-Abascal, E. G., & Martín-Díaz, M. D. (2019). Relations between dimensions of emotional intelligence, specific aspects of empathy, and non-verbal sensitivity. *Frontiers in Psychology, 10,* Article 1066. https://doi.org/10.3389/fpsyg.2019.01066

Fischer, R., & Boer, D. (2015). Motivational basis of personality traits: A meta-analysis of value-personality correlations. *Journal of Personality, 83*(5), 491-510. https://doi.org/10.1111/jopy.12125

Funder, D. C., & Fast, L. A. (2010). Personality in social psychology. In S. T. Fiske, D. T. Gilbert, & G. Lindzey (Eds.), *Handbook of social psychology* (5th ed., pp. 668-697). John Wiley & Sons.

Gardner, W. L., Pickett, C. L., & Brewer, M. B. (2000). Social exclusion and selective memory: How the need to belong influences memory for social events. *Personality and Social Psychology Bulletin, 26*(4), 486-496. https://doi.org/10.1177/0146167200266007

Gerbasi, K. C., Roberts, S. E., Reysen, S., Plante, C. N., & McHugh, R. (2020). The lion, the wolf and the ~~wardrobe~~ fursuit: Do furries attending a furry convention have animal/fursona, furry, and convention themed dreams? In T. Howl (Ed.), *Furries among us 3: Essays by furries about furries* (pp. 62-84). Thurston Howl Publications.

Giluk, T. L. (2009). Mindfulness, big five personality, and affect: A meta-analysis. *Personality and Individual Differences, 47*(8), 805-811. https://doi.org/10.1016/j.paid.2009.06.026

Goldberg, L. R. (1990). An alternative "description of personality": The big-five factor structure. *Journal of Personality and Social Psychology, 59*(6), 1216-1229. https://doi.org/10.1037/0022-3514.59.6.1216

Gosling, S. D., Rentfrow, P. J., & Swann, W. B., Jr. (2003). A very brief measure of the big-five personality domains. *Journal of Research in Personality, 37*(6), 504-528. https://doi.org/10.1016/S0092-6566(03)00046-1

Graham, E. K., Weston, S. J., Gerstorf, D., Yoneda, T. B., Booth, T., Beam, C. R., ... & Mroczek, D. K. (2020). Trajectories of big five personality traits: A coordinated analysis of 16 longitudinal samples. *European Journal of Personality, 34*(3), 301-321. https://doi.org/10.1002/per.2259

Grijalva, E., & Newman, D. A. (2015). Narcissism and counterproductive work behavior (CWB): Meta-analysis and consideration of collectivist culture, big rive personality, and narcissism's facet structure. *Applied Psychology, 64*(1), 93-126. https://doi.org/10.1111/apps.12025

Hakulinen, C., Elovainio, M., Batty, G. D., Virtanen, M., Kivimäki, M., & Jokela, M. (2015). Personality and alcohol consumption: Pooled analysis of 72,949 adults from eight cohort studies. *Drug and Alcohol Dependence, 151,* 110-114. https://doi.org/10.1016/j.drugalcdep.2015.03.008

Hess, G., Schredl, M., & Goritz, A. S. (2017). Lucid dreaming frequency and the big five personality factors. *Imagination, Cognition and Personality, 36*(3), 240-253. https://doi.org/10.1177/0276236616648653

Hyatt, C. S., Zeichner, A., & Miller, J. D. (2019). Laboratory aggression and personality traits: A meta-analytic review. *Psychology of Violence, 9*(6), 675-689. https://doi.org/10.1037/vio0000236

Jenkins, S. T., Reysen, S., & Katzarska-Miller, I. (2012). Ingroup identification and personality. *Journal of Interpersonal Relations, Intergroup Relations and Identity, 5,* 9-16.

John, O. P. (1990). The "big five" factor taxonomy: Dimensions of personality in the natural language and in questionnaires. In L. A. Pervin (Ed.), *Handbook of personality: Theory and research* (pp. 66-100). Guilford Press.

Jordan, M. R., Amir, D., & Bloom, P. (2016). Are empathy and concern psychologically distinct? *Emotion, 16*(8), 1107-1116. https://doi.org/10.1037/emo0000228

Judge, T. A., Heller, D., & Mount, M. K. (2002). Five-factor model of personality and job satisfaction: A meta-analysis. *Journal of Applied Psychology, 87*(3), 530–541. https://doi.org/10.1037/0021-9010.87.3.530

Karwowski, M., & Lebuda, I. (2016). The big five, the huge two, and creative self-beliefs: A meta-analysis. *Psychology of Aesthetics, Creativity, and the Arts, 10*(2), 214-232. https://doi.org/10.1037/aca0000035

Kayiş, A. R., Satici, S. A., Yilmaz, M. F., Şimşek, D., Ceyhan, E., & Bakioğlu, F. (2016). Big five-personality trait and internet addiction: A meta-analytic review. *Computers in Human Behavior, 63,* 35-40. https://doi.org/10.1016/j.chb.2016.05.012

Kooij, D. T. A. M., Kanfer, R., Betts, M., & Rudolph, C. W. (2018). Future time perspective: A systematic review and meta-analysis. *Journal of Applied Psychology, 103*(8), 867-893. https://doi.org/10.1037/apl0000306

Lai, K., Xiong, X., Jiang, X., Sun, M., & He, L. (2020). Who falls for rumor? Influence of personality traits on false rumor belief. *Personality and Individual Differences, 152,* Article 109520. https://doi.org/10.1016/j.paid.2019.109520

Lange, R., Houran, J., Evans, J., & Lynn, S. J. (2019). A review and reevaluation of the revised transliminality scale. *Psychology of Consciousness: Theory, Research, and Practice, 6*(1), 67-89. https://doi.org/10.1037/cns0000153

Lange, R., Thalbourne, M. A., Houran, J., & Storm, L. (2000). The revised transliminality Scale: reliability and validity data from a Rasch top-down purification procedure. *Consciousness and Cognition, 9*(4), 591-617. https://doi.org/10.1006/ccog.2000.0472

Leary, M. R., Kelly, K. M., Cottrell, C. A., & Schreindorfer, L. S. (2013). Construct validity of the need to belong scale: Mapping the nomological network. *Journal of Personality Assessment, 95*(6), 610-624. https://doi.org/10.1080/00223891.2013.819511

Leary, M. R., Twenge, J. M., & Quinlivan, E. (2006). Interpersonal rejection as a determinant of anger and aggression. *Personality and Social*

Psychology Review, 10(2), 111-132. https://doi.org/10.1207/s15327957pspr1002_2
Marengo, D., Sindermann, C., Häckel, D., Settanni, M., Elhai, J. D., & Montag, C. (2020). The association between the Big Five personality traits and smartphone use disorder: A meta-analysis. *Journal of Behavioral Addictions, 9*(3), 534-550. https://doi.org/10.1556/2006.2020.00069
Martingano, A. J., & Konrath, S. (2022). How cognitive and emotional empathy relate to rational thinking: empirical evidence and meta-analysis. *The Journal of Social Psychology, 162*(1), 143-160.
McCutcheon, L., Shabahang, R., Williams, J., Aruguete, M., & Huynh, H. (2021). Dreaming about favorite celebrities in two different cultures. *International Journal of Dream Research, 14*(1). https://doi.org/10.11588/ijodr.2021.1.76309
Merckelbach, H., Horselenberg, R., & Muris, P. (2001). The creative experiences questionnaire (CEQ): A brief self-report measure of fantasy proneness. *Personality and Individual Differences, 31*(6), 987-995. https://doi.org/10.1016/S0191-8869(00)00201-4
Merckelbach, H., Otgaar, H., & Lynn, S. J. (2022). Empirical research on fantasy proneness and its correlates 2000–2018: A meta-analysis. *Psychology of Consciousness: Theory, Research, and Practice, 9*(1), 2-26. https://doi.org/10.1037/cns0000272
Mitsopoulou, E., & Giovazolias, T. (2015). Personality traits, empathy and bullying behavior: A meta-analytic approach. *Aggression and Violent Behavior, 21,* 61-72. https://doi.org/10.1016/j.avb.2015.01.007
Moors, A. C., Selterman, D. F., & Conley, T. D. (2017). Personality correlates of desire to engage in consensual non-monogamy among lesbian, gay, and bisexual individuals. *Journal of Bisexuality, 17*(4), 418-434. https://doi.org/10.1080/15299716.2017.1367982
Mumper, M. L., & Gerrig, R. J. (2017). Leisure reading and social cognition: A meta-analysis. *Psychology of Aesthetics, Creativity, and the Arts, 11*(1), 109-120. https://doi.org/10.1037/aca0000089
Noftle, E. E., & Robins, R. W. (2007). Personality predictors of academic outcomes: Big five correlates of GPA and SAT scores. *Journal of Personality and Social Psychology, 93*(1), 116-130. https://doi.org/10.1037/0022-3514.93.1.116
Oshio, A., Taku, K., Hirano, M., & Saeed, G. (2018). Resilience and Big Five personality traits: A meta-analysis. *Personality and Individual Differences, 127,* 54-60. https://doi.org/10.1016/j.paid.2018.01.048

Ozer, D. J., & Benet-Martínez, V. (2006). Personality and the prediction of consequential outcomes. *Annual Review of Psychology, 57,* 401-421. https://doi.org/10.1146/annurev.psych.57.102904.190127

Pickett, C. L., Gardner, W. L., & Knowles, M. (2004). Getting a cue: The need to belong and enhanced sensitivity to social cues. *Personality and Social Psychology Bulletin, 30*(9), 1095-1107. https://doi.org/10.1177/0146167203262085

Plante, C. N., Reysen, S., Groves, C. L., Roberts, S. E., & Gerbasi, K. (2017). The Fantasy Engagement Scale: A flexible measure of positive and negative fantasy engagement. *Basic and Applied Social Psychology, 39*(3), 127-152. https://doi.org/10.1080/01973533.2017.1293538

Plante, C. N., Roberts, S., Reysen, S., & Gerbasi, K. C. (2014). "One of us": Engagement with fandoms and global citizenship identification. *Psychology of Popular Media Culture, 3*(1), 49-64. https://doi.org/10.1037/ppm0000008

Rentfrow, P. J., & Gosling, S. D. (2003). The do re mi's of everyday life: The structure and personality correlates of music preferences. *Journal of Personality and Social Psychology, 84*(6), 1236-1256. https://doi.org/10.1037/0022-3514.84.6.1236

Reysen, S., & Katzarska-Miller, I. (2013). A model of global citizenship: Antecedents and outcomes. *International Journal of Psychology, 48*(5), 858-870. https://doi.org/10.1080/00207594.2012.701749

Reysen, S., & Katzarska-Miller, I. (2018). *The psychology of global citizenship: A review of theory and research*. Lexington Books.

Reysen, S., Larey, L. W., & Katzarska-Miller, I. (2012). College course curriculum and global citizenship. *International Journal of Development Education and Global Learning, 4*(3), 27-39. https://doi.org/10.18546/IJDEGL.04.3.03

Reysen, S., Plante, C., & Chadborn, D. (2017). Better together: Social connections mediate the relationship between fandom and well-being. *AASCIT Journal of Health, 4*(6), 68-73.

Reysen, S., Plante, C. N., Lam, T. Q., Kamble, S. V., Katzarska-Miller, I., Assis, N., Packard, G., & Moretti, E. G. (2020). Maturity and well-being: Consistent associations across samples and measures. *Journal of Wellness, 2*(2), Article 10, 1-8. https://doi.org/10.18297/jwellness/vol2/iss2/10

Reysen, S., Plante, C. N., Roberts, S. E., & Gerbasi, K. C. (2015). A social identity perspective of personality differences between fan and non-fan identities. *World Journal of Social Science Research, 2*(1), 91-103.

Reysen, S., Plante, C. N., Roberts, S. E., & Gerbasi, K. C. (2020). Cosplayers' and non-cosplayers' involvement in fandom-based drama. *The Phoenix Papers, 4*(2), 28-36. https://doi.org/10.17605/OSF.IO/JZE2P

Reysen, S., Plante, C. N., Roberts, S. E., & Gerbasi, K. C. (in press). Social activities mediate the relation between fandom identification and psychological well-being. *Leisure Sciences*. https://doi.org/10.1080/01490400.2021.2023714

Reysen, S., Plante, C. N., Roberts, S. E., Gerbasi, K. C., & Shaw, J. (2016). An examination of anime fan stereotypes. *The Phoenix Papers, 2*(2), 90-117.

Rhodes, R. E., & Smith, N. E. I. (2006). Personality correlates of physical activity: a review and meta-analysis. *British Journal of Sports Medicine, 40*(12), 958-965. http://dx.doi.org/10.1136/bjsm.2006.028860

Richman, L. S., & Learly, M. R. (2009). Reactions to discrimination, stigmatization, ostracism, and other forms of interpersonal rejection: A multimotive model. *Psychological Review, 116*(2), 365-383. https://doi.org/10.1037/a0015250

Rivers, A., Wickramasekera, I. E., Pekala, R. J., & Rivers, J. A. (2016). Empathic features and absorption in fantasy role-playing. *American Journal of Clinical Hypnosis, 58*(3), 286-294. https://doi.org/10.1080/00029157.2015.1103696

Sayehmiri, K., Kareem, K. I., Abdi, K., Dalvand, S., & Gheshlagh, R. G. (2020). The relationship between personality traits and marital satisfaction: a systematic review and meta-analysis. *BMC Psychology, 8,* Article 15. https://doi.org/10.1186/s40359-020-0383-z

Shaw, J., Plante, C. N., Reysen, S., Roberts, S. E., & Gerbasi, K. C. (2016). Predictors of fan entitlement in three fandoms. *The Phoenix Papers, 2*(2), 203-219.

Shen, X. S., Chick, G., & Zinn, H. (2014). Playfulness in adulthood as a personality trait: a reconceptualization and a new measurement. *Journal of Leisure Research, 46*(1), 58-83. https://doi.org/10.1080/00222216.2014.11950313

Stricker, J., Buecker, S., Schneider, M., & Preckel, F. (2019). Multidimensional perfectionism and the big five personality traits: a meta-analysis. *European Journal of Personality, 33*(2), 176-196. https://doi.org/10.1002/per.2186

Sun, J., Kaufman, S. B., & Smillie, L. D. (2018). Unique associations between big five personality aspects and multiple dimensions of well-

being. *Journal of Personality, 86*(2), 158-172. https://doi.org/10.1111/jopy.12301
Taylor, L. D., & Acic, I. (2021). Magical thinking and fans of fictional texts. *Psychology of Popular Media, 10*(1), 21-27. https://doi.org/10.1037/ppm0000279
Thielmann, I., Spadaro, G., & Balliet, D. (2020). Personality and prosocial behavior: A theoretical framework and meta-analysis. *Psychological Bulletin, 146*(1), 30-90. https://doi.org/10.1037/bul0000217
Tidikis, V., & Dunbar, N. D. (2019). Openness to experience and creativity: When does global citizenship matter? *International Journal of Psychology, 54*(2), 264-268. https://doi.org/10.1002/ijop.12463
Turner, J. C., & Onorato, R. S. (1999). Social identity, personality, and the self-concept: A self-categorization perspective. In T. R. Tyler, R. M. Kramer, & O. P. John (Eds.), *The psychology of the social self* (pp. 11-46). Lawrence Erlbaum Associates Publishers.
Vallerand, R. J., Blanchard, C., Mageau, G. A., Koestner, R., Ratelle, C., Léonard, M., Gagné, M., & Marsolais, J. (2003). Les passions de l'âme: On obsessive and harmonious passion. *Journal of Personality and Social Psychology, 85*(4), 756-767. https://doi.org/10.1037/0022-3514.85.4.756
Vallerand, R. J., Ntoumanis, N., Philippe, F. L., Lavigne, G. L., Carbonneau, N., Bonneville, A., Lagacé-Labonté, C., & Maliha, G. (2008). On passion and sports fans: A look at football. *Journal of Sports Sciences, 26*(12), 1279-1293. https://doi.org/10.1080/02640410802123185
Wilson, K. E., & Dishman, R. K. (2015). Personality and physical activity: A systematic review and meta-analysis. *Personality and Individual Differences, 72,* 230-242. https://doi.org/10.1016/j.paid.2014.08.023

Chapter 19
Purring Motors: Fan Drive and Motivation

Stephen Reysen, Courtney "Nuka" Plante

We've dedicated a lot of space in this book to trying to describe what a furry is, where the furry fandom came from, and what furries do. These questions share a common throughline, the fundamental question of what motivates furries: what drives furries to become furries, why did science fiction and anime fans start the furry fandom in the first place, and what compels furries to produce and consume furry media? The present chapter is focused on answering these questions.

Psychologists have long studied what drives people to do the things they do.[1] Motivation is defined as "a driving force that initiates and directs behavior" (Stangor, 2010, p. 521); it's what compels a person to do something at any given moment instead of carrying on with whatever they were doing. Early psychologists focused on drive states and experiences of discomfort when a basic need wasn't being met (e.g., hunger, which is undesirable and can be sated by seeking food). But motivations need not involve a present state of discomfort: we can be perfectly content but nevertheless strive toward a desired end goal. And, unlike hunger, we may not even be consciously aware of what's motivating us to act.[2]

To understand what drives furries, we'll first examine what leads furries to the furry fandom in the first place. Next, we'll discuss some of the ways psychologists study motivation, with an emphasis on fan studies, and see how we've been able to apply some of these concepts to the furry fandom. We'll then finish up the chapter by talking about furries' values, a related concept that can also help us to understand what might motivate furries.

Routes to Furry

As we've noted elsewhere in this book, most research on the psychology of fans—especially most early work—has focused on sports fans. This work suggests that people are socialized to become sports fans by participating in sports (e.g., in gym class), seeing and watching sports on television, and being surrounded by others who like sports (e.g., parents, friends; see McPherson, 1975). In other words, a liking of sports is almost inevitable,

---

[1] Some might argue that this is the crux of psychology, as a field devoted to the study of human behavior!

[2] Importantly, just because we're unaware of something doesn't mean it can't impact us. A lot of advertising is effective precisely because its impact on the viewer falls largely outside of their attention!

surrounded by it as we are.[3] Smith and colleagues (1981) asked sports fans to identify the people most influential in leading them to follow sports and found that a person's father and friends were the biggest influence, followed to a lesser extent by coaches and the media. Decades later, Wann et al. (2001) similarly found that peers and friends were among the strongest influences on a person's interest in sports (followed by schools and parents). They also noted that a father or brother had a significant impact on their interest in sport. In short, the results suggest a common route to being a sports fan is living in an environment in which others value sports and where sports are easy to access.

So what can this tell us about furries? After all, furry is a fairly niche interest: unlike sports, the most common interest on the planet, most people are not furries. Likewise, there isn't a segment of the nightly news dedicated to talking about the most recent developments in the furry fandom, nor do we dedicate an entire course to being a furry in school in the same way that physical education courses encourage playing sports.

With this in mind, Reysen, Plante, Roberts, Gerbasi, Schroy, et al. (2017) asked samples of furries, anime fans, and fantasy sports fans to "briefly describe how you discovered and became part of [your fan community]." The researchers coded the responses into nine categories including (1) internet (e.g., "Browsing Google I found a furry image, after researching a bit, more I came to enjoy it"), (2) a friend (e.g., "Met a friend of a former roommate who introduced me. Took off from there"), (3) a relationship partner (e.g., "Boyfriend invited me to Anthrocon and I realized my kitten roleplay online was more a part of me than I'd previously thought"), (4) family (e.g., "My older brother was a furry and used to entertain me in his fursuit. I became part of the community when I got my fursuit when I was 7"), (5) media (e.g., "That one episode of CSI"), (6) search for similar others (e.g., "Searching for a place to belong"), (7) fandom (e.g., "I saw fursuits at an anime convention and thought it was cute and fun"), (8) clubs (e.g., "Joined the Wisconsin Fur group at a meet one day"), and (9) other (e.g., "My broad collection of plush animals"). Table 19.1 lists the frequency of each of these different categories in each of the groups of fans. Consistent with past research, fantasy sports fans were overwhelmingly likely to have gotten into their interest in sports through a friend, while anime fans were especially likely to stumble into their interest through a mixture of the

---

[3] As a telling example, nearly 20% of the global population watched the 2022 World Cup Final (Richter, 2023), a number comparable to the number of people who watched the 1969 Apollo 11 moon landing (Hsu, 2019).

internet, anime-themed clubs, exposure to anime in the media, and their friends. In the case of furries, the single-biggest route into the fandom was through the internet, although being introduced to it by a friend and through the media were also common routes.[4]

Table 19.1. Observed (expected) discovery route by fandom (Reysen, Plante, Roberts, Gerbasi, Schroy, et al., 2017).

Route	Furry	Anime	Sport
Internet	326 (283.5)	724 (689)	37 (114.5)
Friend	166 (178.7)	350 (434.2)	169 (72.1)
Partner	35 (18)	19 (43.7)	15 (7.3)
Family	12 (31.8)	61 (77.3)	49 (12.8)
Media	133 (127.8)	333 (310.6)	24 (51.6)
Search	23 (20.1)	51 (48.8)	3 (8.1)
Fandom	24 (11.7)	21 (28.5)	0 (4.7)
Club	51 (104.1)	336 (252.9)	12 (42)
Other	20 (14.3)	25 (34.9)	10 (5.8)

These findings were primarily focused on similarities and differences between fandoms. However, in trying to study routes into the fan interest that may be present for multiple fan groups, we might have glossed over some routes into the furry fandom that are unique to the furry fandom. To address this concern, in a different study we asked a similar question ("Please describe how you came to identify as a furry"), but only to a sample of furries. Reysen et al. (2017a) coded these responses into ten routes to discovery and eventual membership in the furry community, this time using

[4] Table 19.1 lays out data for a statistical analysis called a chi-squared test, which compares expected and observed findings. For example, if you combined all three samples, the internet was the most common way for people to get into their fan interest—but this route was not equally distributed among the three groups. The expected scores in the brackets show how many fans we might expect to pick this route in each group if it were the case that each of these three groups were equally likely to get into their fan interest via the internet. In the case of sports fans, the observed number of fans who said internet was quite a bit lower than expected, meaning that the internet was not an especially strong way for sports fans to get into their interest. With this in mind, the results suggest that the most distinct or characteristic way of getting into the fan interest for sports fans was one's friend, while for anime fans it was the internet, clubs, and, to a lesser extent, the media. For furries, by far the most distinct route into the fandom was through the internet.

categories that were not required to apply to anime fans and sports fans as well. Below are the ten most common themes extracted, along with the percentage of the people falling into that theme and some example responses from participants.

Theme 1: I've Always Been One (26.1%)

The most common theme in participants' responses is that they've always been a furry and that the only "discovery" was to have found a community of their peers, rather than having to discover their interest in furry itself. These responses were also frequently coupled with the idea that they had always had a feeling they were furry.

> *"As a child[,] I started strongly identifying with wolves, especially spiritually. When I stumbled across other people who thought/felt the same way and had built and [sic] entire community around it, I latched on."*

> *"Before exposure to the fandom, I have always felt that something was missing inside myself. It was a similar feeling to knowing that one had forgotten something important but could not remember what. It was during this turbulent stage during puberty that I stumbled on some artwork depicting anthropomorphic animals. It was a revelation to myself at not only how attractive I found the concept of anthropomorphism but also how much I related to and identified with these beings. I felt as though I had finally discovered a forgotten or suppressed aspect of myself. The ease with which I assumed my reclaimed identity was evidence enough for me (as I did not require a long time to agonize about fursona species, I simply became what I was all along). Forgive me if this sounds contrived, but I honestly believe that I am a much happier person now for it."*

> *"I always felt something different & identified w/ anthropomorphic animals from a young age. Once I discovered the fandom it was an eye opener [sic]. I was a furry before I knew about furries."*

Theme 2: Just Happened Across (16.3%)

A second theme revolved around being on the internet and happening across furry-related art or stories, something which jump-started their interest in anthropomorphic animals.

"I accidentally came across furry art while prowling through the internet and became captivated by it. As [I] came to be more and more interested I started to seek out interaction with other people that liked that kind of art. Small pieces in the media brought my attention to conventions and I realized the scope and size of the community. From there[,] I started making friends and began attending conventions."

"Basically stumbled upon the community online, and everything fell into place[.]"

"I first found out about furries by stumbling across anthropomorphic artwork online. I researched further and found out there were events that celebrated this theme and the community. I have been going to at least two furry conventions every year since."

Theme 3: Research Project (14%)

The third theme is similar to the above theme in that fans just happened across the fandom. However, rather than pure chance or looking up a piece of media, this theme reflects searching the internet for more information on a topic (e.g., school projects).

"A project on Norse Mythologies introduced me to fenrir [sic] and I became very interested in creating a modern-day re-telling."

"I have had a strong connection to dragons since 8th grade. Once my family got the internet, I looked up dragons. It wasn't long after this (we got dial-up in the late 90's) that I discovered the fandom. Once I discovered it, I identified with it."

"I found the community while researching a school project. It just felt like it fit already."

Theme 4: Media (13.5%)

A fourth theme involved an interest in a specific piece of media content which led to discovering the fandom. This route, while related conceptually to the second theme, is distinct in that it involves a concerted and active interest in a piece of media already, rather than just stumbling upon furry content by happenstance while doing something else.

"American Werewolf in London & Greek mythology --> internet --> VCL --> Anthrocon site --> fursuits --> [Fursuit builder name omitted] fursuits = full fledged furry[.]"

"I enjoyed The Fox & the Hound as a child. This helped my liking towards foxes, which led me to studying foxes. The internet, anthropomorphism in anime/cartoons[,] and other things led me into the fandom fully."

"I first came into it after seeing some of the serious discussion over Pokémon/Sonic fanart. The eye for detail, the constructive criticism, and the persistence of biological accuracy fascinated me."

"I had no idea why I was so infatuated with these characters, or what that made me. A decade back, I came across MTV's Sex 2k program and it just so happened to be about Furries. I did some research and found that I identified with the fandom[.]"

Theme 5: Friend (12.1%)

The fifth theme is rather self-explanatory: a friend introduced the participant to the fandom.

"A friend introduced me to the fandom, I became intrigued and started to explore it. Before I knew it I was hooked, I came up with my own fursona and have been a furry ever since."

"a [sic] friend showed me furraffinity [sic] and fell in love with the site (and the friend)[.]"

"I had friends that pointed out the fandom to me. Realized very quickly I was a furry."

Theme 6: Love of Animals/Nature (4.9%)

This theme reflects responses in which a person's love for animals and nature more broadly eventually led them to the fandom.

"I was always interested in animals. I took a trip to the zoo in kindergarten [sic]. I played kitty and owner as a child (I was the kitty). I started researching animal related [sic] topics in grade school and

spending time out with the horses and dogs on my grandmothers [sic] farm. I found the furry community on the internet as soon as I had internet access. I studied zoology in university. I've just always been fascinated by other species' (non human) [sic] perspectives of the world."

"I've loved birds all my life. I have found so many others who do too. I now feel that I am "normal" for feeling as strongly as I do. feel [sic] free to "geek out" over my favorite subject!"

"Always loved animals, often thought it would be fun/cool to have animal aspects (tail, senses, etc...) This love translated well into my writing and in my love of webcomics. My favorites always contained animals and the characters of my writing are mostly anthro-animals. It was just a small step from that into furry fandom."

Theme 7: Roleplaying and Second Life (4.2%)

Another route to discovery was through roleplaying and/or Second Life.

"Role playing [sic] on AOL in [the] 1990s (early)[.]"

"By beginning to RP on the Tapestries MUCK, finding artwork I liked, and making friends within the community."

"I had always identified with the fox since I was little. Experiences online, specifically Second Life lead [sic] me to the fandom and got me to consider my connection more seriously[.]"

Theme 8: Different Fandom (3.6%)

Some fans also found their way to the furry fandom through exposure while in a different fandom—a finding overlapping with the fact that many furries are also members of other fandoms (e.g., anime, science fiction; see Chapter 11).

"It happened at a Gen Con convention in 1975. That is where I saw my first anthropomorphic art that wasn't a "cartoon". It had such a strong influence on me, I carried it with me for years before I knew of the existence of the fandom. Finding the fandom was a complete but life changing [sic] accident for me."

"Furry art at World Con 1980[.]"

"I discovered the Star Fox fandom in 1996, and the furry fandom in 1999. I lurked, but did not feel comfortable identifying as a furry until 2008."

"I ran across furtopia [sic] through an anime site and found out about the community[.]"

Theme 9: Porn (3.1%)

This one is also pretty self-explanatory: after stumbling across furry pornography, participants discovered the furry fandom.[5]

"discovered [sic] the porn, found out about there being more to it, became furry[.]"

"I watched a lot of yiff then became a furry and I no longer watch yiff but I am now more of a furry fan than I was then[.]"

Theme 10: Family/Significant Other (2.1%)

The last theme reflects being introduced to the fandom through a family member or relationship partner.

"I began dating a furry, and through him, I came to enjoy the furry fandom as well."

"My GF is a furry artist. She introduced me to the community. It snowballed from there."

"My son is a furry, and I found that I really like the community (and crafting the fursuits & accessories!)"

---

[5] This finding is consistent with research we discuss in Chapter 10 and Chapter 19 showing that while porn use is common among furries, it is rarely the linchpin of a furry's interest in furry media. In this case, only about 3% of furries found the fandom through their interest in furry porn—a number which would be expected to be higher if furry were, first and foremost, a fetish for most furries and which runs counter to stereotypes about furries as driven primarily by sex (see Chapter 21).

A Quantitative Look at Routes into Furry

The above findings were open-ended in nature, meaning that we, the researchers, were responsible for categorizing and organizing the responses. Because this introduces the possibility that our own biases or interpretations may impact the findings, we've also collected quantitative data on the subject. Specifically, we asked fans to rate the extent to which different sources may have influenced their interest in becoming a furry (1 = *definitely not an influence* to 7 = *a very important influence*). As shown in Figure 19.1, many of the most highly-rated influences line up with the themes we identified above, with a few additional categories—suggested to us by furries themselves in conversations at conventions—providing some additional context. For example, while a specific piece of media was a common theme extracted from the open-ended data, the quantitative data goes a step further and shows that this media largely consists of artwork, often animation (with Disney films being one of the most common specific examples).

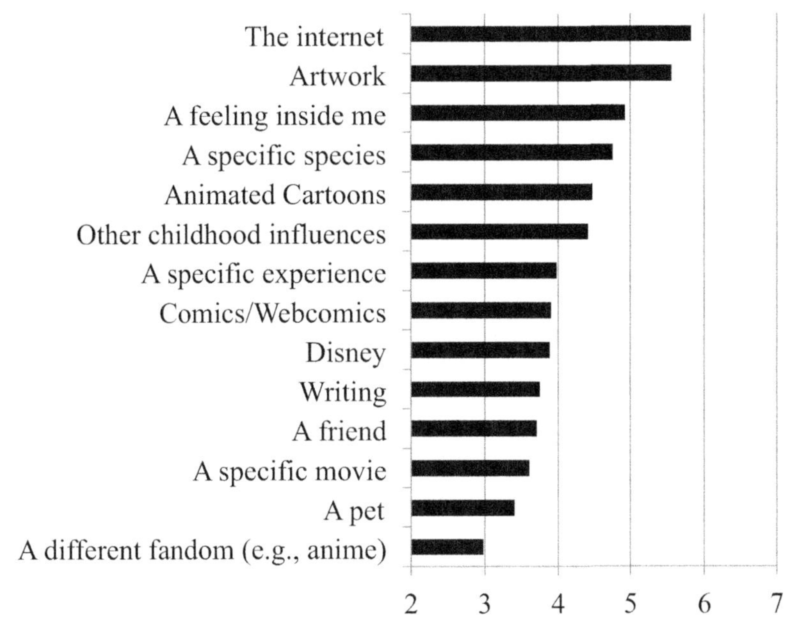

Figure 19.1. Ratings of sources of influence in one's decision to become a furry (7-point scale).

When taken together, these studies reveal a few key points about furries' route into the furry fandom. The first is that many furries describe themselves as stumbling upon the fandom, rather than intentionally seeking out the fandom. The second is that these entryways into the fandom differ quite a bit from past research on sports fans. Indeed, furries more closely match the path of anime fans—another niche, media-based fandom—than they do the path of sports fans—a far more mainstream interest.[6] The third is that furries commonly describe that something "clicked" for them, that they were doing something furry-adjacent and happened across the furry community in the process. This serendipitous occurrence led many to the feeling that they had found their place and their people, a notion that sounds a lot like satisfying a need for belongingness that we'll discuss throughout the rest of this chapter.

On that note, let's shift our focus away from routes into the fandom and more directly onto specific motivations driving furries toward their interest and the furry community.

Wann's Fan Motivations

Daniel Wann is arguably the most well-known fan psychologist. In fact, his work on fan psychology is so well-known that it would be almost impossible to write a paper about fan motivation *without* referencing him at least once. Through his work on sports fans, Wann (1995) proposed eight motivations that he thought drove people to their interest in sports: (1) belongingness (feeling a sense of connection with others in the fandom), (2) family (opportunity to be with family), (3) aesthetics (artistic beauty of the fan interest), (4) self-esteem (interests makes one feel better about themselves), (5) economic (financial gain from being a fan), (6) eustress (excitement or positive stress), (7) escape (opportunity to get away from daily life hassles), and (8) entertainment (pleasurable experience). He developed a measure of these eight different motivations and found that,

---

[6] This may be a product of availability of content or accessibility of the fandom to a mainstream audience: whereas a person would have to actively try to *not* be exposed to sports media, many people are unaware that the furry fandom exists; indeed, one of the most common responses we get from laypersons when describing our work to them is to ask us what the heck a furry is. For this reason, furries may *need* to stumble into the fandom by accident simply because there is less mainstream awareness of the furry fandom than there is of the football fandom—although that may be changing with the growing size of furry conventions, a growing proportion of people who spend time immersed in internet culture (where furries are generally more commonly known), and with the mainstream success of films such as *Zootopia* and shows like *Bojack Horseman* which prominently feature anthropomorphic animal characters.

among sports fans, the highest-rated motivations were entertainment, eustress, belongingness, and self-esteem. These variables were also strongly correlated with fanship (i.e., team identification). In other words, most sports fans were sports fans because it was fun, they enjoyed the rush or thrill of not knowing how a game would turn out, they enjoyed being around other sports fans, and because of the boost they got in their self-esteem through their fan interest (e.g., feeling proud when their team won).

While Wann developed his scale with sports fans in mind, there's no reason why it couldn't also be easily adapted to measure the motivation of other fans as well. To this end, Schroy et al. (2016) administered an adapted version of Wann's scale to a sample of furries, anime fans, and fantasy sports fans. The scale included Wann's original eight motivations along with two plausible-seeming additional motivations (seeking attention from others and a sexual attraction to the interest). As shown in Figure 19.2, furries' highest-rated motivations on this scale included entertainment, escape, and belongingness. These were largely in line with the motivations of anime fans and fantasy sports fans, although furries scored higher on escapism and much higher on belongingness than the other two groups, as well as higher on entertainment than fantasy sports fans but not anime fans. And while furries did score considerably higher on sexual attraction and self-esteem than did either anime or fantasy sports fans, relatively speaking, these particular motivations were fairly low on the list and were by no means the most significant motivators of involvement in the furry fandom.

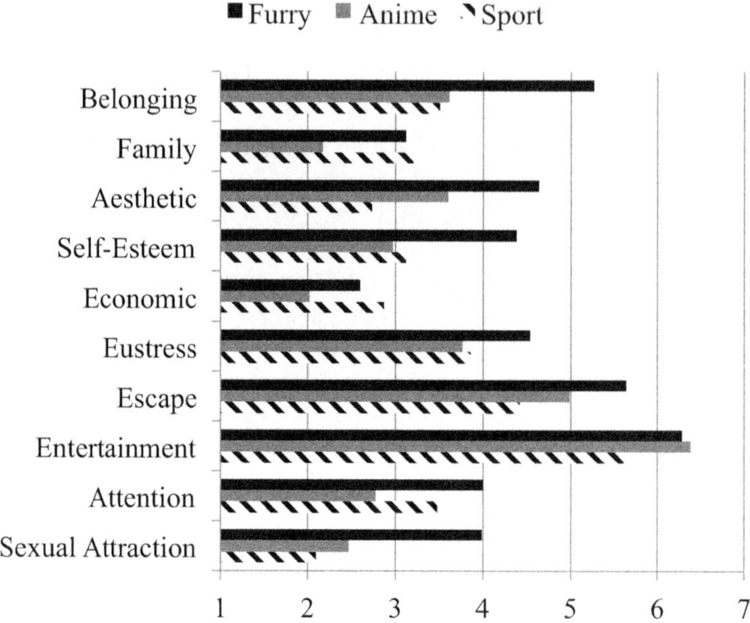

Figure 19.2. Furry, anime, and fantasy sports fans' ratings of motivations to participate in their respective fan communities (7-point scale).

We conducted a follow-up analysis of this data with an analysis called a *regression analysis*. In a nutshell, we ran a pair of statistical models in which participants' scores on all ten of the different motivations were allowed to simultaneously predict either fans' fanship or fandom scores. The results for fanship and fandom are shown in Figure 19.3 and Figure 19.4, respectively. In Figure 19.3, we can see that fanship—an interest specifically in furry content—is most strongly predicted by a desire for belongingness, followed by a much smaller, but still significant drive of sexual attraction; entertainment and family also emerged as fairly weak predictors of fanship. In contrast, fandom scores—an interest in the fan community—were motivated almost entirely by a desire for belongingness, with entertainment being a much weaker secondary motivation.

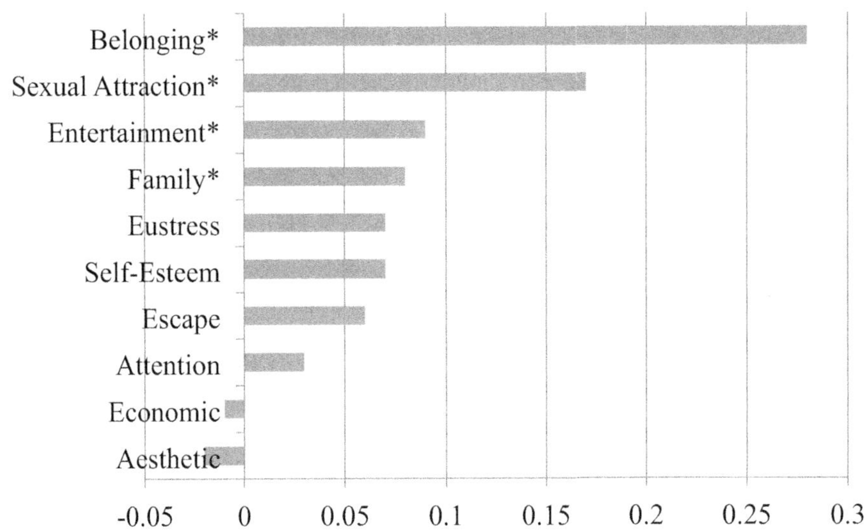

Figure 19.3. Regression with motivations predicting furries' degree of fanship. Standardized betas presented, * $p < .05$.

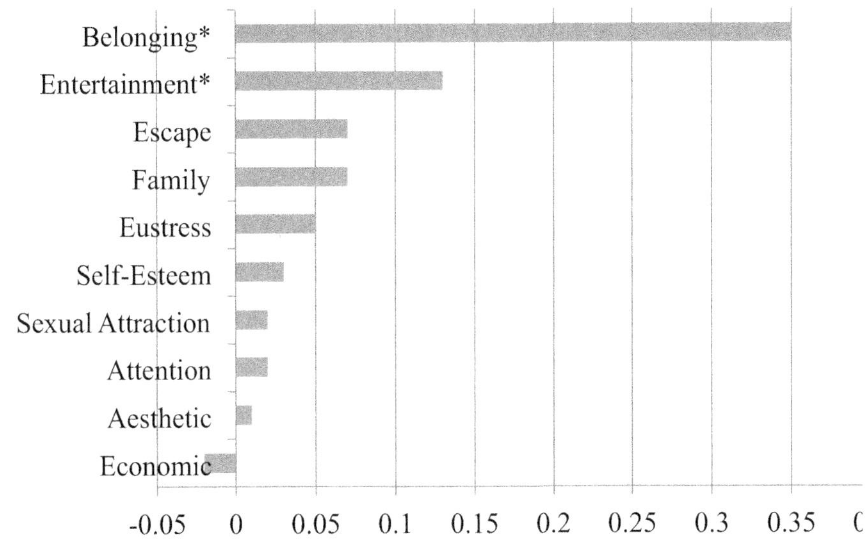

Figure 19.4. Regression with motivations predicting furries' degree of fandom identification. Standardized betas presented, * $p < .05$.

These results converge on findings from sports fans (e.g., Wann, 1995) and from our open-ended questions to furries in showing that belongingness was the biggest driver of furry fandom involvement, as it was for anime and fantasy sports fans. The results also show that there is somewhat of a difference in what motivates a person's general interest in something versus their interest in the fan community—while both were driven predominantly by a need for belongingness, some motivators, like sexual interest, are unique to driving fanship and not fandom. Or, to put it another way, furries' interest in furry media may be at least somewhat driven by an interest in furry porn, but furry porn plays virtually no role in furries' drive to be part of the furry fandom.

Psychological Needs

In the previous section, we looked at motivational variables that were specific to fan interests. However, humans are complex beings driven by a multitude of other factors that apply to far more than just their fan interests. For example, fan communities are just one manifestation of a broader tendency for humans to belong to groups. As such, we can ask whether some of the motivations that drive our broader social behavior may also compel us to join a fan group. To do this, we'll turn to the work of Vignoles et al. (2006) who proposed six key motivations that drive our behavior as a social species: (1) self-esteem (perception of one's self-worth), (2) continuity (seeking a link between past, present, and future self-narratives), (3) distinctiveness (desire to perceive oneself as a unique individual), (4) belonging (felt connection with others), (5) efficacy (felt confidence and competency to meet one's goals), and (6) meaning (sense of meaning and purpose in life). The researchers observed that all else being equal, people identify with groups that satisfy these psychological needs.

Drawing upon this work, we measured these six variables in a sample of furries alongside four additional measures of well-established psychological needs: the need for social support (e.g., Haslam et al., 2018; Smodis-McCune et al., 2022), the need to feel that one's perception of the world is valid (Swann, 1983), the need to feel a sense of control in our lives, and a reduction of perceived uncertainty in the world (Hogg, 2000). Specifically, we asked furries to rate the extent that being in the furry community satisfied each of the ten different needs as a way of measuring what motivates furries to take part in the furry fandom. As shown in Figure 19.5, the biggest motivators were the fandom's ability to satisfy their need for social support, belongingness, distinctiveness, and self-esteem.

Figure 19.5. Mean ratings of psychological needs met through participation in the fandom (7-point scale).

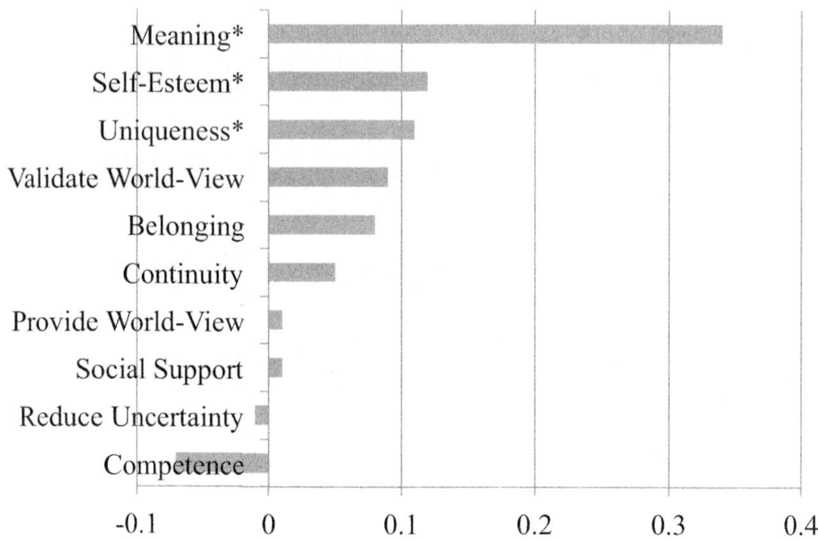

Figure 19.6. Regression with psychological needs predicting furries' degree of fanship. Standardized betas presented, * $p < .05$.

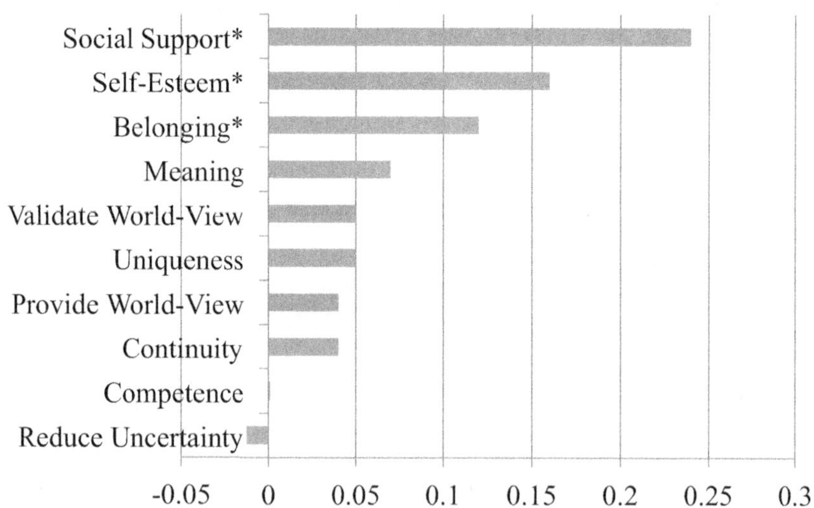

Figure 19.7. Regression with psychological needs predicting furries' degree of fandom identification. Standardized betas presented, * $p < .05$.

Similar to the approach we took with Daniel Wann's motivations, we ran another pair of regression models in which the ten different motivators were allowed to predict fanship and fandom scores. As shown in Figure 19.6, meaning in life was by far the strongest motivator of fanship, followed distantly by self-esteem and a sense of distinctiveness / uniqueness. In contrast, social support, self-esteem, and belongingness were motivators of fandom identification (see Figure 19.7). The results once again illustrate how different factors motivate furries' interest in furry content and their interest in the furry fandom. Or, to put it another way, when asking what motivates furries we need to know whether we're asking what motivates an interest in furry-themed media or what motivates furries to identify as part of the furry community. The results of this study generally align with results presented in Chapter 6, in that fanship seems to be motivated by personal, individual pursuits (meaning, and uniqueness), while fandom is motivated more by things that can only be obtained through group membership (i.e., social support, belonging).

Optimal Distinctiveness

We've noted that belongingness—a desire to be part of a group—is one of the strongest motivators for a furry to identify with their furry interest and with the furry community. However, we also saw that a desire for uniqueness or distinctiveness also motivated furries to identify with the fandom. On its face, this seems like a contradiction: belonging to a group, almost by definition, involves shifting one's identity away from that of an individual to that of the group—the opposite of being unique and distinct. We can better understand these two competing motivations through a framework called optimal distinctiveness theory (Brewer, 1991). The premise of the theory is that people want to stand out from the crowd, but also to fit in with a group, both to a reasonable extent. Intuitively, this makes sense. After all, standing out is fine, but standing out too much can be uncomfortable (e.g., imagine being the only person wearing shorts and a tie-dye t-shirt at a black-tie formal event). In the same vein, it can be exciting to be part of a group, but the feeling of becoming lost in the crowd (e.g., losing one's identity and becoming just another cog in the machine) can be unsettling. To balance out these needs, people seek out groups that fall in the "sweet spot" of satisfying both needs: they give us a sense of affiliation and acceptance, but also let us distinguish ourselves from others.[7] Optimal distinctiveness theory has been

[7] It should be noted that where this "sweet spot" or balance lies will differ from person to person. Some people have a fairly strong need to stand out, and will tend to gravitate toward groups that allow them to stand out from the crowd (e.g., non-

backed by a wealth of research (e.g., Leonardelli et al., 2010) including studies showing that music fans prefer music that's not too popular or unpopular (Abrams, 2009) and that the biggest anime fans also rate themselves as being high on both a sense of belonging and a sense of distinctiveness (Reysen et al., 2017).

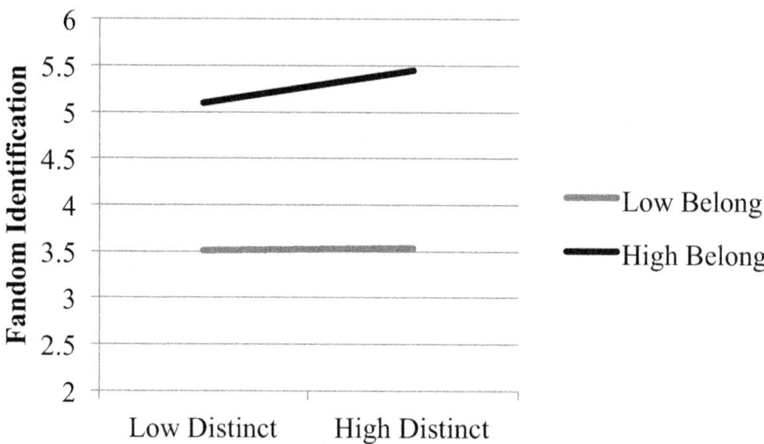

Figure 19.8. Furries perceptions of distinctiveness and belonging interacting to predict the degree of fandom identification.

To test whether this theory helps to explain what motivates furries to identify with the furry fandom, Reysen et al. (2016) asked furries to rate how strongly they felt like they belonged to the furry fandom (e.g., "I feel included and well-integrated into the furry community"), as well as whether they felt the furry fandom was distinct from other groups (e.g., "The furry community is very unique when compared with non-furry groups"). Finally, we, asked furries how strongly they identified with the furry fandom. The results, shown in Figure 19.8, show that the furries who identified most strongly with the furry fandom were those who both felt a strong sense of belongingness and felt that the furry fandom was distinct from other fan groups—supporting optimal distinctiveness theory. In short, the data suggest that at least part of the motivation for furries to be furries is the fact that the

mainstream groups). Conversely, some people have a very low need to stand out, and may prefer to belong to groups that are large or fairly mainstream. Everyone tries to strike a different balance between these two competing needs, with different groups scratching the itch for different people.

furry fandom may satisfy their competing needs to fit in with a group while simultaneously distinguishing themselves from others.

CAPE Model

Scientists love to create classifications, categories, and theoretical boxes and to organize the world within them. This is just as true of biologists, who try to organize all living species into a taxonomic framework, as it is with fan researchers, who try to distinguish between different types of fans. For example, a fan psychologist might try to distinguish die-hard, lifelong fans of a sports team from casual, fair-weather fans who jump on the bandwagon whenever a team is having a good season.[8]

To continue our comparison, biologists use physical traits like an organism's color, size, or shape to distinguish one species from another. In an analogous fashion, fan researchers have proposed a variety of dimensions along which to distinguish one group of fans from another. Some of the proposed variables are motivations, meaning we might be able to distinguish one type of fan from another based on what motivates the fan (e.g., fans motivated by belongingness needs may be different from fans motivated by economic reasons).

In a 2021 book, Plante et al. combed the literature and found 28 different factors that researchers have used to differentiate fans. We combined and condensed these variables using statistical analyses and arrived at a set of four clusters of variables, represented by the acronym CAPE: (1) *commitment* (extent of one's interest in the topic, including loyalty, memorizing knowledge about the topic, participating in fandom activities), (2) *asset* (extent to which one benefits from the interest, including economic benefits or a sense of accomplishment/achievement), (3) *presence* (extent to which the interest absorbs the fan's attention, including escapism, positive stress, and providing novel experiences), and (4) *expression* (extent to which the fandom is significant and meaningful, including fostering personal growth or as a creative outlet). In the remainder of this section, we'll review how these four dimensions are related to the furry community and what they

[8] If you're wondering *why* scientists bother with these boxes and categories, the answer is because these are differences that make a practical difference. For example, knowing that a bird is a member of one species over another helps biologists predict its behavior (e.g., whether it creates nests in trees or on the ground). When it comes to fans, these categories help us predict fan-related behaviors such as purchasing and consumption habits or sticking around through trying times.

can tell us about some of the differences in the way furries think, feel, and behave.

We first examined differences between furries, anime fans, and undergraduate college fans of various interests (e.g., media, sports teams, musical groups) on the CAPE dimensions. As we can see in Figure 19.9, furries stood out the most from the other fans on the dimension of expression, with furries being significantly more likely to see their fan interest as a meaningful means of self-expression than the other groups. This is fairly consistent with some of the distinctions we've noted between furries and other fan groups, such as the fact that most furries create fursonas that represent an idealized version of themselves (see Chapter 7), a feature that lacks a comparable analog in either the anime fandom or in other fandoms (e.g., sports, music). In fact, along with the presence dimension—which was comparable to levels observed in the other fan groups—expression was the highest-rated of the CAPE dimensions for furries, but not for the other fan groups.

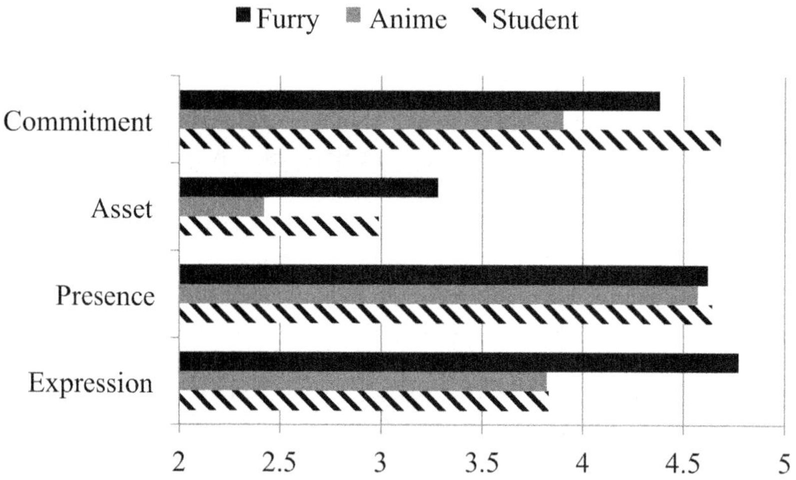

Figure 19.9. Furries, anime fans, and students' mean ratings of the CAPE model of fan interest dimensions.

Next, we ran a series of regression analyses allowing the CAPE variables to predict a wide range of furry-related variables to see whether understanding furries with respect to their CAPE motivations can tell us a bit about how they think, feel, and behave. Table 19.2 shows the results of the analysis for variables related to furry-specific activities, including media consumption, fursonas, fursuiting, elitism, and sexual content. The data show that a furry's commitment score tells us about their engagement in furry-related activities across the board—it was related to both fanship and fandom identification (as well as with being openly furry), with fursuiting and con attendance, spending money consuming furry media, becoming engrossed in furry media, identifying with one's fursona, feeling a sense of higher status among furries, and with the consumption of furry pornography. In other words, commitment-related motivations predict engagement and consumption behavior in furries.

Table 19.2. CAPE model of fan interest dimensions predicting fandom-relevant dimensions.

Variable	C	A	P	E
Fanship	.43**	-.03	.04	.35**
Fandom	.44**	.002	.12**	.19**
Identity Disclosure	.37**	.17**	-.10**	-.03
Years Furry	.30**	-.04	-.12**	-.03
Number of Cons	.22**	.07*	-.02	-.09*
Number Furry-Related Sites	.26**	.01	.07*	-.05
Number Full Fursuit	.17**	.07*	-.11**	-.003
Number Partial Fursuit	.15**	.13**	-.08*	-.04
Frequency Fursuiting Past Year	.27**	.14**	-.07	-.01
Money Spent Last Year	.23**	.13**	-.03	-.08
Attend Cons/Meetups	.34**	.16**	-.02	-.11**
Read/Post Forums	.26**	-.04	.11**	.04
Consume Media/News	.35**	-.07	.11**	.18**
Collect Merchandise	.44**	.02	.004	.05
Talk about Furries	.27**	.09*	.04	.04
Immersion Furry Media	.32**	-.11**	.09**	.23**
Fursona Identification	.20**	.02	.06*	.32**
Intragroup Status	.33**	.28**	-.14**	-.07
Sexual Attraction to Furry Media	.22**	-.12**	.15**	-.04
Frequency View Furry Porn	.14**	-.10*	.14**	-.01

Note. * $p < .05$, ** $p < .01$.

The other variables tell a more nuanced story. Asset-related motivations were associated with being openly furry, going to cons, fursuiting, and spending money on furry content, as well as with status in the fandom. In contrast, these furries also had a somewhat more shallow engagement with furry content and were less likely to view furry pornography. We might suggest that this dimension is tied less to furry content and more to the social elements of the fandom, particularly benefitting from one's status in the fandom. In contrast, presence scores were tied primarily to being a newer, less open furry, as well as with online furry interaction, pornography use, and immersion into furry media. This might suggest a furry whose interaction with the fandom is predominantly online in nature.[9] Finally, the last dimension—expression—is most strongly tied to fanship, fursona identification, and immersion into furry media, and may suggest a furry whose primarily interested in consuming furry media and not interacting with other furries (as indicated by a negative association with convention attendance). These may be furries for whom furry is primarily an individual pursuit, an expression or outlet for their interest without necessarily wanting or needing to become involved with fandom (or, at the very least, not considering this to be as strong a draw as the content or the process of creating a fursona itself).[10]

Table 19.3. CAPE model of fan interest dimensions predicting personality and well-being.

Variable	C	A	P	E
Physical Well-Being	.18**	-.04	-.09**	.002
Psychological Well-Being	.25**	.01	-.14**	-.02
Relationship Well-Being	.24**	.04	-.06	-.06
Fandom Social Support	.22**	.12**	.19**	.21**
Intragroup Helping	.26**	.15**	.04	-.01

Note. * $p < .05$, ** $p < .01$.

[9] This could also simply be a proxy for being a younger furry, with some of our findings from earlier in this chapter suggesting that many furries find furry content first, then begin lurking in furry forums or on furry websites before eventually making it out to furry events and conventions. These may simply be furries who are in the early stages of that process.

[10] We're talking about these dimensions with respect to a hypothetical furry who scored high on one dimension to the exclusion of the others. In reality, most furries are a blend of these four different dimensions, and it would be fairly rare to find a furry who scored high in only one of these dimensions to the exclusion of the other four. Nevertheless, it's useful to help us conceptualize these four dimensions by imagining what a hypothetical furry high on that dimension might be like!

Another analysis allowed the CAPE dimensions to predict measures of well-being. This analysis can help us shed light on stereotypes of furries as maladjusted (described in Chapter 21) by allowing us to see whether there may be ways to predict, based on their underlying motivation, which furries are the most likely to show maladjustment. As shown in Table 19.3, commitment was the dimension most strongly associated with measures of well-being, perhaps owing, as we suggest in Chapter 22, to the fact that commitment motivation was also tied to seeing the fandom as a source of social support and receiving help from the fandom itself. Asset motivation, while also associated with social support and help from the fandom, was not associated with measures of being, nor were expression scores. Presence, on the other hand, was the only dimension negatively associated with well-being and may provide additional context to the above findings. Perhaps furries who struggle with physical or psychological well-being may be the least able to make it out to conventions or otherwise benefit from face-to-face interactions with furries, or perhaps it's the lack of this interaction that contributes to their lower well-being. Future research is needed to delve deeper into these associations, but they do, if nothing else, suggest that the motivations driving a furry may speak volumes as to the nature of their involvement in the fandom and whether it's most likely to be beneficial, harmful, or largely unrelated to their well-being.

Furry Values

In this final section, we'll focus on a concept related to motivation: values. Values are broad, significant beliefs that people use to guide, justify, and direct their behavior (Schwartz, 1992). While not motivation in and of themselves, a person's values shape their actions to be in accordance with their values.[11] Schwartz proposed ten universal values, meaning they can be found shaping behavior in people across cultures:[12] (1) power (valuing status and prestige), (2) achievement (valuing ambition and success), (3) hedonism (valuing self-gratification), (4) stimulation (valuing novelty and excitement), (5) self-direction (valuing exploration and creativity), (6) universalism (valuing social justice and equality), (7) benevolence (valuing helping those

[11] If you think of a person like a rocket, motivation represents thrust, propelling a person forward in a general direction. Values, in this analogy, represent the veins or other devices used to precisely direct the thrust and steer the rocket in a specific direction.

[12] While these values may be present in all cultures, they are not necessarily present to the same extent. People in one culture may, on average, prioritize achievement over benevolence, while another may prioritize benevolence over achievement.

around you), (8) tradition (valuing preservation and maintenance of norms/culture), (9) conformity (valuing societal expectations), and (10) security (valuing safety of self and close others) (Schwartz & Boehnke, 2004).

To see whether furries' values, as a group, differed from others, we compared furries' ratings on a measure of each of the ten values to the ratings of a sample of undergraduate college students, a group generally comparable in age and level of education (see Chapter 13). As shown in Figure 19.10, furries were primarily driven by the values of benevolence, self-direction, and universalism, as were the college students. Significant differences emerged, however, with respect to tradition, conformity, and security—furries scored significantly lower on these measures, in line with furries' generally progressive political views that may include bucking tradition (see Chapter 17) as well as their non-mainstream nature, suggesting they have little interest in adhering to cultural norms. This lack of interest in tradition and conformity may also be an indicator that furries are more open to change, a finding consistent with their tendency to be more open to new experiences (see Chapter 18). Bobowik et al. (2011) found that openness to change is associated with better well-being, Bond et al. (2004) found that it was associated with compromise, collaboration, and problem-solving, and others have found that this openness to change is associated with concern for the environment, prosocial values (Uitto & Saloranta, 2010), and political activism (Vecchione et al., 2015). These last points are consistent with the fact that furries have also been found to be high in global citizenship (see Chapter 17).

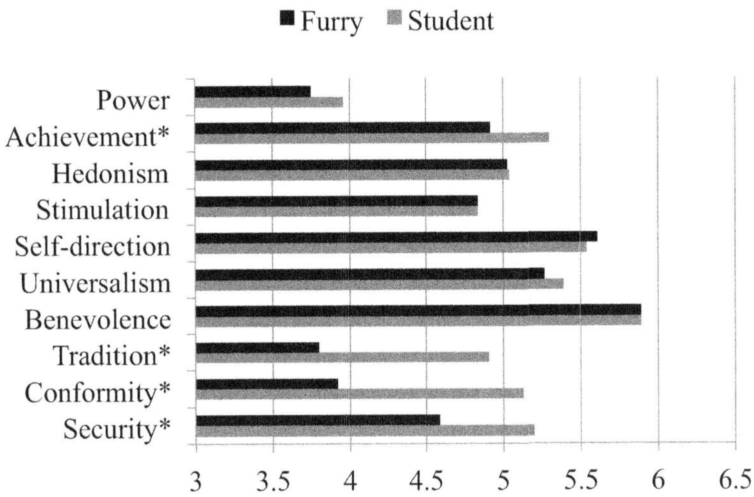

Figure 19.10. Furry and student mean ratings of universal values (* $p < .05$, 7-point scale).

Finally, we can draw upon the social identity perspective (see Chapter 6), which states that when a person's identity as a member of a particular group is on their mind, that group's norms and values become activated. In other words, when furries are reminded of the fact that they are a furry (versus their day-to-day self), they should take on the attitudes, emotions, and personality traits that are stereotypically associated with the group. To test this, we examined furries' ratings on the same ten values, asking them to do so twice: once with respect to their everyday selves and again, thinking about themselves as a furry. As shown in Figure 19.11, the results are generally in line with our finding comparing furries to the undergraduate college students, in that furries saw themselves as less conforming, less concerned with security, and more self-directed when thinking about themselves as a furry than when thinking about themselves in their day-to-day lives. We also found a few other differences: furries were also more likely to endorse the values of hedonism and stimulation and less likely to value achievement when thinking about themselves as furries. While future studies will delve deeper into the specifics of these differences, for now, it's enough to simply point out that furries not only differ from non-furries concerning the values that motivate and guide their behavior but that there is variability within the furry fandom and even within furries themselves in different contexts when it comes to these values. This only adds another layer to the complex and nuanced puzzle of what motivates furries.

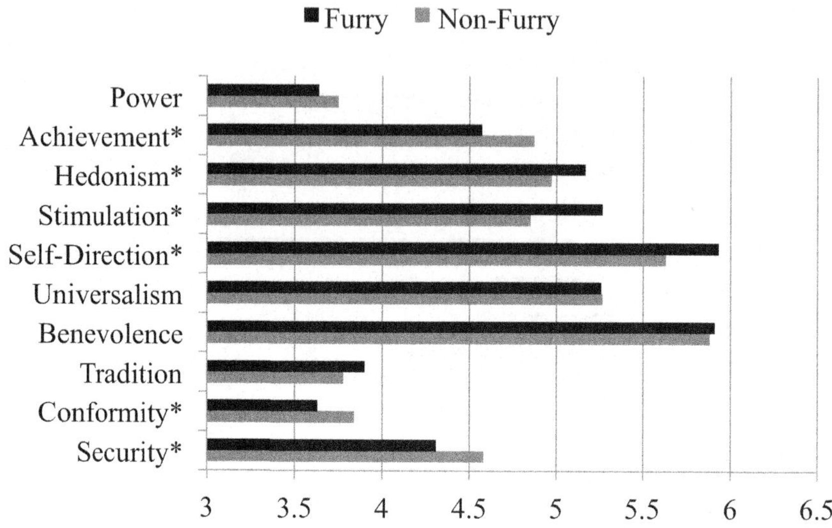

Figure 19.11. Ratings of universal values by furry identity and everyday self-identity (* $p < .05$, 7-point scale).

Conclusion

On paper, it seems like it should be simple to answer the question of what motivates furries, as though we should just be able to say "Furries are furries because they like furry media." But, as we've seen throughout the chapter, the picture of what motivates furries is complex, multifaceted, and differs from furry to furry.

When it comes to how furries find their way into the fandom, their journey seems to differ somewhat from that of other fan groups (e.g., anime and sports fans), with furries being more likely to "stumble" upon the fandom rather than being socialized into it through the friends, family, and groups around them. The internet, exposure to furry media, and a general feeling inside were all among the most frequent roads into the fandom.

As for what compels furries to engage in furry activities and participate in the furry fandom, some of the underlying motivations overlap with those of other fan groups, like an interest in entertainment. Others, like the need to belong, are present in other fan groups (e.g., anime fans, fantasy sports fans), but not nearly to the same extent as they are for furries. We can draw upon models such as optimal distinctiveness theory to show that social psychological motivations play an important role in understanding the duality of furry identification—both as a way to stand out and be distinct and as a way to belong to a community of like-minded others. In a similar fashion, the CAPE model shows us how furries differ from other fans, as well as the ways they differ from one another, and illustrates the impact motivation can have on how furries behave and their well-being.

Finally, we examined how the values furries hold dear may help to distinguish them from other fan groups and may explain what compels a person to choose the furry fandom over other fan groups. We also saw how virtues are malleable and context-specific, changing depending on whether someone is thinking about themselves as a furry or in non-furry spaces.

The present chapter shows us that there are no simple answers when it comes to explaining why furries become furries. Chalking it up to a manifestation of a fetish or a simple preference for one aesthetic over another ignores the plethora of evidence suggesting that furries are driven by a complex array of variables that show the importance of one's furry interest as a way to satisfy important needs for social interaction, entertainment, meaning, self-expression, and, yes, for some, sexual gratification.

References

Abrams, D. (2009). Social identity on a national scale: optimal distinctiveness and young people's self-expression through musical preference. *Group Processes and Intergroup Relations, 12*(3), 303-317. https://doi.org/10.1177/1368430209102841

Bobowik, M., Basabe, N., Páez, D., Jiménez, A., & Bilbao, M. (2011). Personal values and well-being among Europeans, Spanish natives and immigrants to Spain: does the culture matter? *Journal of Happiness Studies, 12*(3), 401-419. https://doi.org/10.1007/s10902-010-9202-1

Bond, M. H., Leung, K., Au, A., Tong, K. K., & Chemonges-Nielson, Z. (2004). Combining social axioms with values in predicting social behaviors. *European Journal of Personality, 18*(3), 177-191. https://doi.org/10.1002/per.509

Brewer, M. B. (1991). The social self: On being the same and different at the same time. *Personality and Social Psychology Bulletin, 17*(5), 475-482. https://doi.org/10.1177/0146167291175001

Haslam, C., Jetten, J., Cruwys, T., Dingle, G. A., & Haslam, S. A. (2018). *The new psychology of health: Unlocking the social cure*. Routledge.

Hogg, M. A. (2000). Subjective uncertainty reduction through self-categorization: A motivational theory of social identity processes.

European Review of Social Psychology, 11(1), 223-255. https://doi.org/10.1080/14792772043000040

Hsu, T. (2019, July 15). The Apollo 11 mission was also a global media sensation. *The New York Times*. https://www.nytimes.com/2019/07/15/business/media/apollo-11-television-media.html

Leonardelli, G. J., Pickett, C. L., & Brewer, M. B. (2010). Optimal distinctiveness theory: A framework for social identity, social cognition, and intergroup relations. *Advances in Experimental Social Psychology, 43,* 63-113. https://doi.org/10.1016/S0065-2601(10)43002-6

McPherson, B. (1975). Sport consumption and the economics of consumerism. In D. W. Ball & J. W. Loy (Eds.), *Sport and social order: Contributions to the sociology of sport* (pp. 243-275). Addison Wesley Publishing.

Plante, C. N., Reysen, S., Brooks, T. R., & Chadborn, D. (2021). *CAPE: A multidimensional model of fan interest.* CAPE Model Research Team.

Reysen, S., & Plante, C. N. (2017). Fans, perceived maturity, and willingness to form a romantic relationship: Application of a short maturity measure. *Communication and Culture Online, 8*(1), 154-173. https://doi.org/10.18485/kkonline.2017.8.8.8

Reysen, S., Plante, C. N., Roberts, S. E., & Gerbasi, K. C. (2015). A social identity perspective of personality differences between fan and non-fan identities. *World Journal of Social Science Research, 2*(1), 91-103.

Reysen, S., Plante, C. N., Roberts, S. E., & Gerbasi, K. C. (2016). Optimal distinctiveness and identification with the furry fandom. *Current Psychology, 35*(4), 638-642. https://doi.org/10.1007/s12144-015-9331-0

Reysen, S., Plante, C. N., Roberts, S. E., & Gerbasi, K. C. (2017a). "It just clicked": Discovering furry identity and motivations to participate in the fandom. In T. Howl (Ed.), *Furries among us 2: More essays on furries by furries* (pp. 111-128). Thurston Howl Publications.

Reysen, S., Plante, C. N., Roberts, S. E., & Gerbasi, K. C. (2017b). Optimal distinctiveness needs as predictors of identification in the anime fandom. *The Phoenix Papers, 3*(1), 25-32.

Reysen, S., Plante, C. N., Roberts, S. E., Gerbasi, K. C., Schroy, C., Gamboa, A., Gamboa, J., & McCarter, T. (2017). Routes to fandom discovery and expression of fan identity in furry, anime, and fantasy sports fans. *The Phoenix Papers, 3*(1), 373-384.

Richter, F. (2023, February 10). Super Bowl pales in comparison to the biggest game in soccer. *Statista*.

https://www.statista.com/chart/16875/super-bowl-viewership-vs-world-cup-final/

Schroy, C., Plante, C. N., Reysen, S., Roberts, S. E., & Gerbasi, K. C. (2016). Different motivations as predictors of psychological connection to fan interest and fan groups in anime, furry, and fantasy sport fandoms. *The Phoenix Papers, 2*(2), 148-167.

Schwartz, S. H. (1992). Universals in the content and structure of values: Theoretical advances and empirical tests in 20 countries. *Advances in Experimental Social Psychology, 25,* 1-65. https://doi.org/10.1016/S0065-2601(08)60281-6

Schwartz, S. H., & Boehnke, K. (2004). Evaluating the structure of human values with confirmatory factor analysis. *Journal of Research in Personality, 38*(3), 230-255. https://doi.org/10.1016/S0092-6566(03)00069-2

Smith, G. J., Patterson, B., Williams, T., & Hogg, J. (1981). A profile of the deeply committed male sports fan. *Arena Review, 5*(2), 26-44.

Smodis-McCune, V. A., Plante, C. N., Packard, G., Reysen, S., & Mendrek, A. (2022). COVID-19 stress moderates the mediational pathway of fandom identification on well-being through problem-focused coping. *The Phoenix Papers, 5*(1), 175-194. https://doi.org/10.31235/osf.io/e6baf

Stangor, C. (2010). *Introduction to psychology*. FlatWorld.

Swann, W. B., Jr. (1983). Self-verification: Bringing social reality into harmony with the self. In J. Suls & A. G. Greenwald (Eds.), *Social psychological perspectives on the self* (Vol. 2, pp. 33-66). Erlbaum.

Uitto, A., & Saloranta, S. (2010). The relationship between secondary school students' environmental and human values, attitudes, interests and motivations. *Procedia-Social and Behavioral Sciences, 9,* 1866-1872. https://doi.org/10.1016/j.sbspro.2010.12.415

Vecchione, M., Schwartz, S. H., Caprara, G. V., Schoen, H., Cieciuch, J., Silvester, J., ... & Alessandri, G. (2015). Personal values and political activism: A cross-national study. *British Journal of Psychology, 106*(1), 84-106. https://doi.org/10.1111/bjop.12067

Vignoles, V. L., Regalia, C., Manzi, C., Golledge, J., & Scabini, E. (2006). Beyond self-esteem: Influence of multiple motives on identity construction. *Journal of Personality and Social Psychology, 90*(2), 308-333. https://doi.org/10.1037/0022-3514.90.2.308

Wann, D. L., Melnick, M. J., Russell, G. W., & Pease, D. G. (2001). *Sports fans: The psychology and social impact of spectators*. Routledge.

Chapter 20
The Animal Within: Animal Attitudes and Therianthropy

Kathleen Gerbasi, Elizabeth Fein, Courtney "Nuka" Plante

In Chapter 5, we saw how difficult it is to nail down a precise definition of what furries are. For some, it's a fan community and a source of social support. For others, it's a form of self-expression and an outlet for creativity. Others, still, consider it to be nothing more than a preference for a particular type of media content. Regardless of how, precisely, one's interest manifests, however, one thing is fairly universal among furries: they have at least a passing interest in the idea of giving human traits to non-human animals.[1,2]

Curious readers and scientists alike may find themselves wondering about the nature and specificity of this interest. For example, given that furries tend to lead fairly active fantasy lives (see Chapter 18), is furries' interest in anthropomorphizing non-human animals simply one expression of a more general interest in anthropomorphizing the world around them—do they anthropomorphize cars, computers, and appliances as well? And given this tendency to anthropomorphize non-human animals, do furries also include them in the rules of human morality—that is, seeing them as autonomous beings and engaging in activism on their behalf? And what happens when the line between "human" and "non-human animal" becomes blurred—are there cases of people who aren't just fans of anthropomorphizing non-human animals, but who would identify themselves *as* non-human animals? These questions are the focus of the present chapter.

Tendency to Anthropomorphize Non-Human Animals

Let's start with the question most directly tied to furry interests: to what extent do furries tend to anthropomorphize non-human animals? The question is simple enough to answer: we asked furries attending a 2013 furry convention to indicate, on a 7-point scale, the extent to which they tended to anthropomorphize non-human animals when they see them. The results, shown in Figure 20.1, show that furries definitely show a tendency toward anthropomorphizing non-human animals, with the average furry scoring 5.5

---

[1] Or, depending on your perspective, giving non-human animal traits to humans, known as zoomorphism!

[2] We use the term "non-human animals" throughout this chapter instead of "animals" because the latter often implies a dichotomy between "humans" and "animals" when, according to biological taxonomy, humans are part of the kingdom animalia. As such, we distinguish humans, who are animals, from other animals which are not humans! It's a bit of a nitpicky detail, but one we feel it's important to make!

on the scale and more than three-quarters of furries scoring above the scale's midpoint. While hardly unsurprising, given that one of the few common threads throughout the furry fandom is a shared interest in anthropomorphizing non-human animals, it is helpful to validate this premise with data.

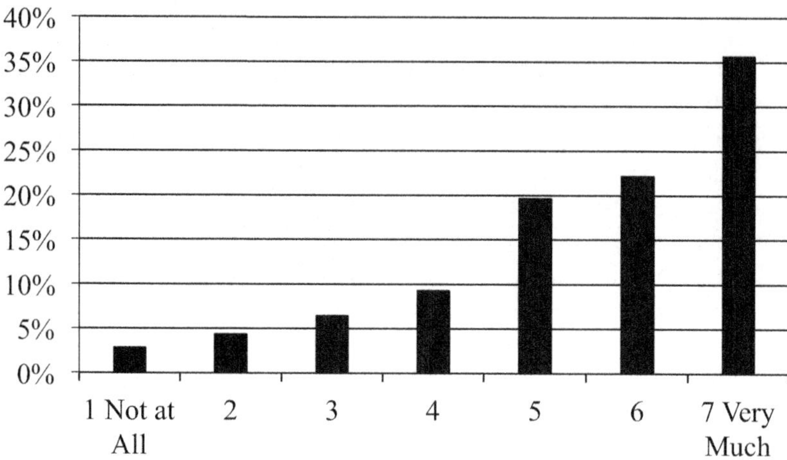

Figure 20.1. Extent to which furries in a 2013 convention study tend to anthropomorphize non-human animals.

While we could end this section here, a critic might argue that these data, in and of themselves, aren't enough to claim that furries have a specific tendency to anthropomorphize non-human animals. After all, these data might mean something entirely different if furries showed a strong tendency to anthropomorphize everything in the world around them and if the tendency to do so with non-human animals was fairly muted by comparison. To test this possibility, we also asked furries in the same study, as well as in an additional convention study and an online study, to also indicate the extent to which they anthropomorphize other things in the world around them (e.g., vehicles, computers, plush animals). We also distinguished between different types of non-human animals (i.e., pets, domesticated animals, wild animals). The results are shown in Table 20.1.

Table 20.1. Average scores of convention-going and online furries on a 1-7 scale of tendency to anthropomorphize various categories. * Category was not asked about in this study.

Category	2013 Con	2019 Con	2020 Online
Animals	5.5	*	*
Pets	*	5.1	*
Domesticated Animals	*	4.1	5.0
Wild Animals	*	4.5	4.5
Vehicles	2.4	2.4	1.6
Computers	2.6	2.4	1.6
Plush Animals	3.6	3.9	4.0
Appliances	1.7	1.9	1.9
Robots	1.9	*	*
Buildings	*	1.5	1.4
The Weather	*	2.2	1.9
Earth	*	2.6	2.2
Non-Playable Characters (Video Games)	*	4.0	3.8
Food	*	1.7	1.4

The data show a fairly consistent tendency for furries to anthropomorphize non-human animals in general, although it's somewhat less consistent whether they tend to do so most with pets, domesticated animals, or wild animals. Importantly, statistical analysis found that this tendency to anthropomorphize non-human animals is stronger than the tendency to anthropomorphize other objects or concepts in the world around them, including objects that are fairly common for people to anthropomorphize (Epley et al., 2007; Kühn et al., 2014; Waytz et al., 2010, 2014).

Further establishing that anthropomorphizing non-human animals is a central part of what it means to be furry, we ran a further set of analyses testing whether it predicts furries' fanship and fandom scores (see Chapter 6). The results of the analyses found that fanship scores were significantly positively correlated with one's tendency to anthropomorphize non-human animals whereas fandom scores were only sporadically or weakly associated with this tendency; in contrast, the tendency to anthropomorphize non-animals was unrelated to fanship and fandom scores. Taken together, these findings suggest that the extent to which one identifies as a furry (e.g., interest in furry content) is tied to their interest in anthropomorphizing non-human animals, as one would predict, but one's tendency to anthropomorphize non-human animals says little about whether one identifies with the furry fandom more broadly. The evidence also shows that being furry is specific to the anthropomorphizing of non-human animals, and not to a more general tendency to anthropomorphize.

As a final test of this fact, in the same 2013 study as above, we also recruited a sample of fantasy sports fans against which to compare furries. The results, shown in Table 20.2, make two important points. First, as predicted, they show that furries do have a stronger tendency to anthropomorphize non-human animals than do other people.[3] Second, they show that this tendency isn't part of a broader tendency to anthropomorphize everything in the world around them; furries did score lower than fantasy sports fans when it comes to anthropomorphizing cars, computers, and appliances. So, while the tendency for furries to anthropomorphize isn't *limited* to only non-human animals, it is a fairly robust difference between furries and non-furries, one that's tied to how furry a person considers themselves to be.

Table 20.2. Average scores of convention-going furries and fantasy sports fans on a 1-7 scale of tendency to anthropomorphize various categories. All scores differed statistically significantly between the two groups.

Category	Furries	Sports fans
Animals	5.5	4.2
Cars	2.4	3.3
Computers	2.6	3.0
Plush Animals	3.7	2.5
Appliances	1.7	2.4
Robots	3.5	2.5

Beliefs and Behaviors Related to Non-Human Animals

Having shown that anthropomorphizing non-human animals is part of what it means to be a furry, it makes sense to ask whether this tendency to look at animals in a distinctly "human" way impacts the way furries think about and behave toward animals. We know, based on prior research, that

[3] This tendency also seems to extend to *plush* animals!

people generally have different sets of moral rules when it comes to humans and non-human entities (e.g., Gray et al., 2007), and tend to consider entities with human-like cognition to be part of our ingroup, warranting better treatment than members of our outgroup (Schultz, 2001; Tajfel & Turner, 1979; Tam et al., 2013). In other words, when we make something more human, we treat it better. This has been shown in several creative studies, including studies showing that people consider it morally wrong to destroy a computer that can play chess (Waytz et al., 2014), are more willing to support conservation efforts when they see pictures of an anthropomorphized Earth (Tam et al., 2013), and, most presently relevant, are more willing to help a dog to get adopted when they've been explicitly instructed to anthropomorphize the dog (Butterfield et al., 2012).

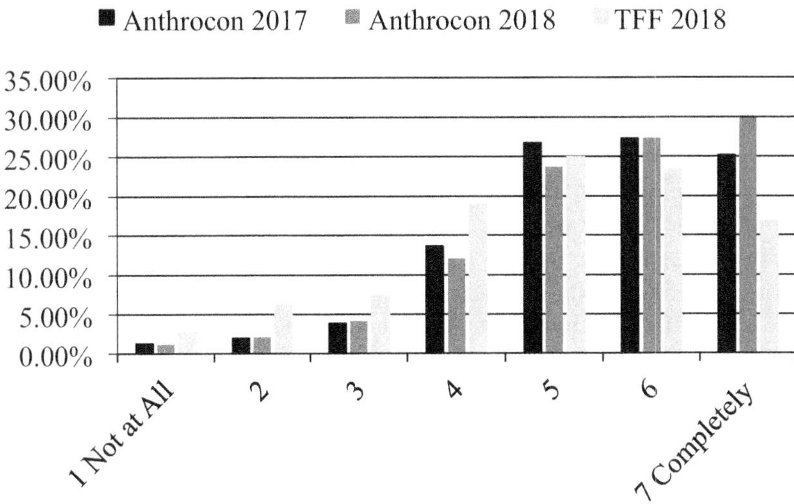

Figure 20.2. Extent to which furries attending three different conventions felt a sense of solidarity with non-human animals.

With this in mind, let's look at whether furries do, indeed, feel a sense of solidarity with non-human animals and care about their well-being. To start, we asked furries across three convention-based studies to indicate to what degree they felt a sense of solidarity with non-human animals—that is, feeling like they're part of the same, shared group. Figure 20.2 shows that the sense of solidarity is strong among furries, with more than 60% of furries scoring above the scale's midpoint across all three studies. Follow-up studies showed that fanship (but not fandom) was positively correlated with this feeling of solidarity, further supporting the idea that part of being a furry is feeling a sense of kinship with non-human animals who you also perceive to share a lot in common with you (i.e., human traits).[4]

But does this sense of connection to non-human animals translate into moral concern for their well-being? We tested this in a 2012 study of online and convention-going furries in which we asked them directly whether they supported animal rights and whether they identified specifically as an animal rights activist. Across the two samples, 79.5-89.7% of furries said that they support animal rights in general, with 10.3-11.5% explicitly calling themselves animal rights activists. Of course, the blanket term "animal rights" is a bit vague, and was left up to the definition of the participant. As such, one participant could have defined animal rights in a very conservative manner, such as not going out of one's way to actively do excessive harm to a non-human animal without reason, while another participant could define animal rights in a much stricter way, such as pushing for non-human animals to have the same right to autonomy and freedom from captivity that humans do.

To measure animal rights concerns more concretely, we gave participants a 28-scale measuring their attitudes toward specific animal rights issues, including the rights of animals used in industry (e.g., ranching, testing products or procedures on animals), the rights of "pest" species (e.g., being okay with killing insects), and the rights of pets[5] (e.g., the morality of keeping an animal in captivity against its will; Taylor & Signal, 2009). The results, shown in Figure 20.3, reveal that while furries are generally supportive of some animal rights issues, it's a fairly mixed bag. For example, while many furries were generally okay with the killing of pest species and with the concept of eating animals for meat,[6] they were also likely to support stronger regulations on the use of animals in research. In other words, there

[4] In fact, in a 2019 study we later found that furries were more willing to include domestic animals into their ingroup than they were to include all of humanity as a whole, further illustrating this sense of solidarity—furries may well feel closer to some non-human animals than they do to other humans!

[5] A set of studies in 2012 and 2013 found that nearly all furries (96.9-97.5%) have had a pet, with 68.0-73.8% saying that they currently have a pet. A more recent 2020 study found that cats are the most common pets among furries (28.9% of furries have a cat), followed by dogs (24.2%), birds (4.2%), and fish (3.8%).

[6] The same study found that 1.6-3.1% of furries were vegetarians, although 9.8-14.9% indicated that they had tried being a vegetarian in the past.

were relatively few furries that were extremely supportive of animal rights issues, but also very few furries who were extremely opposed to them.

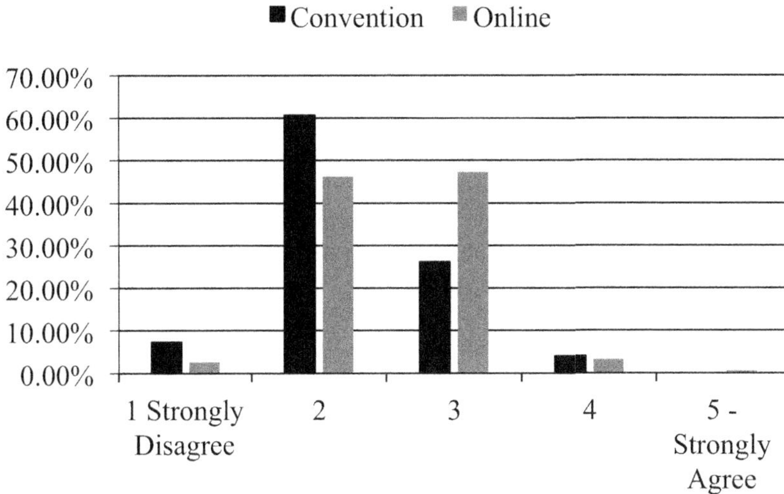

Figure 20.3. Extent to which a 2012 sample of convention-going and online furries endorsed specific animal rights issues on a 28-item scale.

Despite this somewhat mixed bag of attitudes toward animal rights, examples abound of furries acting in support of animal welfare. For instance, in 2011, a small Canadian furry convention with approximately 250 attendees raised more than $10,000 for a wildlife rehabilitation center (Condition Red, n.d.). This is impressive when you consider that, like most furries (see Chapter 13), these attendees were largely teenagers and young adults, many of whom were college-age or working only part-time jobs. Far from being an anomaly, nearly all furry conventions are organized around an animal-themed charity, illustrating the importance of acting to help non-human animals as a value in the furry fandom. Speaking to this point with data, in a 2018 study of convention-going furries, we found that 87.2% of furries said that they had donated to an animal-themed charity in the past. A study in 2019 further found that 62.9% of furries had donated in the past year, with nearly a quarter of participants saying that they had donated more than $100.

Taken together, the data would seem to suggest that, despite being a bit ambivalent when it comes to specific animal rights issues, furries consider themselves to be supporters of animal rights and their charitable behavior would seem to support this idea. We've suggested that this is due, at least in part, to the fact that furries may feel a sense of solidarity with non-human animals. But where does this solidarity come from?

A 2019 study of convention-going furries sheds light on one possibility. The study tested a statistical model in which furries' history of being bullied (see Chapter 21) is associated with a tendency to anthropomorphize non-human animals which, in turn, is associated with a tendency to see non-human animals as part of one's group and even to broaden one's sense of identity to include non-human animals. We found support for the model, which suggests that at least one way in which furries may develop a sense of connection to non-human animals is through a history of being bullied: perhaps being bullied by peers and classmates drove furries away from wanting to be around other people or incentivized them to retreat into fantasy worlds (e.g., books) with non-human characters who, by not being like their human peers, had a certain appeal.[7] This is all speculation for now, and it remains for future studies to test some of the mechanisms, but it does represent one additional pathway into the furry fandom (or, at very least, an explanation for a pathway—where one's interest in furry media might come from), and it is consistent with some past research suggesting that those who feel more lonely are more likely to anthropomorphize inanimate objects around them (Epley et al., 2008).

This final model suggests that, consistent with the idea of bringing humans and non-human animals closer together in one's mind, in addition to anthropomorphizing non-human animals to make them more human, some furries (and non-furries) may also conceptualize themselves in non-human terms, a point which will be our focus for the rest of this chapter.

Therianthropy: Not Entirely Human

We'd wager that almost everyone reading this book has, at least once in their life, imagined what it would be like to be something other than a human being. What would it be like to sport wings or a tail? If you were a dog, what species of dog would you be? What would swimming with a school of fish be like, or running with a pack of wolves, rather than being cooped up in an office or at school all day?

Many furries enjoy imagining themselves as anthropomorphic animal characters as a manifestation of their broader furry interests. They may

---

[7] Another possibility, using a different chain of causation, suggests that perhaps people who tend to anthropomorphize animals and see them as part of their ingroup are simply more likely to be picked on by others, if for nothing else than for being different.

fursuit as these characters or roleplay as them in fandom spaces. But at the end of the day, most furries take off the fursuit or log off and return to their day-to-day, very *human* lives. For most furries, embodying something other than a human is play, an act of fantasy or an expression of creativity, and nothing more.

For others, including some non-furries, identifying with an other-than-human creature runs far deeper. Rather than identifying *with* cats, dogs, or unicorn *characters*, some people identify *as* something not human. They may experience life as a cat trapped in a human body, or a wolf soul reincarnated into a human. They may have memories of being a dragon just as vivid and intense as your own memory of what you had for breakfast this morning.[8] The terms *therian* and *otherkin* are used to describe such people—"therian" for those who identify as an animal that has existed on this planet (e.g., lion, wolf, mammoth), and "otherkin" as a broader term which includes therians, but also includes those who identify as creatures from myths, legends, and other fantastical worlds (e.g., unicorns, gryphons).

To people whose identity resides squarely in being human, it may seem boggling to even imagine what it would be like to identify as anything else. The experience may be more common than you think, however. Prehistoric cave drawings recently discovered in Indonesia dated at over 43,000 years ago depict therianthropes, human-animal creatures (Aubert et al. 2019). People whose sense of self is intertwined with non-human animals can be found throughout history (for a review see McHugh et al., 2019). Some of these characters present with humanoid bodies and a single animal feature, such as the gods of ancient Egypt, like Anubis and Thoth, who had human bodies and non-human heads (jackal and ibis-headed, respectively). The Hindu god Ganesa (Ganesha) similarly has a human body and an elephant's

---

[8] For clarification, we are not making any metaphysical claims about the nature of the soul or about one's essence. Nor are we implying that a person who experiences life as a dragon has anything but human genes. What we're describing here are concepts like identity, the self, perception, and experience—phenomena that reside within the head of the person experiencing them. While we can use science to show that a person is genetically human, the question of whether their soul or essence is that of a non-human entity falls completely outside the realm of science. At best, we can ask them to describe their experiences and conclude that these are, in fact, their experiences. It's not unlike perceiving color: science can tell us that you have the organic hardware to distinguish green from other colors, but it cannot tell us what the experience of green looks like to you, or whether your experience of green is the same as someone else's.

head. The common depiction of angels in Abrahamic tradition, particularly Christian, is yet another example as, artistically, angels of Western cultures are often depicted as beautiful humans with soft bird-like wings,[9] while their demonic counterparts are depicted with goat-like feet and horns.

Other characters are far more animal in form, with very little making them noticeably human beyond the ability to walk on two feet or speak in human languages. One such example is the ancient Egyptian goddess of fertility, Taweret, who has a full hippopotamus body but stands upright on two legs and has human breasts. The Hindu god Hanuman bears features that are more ape-like than human, as do the Australian Aborigine heroes Kurukadi and Mumba, who are described as lizardmen.

Finally, some characters shift their shapes between animal and human, sometimes from one extreme to the other, other times landing on a blended stage in between. Zeus of the Greco-Roman pantheon and Loki of the Nordic traditions are prolific shapeshifters, changing from human-shaped gods to swans, bulls, and horses to seduce, trick, or escape others. Ravens of various Native American traditions likewise changed shapes in numerous tales. Others change their form in specific situations, such as selkies, mermaids, or werewolves. These transitions may result in the character being completely consumed by another form or they may find a middle-ground between animal and human. Although specific characters vary with respect to where they're located between human and animal and regardless of where or when these characters originate, we accept these characters as legitimate features of their culture.

However, when it comes to accepting people who experience life in this way, whose way of being exists between human and other-than-human, therians and otherkin are often marginalized, struggling to find ways to make sense of their experience. With the increasing availability of the internet in the mid-90s, those who felt this way began to find each other and developed a shared language for their experience, beginning on web forums devoted to werewolf lore. Today, people can explore species identities that transcend that of being solely human in communities with like-minded others and are continuously finding ways to better describe their experiences to those who have never had the experience.

---

[9] We should note that biblically accurate depictions of angels are far more Lovecraftian in nature. If you don't know what we're talking about, take a moment to look them up online.

Although social scientists have long been interested in the complex relationship between humans and non-human animals,[10] only a little bit of social scientific research has been done on the lived experiences of therians or otherkin. Grivell et al. (2014) conducted extensive text-based chats and interviews with five (three female and two male) therians selected at random from a group of volunteers recruited from therian internet forums. Their responses were analyzed and interpreted, resulting in three major themes. The first theme is that therians reported experiencing a journey of self-discovery. Most recognized their animal identity in childhood but were also aware of its uniqueness. This awareness typically resulted in a critical quest for evidence to confirm or possibly deny their therian identity. Therians reported experiencing the sensation of "phantom limbs"—being able to feel a body part associated with their "theriotype," such as a tail, wings, or claws. They also reported "mental shifts"—distinct periods where their thoughts, feelings, and sensory perceptions felt closer to that of their theriotype. Such experiences, to them, validate their belief in their therian identity.

A second theme that emerged in the work of Grivell and colleagues is a feeling of a discrepancy between how their body looks on the outside and how they feel on the inside. They felt uncomfortable with a human identity and reported a sort of dysmorphia as a result of the disconnect between their identity and their body.[11]

The final theme to emerge—the therian shadow—refers to the difficulty participants experience when revealing their authentic therian selves to others. They often felt the need to conceal their therianthropy to avoid eliciting negative attitudes from others.

In the course of our work on the furry fandom, we frequently encounter therians. Sometimes they approach us asking us to do a concerted study on the therian experience. Other times, it's to request that we distinguish therians from furries in our work. It's a fair point: across 25 of our studies from 2011 to 2022 we've found that 4.4-16.5% of furries identify as therians

---

[10] In fact, there's an entire field dedicated to this topic called anthrozoology!

[11] If this theme sounds like it bears some resemblance to the experience of some transgender people who struggle with dysmorphia, that might not be a coincidence: 11% of therians and 14% of otherkin identify as transgender and 18% of therians and 36% of otherkin identify as gender-queer, numbers that are substantially higher than that observed in the general population. While we don't mean to suggest a common mechanism or to suggest in any way that the experiences of transgender people and therians / otherkin are the same, it is noteworthy.

(and 3.6-13.9% as otherkin).[12] This means that most furries, by definition, are not therians. It's also a fair bet that many therians, if not most, would not consider themselves to be furries. After all, the two groups are organized around fairly different concepts: furries are *fans* of anthropomorphized animal characters, while therians are people who identify, in whole or in part, with something non-human. Speaking to this point, data from our surveys have shown that therians (65%) are much more likely than furries (11%) to say that they often or nearly always identify with a non-human species and are more likely (86%) than furries (30%) to rate themselves as feeling "less than 100% human".[13,14]

In another, open-ended study of therians (Gerbasi et al., 2017), we asked convention-going participants to describe, in their own words, what the terms "furry," "therian," and "otherkin" mean. We analyzed the content of the 500 or so descriptions we received, counting the frequency with which certain words came up in each description. For furries, the words anthro (93), fan/fandom (57), enjoy (56), community (36), cartoon (33), and art/artistic (26) were commonly used (making up 6% of the total words used to describe furries!). In contrast, none of those words were used a single time in the descriptions of therians or otherkin, except for a single use of the word "community." In contrast, the word "spirit" appeared 47 times and 18 times respectively in the therian and otherkin descriptions, while the word "soul" appeared nine times in the therian description and four times in the otherkin description. "Trapped" also appeared in both the therian and otherkin

---

[12] Variability in this number may stem from the fact that people aren't always aware of what the term "therian" means. Four studies suggest that anywhere from 21.8-32.2% of furries didn't know what a therian was. Whether this means that some of them might be therians if they only knew what the term meant or whether this means that they likely aren't therians if they haven't felt compelled to look into it for themselves, remains to be seen.

[13] Therians (59%) were also more likely than furries (39%) to say that they would choose to become 0% human if they were able to do so.

[14] As a throwback to research we described earlier, we've found that therians, even more than furries, strongly support animal rights and are more likely to engage in behaviors aimed at improving animal rights. This work, which has been published elsewhere, validates what therians say about their tendency to identify with non-human animals: it occurs deep in the mind and can be detected on the order of milliseconds and reaction times in response to a task used to measure the extent to which people identify more strongly with humans or non-human animals; to the extent that therians identified more strongly with animals on this measure, they were also more likely to support and engage in pro-animal behaviors (Plante et al., 2018).

description 7 times, while "belief/believing" occurred 9 times in the therian description and 22 times in the otherkin description.

In short, there is conceptual overlap between furries and therians in that both groups share an interest in non-human animals, but the nature of this interest and how it manifests may be entirely different. While therianthropy and otherkinship are often associated with spirituality and a feeling of being trapped in the wrong body, a furry identity is more often associated with enjoyment, art, fandom, and community. For these reasons, while some therians might be furries and some furries might be therians, most furries are not therians, and, likely, most therians are not furries.[15]

In addition to the collection of some basic survey data on therians, we've also held countless therian and otherkin focus groups, as well as several one-on-one interviews with therians in person at conventions. Through these focus groups, we've largely replicated the three themes in therian participants observed by Grivell and colleagues.

In another study, Clegg et al. (2019) took a quantitative approach to the study of therians, measuring, among other things, well-being, schizotypal personality,[16] and autism in an online sample of 112 therians and 265 non-therians. This study found that therians scored higher than non-therians with respect to their social skills and difficulty with communication on the autism measure, although they did not differ concerning imagination, attention switching, or attention to detail. Therians in the study were also six times more likely than non-therians to have a high autism score and were more likely to have received a mental health diagnosis (40.2% vs. 15.8%), including depression, anxiety, and ADHD. Therians also scored higher on the schizotypy subscales of unusual experiences (e.g., perceptual aberrations), magical thinking, hallucinations, and introverted anhedonia (e.g., they dislike social engagement; Mason et al., 2005). Finally, when it comes to well-being, therians scored lower on measures of relational well-being (e.g., fewer close friends, feeling alone) and lower on environmental mastery (e.g., had more trouble fitting in with others), but they scored higher

---

[15] As an analogy, we can imagine why a soldier might not be an ardent member of the "war movie" fandom. They may see the numerous inaccuracies and oversimplifications of war films as irritating and be put off by fans' enthusiasm for something (i.e., war) that they, themselves, often have to deal with the consequences of (e.g., post-traumatic stress disorder).

[16] Note that this is not the same thing as schizophrenia; schizotypal personality refers to a person who has highly creative or unusual thoughts or behavior.

on the measure of autonomy than the non-therians (e.g., feeling control over the events of one's life).

Other scholars have looked specifically at the experiences of otherkin. For example, anthropologist Devin Proctor (2018) has conducted virtual ethnographic research with otherkin, studying how they negotiate what kinds of evidence feel credible to them. Scholars of new religious movements have also looked at how therian and otherkin experiences are sometimes explained in spiritual ways—though there are also many therians and otherkin for whom the experience has nothing to do with spirituality or religion.

An important topic for us to consider was the relationship (if any) between clinical lycanthropy and therianthropy. In the psychiatric literature, there have been a handful of cases of people who either claim to be non-human animals or who behave as such. This phenomenon, often referred to as lycanthropy or clinical lycanthropy, has been the subject of several comprehensive review articles (Blom, 2014; Guessoum et al., 2021).[17] Keck et al. (1988), for example, established the following operational definition of lycanthropy:

- The individual reported verbally during a period of lucidity or retrospectively, that he or she was a particular animal
- The individual behaved in a manner reminiscent of a particular animal, i.e., howling, growling, crawling on all fours

Using this definition, only twelve cases of clinical lycanthropy were identified in a sample of 5,000 psychiatric reports at McLean Hospital for a 12-year period. For eleven of the twelve patients, lycanthropy was associated with an acute or chronic psychosis as part of another condition (e.g., the most common diagnosis was bipolar disorder, which made up eight of the cases). For all but one of these patients, the lycanthropy was short-lived, ranging from one day to three weeks with a mean duration of about a week. For one patient, however, the lycanthropy had a duration of 13 years. The authors concluded that treatment with antipsychotic drugs typically "cured" lycanthropy in 1-3 weeks, and noted that lycanthropy was NOT associated with any one disorder or neurological abnormality.

By comparison, the extremely limited published peer-reviewed research reports on therianthropy (Clegg et al., 2019; Grivell et al., 2014) reveal that therianthropy and clinical lycanthropy are categorically different. For one thing, Grivell et al. (2014) found that the average length of time their

[17] We should note that clinical lycanthropy is *not* a diagnosis in the *Diagnostic and Statistical Manual*; instead, it's seen as a configuration of symptoms, but not a distinct disorder in and of itself.

participants identified as non-human was on the order of years (10.55 years on average), which is distinctly different from the very short duration of one to three weeks observed in the Keck et al. (1988) report. In addition, nearly 60% of therians in the sample reported having no mental health diagnosis. Likewise, the diagnoses that *were* most commonly reported by therians (depression, anxiety, and ADHD) were dramatically different from the bipolar disorder and schizophrenia present in Keck et al. (1988) cases. Taken together, it's clear that therianthropy and clinical lycanthropy are two very different phenomena!

We should also note that the experience of therianthropy and being otherkin are not identical for all who so identify. For some, the psychological aspects (e.g., having the mentality of a specific non-human species or entity) feel central to their experience, while for others, it is spiritual aspects such as reincarnation or having the soul of a non-human other that characterize the experience (Robertson, 2013). For others, still, physical aspects, such as the experience of phantom limbs, dominate their experience.[18] The identity of each therian or otherkin may contain any or all of these different facets.

Adding to this complexity, we've also considered the impact of situations and environments on the experiences of therians and otherkin. For example, in our open-ended convention and online focus groups of therians and otherkin, many participants reported feeling a deep sense of comfort and belonging in nature, and discomfort in built environments like cities. One of our participants, who identifies as a jackal, told us:

> *"Once you are in the city, you just feel so out of place because it's just such a mix of emotions that have nowhere to be channeled. I wouldn't say depression, but it's like – a deep sorrow. Like a loss of... a loss of self. A loss of – I don't know, just loss. It feels like [the] loss of something. What it is, I couldn't tell you, but... it feels like something is missing. That hollowness is not comfortable. [...] It's to the point that when I go there, and I'm there for more than an hour, I start having, not like a panic attack, but... extreme feelings of dread is a perfect word for it."*

[18] Another way in which therians differ from furries is that therians are six times more likely than non-therians to have experienced phantom body parts, such as paws, a tail, or a muzzle. While experiencing phantom body parts is not uncommon in individuals who've had amputations (Flor, 2002), the experience is not common in the general population—including furries.

On the other hand, many therians and otherkin felt more able to connect with their theriotype while in nature. A fox therian described one such experience:

"...once I got down past the horse pasture and around by some trees I just crouched down on the deep grass [and] just [felt] the cool ground on my hands and feet and I think I just sorta closed my eyes and tried [to] sense everything I could hear, everything I could smell. And as I was doing that I'd swear I could feel my tail behind me, just sorta suspended off the ground, ya know, not so limply drooped to the ground, and not held high but just held straight out. It was a very distressing feeling but at the same time very calming – to get out there, and after a few minutes of that I- I should say the whole time that the human side of the mind is just sort of off in the background - and then after a few minutes of being out there, human side comes back and is just like: well, I can't stay out here all night. I have no choice but to go back. Of course[,] that's depressing, it's like I can't stay out in the woods being me, I have to go back and remain in the human world."

This deep sense of connection with "being me" brings up a bittersweet array of feelings—on the one hand calming, on the other depressing, because of the temporary nature of the participant's sense of belonging in nature.

Challenges such as these, of life in the human world, are often intense for our participants. To this end, we've become interested in how therians and otherkin use mental health services as a means of coping with these difficulties. For the most part, they indicate that they didn't need mental health treatment for their therianthropy—their therianthropy wasn't a problem. Instead, they sometimes sought treatment for other problems, such as depression and anxiety. As one of our research participants put it when asked what he would like mental health professionals to know about therianthropy:

"You're not going to be the one that changes who we are. So, there's no reason to try – just treat us. Leave that alone [...] If we're going to you, we aren't going to you because we're therians, we're going to you because something is making us unhappy."

When seeing a therapist, our participants indicated that they were often hesitant to talk to their therapists about being therian or otherkin for precisely this reason: they were afraid that they would be pathologized, diagnosed, or have treatment forced upon them simply because of who they are. As one participant told us:

> *"I was always really fearful about people finding out, in particular[,] because:[sic] okay, crazy person let's put them away and whatever."*

However, many participants also reported positive experiences working with therapists and other mental health professionals—some of whom were aware that the participant was a therian/otherkin, others who were not. At the time of writing this chapter, we're now working on a guide for therapists and other mental health professionals to help them understand therianthropy and to work with these individuals in a sensitive, well-informed, and welcoming way. As one of our participants put it, it's important for mental health professionals to approach them with a sense of understanding and some familiarity, despite the challenges of doing so:

> *"It's a very real thing for people. And they might – I'm not gonna speak for everybody, but my therapist has looked over it for me and been like: oh that's just part of your like anxiety or whatever like it's it's [sic] a coping mechanism for stuff, and I'm like: no, it's not even close to that for me. But, like I'm not gonna really argue about it because I know what I feel and whatever, and they don't have to understand it. But it would be good if they understand [sic] it. It's very hard to put yourself in somebody's shoes, looking from the outside, it's like that's: insane, how how do they think that, like why do they think that way or whatever."*

Conclusion

Throughout this chapter, we've seen how furries and their interest, based around the concept of anthropomorphized non-human animals, is associated with the way they think, feel, and behave toward non-human animals. We've also contrasted furries and their fan-like interest in non-human animals against therians, a group of people who, while somewhat overlapping with furries, are distinct in their identification *as* non-human animals, in whole or in part. While this work is still very much in its infancy, it's already proven tremendously fruitful and speaks volumes about the need to not only better understand the distinction between furries and therians, but also the need for a concerted research effort to better understand therians and the therian community—to listen to what their needs and wants and to avoid conflating them with furries or trivializing / pathologizing their experience out of ignorance.

References

Aubert, M., Lebe. R., Oktaviana, A. A., Tang, M., Burhan, B., Hamrullah, Jusdi, A., Abdullah, Hakim, B., Zhao, J.-X., Geria, I., Sulistyarto, P. H., Sardi, R., & Brumm, A. (2019). Earliest hunting scene in prehistoric art. *Nature, 576,* 442-445. https://doi.org/10.1038/s41586-019-1806-y

Blom, J. D. (2014). When doctors cry wolf: A systematic review of the literature on clinical lycanthropy. *History of Psychiatry, 25*(1), 87-102. https://doi.org/10.1177/0957154X13512192

Butterfield, M. E., Hill, S. E., & Lord, C. G. (2012). Mangy mutt or furry friend? Anthropomorphism promotes animal welfare. *Journal of Experimental Social Psychology, 48*(4), 957-960. https://doi.org/10.1016/j.jesp.2012.02.010

Clegg, H., Collings, R.& Roxburgh, E. (2019). Therianthropy: Wellbeing, schizotypy, and autism in individuals who self-identify as non-human. *Society & Animals: Journal of Human-Animal Studies, Vol 27*(4), 403-426. https://doi.org/10.1163/15685306-12341540

Condition Red. (n.d.). *Wikifur*. http://en.wikifur.com/wiki/Condition:_Red.

Epley, N., Waytz, A., & Cacioppo, J. T. (2007). On seeing human: A three-factor theory of anthropomorphism. *Psychological Review, 114*(4), 864-886. https://doi.org/10.1037/0033-295X.114.4.864

Epley, N., Akalis, S., Waytz, A., & Cacioppo, J. T. (2008). Creating social connection through inferential reproduction: Loneliness and perceived agency in gadgets, gods, and greyhounds. *Psychological Science, 19,* 114-120. https://doi.org/10.1111/j.1467-9280.2008.02056.x

Flor, H. (2002). Phantom-limb pain: characteristics, causes, and treatment. *The Lancet, Neurology Volume 1(3)*, 182-189. https://doi.org/10.1016/S1474-4422(02)00074-1

Gerbasi, K. C., Fein, E., Plante, C. N., Reysen, S., & Roberts, S. E. (2017). Furries, therians and otherkin, oh my! What do all those words mean, anyway? In T. Howl (Ed.), *Furries among us 2: More essays on furries by furries* (pp. 162-176). Thurston Howl Publications.

Gray, H. M., Gray, K., & Wegner, D. M. (2007). Dimensions of mind perception. *Science, 315,* 619. https://doi.org/10.1126/science.1134475

Grivell, T., Clegg, H., & Roxburgh, E. C. (2014). An interpretative phenomenological analysis of identity in the therian community. *Identity: An International Journal of Theory and Research, 14*(2), 113-135. https://doi.org/10.1080/15283488.2014.891999

Guessoum, S. B., Benoit, L., Minassian, S., Mallet, J, & Moro, M. R. (2021) Clinical lycanthropy, neurobiology, culture: A systematic review. *Frontiers in Psychiatry, 12,* 718101. https://doi.org/10.3389/fpsyt.2021.718101

Keck, P. E., Pope, H. G., Hudson, J. I., McElroy, S. L, & Kulick, A. R. (1988) Lycanthropy: Alive and well in the twentieth century. *Psychological Medicine, 18(1)*, 113-20. https://doi.org/10.1017/s003329170000194x

Kühn, S., Brick, T. R., Müller, B. C. N., & Gallinat, J. (2014). Is this car looking at you? How anthropomorphism predicts fusiform face area activation when seeing cars. *PLoS ONE, 9*(12), e113885. https://doi.org/10.1371/journal.pone.0113885

Mason, O., Linney, Y., & Claridge, G. (2005) Short scales for measuring schizotypy. *Schizophrenia Research, 78,* 293-296. https://doi.org/10.1016/j.schres.2005.06.020

McHugh, R. M., Roberts, S. E., Gerbasi, K. C., Reysen, S., & Plante, C. N. (2019). Of gods and gorgons, demons and dogs: Anthropomorphism and zoomorphism through the ages. In T. Howl (Ed.), *Furries among us 3: More essays on furries by furries* (pp. 141-163). Thurston Howl Publications.

Proctor, D. (2018). Policing the fluff: The social construction of scientistic selves in Otherkin Facebook groups. *Engaging Science, Technology, and Society, 4,* 485-514. https://doi.org/10.17351/ests2018.252

Robertson, V. (2013). The beast within: Anthrozoomorphic identity and alternative spirituality in online therianthropy movement. *Nova Religio: The Journal of Alternative and Emergent Religions, 16,* 7-30. https://doi.org/10.1525/nr.2013.16.3.7

Schultz, P. W. (2001). Assessing the structure of environmental concern: Concern for self, other people, and the biosphere. *Journal of Environmental Psychology, 21,* 1-13. https://doi.org/10.1006/jevp.2001.0227

Tajfel, J. C., & Turner, J. C. (1979). An integrative theory of intergroup conflict. In W. Austin & S. Worchel (Eds.), *The social psychology of intergroup relations* (pp. 33-47). Brooks/Cole.

Tam, K.-P., Lee, S.-L., & Chao, M. M. (2013). Saving Mr. Nature: Anthropomorphism enhances connectedness to and protectiveness toward nature. *Journal of Experimental Psychology, 49,* 514-521. https://doi.org/10.1016/j.jesp.2013.02.001

Taylor, N., & Signal, T. D. (2009). Pet, pest, profit: Isolating differences in attitudes towards the treatment of animals. *Anthrozoös, 22*(2), 129-135. https://doi.org/10.2752/175303709X434158

Waytz, A., Cacioppo, J., & Epley, N. (2014). Who sees human? The stability and importance of individual differences in anthropomorphism. *Perspectives in Psychological Science, 5*(3), 219-232. https://doi.org/10.1177/1745691610369336

Waytz, A., Morewedge, C. K., Epley, N., Monteleone, G., Gao, J-H., & Cacioppo, J. T. (2010). Making sense by making sentient: Effectance motivation increases anthropomorphization. *Journal of Personality and Social Psychology, 99*(3), 410-435. https://doi.org/10.1037/a0020240

Chapter 21
Haters Gonna Hate: Furry Stigma

Stephen Reysen, Courtney "Nuka" Plante

Furries—aren't they those crazy folks who dress up like animals to do weird sex stuff?

If you've ever heard a conversation about furries online, in mainstream media, or just between two people on the bus, chances are fairly good that, at least once during the conversation, someone brought up mental health, sexual deviance, or both. Examples of this point abound in popular media. A now-infamous *CSI* episode called "Fur and Loathing"[1] portrays an orgy at a furry convention and a character named Sexy Kitty who initially refuses to speak to the police without their fursuit head on (Zuiker et al. 2003). A *Vanity Fair* article entitled "Pleasures of the Fur" defines the terms "yiff,"[2] "spooge,"[3] and "furvert"[4] without properly defining what a furry is (Gurley, 2001). An episode of *1000 Ways to Die* with the cringe-inducing title of "Em-bear-assed" defines furries as "people who like to put on animal costumes and get together for fun things like group sex" before telling a story about someone who was killed by a bear while on drugs and wearing a fursuit (McMahon et al., 2009).

Unfortunately, you don't have to limit your attention to fictional media to find examples of furries being the target of vitriol. In 2022, a senator from Nebraska, Bruce Bostelman, brought up furries during a legislative debate, including the roundly debunked claim that furries in high schools were demanding to use litter boxes[5] and were socially stunted, refusing to speak to their teachers except through barks and meows (The Guardian, 2002). Later

---

[1] Words cannot express our disappointment at the fact that such a clever title was wasted on such a bad episode!

[2] A piece of furry jargon used to refer to sex or sexual content, often used in a tongue-in-cheek manner by furries.

[3] A term used to describe semen, usually with a comedic connotation.

[4] A term used to describe a furry pervert, almost always used in an ironic way or by furries intending to poke fun at popular conceptualizations of furries.

[5] To be clear, there *have* been instances where kitty litter has been provided in classrooms, although the reason is far more tragic: because of the frequency of school shootings in the U.S., some school districts have put buckets of kitty litter into classrooms as a place for children to use the bathroom during active school shooting events (Bates, 2019).

that year, a Republican gubernatorial candidate blamed furries for mass shootings and made the banning of furries from schools part of her campaign (Pennacchia, 2022; Taylor, 2022). And in the wake of growing anti-LGBTQ+ sentiment and legislation in the U.S., furries, of whom the majority are LGBTQ+ (see Chapter 15 and Chapter 16), frequently find themselves in the crosshairs (Dickson, 2023).

These are just a few examples of the stigma furries routinely face. Stigma refers to the devaluing of a group by a society, usually based on one aspect of that group (sometimes real, sometimes presumed) being devalued (Major & O'Brien, 2005). Stigmatized group members frequently face negative stereotypes, prejudice, and discrimination as a result of this stigma. Markers of a stigma can be controllable (e.g., a person can choose to wear or not to wear a t-shirt espousing a stigmatized political position) or uncontrollable (e.g., being born with dark skin) and can be visible (e.g., race) or invisible (e.g., sexual orientation). According to Erving Goffman's (1963) groundbreaking work on the sociology of stigma, people will often use someone's membership in a stigmatized group as justification for devaluing, discriminating against, and ostracizing or attacking them, with obvious (and not so obvious) negative outcomes for the stigmatized (Major & O'Brien, 2005).

By far the largest area of research on the outcomes of stigma has examined the association between being part of a stigmatized group and well-being. In a meta-analysis of 144,246 participants, Schmitt et al. (2014) found that perceived societal discrimination is associated with worse well-being, including lower self-esteem and life satisfaction, higher depression, anxiety, and distress. Students who are members of stigmatized groups tend to perform more poorly in school than students who are not stigmatized (Guarneri et al., 2019; Major & O'Brien, 2005) and stigmatized group members show poorer physical health compared to non-stigmatized group members (see Major & O'Brien, 2005).

In this chapter, we'll focus our attention on what it means for furries to be stigmatized. We'll begin by laying out evidence—beyond anecdotes from headlines and violent rhetoric from online forums—showing that furries are stigmatized and recognize this stigma. Next, we'll describe research showing some of the reasons why furries are stigmatized as well as the consequences of this stigma for furries, including research showing that furries experience a significant amount of bullying. Finally, we'll discuss three ways that furries cope with this stigma—selective disclosure, denial of personal discrimination, and identification with the stigmatized group.

Stigma Directed Toward the Furry Fandom

Let's start by saying, unequivocally, that yes, furries are stigmatized. We've measured this a few different ways over the years, each time finding consistently that furries are held in fairly low regard by others, be it members of other fan groups or in a routine sample of fairly typical people. For example, Roberts et al. (2016) asked 150 fantasy sports fans to rate how they felt toward anime fans, bronies, and furries on a 101-point scale, from 0 = *extremely negatively* to 100 = *extremely positively*. Higher scores on this scale represent positive prejudice toward the group while lower scores represent negative prejudice.[6] The mean ratings showed that furries (M = 22.76) and bronies (M = 21.83) scored significantly lower than anime fans (M = 37.16), although all three fan groups were judged negatively (below the midpoint of the measure).

In an even more striking example of prejudice toward furries, Reysen and Shaw (2016) created a list of 40 popular fandoms split into four categories: sports (e.g., football, baseball), music (e.g., Jimmy Buffet, David Bowie), media (e.g., anime, *Star Trek*), and hobbies (e.g., cooking, video games). U.S. undergraduate college students rated their degree of prejudice toward fans of each of the fan interests (1 = *cold* to 10 = *warm*). The results showed that furries tied with bronies as the second lowest-rated fan group from the list (scoring only slightly above fans of the Insane Clown Posse; see Figure 21.1). Far from being a fluke, in another study (Plante & Reysen, 2023), participants gave virtually the same ratings, this time putting furries at the very bottom of the list. In short, across studies using different measures of prejudice and different samples of participants, we consistently find negative prejudice (i.e., stigma) directed toward furries.

---

[6] The terms "positive prejudice" and "negative prejudice" simply refer to the valence of a person's attitudes toward a group's members based solely on the fact that the person is a member of this group—this is prejudice. When the term prejudice is used in common parlance, people are usually referring to negative prejudice (i.e., disliking members of a group because of their group membership), but positive prejudice is also a thing. And while the effects of negative prejudice are more readily apparent, one should be cautious any time their attitudes and behavior toward a person are based solely on that person's group membership—even when the attitude is positive. For example, research suggests that positive prejudice and the endorsement of positive stereotypes reinforces the use of stereotypes and prejudice, justifying or opening the floodgates for negative prejudice (e.g., Kay et al., 2013).

Do Furries Know They Are Stigmatized?

It's one thing to show that furries are stigmatized, but it's another thing to show that furries *know* they're stigmatized. After all, while some of the detrimental effects of stigma stem are a direct consequence of the stigma (e.g., being harassed, attacked, ostracized), others require the person to be aware that they're stigmatized—a person is unlikely to feel anxiety about being targeted for being a furry if they don't realize that people dislike furries.

To this end, we designed a study to test whether furries were accurate in their perception of how much stigma is directed toward them. To do this, Reysen et al. (2017) recruited anime fans at A-Kon, an anime convention in Dallas, Texas, and furries at Anthrocon, a furry convention in Pittsburgh, Pennsylvania. Both groups estimated how positively or negatively they expected the other fan group to feel about them, as well as their own feelings toward the other group. Ratings were made on a 101-point scale, from 0 = *extremely positive* to 100 = *extremely negative*.[7]

The results (Figure 21.2) show that anime fans rate furries fairly negatively ($M = 54.26$, above the midpoint of the measure), while furries rate anime fans fairly positively ($M = 26.87$). This latter result is understandable, since a good chunk of furries also like anime (see Chapter 11). As for anime fans, they expected furries to like them ($M = 35.08$), although they tended to underestimate how much furries actually liked them. In contrast, furries thought anime fans would like them around the midpoint of the measure ($M = 46.20$), underestimating anime fans' dislike of furries. In other words, anime fans seem to overestimate the degree of prejudice toward them while furries, recognizing that people might have mixed feelings about them as a group, underestimated the degree of prejudice directed toward them—although they were more accurate in their perception than were anime fans.

---

[7] Note here that in this study, the scale was reversed—higher scores indicate more negative prejudice.

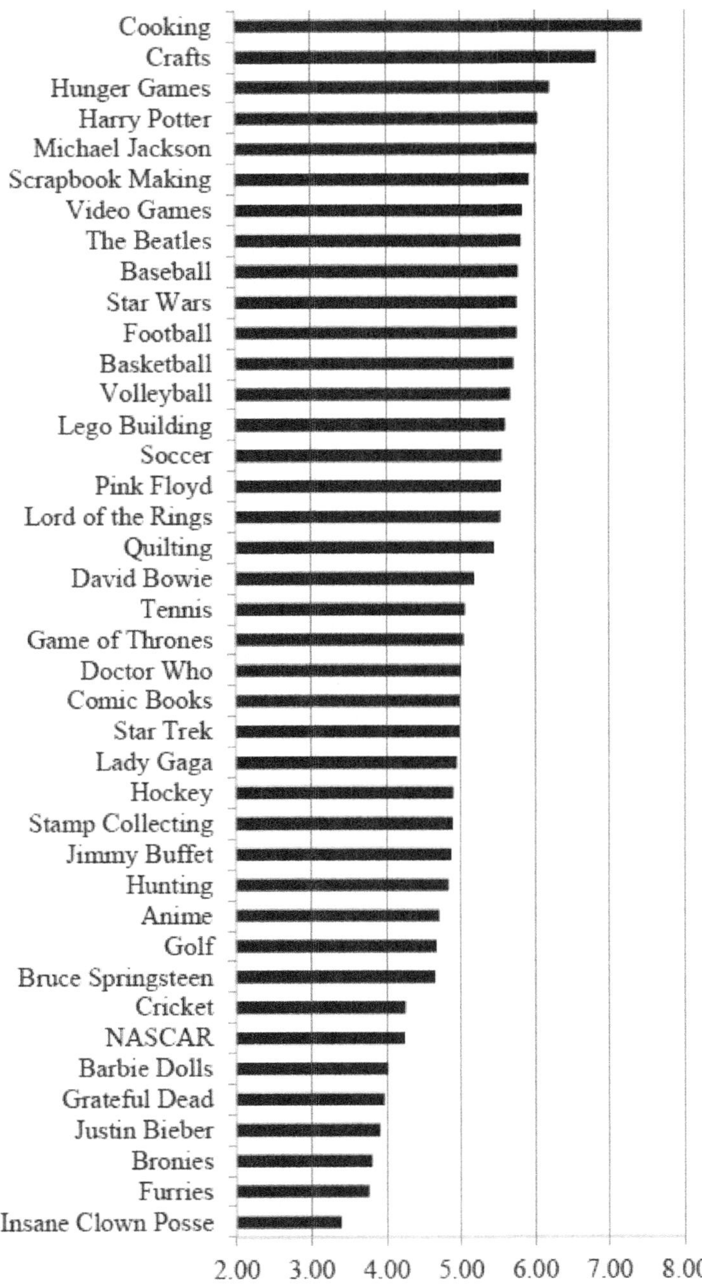

Figure 21.1. Ratings of different fan groups (1 = *cold*, 10 = *warm*).

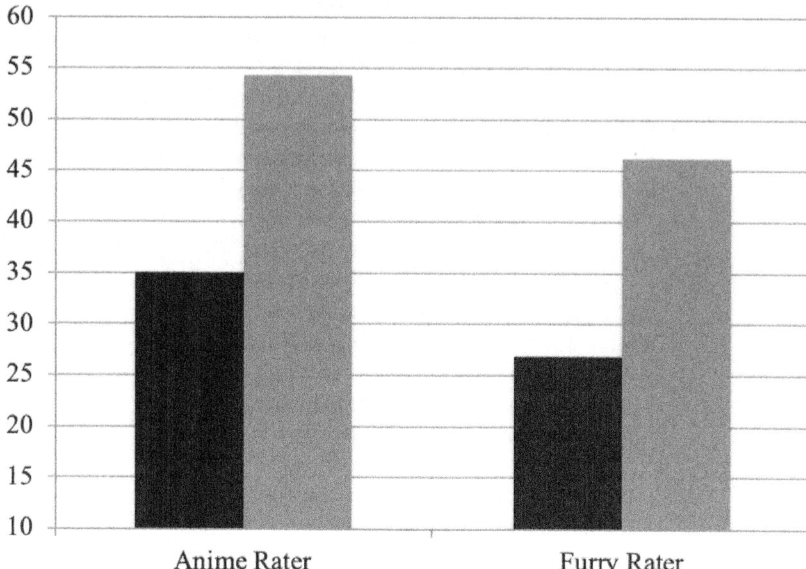

Figure 21.2. Perception of outgroup rating the ingroup and ingroup rating prejudice toward outgroup (0 = *warm*, 100 = *cold*).

Why is There a Stigma Toward Furries?

Reysen and Shaw (2016) proposed that the reason some fandoms are stigmatized is because they deviate from the prototype of what a fan is and are therefore viewed as abnormal. Prior research shows that things that deviate from the prototype or norm tend to be viewed more negatively. For example, Devos and Banaji (2005) found that the prototype for "American" is White (as opposed to other ethnicities / races). Because of this, non-White Americans are viewed as less prototypical, less American, and face greater discrimination as a result (Devos & Mohamed, 2014). In another example, heterosexual sex in the missionary position is the prototypical sexual act (Reysen et al., 2015). People who engage in other sexual acts (e.g., fisting), which are perceived by people as being fairly uncommon, are rated more negatively.

In line with this prior research, Reysen and Shaw (2016) proposed that, when it comes to fans, the prototype that comes to most peoples' minds is "sports fan"—with the specific type of sport varying from country to country (e.g., football, basketball, or baseball in the U.S., hockey in Canada, cricket in India). As a result, sports fans are likely to be seen as the most "normal," while anything deviating from a sports fan is likely to be seen as "abnormal" or "weird"—especially so the more it differs from being a mainstream interest like sports. To test this, the researchers surveyed U.S. undergraduate college students and asked them to describe what they thought of when they thought of a "fan." Participants also rated the 40 fan groups shown in Figure 21.1 concerning how prototypical the groups were considered to be (1 = *definitely not a stereotypical fan*, 7 = *definitely a stereotypical fan*), how normal it was to be a fan of that interest (1 = *not normal*, 7 = *very normal*), and prejudice toward members of that group (1 = *cold*, 10 = *warm*).

Open-ended responses from the study showed that when asked to describe a "fan," just over half of the participants (50.8%) described a sports fan, while another large chunk (20.8%) provided a general description that could be applied to any fan group. In other words, the results support the idea that, for most people, sports fans are the default prototype of a fan, the fan group against which other fan groups are compared. Similar to prior results, furries were rated low (i.e., high in negative prejudice directed toward them). More importantly for the present question, however, the researchers looked at data across the 40 different fan groups and saw that the more prototypical groups were seen as having the most normal fans and that the groups seen as having the most normal fans were viewed the most positively. In other words, the more a particular fan group differs from the prototype of a fan, the less normal they seem, which predicts negative prejudice toward that group and its members.

We recently revisited this study by delving more deeply into the mechanisms driving this link between non-prototypicality and prejudice (Plante & Reysen 2023). We again surveyed U.S. undergraduate college students and asked them to rate the same 40 fan groups on the same measures of perceived prototypicality and prejudice. This time, however, we also asked participants to rate the extent to which each fan group elicited negative feelings in them (e.g., discomfort, disgust) and the extent to which they held negative beliefs about members of those groups (e.g., they're dysfunctional, their interests are impure and tainted by other motivations, like sex). The results of this study again showed that furries were seen as non-prototypical and the subject of considerable negative prejudice. More importantly, we tested, and found support for, a statistical model which showed that this link was driven by the negative feelings and negative beliefs that people had toward furries. In effect, the more any fan group deviates from the prototypical sports fan, the more people feel negative emotions toward the group (e.g., they're gross, they make me uncomfortable), something which, in turn, predicts the endorsement of negative beliefs about the group (e.g., they're dysfunctional, they've got weird sexual interests) and, ultimately, negative prejudice toward the group.

These findings are consistent not only through the negative prejudice we commonly see in media stories and popular discourse about furries, but also in the specific content of these stories: furries are typically decried as being weird, dysfunctional, or out of touch, and as being sexual deviants.

Outcomes of Stigma

As we noted earlier, stigma carries with it a variety of negative outcomes such as lower well-being and poorer academic performance (Guarneri et al., 2019; Major & O'Brien, 2005; Schmitt et al., 2014). Across multiple studies we've tested whether this was the case with furries, asking them to rate their degree of experienced discrimination ("I feel that I am treated differently (worse) when people know I am a furry") and then testing whether their responses to this question correlations with measures that indicate negative outcomes. As Table 21.1 shows, greater stigma is associated with a wide range of undesirable outcomes.

Table 21.1. Correlations between perceived personal stigma and other variables.

Variable	Stigma
Fandom is under Threat	.24**
Fan Entitlement	.13**
Species Ingroup Projection	.20**
Identity Disclosure	-.19**
Self-Esteem	-.23**
Satisfaction with Life	-.21**
Depression	.15**
Negative Emotions	.19**
Identity Integration	-.23**
Identity Differentiation	-.16**

Note. ** $p < .01$.

For one thing, furries who were the target of stigma (i.e., experienced discrimination) were more likely to believe that the fandom and the people in it were under threat. The anxiety that comes with this perception of always potentially being targeted may explain why furries were also less likely to disclose their identity as a furry, felt lower self-esteem (an indicator of their perceived value or worth in the eyes of others), were less satisfied with their life, and were higher in depression and other negative emotions. Perceived stigma was also negatively associated with maturity (i.e., identity integration and differentiation), suggesting how being targeted because of some aspect of one's identity can make it harder for a person to mature into a fully realized person with a stable and positive sense of identity. Finally, we find that furries who perceived greater stigma were also more likely to feel a greater sense of entitlement in the fandom (e.g., believe that they deserve special treatment from artists) and were more likely to experience species ingroup projection—the belief that one's fursona species is the norm in the fandom and that other species are lesser. While these latter two findings might seem a bit out of place (e.g., is the bullied becoming the bully?), one possibility is that furries who "suffer" to be a furry may feel a sense of elitism in furry spaces—the idea that they are particularly stellar and laudable furries for sticking with the furry fandom and demonstrating loyalty despite this stigma. We'll be exploring this possibility in future research.

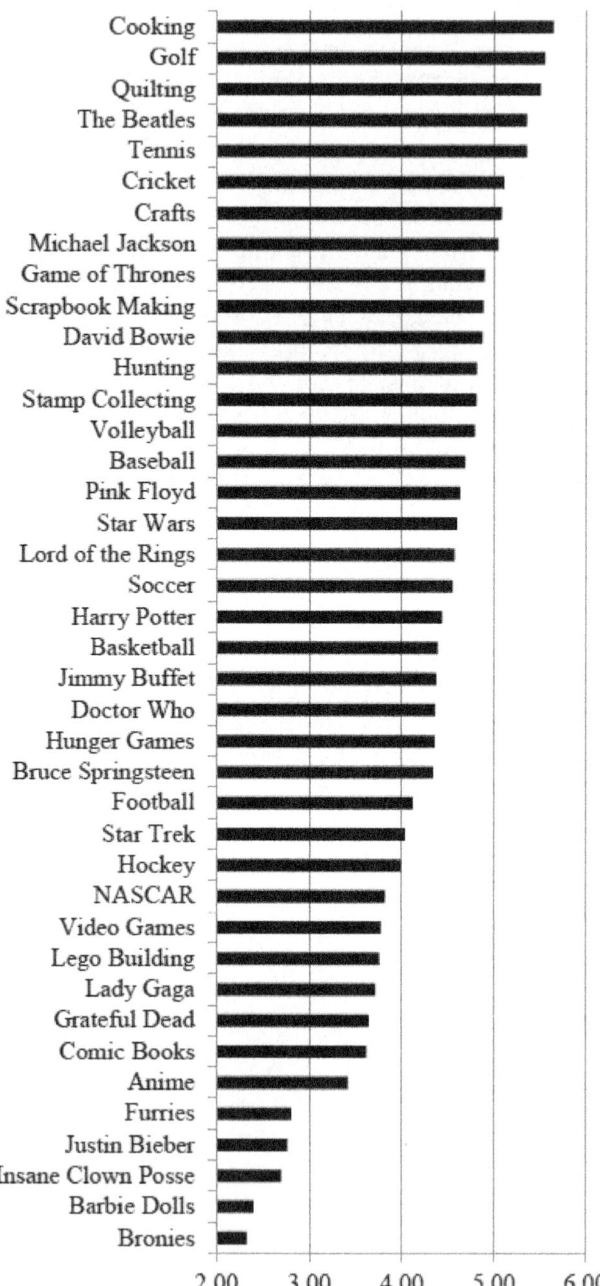

Figure 21.3. Perceived maturity of fans.

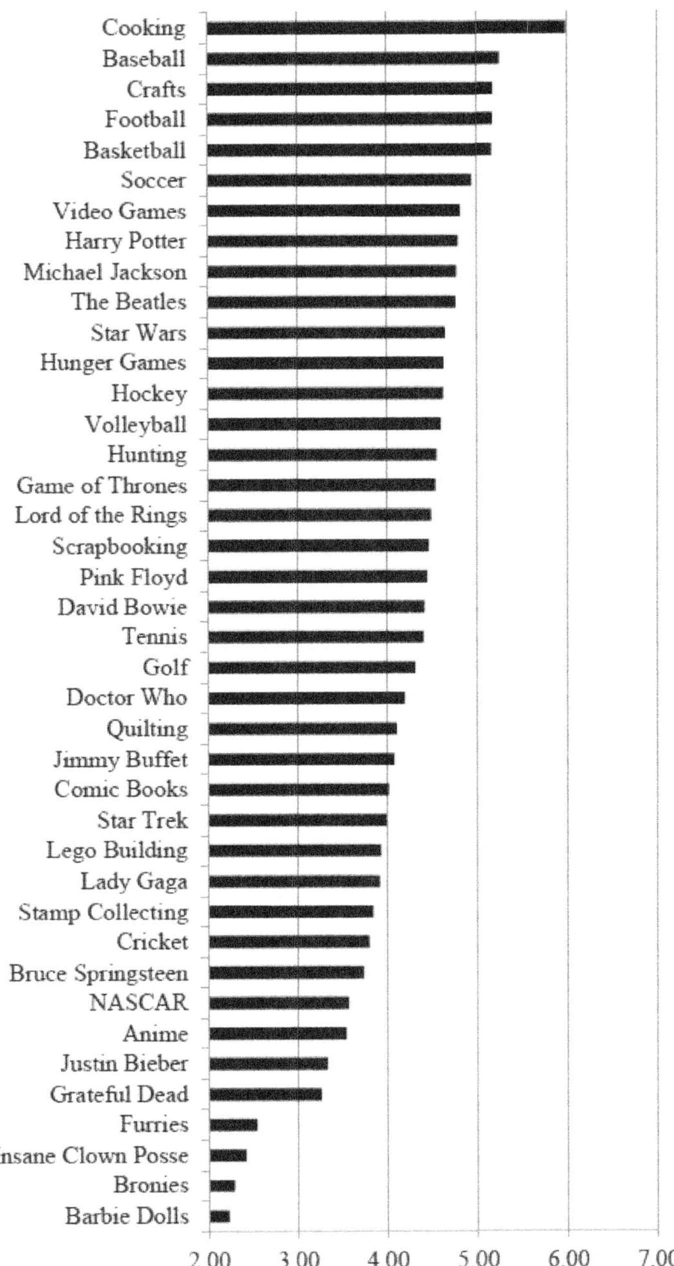

Figure 21.4. Willingness to date fan of the interest.

Another study we conducted highlighted some other potentially undesirable outcomes that come from belonging to a stigmatized group (Reysen & Plante, 2017). In this work, undergraduate college students were again asked to rate the 40 fan interests mentioned in Figure 21.1. These 40 groups were rated on whether the fans were believed to be mature and the participant's willingness to date someone with that fan interest. As shown in Figure 21.3, furries were rated 5th from the bottom with respect to their perceived maturity (just above Justin Bieber fans) and were rated 4th from the bottom in terms of participants' willingness to date them (Figure 21.4). Likewise, perceived maturity scores and willingness to date were positively correlated, meaning that furries' lack of perceived maturity was tied to participants' unwillingness to date a furry. These, coupled with the above findings, illustrate just some of the ways—some more obvious and some more subtle—that the stigma furries face can lead to tangible negative consequences. But we can perhaps illustrate this point most clearly by looking at the extent to which furries experience bullying.

Furries as the Target of Bullying

Bullying is defined as aggressive behavior that's intentional, recurring, and in which there is a power imbalance wherein the victim is unable to defend themselves (Olweus, 2013). A review of the literature shows that bullying unequivocally harms those who are bullied. For example, students who are bullied experience increased depression, academic difficulties, and anxiety, the effects of which can extend into adulthood (Juvonen & Graham, 2014; McDougall & Vaillancourt, 2015). A review of workplace bullying similarly shows that bullying is not only prevalent in adulthood, but it has the same effects as it does in childhood, including harming one's mental and physical health (e.g., depression, anxiety) and hurting vocational outcomes (e.g., absenteeism, turnover, lower productivity; Fitzpatrick et al., 2011). While you might be tempted to think that you could hide from bullying by retreating to online spaces, studies suggest that cyberbullying is just as prevalent and has the same outcomes as in-person bullying (Olweus, 2013).

Cook and colleagues (2010) conducted a meta-analysis to examine who is the most likely to become a bully, a victim of bullying, and who becomes both. The results showed that victims tend to be unpopular or low in status, often felt rejected and isolated, and are unable to "inhibit socially unacceptable behaviors" (p. 67). In effect, people who stray from the norm—be it at school, at work, or online—are often easy targets for bullies (Juvonen & Graham, 2014).

Given what we've seen earlier in this chapter—that furries are people with a fairly non-prototypical interest who are generally perceived as weird and dysfunctional—and given that people who deviate from the norm often find themselves stigmatized and targeted by bullies, we tested whether furries were especially likely to have a history of being bullied. In studies comparing furries to anime fans we've found that furries were especially likely to have been bullied between the ages of 11 to 18 (Reysen et al., 2021). We've also compared furries to a community sample (i.e., a sample of non-furry Americans), asking both to rate the frequency with which they were physically bullied, teased, and hit when they were a child using a 4-point scale, from 1 = *never* to 4 = *often*. As shown in Figure 21.5, while a history of being bullied when you were younger is unfortunately common in the general population, furries experience significantly more of it, regardless of the specific type of bullying being considered.

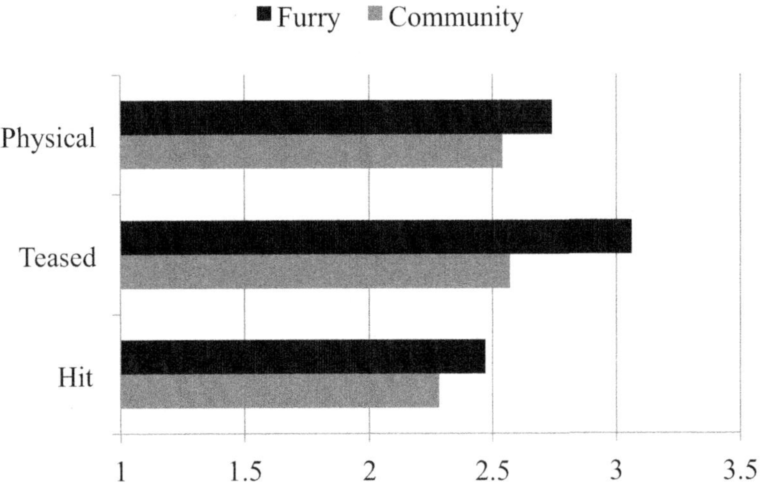

Figure 21.5. Frequency of different types of bullying experienced by furries and non-furries.

While furries were bullied more often than non-furries, these findings don't differentiate who was doing the bullying. Additionally, these items only referenced bullying experienced as a kid, not as an adult. To address these concerns, we asked furries in another study to rate the frequency and type of bullying they've experienced in the past five years (1 = *never*, 5 =

frequently), and to indicate whether the bullying was directed at them from other members of the furry fandom (with whom furries presumably interact a fair bit) or from non-furries. As shown in Figure 21.6, regardless of the type of bullying being considered, furries were more frequently bullied by non-furries than they were by furries.[8] The results also suggest that there is not a large amount of bullying within the past five years, given that all the means were well below the scale's midpoint, meaning that most of the bullying furries have experienced took place in their childhood or early teenage years—often before many of them identified as furry or even knew what the furry fandom was!

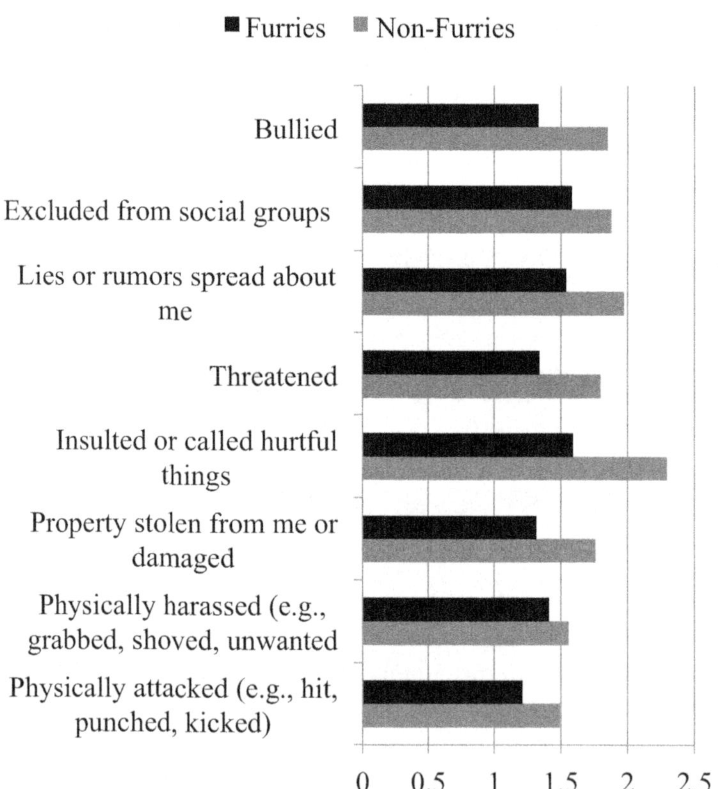

Figure 21.6. Frequency of being bullied by furries and non-furries.

[8] This is not to downplay or suggest that bullying doesn't happen in the furry fandom, of course. However, as we've seen in Chapter 21, many furries consider the fandom to be a refuge from the stigma and hate they experience in day-to-day life.

We grouped these eight "bullying from non-furry" items together into a single measure of bullying and tested them to see whether being bullied is associated with important measures related to well-being. As shown in Table 21.2, those who were bullied more frequently were more likely to be experiencing difficulties in day-to-day life, struggled with communication, and had become more insensitive toward others.[9] Being bullied is also associated with reduced physical and psychological well-being, a greater need to belong to a group of others (a possible byproduct of ostracism), and with signs of impulsive or risk-taking behavior (e.g., overspending, risky sexual or drug use behavior) suggesting a lack of concern with one's own well-being.

Table 21.2. Correlations between the frequency of being bullied and other variables.

Variable	Bullied
Difficulties in Daily Life	.26**
Difficulties Communicating with Others	.19**
Being Insensitive toward Others	.25**
Physical Well-Being	-.26**
Psychological Well-Being	-.16**
Overspending in Day-to-Day Life	.32**
Overspending at Conventions	.32**
Risky Behaviors	.17**
Need to Belong	.20**

Note. ** $p < .01$.

Coping and Disclosure

When asked, most furries indicated that they don't believe that furry is something biological or innate (Plante et al., 2015). In other words, most furries see being furry as a choice. Moreover, being a furry is something that a furry can generally hide from others, unlike, say, their race or having a visible disability. Since being a furry is stigmatized, one might ask whether furries can avoid the negative consequences we've highlighted above by

[9] In all three of these cases it's possible that these issues may have preceded the bullying (e.g., made a person a bigger target for bullying), though it's easy to see how these could also have emerged as a consequence of bullying—struggling due to anxiety caused by bullying, as well as finding it difficult to trust or empathize with others after a history of being bullied by others.

hiding the fact that they're furries from others. After all, how can one be targeted for being a furry if someone doesn't know that you're a furry?

The idea isn't a new one to furries, many of whom do, indeed, hide their furry identity from others in their lives. We asked furries, as well as anime fans and fantasy sports fans, to rate the extent to which they disclose their furry identity to others on a 7-point scale (with higher numbers indicating greater disclosure). As shown in Figure 21.7, furries were the least likely to disclose their fan identity to others, including their family, friends, peers, supervisors, and new people that they met—or, to put it another way, they were the most likely to conceal this part of their identity from others. Furries were the most likely to disclose their furry identity to their friends—likely because, as we saw in Chapter 13, about half of a typical furries' friends are, themselves, furries. Their friends aside, furries expressed significant reluctance to disclose their furry identity to others, including those in their own families—the data suggest that while furries tend to disclose to at least some members of their family, many do so only to a limited extent.[10] Likewise, many furries choose not to disclose their furry identity to their work peers or supervisors, often out of fear that it may hurt their career prospects.[11]

---

[10] We've heard numerous stories from furries who've told one of their siblings or one of their parents about their furry identity while choosing to keep it a secret from others in their family for fear of negative repercussions. This is especially likely in younger furries, who may have more reason to fear backlash from their families due to the power their families may have over them (e.g., if they're living with their parents, the fear of being kicked out into the street and being left homeless).

[11] Numerous furries working as soldiers, police officers, teachers, in businesses, or in the public sector have told us that they risk being fired if anyone in their workplace were to find out that they were furry. Their fear is not wholly unfounded either: in 2017, a Connecticut councilman was forced to resign by the mayor after it was discovered that he was a furry (Miller, 2017).

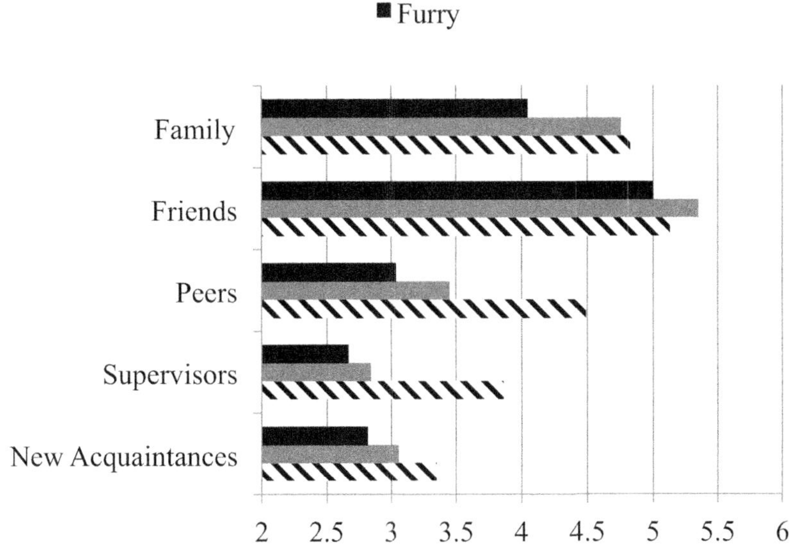

Figure 21.7. Degree of disclosure of fan identity to others (7-point scale).

On the surface, one might think that concealing a stigmatized identity seems like a good strategy to dodge the stigma and detrimental outcomes that come with being the target of discrimination. However, psychological research has shown that this isn't the case: being forced to conceal an aspect of one's identity (e.g., sexual orientation) is associated with poorer mental health (Pachankis, 2007), in part because of the chronic anxiety associated with worrying about being discovered and constantly having to self-monitor (e.g., to make sure you don't accidentally out yourself; Meyer, 1995). We've tested this idea in furries, showing that furries who were forced to conceal their furry identity experienced lower self-esteem (Plante et al., 2014), while those who were able to be more freely and openly furry experienced higher self-esteem and satisfaction with life (Mock et al., 2013). We've also tested, and found support for, a model that argues that those who identify more strongly with the furry fandom experience greater self-esteem and life satisfaction, in part, because they are more able to be open and disclose their interest rather than having to keep it hidden (see Figure 21.8; Reysen et al., in press).

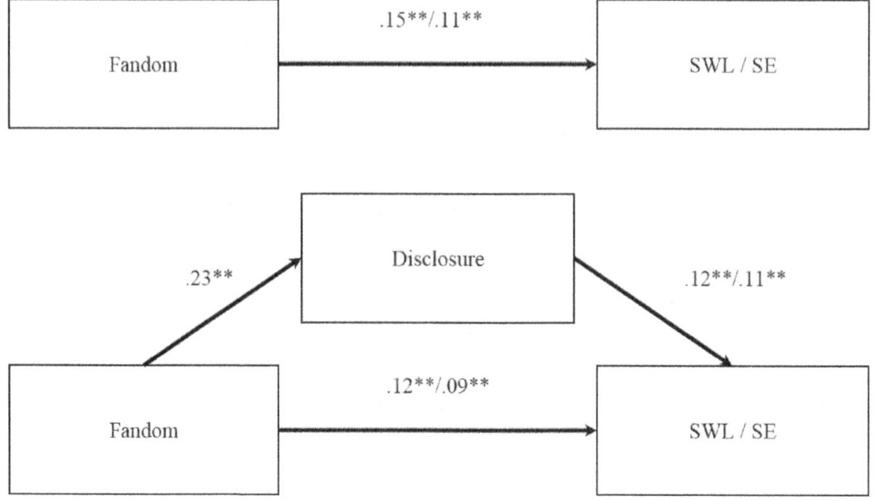

Figure 21.8. Furry identity disclosure mediating the relationship between fandom identification and satisfaction with life (SWL) and self-esteem (SE). Standardized betas are presented. ** $p < .01$.

Coping and Denial of Personal Discrimination

Another way to cope with stigma is to simply deny that you've personally been affected by it. This phenomenon was first observed by Faye Crosby (1984) when she observed that working women in Boston acknowledged that women in general were discriminated against at work. Nevertheless, these same women did not consider themselves to have been discriminated against. Crosby knew that the women in the study were likely facing discrimination at work, yet they did not report this being the case in the study. In effect, those who are the targets of discrimination due to being stigmatized may deny this discrimination to avoid the anxiety that accompanies this awareness: they argue that "my group is discriminated against, but I haven't been discriminated against."

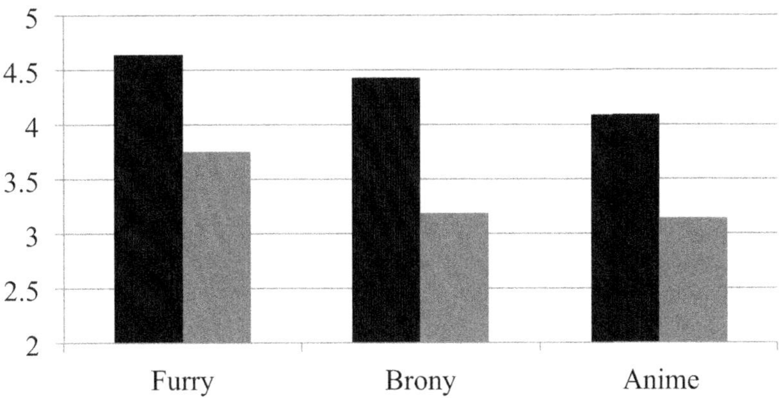

Figure 21.9. Ratings of group and personal discrimination (7-point scale).

To test this possibility, we administered measures of group ("Furries are discriminated against") and personal discrimination ("I have felt discriminated against because I am a furry") on a 7-point scale (higher scores indicate greater discrimination). As shown in Figure 21.9, fans from all three groups indicated that their group had experienced greater discrimination than they, themselves, had. Indeed, we also administered these measures to undergraduate college students and found the same effect regardless of what they were a fan of (e.g., music, sports). What is also notable in the figure is that furries rated higher on both group and personal discrimination, suggesting again that furries are aware of the stigma they face, even if they downplay their own experience of discrimination.[12]

---

[12] One explanation for this phenomenon comes from the human tendency to strategically make downward social comparisons—that is, to compare ourselves to those doing worse off than we are—in order to feel better about ourselves (Wills, 1981). In this regard, a furry who feels bad about being part of a stigmatized group (furries) might point to a furry who's received more discrimination than they have to avoid some of the anxiety they might otherwise feel: "Sure, I have it bad because my coworkers tease me, but Steve got fired from his job for being a furry, so I guess I don't have it too bad!" Another possibility is that furries might not feel like their experience of discrimination is valid, in much the same way that others who've experienced violence or harassment might not feel their case "counts" because it doesn't align with their prototype of what such a case ought to look like

Coping and Group Identification

A third, somewhat paradoxical response to stigma is to identify more strongly with the stigmatized group. According to the rejection identification model (Branscombe et al., 1999), those belonging to stigmatized groups who might not find it easy to conceal their identity, or who might simply prefer not to do so, may instead identify more strongly with the group and draw upon the social support provided by the group as a means of coping with the stigma of being a group member. While this work has been studied largely in the context of race or sexual minorities, we've also found evidence that the model can apply to fan groups as well. For example, we've found, in a sample of bronies, that those who perceived the brony fandom as more stigmatized were also more likely to strongly identify as bronies themselves (Chadborn et al., 2016). Likewise, in a sample of undergrads with a variety of fan interests, those whose fan interests were perceived as being the most stigmatized were also more likely to identify with their fan group (Tague et al., 2020). More importantly, this latter study also found that perceptions of stigma were associated with a greater sense of belongingness to their respective fandoms, suggesting that a fandom's social functions—including providing members with a sense of positive identity and social support network—may represent a defense against stigma.

While we've not directly tested these hypotheses in the furry fandom, there is little reason to believe that furries would be unique or distinct among fandoms in this regard. Moreover, even though we've never directly tested this hypothesis in furries, open-ended interviews and focus group data support this idea that, for many furries, despite the stigma and discrimination they experience for being a furry, the fandom is nevertheless a source of social support for them, and the very thing which helps them to cope with the consequences of being targeted, be it for having unusual fan interests or for being LGBTQ+ (Roberts et al., 2015).

Conclusion

Throughout this chapter, we've made the case that furries are members of a stigmatized fan community, a community targeted, in part, because of its non-prototypicality as a fan group. Because furries' interests deviate from typical fan interests, people experience negative emotional responses to them and believe in misconceptions about furries as maladjusted or motivated by sexual deviancy. Furries are well aware of the stigma they face and are fairly

---

(Sanmuhanathan, 2021). For example, they might tell themselves: "Yeah, sure, I've been teased and ridiculed for being a furry, but it's not *real* bullying until someone hits me—that hasn't happened to me!"

accurate in predicting the degree of stigma directed toward them. In line with past research, this stigma carries a number of negative consequences for the physical and psychological well-being of furries, often as a direct or indirect result of experiencing bullying and harassment. Furries, like members of other stigmatized groups, have turned to a variety of strategies to cope with this stigma, including hiding their identity as furries from others, denying personal discrimination, and turning inward toward the furry community as a source of resilience and social support.

Perhaps the most remarkable observation we've made in over a decade of studying furries is that, despite the significant stigma they routinely experience, they are resilient as a community. Furries can frequently be found mocking and parodying efforts to stigmatize them, embracing and redirecting the negativity rather than retreating from it. The ability to do this likely stems from the fandom's solidarity and the close-knit sense of belongingness the fandom provides for many members (see Chapter 19), many of whom see the furry fandom as the first place that they've been able to find acceptance after a childhood of ostracization for being different—either in hobby or in other facets of their identity (e.g., being LGBTQ+). This closeness and the resilience it provides has been the subject of many of our studies, and will undoubtedly continue to be a source of research questions and interest in the future.

References

Bates, J. (2019, August 21). Colorado school district providing kitty litter buckets for kids to use the bathroom during lockdowns. *Time*. https://time.com/5658266/colorado-district-kitty-litter-buckets-lockdowns/

Branscombe, N. R., Schmitt, M. T., & Harvey, R. D. (1999). Perceiving pervasive discrimination among African Americans: Implications for group identification and well-being. *Journal of Personality and Social Psychology, 77*(1), 135-149. https://doi.org/10.1037/0022-3514.77.1.135

Chadborn, D., Plante, C. N., & Reysen, S. (2016). Perceived stigma, social identity, and group norms as predictors of prosocial giving in a fandom. *International Journal of Interactive Communication Systems and Technologies, 6*(1), 35-49. https://doi.org/10.4018/IJICST.2016010103

Cook, C. R., Williams, K. R., Guerra, N. G., Kim, T. E., & Sadek, S. (2010). Predictors of bullying and victimization in childhood and adolescence: A meta-analytic investigation. *School Psychology Quarterly, 25*(2), 65-83. https://doi.org/10.1037/a0020149

Devos, T., & Banaji, M. R. (2005). American = White? *Journal of Personality and Social Psychology, 88*(3), 447-466. https://doi.org/10.1037/0022-3514.88.3.447

Devos, T., & Mohamed, H. (2014). Shades of American identity: Implicit relations between ethnic and national identities. *Social and Personality Psychology Compass, 8*(12), 739-754. https://doi.org/10.1111/spc3.12149

Dickson, E. J. (2023, May 25). Furries now have serious beef with Ron DeSantis. *Rolling Stone*. https://www.rollingstone.com/culture/culture-news/furries-beefing-ron-desantis-1234742107/

Fitzpatrick, M. E., Cotter, E. W., Bernfeld, S. J., Carter, L. M., Kies, A., & Fouad, N. A. (2011). The importance of workplace bullying to vocational psychology: Implications for research and practice. *Journal of Career Development, 38*(6), 479-499. https://doi.org/10.1177/0894845310390035

Goffman, E. (1963). *Stigma: On the management of spoiled identity.* Prentice-Hall.

Guarneri, J. A., Oberleitner, D. E., & Connolly, S. (2019). Perceived stigma and self-stigma in college students: A literature review and implications for practice and research. *Basic and Applied Social Psychology, 41*(1), 48-62. https://doi.org/10.1080/01973533.2018.1550723

Gurley, G. (2001, March). Pleasures of the fur. *Vanity Fair*. Retrieved from http://vanityfair.com/culture/features/2001/03/furries200103?currentPage=1

Juvonen, J., & Graham, S. (2014). Bullying in schools: The power of bullies and the plight of victims. *Annual Review of Psychology, 65*(1), 159-185. https://doi.org/10.1146/annurev-psych-010213-115030

Kay, A. C., Day, M. V., Zanna, M. P., & Nussbaum, A. D. (2013). The insidious (and ironic) effects of positive stereotypes. *Journal of Experimental Social Psychology, 49*(2), 287-291. https?/doi.rog/10.1016/j.jesp.2012.11.003

Major, B., & O'Brien, L. T. (2005). The social psychology of stigma. *Annual Review of Psychology, 56,* 393-421. https://doi.org/10.1146/annurev.psych.56.091103.070137

McDougall, P., & Vaillancourt, T. (2015). Long-term adult outcomes of peer victimization in childhood and adolescence: Pathways to adjustment and maladjustment. *American Psychologist, 70*(4), 300-310. https://doi.org/10.1037/a0039174

McMahon, T. (Writer, Director), Arnarson, H. A. (Writer), & Miller, G. (Writer). (2009). Death over easy: Em-bear-assed [Television series episode]. In Original Productions (Producer), *1000 ways to die*. Spike.

Meyer, I. H. (20023). Prejudice, social stress, and mental health in lesbian, gay and bisexual populations: Conceptual issues and research evidence. *Psychological Bulletin, 129,* 674-697. https://doi.org/10.1037/0033-2909.129.5.674

Miller, J. R. (2017, September 8). Councilman resigning after secret 'furry' life revealed. *New York Post.* https://nypost.com/2017/09/08/councilman-resigning-after-secret-furry-life-revealed/

Mock, S. E., Plante, C. N., Reysen, S., & Gerbasi, K. C. (2013). Deeper leisure involvement as a coping resource in a stigmatized leisure context. *Leisure/Loisir, 37*(2), 111-126. https://doi.org/10.1080/14927713.2013.801152

Olweus, D. (2013). School bullying: Development and some important challenges. *Annual Review of Clinical Psychology, 9*(1), 751-780. https://doi.org/10.1146/annurev-clinpsy-050212-185516

Pachankis, J. E. (2007). The psychological implications of concealing a stigma: A cognitive-affective-behavioral model. *Psychological Bulletin, 133*(2), 328-345. https://doi.org/10.1037/0033-2909.133.2.328

Pennacchia, R. (2022, May 16). Furries to blame for Buffalo shooting, say Stew Peter and Kandiss Taylor. *Wonkette.* https://www.wonkette.com/martha-speaks-buffalo-shooting

Plante, C. N., & Reysen, S. (2023). "They're just weird": Cognitive and affective mediators of the association between perceived non-prototypicality of, and prejudice toward, fan culture. *Psychology of Popular Media.* Advance online publication. https://doi.org/10.1037/ppm0000440

Plante, C. N., Roberts, S., Reysen, S., & Gerbasi, K. (2014). Interaction of socio-structural characteristics predicts identity concealment and self-esteem in stigmatized minority group members. *Current Psychology, 33*(1), 3-19. https://doi.org/10.1007/s12144-013-9189-y

Plante, C. N., Roberts, S. E., Snider, J. S., Schroy, C., Reysen, S., & Gerbasi, K. (2015). 'More than skin-deep': Biological essentialism in response to a distinctiveness threat in a stigmatized fan community. *British Journal of Social Psychology, 54*(2), 359-370. https://doi.org/10.1111/bjso.12079

Reysen, S., & Plante, C. N. (2017). Fans, perceived maturity, and willingness to form a romantic relationship: Application of a short maturity measure. *Communication and Culture Online, 8*(1), 154-173. https://doi.org/10.18485/kkonline.2017.8.8.8

Reysen, S., Plante, C. N., Chadborn, D., Roberts, S. E., & Gerbasi, K. (2021). *Transported to another world: The psychology of anime fans*. International Anime Research Project.

Reysen, S., Plante, C. N., Roberts, S. E., & Gerbasi, K. C. (2017). Accuracy of perceived prejudice toward one's fan group. *The Phoenix Papers, 3*(1), 122-129.

Reysen, S., Plante, C. N., Roberts, S. E., & Gerbasi, K. C. (in press). Social activities mediate the relation between fandom identification and psychological well-being. *Leisure Sciences*. https://doi.org/10.1080/01490400.2021.2023714

Reysen, S., & Shaw, J. (2016). Sport fan as the default fan: Why non-sports fans are stigmatized. *The Phoenix Papers, 2*(2), 234-252.

Reysen, S., Shaw, J., & Brooks, T. R. (2015). Heterosexual missionary as the sexual default and stigmatization of perceived infrequent sexual activities. *Advances in Social Sciences Research Journal, 2*(5), 93-104. https://doi.org/10.14738/assrj.25.1181

Roberts, S. E., Plante, C. N., Gerbasi, K. C., & Reysen, S. (2015). Clinical interaction with anthropomorphic phenomenon: Notes for health professionals about interacting with clients who possess this unusual identity. *Health & Social Work, 40*(2), e42-e50. https://doi.org/10.1093/hsw/hlv020

Roberts, S. E., Plante, C. N., Reysen, S., & Gerbasi, K. C. (2016). Not all fantasies are created equal: Fantasy sports fans' perceptions of furry, brony, and anime fans. *The Phoenix Papers, 2*(1), 40-60.

Sanmuhanathan, N. (2021, March 2). I'm a sexual assault counselor. Here's why it's so hard for survivors to come forward, and what happens when they do. *The Conversation*. https://theconversation.com/im-a-sexual-assault-counsellor-heres-why-its-so-hard-for-survivors-to-come-forward-and-what-happens-when-they-do-156038

Schmitt, M. T., Branscombe, N. R., Postmes, T., & Garcia, A. (2014). The consequences of perceived discrimination for psychological well-being: A meta-analytic review. *Psychological Bulletin, 140*(4), 921-948. https://doi.org/10.1037/a0035754

Tague, A. M., Reysen, S., & Plante, C. N. (2020). Belongingness as a mediator of the relationship between felt stigma and identification in fans. *Journal of Social Psychology, 160*(3), 324-331. https://doi.org/10.1080/00224545.2019.1667748

Taylor, K. [@KandissTaylor]. (2023, March 23). *The furry days are over when I'm governor. Public school is for academics not fairy tales*

[Tweet]. Twitter. https://twitter.com/KandissTaylor/status/1506603753008472064

The Guardian. (2022, March 29). *Republican retracts false claim schools placing litter boxes for 'furry' students.* The Guardian. https://www.theguardian.com/us-news/2022/mar/29/nebraska-lawmaker-litter-boxes-claim-debunked

Wills, T. A. (1981). Downward comparison principles in social psychology. *Psychological Bulletin, 90*(2), 245-271. https://doi.org/10.1037/0033-2909.90.2.245

Zuiker, A. E. (Writer), Stahl, J. (Writer), & Lewis, R. (Director). (2003). Fur and loathing [Television series episode]. In J. Bruckheimer (Producer), *CSI: Crime Scene Investigation.* CBS Paramount Network Television.

Chapter 22
The Kids are Alright: Furry Well-Being and Mental Health
Stephen Reysen, Courtney "Nuka" Plante

Psychology, as a field of study, focuses on the mind and behavior. It's a broad field whose topics range from animal training to cult indoctrination, from personality assessment to visual perception, from language learning to neuronal activity in the brain. Despite this wide scope, however, the study of well-being is, hands down, the bread and butter of psychological research.[1] It's the backbone of psychology insofar as, sooner or later, almost every other field of psychology circles around to discuss its implications for well-being. This, coupled with the fact that one of the most common questions we're asked by laypersons about furries is "Are furries okay?", is why we've included measures of well-being in our research on furries for about as long as we've been doing research on furries. Indeed, over the years we've collected so much data on furry well-being that we could easily make this chapter into its own book! To keep this book from becoming a two-volume set, we'll be succinct and focus this chapter just on the main points. We'll begin with a short introduction to well-being and how to measure it.[2] Next, we compare furries to other groups on measures of well-being—since knowing how well furries are doing is a bit meaningless without a point of comparison. Finally, we discuss the prevalence of mental illness in furries and how it stacks up against other fandoms before briefly considering some of the variables that help us predict which furries tend to score highest on measures of well-being.

What is Well-Being?

Chances are, you've already got a pretty intuitive understanding of what well-being is: it's the state we're all striving toward, how we would like to be doing if given the choice.[3] But philosophy and psychology have a long history of deliberating over what, precisely, comprises a person's well-being. For example, McDowell (2010) describes well-being as "contentment, satisfaction, or happiness derived from optimal functioning" (p. 70). This definition implies that well-being is something people judge for themselves

---

[1] As a testament to this fact, there's an entire subdiscipline of psychology dedicated to discovering what makes people happy and thriving—positive psychology!

[2] As it turns out, well-being isn't as simple and singular a concept as you might think!

[3] I always imagine it as how I *wish* I was doing when I'm feeling sick or having a really rough day.

based on how they're functioning at that moment. Someone who's dealing with chronic pain could, to an outsider, be seen as doing fairly poorly in terms of well-being, but if they're comparing themselves to others in worse situations, they might feel they're doing pretty well! Alternatively, you could be in perfect physical health, but feel incomplete and unsatisfied with your daily life. Even someone who's completely devoid of any illness or disease and who's balancing life quite well might decide that merely existing without problems is insufficient—that unless they're thriving and continuously growing, they're not doing well.[4]

Ultimately, there's no perfect, universally agreed-upon way to assess well-being. As a result, researchers have proposed countless measures and dimensions along which to measure well-being, each one tailor-made to measure well-being as it's conceptualized in each researcher's own model or framework. Illustrating just how many different conceptualizations we're talking about, Linton et al. (2016) examined 99 different measures of well-being and identified 196 distinct dimensions. Of course, they recognized that some of these different dimensions overlapped with one another, so they condensed and categorized them down to a smaller, more manageable set of six broad clusters (e.g., mental well-being, spiritual well-being).

Other researchers have statistically examined the relationships between these dimensions and suggested that there may be as few as two main dimensions when it comes to well-being. We generally refer to these as *subjective* well-being ("evaluation of life in terms of satisfaction and balance between positive and negative affect"[5]) and *psychological* well-being ("perception of engagement with existential challenges of life;" Keyes et al., 2002, p. 1007).[6] In their study, Keyes et al. measured well-being in various ways in a group of people and found that they clustered together into one dimension tapping into subjective well-being (e.g., positive affect, life satisfaction) and one tapping into psychological well-being (e.g., personal growth, purpose in life) (Keyes et al., 2002). When Compton et al. (1996) similarly administered various measures of well-being to students and

---

[4] This isn't even mentioning the fact that philosophers have opined for millennia about what it means to live the good life: is it hedonism—maximizing pleasure and minimizing pain—or being fully immersed and engaged moment to moment? Or is it something different entirely, like maximizing one's productivity and generativity?

[5] "Affect" is the fancy psychological word for "feelings" or "emotions."

[6] Other researchers use different terminology to refer to these same two dimensions. For example, Ryan and Deci (2001) call these two dimensions hedonic well-being (e.g., happiness) and eudaimonic well-being (living up to one's potential).

community members, they found the same loading onto these two dimensions, subjective well-being (e.g., happiness, satisfaction with life) and psychological well-being (e.g., maturity, self-actualization).

Since there are no perfect, universally agreed-upon measures of well-being, we tend to call all of these various constructs, as well as related constructs like self-esteem,[7] indicators of well-being, recognizing that, despite the small differences between the different constructs, they all tend to be fairly positively correlated with one another—in other words, when you're high on one measure of well-being, it can safely be assumed that you would also score high on dozens of other, similar measures of well-being.[8]

Fandom Comparisons

So, how does furries' well-being stack up against other fans? Our first such comparison was between furries, anime fans, and fantasy sports fans in a large-scale study that employed various measures of well-being (e.g., life satisfaction, self-esteem, anxiety). As shown in Figure 22.1, furries and fantasy sports fans did not differ with respect to life satisfaction or self-esteem, although both groups scored significantly higher than anime fans. Furries and anime fans did not differ when it came to depression and anxiety, though both groups were significantly higher than fantasy sports fans. Lastly, furries reported more stress than either anime or fantasy sports fans (who did not differ from one another). Finally, we should note that furries scored

---

[7] We'll take this moment to get on a soapbox: we believe that self-esteem is also an indicator of well-being. It's a theoretical argument we've gotten into with other researchers in the past. On the one hand, yes, technically self-esteem—a general evaluation of one's overall self-worth—is a construct distinct from well-being—it's not the exact same thing as how one's life is going. However, in studies that have measured both well-being and self-esteem, the two are almost always moderately to strongly correlated (e.g., Kashdan, 2004; Lyubomirsky et al., 2006; Paradise & Kernis, 2002). When included in analyses of well-being, self-esteem usually clusters together with other measures of subjective well-being (Compton et al., 1996), and in a large study across 31 nations, self-esteem was nearly always positively correlated with satisfaction with one's life (Diener & Diener, 1995). In other words, we've included furry self-esteem in this chapter as a measure of well-being—arguably a proxy measure for it—and are letting you, the reader, know that not all psychologists would agree with this decision.

[8] This has frequently been our approach to measuring well-being: While any individual measure of well-being might have quirks or idiosyncrasies, if you measure well-being in three different ways and they all come out showing the same general trend, you can be reasonably sure you're measuring general well-being and not something oddly specific to one particular measure.

above the midpoint of the measures for life satisfaction and self-esteem, and lower than the midpoint on depression, anxiety, and stress. This suggests furries generally report fairly good well-being on average, with differences between furries and other fan groups being fairly small differences of magnitude rather than big, categorical differences. In other words: furries seem to be doing about as well as other fan groups, despite stigma and popular misconceptions suggesting otherwise (see Chapter 21 for more on this).

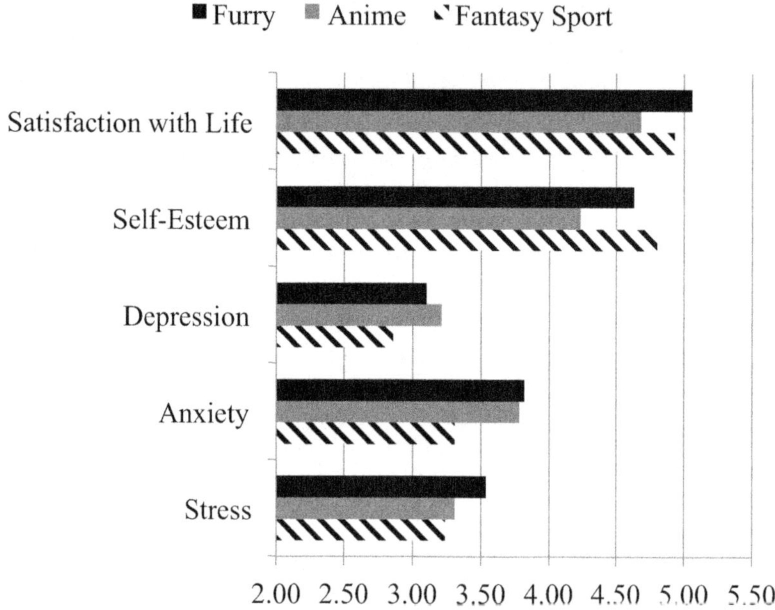

Figure 22.1. Mean comparisons of well-being indicators for furries, anime fans, and fantasy sports fans (7-point scale).

As we noted earlier, there are two basic dimensions of well-being: subjective and psychological. Because psychological research has generally focused on subjective well-being (e.g., happiness, satisfaction with life), Ryff (1989, p. 1072) proposed six dimensions of psychological well-being: autonomy ("self-determining and independent; able to resist social pressures"), environmental mastery ("competence in managing the environment; controls complex array of external activities"), personal growth ("a feeling of continued development"), positive relations with others (having "warm, satisfying, trusting relationships with others"), purpose in life ("has goals in life and a sense of directedness"), and self-acceptance ("a positive attitude toward the self"). Wanting to move beyond measures of subjective well-being, we've also conducted studies that measured each of Ryff's six dimensions of psychological well-being, doing so in samples of furries, anime fans, and undergraduate college students for comparison (Reysen et al., 2020).

As shown in Figure 22.2, furries' scores were generally comparable to the two comparison groups, not standing out as being especially high or low with the possible exception of the personal growth and positive relations category, where they scored significantly higher than the other groups. Furries also scored above the midpoint on all of the dimensions suggesting that, overall furries have fairly good psychological well-being. Indeed, one of the more surprising findings from this study was that, on many of the dimensions, furries were more psychologically well-off than college students.[9]

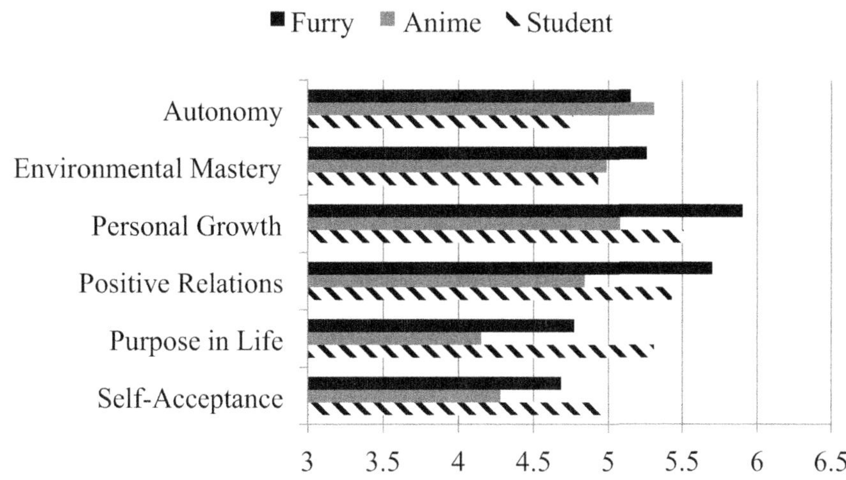

Figure 22.2. Mean comparison between furries, anime fans, and U.S. college students on dimensions of psychological well-being (7-point scale).

At this point, you may be wondering if anime fans are doing okay. Across most of our measures of well-being, they seem to be scoring lower than furries. We wanted to see whether we could account for some of these differences by asking whether the number of friends both groups have might

[9] In Chapter 13, we note that most furries are, themselves, college students or former college students, making this a fairly apt comparison.

account for these differences, given that furries are highly motivated to participate in the furry fandom by belongingness and given the fandom's norms of acceptance and tolerance (see Chapter 17 and Chapter 19). To test this, we ran a mediation model (shown in Figure 22.3), in which we found, first and foremost, that furries scored higher than anime fans on a measure of life satisfaction. Next, we tested whether furries and anime fans had comparable numbers of friends and found that furries, on average, did have more friends ($M = 11.38$) than anime fans ($M = 9.20$). We also found that those who had more friends tended to be more satisfied with their lives, on average. Putting the whole model together, at least some of the difference in life satisfaction between furries and anime fans can be accounted for by the fact that furries have more friends on average. This finding highlights the importance of social connections for one's well-being, a theme that will continue to pop up throughout this chapter.

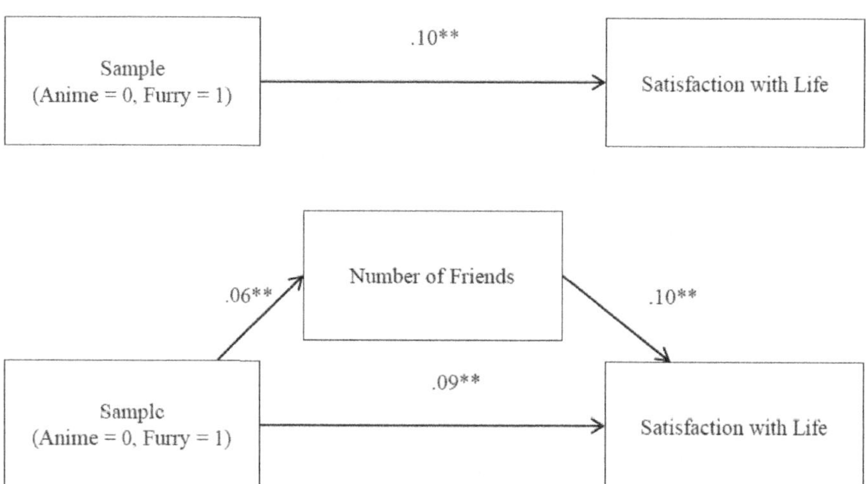

Figure 22.3. Sample comparison predicting satisfaction with life through the number of friends. Standardized betas are presented. ** $p < .01$.

Mental Health Diagnoses

One way a doctor could assess a patient's physical health would be to test for the presence or absence of disease, infection, or dysfunction. In a somewhat analogous fashion, another way we can indirectly assess mental health is to test whether a person has been diagnosed with a mental health problem.[10] With this in mind, we asked a sample of furries, bronies, and anime fans whether they had ever been diagnosed by a licensed practitioner with one or more psychological conditions (Reysen et al., 2018). We then coded the responses into major groupings of disorders: mood disorders (e.g., depression, bipolar), anxiety disorders (e.g., panic disorder, generalized anxiety disorder), attention-deficit/hyperactivity disorder (ADHD), and autism spectrum disorder.[11]

The results of this study found that furries and anime fans did not differ when it comes to the percentage of fans diagnosed with a mood disorder, although both had a higher prevalence rate than was observed in bronies (see Figure 22.4). Anime fans reported more anxiety disorders than bronies, while furries fell somewhere in-between and did not differ significantly between the two groups. Furries reported a significantly higher prevalence of ADHD than did bronies, who, themselves, were more likely to have ADHD than anime fans. Finally, furries and anime fans did not differ when it came to having a diagnosis of autism spectrum disorder, although both were significantly below bronies.[12]

---

[10] We should note that we didn't use this, by itself, as an indicator of mental health. For example, we've never said "this person has been diagnosed with an anxiety disorder, therefore they must have worse mental health than a person who has not been diagnosed." For one thing, this ignores the fact that some folks might be diagnosable with a condition but simply have never been diagnosed. Moreover, a person with a mental illness who's managing it well may well be functioning better than someone who has not been diagnosed with a mental health condition but who is nevertheless struggling to cope with day-to-day life for a myriad of reasons. Instead, we look at mental health as a moderating factor—a possible risk factor or aggravating/amplifying force—when it comes to problems with well-being, rather than being an indicator of mental health in and of itself.

[11] Again, we reiterate that, in and of itself, being neurodivergent is not an indicator of problems with well-being. In fact, in many cases problems with well-being in neurodivergent people have less to do with someone being neurodivergent and more to do with their living in a society in which neurodivergence is stigmatized or punished through systemic barriers and arbitrary cultural norms.

[12] In other studies with furries we've seen rates of autism spectrum disorder diagnosis vary, sometimes going as high as 13.2%.

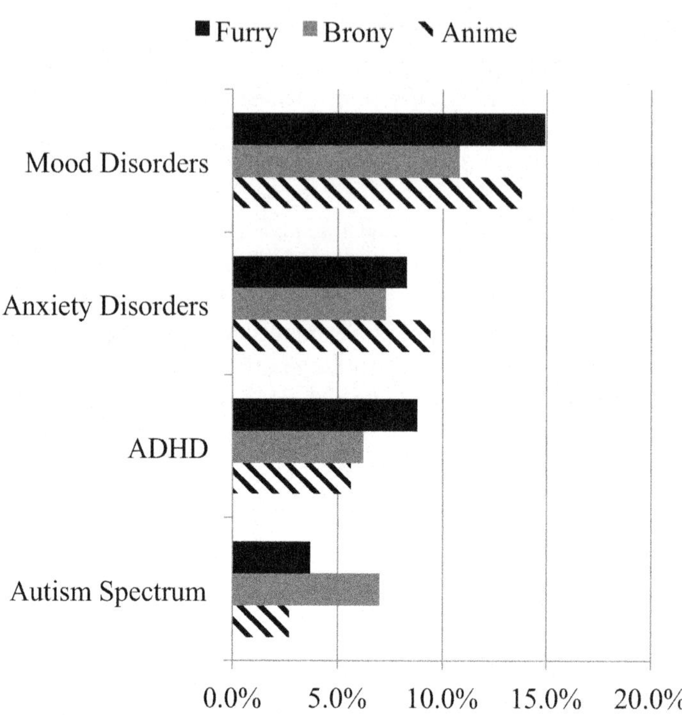

Figure 22.4. Prevalence of disorders in furry, brony, and anime fandoms.

We also compared the prevalence of each of these disorders with U.S. lifetime prevalence rates.[13] All three fan groups showed a lower prevalence of mood disorders, anxiety disorders, and ADHD than the U.S. lifetime prevalence rates. In contrast, all three groups showed higher rates of autism spectrum disorder than is observed in the general U.S. population.[14] All in

---

[13] By no means is this a great comparison—for one thing, the average furry is significantly younger than the average American (see Chapter 13) meaning, if nothing else, they have had less time to have been diagnosed. Nevertheless, it's the best data we have available to make comparisons between mental illness in the furry fandom compared to the general population as a whole—a comparison laypersons seem determined to make.

[14] An important caveat when interpreting this finding is to keep in mind that one of the diagnostic criteria for autism spectrum disorder is a specific, restricted, or repetitive behavior or interest. What is a fan, if not a person with a very specific interest in something? We're not meaning to suggest that all fans are on the autism

all, these findings suggest that the relative number of people who've been diagnosed with a mental illness is relatively low in the furry fandom (except in the case of autism) compared to the U.S. population, meaning that, if nothing else, furry is not defined by, or especially susceptible to, diagnosable mental health problems.[15]

Fanship versus Fandom

As we discussed in Chapter 6, we regularly make a distinction between fanship (the degree of one's psychological connection with a fan object) and fandom (psychological connection with other fans as a group) in our research (Reysen & Branscombe, 2010). This distinction is especially important when it comes to predicting fan well-being (Edwards et al., 2019; Reysen et al., 2021). Based on studies showing that identifying with a particular sports team (i.e., fanship) was associated with fan well-being, Daniel Wann (2006) argued that this association was because fans who identified more strongly with a sports team also formed social connections to other fans and that this was driving the link with higher well-being. However, in three studies testing the model, he was unable to find support (Wann et al., 2015; Wann et al., 2011). In 2017, however, we did find support for the model, not in a sample of sports fans but rather in a sample of anime fans and the face-to-face friendships (but not online friendships) that they made through their interest in anime (Reysen et al., 2017).

In other studies, researchers have similarly found a link between identifying with a sports team and well-being. For example, in a 2017 study, Wann and his colleagues found a link between identifying with a sports team and feeling a sense of belonging in life, one that was driven by the fact that being a fan provided them with a sense of belonging to the fan community. Likewise, in a sample of Japanese football fans after a natural disaster, Inoue et al. (2015) found that fans' perceived social support was a driver of the relationship between team identification and feeling a sense of cohesion in one's community and found, in another study, that team identification and life satisfaction were driven by the sense of belonging provided by the fan interest (Inoue et al., 2020).

---

spectrum, but rather that people on the spectrum may find kinship with others who share a similar fascination or passion for an interest (see Chapter 23).

[15] This is based on a premise we talk about in Chapter 21 and in a published psychological article showing that people tend to dislike those with unusual fan interests, in part, because of a presumption of dysfunction (among other things; Plante & Reysen, 2023).

As we point out in Chapter 6 and what was readily apparent in the previous paragraphs, most fan research in psychology focuses on sports fans. We also pointed out in Chapter 6 that most fan research focuses on fanship while omitting fandom. This is an important oversight: when pitted against each other, fandom—the more social component of fan identity—is a better predictor of well-being than fanship in samples of bronies (Edward et al., 2019), anime fans (Reysen et al., 2021), and furries (see Chapter 6 on fanship / fandom). This is because being a fan, despite seeming trivial, is an important group identity (Tajfel & Turner, 1979; Turner et al., 1987), one which is tied to better well-being, since humans are a social species and benefit from social support and coping resources provided by our groups (Haslam et al., 2018; Haslam et al., 2008, 2009). Indeed, belonging to more groups is often related to better well-being (e.g., Haslam et al., 2008), something just as true for fandoms as it is for other groups; in a sample of bronies, belonging to multiple fandoms was found to predict lower loneliness (Reysen, Plante, & Chadborn, 2022).

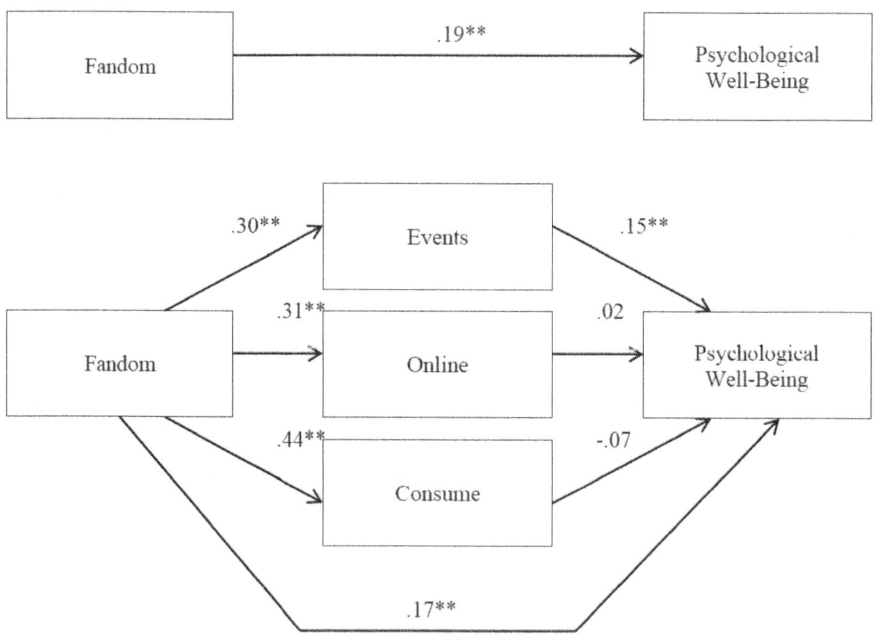

Figure 22.5. Mediation model of fandom predicting psychological well-being through fan activities in a sample of furries. Standardized betas are presented. ** $p < .01$.

But is this true for furries? The short answer is yes—furries are, in this regard, no different than any other group. In samples of U.S. undergraduate college students, furries, and anime fans, Reysen et al. (in press) found that fandom was a better predictor of psychological well-being than fanship. The groups did differ when it comes to what's driving this effect, however. In the students, the more friends they knew who were also fans of their favorite fan interest drove the relationship. In furries and anime fans, the effect was driven by attending in-person events, and not by online engagement or consumption of media (see Figure 22.5). In other words, for fans in general, social connections are a primary driver, or source, of fans' well-being, with data on furries and anime fans specifically suggesting that face-to-face interactions make it easier to forge these sorts of supportive social connections than online interactions.[16]

We've similarly shown the importance of interacting with other fans as an important part of well-being in furries and in other fan groups. For example, for furries, disclosing one's furry identity to others is associated with better well-being (Mock et al., 2013; Plante et al., 2014), in part because being able to be yourself around other people allows you to live more authentically and to avoid the anxiety of having to hide aspects of yourself from others. Other studies show that fans rate their well-being higher when they do so while at a fan event than they do if they're doing so at home (Ray et al., 2018; Wann et al., 2008), suggesting that being around fellow fans is beneficial for one's well-being. In fact, furries often talk about a condition called "post-con depression" which occurs after returning home from a furry convention, a finding that was tested and shown to be true (Plante et al., 2016; Roberts et al., 2017)! In other words, fans are generally at their best when they are surrounded by other fans, and show signs of reduced well-being when deprived of the chance to interact with other fans. This may be why many fans openly display symbols of the group (e.g., clothing) to signal to other potential fans in their day-to-day life as a way to make new friendships (Chadborn et al., 2017).[17]

---

[16] This isn't to say that it's impossible to forge significant and meaningful connections with other fans online (e.g., through forums, VRChat, and chat groups)—but it may be easier to do so face-to-face. After all, humans evolved in a time before online media existed, and so our instincts (e.g., learning to trust) are particularly attuned to in-person interaction.

[17] This presents a bit of a conundrum for furries, who are a stigmatized group. On the one hand, they may benefit from finding other fans, but, on the other hand, having other people find out that you're a furry might lead to stigma and ostracism. One

Intragroup Helping

Consistent with the social identity perspective discussed in Chapter 6, all else being equal, people tend to help members of their own group more than they'll help strangers or members of other groups (e.g., Balliet et al., 2014). This behavior holds just as true for fan groups as it does for other important group identities (e.g., race, gender, religion). For example, Platow et al. (1999) set up three charity donation tables at a sports event. The workers at the tables wore scarves that either matched the colors of one of the two teams playing or a neutral color. Fans gave more money to the donation table where the workers had scarves matching the colors of the home team. In another example, Levine et al. (2005) had participants think about their fan identity before asking them to walk to another building on their college campus. On the way to the next building, the participants saw someone fall and hurt themselves (this was a confederate—a person working for the experimenters). The confederate was either wearing a shirt with the participant's favorite team symbol, a rival team, or no symbol (i.e., neutral). Participants were more likely to stop and help the person wearing a shirt that had their favorite team logo compared to helping the person wearing a rival team's shirt or neutral shirt. In short—people help members of their own group—including fans helping other fans.

As you might expect, helping is beneficial—being helped by someone improves your well-being relative to not being helped (e.g., having someone lend you money in a time of need). Somewhat unexpectedly though, helping behavior also benefits the person *doing* the helping. For example, when participants in a study were asked to recall a time when they spent money on someone else (vs. themselves) they reported higher levels of happiness (e.g., Aknin et al., 2013).[18] The link between helping others and one's well-being extends beyond giving money as well. In a meta-analysis, acts of kindness were positively associated with subjective well-being (Curry et al., 2018). Volunteering one's time is associated with higher subjective well-being (Magnani & Zhu, 2018) while engaging in prosocial activism is related to subjective and psychological well-being (Klar & Kasser, 2009).

With this in mind, Reysen, Plante, Chadborn, Roberts, and Gerbasi (2022) surveyed bronies, anime fans, and furries to examine helping within one's fan group as a predictor of well-being. The results for furries showed

---

solution is to use symbols that are meaningless to non-fans, but known widely within the group (e.g., the logo for a popular furry website or company).

[18] Anyone who's a fan of giving a gift to someone recognizes this phenomenon: there's joy to be had in doing a kind deed for someone!

that greater fandom identification led to greater intragroup helping (the more of a fan you are, the more you help other fans) and that this was associated with greater psychological well-being (see Figure 22.6). Similar results were obtained for the other two fan groups as well, suggesting that this psychological process is not unique to furries, but rather is a general principle when it comes to fan groups in general (or any group, really). Not only do people benefit directly from receiving or giving help, but the exchanging of help may also open up opportunities to strengthen and deepen friendships or to build new friends who'll be there for you in a time of need, a source of resilience and coping in the long run.

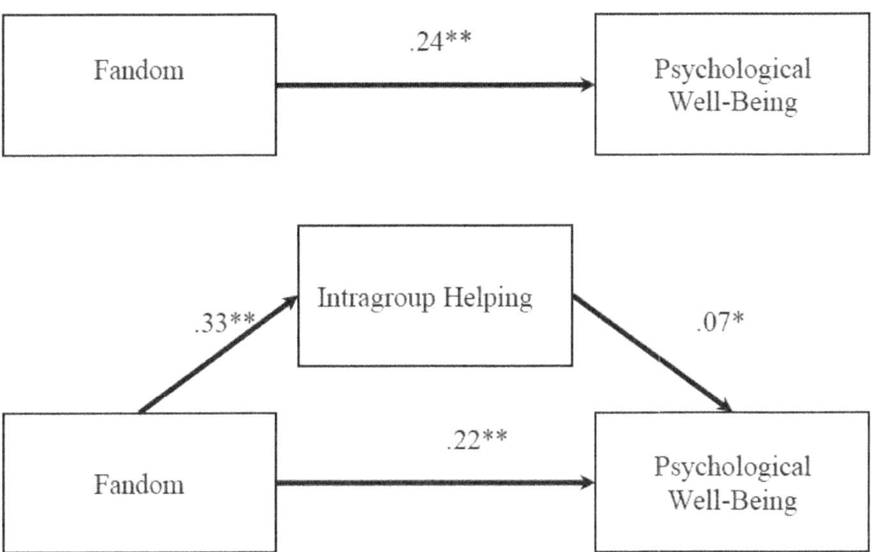

Figure 22.6. Mediation of the relationship between identification with the furry fandom and psychological well-being through intragroup helping. Standardized betas are presented. * $p < .05$, ** $p < .01$.

COVID-19

The evidence we've reviewed to this point shows that face-to-face interactions with other fans contribute to fans' well-being. So what happens when those face-to-face interactions are suddenly taken away? This is exactly what occurred during the global COVID-19 pandemic as countries went into lockdown, canceling conventions, and local gatherings and forcing people into isolation for months at a time. In the midst of this, we asked furries to complete measures of fandom identification, the extent to which people had adopted healthy coping strategies, stress due to COVID-19, and psychological well-being (Smodis-McCune et al., 2022). We tested a model in which the link between fandom identification and well-being was driven by adopting healthy problem-focused strategies (e.g., talking to other people, avoiding things like drinking) and asked whether the model worked differently for those low and high in stress related to the pandemic. The results supported the model, showing that the more stress a person was under, the stronger the link was between fandom, healthy coping styles, and well-being—those who were experiencing the most stress were leaning the most on the fandom to help them cope.

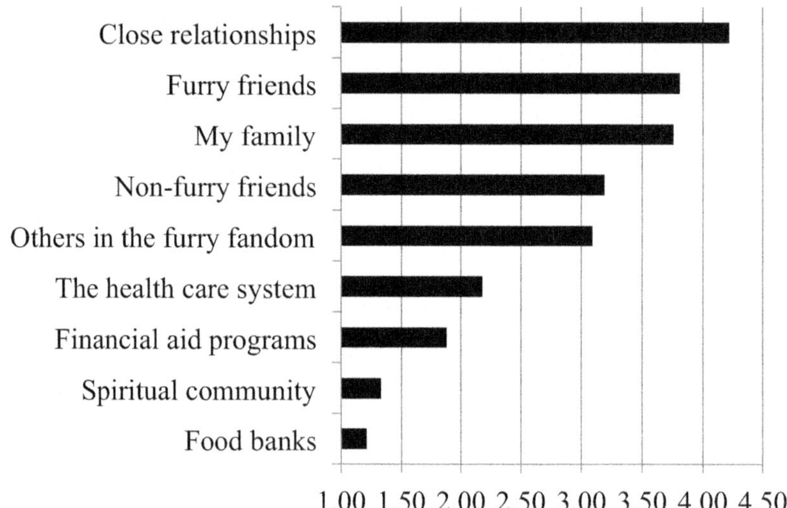

Figure 22.7. Ratings of sources of resources during the COVID-19 pandemic (7-point scale).

In a different study from 2020, we asked furries to rate the extent to which they relied on different resources to help them get through the COVID-19 pandemic (from 1 = *not at all* to 7 = *frequently*). As shown in Figure 22.7, furries' furry friends were the second-most common source of support, behind only close relationships (e.g., significant other). In fact, furries were about as likely to turn to their fellow furries as they were to turn to their family as a source of coping and support, illustrating how vital fellow furries are as a source of coping, support, and well-being in times of crisis. Even though furries were unable to congregate in person at conventions as they would have liked, they nevertheless benefitted from the connections they had forged in the fandom through their interaction with other furries online.

A Short Aside on Fursonas

A few years ago we noticed a small association between the number of fursonas that a furry had over their lifetime and their degree of self-esteem: more fursonas was related to lower self-esteem.[19] One reason we hypothesized for this relationship may be furries' degree of self-concept clarity. *Self-concept clarity* is defined as "the extent to which the contents of an individual's self-concept (e.g., perceived personal attributes) are clearly and confidently defined, internally consistent, and temporally stable" and positively related to self-esteem (Campbell et al., 1996, p. 141). In other words, a person with high self-concept clarity has a fairly clear and consistent sense of identity across situations, whereas a person low in self-concept clarity may struggle with questions of who they are and may find their thoughts and behaviors especially dictated by the situation around them.[20] If a furry is constantly changing their fursona, and if we assume that most fursonas are a reflection of the furry who created them (see Chapter 7 on this), this may be a sign that the person has a somewhat unstable self-concept.

To test this possibility, we asked a sample of furries how many fursonas they've had across their lifetime, as well as questions about their self-concept clarity and self-esteem. The results revealed that having fewer fursonas in one's life predicted higher self-concept clarity which, in turn, was associated with higher self-esteem, consistent with our hypothesis (see Figure 22.8).

Not long after talking about these results at Alamo City Furry Invasion in San Antonio (Texas), a furry approached us asking if the same is true for furries who have multiple fursonas at once (e.g., different fursonas for different aspects of one's personality).[21] As we usually do, we followed up

---

[19] You may recall, from Chapter 7, that most furries currently have a single fursona at any given time. And, while most furries have only ever had one fursona, it's also fairly common to have changed their fursona over time, though most only do so once or twice at most.

[20] Of course, as a social species, we're all affected, to one extent or another, by the situations around us. But for people with low self-concept clarity, they may be especially susceptible to situational influences.

[21] Most furries who've reported having more than one fursona ever tend to adopt fursonas in a serial fashion—identifying with one until it no longer represents them, before switching to another. A minority of furries do hold multiple fursonas, simultaneously.

the question with another study to get an answer. In the next study, we measured the number of fursonas participants have had over one's lifetime as well as how many fursonas they currently have. First off, we replicated the previous finding, showing that having more fursonas in the course of one's life was associated with less self-concept clarity and lower well-being. However, the same effect was *not* found for the number of fursonas a person currently has. In other words, the number of fursonas you've adopted and changed over time may be a sign of lower self-concept clarity, but holding multiple fursonas at once to represent different facets of yourself does not seem to be a sign of low self-concept clarity.[22]

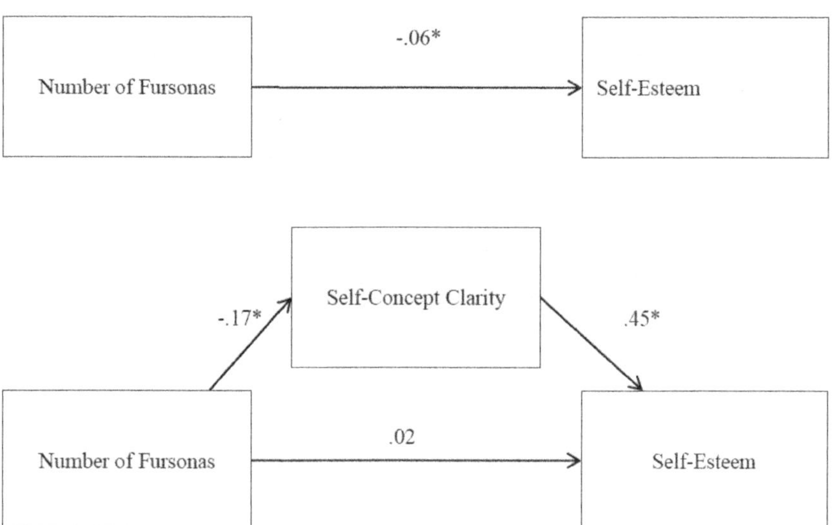

Figure 22.8. Number of fursonas in one's lifetime predicting self-esteem through self-concept clarity. Standardized betas are presented. * $p < .05$.

Conclusion

We've seen that well-being is a more complex and nuanced concept than it seems at first glance—countless researchers have come up with various ways to study it, and we'd prefer not to wade into that particular minefield and take a stance on what the "true" way to measure well-being is. Instead, across numerous studies comparing furries to other groups of interest, we've

[22] This aside is dedicated specifically to that one furry from Alamo City Furry Invasion who asked us this question—it may have taken us a few years to get you your answer, but we got it in the end!

made a point of assessing well-being in a variety of ways to determine whether the link between furry fandom identification and well-being is genuine or simply a quirk of one particular measure of well-being. The results overwhelmingly show that, yes, identifying with the furry fandom (rather than just identifying as a fan of furry content) is tied to one's well-being however you measure it, and that, despite misconceptions about furries as being maladjusted or dysfunctional, furries' well-being is comparably high to other groups, including other fans and undergraduate students. Given furries' relatively young age, it's unsurprising that furries tend to be less diagnosed with a variety of mental illnesses (although they were more likely to have been diagnosed on the autism spectrum, a finding likely based on their being fans, not furries, specifically).

Reasons for the link between being a furry and well-being are varied, although most have to do with the social benefits that accompany being a furry, including having more friends, being able to interact with more fellow furries in person, being better able to receive help from furries, especially during times of need (e.g., a global pandemic), and being able to adopt healthier coping strategies (e.g., turning to friends for support rather than turning to drugs and escapism). We also discussed an unexpected link between furry and well-being—the extent to which one's fursona may be a sign of self-concept clarity—illustrating just how deep the well of questions regarding the link between furry and well-being runs. As we said at the start of this chapter, we've only just scratched the surface when it comes to the link between the furry fandom and well-being, though, overall, we can comfortably conclude that the results of numerous studies point to being part of the furry fandom as being beneficial overall for most furries' well-being, a finding which contradicts lay beliefs furries and maladaptation (see Chapter 21).

References

Aknin, L. B., Barrington-Leigh, C. P., Dunn, E. W., Helliwell, J. F., Burns, J., Biswas-Diener, R., Kemeza, I., Nyende, P., Ashton-James, C. E., & Norton, M. I. (2013). Prosocial spending and well-being: Cross-cultural evidence for a psychological universal. *Journal of Personality and Social Psychology, 104*(4), 635–652. https://doi.org/10.1037/a0031578

Balliet, D., Wu, J., & De Dreu, C. K. W. (2014). Ingroup favoritism in cooperation: A meta-analysis. *Psychological Bulletin, 140*(6), 1556-1581. https://doi.org/10.1037/a0037737

Campbell, J. D., Trapnell, P. D., Heine, S. J., Katz, I. M., Lavallee, L. F., & Lehman, D. R. (1996). Self-concept clarity: Measurement, personality correlates, and cultural boundaries. *Journal of Personality and Social Psychology, 70*(1), 141-156. https://doi.org/10.1037/0022-3514.70.1.141

Chadborn, D., Edwards, P., & Reysen, S. (2017). Displaying fan identity to make friends. *Intensities: The Journal of Cult Media, 9,* 87-97.

Compton, W. C., Smith, M. L., Cornish, K. A., & Qualls, D. L. (1996). Factor structure of mental health measures. *Journal of Personality and Social Psychology, 71*(2), 406-413. https://doi.org/10.1037/0022-3514.71.2.406

Curry, O. S., Rowland, L. A., Van Lissa, C. J., Zlotowitz, S., McAlaney, J., & Whitehouse, H. (2018). *Journal of Experimental Social Psychology, 76,* 320-329. https://doi.org/10.1016/j.jesp.2018.02.014

Diener, E., & Diener, M. (1995). Cross-cultural correlates of life satisfaction and self-esteem. *Journal of Personality and Social Psychology, 68*(4), 653-663. https://doi.org/10.1037/0022-3514.68.4.653

Edwards, P., Chadborn, D. P., Plante, C., Reysen, S., & Redden, M. H. (2019). *Meet the bronies: The psychology of adult* My Little Pony *fandom*. McFarland & Company.

Haslam, C., Holme, A., Haslam, S. A., Iyer, A., Jetten, J., & Williams, W. H. (2008). Maintaining group memberships: Social identity continuity predicts well-being after stroke. *Neuropsychological Rehabilitation, 18*(5-6), 671-691. https://doi.org/10.1080/09602010701643449

Haslam, C., Jetten, J., Cruwys, T., Dingle, G. A., & Haslam, S. A. (2018). *The new psychology of health: Unlocking the social cure*. Routledge.

Haslam, S. A., Jetten, J., Postmes, T., & Haslam, C. (2009). Social identity, health and well-being: An emerging agenda for applied psychology. *Applied Psychology: An International Review, 58*(1), 1-23. https://doi.org/10.1111/j.1464-0597.2008.00379.x

Inoue, Y., Funk, D. C., Wann, D. L., Yoshida, M., & Nakazawa, M. (2015). Team identification and postdisaster social well-being: The mediating role of social support. *Group Dynamics: Theory, Research, and Practice, 19*(1), 31-44. https://doi.org/10.1037/gdn0000019

Inoue, Y., Wann, D. L., Lock, D., Sato, M., Moore, C., & Funk, D. C. (2020). Enhancing older adults' sense of belonging and subjective well-being through sports game attendance, team identification, and emotional support. *Journal of Aging and Health, 32*(7-8), 530-542. https://doi.org/10.1177/0898264319835654

Kashdan, T. B. (2004). The assessment of subjective well-being (issues raised by the Oxford happiness questionnaire). *Personality and Individual*

Differences, 36(5), 1225-1232. https://doi.org/10.1016/S0191-8869(03)00213-7

Keyes, C. L. M., Shmotkin, D., & Ryff, C. D. (2002). Optimizing well-being: The empirical encounter of two traditions. *Journal of Personality and Social Psychology, 82*(6), 1007-1022. https://doi.org/10.1037/0022-3514.82.6.1007

Klar, M., & Kasser, T. (2009). Some benefits of being an activist: Measuring activism and its role in psychological well-being. *Political Psychology, 30*(5), 755-777. https://doi.org/10.1111/j.1467-9221.2009.00724.x

Levine, M., Prosser, A., Evans, D., & Reicher, S. (2005). Identity and emergency intervention: How social group membership and inclusiveness of group boundaries shape helping behavior. *Personality and Social Psychology Bulletin, 31*(4), 443-453. https://doi.org/10.1177/0146167204271651

Linton, M. J., Dieppe, P., & Medina-Lara, A. (2016). Review of 99 self-report measures for assessing well-being in adults: exploring dimensions of well-being and developments over time. *BMJ Open, 6*(7), e010641. http://dx.doi.org/10.1136/bmjopen-2015-010641

Lyubomirsky, S., Tkach, C., & DiMatteo, M. R. (2006). What are the differences between happiness and self-esteem? *Social Indicators Research, 78*(3), 363-404. https://doi.org/10.1007/s11205-005-0213-y

Magnani, E., & Zhu, R. (2018). Does kindness lead to happiness? Voluntary activities and subjective well-being. *Journal of Behavioral and Experimental Economics, 77,* 20-28. https://doi.org/10.1016/j.socec.2018.09.009

McDowell, I. (2010). Measures of self-perceived well-being. *Journal of Psychosomatic Research, 69*(1), 69-79. https://doi.org/10.1016/j.jpsychores.2009.07.002

Mock, S. E., Plante, C. N., Reysen, S., & Gerbasi, K. C. (2013). Deeper leisure involvement as a coping resource in a stigmatized leisure context. *Leisure/Loisir, 37*(2), 111-126. https://doi.org/10.1080/14927713.2013.801152

Paradise, A. W., & Kernis, M. H. (2002). Self-esteem and psychological well-being: Implications of fragile self-esteem. *Journal of Social and Clinical Psychology, 21*(4), 345-361. https://doi.org/10.1521/jscp.21.4.345.22598

Plante, C. N., & Reysen, S. (2023). "They're just weird": Cognitive and affective mediators of the association between perceived nonprototypicality of, and prejudice toward, fan culture. *Psychology of*

Popular Media. Advanced online publication. https://doi.org/10.1037/ppm0000440
Plante, C. N., Reysen, S., Roberts, S. E., & Gerbasi, K. C. (2016). *Furscience! A summary of five years of research from the International Anthropomorphic Research Project*. Furscience.
Plante, C. N., Roberts, S., Reysen, S., & Gerbasi, K. (2014). Interaction of socio-structural characteristics predicts identity concealment and self-esteem in stigmatized minority group members. *Current Psychology, 33*(1), 3-19. https://doi.org/10.1007/s12144-013-9189-y
Platow, M. J., Durante, M., Williams, N., Garrett, M., Walshe, J., Cincotta, S., Lianos, G., & Barutchu, A. (1999). The contribution of sport fan social identity to the production of prosocial behavior. *Group Dynamics: Theory, Research, and Practice, 3*(2), 161-169. https://doi.org/10.1037/1089-2699.3.2.161
Ray, A., Plante, C. N., Reysen, S., Roberts, S. E., & Gerbasi, K. C. (2018). "You had to be there": Convention attendance and well-being in anime fans. *The Phoenix Papers, 3*(2), 20-30.
Reysen, S., & Branscombe, N. R. (2010). Fanship and fandom: Comparisons between sports fans and non-sports fans. *Journal of Sport Behavior, 33*(2), 176-193.
Reysen, S., Plante, C. N., & Chadborn, D. (2022). Perceived permeability of group boundaries as a mediator between belonging to multiple fandoms and loneliness. *Popular Culture Studies Journal, 10*(1), 315-333.
Reysen, S., Plante, C. N., Chadborn, D., Roberts, S. E., & Gerbasi, K. (2021). *Transported to another world: The psychology of anime fans*. International Anime Research Project.
Reysen, S., Plante, C. N., Chadborn, D., Roberts, S. E., & Gerbasi, K. C. (2022). Intragroup helping as a mediator of the association between fandom identification and self-esteem and well-being. *Leisure/Loisir, 46*(3), 321-345. https://dx.doi.org/10.1080/14927713.2021.1971553
Reysen, S. Plante, C. N., Chadborn, D., Roberts, S. E., Gerbasi, K. C., Miller, J., Gamboa, A., & Ray, A. (2018). A brief report on the prevalence of self-reported mood disorders, anxiety disorders, attention-deficit/hyperactivity disorder, and autism spectrum disorder in anime, brony, and furry fandoms. *The Phoenix Papers, 3*(2), 64-75.
Reysen, S., Plante, C. N., Lam, T. Q., Kamble, S. V., Katzarska-Miller, I., Assis, N., Packard, G., & Moretti, E. G. (2020). Maturity and well-being: Consistent associations across samples and measures. *Journal of*

Wellness, 2(2), Article 10, 1-8. https://doi.org/10.18297/jwellness/vol2/iss2/10

Reysen, S., Plante, C. N., Roberts, S. E., & Gerbasi, K. C. (2017). Anime fans to the rescue: Evidence of Daniel Wann's team identification-social psychological health model. *The Phoenix Papers, 3*(1), 237-247.

Reysen, S., Plante, C. N., Roberts, S. E., & Gerbasi, K. C. (in press). Social activities mediate the relation between fandom identification and psychological well-being. *Leisure Sciences*. https://doi.org/10.1080/01490400.2021.2023714

Roberts, S. E., Chong, M.-M., Shea, S., Doyle, K., Plante, C. N., Reysen, S., & Gerbasi, K. C. (2017). The highs, the lows, and post-con depression: A qualitative examination of furries' return home following an anthropomorphic convention. In T. Howl (Ed.), *Furries among us 2: More essays on furries by furries* (pp. 129-141). Thurston Howl Publications.

Ryan, R. M., & Deci, E. L. (2001). On happiness and human potentials: A review of research on hedonic and eudaimonic well-being. *Annual Review of Psychology, 52*(1), 141-166. https://doi.org/10.1146/annurev.psych.52.1.141

Ryff, C. D. (1989). Happiness is everything, or is it? Explorations on the meaning of psychological well-being. *Journal of Personality and Social Psychology, 57*(6), 1069-1081. https://doi.org/10.1037/0022-3514.57.6.1069

Smodis-McCune, V. A., Plante, C. N., Packard, G., Reysen, S., & Mendrek, A. (2022). COVID-19 stress moderates the mediational pathway of fandom identification on well-being through problem-focused coping. *The Phoenix Papers, 5*(1), 175-194. https://doi.org/10.31235/osf.io/e6baf

Wann, D. L. (2006). Understanding the positive social psychological benefits of sports team identification: The team identification-social psychological health model. *Group Dynamics: Theory, Research, and Practice, 10*(4), 272-296. https://doi.org/10.1037/1089-2699.10.4.272

Wann, D. L., Hackathorn, J., & Sherman, M. R. (2017). Testing the team identification-social psychological health model: Mediational relationships among team identification, sports fandom, sense of belonging, and meaning in life. *Group Dynamics: Theory, Research, and Practice, 21*(2), 94-107. https://doi.org/10.1037/gdn0000066

Wann, D. L., Martin, J., Grieve, F. G., & Gardner, L. (2008). Social connections at sporting events: Attendance and its positive relationship

with state social psychological well-being. *North American Journal of Psychology, 10*(2), 229-229.
Wann, D. L., Waddill, P. J., Brasher, M., & Ladd, S. (2015). Examining sports team identification, social connections, and social well-being among high school students. *Journal of Amateur Sport, 1*(2), 27-50. https://doi.org/10.17161/jas.v0i0.4931
Wann, D. L., Waddill, P. J., Polk, J., & Weaver, S. (2011). The team identification-social psychological health model: Sports fans gaining connections to others via sports team identification. *Group Dynamics: Theory, Research, and Practice, 15*(1), 75-89. https://doi.org/10.1037/a0020780

Chapter 23
Autism in the Furry Fandom: Opportunities, Barriers, and Recommendations

Elizabeth Fein, Amy Adelman

In Chapter 22, we discussed well-being and mental health in the furry fandom. As part of that conversation, we reviewed data showing that autism is significantly more prevalent in the furry fandom than it is in the general population. While autism is not a defining feature of the furry fandom (or of any fandom, for that matter), we did speculate that autistic people[1] may be especially drawn to fandoms like the furry fandom as an outlet for a strong, specific interest they may have and to be surrounded by like-minded others. For this reason, we've been studying autism and neurodivergence in the furry community over the past few years as part of an ongoing ethnographic study aimed at letting autistic people speak for themselves and elevating those voices to the forefront of conversations in the fandom. In this chapter, we report on some of the study's findings. We'll begin by briefly reviewing what autism is, describing the link between autism and the furry fandom, and going over the logistics of the ethnographic study. Next, we'll discuss the features of the furry fandom that make it especially appealing to people on the autism spectrum. Finally, we'll discuss some of the barriers to fandom participation that our participants pointed out and recommend some initiatives to begin addressing these barriers.

What is Autism?

The autism spectrum is extremely broad, and what it means to be "on the spectrum" (or to "have autism" or to "be autistic") is different for different people. Despite the considerable variability in how it manifests, we can point to a few general facts about autism.[2] For one thing, autism affects people

---

[1] Some readers may be put off by the use of the term "autistic people" because clinicians generally adopt person-first language to avoid dehumanizing clients (e.g., a "person with schizophrenia" rather than "a schizophrenic"). For this reason, readers might be tempted to use the term "person with autism." However, the term "autistic person" has been promoted by many autistic people as preferable because it is identity-focused, recognizing autism as a significant part of who they are, rather than as something that needs to be "cured" (Marschall, 2023).

[2] Note that everything we discuss in this chapter represents a broad strokes, generalized approach to autism. There is no such thing as an "average autistic person," nor would we expect everything we say here to apply to every autistic person.

from very early on in life and continues to affect them throughout their entire lives,[3] even if the way it affects two different people may differ from one another or even change over time. Autism tends to affect people in three main areas: social interactions and relationships, a preference for routine, repetition, or sameness, and differences in sensory sensitivity ranging from seeking out certain sensory input (e.g., oooh, shiny) to avoiding certain kinds of sensory input (e.g., ugh, florescent lights!). Autistic author Nick Walker defines autism as follows:

> *Autism is a genetically-based human neurological variant. The complex set of interrelated characteristics that distinguish autistic neurology from non-autistic neurology is not yet fully understood, but current evidence indicates that the central distinction is that autistic brains are characterized by particularly high levels of synaptic connectivity and responsiveness. This tends to make the autistic individual's subjective experience more intense and chaotic than that of non-autistic individuals: on both the sensorimotor and cognitive levels, the autistic mind tends to register more information, and the impact of each bit of information tends to be both stronger and less predictable.[...] Autism produces distinctive, atypical ways of thinking, moving, interaction, and sensory and cognitive processing.*

As a consequence, many people on the autism spectrum become easily overwhelmed in highly stimulating, chaotic environments and may seek quiet, order, or routine as a refuge.[4] Autistic people also tend to have a range of differences in the ways their brains process information: some may have difficulty recognizing faces, others may process verbal or auditory information more slowly, while others still are extremely sensitive to visual patterns. People on the autism spectrum also often have difficulty displaying and interpreting nonverbal social cues, such as body language, tone of voice,

---

[3] In other words, autism isn't something a person "grows out of," nor is it a "fad" or something they develop in their 20s. While it may take awhile for a person on the spectrum to be diagnosed—if they even seek diagnosis at all—they have likely been neurodivergent their entire life and have simply been good at masking (e.g., passing as neurotypical).

[4] To be clear, neurotypical people can also become overwhelmed in highly stimulating, chaotic environments, as anyone who's been to a child's birthday party can attest! But autistic people may have a lower threshold for being overwhelmed or be especially prone to overstimulation from particular stimuli.

facial expressions, and non-literal social communication (e.g., sarcasm). As a result, social interaction is often more difficult for them, making social relationships more of an effort, making school more of a struggle, hurting their job prospects, and generally impeding their ability to find a way to fit into a neurotypical society. For this reason, social isolation can be a significant threat to their quality of life.[5]

What's the Connection Between Autism and the Furry Fandom?

While people on the autism spectrum often struggle to find a place to belong, some find community, connection, and friendship through creative subcultures organized around shared interests. The furry fandom is one such example. Across several of our online and in-person studies of furries, 10–15% identify themselves as being on the autism spectrum—a number that includes those who've been formally diagnosed with autism, those who feel they're on the spectrum despite not having been formally diagnosed,[6] and those who are unsure whether they agree with the autism diagnosis they've received. For most of these people, their desire to be part of the furry fandom is motivated by the same thing that compels neurotypical furries to be part of the fandom: for entertainment, social connection, and as a source of social support.

About the Research Project

We've been interested in studying autism in the furry fandom because of its high prevalence of autistic people (relative to the general population). Moreover, conversations with autistic furries have suggested that furry may be an interest that's especially appealing for autistic people. For this reason,

---

[5] A common misconception is that autistic people are asocial and would prefer to be left to their solitude. Not only is this unfeasible (sooner or later you need to get groceries, deal with a landlord, or correspond with the government), but it overlooks the fact that autistic people are human beings too, with the same instinctive drive to be social. Just because they may find one or more aspects of social interaction difficult doesn't mean they don't share the same drive to interact with others!

[6] There are multitudinous reasons why an autistic person may not seek out formal diagnosis. One reason is because they lack the resources (e.g., money) to see a clinical psychologist and be formally diagnosed. Another is because they distrust or fear mistreatment from psychologists, whom they expect will try to "cure" their autism by trying to change who they are. A third reason is because they are opposed to the pathologizing or medicalizing of autism—the very premise of diagnosis is that neurodivergence is a problem. In contrast, many autistic people see their neurodivergence as a difference and nothing more, with any problems stemming not from being autistic but rather from being neurodivergent in a stubbornly unaccommodating and misunderstanding neurotypical world.

we've been studying autism in the furry fandom for years to learn from furries themselves how to better support and include people on the autism spectrum.

The project, an ethnographic study, involved a combination of nine focus groups (each of which had between three and ten participants) and 11 individual interviews, conducted in person at several large and small furry conventions in the U.S. and Canada. Any attendee over the age of 18 was welcome to participate in the focus groups, regardless of whether or not they identified as a person on the autism spectrum or had friends or family members on the spectrum. Of the 78 total people who participated, 37 reported having been diagnosed with an autism spectrum condition, 20 reported that they had never been formally diagnosed but thought they might be on the autism spectrum; 12 identified primarily as close family members of someone on the autism spectrum but not on the spectrum themselves, and 9 fell into none of the above categories.

The focus groups and interviews were organized around the following questions:

- Why participants thought that so many furries were on the autism spectrum relative to the general population?
- Are there things about the furry fandom that participants thought were particularly appealing for people on the autism spectrum?
- Does autism affect participants' involvement in the furry fandom and, if so how?
- Had participants met people on the autism spectrum through the furry fandom?
- What are some of the things that make it easy/difficult for people on the autism spectrum to participate in the furry fandom?

The interviews and focus groups were audio recorded and transcribed verbatim and were then thematically analyzed using the software program NVivo. The research team then identified significant themes in the responses and coded the responses according to those themes.

What Motivates People on the Autism Spectrum to Participate in the Furry Fandom?

Participants identified many reasons why the furry fandom might have such a high rate of people on the autism spectrum. The most common reason stated was the fandom's inclusive, accepting nature.

"I think what makes the fandom so appealing is most often the inclusiveness we have. We're a very diverse people. Doesn't matter what

gender, race, religion, even all the species, we all accept each other for who we are."

"It's difficult to be in a society where everyone thinks differently from you. And kinda in a different method of interpreting the world and understanding what's around you. And what I see in the community here is that you can throw that all aside and however you wanna interpret the world or interact with becomes acceptable. So you don't have to try to fit another way of thinking. So you can really just be yourself, basically."

Participants suggested that this inclusive nature is likely the result of many people in the furry community having had some experience of social exclusion or marginalization themselves, inspiring them to be accepting of others to avoid propagating the marginalization. This includes being accepting of those whose social behavior may come across as unusual.

"There's so much respect for people that are not quote-unquote normal, because I think most people in this fandom, at some point or another[,] have felt outcast, and they don't want anyone else to feel that way."

Beyond being an inclusive place, participants also indicated that the content of the fandom itself was also appealing to many people on the autism spectrum, with many stating that they had typically found animals easier to understand than humans.

"People who are on the autism spectrum, [it] may be that more of them just relate to animals more than humans. Because I've personally felt that, where it's like 'oh, wow, look at that human, they act completely different from me' but like look at a cat, now I see a lot of mannerisms in myself that I can see in a cat. I know how a cat speaks, but I don't know how a human speaks. So, maybe there's just a bunch of autistic people who identify more with other species than humans."

In a similar vein, some participants felt that if they could build a bridge between animals and humans through an interest in anthropomorphic animals, it might help them to forge deeper human connections.

"I understand the importance of being around people now; I didn't understand it in the past. But being around animals – at one point I would

[have been] perfectly fine with being, like, on an island, by myself, for the rest of my life, just around some wild animals. I thought that would be cool. It's kinda relieving to be able to bring it one step towards people."

For other participants, the artistic, creative side of the fandom was part of the draw.

"I know what made the fandom appealing to me, such as the diversity and the creativity that we have here."

"A lot of those kids [on the autism spectrum] tend to have some sort of artistic, creative side, whether that's musical, theatrical, drawing, painting. So I feel like those two things [creativity and animals], connected, make that connection to that furry fandom even stronger."

Many participants also noted that the draw of the furry fandom wasn't just in the content itself, but also the fact that many common fandom activities encourage participation for people on the autism spectrum. Such activities include board games, karaoke, and fursuit dances as structured opportunities which gave participants a chance to engage in shared activities, try new things, and put themselves out there in a supportive environment that minimized the chances of embarrassment.

"I've never liked to dance. I hated to dance, and I never wanted to participate in anything like that. And coming to [convention] last year in suit I just decided: you know what? I don't even have to be me. I can be something else for a moment. And I can go out to that dance and just pretend like I'm dancing. Pretend, you know, blend in with what everybody else is doing. And then, after I gave myself a chance to do that, it was like 'Wow, this is why these people are enjoying this. I now like it too'. And I love to dance now, and I dance all the time. And I went to the rave two nights ago and had a blast.[...] I prefer to dance in my fursuit, but I'm capable and do enjoy doing so without my fursuit now."

One such activity that encourages participation is the act of creating and roleplaying as one's fursona. Doing so gave participants a chance to safely experiment with being more outgoing and confident despite any negative past social experiences they may have had.

"When I was creating my character, um, I noticed that one of the main qualities I gave him—this was after some introspection—was confidence.[...] And I think that's what a lot of us here do in the furry community is we create an image of ourselves that we want other people to see, that the average society might not necessarily see that. But, in the furry community, we take everything at face value, basically. We see a person and that's who they say they are and we trust in that. And, even if it isn't true at the moment, it eventually becomes a reality. And I think that's what allows people on the autism spectrum to communicate within the community so easily compared to other aspects of society."

Creating a fursona was also seen by participants as a way for people on the spectrum to practice new ways of reacting to difficult situations.

"Sometimes when I'm feeling stressed or overstimulated, and having trouble dealing with that stress and being present in the moment, I think about my fursona and imagine what he would do, and use that as a way to get through a situation and process it differently. So I think that identifying with a fursona or animal alter ego is something that is, that can be, therapeutic for people on the autism spectrum."

Related to fursonas, fursuits are physical manifestations of a person's fursona. In addition to giving furries a chance to embody their fursonas in fandom spaces, they offer some very specific benefits for people on the autism spectrum. For those who have sensory sensitivities, fursuits can provide a buffer against sensory input, while also providing sensations of weight and pressure that some find calming.[7]

"If I was going to put a suit on, I would be a lot more social and willing to go up to people and hug people, 'cause I don't normally like to be touched, so, but if I'm in a suit, I'd be perfectly fine with that."

---

[7] We can't help pointing out that the aspects of wearing a fursuit that many neurotypical fursuiters find unappealing (their weight, the insensitivity that comes with having a layer of foam and fur between you and whatever you're seeing / hearing / touching) are the exact features that may make it so appealing to some neurodivergent furries! It's a great demonstration of how the same act can mean different things, and be used for different functions, by two different people, and only reinforces what we pointed out in Chapter 19, that furries are diverse when it comes to what motivates them to participate in the furry fandom!

In addition to providing a sensory buffer against external stimuli, fursuits can also provide a metaphorical buffer against the social judgment that many on the spectrum experience.

> *"I take everything personally[...]Those sort[s] of things don't roll off my shoulders. Whereas I put my fursuit on, and it just goes whoosh! and it helps – it's almost like it's like a second skin sort of thing. It's a harder kind of outer shell that takes the hit for me."*

Some pointed out that fursuit nonverbal communication is simplistic and deliberate and takes away the expectation for verbal communication. All of these things were a relief to many on the spectrum who typically struggle with the speed and nuance of everyday verbal and nonverbal social communication.

> *"Fursuiters tend – since they don't have the expression in the face – they tend to be more gesture-based and physical. And I think that's pretty appealing [for people on the spectrum] 'cause you have to perform, where you can get by with the most basic emotion that's easy to read, and there's no ambiguity there."*

Participants also pointed out that the consistent positivity of most fursuit expressions, along with the consistently positive response they evoke from others, took the pressure off of them to constantly have to make eye contact, assess the facial expressions of others, and change their facial expressions accordingly—all of which can be tiresome and anxiety-provoking for people on the spectrum.[8]

> *"People who are on the spectrum, it's very difficult for them to make eye contact with people. You know, it's kind of one of my problems. [...] But when you're looking at a fursuit, and a mask, it's only got one expression, and you don't need to worry about, you know, what's going on behind the*

---

[8] While he's not on the autism spectrum, one of this chapter's editors *can* attest to the fact that the first time he gave a guest lecture on furries while in his fursuit to a class of around 60 students, he dealt with the anxiety by keeping his eyes closed for most of the lecture. It was remarkably liberating to be able to interact with others without any need to think about the expression on his own face, so much so that the memory of it has stuck with him all these years later!

mask. It's always smiling. It's always happy. It's always charming and bright.[...]And when I put on a fursuit, at one of the conventions that I went to, everybody around me had a smile. They wanted to come up to me. They wanted to get pictures[...] That is a good confidence boost right there."

Another appeal of the furry fandom for those on the autism spectrum is how online and in-person socializing are frequently blended together. Many people on the spectrum find online socializing easier because it doesn't require nonverbal communication the way face-to-face interaction does. Furries commonly interact both online and in person, which helps participants on the spectrum to initially form social connections online, where they feel more comfortable, before continuing to grow these relationships in person. Moreover, online interactions make it necessary to make emotional nuance explicit (rather than inferring it through tone or facial expression), something which is sometimes carried over into in-person interactions in furry spaces.

"I would also like to point out that a huge, huge portion of the furry community is online. Like I know that we're at the convention right now, but online is entirely text-based. You don't have to worry about "Am I doing the right body language? Am I reading that body language right? What is that facial feature?" How you communicate only and entirely in text is a little different, and I find that it's much easier to read that, and people have to be much more explicit or have like, ascii [sic] emoticons, or something to convey tone that is much more difficult to do on the fly in real life. And I feel like that kind of carries over when people in the furry fandom meet in real life."

As a result of these and other inviting aspects of the furry fandom, many furries on the autism spectrum benefit from their participation in the fandom. One such benefit, already mentioned above, is decreased social anxiety at furry events.

"At furry conventions, I noticed that I have almost no social anxiety like I normally do."

Free from this social anxiety, autistic furries are more likely to expand their social repertoire, develop social skills, and forge social connections in ways that would have been hard for them to do otherwise.

> *"When I first joined the [fandom], that would be one of the few times in my life where I have found people who are of like mind, of same mind who I could be more open with, unlike the bullies and the other students that were at my schools[...] I had very, very few friends during the schooling."*

> *"That's something great about this fandom that makes it so easy for people with autism to get into it. It's very accepting, and, like, it's chill with whoever you are and whatever you like. It's like, "hey you're awesome no matter what". Looking back at my first con which was Anthrocon 2017, I was very different. I was very timid, shy, I was not as confident in how I spoke[...] Being able to portray yourself as someone that you want to be and something you really admire, being able to turn yourself into that over time, it's just, it's something really positive about this fandom."*

While it's easy to trivialize any benefits that may come from interacting with the furry fandom because of its fantastical / cartoonish content, many participants emphasized the significance of the benefits they've received, with some pointing out how the social support they received through the furry community had saved their life.

> *"Honest to God, without the support from the furry community, I probably would have offed myself a couple years ago. [...]Pretty much if I didn't stay home and play video games all day, I would have ended up dead in in [sic] a bathroom at school, cause [sic] it was that bad. I think without the support of the furry community, I probably would have. Even when you're at that low, it's nice knowing that people do care."*

Parents and family members of youth on the spectrum spoke about how happy they were to see their family members having positive experiences and forming social connections with others. In our focus groups, they were often tearful as they described watching their family member go off to have fun with others like them.

"You're so connected to your child, you can see how emotional you are getting 'cause you feel like you're helping your son to find something to connect to, and, which he may not necessarily get at when he was growing up: finding friends, keeping friends, interacting, and being invited to things. There are things that parents kinda look for, 'cause they want their child to be socialized and to have friends, and because we're not gonna be here all the time, so I worry about what that future brings."

Taken together, these results illustrate how deeply rewarding and fulfilling the furry fandom can be for people on the autism spectrum. It provides ample opportunity for social connection, skill-building, self-confidence, and fun. Contextualized thusly, it comes as no surprise why autistic furries are drawn to fandoms, both broadly and to the furry fandom specifically.

Barriers to Participation and Recommendations

While participants emphasized how accessible, welcoming, and transformative the furry fandom can be, they also mentioned some of the hurdles that can sometimes make it difficult to participate in the ways they want. In the following sections, we discuss some of these barriers to participation. Rather than just pointing out limitations, however, we'll take a proactive stance and suggest recommendations for those who run furry events, recommendations which come from participants themselves, with only a small amount of shaping based on our research and expertise.

Problem: "It Can Be Overwhelming"

In the hot, crowded, exciting, and highly social environment of a furry convention, it's easy for someone on the spectrum to get overwhelmed. Large crowds in particular may be difficult to navigate, both because of the intense social processing demands they pose and because people on the spectrum sometimes have problems shifting attention and processing visual-spatial information. As such, one can imagine the difficulty they may have charting a course through a fast-moving crowd to get to a booth in the dealer's den or trying to find someone to ask for directions to the lost-and-found with a noisy fursuit parade going by.

"What are some things that are difficult? Well, the fact that there are many people. It's a crowd. Especially at the conventions. It can be overwhelming. But usually like when it happens, I just focus on one direction. If I see someone I know, it's even better. For example, I know I have to go at [sic] the one panel. Well[,] I just focus on it. I don't look at

people, just go at the panel. Enjoy the panel. And then I go in the one direction again."

Some participants pointed out that clear signage and clear pathways can help, especially when others respect these principles.

"The number one thing I wish people would do to better accommodate people with autism is stop loitering in the walkways, get off to one side. So that people who want to move around or go someplace else can move. That's the easiest thing they could do, I think, to make this space friendlier."

Feeling overwhelmed can have entirely different origins at a furry convention, however: those sensitive to heat may find fursuiting to be a challenge.[9]

"It's unbearably hot[...]that for me is quite a hard thing, 'cause my heat tolerance isn't the best."

Regardless of its source, it doesn't take long to become overwhelmed, and it can happen without much warning. Under these circumstances it can be hard to find a place to recover—for example, your hotel room might be too far away or inaccessible behind a half-hour line for the elevator[10]—and you might not be able to explain to others what you need and why you need it.

"You might be able to go out and then socialize! Be [sic] nice! Have [sic] fun! But when you're done, you're done. You can't handle any more [sic]. And then people like to: "hey[sic], why are you – what's up?", you know,

---

[9] In fact, overheating in fursuit is a common enough problem at furry conventions that most have a "headless lounge," complete with water bottles, fans, and drying racks to allow fursuiters to quickly get out of suit and cool down in a spot away from the main convention space.

[10] This will be an all-too-familiar experience for anyone who's been to a furry convention of even moderate size. Despite being to dozens of furry conventions in different hotels, we can count on one hand the number of conventions that have done a reasonably good job managing elevator traffic to and from the hotel rooms. It's not uncommon for con attendees to plan their schedule around minimizing the number of times they have to return to their room because of this.

like "you [sic] were just fine a minute ago". And it's like - it's just too much. I can't handle it anymore."

Recommendation: Quiet Room

When people are overstimulated by sensory input and/or intense, ongoing social interaction, they often benefit from a retreat to a quiet, low-stimulation environment to chill out and recharge. Both those on the spectrum and those who have close friends, partners, or family on the spectrum often suggested that cons create a "quiet room" where participants can go when feeling overwhelmed. This was, by far, the most common suggestion we received for how to improve the experience of people on the spectrum at cons.

"In the last con I went to which was in April, they installed this new thing, which was basically they just had a room and it was completely quiet. They had, like, soundproofing on the walls, and they had stereo headphones that you could put on, and you could put on music, or you could just sit there and color, and it was very peaceful, and you could even like, they had beanbags and stuff, and you could just take a nap. And it was really, really nice. So, that would be wonderful."

Participants made several suggestions for how to make such a quiet room maximally effective, including:

- The room should be clearly advertised in the con booklet as a quiet space for those who need a quiet space to recharge, and it should be monitored/supervised to ensure it's used exclusively for this purpose (and not as a place to socialize with others)
- The room could be equipped with comfy chairs and/or beanbag pillows and comforting stuffed animals, headphones and/or earplugs, quiet activities such as coloring or small items to fidget with, and some basic necessities such as water, snacks, or tissue boxes
- To accommodate those with sensory sensitivities, the room would ideally have dimmable lights, avoid bright colors, and those monitoring the room could be asked to refrain from wearing strong perfumes and scents
- The room could contain cubicles or a few tent-like structures for those who need some time to be alone, although there should also be space for those who need someone to be with them (e.g., the room's main space)
- It should be located somewhere that's easy to find on a map, easily accessible from the main social spaces of the con, but also not adjacent to

loud or noisy areas. It would also be best if participants did not need to navigate elevators or escalators while trying to access this room

- People would ideally be allowed to remain in the room for as long as they need to, without time limits
- It would be helpful to have staff members check on the room occasionally, or even assign a staff member to the room itself to make sure it remains clean and tidy. Ideally, the staff member would some basic training in how to communicate effectively with people on the spectrum and with those who are feeling overwhelmed or distressed, although they would not be expected to take on a therapeutic role—their job is just to make sure the space remains available and accessible for those who need it

The above suggestions represent an ideal quiet space at a con, and we realize that many conventions will not have the resources to perfectly implement this idea. Even an approximation of this idea, something as simple as a plain, quiet room off to the side where no events are scheduled and which has been allocated simply as a quiet space would go a long way to helping attendees better enjoy the lively atmosphere of a furry convention with the comfort and security that comes from knowing they've got a place to go if it becomes a little too much for them.

Problem: "Despite the tools that the furry fandom can give to deal with interacting with people, at the end of the day, you still have to interact with them. It can still be hard."

Many participants noted that, despite how the fandom helped them with their social problems, they still experience difficulties with communication: trouble understanding others, trouble making themselves understood, and anxiety about how they'll be interpreted by others. While the furry fandom helps to reduce some of the challenges faced by people on the autism spectrum, the problems don't disappear completely.

> *"One of the things that's a little difficult is: a lot of what I'd struggled with is the body language of people— communicating with people and trying to read moods or how they use their body or their faces to portray how they feel. It's kind of daunting."*

Participants often report feeling anxious about encountering negative responses to their social communication blunders despite seeing the fandom overall as an accepting and nonjudgmental space.

"I always worry, like, are people being turned off because I – am I geeking out? And I am[,] I talking too much about this one thing? Am I talking too much? And so the self-consciousness—with any social interaction—it doesn't disappear entirely."

Participants note that once furries learn about these social communication challenges, they're often able and willing to be supportive.

"The friends that I met early on in the community, they were a little apprehensive of me at first, because I spoke very literally—very very literally. [...] And because of that, it made communicating a bit difficult, early on. But, I was very fortunate in that the people I met, though, once I told them like 'hey [sic] - I don't get this stuff sometimes, and if I misspeak just tell me', I was so fortunate that their response to that was, 'I will gladly work with you with whatever you need.'"

"Sometimes I don't always understand what other people mean, but after that[,] I just say, 'I'm Asperger, I have a problem understanding. Can you be more clear?' So usually they understand."

While the social communication challenges that come with autism, as well as other conditions (such as ADHD, dyslexia, auditory processing disabilities, and speech impediments), don't go away entirely in the furry fandom, they do become less of a problem, particularly when others around them are familiar with these challenges and have signaled that they are willing to help.

Recommendation: Education for the Fandom about Autism and Related Conditions

Participants suggested it would be helpful to hold a panel where participants could learn more about autism and related conditions from an accepting, nonjudgmental standpoint. In particular, when asked what they wished others in the fandom knew about their condition, participants on the autism spectrum mentioned several things:

- Some people have a hard time understanding rhetorical questions and sarcasm, and tend to take things literally
- Some people have a hard time recognizing and remembering faces (even if they can recognize and remember fursuits)
- Sometimes social conflicts arise because of misread social cues, rather than because of genuine disagreements or bad intentions

- When someone needs to leave a social situation quickly, it might be because they have become rapidly overwhelmed by external stimuli that they can no longer effectively process—it's nothing personal
- Just because someone was able to handle a situation effectively and comfortably in the past (even the very recent past), it doesn't mean that they can do so right now. Their internal and external circumstances may have changed in significant ways, and those changes may not be obvious to those around them
- People's experiences of time differ. While one person might be able to focus on the present moment, another may need to plan for the future to feel safe and secure
- People's thought patterns and thought processes differ, so what might be useful advice for one person might not be a useful coping strategy for another

Some participants also mentioned that it might be helpful for convention staff and security to have some basic training in how to interact effectively with a person on the autism spectrum who is in distress.

Recommendation: Celebrate Neurodiversity Ribbon

In addition to helping to raise awareness of neurodiversity in the fandom, many participants, both those on the spectrum and parents of youth on the spectrum, mentioned that it might be helpful to have a way to identify those who are familiar with autism and who can support the social and communication needs of neurodiverse people, or to help neurodivergent people to smooth over or avoid awkward social situations.[11]

> *"I would love it if there were some form of identifier for people who were autism friendly[...]That would identify for me, as a parent [of a person on the autism spectrum], saying, 'Oh this person understands, this communication is going to be a little bit of a challenge.' It occurred to me when you're talking about artists, they might not understand where we're coming from, when we're being real particular about something [when arranging a commission]. I would be more apt to even talk to an artist if I saw some identifier saying, 'I get it,' even if they're not on the spectrum themselves. So some sort of identifier. I don't know how you guys feel about that but as a parent that would help me out."*

---

[11] The term "neurodiversity" (when talking about a group, or "neurodivergent" when talking about an individual) is often used to describe the ways that people's brains are different in a way that recognizes and appreciates the difference without pathologizing it.

"For some people, like for me, I have trouble articulating quickly that I have problems with communication, so I think having a ribbon that just said 'neurodivergent' is kind of like having a button that says, 'Ask me about this...' So to me, that would be helpful. I know that's going to apply to everyone because not everyone wants to share that. But then you don't have to take a ribbon if you don't feel comfortable with it."

In several of the focus groups, participants discussed whether it would be better to have a ribbon specifically for people who identify as neurodivergent and another for people who are "neurodiversity friendly," or whether it would make more sense to have an image that functions like a Pride flag (used by both people who are LBGTQ and those supportive of LGBTQ people, without specifying which one you are). The consensus overall was that it would be best to have a ribbon that indicates the person is familiar with neurodiversity in some way, without suggesting people disclose whether or not they identify as "neurodivergent" themselves.

We recommend that the con offer a ribbon – perhaps a rainbow Möbius strip (a common symbol for neurodiversity) drawn as interlinked rainbow animal tails—with the phrase "Celebrate Neurodiversity."[12] The convention program and informational flyers could then explain the ribbon by saying something like:

"Our brains work in different ways, and some of us have different ways of communicating. Some of us might take a little longer to speak, or a little longer to understand what you say. Some of us talk about things we're interested in for a really long time, and have a hard time shifting gears quickly. Some of us love talking to lots of people—others get worn out quickly by social interaction and might have to disappear into our burrows if we feel overwhelmed. These differences are part of what makes our community so special—a place where cats and dogs and wolves and foxes and dragons and rabbits can all hang out together."

---

[12] Some readers might be familiar with images of puzzle pieces as a symbol of autism. To put it mildly, this symbolism is controversial, in no small part because of its affiliation with the organization Autism Speaks and its position, over the years, that autism is something that needs to be fixed or cured, its treatment of autism as a burden for parents, and its tendency to speak on behalf of autistic people rather than allowing for autistic self-advocacy.

"If someone's wearing a 'Celebrate Neurodiversity!' ribbon it means they know and appreciate that brains can work in a lot of different ways. If you're curious about how someone decided to wear a Celebrate Neurodiversity ribbon, try saying 'I like your ribbon!' and maybe they'll tell you more about why they're wearing it."

Several participants also mentioned that the furry fandom is already making inroads to support those with physical, perceptual, and communication differences because of its commitment to inclusiveness—in part because they're so accustomed to accommodating fursuiters, whose mobility, vision, and hearing, or ability to speak is often quite limited! Providing more education to the fandom about the ways people's brains, bodies, and communication styles differ and giving furries a way to signal that they understand and are willing to help will help people on the autism spectrum see and know that they can count on that support from their community.

Problem: "I don't know how to properly interact with all these people because I literally don't hardly know any of them."

Many participants on the autism spectrum reported that they have difficulty knowing how to socialize in larger groups, specifically when it comes to initiating conversations with strangers or getting involved in group conversations.

Participant: *It's kinda hard because I don't really know when to step in or when to make an interaction, something like that. It's really hard for me because I, well, I do have autism, and I don't know how to properly interact with all these people because I literally don't hardly know any of them.*
Researcher: *When does it work well for you?*
Participant: *Well when I know somebody, I guess. I can easily walk over to them and say, 'Hey I know you from this place' or something like that.*
Researcher: *And what makes it harder?*
Participant: *When I don't really know them because, well, they have a lot of other friends, and they don't really have time for somebody like me who they don't know.*

As a result, many autistic furries often felt lost or on the fringes in large social gatherings.[13]

> *"I've just never been very social[,] to begin with, and it can be hard for me to be the first one to start talking, or, you know, to speak up[...]Never quite sure what to say, unless, you know, someone like asks me a question, or we're already part way down some sort of conversational path, and I, you know, have a point to make.[...]Large groups have always made me nervous."*

Sometimes, this anxiousness stems from the misperception that everybody else knows each other and is already perfectly comfortable with one another.

> *"You'd be surprised at how many people are like: 'I'm just feeling shy because everyone else knows each other and I don't really know how to come in' and I'm like, all you need is someone to go, 'hey, come here. You can sit with us.' And that's what I try to do. [...]'Cause that's how I came in. I was scared. I didn't know where to come from. At my first meet, this little teeny meet. And I was terrified because I knew the person who took me there to go with 'cause I wanted to at least have someone I knew, but I literally – I went up and I was like 'I gotta get some courage,' and I talked to this one girl. Who happened to be my best friend now for four years."*

For some, having at least one good friend available to make introductions makes a huge difference when it comes to breaking the ice.

> *"When I first joined, I was kind of nervous to know anyone. And what actually helped me get into that was actually getting to meet a few people and actually them encouraging me to go out and have fun, and it turned out to be a really fun time."*

It's also generally easier to introduce oneself to individual furries than it is to inject oneself into larger group conversations.

---

[13] Not to sound like a broken record, these feelings are hardly unique to just neurodiverse furries; they're also commonly experienced by neurotypical furries! We've observed countless furries wandering around their first furry convention by themselves, too nervous to introduce themselves to others around them.

"I have some challenges too, such as being with big groups. So, I try to interact with a single individual at a time, in order to feel that I have the interaction that I need in order to bond a friendship."

Once a connection is made, interaction tends to become much easier.

"It's hard to, like, talk first, but once you do it gets easier. And then, like I said, it just spirals. It's like I get more confidence and then I can start talking to more people, and it feels comfortable doing that."

Recommendation: Small group events targeted toward people on the autism spectrum and those with other social communication differences.

To help people who struggle to meet people in large group settings like furry conventions, we recommend that cons consider hosting a "NeurodiFURsity Meet-and-Greet", where people with social communication challenges can connect with each other in smaller groups and where they don't have to wonder whether others around them are interested in talking with them.

"I think it might be helpful to have opportunities or sessions that people can go to that were smaller in number, that would help folks on the spectrum to feel a little bit easier or without hesitation. Because it's not easy, still."

The event might feature structured opportunities to talk with one other person at a time, with some participants suggesting something like a "speed dating" format where people get paired at random with other panel attendees for a short conversation, perhaps while choosing from a list of conversation topics.[14]

"If there were a session here that was written up, and it mentions that it's a session for folks on the spectrum to have an opportunity to meet people – but in this group session, it would be a one-on-one opportunity for a few minutes here and there in a more calm area, quiet area."

---

[14] In fact, some of our participants mentioned that our focus groups functioned in this way for them: giving them a chance to have a structured conversation in a small, quiet group.

Events like this would allow for people on the spectrum to connect and potentially strategize experiences and recommendations from their own experience. It would also have the potential to create a greater sense of belonging.

> *"I think part of it's like, if you realize you're not alone, it helps you. 'Cause sometimes you think 'oh [sic] it's just me, I'm the only one who's like freaking out, I'm the only one having problems' and you just build up this entire situation, so it's like you do like a meet-and-greet, see these other people like you, it's sometimes then easier."*

For this reason, we recommend that furry conventions consider creating opportunities for people who identify as neurodivergent to meet and socialize with each other.[15] These sorts of small-group, structured opportunities for people to interact one-on-one without the fear of questioning whether the other person wants to talk to you or struggling to think about what to talk about would help those who struggle with this initial hurdle to making friends. We would also recommend that any events like this be scheduled early on in the programming to allow attendees to benefit from the connections they've made by being able to interact with their newfound friends throughout the rest of the convention.

Recommendation: Volunteer guides

Another recommendation is to create a list of volunteers who are available to hang out with shy newcomers and show them around.

> *"During my first convention I was drowning, and I met up with someone during a writing panel who offered to just escort me around. And that, just having someone there who I could just rely on, I could just talk to them, that really helped me, so I didn't have to focus on everything around me."*

> *"Having someone who can sort of guide you around can be a huge help."*

There was a lot of discussion within the groups about how to set up such a listing, where to host it, and how people could join it, although no clear consensus about best practices emerged other than a sense that it might be similar to how people volunteer themselves as fursuit handlers. The

---

[15] Also, let's be real: The word "neurodifursity" is too good to pass up!

mechanics of how to handle this effectively will almost certainly differ from event to event. The important thing would be to ensure that anyone coming to a con and feeling shy about meeting new people could have at least one person they could buddy up with, someone to introduce them to others and to generally be a friend among the crowd.

Recommendation: Friendly Bench

Another related recommendation made by one of the editors of this chapter is to designate a bench or other such spot in the main convention space where attendees can sit if they want someone to strike up conversations with them. As opposed to informal hangout spaces such as the "Zoo," where people can go for all sorts of reasons, the Friendly Bench is explicitly marked as a place designated for people who want to meet and chat with other people they don't know. Indeed, one of the biggest points of anxiety when approaching someone to say hello is wondering whether that person is interested in talking to anyone. The friendly bench removes this ambiguity from the situation and encourages people to be more confident in striking up a conversation with a stranger. On the flip side, altruistic furries who want to help lonely or shy furries socialize can keep an eye out to see if anyone is sitting on the bench alone.

Problem: "I've been trying to go since I turned 18….Budgetary and financial reasons blocked me."

Many of our participants indicated that financial factors often kept them from participating in the fandom in all the ways that they wanted to.

> *"If you're not well off, and you don't make a lot of money, it's just hard and it's stressful."*

While money is often a restricting factor for many furries, given both the cost of fursuits and conventions (see Chapter 8), as well as the fact that many furries are young and in college (see Chapter 13), people on the autism spectrum often have the *additional* difficulty of struggling to find and keep employment. Parents of youth on the spectrum, in particular, often reported feeling torn between alarm at the cost of fursuits and appreciation for the social benefits they provide.

> *"I helped her buy her first [fursuit head]. I think it was nine hundred U.S. dollars - and I was gob-smacked. And I said, "Oh my god. Nine hundred." [...]Her dad was a bit deterred at the price, but I said, 'It's her money. Let her buy what she wants.' [...]She's very introverted, very quiet, but*

when she puts her mask on, her costume on, she becomes very exuberant, and she'll pose for pictures, and you know I never see her do that in her life. And so I think, for her—and for me—it's great to see her show different emotions."

Recommendation: Explore funding/discount opportunities for people on the spectrum

This was another one of the issues where few clear solutions emerged from our discussions. As a research team, we wondered whether there might be opportunities to create or find financial support for people on the autism spectrum who want to attend cons or purchase a fursuit but who are unable to do so due to a lack of financial resources. One challenge to a formal discount or scholarship program is that many people affected by autism or similar social communication challenges do not have a formal autism diagnosis, especially those who simply can't afford to get diagnosed. Another challenge is that discount programs targeted toward one group risk the appearance of inequity towards other groups who might also benefit from such support (e.g., furries who are from groups that are marginalized in other ways).[16]

Another option is to address this problem through informal collaborations: for example, a fursuit maker might be willing to work at a reduced cost with networks of therapists/clinicians who work with people on the autism spectrum. Another option might be to create a scholarship fund for people on the spectrum to receive assistance toward the cost of travel to a furry convention. While it might seem far-fetched at first to suggest that external sources might be willing to finance an endeavor like this, as the benefits of the furry community and of fursuiting for people on the spectrum become more widely known, those outside of the community may become more willing to financially support it.

Lastly, it's important to note, as many participants did, that purchasing an expensive fursuit or even attending a large national convention isn't necessary to be a part of the fandom. The continued proliferation of local events, the openness of the community to less elaborate forms of fursuiting, and the willingness of many members of the community to let friends try their suits on all help make these opportunities more available to a wider

[16] One might suggest that furries could raise money through charity drives for such a fund, given that furries are legendary fundraisers—nearly every furry convention includes a charity auction at the core of its programming. These charity efforts, however, are traditionally targeted towards animal welfare organizations.

range of people. The problem isn't a lack of money itself, it's a lack of access. As such, monetary solutions are far from the only option![17]

Problem: "To me, this is very strange"

Parents and other family members of youth on the autism spectrum occupy a unique position in the fandom. They're often learning about a new and unfamiliar culture and may feel uncertain about whether to support their family member's participation in that culture or, if they want to support it, they may not know how to support it. This is especially likely to be the case if they are a novice when it comes to the furry fandom. Speaking to this idea, family members of people on the spectrum often reported an initial sense of confusion or even unease about the fandom, one that generally dissipated once they became more familiar with the fandom.

> *"To me, this is very strange. That's why I came to see what it was about, why my son was so involved in it. But it makes more sense now to me. You know, the way he sees things, that's what I'm seeing now! Okay, I don't understand: why is this person dressed like this? Why does this person act like that? 'Cause that's not the way that I would interpret things. But he's very comfortable with it, and he's comfortable here. I think a lot of [the attention] needs to go to education, to people like me."*

Even so, parents still sometimes wonder how to help their child stay safe in what is in many ways an unfamiliar culture, especially given the centrality of the Internet.

> *"Can I ask a question? One of the things that that [sic] I really worried about, is like you were saying, you chat online with your friends – my [family member] doesn't have friends who he physically interacts with unless he's here. It's all online. And I worry all the time that there are gonna be people who take advantage of him. Can somebody talk to me about that, whether that's a legitimate concern?"*

---

[17] Another possible solution, for example, might be to solicit donations of "retired" fursuits to be tried on or shared with furries at a convention who are unable to afford their own fursuit but would still like the opportunity to try fursuiting for themselves. It wouldn't cost much—perhaps the cost of a good disinfectant spray to maintain good hygiene practices when sharing a fursuit!

They struggled with how they could continue the learning process that they and their family members were both having at furry events once they returned home.

> *"You don't know how much I wish there was a group like this near where we live where I could come and talk to people to figure out: [...]What am I doing that's helpful? What am I doing that's not helpful? I really wish there was some place [sic] I can go to talk with people!"*

Recommendation: Consider informational get-togethers for local parents throughout the year

This was another area where our group discussions did not produce a lot of clear answers. However, our research team had some thoughts on the matter. Furry conventions like Anthrocon offer welcoming and informative panels and events for parents accompanying their children to the con. However, these events only occur at some conventions, and even if when they do take place, they only occur at the convention, once a year. Get-togethers during the year for parents whose children are interested in the furry fandom might be helpful, especially for parents and family members of neurodivergent furries. Some sort of "Neurodiversity in the Furry Fandom" meetup in Pittsburgh or other major con-hosting cities, ideally before the convention itself, would allow parents to learn more about the event that their child wants to attend and can help the family prepare for the event, anticipate their child's needs, and even help them make friendships beforehand that they can nurture during the convention itself. And if demand in a single city is somewhat low, there's no reason why such a meet-up couldn't be offered virtually as well via videoconferencing.[18]

Problem: "The hard thing is, she can't tell anyone about it."

One concern, related to the above problem, that's frequently raised by parents and family members of people on the spectrum, is the societal stigma directed toward furries (see Chapter 21). Participants wondered whether this stigma was making it harder for their family members to benefit from the social support they find within the fandom and whether it could be used to benefit the rest of their lives, or whether they're forced to separate their furry interests from their day-to-day life.

---

[18] Once again, this is a suggestion with utility beyond parents and family members of neurodivergent furries: organizations such as Moms of Furries have shown that there is demand for events and resources aimed at parents with furry children.

"The hard thing is: she can't really tell anyone about it. And she makes these, you know, great costumes, and I'm always wanting to show my friends. You know, 'Look at these amazing things she made!' And my one friend is totally fine with it. But anybody else would kinda be like, you know, 'What are you doing? Why are you encouraging this kinda thing?'"

"I think the hardest is, and I noticed this with his school when he started coming up: that his peers were kinda at first mocking, you know, 'Oh man, I can't believe you're doing that.'"

Recommendation: Continued efforts to correct misperceptions and raise awareness about the fandom

As we've shown elsewhere in this book, popular stereotypes and misconceptions about furries make it difficult for them to integrate their fandom experiences—including the benefits they get from the fandom—into the rest of their life. Fortunately, the tide appears to be turning, including more recent positive coverage of the fandom in outlets like CNN and Rolling Stone, greater and more diverse participation in the fandom, and a more realistic picture of furries making their way into cultural awareness as furries gain control over their narrative (e.g., social media, fandom-produced documentaries). It's our hope that books like this one, the presentation of our research in academic journals, and the spreading of our work in popular media outlets will also help to raise cultural awareness about furries—both what they are and the fandom's benefits—both for autistic furries and for furries more generally.

Conclusion

The work represented here represents only a fraction of the questions that have arisen as we dig deeper into the topic of autism and neurodiversity in the furry fandom. The input of so many neurodiverse furries and their family members has helped to shed light on some of the unique problems they face in the fandom, as well as some potentially fruitful solutions. More importantly, they've also highlighted the reason why it's worth pushing so hard to make the fandom an inclusive place for neurodivergent furries—the benefits they've reported from the fandom make it clear that the furry fandom is absolutely a net positive for them. Moreover, learning about the needs and recommendations of neurodiverse furries has also helped shed light on some novel ways to benefit not just them, but the furry community as a whole—many of the recommendations they've made would almost certainly be welcomed by the furry fandom as a whole!

We look forward to continuing this research in the future, both as a way to find new questions and answers about neurodiversity in the furry fandom, but also as a way to give voice to those who have so much to teach us about the fandom and, yet, so often go unheard.

References

Marschall, A. (2023, January 12). Should you say "person with autism" or "autistic person"? *Verywellmind.* https://www.verywellmind.com/should-you-say-person-with-autism-or-autistic-person-5235429

Chapter 24
Furry Identity, Furry Capital, and Intrasonas: Merging Quantitative, Qualitative, and Anthropological Findings to form the Furry Fandom Identity Resolution Model (FFIRM)

Sharon E. Roberts

My foundational conceptions of *identity, identity formation*, and *identity resolution* are rooted in a theoretical framework initially put forward by Erik Erikson (1959, 1968, 1978) in the mid-20th century and further developed by other sociologists and psychologists over the next 50 years. *Identity* refers to an awareness of one's coherent sense of self that persists across space and time. A foundational feature of the Eriksonian definition of identity is that a *core* part of the person develops in youth and remains relatively consistent throughout adult life.

A person's identity emerges via a developmental activity called *identity formation,* which is broadly defined as the process by which an individual synthesizes adult roles, personal identifications, behaviors, and values—developmentally achieved within the context of a larger community that recognizes and validates the individual (Erikson, 1959, 1968). This is contrasted with *identity resolution*, which describes the completion of identity-related developmental tasks—resulting in the long-term commitments to adult roles and identifications that connect individuals to a larger community while simultaneously distinguishing them from others in that community (Roberts, 2007).

In our conception of its measurement, identity resolution includes the sub-elements of "self-identity formation (integration and differentiation) and social-identity formation (work roles and worldview)" (Roberts & Côté, 2014, p. 225). In other words, individuals going through the transition to adulthood must complete the developmental tasks associated with figuring out who they are and what they believe as it relates to (1) how this core sense of self fits within a larger community (*integration*) but (2) is simultaneously unique or niche within that community (*differentiation*) (Adams & Marshall, 1996), while (3) acquiring educational credentials or skills required for self-sustenance (*work roles*), and (4) developing a honed *worldview* that conveys purpose and meaning. Moreover, this understanding of identity not only incorporates concepts of *exploration* of—and *commitment* to—adult roles (Marcia, 1968, 1980), it highlights the *awareness* of that subjective sense of self and continuity (*ego identity*), behavioral continuity in interpersonal engagements (*personal identity*), and having one's social roles and statuses be recognized by a larger community (*social identity*) (Côté & Levine, 2002).

This theoretical model of identity formation incorporates elements of several disciplines, such as developmental psychology, social psychology, and sociology. I've used this framework in my academic career to study various concepts: education-to-work transitions in youth, risk-taking behaviors, eating disorders, and, of course, furries. For most of these topics, the strategy has been to measure various levels of identity formation or identity resolution and model how scores on these identity scales relate to other measured variables, such as parenting styles, preparedness for university, the frequency of episodic drinking, and mental health outcomes, like anxiety.

An Important Caveat: The "Furry Identity"

A *Daily Beast* reporter once asked me to clarify what I meant when I said people "identify as furries" or "furries identify with their fursonas." For me, the *furry identity* refers to *an individual's sense of self-awareness and feelings of belonging in a community that results from participation in the furry fandom*. In that definition, I'm adapting elements of a neo-Eriksonian approach to describe identity formation and meaningful self-discovery through anthropomorphic and community connections that many furries—but not all—experience because of being part of the furry fandom. When I speak of people *identifying as furries*, I am referring to their *felt* and *meaningful* association with the furry fandom, and when I say that "*furries identify with their fursonas*," I'm describing the meaningful connection that some furries develop with their fursonas that may *facilitate* exploration, self-reflection and awareness, and human growth. This identity work occurs because of a *voluntary* involvement in the community—an achieved status of *choice*. Thus, the furry identity is a type of content—*a social role*—that *supports* the identity developmental *process*.[1]

Importantly, the *furry identity* is *not* an orientation in *my* use of the term. It is *not* a protected status. It's a particularly meaningful fan identity that incorporates creative self-reflection and connection to something larger than the self. In the same way, someone might identify as a *Star Trek* fan and experience personal and meaningful *benefits* from the related activities—attending conventions, connecting with others in-person and online, and benefiting from any resulting self-reflection, sense of belonging to a community, and subsequent growth as a person that comes from being

---

[1] See Côté and Levine (2015, pp. 15-18) for a nuanced description of the differential dimensions of identity and self.

affiliated with a community. It's the furry *fandom*.[2] However, the terminology is also a bit tricky because there are other adaptations of the word *identity* that have more ascribed—and legally protected—status and meaning, such as *gender identity* and *racial identity*. In my current use of the term, the *furry identity* is *not* equivalent to these other statuses. It *is* important to note, though, that many furries *do* occupy protected statuses, such as being part of the 2SLGBTQI+ community.[3]

Identity Resolution in the Prolonged Transition to Adulthood

Knowing *who* you are is a key developmental task of adolescence and youth. Hundreds of researchers have espoused the benefits of identity formation and its relationship to a myriad of well-being outcomes. My dissertation research examined the benefits of identity resolution for mental health outcomes—the findings showed that the relationship between a well-developed, coherent sense of self and good mental health was strong (Roberts, 2007). However, the task of forming a coherent sense of self is taking longer than ever in Westernized societies. Some developmental psychologists have thought the shift to be so profound that they have termed a new developmental period between adolescence and adulthood—*emerging adulthood* (Arnett, 2000, 2004). And, while some proponents of emerging adulthood have described the lengthened transition to adulthood in benign terms, other researchers have expressed concerns that if identity formation stagnates, then it can have grave developmental consequences for the individual (Côté & Allahar, 2011; Côté & Levine, 2002, 2015; Roberts & Côté, 2014).

But *why* is the task of identity development becoming more difficult in contemporary Western societies? And what does this have to do with furries?

To answer these questions, I need to explain a bit more about identity development throughout human history and how it changed drastically to become a more daunting task—initially with the industrial revolution and then even more so with the information revolution.[4] You might wonder what

[2] However, I *do* think that the furry fandom, for some, offers its participants an exceptional opportunity for growth and connection to others that is life changing—more so than my own casual affiliation with being a Trekker. It was *this* aspect of the furry fandom that I will address in this chapter.

[3] 2SLGBTQI+ Two-Spirit (Indigenous), Lesbian, Gay, Bisexual, Transgender, Queer, Intersex

[4] As a sociologist, I have grave concerns for the consequences of the impending AI revolution for many reasons, but the greater disconnection of humans from experiencing meaningful interactions is certainly on the list.

this sociological theory has to do with furries, but, later in the chapter, I will propose a theory to explain how the furry fandom provides an antidote of sorts to the conditions of late-modern society for some furries. In order to explain what hardships the fandom is relieving, I first need to describe the problem.

In pre-industrial societies, people's sense of themselves came from their identifications with others in their community (Côté & Levine, 2002). For example, in pre-modern societies, most people had their "futures" established for them by their community's expectations, which were grounded in ancestral responsibility. They typically followed a pre-determined path rooted in family status, occupation, and gender roles. As Durkheim (1893) described it, there was a sameness of experience that held society together—he called it *mechanical solidarity*. The strong bonds of community that were rooted in primary group relations guided people's lives and shaped their actions—there was no need to "figure out" what a person was "going to be" when they "grew up" because existing structural expectations and norms already dictated the answers (Côté & Levine, 2002).[5]

However, the industrial revolution would permanently disrupt this kind of simple society as it ushered in an era of new work roles that required specialized skills (Durkheim called it a *complex division of labor*), selling one's labor for wages, more extensive education for children and youth, more migration into cities, less connection with others (i.e., a community of strangers), and smaller family sizes. The dominant influence of primary groups and close-knit communities on individuals in pre-modern societies shifted in modern societies to secondary groups that were impersonal. These new conditions of society led to greater isolation and increased the potential for anomie.[6] This was an extraordinary amount of change that occurred in a relatively short period of time, and as we moved past the industrial revolution and through the information revolution that began in the 1950s, each of these conditions deepened in their consequence as we entered the era of late-modernity (Côté & Levine, 2002).

Simultaneously, the emerging societal focus on individualism—where people have the "freedom" to "choose" their path in life—assigned

---

[5] To be clear, there was also *significant* inequality in pre-modern societies.

[6] Emile Durkheim's theory of anomie—a state of *normlessness*, where norms are defined as culturally appropriate expectations of behaviour that shape people's way of life—that was proposed in 1893 seems to have growing merit with every passing year (see English translation in Durkheim, 2014).

responsibility to the individual to pave their own path towards prosperity.[7] Exacerbating the situation *further* is the advancement in technology that places increasing pressures on youth to earn post-secondary credentials to be competitive in the job market (Côté & Allahar, 2011). While considered liberating for some, the ubiquity of "individual choice" in modern societies consequently ushers in new developmental vulnerabilities for identity formation (Schwartz, 2000), as "people lack a sense of self-determination rooted in a community of others, which was the basis of human identity throughout history" (Côté & Levine, 2002, p. 2).

Taken together, contemporary, Westernized societies have created the conditions where youth—if privileged enough—are often strong-armed into developmental moratoriums while they earn credentials to be competitive for jobs, manipulated by consumerism, and distracted by social media—all against the backdrop of too much choice, too little guidance, and a culture consumed with individualism (Côté & Allahar, 2011). Moreover, these societal and economic conditions resulted in a lengthened transition to adulthood—an ever-increasing protraction of the time it takes to become an independent and self-sufficient member of adult society with a fully-formed sense of self. This leaves members of post-industrial societies metaphorically—and sometimes literally—meandering about and looking for things to help them create meaning in their lives[8] or simply distract them sufficiently from dealing with their challenging realities of social isolation (Côté, 2000), which was further exacerbated by the pandemic. It is all taking its toll on human development, broadly, and on identity formation, specifically.

Various sociologists and psychologists[9] have been sounding the horn for some time regarding the harmful effects of late-modern society on the wellbeing of individuals. Researchers in the field have written about their

---

[7] In this type of environment, the focus on individual prosperity and the assumption of total agency also obscure the remaining structures (race, gender, socioeconomic status, age) that largely dictate our social standing in the world and act as invisible facilitators or barriers to opportunities (i.e., hidden but significant causes of inequality).

[8] It is one of the reasons, I think, that people get easily sucked into fads, celebrity obsession, extreme politics, cults, conspiracy theories, social media, etc.—isolated people are desperate to belong to something that is bigger than themselves (see *mass society* theory; Kornhauser, 1959).

[9] Erik Erikson, Anthony Giddens, James Côté, Anton Allahar, Steve Berman, Marilyn Montgomery, Paivi Fadjukoff, Seth Schwartz, to name only a few.

concerns regarding the consequences of youth not developing a core sense of self (e.g., Côté & Levine, 2002, 2015)—whether that be the result of consumer-driven distraction, loss of connection to a community of others who validate us, facing a tyranny of choices but lacking the guidance to pave a path forward (Schwartz, 2000), or even simply a belief that a core sense of self is simply no longer a necessary developmental outcome and that the fragmentation of self is liberating (Gergan, 1991). Interventions are needed, and the furry fandom may be a unique example of how people can cope with or compensate for the normative inadequacies of contemporary society. As such, the question of what youth in post-industrial societies do with leisure time during the prolonged transition to adulthood was of key concern to me, and I became interested in the identity development of furries as they participated in the furry fandom.

The Identity Issues Inventory

When I joined the International Anthropomorphic Research Project in 2011, one of my first queries of interest was to take the measure I had developed as part of my doctoral studies and apply it to the furry fandom. I was interested in seeing how people scored on the *Identity Issues Inventory (I_3),* which measures identity resolution (Roberts & Côté, 2014).[10] The I_3 has been translated into at least four languages and has been shown to be an effective tool for assessing identity resolution in many countries across the globe. It has the capacity to measure self-identity tasks (*integration* and *differentiation*) and social-identity tasks (*work* and *worldview*) while encompassing three levels of identity formation (*ego*, *personal*, and *social*). The full scale is comprised of 48 items (6-point Likert).[11] In this chapter, unless otherwise specified, the results of the I_3 are presented as an average out of 6 for each of the four subscales, out of 12 for self-identity tasks and social-identity tasks, and out of 24 for total identity resolution.

---

[10] At the time, I was a total furry-fandom outsider. I'm already on the record (see Roberts, 2022) stating that, when I started studying furries, I had nothing more to go on other than what I had learned from the infamous *CSI* episode. However, as someone who thrives on having an open mind and being open to new experiences, I decided to *not* take a leap of faith, but rather, take in the science and let the data tell me what conclusions I needed to draw about furries, in general, and identity formation in the furry fandom, specifically.

[11] Scales run from 1 to 6 (strongly disagree, disagree, somewhat disagree, somewhat agree, agree, strongly agree).

The Furry Fandom—Identity Resolution Data

General Performance of the I_3 in Furry Samples

Over the years, we've seen consistent findings related to the performance of the I_3. Across 14 online and convention samples that we gathered over 2011-2019, furries' average *integration* scores on the I_3 scale were consistently above the midpoint (3.5) and averaged 4.28 (4.0-4.5). Similar trends were found for *differentiation,* which averaged 4.20 (3.8-4.5). Across nine online and convention samples in the same timeframe, furries' *work* scores were also consistently above the scale's midpoint, with an average score of 4.19 (3.9-4.5), and *worldview* scores at 4.17 (3.6-4.7) were similar, too. Overall, this shows a remarkable consistency of the I_3's measurement in the furry fandom. The slight variability in the four subscales is also consistent with data previously gathered from non-furry samples that have documented slightly elevated integration scores and slightly lower worldview scores. Also consistent with our previous research, a 2017 online study found that all four subscales of the I_3 were positively associated with measures of psychological well-being.

However, the I_3 scores—by themselves, as numbers—don't inherently mean anything because we have yet to develop large-scale, nationally representative threshold metrics. From the studies we *have* completed, we can expect the I_3 scores of a sample to fluctuate as a product of other demographic variables. For example, we would expect to see that the I_3 scores would be higher in older (30+) people because they have—presumably—developed a core-sense of knowing themselves as they age, or we might expect that the subscale representing *work* scores would be lower for those who were still engaged in post-secondary education. Thus, because we know that the furry fandom largely remains a "young" fandom, we could expect to see lower I_3 scores than a control group that was comprised of older participants. The question then becomes, what happens to the I_3 scores if you factor in—account for—these other variables by controlling for them statistically? Will furries' I_3 scores be different than various control groups? Is there something about the furry fandom that facilitates identity growth?

Identity Resolution in Furries versus Non-Furries

Our next task was to see if we could detect any differences between a furry sample and a non-furry sample. As such, we collected data from a sample of 942 furries (with an average age of 26) and a control group of 782 non-furries (average age of 32). Using the measures of *integration* and *differentiation* and controlling for age, sex, income, liberalism, and education, we were able to compare identity scores for the two groups and found that furries had significantly higher scores on the I_3 and that cis-male identifying furries, in particular, seemed to benefit the most from participation in the fandom. This was an interesting finding because, in non-furry samples, *some* emerging data indicate that cis-men seem to be struggling with the tasks of identity formation (have lower scores) more so than cis-women. However, we wanted to see if the identity benefits for furries over non-furries were related to being a part of *any* fandom or if it was unique to the *furry* fandom.

Identity Resolution in Furries, Anime Fans, and Fantasy Sports Fans

Specifically, we wanted to examine the effects of self-created and other-created fantasy identities by studying three fan groups: furries, anime, and fantasy sports fans. Furries, who are bonded in the furry fandom by an interest in anthropomorphism, typically create a non-human animal-based identity called a *fursona*, which is often an idealized version of themselves. Anime fans, who typically enjoy Japanese-style animation, may cosplay as a favorite character (or multiple characters) in popular culture that is most often created by someone else (e.g., a comic book or movie character). Fantasy sports fans are usually fans of sports who engage in league competitions by becoming the "manager" of their own fantasy team. They pick players, and, based on the actual events of sporting teams, their teams compete in the fantasy league. (Fantasy) sports fans were chosen as the control group for this study because of the ubiquity of sports in North American culture.

We developed three customized, but conceptually identical, surveys so that they were suitable to administer to furries, anime fans, and fantasy sports fans and used 24 items of the I_3 to measure *integration, differentiation*, and *total self-identity tasks*.[12] In total, we surveyed 4,611 participants—1,031 furries from Anthrocon in Pennsylvania (with an average age of 26.8), 3,159 anime fans from A-Kon in Texas and online (average age of 23.3), and 421 fantasy sports fans online using Mechanical Turk (average age of 31.9).

We then conducted several general linear models and found that there was evidence to support our hypothesis that furries (controlling for age, sex, and fan commitment) had significantly higher scores—about 3 points—on the (total self-identity tasks) I_3 than anime fans, and almost 6 points more than fantasy sports fans. Overall, the analyses for the whole sample also showed that cis-males had lower scores than cis-females by about 2 points on the I_3, older age was a significant predictor of higher I_3 scores (about half a

[12] Total self-identity task scores ranged from 6-144.

point per year), and low levels of fan commitment were associated with *lower* I_3 scores by just over 6 points. All things considered, being a furry (compared to being an anime fan or fantasy sports fan), being cis-female,[13] being older in age, and having high levels of fan commitment each uniquely and significantly explains variability in participants' I_3 scores.

Identity Resolution in Furries: What's Happening?

So, what is going on in the furry fandom? In order to understand a bit more of the diversity of identity resolution in furries, we conducted a study examining the factors associated with self-identity tasks (summing integration and differentiation),[14] social-identity tasks (summing work and worldview),[15] and total identity (summing the four I_3 subscales).[16] The analysis included the data of 2,360 furries, and the results yielded some fascinating, preliminary insights into the factors that contribute to identity resolution in furries.

Using a combination of regression and general linear models, we assessed the unique influence of several variables. We included an overall measure of relative wellbeing by asking people to compare themselves to others in their country and report their relative standing (*ladder*, Likert-type scale from 1 = *worst off* to 10 = *best off*), identification with the furry fandom (*identification*, 1 = *strongly disagree* to 7 = *strongly agree*),[17] and *age*.[18]

---

[13] There was not enough transgender data across the three samples to conduct a more thorough and inclusive gender analysis.

[14] Total self-identity task score out of 12.

[15] Total social-identity task score out of 12.

[16] Total identity scores out of 24.

[17] In this analysis, a series of tests indicated that that being emotionally connected to the furry community (fandom, Likert-type scale from 1 = *strongly disagree* to 7 = *strongly agree*), identifying with being a furry (fanship, 1 = *strongly disagree* to 7 = *strongly agree*), and being emotionally connected with one's fursona (character, 1 = *strongly disagree* to 7 = *strongly agree*), if entered as three separate independent variables, were scoring too similarly to each other when used to predict identity. Within-subjects tests revealed no significant differences between fanship and fandom scores in this sample, and the fandom and fanship measures were highly correlated (r = .66). Also, regression analyses indicated that when fanship and fandom were entered sequentially into the model, fanship made no unique contribution (as would be indicated by a significant R2 increase), and preliminary tests via regression indicated that there may be concerns with multicollinearity in this analysis if the three variables were all used as independent variables. As such, the decision was made to combine the measures into a single item (Cronbach's alpha .84).

Participants were asked a series of questions about their furry-related fantasy engagement, including the extent to which their furry-themed fantasies involved them reimagining themselves as *different* from their day-to-day lives. We incorporated into the analyses two items that asked about the degree of felt difference between the self and the object of furry-themed fantasy. First, furries were asked about imagining themselves as a "better or more ideal" version of their current self (*ideal,* 1 = *never* to 7 = *always*) and, second, about imagining the self as a more "unlikeable or worse" version than their current self (*worse,* 1 = *never* to 7 = *always*). We also included a scale of being open about being a furry with family, friends, and day-to-day acquaintances (*open,* 1 = *strongly disagree* to 7 = *strongly agree*). Two categorical measures were also included. The first was an assessment of *autism*[19] and the second assessed the effects of *gender* using a variable that asked participants to indicate the *best* category that described them (cis-man, cis-woman, trans-man, trans-woman, and non-binary/gender fluid).[20]

Table 24.1 shows both the unstandardized and standardized coefficients[21] for the predictor variables for self-identity tasks, social-identity tasks, and total identity resolution as measured by the I_3. Broadly speaking, the overall results indicate that the independent variables (*ladder*, *identification*, *age*, *ideal*, *open*, *worse*, *autism*, and *gender*) each uniquely and significantly predict identity resolution—higher scores of relative well-being, greater identification with the fandom, being older, and being open about being a furry all uniquely predicted higher scores of self-identity tasks, social-identity tasks, and the total measure of identity. The two variables that measured furry-themed fantasy—fantasy about being *different* from the current self as a better / more ideal version of self and as a more unlikable / worse version of the self—predicted *lower* scores of identity. Finally, the variable *autism* was a significant predictor of identity resolution in all three models, but *gender* significantly predicted self-identity tasks (driving significance in total identity resolution, too) and not social-identity tasks.

So, what do these findings mean for predicting self- and social-identity resolution?

---

[18] Recategorized: 18-19, 20-25, 26-29, 30-45, 46+; these were more consistent with previous research using the I_3.

[19] Not on the spectrum, on the spectrum, and unsure if on the spectrum, where unsure was the reference category.

[20] For the gender variable, genderfluid / non-binary was the reference category.

[21] Please see the endnote for a lay explanation of unstandardized and standardized beta co-efficients.

Table 24.1. Regression: Unstandardized and standardized beta coefficients predicting identity tasks.

Variable	Self-Identity Tasks /12		Social-Identity Tasks /12		Total Identity Score /24	
	Unstand. Beta	Stand. Beta	Unstand. Beta	Stand. Beta	Unstand. Beta	Stand. Beta
Intercept	3.86**		3.91**		7.77	
Ladder	.18**	.17**	.31**	.28**	.50**	.24**
Identification	.39**	.24**	.26**	.15**	.65**	.21**
Age	.22**	.12**	.32**	.17**	.54**	.16**
Ideal	-.14**	-.13**	-.09**	-.08**	-.23**	-.11**
Openness as a furry	.20**	.17**	.11**	.10**	.31**	.14**
Worse	-.13**	-.11**	-.08**	-.07**	-.22**	-.10**
Autism						
Yes	.52*	-	.54*	-	1.06*	-
No	.72**	-	.84**	-	1.56**	-
Unsure (ref category)	0	-	0	-		-
Gender						
Cis-Man	.75**	-	.49		1.23**	-
Cis-Woman	.70**	-	.39		1.09*	-
Trans-Woman	.57*	-	.29		.86*	-
Trans-Man	.53*	-	.45		.98*	-
Genderfluid/non-bin (ref)	0		0	-	0	-
Adjusted R^2	.19		.18		.21	

Note. In the third model, total identity, the intercept is higher because it is adjusted for the 24-point scale. There were also significant differences between being on the spectrum (yes) and not being on the spectrum (no) for social-identity tasks. Both *yes* and *no* categories were significantly higher than the reference group, *unsure*. Gender categories (cis-man = cis-woman = trans-man = trans-woman) were all significantly higher than the non-binary/gender fluid category, but they were not significantly different from each other.

Ladder. Non-furry people who describe themselves as "further up the ladder" on this measure tend to be more settled in adulthood roles. Similarly, furries who see themselves as "better off" relative to others replicate this finding and have higher scores on identity resolution. In our analyses, these trends were strongest for social-identity resolution, which encompasses *work roles* and *worldview*. The results are also consistent with findings that people from lower-class backgrounds may face additional barriers with identity formation (e.g., Côté & Levine, 2015; Phillips & Pittman, 2003; Yoder, 2000).

Age. Like non-furry samples, as furries age, they continue to make significant identity gains—a finding that is consistent with previous research. Using the overall identity I_3 score as the outcome variable, subsequent analyses (estimated by the model and holding the other variables constant) indicate that there are significant gains in identity that are made as people age through emerging adulthood—18-19 (15.82), 20-25 (16.40), and 25-29 (17.26)—but then level off in middle adulthood (30-45 = 17.40; 46+ = 18.00). This indicates that furries—like other non-furries—are gaining a more honed sense of who they are during this important developmental period of life.

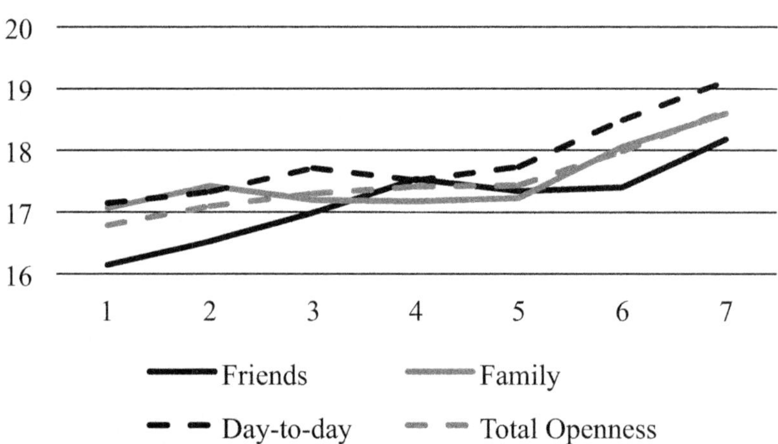

Figure 24.1. Openness.

Furry Identification. Strongly identifying with the fandom was especially important for self-identity resolution, but it was also a significant predictor of social-identity resolution, too. This makes sense because self-identity is represented by feelings of fitting into a larger community (integration) while also feeling unique (differentiation). The findings indicate that the more a person identifies with being a furry, is connected to the fandom, and identifies with their fursona, the higher they score on identity resolution. Furthermore, being open about being a furry was an important predictor of identity, which indicates that living authentically and openly is important for identity—something that is consistent with past research, too. Additional sub-analyses revealed that being open with friends and people in day-to-day life accounted for the biggest increases in identity resolution. Figure 24.1 shows the link between openness about being a furry with friends, family, and people in day-to-day life and total identity resolution scores.

The graph shows that, overall, lower scores of openness related to being a furry are associated with lower rates of identity resolution, and higher rates of disclosure are associated with more identity resolution. Those who can live most openly in their day-to-day lives (about 20% of the sample score 6-7 on the measure) are associated with the greatest identity benefits, while not being able to live authentically with friends about being a furry (about 11% of the sample score 1-2 on the measure, and, on average, had been in the fandom for significantly fewer years) predicts lower identity resolution. For most participants, openness with family has little variable effect (similar outcomes for those scoring 1-5)—unless the openness is relatively high (about 41% of the sample score a 6-7), in which case it predicts more identity resolution. All things considered, although furries tend to be the least open with people in their day-to-day lives and family, when they *are* open, they tend to also have higher levels of identity resolution. However, when furries are not open with their friends about being a furry, the negative effect is particularly pronounced, something that seems to be remedied for many furries by spending more years in the fandom.

Fantasy. Regarding the role of fantasy, furry-themed fantasies that emphasize the *difference* between the current self and the ideal self, and fantasies that result in imagining the self as *more unlikeable* or worse were both related to lower scores of identity resolution. This also means the inverse is true: people who score *lower* on having fantasies that see themselves as markedly different from their current self (i.e., they are *not* different) and people who score *lower* on fantasies depicting themselves as worse (i.e., they are *not* unlikable) would score *higher* on identity resolution. This is evidence that engaging in positive fantasy about furry-themed content that is consistent with the self and positive can predict beneficial identity outcomes, and they replicate previous findings about the effects of positive fantasy (Plante et al., 2017). The results are also consistent with an understudied, but growing, body of research that highlights the problems associated with developing a *negative identity* (Hihara et al., 2018).

Autism. Autism was a significant predictor of identity resolution in all three models. While the relative trends were consistent for not being on the spectrum (no = highest identity scores), being on the spectrum (yes = middle position), and feeling unsure about being on the spectrum (unsure = lowest identity scores), across the three measures of identity (self, social, and total identity tasks), they were not *uniformly* significant across the three models. Participants who were unsure if they were on the spectrum had estimated margin means scores[22] that were significantly lower (self 7.97, social 8.23, total 16.03) than those who said they had a diagnosis of autism (self 8.49, social 8.76, total 17.08). Participants in the *unsure* category also scored significantly lower on identity resolution than those who were not on the spectrum (self 8.70, social 8.98, total 17.58). We also detected a significant difference between those who were on the spectrum and those who were not on the spectrum for social-identity tasks (yes = 8.76 vs. no = 8.98), but not self-identity tasks (yes = 8.49 vs. no = 8.70). The significant difference between the yes and no autism categories in social-identity tasks was due to the slightly higher work and worldview scores for people who were not on the spectrum. All things considered, this suggests that neurodiversity may present additional challenges with resolving identity, which needs to be investigated further in future studies because of the large number of furries that are on the spectrum (approximately 15%). However, it also appears that the I_3 is tapping into the uncertainty (lower resolution) associated with being unsure if one is autistic or not.

Gender. Finally, gender was assessed, and some very interesting preliminary findings were revealed—largely that identity resolution is not particularly impacted by gender—including trans-men and trans-women. This is an interesting finding because previous research (e.g., Anderssen et al., 2020) shows transgender identity (both binary and non-binary) is often associated with a host of poorer wellbeing outcomes compared to cis-gender participants—largely because of discrimination. However, this was not the case in the furry sample. First, when the overall variable was included in the three models, it did not significantly predict differences in social-identity tasks at all.[23] And, in the case of self-identity (which was driving the

[22] Estimates that are calculated adjusting for all the variables in the model.
[23] In the raw data, where other variables are not accounted for, gender differences are found between cis-men and non-binary / genderfluid categories (others non-significant) for social-identity tasks. However, in the more complex analyses that include multiple independent variables, the finding becomes non-significant.

significant effects of total identity), when the effects of the other variables are accounted for in the model, it appears that lower total I_3 scores are significant only for those who are non-binary / genderfluid (16.06) compared to everyone else; there is no significant difference in the (estimated margin means) identity resolution of cis-men (17.30), cis-women (17.15), trans-women (16.94), and trans-men (17.04). It appears that the lower scores of self-identity resolution for non-binary/genderfluid people are driving any differences being detected in the models. Our future studies will be able to determine if this finding is unique to furries or remains constant in anime and sports fans.

Further studies will allow us to investigate these complex relationships. Overall, it appears that various aspects of identifying with the furry fandom are more strongly associated with the self-identity subscales on the I_3 than the social-identity subscales. This finding makes sense if we recognize that the main benefit of participating in the furry fandom is that it provides a mechanism for furries to build connections with others around their interest in anthropomorphic media. But what *exactly* are the mechanisms at play? Why does identification with *the furry fandom* yield such benefits for identity development—more so than other fan groups?

Formal and Informal Furry Norms: Anthropological and Sociological Insights

Over the past decade, so many members of the furry community have gifted our research team with rich insight into their lives.[24] In addition to collecting data from tens of thousands of furries, we have also been given permission and/or invited to have a presence at many fandom events and be

---

[24] They have done this through their incredible participation in our research projects, the likes of which I have never experienced anywhere else in my tenure as a researcher. A quick anecdote: I was recently part of a project related to understanding university students' felt sense of preparedness for academia. I worked with faculty members from several large universities in Southwestern Ontario. When discussing our response rates, one of my colleagues seemed delighted that we had obtained a 5% response rate. As part of the IARP conducting studies on furries, we regularly obtain response rates of more than 50% on our paper surveys that we hand out at conventions… It was a reality check for me on how exceptionally and generously engaged the furry community is with research. Furries regularly answer Furscience surveys that have 300 or more questions on them. Not only are the responses numerous, when they include qualitative responses, they are often *detailed.* Clearly, furries have invested significant time in facilitating our understanding of their community, and we are grateful to the furry community for sharing their lives with us.

included in furry online spaces. While the quantitative data show that there is a relationship between being part of the furry fandom and identity resolution, using the anthropological-like opportunity to be immersed in the furry community has allowed me to gain a privileged glimpse into the nuances of furries' varied interactions.

As a sociologist, I was struck by the amount of normative structure—both formal and informal—that exists in the furry fandom. The community expends a great deal of energy to help guide members on how to participate in the fandom both in-person at conventions and in online spaces. In the next sections, I will present an analysis of various components of the furry fandom and argue that they provide many benefits for its participants. I will document how these benefits can support both social-identity tasks and self-identity tasks in the overall development of identity formation. Specifically, under the broad categories of *community* and *fursona* fall a variety of skills development, encouragement, and validation that support both inclusion and individuation and may explain why we observe greater identity resolution in the furry fandom.

Community

First and foremost, when people join the furry fandom, they are joining a *community*. The fandom creates a vision and purpose of connection that has become a safe place of belonging that is helpful to many of its members. Connections are made and encouraged in online spaces (social media, Discord, furry artwork websites),[25] local meetups, and conventions. The community offers connections to others that are meaningful and create an atmosphere of inclusion, creates in-group feelings with unique language, acts as a self-correcting system, and actively targets the development of life skills.

Inclusion. One of the things that I hear repeatedly through interviews—and is supported by the quantitative data—is that the furry fandom is fiercely defensive of its position as an *inclusive* community. Inclusion in the fandom is a conscientious and active choice that people make while being part of the community. It resides as a communal goal, and there is omnipresent intolerance for people who act intolerantly. It is in these environments that furries begin to feel safe to be their most authentic selves and have that

[25] People should always exercise caution when engaging with strangers online. Parents should always use their best judgement when overseeing their children's online and in person activities, and the furry fandom should not be exempted from parental scrutiny.

authentic self be validated by a community that *sees* the real them (this finding was replicated across multiple studies).

My interviews on bullying gave me some insight into this. Many furries have experienced bullying in their lives—about twice the rates of non-furry samples. The interviews reveal that furries' experiences of being bullied are part of the reason that they are so fiercely protective of fandom spaces where vulnerable others can gather, whether that be at conventions or in online spaces. I observed a deep sense of generativity—the desire to help the next generation grow and thrive—from older furries regarding this issue. Some of the older furries—particularly those who are part of the 2SLGBTQI+ community—express how they experienced hardship around sexual orientation in a world that wasn't kind. The interviews revealed the personal meaning these furries derive from creating a space (e.g., online, conventions) where younger furries don't have to fear being their authentic selves. I interpret this generativity as a type of post-traumatic growth. In this way, not only is the focus on inclusion in the community helping younger furries in their development, but it is also providing furries who are in later phases of psychosocial development with an outlet to fulfill their human needs and have a purpose beyond the self.[26] The functionality of this should not be understated. Contemporary Westernized societies have become incompatible with large families and close communities, so accessing an outlet for this kind of growth is an asset to fundamental human wellness.

Language. As a non-furry outsider, coming into the fandom as a researcher gave me insights into how various ubiquitous phenomena *in* the fandom are also *completely* unique *to* the fandom. The furry fandom has developed its own vernacular that supports member inclusion and, subsequently, identity development. When I started the research, I didn't quite understand it, but furries were both patient with me and eager to share their language and culture. The uniqueness of the terms facilitates an "in-group" environment, where people can feel included because they "get" the meaning or joke. In fact, the adoption of furry monikers during the research—hello *Furscience*—was a way for us as researchers to give a wink and a nod to the community, too, as we went about disseminating our findings to the public. While the unique elements of language (often creating

[26] Erikson's work included an 8-stage model of psychosocial development. Stage five is identity versus confusion, and fidelity is the virtue acquired through resolution. Stage seven is generativity vs stagnation, and the virtue developed is care. While the focus of this chapter is on identity, the link to fandom and generativity is intriguing, too.

a furry pun and unique fursona names) operate functionally as a mechanism for creating in-group dynamics, they aren't used as a tool to create a hierarchical order within the fandom—although understanding the vernacular *does* give away that *Pink Fuzzy Bunny* who demands a litter box be placed in a bathroom is almost certainly trolling. The language is an overt, tangible mechanism for developing a sense of integration (belonging) while simultaneously having one's uniqueness validated (differentiation) within the community.

The Self-Correcting System. As a sociologist, it has been fascinating to observe the teaching and adherence of structural norms in the fandom, the dedication to intergenerational relationships and mentoring, and the community's commitment to being a self-correcting system. There are normative expectations of behavior in the fandom—some are as simple as "Don't make us look bad!" However, the mechanics behind the security at conventions were both unexpected and impressive. While a big convention like Anthrocon, which fosters an excellent relationship with the hosting city, may have a small, uniformed police presence at their convention, too, most of the security at conventions is provided by fan-friendly security, like *The Dorsai Irregulars*,[27] or a well-prepared team of furry volunteers. They wear visible clothing denoting their security status, and many are connected to their operational headquarters via two-way radios. It is *organized.* In these environments, especially the smaller conventions, furries tend to adopt strategies for oversight that closely resemble community policing, where they can address and deescalate problems proactively. The more intimate approach to security emphasizes the importance of community while providing a layer of safety. The various convention organizers also communicate with each other regularly to stay abreast of any possible issues or problematic attendees. Fascinatingly, the head of security at a convention once told me that during his post-event debrief with the venue, the hotel manager declared that, compared to the rather incident-free furry convention, they'd had *significantly more* problems with the recent *librarian's* convention.

Inevitably, though, distressing behavior can occur. Unlike other groups that sometimes try to cover up the evidence, furries tend to look out for each other by making people aware of what is happening. Grievous behavior can be met with shaming, ostracism, or banishment. In extreme (and rare) cases, where legal action is required, the community's rebuke is often fast and

[27] https://www.di.org

public. At one convention I attended, a known offender was spotted, reported, and removed from the property before any incident could occur.

In less severe cases of deviance, though, the fandom practices varying degrees of *reintegrative shaming* (Braithwaite, 1989), which has been theorized to be effective for correcting poor behavior. Depending on the nature of the conduct, subsequent chances for reintegration and inclusion often occur. In this way, community-based components of the fandom emulate elements of *authoritative parenting*—expectations of participants are warm and welcoming but balanced with strictness and expectations regarding appropriate behavior. I studied the effects of parenting styles on identity formation during adolescence for my master's thesis, and this combination of warmth and strictness in parenting is associated with gains in identity formation as well as a host of well-being outcomes (Steinberg, 2001). To me, it is conceivable that those same principles can be applied to a community and its members, especially when intergenerational care and norm development are so foundational to the community's identity.

Skill Development at Conventions. Conventions can become a meaningful way to develop skills, as the programming is specifically designed to help facilitate a sense of community and inclusion in the fandom. Panels are dedicated to topics like "so this is your first convention" that explicitly convey to newcomers the ropes of being at a convention. As a sociologist, I observed that these panels serve as institutionalized methods for teaching the community about the norms and expectations of participating in convention activities, community development, and skill enhancement. Some panels are dedicated to group performance activities, such as fursuiting, while others offer instructions on how to overcome personal barriers, such as shyness and anxiety. Some panels are dedicated to work-related skills, such as artistry, writing workshops, advice on publishing, and offering guidance on how to navigate post-secondary education. There are also many panels that are dedicated to creating inclusive and validating spaces for unique subgroups, whether that be a species of fursona (e.g., snow leopard) or sexual orientation (e.g., asexuality). Table 24.2 documents some examples of convention panels held at Anthrocon.

This is only a small selection of the incredibly diverse programming available. The panels are typically run by furries who have experience or expertise in an area and want to connect with others about that interest. The programming schedule is usually made available before the convention, and often furries will indicate their intention to attend specific events by creating a schedule of panels. The public displays of interest can be validating for the host as well as the attendees.

Table 24.2. Examples of Anthrocon convention programming.

Title of Panel	**Description**
So this is your first fur con	Is this your first time at a fur con? Or even just your first time at AnthroCon? Well come on in and learn the do's and Don'ts of being at a fur con. From dealing with fursuits to the 6/2/1 rule. A great way to start your convention and learn the best way to have a good time.
Public Fursuiting 101	Ever wanted to fursuit in public, host a fursuit outing, or do both, but were unsure how to go about it? Come to this exciting (and sometimes humorous) panel and learn the ins and outs of fursuiting in public!
Overcoming Shyness and Anxiety	This panel is geared toward the shy, anxious, and or socially awkward folk in the fandom. Do you have trouble making friends? Talking to artists? Finding communities? Going about your day? Then stop by and get some advice on where to start!
Out of the Spectrum: An Asexual Experience	[Redacted] and [Redacted] are pleased to present our informative panel about the asexual spectrum: OSAAE! This panel will be mostly focused on exploring the asexuality spectrum, exploring the relationship between those on the spectrum and the labels we use to define ourselves, as well as our personal experiences on the asexuality spectrum and how it affects our relationship with each other and friends. We will also provide a few general guidelines on how to communicate with others using these labels and the most important tools those outside of the spectrum have for understanding the asexual experience and end with a Q&A for any inquisitive folks looking to learn more. Please join us on this informative, entertaining, and explorative journey into the world of asexuality!
How Can We Organize the Furry Fandom?	Current events are stressful, and we could all use a break. But what constructive things could the furry fandom offer us in such trying times? In this newly

	updated and illustrated talk, we explore what makes furry special, what we can currently do to make a difference in today's world, and what exciting and hopeful futures we may build thanks to the best parts of the fandom.
Fursuit Character Development and Improv	The way you move and interact in your fursuit conveys the personality of the character you are trying to create. This panel teaches basic performance skills and includes improv exercises to practice these skills.
World's Worst Singalong	Sing along to popular and unpopular tunes with your fellow furs.
BIPOC Furry Meet and Greet:	A space for BIPOC (Black, Indigenous, and People of Color) to meet one another and share experiences and resources. The meet and greet will be a space where panelists will discuss their art, writing, and experiences in the furry fandom along with time for all those attending to participate and share their art and experiences with others. This panel will also briefly present on current research on queer and trans people of color in the furry fandom from furry doctoral researcher Sibyl.
Low Stimulation Room	Sometimes we need a quiet place to just re-collect ourselves. Please keep this space for individuals who need a moment to collect themselves.
Anthrocon Discord Server Meetup	Bring your memes and emojis and come join other users from the Anthrocon Discord Server for an in-person meetup.
Guide to Self-Publishing	In the modern world, there are so many ways to get your work out there. Whether it's serving a niche market, or simply choosing to go it yourself and reap more of the exact rewards, self-publishing through various sites and markets can be the right choice for many authors. We'll discuss how to get started, where to put your work and the extra bag of tricks you'll need for self-publishing success.
Badge Workshop	Bring your art supplies and make some badges as souvenirs for you and your friends! Some art supplies will be provided.
Finding a College	Furries are everywhere, even right under your nose!

Furry Group	Join us in finding out how you can find a fur group in college or how to create your own!
Doodling for Better Mental Health	Come join our Guest of Honour [Redacted] as she talks about doodling for better mental health. Dealing with stress, anxiety, PCD – there are ways that we can doodle ourselves out of those feelings.
The Dos and Donts of Owning Your First Fursuit	You've got the suit - now how do you take care of it? Come and let [Redacted] give you some advice from years of experience.
Cheetah/Snow Leopard Meet-Up:	Are you a cheetah? Part-cheetah? Cheetah-friendly? Come join us for an in-person meetup. (Sneps are okay too...)
Ancient Fursuiting: A Brief History of Animal Costume, Disguise and Ritual	Wearing animal costumes has a long and rich history. In this presentation and discussion, a Classical Studies professor will walk through how and why people in ancient Greece and Rome dressed as non-human animals, what that can tell us about their attitudes towards humanity and animality, and how that can deepen our understanding of the motivations for and experience of fursuiting today.
How to be Queer	This panel is for all those who are new to the wonderful rainbow world of the LGBTQ+ Community. I will be hosting a safe space for people to learn unfamiliar terminology that is often used in the LGBTQ+ Community, as well as being able to ask questions in an understanding environment.
University Furs Furmeet	Do you go to university? Want to talk to others of similar majors? Or maybe you'd like to make connections or ask for advice for college! If so, this is the panel for you!

Note. Source: https://anthrocon2022.sched.com/ (used with permission). Anthrocon is a registered service mark of Anthrocon, Inc., and is used with permission. Anthrocon is not a sponsor of this publication and the use of its programming materials herein does not imply endorsement by Anthrocon, Inc.

Fursonas

As described in the last section, the community provides many benefits to the members of the furry fandom. The community also provides normative structures that support the development of furries' fursonas, which in turn help reinforce stability in the community. This ultimately gives people a sense of participating in—and belonging to—something greater than themselves. Moreover, many of the fandom's cultural norms are, in part, owed to fursonas. The next section will describe the norms of fursonas, the utility of furry art, the exploration of fursona details, the use of fursona as an externalizing tool for problem-solving, and how fursonas can lead to growth.

Fursona Norms in Fandom Spaces

Demonstrations of how to develop and talk about fursonas are ubiquitous in the furry fandom. There is a normative—almost given—expectation that fursonas will be developed and used in communication with others. For example, when attending a furry convention, part of the registration process includes providing a badge name that must be worn at *all* times in con space.[28,29] However, the name displayed on the badge is typically a fursona (or other creative) name that attendees will use to interact with each other.

In addition to the attendee badge, many furries don one or more laminated badges of fursona artwork that dangle from a lanyard or wear furry paraphernalia. It is normative and acceptable for someone to begin a conversation with another attendee by commenting on a badge, fursona detail, fursuit, item of furry-themed clothing, ears, or tail. The ubiquity of the fursona and related physical objects help establish cultural norms surrounding their use for interactions while fostering a culture of inclusivity with easy "ins" to begin a dialogue with others.

In both in-person and online venues, I have witnessed people make themselves vulnerable by saying something akin to "I'm new here and hoping to make some friends." Responses are almost invariably some combination of "welcome!" and conversations that begin with "my fursona is X" or "my species is Y." These acceptable engagement strategies can remove communication barriers that are often experienced when amongst strangers. In one focus group, a young furry in her 20s said (paraphrased):

---

[28] Conventions require government-issued ID be produced to pick up registration badges. The information is linked to a registrant ID number that is printed on the badge with the username.

[29] Convention security personnel are posted at entry points and will refuse access to convention spaces unless a badge is prominently displayed. A forgotten badge must be retrieved, or else access is denied. (EE4MB)

"When I'm outside of the fandom, I don't speak to anyone. Ever. But here, I'm comfortable, and I can have conversations with people."

Moreover, the structure and rules around interactions using fursonas may be especially beneficial to furries on the spectrum, and the fandom's established norms can help ease anxiety.

Not only do fursonas connect furries around a common interest with like-minded others and enhance their sense of belonging to a community, but they simultaneously validate the unique components of the fursona identity. Moreover, when people articulate the details of their fursonas, they are creating opportunities for further development in the process. This became evident in my analyses of the functions of fursona art.

Fursona Art as Identity Exploration and Commitment

Anthropomorphic artwork is a huge part of the furry fandom, and much of the content features fursonas. For those furries who are not artistically gifted, they may commission an artist to create an image of their fursona. This requires that the patron articulate out loud very specific details about the fursona. Experienced artists may ask a series of questions about the character to elicit more details and improve accuracy—like a sketch artist. Sometimes the details of a fursona character are documented via a reference sheet. These are like blueprints for a character that signify little, but important, features of the character from multiple angles. Reference sheets are useful for art and fursuit commissions, as they increase the fidelity of artistic representations. If furries are artistically talented themselves, they may enjoy developing their characters via drawings. The details of the fursonas and the contents of the images, of course, need to be fleshed out in the process. Thus, using artwork to develop representations of the character can push the person to explore and commit to the details of the character and what they mean.

My studies also indicate that fursonas and creative furry art can give cover to people who want to explore their gender identity and sexual orientation. Both general audience and adult-themed art can be highly functional as a mechanism for exploring how one feels about important, but often sensitive, issues of identity as they contemplate their fursona in different roles, shapes, and situations. Furries may also share these fursona details or art with someone else to gauge their response on an issue that they are exploring—after all, it's not *them* who is [explored trait], it's *their fursona*. For other furries who are exploring elements of their sexual orientation or gender identity in non-furry social environments that are hostile towards diversity, this may be a safer way to *test the waters* on important issues of personal identity before they commit to what feels right for them.

Exploration of the Fursona Details

Furthering this last point, the details of the fursona convey important information to the self and others in the community. There is often significant emphasis placed on the associated meaning of the chosen species (or combination of species). Visual details and personality characteristics of the fursona are often chosen with care and are meaningful. For example, in one interview, a participant explained his relationship to his fursona in the following way:

> *"I [developed a] fursona 4 years ago. It's a wolf with orange eyes that glow. I chose a wolf... I'm noble and everything. I'm a cancer survivor of over 23 years, so the orange eyes are the fire that keep [sic] me going."*

Meaningful Reflection and Personal Growth

The details of fursona characteristics may continue to develop over time. When I've talked to furries about the evolution of their fursona, they sometimes say things like (paraphrased):

> *"When I joined the fandom, I first picked a fox for my fursona. I think I picked a fox because I thought it would help me to fit in when I joined the fandom because it's a popular species. However, after thinking about it more over two years, I think a hare is a better fit for me."*

In these conversations, the participant then describes the characteristics that they either have in common with the species or admire and aspire to be more like. In one interview, a furry described the three fursonas that he had developed sequentially. The first one was his fursona when he was a younger man, and for him, the species was aesthetically beautiful. At that time in his life, he was contending with body image issues, and the species selected represented more of what he wanted to be but in his mind was not. As he aged, the species changed and so did his relationship with his fursona. His current fursona represents strength, resilience, and wisdom, which in my observation of this remarkable, established, and articulate person, is an excellent representation of who he is at this point in his life.

The Fursona as an Externalizing Agent

In the non-furry world, there are many approaches that therapists take to help their clients gain perspective on situations in their lives. One popular approach is narrative therapy, which operates on the assumption that externalizing the problem from the individual—separating the identity from the problem—and creating a new construction of life, will help to resolve the issue (White & Epston, 1990). Monk and Gehart (2003) summarize it as such:

> *"Perhaps narrative therapy's most distinctive feature, externalizing conversation, creates space between clients and problems to counteract oppressive, problem-saturated stories, thereby altering clients' relations to problems."* (p. 25).

In narrative therapy, externalizing issues involves locating the challenges and separating them so that they become an *external* part of the person (as opposed to an internal part of a person). By deconstructing and externalizing problems (i.e., flaws) associated with individual identity and then reconstructing these problems as externalized identities, the individual begins to relate to alternative realities that reframe the individual via the narrative of their and relate to the new identity they have formed for themselves (Gehart, 2013).

From conducting interviews with participants about their experiences as furries, I both recognized and admired the externalizing potential of fursonas and how they could ease the process of self-reflection by cultivating a therapeutically safe distance from the issues of consideration. Here is how one participant described the process of using the fursona as a tool for active reflection:

> *"My fursona is a representation of myself. Sometimes what I do with my fursona is put him into a situation I'd like to see and think about how I'd react and how my fursona acts."*

Thus, fursonas can be used by furries to aid in problem-solving strategically and practically. Some of these strategies could be described as *furry therapy,* where a respected and meaningful fursona can help the individual externalize problems, reveal what is important to the person, and, ultimately, reveal a nuanced *awareness* of their *own* growth towards *becoming* their idealized version of self.

Identity Growth

All things considered, the fursona can have significant and positive implications for furries. We also have quantitative data that directly point to the utility of the fursona for identity development. For example, across many studies, furries generally agree that their fursona represents an idealized version of themselves, generally agree their fursona also represents their *actual* selves, and largely disagree that their fursona represents the worst parts of themselves. By talking about fursonas with other furries, a type of "correspondence" can be reinforced between the objective (how others see us) and subjective identities (how we see ourselves) of furries, which is crucial for identity formation (Côté & Levine, 2002).

Moreover, by engaging with others using fursonas, personal growth opportunities experienced through the fursona may translate to other real, tangible benefits for the individual, too. For example, someone who is shy, anxious, or autistic may benefit from the structured exchanges with others about their fursonas. In the process, they gain experience and confidence because of the positive interactions.

The Community and Fursona: Encouragement and Validation for Growth

Stepping outside of one's comfort zone can be challenging and anxiety-producing for some people. However, the fandom can gently encourage members to push themselves beyond their comfort zones. There are a couple of ways that this can happen. One is with the fursona, which permits reflexivity of the self and a safer way for people to validate versions of the self-being tried out through the fursona's identity exploration (e.g., gender identity and sexual orientation). Convention spaces offer another opportunity for going beyond the comfortable, whether it be letting loose at the rave, participating in a dance contest, running a panel of interest, or engaging in some kind of public speaking event.

Dr. Samuel Conway, who is the CEO of Anthrocon, once recounted to me one of his favorite stories that exemplified how he sees the fandom. Basically, a very shy person got up on stage, froze, and then ran off the stage. In any other environment, it is conceivable that such a scene might be met with laughter and admonishment, but not in *his* fandom. Instead, the crowd delivered rousing encouragement to the young person, who mustered the bravery to come back on the stage and perform to a cheering and reassuring ballroom of fellow furries. A broader goal of many furry events is to make people feel comfortable and welcome in ways that the rest of the world does not often accommodate—much less facilitate.

I have experienced this encouragement and warm welcome firsthand, too. When I brought a colleague of mine to his first furry convention at CanFURence, we were invited to speak at the opening ceremonies. Many of the convention people were familiar with me and Furscience because we had been attending the convention since its inception in 2016. My colleague took the microphone, rather tentatively, to introduce himself. He said a few words about who he was and gave a few demographic pieces of information about his lived experiences[30] and research expertise. To both of our utter amazement—and honestly to my joy—hundreds of people in a ballroom started chanting "One of us! One of us! One of us!" to greet my colleague and let him know that he was welcome to be a part of this fandom space. It has been close to half a decade since this happened, and I can still remember the feelings of gratitude I experienced for this amazing group of people who were doing what they could to make my colleague feel comfortable and included in a space that he entered three hours earlier as a total outsider.

My point in bringing up these two anecdotes is that they represent what I see also happening at the micro-level with people in the fandom. People who are shy, new, or don't feel like they quite fit in with the rest of the world are extended an opportunity and invitation to become something bigger than they were when they arrived, to leave feeling more included and more confident than when they started. It's not perfect. Bad things and experiences happen, too. People can go to a convention with high expectations and leave disappointed, and whenever large crowds congregate, there is the potential for things to not go exactly as planned. However, my overall takeaway from engaging in more than a decade of research in this community—quantitative and qualitative work that spans psychological, sociological, social work, and anthropological approaches—is that the fandom gives more than it takes for most people. It's giving people a way to engage in deep and safe reflection aided by the development of a fursona and a community that accepts that as a credible currency for communication. My interviews with older furries, especially, indicate that the history of bullying, the significant marginalization, and the occupation of diverse identities, make people want better for the next generation—an expression of generativity that I'm most interested in exploring further in future research projects.

---

[30] In the social work field, it is standard practice to disclose one's social locations before research (i.e., gender identity, sexual orientation, race, etc.).

A Tentative Framework: The Furry Fandom Identity Resolution Model (FFIRM)

I hope readers will be able to see the connections among how the community, fursona, and other fandom-related elements are working in tandem to create an antidote to the developmental hardships ushered in by late-modern society. Remember, in our theoretical understanding of *identity resolution*, self-identity tasks, and social-identity tasks encompass an *awareness* of the subjective sense of self and continuity (ego identity), *behavioral continuity* in interpersonal engagements (personal identity), and having one's social roles and statuses be *recognized by a larger community* (social identity). This process is facilitated by the actions of *exploring* and *committing* to adult roles. However, identity resolution is harder than ever in contemporary Western societies. We often miss feeling like we are *integrated* into *something* larger than ourselves. While strong messages of individualism may lead to searching for a unique sense of a *differentiated* self, the optimal developmental results are commonly sidelined by consumerism and fast fashion that is superficial, and does not foster deeper self-reflection. Moreover, the lengthened transition to adulthood means that we struggle to gain skills and take on adult *work roles* that allow for self-sufficiency. Finally, the ability to commit to values that are a part of something *bigger* than us—a coherent *worldview*—can be challenging without a greater social structure to give us guidance.

Our everyday existence is inundated with interactions that are impersonal or superficial, which can leave us feeling isolated and lonely. We repeatedly face too many choices but lack the guidance to help us navigate them. Unsurprisingly, these social conditions can culminate in an inability to meaningfully connect with others or receive recognition and feedback for emerging versions of the self as they are explored. However, the furry fandom helps to provide a type of antidote to the social and developmental conditions of late-modern society by giving furries community, a sense of purpose, structured exploration, a space for genuine authenticity, emotional and psychological support, encouragement for growth, personalized therapeutic tools, and a mechanism to actively engage in the hard work of meaningfully exploring and committing to a vision of self—all in a safe space that fiercely protects inclusion.

Furry Identity, Furry Capital, and Intrasonas: To be Continued…

After much reflection on the identity-related processes in the furry fandom, I developed a preliminary, fandom-based model of identity formation, the Furry Fandom Identity Resolution Model (FFIRM; see Figure 24.2).

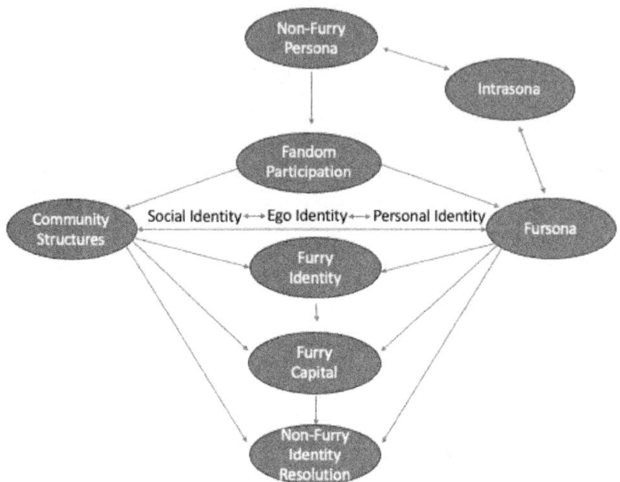

Figure 24.2. The Furry Fandom Identity Resolution Model (FFIRM).

The FFIRM is based on quantitative analysis about the relationships among fandom variables, qualitative interviews, and focus groups that have shed light on the meaningful interactions furries have with others in the community, and ethnographic observations of the normative structures that guide people in the furry fandom. It highlights the importance of people participating in the fandom, becoming involved in the community, and developing a fursona, which can facilitate the emergence of a robust sense of self that I am terming the *intrasona*. Under the right conditions, individuals who participate in the furry fandom can develop a *furry identity*, gain *furry capital*, and ultimately benefit from a strengthened, resolved, non-furry identity.

Furry Identity

I began the chapter by advancing a definition of *furry identity*, which refers to *an individual's sense of self-awareness and feelings of belonging in a community that results from participation in the furry fandom*. The definition encompasses a neo-Eriksonian identity approach and focuses on the meaningful self-discovery and community connections gained from participating in the fandom. In this interpretation, the *furry identity* is, in part, a type of *chosen*—sociologists would call it *achieved*—social identity.

However, like some *ascribed* social identities that are stigmatized, being a furry may elicit a salient need in individuals to understand *how* they fit into the stigmatized group, which subsequently triggers an extensive exploration of what it *means* to be a *person* in the community (Phinney & Rosenthal, 1992). Thus, furry identity is the product of meaningful participation in the furry fandom as it is channeled through (1) community experiences that establish strong norms and structures and (2) the development of one or more fursonas that are meaningful to the individual and facilitate interactions with others, exploration, and validation. The community and fursona factors reciprocally reinforce each other and support ego, personal, and social identity growth.

Furry Capital

In the FFIRM I'm proposing, high levels of furry identity have both direct and indirect benefits to the individual, including the potential growth of *furry capital.* I define furry capital as *the individual, group, and societal level benefits and skills that arise from engagement in the furry fandom*, particularly as they relate to social, relational, interpersonal, emotional, and psychological well-being. In addition to supporting the development of the furry identity (self-awareness and sense of belonging), robust and meaningful participation in the furry fandom via engagement with a responsive community and the fursona may also directly increase furry capital (transferable benefits and skills), too.

The benefits and skills developed from participation in the furry fandom via community and fursonas have relevance beyond the fandom, too. For example, navigating the uncertainty of a stigmatized identity can facilitate the development of important moral reasoning capabilities and self-efficacy (Côté & Levine, 2002, 2015; Phinney & Rosenthal, 1992). The fandom's strong contingent of 2SLGBTQI+ and other marginalized individuals may cultivate a safe environment to negotiate sexual orientation and gender identity, which consequently creates a social justice mindset that permeates non-furry worldviews. The use of fursonas helps to develop communication skills and personal problem-solving techniques. Self-esteem can emerge as a result of skill mastery (e.g., art) and deep attachment to the products of creative labor. Engagement in both the community and fursona can foster the courage required to live authentically, develop autonomy, and better resist the seduction of consumerism as a method for expressing oneself. Ultimately, furry capital may ease the challenges of navigating work, school, and personal relationships outside of the fandom, too, and support the resolution of a robust adult (non-furry) identity.

Intrasona

Another theoretical concept that may factor into the FFIRM and contribute to identity formation is the *intrasona.* I've picked this term (*intra* - Greek for within) because it implies an amelioration of dissonance—*the co-existence of selves, where the fursona (or essence) and persona are intrinsically linked and validated.*[31,32] Our research has explored various ways that furries' fursonas and personas can relate to each other. Often, the fursona is an idealized version of self, but the degree of similarity between the fursona and persona can be variable. For some furries, the fursona and persona grow closer together over time and may blossom into a new representation of self with high relevance to the individual. This *intrasona* informs both the fursona and persona with a fidelity of self that persists *both* inside and outside of the fandom. While I think it is more common that the persona takes on traits of the fursona over time, an intrasona might also emerge as a product of personal self-reflection that leads to a subsequent desire to modify an existing fursona so that it more accurately represents the emerging sense of self.

There may be cases where a furry with low levels of identity resolution develops an ideal sense of self through a fursona but experiences frustration because they are aware of the significant gap between the idealized self and their own sense of being—which our research indicates is associated with lower well-being outcomes. This is the situation where the fandom community can be especially valuable as a mechanism to facilitate growth. As people engage with others using the fursona, they gain experience, validation, and increasing comfort with themselves. My hope is that, with time, the gap between the idealized version of self, which is represented by the fursona, and the persona will close and a robust intrasona will emerge. My greater concern resides with the furries who have low levels of identity resolution and/or possess a negative identity *and* develop a fursona with *negative* attributes or characteristics. Our data detect correlations among negative fursonas and lower scores of wellbeing, like self-esteem. Moreover, my research in non-furry samples indicates that if people stagnate in identity development past the age of 30, then they tend to suffer from more mental

---

[31] I included the word *essence* because I think the concept of the intrasona might become relevant to our work with therian and otherkin communities, too. However, while the origins of therian / otherkin identities are less understood, they are fundamentally different from furries' experiences of a fursona.

[32] I also like the implied authenticity and nod to developmental growth that stems from active identity work.

health challenges (Roberts & Côté, 2014). By merging these two research findings, we can conceive of the situation where a person with unresolved identity will not experience the potential for positive developmental growth in the same way that others with lower identity resolution do when they create a fursona with positive attributes. Moreover, the deleterious effects of demonstrating poor identity resolution expressed through negative fursonas may become more pronounced in middle and late adulthood.

Some furries may change their fursona when another need becomes apparent, such as desiring new personality character traits, questioning gender identity, exploring sexual orientation, or a solution to boredom. Yet, for other furries, as they acquire the desired characteristics of a fursona through practice and engagement with others, they may no longer rely on—or connect with—a fursona as they once did. While some furries will keep the fursona in its current form or a slightly tweaked version, others may begin exploring a new or additional fursona that has variable personal meaning attached to it because the *need* for meaning is satiated.

There are also furries that join the fandom who have already completed the work of developing an adult identity. In this case, a meaningful fursona might simply represent a nod to the existing self with slight modifications (e.g., "My fursona *is* me, he just has a six-pack"[33]). The intrasona is predominantly driven by the non-furry persona. Furries may also create a fursona that is intentionally *radically* different from the persona, so no intrasona will emerge. In this case, the fursona is not so much contributing to identity development but, rather, may benefit the person by simply being an outlet for creativity in a world that often stifles it or by providing a fun avatar to facilitate engagement with others in the community. In this situation, people may still benefit from the development of a furry identity (awareness of belonging) and furry capital (skill development), it just may not affect a well-established sense of non-furry identity.

Limitations and Future Directions

There are some limitations to this thesis and permutations of fursona development that are currently unaccounted for in the FFIRM. That is because understanding furries' relationships with their fursonas is complicated. Many furries only have one fursona for their entire lives, but other furries have multiple fursonas—some sequentially and some simultaneously. When furries develop sequential fursonas or multiple fursonas, there may be greater affinity and closeness with the old fursona, the

[33] That's a real quote.

new fursona, *or* both. The new fursona could be more differentiated than the persona *or* more similar. Sequential and multiple fursonas could mean that furries experience all of the above. Future research will be focused on understanding the evolution of fursonas and developing these ideas further.

Further discussion is warranted regarding the directionality of the arrows in the FFIRM. In its current conception, participation in the fandom leads to furry identity, furry capital, and non-furry identity resolution for some furries. Participation in the fandom also holds the potential to foster the development of an intrasona, which can impact the persona and fursona bidirectionally. As our research findings continue to inform various parts of the FFIRM, and as we collect more longitudinal data, we will revisit our hypothesized directionality of the arrows in the FFIRM.

Future research should also assess how furry capital relates to other models of capital. For example, Côté's *Identity Capital Model (ICM)*[34] highlights that "certain context-specific resources are particularly important in societies where many roles and statuses are no longer strictly ascribed, but there is little structure to replace the ascriptive processes" (Côté, 2016, p. 5). Perhaps furry capital is a contextually specific form of identity capital that provides benefits through *social capital* (Putnam, 2000) connections, which in turn support various self-identity strengths, like integration and differentiation. Whether furry capital is re-conceptualized as a unique resource/barrier under the existing identity capital model, overlaps fully or partially with other elements already encompassed by the ICM (like social capital), or situates itself adjacent to existing concepts of capital altogether remains a question. Côté and Levine (2015) also argue that there is a need for greater focus on understanding the social contexts of identity development. The ability of the furry fandom to support ego, personal, and social identities, facilitate transcendence of connections from place to space, and generate a mechanism for creating, nurturing, and validating reflection that culminates in identity exploration and commitment to both self and societal concepts is something that I look forward to exploring further.

In conclusion, the furry identity, furry capital, and intrasona ideas tap into the notion that the furry fandom, for some, can help mobilize a person's best self and lead to skill acquisition, social benefits, opportunities, and personal fulfillment. While the model proposed here describes what I theorize is happening when people participate in the furry fandom, the basic structure of the FFIRM could also apply to other fandoms or leisure activities that offer

---

[34] Chapter 6 in Côté and Levine (2015) is a great introduction to the concept and written for a general audience.

the opportunity for connection with like-minded others and are facilitated by meaningful, self-created characters. Ultimately, more time, data, and observations are needed to map out the theoretical model of what is happening in the furry fandom and how it relates to identity resolution.

References

Adams, G. & Marshall, S. (1996). A developmental social psychology of identity: Understanding the person-in-context. *Journal of Adolescence, 19,* 429-442. https://doi.org/10.1006/jado.1996.0041

Anderssen, N., Sivertsen, B., Lønning, K. J., & Malterud, K. (2020). Life satisfaction and mental health among transgender students in Norway. *BMC Public Health, 20,* Article 138. https://doi.org/10.1186/s12889-020-8228-5

Arnett, J. J. (2000). Emerging adulthood: A theory of development from the late teens through the twenties. *American Psychologist, 55*(5), 469-480. https://doi.org/10.1037/0003-066X.55.5.469

Arnett, J. J. (2004). *Emerging adulthood: The winding road from the late teens through the twenties*. Oxford University Press.

Braithwaite, J. (1989). *Crime, shame and reintegration*. Cambridge University Press.

Côté, J. E. (2000). *Arrested adulthood: The changing nature of maturity and identity*. NYU Press.

Côté, J. (2006). Identity studies: How close are we to developing a social science of identity?—An appraisal of the field. *Identity, 6*(1), 3-25. https://doi.org/10.1207/s1532706xid0601_2

Côté, J. E. (2016). *The identity capital model: A handbook of theory, methods, and findings*. Unpublished manuscript, Department of Sociology, The University of Western Ontario, London, Ontario, Canada.

Côté, J. E., & Allahar, A. (2011). *Lowering higher education: The rise of corporate universities and the fall of liberal education*. University of Toronto Press.

Côté, J. E., & Levine, C. (2002). *Identity formation, agency and culture: A social psychological synthesis*. Laurence Erlbaum Associates Inc.

Côté, J. E., & Levine, C. (2015). *Identity formation, youth, and development: A simplified approach*. Psychology Press.

Durkheim, E. (2014). *The division of labor in society*. Simon and Schuster.

Erikson, E. (1959). *Identity and the life cycle. Selected papers by Erik Erikson*. International University Press.

Erikson, E. H. (1968). *Identity: Youth and crisis*. Norton.

Erikson, E. H. (1978). *Adulthood.* W. W. Norton.

Gergen, K. J. (1991). *The saturated self: Dilemmas of identity in contemporary life*. Basic Books.

Gehart, D. R. (2013). *Mastering competencies in family therapy: A practical approach to theory and clinical case documentation*. Cengage Learning.

Hihara, S., Sugimura, K., & Syed, M. (2018). Forming a negative identity in contemporary society: Shedding light on the most problematic identity resolution. *Identity, 18*(4), 325-333. https://doi.org/10.1080/15283488.2018.1524329

Kornhauser, W. (1959) *The politics of mass society*. Free Press.

Marcia, J. (1964). *Determination and construct validity of ego identity status*. Unpublished doctoral dissertation. University of Michigan, Ann Arbor, Michigan, USA.

Marcia, J. E. (1980). Identity in adolescence. In J. Andelson (Ed.), *Handbook of adolescent psychology* (pp. 159-187). Wiley.

Monk, G., & Gehart, D. R. (2003). Sociopolitical activist or conversational partner? Distinguishing the position of the therapist in narrative and collaborative therapies. *Family Process, 42*(1), 19-30. https://doi.org/10.1111/j.1545-5300.2003.00019.x

Plante, C. N., Reysen, S., Groves, C. L., Roberts, S. E., & Gerbasi, K. (2017). The fantasy engagement scale: A flexible measure of positive and negative fantasy engagement. *Basic and Applied Social Psychology, 39,* 127-152. https://doi.org/10.1080/01973533.2017.1293538

Phillips, T. M., & Pittman, J. F. (2003). Identity processes in poor adolescents: Exploring the linkages between economic disadvantage and the primary task of adolescence. *Identity, 3*(2), 115-129. https://doi.org/10.1207/S1532706XID030202

Phinney, J. S., & Rosenthal, D. A. (1992). Ethnic identity in adolescence: Process, context, and outcome. In G. R. Adams, T. P. Gullotta, & R. Montemayor (Eds.), *Adolescent identity formation* (pp. 145-172). Sage Publications, Inc.

Putnam, R. (2000). *Bowling alone: The collapse and revival of American community*. Simon and Schuster.

Roberts, S. E. (2007). *Identity stage resolution in the prolonged transition to adulthood: Development and validation of the Identity Issues Inventory* (Doctoral dissertation). University of Western Ontario.

Roberts, S. E., & Côté, J. E. (2014). The identity issues inventory: Identity stage resolution in the prolonged transition to adulthood. *Journal of Adult Development, 21,* 225-238. https://doi.org/10.1007/s10804-014-9194-x

Schwartz, B. (2000). Self-determination: The tyranny of freedom. *American Psychologist, 55*(1), 79-88. https://doi.org/10.1037/0003-066X.55.1.79

Steinberg, L. (2001). We know some things: Parent–adolescent relationships in retrospect and prospect. *Journal of Research on Adolescence, 11*(1), 1-19. https://doi.org/10.1111/1532-7795.00001

White, M., & Epston, D. (1990). *Narrative means to therapeutic ends*. W.W. Norton & Company.

Yoder, A. E. (2000). Barriers to ego identity status formation: A contextual qualification of Marcia's identity status paradigm. *Journal of Adolescence, 23*(1), 95-106. https://doi.org/10.1006/jado.1999.0298

Endnote

The unstandardized coefficients state the magnitude (further away from zero is stronger) and direction (positive/increase or negative/decrease) of the relationship between an independent variable (e.g., *ladder* score) and the dependent/outcome variable (identity score). Increasing the independent variable by one unit (e.g., increasing by a point on the ladder scale), means that your predicted score on the dependent variable (*self-identity*) will increase by the unstandardized beta value (the *ladder* unstandardized beta is .18). The influence of *ladder* in the three models—self-identity (possible scores of 2-12), social-identity (possible scores of 2-12), and total identity (possible scores of 4-24)—shows that as you go up each point on the ladder measure (1-10), we can predict a .18 increase on the score of self-identity tasks, a .31 increase on social-identity tasks, and .50 increase on total identity tasks (when all of the other independent variables are held constant in the model). So, someone who scores low on *ladder* (they check 2 on the ladder question) would be predicted to have .36 increase in their self-identity score, but someone who scores higher on *ladder* (they check the 10) would be predicted to have a 1.8 increase in their self-identity score. Higher scores on the ladder mean predicting a higher score on identity. This interpretation applies to the continuous (or scaled) independent variables in the model—*ladder, identification, age, ideal, openness,* and *worse*. For the categorical variables (*autism* and *gender*), unstandardized betas allow for a comparison against a designated reference category (*unsure* if they are on the spectrum and *genderfluid / non-binary*). So, a trans-woman is predicted to score .57 points higher on her self-identity tasks than a non-binary/genderfluid person (set to zero), and a cis-woman is predicted to score .70 points higher (significantly higher) than a non-binary/genderfluid person on the identity measure. To interpret the autism data, someone who is *not* on the spectrum will score .72 points higher on self-identity than someone who is unsure (set to zero), and someone who *is* on the spectrum will score .52 units higher than someone unsure. Standardized coefficients are calculated so that you can compare the relative impact of each independent variable (ladder, identification) on the dependent variable (identity score). This is handy when the independent variables use different metrics, such as *identification* being measured with a 1-7 scale but *ladder* being measured with a 1-10 scale. If we just used the unstandardized coefficients, then it would be hard to compare the beta scores against each other because they don't use the same unit of measurement. However, we can do a fancy calculation to get something called a standardized beta (.17 for *ladder* and .24 for *identification* in the self-identity model). This allows us to see that *identification* is more impactful than *ladder* in predicting self-identity, but in the case of social-identity tasks, *ladder* is more impactful than *identification*. These are very useful for seeing the relative importance of variables in the model when examining continuous variables. However, standardization is less appropriate for interpreting categorical variables, so they are not reported.

Acknowledgements

Thank you to my mentor, Professor James Côté, for reviewing this chapter. This research is supported in part by funding from the Social Sciences and Humanities Research Council.

Conseil de recherches en sciences humaines du Canada

Canada

Part 5

Curtain Call

Chapter 25
An Ongoing Tail: Where Do We Go From Here?
Courtney "Nuka" Plante

As we get to the end of this book, I'm reminded of a question I was once asked by a furry as I was packing up after a presentation of our findings at a furry convention: when will you be done?

I can't help but smile at the question as I look back at more than a decade of research on furries because I realize, in hindsight, that I can't think of a single time in all those years when I've felt closer to being done than when I first started. That's just part of what it means to be a scientist: every answer you find introduces you to two new questions. Or, to put it another way, the more know about a subject, the more you understand how much you *don't* know about it![1]

This process of trying to answer a relatively simple question, only to discover that the rabbit hole goes far deeper than we could have imagined has been the recurring story of Furscience.[2] As you've seen throughout this book, just figuring out the right way to ask the question in the first place can be fraught with mistakes and false starts (e.g., our oversimplified studying of gender by asking furries to choose "male" or "female" comes to mind; see Chapter 15). And once we do get an answer (e.g., the most common fursona species is the wolf, see Chapter 7) and disseminate it to furries, scholars, and the general public, it's not long before they come back to us with an ever better question (e.g., "yes, but *why* wolves?").

The result of this is two-fold. First, it means we'll never run out of research ideas. As it is, many members of the Furscience team keep pages-long lists of ideas and questions for future studies, some of which come from their own reading of the academic literature and others which come from furries or laypersons asking about our prior findings. Even as we churn through a handful of those questions with each survey, we almost inevitably end up adding more questions to those lists than we were able to answer. If nothing else, this at least means we'll never run out of things to study!

The second result—and the far more important one—is that the state of our knowledge of furries is, and will always be, in a state of change. Of

---

[1] Indeed, psychologists even have a name for this: the Dunning-Kruger effect! (Dunning, 2011).

[2] As we stated in Chapter 3, Dr. Gerbasi, the first member of the Furscience team to do furry research, started in this exact manner—trying to answer a simple question about the veracity of furry stereotypes printed in a *Vanity Fair* article!

course, some of our findings are robust enough across abundant studies that we can be reasonably sure they won't change or, if they do, it'll be in a relatively slow fashion. For example, the average furry's age hasn't changed much in the past ten years, so we can be reasonably sure that five years from now, most furries will continue to be in their late teens and early to mid-twenties (see Chapter 13). Others, however, will likely be obsolete within just a few years of this book being published! For example, in the past five or six years alone we've seen a marked increase in the number of furries who identify as transgender, non-binary, or genderqueer, a number that's likely to continue increasing as broader cultural norms become more include and as the next generation develops an improved vocabulary and theoretical framework within which to understand and elaborate on their gender identity. By the time you're reading this, our numbers on the prevalence of transgender people in the fandom—or the terminology used to describe them or even the very concept of gender itself—may be obsolete.

Throughout this book, we've encouraged readers not to think of this book not as the final, unwavering truth about furries, but rather to think about it as a snapshot in time. We tend to think of it as a glimpse of what the state of furry research was like in a given moment with the caveat that any future study could upend our understanding of any of these topics. While we can't exactly call it a living document, we can predict—as confidently as we're able to—that there will almost certainly be a second edition of this book, and that it will involve all manner of updates and additions to what we've presented here.[3]

So what does the future look like for Furscience and our research? While it's hard to know when serendipity will strike and send a researcher careening down an entirely new line of research, we can note several lines of research that we're particularly interested in pursuing in the upcoming years. For one thing, we're still very interested in understanding how furries use fandom spaces and the fantasy theme of furry content to shape and develop a coherent, positive, stable sense of identity. We'd like to run more studies that more directly address the processes involved, including seeing, perhaps longitudinally, whether we can track changes in how furries see themselves over a long period of time.

A second line of research we're particularly interested in pursuing is a better understanding of the role that the internet will play in fandom dynamics and furry behavior. In recent years, we've seen how much furry

---

[3] Although if the book gets much longer, we may well need to split it into a two-volume set!

discourse has shifted away from occurring primarily in forums to, instead, taking place on social media, groups such as Telegram, and, perhaps most recently, programs like VRChat. Numerous furries have eagerly told us how being able to interact with other furries in virtual reality, when they can walk around as their fursonas, is their favorite furry-related behavior. To this end, at the time of writing this book, we're in the process of running a pair of studies that assess VR use among furries and which are beginning to delve into questions of which furries are the most likely to use VR, why they use VR, and how interaction in virtual spaces compares to interaction in real-world spaces.[4]

Another area of great interest for our research is the growing role of politics and activism in fandom spaces. As the number of transgender furries is expected to go up in the future, and as this continues to be a highly-charged topic in popular political discourse, we fully expect the furry fandom to become a space not only for escapism but for political organization and activism. Tensions may grow between furries who would prefer the space remain politically neutral and a growing majority of furries for whom a non-political furry fandom is simply not possible. The dynamics of this shift in the fandom would be fascinating to document.

We would also like to better study furries whose voices are frequently underrepresented in fandom spaces and our research. In the past few years, we've seen how incredibly fruitful it has been to conduct qualitative studies that get at the rich details and lived experiences of racialized furries, autistic furries, and transgender furries. In addition to following up on the multitudinous questions raised by these interviews directly, we'd also like to use the lessons we've learned from this approach to find and study other frequently overlooked or silenced groups within the furry fandom. For example, several furries have recently brought to our attention the fact that our convention and online surveys often miss furries with disabilities or older furries who might, for reasons of being a bit removed from the main fandom or who are simply more insular in their interactions with other furries, might not have the opportunity to do our surveys. We would also like to find a way to study furries under the age of 18—ideally studying furries as young as 13 or 14, just as they're getting into the fandom, to better understand the dynamics of being a minor in the furry fandom and to better understand the early years of being a furry—the transition from being a fan of furry media to becoming an active member of the furry fandom.

---

[4] As a long-time fan of the cyberpunk genre, I must resist the urge to use the term "meatspace" to refer to the real world!

Regardless of where our future studies take us, we're confident that Furscience will continue to be dedicated to using science to help others—furry and non-furry alike—to better understand the furry fandom and to help dispel stigmatizing misconceptions about furries. We hope that this book has helped you in this regard, and thank you—whether you're a furry who participated in our studies directly or is simply trying to learn more about this fandom of theirs, a parent of a furry trying to better understand your child's new interest, a scholar and potential future collaborator who's critiquing our work through another theoretical perspective, or a journalist doing your due diligence and trying to write the most accurate piece about furries that you can. This book, and, indeed, our research and the incredible journey it's been over the past decade, wouldn't have been possible without you.

References

Dunning, D. (2011). The Dunning-Kruger effect: On being ignorant of one's own ignorance. *Advances in Experimental Social Psychology, 44,* 247-296. https://doi.org/10.1016/B978-0-12-385522-0.00005-6

Author Biographies

Kathleen Gerbasi

Kathleen Gerbasi is a recently retired social psychologist and anthrozoologist. She was the principal author of the first peer-reviewed, published scholarly study of furries. She currently studies the furry fandom as well as therian and otherkin identities.

Courtney "Nuka" Plante

Courtney, or Nuka, as he's known by his friends and fellow furries, is a social psychologist who graduated with a PhD in 2014 from the University of Waterloo and who is currently an Associate Professor of Psychology at Bishop's University in Sherbrooke, Quebec, Canada. He's been a furry "officially" for more than 15 years, although his interest in furry media goes back even longer than that. Nuka's research interests include stigma, group identity, and fantasy and how all of these processes operate in the context of fan cultures, including furries, bronies, anime fans, and *Star Wars* fans. He also studies the impacts of media more broadly on the way we think, feel, and behave. This is his fifth book based on his research.

Stephen Reysen

Stephen Reysen is a Professor of Psychology at Texas A&M University-Commerce. His research interests include topics related to personal (e.g., fanship) and social identity (e.g., fandom).

Sharon E. Roberts

Sharon E. Roberts is an Associate Professor at Renison University College at the University of Waterloo in Canada. Her educational background is interdisciplinary: Psychology (BAHns), Sociology (MA, PhD), and Social Work (MSW). She is one of the co-founders of the IARP / Furscience.

Elizabeth Fein

Elizabeth Fein, Ph.D. is Associate Professor and Chair of the Psychology Department at Duquesne University. She is the author of *Living on the Spectrum: Autism and Youth in Community* (NYU Press, 2020) and co-editor, with Clarice Rios, of *Autism in Translation: An Intercultural Conversation on Autism Spectrum Conditions* (Palgrave, 2018). A psychological anthropologist and licensed clinical psychologist, her work focuses on the intersection of psychology and culture. She sings with the synthpop band Take Me With You and DJs with the Treasure team in Pittsburgh, PA.

Frances H. I. Henry

Frances is a visiting associate professor in history at King's University College at Western University, Canada. She received her PhD in History from Western University in 2019. Her research focuses on homosexuality in early modern Europe, particularly the intersections of sexuality, gender, religion, and law. She is in the process of turning her thesis into a book.

Anna Renee Henry

Anna Renee Henry is a graduate student in sociology at the University of Guelph, Canada. Her research focuses on disability (particularly mental illness) and stigma. As an undergraduate at Renison University College at the University of Waterloo, she worked closely with Dr. Sharon Roberts as a member of Furscience. She continues to work with them on numerous forthcoming publications.

Thomas R. Brooks III

Dr. Thomas R. Brooks is an Assistant Professor of Psychology at New Mexico Highlands University. He is the supervisor of The Human Connection Lab, where he and his students investigate the psychological principles of how humans make and maintain relationships in romantic, technological, metaphysical, and educational contexts. Thomas is one of the authors of the book: *CAPE: A Multidimensional Model of Fan Interest.*

Camielle Adams

Camielle or "Cami" is a passionate and deeply sensitive writer who can usually be found with her nose buried in a book. She is a magna cum laude graduate of Tuskegee University and a current graduate student of the University of Calgary where she studies Political Science. She is currently studying the relationship between social media and right-wing domestic terrorism.

Printed in Great Britain
by Amazon

36015111R00436